C0-AWN-220

Treuhandanstalt
The Impossible Challenge

Treuhandanstalt

The Impossible Challenge

Edited by
Wolfram Fischer
Herbert Hax and
Hans Karl Schneider

Scientific subeditors
Hartmut Maaßen and
Jutta Wietog

Akademie Verlag

This book was first published in German: Treuhandanstalt. Das Unmögliche wagen. Forschungsberichte herausgegeben von Wolfram Fischer, Herbert Hax und Hans Karl Schneider, Akademie Verlag, Berlin 1993.

1st English edition

Library of Congress Card Number pending

Die Deutsche Bibliothek - CIP-Einheitsaufnahme

Treuhandanstalt ; the impossible challenge / ed. by Wolfram
Fischer ... - 1. ed. - Berlin : Akad. Verl., 1996
ISBN 3-05-0022746-0
NE: Fischer, Wolfram [Hrsg.]

Akademie Verlag is a member of the VCH Publishing Group.

Printed on non-acid paper.
The paper used corresponds to both the U.S. standard ANSI Z. 39.48 – 1984
and the European standard ISO TC 46.

Satz: PreMedia, Malteserstraße 120, 12249 Berlin
Printing: GAM Media GmbH, Berlin
Bookbinding: Lüderitz & Bauer GmbH, Berlin

Printed in the Federal Republik of Germany

Akademie Verlag GmbH
Postfach
D-13162 Berlin
Federal Republic of Germany

VCH Publishers, Inc.
220 East 23rd Street
New York, NY 10010-4606

Contents

Part A The history, legal framework, and organisational structure of the Treuhandanstalt (THA)

Part B The Treuhand's working priorities

Part C The effects of the Treuhand's work

The main German laws affecting the work of the THA

(The short form shown underlined in the English explanation is the term used in the body of the text.

BInvG — *Gesetz über besondere Investitionen in der Deutschen Demokratischen Republik (Investitionsgesetz) vom 23. 9. 1990, BGBL. II. S. 885, 1157, geändert durch das Gesetz zur Beseitigung von Hemmnissen bei der Privatisierung von Unternehmen und zur Förderung von Investitionen (Hemmnisbeseitigungsgesetz) vom 22. 3. 1991, BGBL. I S. 774.*
Law on special investments in the German Democratic Republic **(Investment Act)** of 23rd September 1990, Bundesgesetzblatt II page 885, 1157, as amended by the Law for the Removal of Obstacles to the Privatisation of Companies and for the Promotion of Investment **(Removal of Obstacles Act)** of 22nd March 1991, Bundesgesetzblatt II page 774.

DMBilG — *Gesetz über die Eröffnungsbilanz in Deutscher Mark und die Kapitalneufestsetzung (D-Markbilanzgesetz) vom 22. 9. 1990, BGBl. II S. 889, 1169, 1245, zuletzt geändert durch das Gesetz zur Änderung des Vermögensgesetzes und anderer Vorschriften (Zweites Vermögensrechtsänderungsgesetz) vom 14. 7. 1992, BGBl. I, S. 1284.*
Law on the Opening Balance Sheet in Deutschmarks and the Redefinition of Capital (Opening DM Balance Sheet Act) of 22nd September 1990, Bundesgesetzblatt II page 889, 1169, 1245, as most recently amended by the Act for the Amendment of the Property Act and other regulations **(2nd Law Property Amendment Act)** of 14th July 1992, Bundesgesetzblatt I, page 1284.

EGAktG — *Einführungsgesetz zum Aktiengesetz in der Fassung vom 14. 7. 1992, BGBl. I, S. 1283.*
Introductory Act to the Companies Act (on AG-companies) of 14th July 1992, *Bundesgesetzblatt* I, page 1283.

EGBGB — *Einführungsgesetz zum Bürgerlichen Gesetzbuche vom 18. 8. 1896, RGBL., S. 604, zuletzt geändert aufgrund des Einigungsvertrages vom 31. 8. 1990 (BGBl. II, S. 889, 941), Gesetz über die Spaltung der von der Treuhandanstalt verwalteten Unternehmen vom 5. 4. 1991 (BGBl. II, S. 854), Zweites Vermögensrechtsänderungsgesetz vom 14. 7. 1992 (BGBl. I, S. 1257), Gesetz vom*

	21. 12. 1992 (BGBl. S. 2116) und Gesetz vom 21. 12. 1992 (BGBl. II. S. 889). Introductory Act to the Civil Code of 18th August 1896, Reichsgesetzblatt page 604, as most recently amended on the basis of the Unification Treaty of 31st August 1990 (Bundesgesetzblatt II, 889, 941), Law on the splitting of companies administered by the THA (Splitting Act) of 5th April 1991 (Bundesgesetzblatt II, page 854), Second Property Law Amendment Act of 14th July 1992 (Bundesgesetzblatt I, page 1257), Law of 21st December 1992 (Bundesgesetzblatt I, page 2116) and Law of 21st December 1992 (Bundesgesetzblatt I, page 2117).
EV	*Vertrag zwischen der Bundesrepublik Deutschland und der Deutschen Demokratischen Republik über die Herstellung der Einheit Deutschlands (Einigungsvertrag) vom 31. 8. 1990, BGBl. II, S. 889.* Treaty between the Federal Republic of Germany and the German Democratic Republic on the creation of German unity **(Treaty of Unification)** of 31st August 1990, *Bundesgesetzblatt* II, page 889.
GesO	*Gesamtvollstreckungsverordnung vom 6. 6. 1990, GBl. DDR I, S. 285, geändert und umbenannt in Gesamtvollstreckungsordnung durch Anlage II Kapitel III Sachgebiet A Abschnitt II Nr. 1 des Einigungsvertrages vom 31. 8. 1990 in Verbindung mit Artikel 1 des Gesetzes vom 23.9 1990, BGBl. II, S. 885, 1153, in der Fassung der Bekanntmachung vom 23. 5. 1991, BGBL. I, S. 1185.* Compulsory Enforcement (= bankruptcy) Order of 6th June 1990, East German *Gesetzblatt* I, page 285, as amended and renamed the Total Compulsory Enforcement Ordinance **(Bankruptcy Order)** by Appendix II Chapter III Specialist field A Section II Clause 1 of the Treaty of Union in conjunction with Article 1 of the Law of 23rd September 1990, *Bundesgesetzblatt* II, page 885, 1153, as promulgated on 23rd May 1991, *Bundesgesetzblatt* I, page 1185.
InVorG	*Gesetz über den Vorrang für Investitionen bei Rückübertragungsansprüchen nach dem Vermögensgesetz (Investitionsvorrangsgesetz) vom 14. 7. 1992, BGBl. I, S. 1268.* Act on the priority of investment in claims for restitution under the Property Act **(Investment Priority Act)** of 14th July 1992, *Bundesgesetzblatt* I, page 1268.
KVerfG	*Gesetz über die Selbstverwaltung der Gemeinden und Landkreise (Kommunalverfassungsgesetz) vom 17. 5. 1990, GBl. DDR I, S. 255.* Law on the autonomous administration of municipalities and rural counties **(Communal Constitution Act)** of 17th May 1990, East German Gesetzblatt I, page 255.

KVG

Gesetz über das Vermögen der Gemeinden, Städte und Landkreise (Kommunalvermögensgesetz) vom 6. 7. 1990, GBl. DDR I, S. 660, zuletzt geändert durch Gesetz vom 13. 9. 1990, GBl. DDR I, S. 1537.
Law on the Property of Municipalities, Towns, and Rural Counties **(Communal Property Act)** of 6th July 1990, East German *Gesetzblatt* I, page 660, as last amended by the Law of 13th September 1990, East German *Gesetzblatt* I, page 1537.

LAnpG (LwAnpG)

Landwirtschaftsanpassungsgesetz vom 29. 6. 1990, GBl. DDR I, S. 642, geändert durch das Gesetz vom 3. 7. 1991, BGBl. I, S. 1410, zuletzt geändert durch das Gesetz zur Änderung des Vermögensgesetzes und anderer Vorschriften (Zweites Vermögensrechtsänderungsgesetz) vom 14. 7. 1992, BGBl. I, S. 1283.
Agricultural Adaptation Act of 29th June 1990, East German *Gesetzblatt* I, page 642, as amended by the Law of 3rd July 1991, *Bundesgesetzblatt* I, page 1410, as last amended by the **Second Property Law Amendment Act** of 14th July 1992 (*Bundesgesetzblatt* I, page 1283).

PrHBG

Gesetz zur Beseitigung von Hemmnissen bei der Privatisierung von Unternehmen und zur Förderung von Investitionen (Hemmnisbeseitigungsgesetz) vom 22. 3. 1991, BGBL. I S. 766, zuletzt geändert durch das Gesetz zur Änderung des Vermögensgesetzes und anderer Vorschriften (Zweites Vermögensrechtsänderungsgesetz) vom 14. 7. 1992, BGBl. I, S. 1283.
Law for the Removal of Obstacles to the Privatisation of Companies and for the Promotion of Investment **(Removal of Obstacles Act)** of 22nd March 1991, *Bundesgesetzblatt* II page 766, last amended by the **Second Property Law Amendment Act** of 14th July 1992 (*Bundesgesetzblatt* I, page 1283).

SpTrUG

Gesetz über die Spaltung der von der Treuhandanstalt verwalteten Unternehmen vom 5. 4. 1991 (BGBl. II, S. 854).
Law on the splitting of companies administered by the THA **(Splitting Act)** of 5th April 1991 (*Bundesgesetzblatt* II, page 854).

StaatsV

Vertrag über die Schaffung einer Währungs-, Wirtschafts- und Sozialunion zwischen der Bundesrepublik Deutschland und der Deutsche Demokratische Republik (Staatsvertrag) vom 18. 5. 1990, BGBl. II, S. 537
Treaty creating Monetary, Economic, and Social Union between the Federal Republic of Germany and the German Democratic Republic **(State Treaty)** of 18th May 1990, *Bundesgesetzblatt* II, page 537.

THA-KredG

Gesetz zur Regelung der Aufnahme von Krediten durch die Treuhandanstalt vom 3. Juli 1992, BGBl. I, S. 1190 Law regula-

	tion the Credit Line to be taken out by the THA (**THA Credit Act**) of 3rd July 1992, *Bundesgesetzblatt* I, page 1190.
THG	*Gesetz zur Privatisierung und Reorganisation des volkseigenen Vermögens (Treuhandgesetz) vom 17. 6. 1990, GBl. DDR I, S. 300, geändert durch Gesetz vom 22. 3. 1991, BGBl. I, S. 766.* Law on the Privatisation and Reorganisation of state-owned Property (**Treuhand-Act** or simply **THG**) of 17th June 1990, East German *Gesetzblatt* I, page 300, as amended by the Act of 22nd March 1991, *Bundesgesetzblatt* I, page 766.
1. DVO	*Erste Durchführungsordnung zum Treuhandgesetz vom 15. 8. 1990. GBl. DDR I, S. 1076.* **First Implementation Ordinance** to the THA-Act of 15th August 1990, East German *Gesetzblatt* I, page 1076.
2. DVO	*Zweite Durchführungsordnung zum Treuhandgesetz vom 22. 8. 1990, GBl. DDR I, S. 1260.* **Second Implementation Ordinance** to the THA-Act of 22nd August 1990, East German *Gesetzblatt* I, page 1260.
3. DVO	*Dritte Durchführungsordnung zum Treuhandgesetz vom 29. 8. 1990, GBl. DDR I, S. 1333.* **Third Implementation Ordinance** to the THA-Act of 29th August 1990, East German *Gesetzblatt* I, page 1333
4. DVO	*Vierte Durchführungsordnung zum Treuhandgesetz vom 12. 9. 1990, GBl. DDR I, S. 1465, geändert auf Grund der Vereinbarung vom 18. 9. 1990, BGBl. II, S. 1239.* **Fourth Implementation Ordinance** to the THA-Act of 12th August 1990, East German *Gesetzblatt* I, page 1465, as amended by the Agreement of 18th September 1990, *Bundesgesetzblatt* II, page 1239.
5. DVO	*Fünfte Durchführungsordnung zum Treuhandgesetz vom 12. 9. 1990, GBl. DDR I, S. 1466* **Fifth Implementation Ordinance** to the THA-Act of 12th August 1990, East German *Gesetzblatt* I, page 1466.
TreuhAS	*Satzung der Treuhandanstalt vom 18. Juli 1990, GBl. DDR I, S. 809* **Articles of Association** of the THA dated 18th July 1990, East German *Gesetzblatt* I, page 809.
UmwVO	*Verordnung zur Umwandlung von volkseigenen Kombinaten und Betrieben und Einrichtungen in Kapitalgesellschaften (Umwandlungsverordnung) vom 1. 3. 1990, GBl. DDR I, S. 107, geändert durch §12 Nr. 9 Änderungs- und Aufhebungs-VO vom 28. 6. 1990, GBl. DDR I, Nr. 38, S. 509.* Ordinance on the conversion of state-owned industrial combines, companies, and organisations into joint-stock companies (**Con-**

version Ordinance) of 1st March 1990, East German *Gesetzblatt* I, page 107, as amended by Article 12 Clause 9 of the Amendment and Cancellation Ordinance of 28th June 1990, East German *Gesetzblatt* I, no. 38, page 509.

URüV

Verordnung zum Vermögensgesetz über die Rückgabe von Unternehmen (Unternehmensrückgabeverordnung) vom 13. 7. 1991, BGBl. I, S. 1542.
Ordinance to the Property Act on the restitution of ownership of companies **(Company Restitution Act)** of 13th July 1991, *Bundesgesetzblatt* I, page 1542.

VermG

Gesetz zur Regelung offener Vermögensfragen (Vermögensgesetz) vom 23. 9. 1990, BGBl. II, S. 889, 1159, geändert durch das Gesetz zur Beseitigung von Hemmnissen bei der Privatisierung von Unternehmen und zur Förderung von Investitionen (Hemmnisbeseitigungsgesetz) vom 22. 3. 1991, BGBL. I S. 766 geändert durch das Gesetz zur Änderung des Vermögensgesetzes und anderer Vorschriften (Zweites Vermögensrechtsänderungsgesetz) vom 14. 7. 1992, BGBl. I, S. 1257.
Law to regulate unsettled property questions **(Property Act)** of 23rd September 1990, *Bundesgesetzblatt* II, page 889, 1159, as amended by the Law for the Removal of Obstacles to the Privatisation of Companies and for the Promotion of Investment **(Removal of Obstacles Act)** of 22nd March 1991, *Bundesgesetzblatt* II page 774, as amended by the Act for the Amendment of the Property Act and other regulations **(2nd Property Law Amendment Act)** of 14th July 1992, *Bundesgesetzblatt* I, page 1257.

2. VermRÄndG

Gesetz zur Änderung des Vermögensgesetzes und anderer Vorschriften (Zweites Vermögensrechtsänderungsgesetz) vom 14. 7. 1992, BGBl. I, S. 1257.
Act for the Amendment of the Property Act and other regulations **(2nd Property Law Amendment Act)** of 14th July 1992, *Bundesgesetzblatt* I, page 1257.

VZOG

Gesetz über die Feststellung der Zuordnung von ehemals volkseigenem Vermögen (Vermögenszuordnungsgesetz) vom 22. 3. 1991, BGBl. I, S. 784, geändert durch das Gesetz zur Änderung des Vermögensgesetzes und anderer Vorschriften (Zweites Vermögensrechtsänderungsgesetz) vom 14. 7. 1992, BGBl. I, S. 1280.
Law for determining the categorisation of formerly state-owned property **(Property Assignment Act)** of 22nd March 1991, *Bundesgesetzblatt* I, page 784, amended by the Act for the Amendment of the Property Act and other regulations **(2nd Property Law Amendment Act)** of 14th July 1992, *Bundesgesetzblatt* I, page 1280.

Abbreviations

ABM	Arbeitsbeschaffungsmaßnahmen
ABS	Arbeitsförderung, Beschäftigung, Strukturentwicklung
AcP	Archiv für civilistische Praxis (Zeitschrift)
AFG	Arbeitsförderungsgesetz
AG	Aktiengesellschaft
AiB	Arbeitsrecht im Betrieb (Zeitschrift)
A-Interview	Interviews which were made by Dietmar Rost under the scientific responsibility of Professor Martin Kohli
AktG	Aktiengesetz
AP	Arbeitsrechtliche Praxis
ArbGG	Arbeitsgerichtsgesetz
AROV	Amt zur Regelung offener Vermögensfragen
ATLAS	Ausgewählte Treuhandunternehmen vom Land angemeldet zur Sanierung
AuA	Arbeit und Arbeitsrecht
BAG	Bundesarbeitsgericht
BAROV	Bundesamt zur Regelung offener Vermögensfragen
BB	Betriebs-Berater (Zeitschrift)
BeschFG	Beschäftigungsförderungsgesetz
BetrVG	Betriebsverfassungsgesetz
BezG	Bezirksgericht
BHEI	Beratungshandbuch Eigentum und Investitionen in den neuen Bundesländern
BHO	Bundeshaushaltsordnung
B-Interview	Interviews made by the individual authors
BR-Drucks.	Bundesratsdrucksache
BT-Drucks.	Bundestagsdrucksache
BVerfGG	Bundesverfassungsgerichtsgesetzt
BVVG	Bodenverwertungs- und -verwaltungsgesellschaft mbH
DB	Der Betrieb (Zeitschrift)
DtZ	Deutsch-Deutsche Rechts-Zeitschrift
DWiR (DZWiR)	Deutsche Zeitschrift für Wirtschaftsrecht
DtZ	Beutsch-Deutsche-Rechts-Zeitschrift
DVBl	
EGAktG	Einführungsgesetz zum Aktiengesetz
EGBGB	Einführungsgesetz zum Bürgerlichen Gesetzbuch (*e*)

EzA	Entscheidungssammlung zum Arbeitsrecht
GK-AFG	Gemeinschaftskommentar zum Arbeitsförderungsgesetz
GK-BetrVG	Gemeinschaftskommentar zum Betriebsverfassungsgesetz
GmbHG	GmbH-Gesetz
GO-BT	Geschäftsordnung des Bundestages
GO-THA	Geschäftsordnung Treuhandanstalt
GO-V	Geschäftsordnung der Volkskammer der Deutschen Demokratischen Republik
HGrG	Haushaltsgrundsätzegesetz
HAS	Handbuch des Arbeits- und Sozialrechts
IAB	Institut für Arbeitsmarkt- und Berufsforschung der Bundesanstalt für Arbeit
JUS	Juristische Schulung
KG	Kammergericht
KoKo	Kommerzielle Koordinierung
KR	Gemeinschaftskommentar zum Kündigungsschutzgesetz
KreisG	Kreisgericht
KSchG	Kündigungsschutzgesetz
LAROV	Landesamt zur Regelung offener Vermögensfragen
LPG	Landwirtschaftliche Produktionsgenossenschaft
MBI	Management Buy-In
MBO	Management Buy-Out
NJW	Neue Juristische Wochenschrift
NZA	Neue Zeitschrift für Arbeits- und Sozialrecht
OVG	Oberverwaltungsgericht
RGRK	Das Bürgerliche Gesetzbuch – mit besonderer Berücksichtigung der Rechtsprechung des Reichsgerichts und des Bundesgerichtshofs (Kommentar)
THA	Treuhandanstalt
TLG	Liegenschaftsgesellschaft der Treuhandanstalt mbH
UrTHA	Ur-Treuhandanstalt
VEB	Volkseigener Betrieb
VEG	Volkseigenes Gut
VIZ	Zeitschrift für Vermögens- und Investitionsrecht
VwGO	Verwaltungsgerichtsordnung
WM	Wertpapier-Mitteilungen (Zeitschrift für Wirtschafts- und Bankrecht)
WRV	Weimarer Reichsverfassung
ZGR	Zeitschrift für Unternehmens- und Gesellschaftsrecht
ZIP	Zeitschrift für Wirtschaftsrecht

Preface

by Wolfram Fischer

From the summer 1990 to the end of 1994, a period of four and a half years, the *Treuhandanstalt* (THA) was the principal agent in the transformation from a centrally planned economy to a market economy in Eastern Germany. The THA was founded in its original form on March 1st 1990, by a decree of the last communist majority government of the GDR, led by Hans Modrow, in order to introduce decentralised management of the economy and secure thereby the bulk of the "property of the people". Privatisation was to be limited to small enterprises which had been nationalised in 1972. Larger production units were to be entrusted to the THA, while joint ventures with up to 49% "foreign" ownership – including West German companies or individuals – were to be allowed.

The first and only freely elected parliament (*Volkskammer)* of the German Democratic Republic replaced this decree with an act of law dated 17th June 1990. This reformulated the goals to be achieved and aimed at total privatisation, including the restitution of property to former owners. Thus the *Treuhandanstalt* in its present form came into being. It was, this has to be stressed, a creation of the GDR during the last phase of its existence, not of the Federal Republic of Germany, though the de Mazière government took West German advice in formulating the necessary legislation. The Treaty of Unification of 31st August 1990 confirmed the validity of the act following the reunification of both parts of Germany, and it therefore remained in force after the third of October 1990, the official date of reunification.

Having accomplished its main task, the *Treuhandanstalt* will from 1995 onwards be replaced by a federal institute attached to the Ministry of Finance, the Federal Institute for the Administration of Special Assets arising from the Unification Process, *Bundesanstalt für vereinigungbedingtes Sondervermögen (BVS).* This will administer those remains of the former "property of the people" (*Volkseigentum*) which could not be sold before the end of 1994, and also the property belonging to former political parties of the GDR and to the ill-famed "commercial coordination" (*Kommerzielle Koordinierung* or *KoKo*) companies which were created secretly by the GDR government in several European countries to hold hard currency. The BVS will also administer tens of thousands of contracts which were concluded by the THA and ensure that the new owners of companies will honour their obligations.

The *Treuhandanstalt* was set an almost impossible task, and a high degree of imagination and initiative was needed to achieve it. Nearly all the procedures to be followed had to be invented. The THA was faced with an avalanche of decrees, laws and law amendments from government and parliament, some of which it had itself initiated in order to be able to carry out its activities. Operations had to begin immediately, since the East German economy was in decay, and excessive bureaucracy had to be avoided. At the same time however, the THA organisation had to be built up from nothing. The first couple of hundred managers and employees came from East Germany, mainly from the GDR ministries the THA was to replace, and were appointed by the

East German government, as were the first top managers from the West, such as Detlev Rohwedder, the first chairman of its administrative council, who took up the position of President of the THA on 20th August 1990 and who was murdered in his Düsseldorf home at Easter 1991.

From Spring 1990 to the end of 1993, the number of THA staff grew from a few dozen people working in provisional offices with a few telephones, typewriters and secretaries (without computers or fax) to more than 5,000 working within a sophisticated organisational structure with its headquarters in the former House of Ministries of the GDR (originally built in the 1930's to house Hermann Goering's Air Ministry), close to Potsdamer Platz and immediately in front of the Wall. Several hundred people were employed in the fifteen regional offices. From the end of 1993 the number of staff has been reduced parallel with the reduction in work still to be done.

At the outset, some 8,000 industrial units, ranging from large combines (*Kombinate*) – socialist trusts with thousands of employees and production units in all parts of East Germany – to small units such as bookshops and pharmacies, had to be registered as companies in accordance with western legal practice. A DM opening balance sheet had to be prepared and concepts developed for the future of the company. It soon became clear that practically none of these units would be able to exist in a competitive environment. Few companies had products that could be sold in the West. Production machinery was in a lamentable condition, capital reserves were non-existent, companies were burdened by large debts imposed upon them by the former government, and skills were totally lacking in the marketing, controlling and legal fields.

To prevent an economic disaster, the staff of the THA and their outside advisers had to act quickly. Though legally an institution under public law, the THA was in the main run as a business. Experienced managers and lawyers from the West soon took over the leading managerial positions, and many young graduates from West German business and law schools chose to make the THA the starting point for their careers, while some senior civil servants, on leave from their ministries in West Germany, attempted to lay down the necessary legal and organisational foundations, develop procedures and documentation systems in order to allow the Ministry of Finance, the German parliament (*Bundestag*) and the Federal Audit Office to control the work and the finances of the THA. The bulk of THA employees nevertheless remained East German.

Originally, some East German experts had wanted the world to believe that the GDR economy when privatised would be worth more than a trillion DM. Even western experts and Rohwedder himself in Summer 1990 believed that about 600 million DM could be gained by selling the bulk of the industrial units to western firms. It soon became obvious that no overall profit, but rather losses would be made, although some profitable sales were concluded. The most spectacular, after four years of bargaining, was the sale of most of the electrical powerstations, the electricity transfer network and the lignite mines in the Lausitz area to a group of West German electricity producers for ten billion DM in September 1994. In all it is estimated, however, that the THA will not end up with a surplus, but with a debt of about 275 billion DM, to be carried by the German taxpayer. It will be one of the tasks of the above mentioned successor organisation of the THA to administer this huge debt.

By the middle of 1994 the original total of 8,000 industrial units had grown to more than 14,000 as a result of splitting the *Kombinate* into smaller companies. By now – Autumn 1994 – most of them have been either sold, returned to their original owners, turned over to local authorities or liquidated. 6,139 units were totally privatised, while in 274 enterprises the THA retained a minority shareholding. 2,667 of the firms privatised were sold to their former managers in a management buy out. In 7,374 cases, parts of former industrial units were sold. 1,585 businesses were returned to their former owners, 268 to local authorities. More than 3,500 units had to be liquidated. It is remarkable that even under these circumstances nearly a third of 333,000 jobs could be saved. In only 119 cases has the legal procedure of liquidation already been completed.[1] It will be the task of the successor organisation to follow carry out the remains of the process.

Many of the privatisation contracts include penalty clauses relating to investments and employment. By the middle of 1994, undertakings to invest 200 billion DM and guarantee 1,460,883 jobs had been made. The sales proceeds amounted to 52.7 billion DM. 839 enterprises were purchased by non-German investors, who paid a total of 5.6 billion DM and gave undertakings to employ 148,354 people and invest 19.8 billion DM. Swiss persons or companies purchased the highest number of firms, 138 in total, mainly middle-sized companies, and paid 350 million DM. Investors from France purchased only 88 enterprises, paid however 1.447 billion DM, promised 25,422 jobs and 5.454 billion DM of investments. The French are, therefore, the largest foreign investors in East Germany, followed by the British and Americans.[2]

In addition to the larger industrial units, as part of the so-called "small privatisation" action, the THA privatised around 25,000 restaurants, hotels, pharmacies, bookshops and cinemas, and 38,000 pieces of real estate. This amounted altogether to nearly 82,000 cases of privatisation.

Some businesses which could not be sold but were still deemed viable were formed into groups to be managed in a so-called "Management KG" holding company. It is expected that most of these will be sold to private owners in due course.

The work of the *Treuhandanstalt* has been watched closely, not only by government agencies and parliamentary bodies but also by the general public represented by the media. The THA featured constantly in newspaper and TV reports, and these were rarely favourable. The THA's work was often termed a "sell out" of the property of the people of East Germany to Western capitalists, and much mention was made of the "enrichment of insiders", be it of the *nomenklatura* of the old GDR or the West German business elite. Some unfortunate cases where investors could or would not keep their promises affected the THA's standing, and the few cases of corruption and misuse of insider knowledge had a further adverse affect on public opinion.

The authors of this book do not follow the popular view. The story which they have to tell is a quite different one. It deals with the courageous and often risky attempt to save whatever could be saved from a bankrupt political and economic system. The authors are scholars from different backgrounds: lawyers, historians, sociologists and political scientists – mainly however economists and business administrators. They were asked by the THA in late 1992 to carry out research on its work from different angles and to lay some groundwork for a scholarly evaluation whilst operations were still in full swing. Most of the research was carried out in the spring and summer of 1993. Some of the facts presented in this book will seem, therefore, outdated by now. Some more recent ones have accordingly been included in this preface. Not outdated are, however, the basic findings and the arguments put forward. The authors differ in their judgements as to the performance of the THA and the legal basis of its work, as is to be expected when scholars of different origins, perspectives and personal opinions are brought together.

Work on the book was coordinated by three editors, an economist, Hans K. Schneider, Professor emeritus of the University of Cologne and former Chairman of the Board of Economic Advisors to the Federal Government of Germany; a business adminstrator, Herbert Hax, professor at the University of Cologne and present chairman of this advisory body; and an economic historian, Wolfram Fischer, professor at the Free University of Berlin and Chairman of the Berlin Historic Commission, *Historische Kommission zu Berlin*.

The editors and authors wish to thank the *Treuhandanstalt* and its President, Ms Breuel, for granting them the opportunity to observe history in the making and to draw upon the valuable information provided by THA staff at a time when their work was occupying them far outside of normal working hours, and for not interfering with the independent judgements of the authors. The English translation of this book will, I am sure, serve to spread throughout the world knowledge of a dramatic episode in modern history and of an economic and social transformation process of unprecedented scale.

Berlin, September 1994 Wolfram Fischer

Introduction

by Wolfram Fischer, Herbert Hax, and Hans K. Schneider

Daring the impossible. This is how the editors of this volume see the task facing the *Treuhandanstalt* (also called THA or Treuhand), the public trustee institute of the German federal government entrusted with privatising the state-owned companies and property of the defunct German Democratic Republic (GDR). This task is being carried out in an environment shaped by a myriad of political and other interests; it amounts to nothing less than the virtually complete transfer of all the state-owned means of production into the free market economy. When the institute was set up, a central administration organisation, of all things, was entrusted with the task of liquidating a centrally planned economic system. This fundamental change exposed the formerly state-owned companies to competition and open markets for the first time, and revealed the dire straits into which their competitiveness had sunk, particularly in heavy industry, the core of they GDR economy. The range of activities the Treuhand could undertake to help those companies was very limited, if one adheres to the economic criteria on which its task was based. On the one hand there was the statutory task itself and limited room for manoeuvre; on the other was the property it had to sell; between these elements existed a tension which appeared impossible to dispel. The amount the Treuhand can actually do to fulfil its task must therefore inevitably lag far behind the expectations and demands of the general public and, particularly, those affected by its work.

The article by *H. M. Kepplinger* in this volume shows that the Treuhand has received predominantly bad press. The media tend to focus on failed attempts at privatisation, fraudulent dealings, and spectacular individual cases, such as the dogged resistance of the miners in Bischofferode against the shutdown which was decided upon by the Treuhand and approved by the Federal Ministry of Finance and even the miners' own trade union. Such reporting has given rise to a distorted picture in the public's mind. A number of articles in this volume attempt to correct this picture by presenting figures to show that the vast majority of privatisations, particularly those of smaller companies, have been completed relatively smoothly in just a few years and, as far as one can see at the moment, may be considered success stories (see: articles by *K.-D. Schmidt, J. Schwalbach, P. Klemmer*). Considering the odds the Treuhand was up against – including the globally bad business climate in recent years, the even more severe recession affecting western Germany from the summer of 1992 onwards, and newly emerging competition from many locations in Central and Eastern Europe – one cannot deny that the Treuhand deserves recognition for its privatisation work so far.

The Treuhand holds a key position in the transformation of the former communist GDR economy into the free market economy of the Federal Republic of Germany. Its long-term goal is clear and undisputed: it is to contribute to the creation of a new, efficient economy in the eastern part of Germany which gives working people the same opportunities their counterparts in western Germany enjoy. However, the right methods for achieving that goal are unknown; these are uncharted waters. There is no experience that tells us how to change a centrally planned ecnomy from top to bottom into a market economy, no wealth of information from which we can extract an equation for making the new market economy efficient and acceptable to the general population.[1] Right up to the end of the 1980's, economists and social scientists from all over the world thought it most unlikely that the communist-style planned economy in the GDR could be rolled back at all. As the shortcomings of central planning became increasingly evident, economists began to look for ways not to change the system, but rather to effect economic reforms within the existing system. This academic discussion did not produce the idea of a public trustee institute.

A new institution, created specifically for the one task of transferring the greatest possible proportion of state-owned production facilities into private hands as quickly as possible, and thus building up an economy regulated not by the state but by the market, was certainly not the focal point of the plans produced by the Modrow government when it set up the Treuhand (see: article by *W. Fischer/H. Schröter*). Rather, the Original-Treuhand took charge of its companies without any clear mandate to pursue market-economy goals and standards. At that time, the dream of creating a revised edition of the old communist economy was still very much alive, and that was exactly what the Treuhand's communist initiators intended to do. Their discussions indicated that the Treuhand would facilitate a limited, tightly-controlled opening up to a market economy. Its primary function would be to ensure that the state would continue to exert the greatest possible influence on the economy. In this manner, the door to a kind of "third route" – one between communism and the market economy – could be kept open.

This policy was reversed on 17th June 1990, when the new, democratically elected GDR *Volkskammer* (People's Chamber, the parliament) passed the Public Trustee Act (Treuhandgesetz), which issued the first unambiguous statements about the purpose of the Treuhand. This act was kept in force under Article 25 of the Treaty of Unification: "The Treuhandanstalt shall have the task, within the confines of the provisions of the Treuhand Act, of restructuring companies previously owned by the state to make them competitive and to privatise them." The institute was thus not given the status of an ultimate holding company with long-lasting tasks, rights, and duties, a fact that has led to widespread criticism. However, the decision was right if only because a conglomerate holding company embracing some 8,000 subsidiaries would have been ungovernable from the start. The decision to set up the Treuhand as an intermediate owner meant to transfer companies and other formerly state-owned assets under its administration into private hands – and thus into private responsibility (or, in some cases, to the relevant local authority) – was the only possible route to take. Integration into the market economy would otherwise have been doomed to failure from the outset.

The reorganisation and restructuring of Treuhand companies added considerably to their numbers. By the end of July 1993, the original number of 8,000 companies had risen to 13,100. By

1 However, see the book by Peter Dietrich Propp (of which economists have apparently taken little notice), *Zur Transformation einer Zentralverwaltungswirtschaft sowjetischen Typs in eine Marktwirtschaft*. Osteuropa-Institut an der Freien Universität Berlin, Wirtschaftswissenschaftliche Veröffentlichungen, edited by Karl C. Thalheim, 1964. Reprint Edition Deutschland Archiv. Cologne 1990, with a foreword by Gernot Gutmann. He points out that "most of the conclusions drawn at that time for a process of transformation of the GDR economy apply with equal force today. The writer's views appear extraordinarily up to date in 1990."

that time, the Treuhand had sold a total of 12,806 companies or parts of companies to new owners, or handed them back to their previous owners, thus realising sales proceeds amounting to DM 44.1 billion. On 1st July 1993 it still had 741 companies, employing a total of 204,427 people, on its books.[2] Further privatisations were carried out during the course of the summer, so that by the end of August the Treuhand was only holding 635 companies.[3] A solution should be found for nearly all the rest by the end of 1994. The overall results of the programme of privatisation and reprivatisation in less than three years are thus very remarkable, even on the basis of the criteria of the privatisation route taken. Even at this early stage, with the sale and reprivatisation of most of the old GDR companies just recently completed, it can be seen that gloomy forecasts of a privatisation flop which were still being made in the previous year were proved wrong. Even in privatising agricultural and forestry land, the Treuhand made faster progress than most people had expected (see: articles by *K.-D. Schmidt, H. Willgerodt, K. König*).

The particularly *German* way of transferring the communist GDR economy via the Treuhand into the free-market system was not the result of a plan but of political developments. This method spurred a broad level of interest but also wide-ranging criticism in Germany and abroad.[4] Some politicians predicted that the Treuhand would degenerate into a long-term state holding company, thereby blocking the road to a competition-driven market economy. The speed at which privatisation was conducted disproves this criticism to a great extent, but cannot neutralise it completely as long as it is unclear what the Treuhand will do with the companies still in its portfolio, and as long as influential political groups continue to demand greater involvement by the state.

Another body of criticism claims that rigorous decentralisation would be better for competition than the highly centralised privatisation programme of the Treuhand and its branches. This could hold true for companies in the service sector and also for small and medium-sized companies in the manufacturing industry. However, in these areas as in others the Treuhand has pursued a generally decentralised route by transferring operational business to its branches. With the large formerly state-owned corporations, indeed, there would have been little point in considering any other route than a centrally operated privatisation programme, and this was exactly the route taken by the other ex-communist countries of Central and Eastern Europe. It would also have been difficult to apply a general solution such as the broad distribution of share ownership to the population. This method of privatising by using, for example, vouchers, is often praised as the ideal way to achieve a broad scale distribution of the ownership of formerly state-owned assets. It is seen by some as a method which is superior to the Treuhand approach, especially for medium-sized and extremely large corporations. The voucher system, however, does not address the problems of how to make resolute decision-makers out of the new owner-

---

2 This includes the companies in the so-called "Management-KG" scheme. See: *Treuhandanstalt Informationen* 19 (July/August 1993), page 8. The actual total number of companies was still 1,668, but various different kinds of solutions seemed to have been found for 927 of them.

3 The total stock of companies at the end of August 1993 was 1,392 according to the Documentation and Data Management Department of the Treuhand. The number of companies sold and of those still on offer changes constantly because they are continually being split up or merged together, and occasionally because companies already sold had to be taken back; another cause is the "tidying up" of the data bank, so it is not possible simply to subtract the number sold from the number previously in stock. Solutions were already in sight for 757 companies.

4 See: Rüdiger Liedtke (editor), *Die Treuhandanstalt und die zweite Enteignung der Ostdeutschen*. Berlin 1993.

managers, or how to recruit efficient management or raise equity capital. These are exactly the three bottle-neck problems which a company must solve if it is to secure and defend its position successfully against competitors.

Compared to western German companies – enterprises which have developed out of extensive exposure to tough international competition – the industrial companies taken over by the Treuhand were almost without exception in a wretched condition (see: article by *J. Schwalbach*). Their production facilities were outdated, their products were not competitive, their working operations inefficient. Far too many people were employed in each company, and the level of qualification and motivation of the employees was not always up to the level of the western competition. The need for restructuring the communist legacy financially and operationally proved to be enormous.

The maintenance of these outdated companies, with their hardly modernised product ranges, and the creation of new successful companies were made all the more difficult by the collective agreement to raise eastern German wages to western German levels by 1995. This set off a "wages shock"; most companies simply could not afford the hike. Neither side in the collective bargaining between unions and employers' associations paid any heed to the insistent urgings of the Council of Economic Advisors to set wages in some relation to the various levels of efficiency in eastern German companies.[5] This led to production costs per-unit which were far above the western German level (and western German production costs are quite high in international comparison). In those cases in which the sale value of companies had not already been reduced almost to zero by products which simply could not be marketed, these excessive costs cancelled out the value of the capital stock in one blow and led to correspondingly low sale prices from privatisation.

Eastern Germany does not offer an attractive palate of factors which give it a significant comparative advantage as an industrial location over its domestic and international competitors. Not until great progress has been made in the improvement of infrastructure in the next few years will the east catch up with competing locations in the west. The quality of labour as an economic factor is no higher than in the competing western companies; nor are there any natural resources of any relevance which make the east more attractive as an industrial location. The negative side of the balance of factors affecting location is represented by considerable environmental pollution. In the competition with other industrial locations to attract capital and highly qualified labour, the prices of the geographically defined factors of production are of crucial importance, especially wages paid to the local labour. Wages which are too high in proportion to productivity repel the capital looking for investment. The effect of this on privatisation is seen in correspondingly low sale prices, and on newly formed companies in their lower levels of investment. So, once again, the state has to come rushing to the companies' aid in order to put right a mistake made in wage negotiations, and has to accept privatisation sales in some cases with no payment of any purchase price at all. It must also pay off the hefty debts of some Treuhand companies and assist investment by paying larger subsidies.

In line with its statutory task, the Treuhand decided to give priority to a strategy of *restructuring through privatisation*. This approach is based on the view that as a general rule the final,

5 See: Sachverständigenrat zur Begutachtung der gesamtwirtschaftlichen Entwicklung (i. e. the Council of Economic Advisors), *Auf dem Weg zur wirtschaftlichen Einheit Deutschlands. Jahresgutachten 1990/91.* Stuttgart 1990, Note Points 404 et seq., and in particular Point 410.

new owner, and not the Treuhand as the intermediate owner, should be best able to conceive and implement an effective restructuring strategy. It would most probably turn out to be a misplaced investment if the Treuhand were to invest funds in a restructuring programme which the later owner would have tackled quite differently. The more progress the process of privatisation made, the clearer it became that virtually no more purchasers could be found for the remaining companies still in need of restructuring, and thus the companies concerned, their employees, the trade unions, the state governments and local communities started demanding more and more urgently to be allowed to take restructuring into their own hands in order to give the companies a chance of surviving and, if at all possible, of being privatised.

It is not always clear in this context what "restructuring" should be taken to mean. It is definitely not enough to forgive the company its debts or facilitate the technical modernisation of its equipment. As shown in more detail in the article by *J. Schwalbach*, restructuring covers measures to improve a company's output and productivity as well as its financial structure; it also encompasses other measures in the legal and organisational fields. Restructuring to improve productivity is of the greatest significance to the Treuhand: this requires an entrepreneurial concept which provides the prospect of the company holding its own in the market in future, only after this concept has been defined loan and equity capital can be obtained to finance the necessary investments and create all in all a durable financial basis.

The basic decision to look for a route to restructuring primarily via privatisation was based on the view that it was not going to be possible to initiate the restructuring of thousands of companies effectively by means of a bureaucratic organisation such as the Treuhandanstalt. Privatisation mobilises entrepreneurial potential and guarantees at the same time that all investments will be strictly oriented to the goal of market success and thus of profitability. In the case of restructuring initiated while the company is still in the THA's hands, there is hardly any way of preventing political aspects from influencing the decision. This leads to decisions about whether or not a company is worth to be restructured sometimes being based on political rather than purely economic criteria. The upshot is that some investments are made on the pretext of restructuring when in fact they are just meant to keep the company in existence, even if there are no well-founded prospects of its ever returning to profitability. Such companies remain permanently dependent on subsidies.

The Treuhand has helped many of its companies to modernise and upgrade their plants by granting bank guarantees or even direct loans. Exactly how much money the Treuhand poured into this so-called "initial restructuring", and how much went merely to cover losses is very hard to establish. The total identified by the Treuhand for restructuring in 1992 – almost DM 11 billion – is probably far above the mark in any case (see: article by *J. Schwalbach*). Restructuring programmes are sure to be unavoidable to a limited extent if one wants to remove the most obvious barriers to improving productivity and to prevent stoppage of operations, at least in those companies which appear to be worth to be restructured. However, this is not the whole point at the moment. In regions where there is a concentration of unsold production locations producing at a loss, the people affected and politicians of all parties are demanding that the Treuhand change its policy: they say the institute ought to take an active part in making the core businesses in the region viable again by means of a top-to-bottom restructuring programme, thus retaining the old economic basis.

Demands have been raised with increasing energy over the last years for a new, active industrial policy which involves the Treuhand and its companies. These demands include the new regional policy in eastern Germany but also have more general implications; it is intended to counteract the de-industrialisation of eastern Germany by initiating not only the broad scale restructuring of industrial companies which *deserve* to be preserved, even if from the businessman's point of view they are not *capable* of being preserved, but also the development of entirely new industries. The idea being paraded for this new policy is that the purely business point of view, because it is too short-term, should give way to a macro-economic approach.[6] This discussion has not yet produced any convincing criteria to show what aspects might be wrong for business but right for the economy. The plea for the preservation of industrial cores is obviously based on political value-judgements. The politicisation of these decisions holds considerable economic dangers. If the criteria for restructuring old companies and establishing new ones are defined not by the stringent demands of competition but through political bargaining, then restructuring will be condemned to failure from the start; and the results will be either a costly reversal of policy down the road, or the dogged embrace of a new policy of bottomless subsidies.

The search for a new way to restructure old industrial regions will continue to be the greatest and the most difficult task in rebuilding the economic basis of eastern Germany. No paradigms can yet be discerned from the attempts made so far for a new regional policy which could be described already as having a chance of success. The question remains open as to the extent to which a new version of the experiments successfully conducted in other countries in building up new regional economic bases "from the bottom up" could provide the key to the "new role of the state" (see: *H. Kern/Ch. F. Sabel*).

This volume is divided into three sections:

The *first section* covers the initial development of the Treuhandanstalt during the final days of the GDR: the overall framework of state and private law to which it was subject as defined by laws, treaties, and the transfer of the West German legal system to the east; its organisational and personnel construction; and the political environment in which it had to operate.

The Treuhand was the brainchild of the collapsing GDR. Its original structure was concocted by the last communist government under Modrow, but even its present-day form was shaped by a law passed by the *Volkskammer*, the East German parliament, and not by the *Bundestag* in Bonn. Its status was confirmed by the Treaty of Unification. It would be superfluous to ask now whether the Treuhand was the best of all imaginable solutions. As with the rushed currency reform and indeed unification itself, great haste was necessary, not only to make the best use of a favourable moment but also to create structures and institutions to facilitate an orderly transfer to a parliamentary system of government and a free market economy before the imminent collapse of the entire communist state and economic system finally happened. There are many who consider that such a period of chaos should have produced more creative solutions. Be that as it may, these times might have also turned into a "might is right" era, setting off a fight of every man for himself. The Treaty of Unification, the monetary, economic, and social union, and indeed the Treuhand itself all made a controlled, legal, and bloodless transformation possible.

One pre-requisite for the transformation was the rapid passing of numerous laws and ordinances, some of which had to be supplemented or changed very quickly (see: article by

6 One example is the Darmstädter Thesen from IG Metall (the trade union for the metal-working industry), *Zur solidarischen Finanzierung und sozialen Gestaltung der deutschen Einheit,* dated 10th October 1991, Thesis 8.

M. Kloepfer). It is here not possible to give the ministries, legal advisors, and parliamentarians their due for this achievement, but only to outline the results where they are relevant to the work of the Treuhand. A host of problems arose under civil law, as *H. P. Westermann* explains in his article. The GDR hardly possessed even the vestiges of civil law on property, companies, or trade which had developed during the time of the German Empire and had continued to develop in West Germany. Its "usufruct rights", reminiscent of the feudal age, and often defined only very vaguely, could not be simply transferred into the legal structure valid for all of Germany as of 3rd October 1990. Legal uncertainty arose, however, not only from doubts over categorisation but, far more, from a totally different system of courts of law in which there was no administrative or labour court, and from a dearth of lawyers adequately qualified to work in a state governed by the rule of law. The adaptation of real-life conditions to fit the legal standards taking effect during the transitional phase led to great doubts and uncertainties in legal questions. It was in this environment that the Treuhand had to quickly and efficiently make decisions which were often of great significance, but which had to be legally watertight.

The huge number of tasks to be tackled called for an organisation of a size and nature for which there was no precedent. The construction of an institute under public law which ought never to have been set up in the GDR, because there was no room in that country's legal system for any such institution, and which at the same time had to carry out business-like tasks of Herculean dimensions for which an institution existing under public law definitely does not create the best conditions, will some day be described as an incredible and unique example of improvisation – a successful one, let us hope – in which a wealth of imagination and flexibility, a willingness to make decisions, and indeed courage, were called for such as is seldom encountered under normal circumstances.

Obviously, structures arose in the process that were not the best possible ones, and the search was directed more towards finding people for specific jobs than towards setting up the right legal and regulative framework. Recruiting staff, rapidly developing an *esprit de corps* within the institute, and the astonishingly rapid construction of a formal organisation with clearly defined lines of responsibility and procedures, form the subject dealt with by *W. Seibel* in this volume.

The analysis by *R. Czada* shows how this new institution found its way through and came to grips with an environment of complex and varied interests. The Treuhand is simultaneously a public institute and a commercial company reporting to the ministry of finance of a federal government. But it is also a major player in the newly forming eastern German states, an environment in which employers' associations and trade unions demand a major hand in all decisions, in which millions of people want to keep their jobs, in which there was a shortage of thousands of managers and lawyers, and where billions needed to be invested. Therefore the Treuhand had to make compromises and build up relations with many different interest groups; in this manner it rapidly became a key institution in the political network of the Federal Republic in which decisions were hammered out daily between many different protagonists.

The *second section* of this volume is devoted to the main activities of the Treuhand: restructuring, privatisation, reprivatisation (or restitution), communalisation (handing assets over to the local authorities), and the winding up of companies not capable of being restructured.

Restructuring and privatisation are closely linked to one another. Privatisation is regarded as the most promising route to restructuring; however, if a company is not immediately in line for privatisation, the door to restructuring must at least be kept open. Problems involved in the notion of giving restructuring priority over privatisation efforts stem from the fact that much time is needed for privatisation, so a decision has to be made in each individual instance as to whether a company can be restructured effectively and eventually privatised. One must ask whether it is worthwhile to invest funds to keep that company in existence for the time being or even to finance the first steps of restructuring before the company is privatised. The article by *J. Schwalbach* shows how the Treuhand operates in such cases. The central points are the examination of the company's suitability for restructuring, the categorisation upon which this is based, and the management of the restructuring process. The basic difficulty which becomes apparent here again is in fact that decisions relating to restructuring which have to be made before privatisation have to be kept free of political influences and considerations, and the danger has to be obviated of allowing restructuring efforts to deteriorate into a policy of eternal subsidies for companies incapable of surviving on their own.

The *Treuhandgesetz* (Treuhand Act, or Public Trustee Act) made the institute responsible for privatisation without tying it down to any specific method of operation. The article by *K.-D. Schmidt* illustrates the privatisation strategies developed by the institute and discusses them critically. The Treuhand's methods have often been judged sceptically, the main point of criticism being that it does not utilise to any great extent auctions or activities similar to auctions. However, it should be borne in mind that an auction is only possible when the sole point remaining to be settled is the price, and that privatisation, on the other hand, requires investors to submit complex business strategies for restructuring the company. These strategies can vary from one potential buyer to another, so the Treuhand has to arrive at a solution by negotiating with serious potential buyers. This is particularly important because the Treuhand is not only interested in achieving the highest possible price, but also, and to a very great extent, it wants to ensure that jobs are preserved and investments made.

Privatisation can take the form of reprivatisation or restitution, meaning that property is returned to its previous owner. The principle underlying this activity – that the restitution of property to its rightful owner should have priority over their being paid compensation – is very controversial. Many say this rule creates an unclear situation which seriously inhibits other investors. In fact, the principle of "restitution before compensation" is actually only applied with considerable limitations. Property confiscated between 1945 and 1949 is excluded, and the Treuhand has been given the opportunity, through a number of statutory regulations, to grant restitution claims a lower priority if they get in the way of the investment plans of other potential owners. On the other hand, reprivatisation offers an opportunity to activate the entrepreneurial potential of the former owners and to promote the development of an efficient commercial class of small and medium-sized businesses in eastern Germany. *H. Willgerodt* submits the reprivatisation work of the Treuhand to a critical analysis in his article, and concludes that reprivatisation has generally been seen as a necessary evil; restitution to the previous owners has been hindered in many different ways, and difficulties have prevented the restructuring of reprivatised companies. The main cause of this is statutory regulations; these have had a significant effect on the work of the Treuhand.

The assets held by the Treuhand include a large number of properties which are needed immediately by the various organs of public administration – especially local governments – in order for them to operate properly. In addition to this, there are claims by public offices for the restitution of assets which have been confiscated without compensation. These problem areas are covered in the article by *K. König*. This field is bedevilled by problems such as the definition of public responsibility as it pertains to administrative tasks and financial property. *König*'s conclusion is that the Treuhand has not devised innovative solutions to the questions of demarcation between the public and the private sectors, however he also raises some doubts as to whether it would have been within the Treuhand's power to depart from conventional divisions of responsibility.

The only option available to the Treuhand in the cases where companies cannot be effectively restructured and thus cannot be privatised is to wind them up. Treuhand organisation and working methods in this area are described in *E. Wandel*'s article. It is in the winding up of companies that the destructive side of the economic revolution becomes the most apparent, but a closer examination reveals that the Treuhand demonstrates not just destructive but also highly constructive characteristics. Winding up also means that the resources that had previously been put to unprofitable use are made available for other purposes. The Treuhand has frequently succeeded in hiving off parts of companies and selling them as complete units; land and buildings that can hence be used for other commercial purposes. In this manner the Treuhand has succeeded in preserving a considerable proportion of the jobs which existed when the liquidation process started.

The Treuhand's privatisation strategy has led to very unique and specific types of contract formulation, and *H.-U. Küpper*'s article is devoted to this subject and to contract management. Typical clauses in Treuhand contracts relate to jobs, investment, collateral to be provided by the purchaser, and the particulars of dividing responsibilities and risks – such as environmental clean-up – between the Treuhand and the purchaser. This kind of contract formulation makes contract management a necessary activity which will continue for many years even after privatisation has run its course. The adherence to all contracts will need to be monitored, and in many cases it will be necessary to take up negotiations again to revise the contracts to suit changed circumstances.

The *third section* deals with the outward effects of the Treuhand's work, to the extent that they can already be identified today. The article by *G. Hedtkamp/H. Clement* goes beyond this question and analyses the delay and hesitancy with which the Treuhand as well as the federal government have reacted to the economic consequences of the collapse of Eastern Europe. It was very late in the game before the management levels in the THA and in the Treuhand companies realised that the old, centrally-planned sales channels in the communist system had become worthless under the new circumstances. It was illusory to hope that trade with Central and Eastern European countries could be revived merely by overcoming a few financial bottlenecks and temporary adjustment difficulties; what was needed was a top-to-bottom reorientation of sales, production, and purchasing in the formerly communist countries. The necessary redirection of export efforts did not take place in the Treuhand companies until much too late, or at least much later than in the Central and Eastern European countries. This showed once again that an economic policy meant to ease the pressure of immediate and direct competition and thereby provide more time for adaptation only hinders adaptation in the long run.

The article by *J. Müller* pursues the structural effects of Treuhand privatisations. Starting with the GDR company structures as they existed in 1989 and the predominance of the main sectors, he examines sectoral adaptation and takes a macro-economic look at the changing of company structures within each industry. Treuhand privatisations are approached differently and have different effects in various sectors; particular emphasis is placed on the rejuvenation of small and medium-sized companies, although the author judges their chances of success in the market for industrial products somewhat sceptically. The decision to restructure or, in some cases, close down some of the larger corporations in the "core industries" should not, in the writer's opinion, be based solely on business management criteria, but should also take into account the opportunity costs for the economy as a whole. *Müller* calls not only for the most rapid possible restructuring of the remaining core industries, but also for further support in the form of job creation schemes for a transitional period. He ends by assessing the restructuring policy of the Treuhand, and comes to the conclusion that it was all in all quite successful.

In this publication we had originally planned to examine the regional effects of the Treuhand's work using specific examples; this idea had to be abandoned because of lack of reliable statistics. Instead, *P. Klemmer* examines on a regional basis the Treuhand's success in its privatisation programme under the heading of "Regional aspects of the THA's privatisation work". His criterion is the degree of successful privatisation as a percentage of the privatised companies and jobs. Almost 10 % of the Treuhand's privatisation success can be explained by the regional factors included in the analysis. The sequence into which the individual regions are arranged – by the (positive) difference between effective value and the value that could be expected from privatisation on the basis of statistics – is consistent and provides a catalyst for a more detailed analysis.

The most difficult challenges facing the Treuhand are those companies in its portfolio for which no buyer could be found to date, but which cannot be closed down because the economies of entire regions are based on them. *H. Kern* and *Ch. F. Sabel*, in their article, "The Treuhandanstalt – a trials ground for developing new company forms" examine three totally different approaches to a solution on the basis of three projects: ATLAS, EKO, and Management-KG's. The attempt to solve the problem of too much state involvement by means of an approach combining more market expertise with more political supervision cannot yet be assessed; it is still too early. The authors see the difficulties of privatisation through restructuring very clearly: in these co-operative approaches to restructuring, each of the parties actively involved is motivated to make the "best business deal for here and now" (on the assumption that any deal could be the last one). In this manner companies and institutions learn a great deal about the negotiation processes but not necessarily enough about taking business-minded action, which is exactly what is needed.

"The public image of the THA" is examined in *H. M. Kepplinger*'s article. The press reaction to the Treuhand's work is analysed qualitatively and in detail on the basis of three case histories, one each on liquidation, restructuring, and privatisation (the companies being Robotron, Orwo, and Freital respectively). The remarkable points here are, firstly, the great differences between the pictures painted by the eastern and the western German press, and secondly, the systematic distortion in reporting, as already mentioned above. The quantitative analyses deal with topics and trends in press reporting. Publications specialising heavily in business, sometimes as authorities in this field, not only take up quite different main subjects from those in other newspapers; they tend overall to make a more favourable assessment of the Treuhand.

The effects on the labour market and the "Regulation of the social effects of the THA's work by labour law" are the subject of the article by *P. Hanau*. More than half of the four million people originally employed in Treuhand companies had to be dismissed by early 1993; this was quite inevitable in light of the high level of over-employment in these companies. The route chosen by the Treuhand for arranging the details of the job reductions, however, is not accepted as the best possible one by *P. Hanau*. The author goes into detail on the complexity and diversity of the labour-law regulations applicable to the sale of companies, to mass redundancies and "social plans" (which cover mainly compensation, but also redeployment and outplacement in cases of mass redundancy). His particular attention is devoted to the Treuhand's involvement in job creation schemes and works agreements, and to regulations based on collective agreements. He ends by drawing up a "net outcome" under social law and in social terms.

This volume contains 17 articles on various subjects, which are augmented and rounded off by a statistical appendix drawn up by *U. Maurer* and *W. Glöckler*. The statistical tables provide comprehensive information on the effects of the profound economic and structural change, the trends in income from wages, and the economic situation of a cross section of private households in eastern Germany. Further tables report in detail on the success of the privatisation programme (the number of companies privatised, the proceeds from their sales, undertakings to preserve or create jobs and to invest), and on the Treuhand's company portfolio as of 30th June 1993. The Statistical Office of the Federal Republic has rapidly constructed a national accounting system for eastern Germany as well as a wide range of other detailed figures; this represents a commendable achievement. Admittedly, it is perhaps not possible to offer a complete statistical report of all aspects of an economy in the process of transition and re-creation, but we do know that the investments triggered off by privatisation are only the beginning. Ultimate success or failure will depend on the comparative economic conditions which determine the crucial flow of follow-up investments, and on the range of new jobs that will develop as a result of this process.

This volume is a first interim report on the great experiment called "Treuhandanstalt". Sales successes, measured on the criteria of the number of privatised companies and the contractual undertakings of the purchases to preserve jobs and undertake investments, are still no evidence that success will prove durable. Privatisation *per se* is obviously no guarantee that the companies, once in the market, will flourish; but such a guarantee of success does not exist anywhere. Time will tell how the new (or the previous rightful) owners handle the companies acquired from the Treuhand and how successful they will be.

Mistakes, failures, and even criminal activities relating to the Treuhand's work have drawn considerable attention from the general public. However, its work must not be measured solely, or even largely, from such events. The task with which the Treuhand has been entrusted is more difficult than anyone could have imagined. It is incredibly more complicated than the restructuring of a company which has grown up in an environment of competition. Western companies, with their institutional knowledge of markets and production, their reserves of fixed and human capital, and their footholds in the market stand an infinitely better chance of being restructured effectively from the outset. The task of transferring an ex-communist economy into the market economy, moreover, was entrusted to an institution which had to be created from scratch in just a few months. How, one may ask, could anyone have avoided the mistakes and failures suffered by such a gigantic but overtaxed organisation? Or prevented criminal elements from exploiting the chaos inherent in innovation?

The Treuhand intends to complete its core task – the privatisation of the companies and other productive assets entrusted to it – by the end of 1994. Once the core task has been completed, totally new ones will become necessary which will have to be implemented by the end of 1994 at the latest, as that is the date when the legal basis for the financing of the Treuhand is set to expire. At the same time this will bring to an end a development which has been marked by the continual decline of the Treuhand's significance in economic policy for the new eastern German states, and by the transition to normality in the division of responsibility between the states and the federal government of Germany. In the interests of the greatest possible efficiency and flexibility, solutions will be sought on the basis of private law. For the work still to be done, the Treuhand's organisation has to be changed. The decision as to precisely what form this organisation is to take and exactly what its responsibilities will be, however, rests not with the executive bodies of the Treuhand, but with the federal government of Germany.

Once the core task has been completed, there will be three major responsibilities remaining:

a) the administration and sale of plots of land for commercial, residential, and other purposes. Unlike the privatisation of companies, this is a long-term task, affecting not only the land owned by the Treuhand directly but also those plots which were initially part of Treuhand companies but which were carved off either prior to privatisation or as part of the liquidation process to be sold off separately;
b) the administration and sale of agricultural and forestry land, for some of which sale procedures are already planned but which are not expected to be completed for a number of decades;
c) contract management, i. e. monitoring and supervising concluded contracts for the sale of companies and parts of companies and for the sale of land. In addition to checking the punctual receipt of payments and examining claims for government-assisted financing of the removal of environmental contamination, this principally means making sure that commitments to preserve and create jobs and make investments are being adhered to.

In addition to the above, a number of other tasks will not yet have been completed by the end of 1994. These in particular include the sovereign tasks of the Treuhand, such as dealing with the remaining assets of the communist and other satellite parties and so-called "mass organisations" of the former GDR, marketing Treuhand experience and know-how to Central and Eastern Europe, and regulating the financing of Treuhand losses. A certain volume of supervisory tasks will probably remain involving those companies which are not yet privatised but which are capable of being restructured, including particularly the supervision of "Management-KG" companies, companies in liquidation, and, depending on the outcome of certain decisions still pending, a few major conglomerates capable of being restructured but which for special reasons are not privatised by the end of 1994.

The authors and the editors owe their thanks to a large number of people inside and outside the Treuhand who made themselves available for interviews, assisted in the search for information or verification, or helped to correct mistakes. A special debt of gratitude is owed to Dr Hartmut Maaßen, who was responsible within the Treuhand for supervising the production of these articles, to Ms Jutta Wietog MA, head of the clearing office set up by the Treuhand to facilitate the flow of information from the operational staff to the researchers, and to her various assistants. These people also shouldered responsibility for the editorial design of this publication under a very tight timetable. The authors and editors of course accept the blame for any errors which may remain uncorrected despite these efforts.

Part A

The history, legal framework, and organisational structure of the Treuhandanstalt (THA)

The origins of the Treuhandanstalt

by Wolfram Fischer and Harm Schröter

I. Introduction[1]

The *Treuhandanstalt* (also called the Treuhand or THA), came into being in the dying days of the German Democratic Republic (GDR). Founded in its original form by the last communist government under Hans Modrow, it was given its present form by a legislative act of the first freely elected *Volkskammer*, the GDR Parliament, while the government under Lothar de Maizière was in power. Its fathers and midwives attributed various different tasks to it. Some of them saw it as a means towards a "better socialism", a system without a central planning authority and with clear elements of a free market economy, but retaining the basic socialist principle of state ownership of the means of production in all central aspects of the economy. Others wanted to use it to create a "social and ecological market economy" in which, likewise, important areas were to remain in state ownership but with the majority of the companies handed over to the eastern German population with the aid of share certificates, or vouchers. They were looking for a "third route" between socialism and capitalism. However, in the summer of 1990, under the pressure of events, the clearest alternative to the present system became evident, namely, one headed towards the conversion of a planned economy into a market economy with the highest possible level of private ownership. The Treuhand was to be the most important vehicle for this route. It was therefore given a mandate completely opposite of the mission entrusted to the *Deutsche Treuhand Verwaltung*, the German Trustee Administration created during the early years of the GDR to promote the conversion *into* a socialist economy. The Treuhand thus became an important connecting link between the vanishing GDR and the Federal Republic of Germany. Its history embodies, as if under a magnifying glass, both the economic and political collapse of the GDR and the difficulties of the transition into the economic and social system of West Germany. The Treuhand can thus rightly be described as one of the "most sensitive subjects in German post-war history".[2]

The Honecker government had reduced the GDR to ruin in economic and in other terms. The Treuhand, with whose aid the Modrow government intended to avert imminent bankruptcy, became as events developed an instrument for winding up companies in hopeless situations. The fact that the institute was originally designed to actually create a new, competitive socialism can be regarded as one of history's frequent involuntary ironies. The aim of the following article is to trace the creation of the Treuhand, to clarify the intentions and the influence of the various players who came and went, and thus at the same time to contribute to the understanding of events surrounding the emergence of a united Germany.

---

1 The authors wish to thank all those who contributed to this article with interviews, material, pointers, and constructive criticism.

2 Luft, *Treuhandreport*, page 11.

II. The roots of the Treuhand: The first route and the search for a third

Soon after the first preliminary considerations cropped up on the subject of a Treuhand-type agency, basic political positions began to take shape which culminated in the Treuhand Act of 17th June 1990. Apart from the proposals which came from West Germany, two major hypotheses considered at that time are clearly distinguishable; one belonged to the citizens' movement, and the other to the GDR government.

1. The citizens' movement and the SPD

The idea for setting up a trustee agency to administer state assets is generally attributed to Wolfgang Ullmann, the representative of the *Demokratie Jetzt* (Democracy Now) movement at the Round Table (a non-partisan parliamentary body which advised the GDR government during the months preceding unification). However, when Ullmann raised the proposal for discussion by the Round Table on 12th February 1990, he was only acting as the spokesman for the citizens' movement, a small faction of which for some time had been discussing the eminent economic and social collapse of the GDR.

This group of people, originally consisting of the engineer Matthias Artzt, the physicist Gerd Gebhardt, and the theologian Ullmann, had been meeting occasionally since mid-1989 to discuss questions of social policy.[3] They were unanimous in their rejection of the existing form of socialism, in their conviction that the social system of the GDR was at the end of its tether, and in their prognosis that the powers in charge of the state had no idea how to remedy the situation. Working from the basis of their scientific work in chaos research, Artzt and Gebhardt took the view that a chaotic phase of political disorientation was immediately imminent in which it would be possible to effect great changes with relatively modest resources. On the strength of this belief and their other shared convictions, the group stood ready to act as a kind of nucleus from which a new social policy could grow and take shape.

The group attracted other members, and on 11th November 1989, two days after the GDR border was opened, they were able to finalise a paper entitled "The Future through Self-Organisation" which presented a liberal social-policy theses.[4] Although cautious and academic in style, the paper argued in favour of the concepts of private property and a free-market system with social obligations. Their second strategic aim was to enable the citizens of the GDR to take over as much of the existing state property as possible. The group was well aware of the ramifications of their demands, but still wanted to "wrench the decision-making power from the state"[5] with

3 B-interview (for A-interviews and B-interviews see page XVI) with Dr Artzt, Dr Gebhardt, and Günter Nooke on 30th October 1992 and 2nd April 1993, and Stefan Kapferer's interview with Günter Nooke on 28th August 1992.

4 Artzt, Gebhardt, Lehmann, Schönfelder, and Wolf, *Zukunft durch Selbstorganisation.*

5 Dr Artzt in a B-interview on 30th October 1992.

the aid of private property. Both sides, the citizens' movement and the GDR regime, took such ideas perfectly seriously.[6]

The group established itself on 6th December 1989 as the "Free Research Community for Self-Organisation" in order to lay the basis for longer-term work as political consultants. This foundation should be seen in conjunction with the creation of the Round Table, which met for the first time on the very next day. The Free Research Community for Self-Organisation sent Ullmann as its representative. The other members were to represent an organisational body of consultants both for Ullmann and for the citizens' movement in general. In pursuing its goals, the Research Community also looked for advice abroad.[7] The idea soon emerged that the GDR would be needing a kind of "administrator of the estate" after its demise. In the first half of February 1990, the Research Community prepared a detailed proposal for the foundation of a trustee institute which was to take over the entire GDR state property and divide it into four shares. One quarter was to be privatised by distributing vouchers to the population at large, about 10 % was intended for an "institute for all non-commercial fields, such as the arts", and the third and fourth shares, as of yet undefined, were to be transferred into the state's possession to be used for the improvement of basic ecological and infrastructural conditions of human existence as well as for solving economic problems such as settling debts and claims for restitution.[8] Once the paper had been prepared, Ullmann presented it on 12th February to the Round Table, where it was received positively. The media also devoted considerable attention to the proposal.[9]

The Free Research Community for Self-Organisation, which produced the pioneer thinking on which "Democracy Now" was based, openly attacked the fundamental concept of socialism and thus the whole existence of the GDR, bringing not only the economic but also the social transition to a market economy onto the agenda. Their proposal that a trustee institute should be founded grew out of the wish to create an instrument which could completely transform the fundamental organisation of the East German economy.

None of the opposition groups in the Round Table had anything like this head-start in the matters of economic reform. The entire economic thinking in East Germany had after all been concentrated for many years on the SED (the "Socialist Unity Party of Germany", which, until the Wall fell, dominated the central government of the GDR). There was a total absence of economic experts and knowledge in the opposition groups, and their ideas on economic policy were correspondingly vague. The *Demokratischer Aufbruch* (Democratic Renewal) party demanded "the privatisation of the majority of existing state companies". Unlike the citizens' movement, the SPD (the Social Democratic Party, a new party in the GDR modelled after the West German SPD) stuck firmly to the idea of a *partial* socialisation of property, particularly of land, to an

---

6 The "strictly secret" information provided by the Ministry for State Security (the "*Stasi*") on 2nd October 1989 to the state leadership (Honecker, Stoph, etc.), pointed in the first of a number of points to such endeavours: MfS, ZAIG No. 434/89, Document no. 32, printed by Mitter and Wolle (editors), *Ich liebe euch doch alle!*, page 184.

7 Among those consulted were representatives of the Financial Times, the Matuschka (management consultancy) Group, the Japanese trading house Marubeni, and the World Lutheran League.

8 Claims for restitution were defined as also including claims for compensation of all kinds.

9 See: press reports and the programme on East German television featuring Artzt and Gebhardt on 20th February 1990.

even greater extent than the Modrow government did.[10] A similar position was taken up by the New Forum and, before the end of December 1989, by the Round Table's Working Group on Economic Issues.[11]

2. The GDR government

The establishment of the Original-Treuhand, however, was the work of the Modrow government. The institute represented the end of a process of erosion in social policy during the course of which, as a result of political and economic pressure, the socialists' "commanding heights of the economy" (Lenin) had to be cleared away one after another. In the end it was the socialist government itself that called in the undertaker to bury socialism, the experiment of the century, as painlessly as possible.

The GDR leadership had been aware of the growing economic difficulties for years. Calculations on the balance of payments made already in 1988 showed that the GDR needed to reschedule its debt payments within four or five years at the latest.[12] In view of political developments in the other socialist states, however, there was almost a complete total taboo on any public discussion of this point. Nevertheless, in party circles, at East Berlin's Humboldt University, and elsewhere, discussions on economic reform had taken place. The Rector of the *Hochschule für Ökonomie,* Professor Christa Luft, touched on questions of economic reform in her inaugural address in October 1988. Admittedly, the concentration was still on improving the efficiency of the centrally planned economy. Luft said that, at a time "when the historical process of radical political, economic, intellectual and cultural change" was making its mark, she wanted to make socialism more efficient and flexible by exploiting the "advantages in time innovative processes of structural change", revealing "the potential driving force of socialist ownership", gaining "the stimuli to innovation which are typical of socialism", and making better use of "the potential for productivity and efficiency inherent in the international division of labour". All the same, the speech contains the demand for an "uncompromising recognition and implementation of international criteria", meaning that the "strategies and mechanisms for mastering scientific-technical progress" which were used in the "advanced capitalist industrial countries" were to be "carefully studied". There was no mention of reforming the entire economic system.[13]

As soon as Honecker had been replaced by Egon Krenz as Chairman of the Council of State (the East German cabinet), the economic disaster was publicly debated. On 31st October 1989,

10 See: Bogisch and Pawliczak (editors), *Denkmodelle zur künftigen Wirtschafts-, Umwelt- und Sozialpolitik; Wirtschaftliches Programm der Sozialdemokratischen Partei Deutschlands,* page 8 et seq., undated, but prior to 1st March 1990; one copy of each was given to the authors by Frank Bogisch.

11 For *Demokratischer Aufbruch* see: Fred Ebeling in "*Neues Deutschland*" (the East German party newspaper) of 21st February 1990. For the SPD see: *Wirtschaftspolitische Grundsätze der SPD*, page 2 et seq. At the same time the SPD proposed equal treatment for all forms of ownership: Gutmann and Klein, *Skizzen zu Reformen des Wirtschaftssystems in der DDR*, page 37. The Neues Forum wanted communal ownership of all companies employing more than 300 people; see: Neues Forum (editor), *Wirtschaftsreform der DDR; Erklärung der Arbeitsgruppe Wirtschaft des Runden Tisches*, page 10.

12 B-interview with Dr Grabley, former Secretary of State in the Ministry of Foreign Trade, on 1st April 1993.

13 Luft, Antrittsrede, pages 12 to 17.

the Politburo of the Central Committee of the SED even received an analysis which Krenz had commissioned. It was in an impenetrably complicated form and was labelled "Top Secret", but it did address the imminent economic collapse of the GDR: "Even if all of these measures are carried out with great urgency and quality, the ... [prospect of an] export surplus with the NSE[14] presented here and necessary for the GDR's solvency is not discernible. In 1985 it would still have been possible if great efforts had been exerted. This opportunity no longer exists today. Even calling a halt to public borrowing in 1990 would require a drop in living standards of 25 to 30 % and make the GDR ungovernable."[15]

The party newspaper *Neues Deutschland* carried the first lengthy article, on 3rd November 1989, on "Economic Reform; An Element in the Renewal of Socialism", written by Wolfgang Heinrichs and Wolfram Krause.[16] The article called for a "policy of total change" which should have its effect in the economic sphere, and insisted that "a functioning market mechanism [was] indispensable". The article stated we "should not be afraid ... to break new ground in the economic sphere", but what it really promoted was a market economy without the driving force of private ownership.

But even this aim went too far for Modrow. He preferred to search for a third route between a planned and a market economy, and assumed that the GDR would continue to exist for a number of years. His government declaration of 17th November 1989, which called for a "better kind of socialism", lagged behind the demands already being made for a functioning market mechanism.[17] It linked the achievement principle for necessary economic reform to an improvement in central planning, and took an overall optimistic stance: "But the economic substance of our socialist state is powerful and strong enough, to produce stabilisation within a foreseeable period of time". The discrepancy between this and the assessment in the "top secret" paper from the Politburo seems to indicate that Krenz had withheld this paper from Modrow.[18] However, Modrow had been informed of it in general terms from other sources. On 1st November 1989 he

14 Non-Socialist Economies.

15 Schürer, Beil, Schalck, and others, *Geheime Verschlußsache b5 1158/89*, page 1119; see also: Luft, *Treuhandreport*, page 17. Under the division of responsibilities at that time, the Chairman of the State Planning Commission, the Minister of Foreign Trade, and the Minister of Finance took a major hand in the preparation of the document, but not Krenz himself, however he was just as convinced as the others of the need for reforms: B-interview with Egon Krenz on 19th August 1993.

16 Wolfram Krause was Deputy Chairman of the State Planning Commission during the 1970's and also Party Secretary in this institution for a time. He drew the attention of the Bureau of the Central Committee in the middle of 1978 to the increasing contradictions in the GDR economy, and was then removed from the Planning Commission as being "no longer trustworthy" or acceptable for top party and economic functions. During the years that followed he worked in an inconspicuous position in the District Committee of the Berlin SED. Wolfgang Heinrichs was the Director of the Institute for Economic Sciences in the Academy of Sciences of the GDR.

17 In a B-interview on 26th January 1993, Dr Modrow emphasised that his government declaration was "genuine" and entirely in accordance with his own convictions.

18 Ms Luft, who was the member of Modrow's cabinet responsible for the economy, did not gain knowledge of it until three years later, and by accident at that. See: Luft, *Treuhandreport*, page 17. In a telephone B-interview on 5th March 1993 she stressed this lack of information once again. According to Krenz this was not due to inadequate coordination but a failure of the bureaucratic apparatus, see: B-interview with Egon Krenz on 19th August 1993.

had received a joint memorandum from the State Planning Commission, Minister of Foreign Trade Beil, and the representatives of the State Bank of the GDR and the Ministry of Finance, Mr Polze and Dr König, which declared that "in 1990 the top limit" for obtaining credit would be reached and, consequently, "(the state) will become insolvent in 1991".[19] Consequently, Modrow must have been aware that it was not possible to stabilise the economy without outside help, so his interpretation of the situation can only be regarded as self-serving optimism. The dangerously precarious financial situation of his government was explained to him both before and after his declaration.[20]

The realisation, however, that fundamental economic reforms were necessary formed one of the cornerstones of Modrow's government. He therefore handed responsibility for the economy to Christa Luft, who was known to be a reformer, and appointed her as his deputy. It was important for him that Ms Luft had not been integrated into the existing hierarchy of economic planning, but belonged to the Academy of Economics, which was where the discussion on an economic reform within the system had made the most progress. Ms Luft herself harboured misgivings as to the willingness of the dominant *cadres* (elitist groups of influential officials) of the official economic system to indulge in reform. For this reason she did not seek support from the Planning Commission, but rather on 8th/9th November created the "Working Group on Economic Reform in the Council of Ministers of the GDR" and appointed Wolfram Krause to chair it.[21] The government's lack of confidence in the ability of the State Planning Commission to reform itself was justified, but it was not immediately possible to dissolve this commission because of the concentration of information it contained. There was no mistaking the gulf between the government and the commission members left over from the Honecker administration, but the conviction nevertheless remained that many affairs would still need to be regulated by the state.[22]

The Modrow government was unrealistic about the time it had for implementing reform, and this illusion was strengthened in part by influential personalities from the West.[23] It thus decided

19 Quoted from written information from Dr Grabley dated 10th April 1993.

20 Shortly after he had taken over the government, a paper was prepared for Modrow by the Minister of Foreign Trade Beil, his Secretary of State Grabley, Schalck-Golodkowski (until 1989 Secretary of State in the Ministry of Foreign Trade and in addition to this head of the GDR group of companies "*Kommerzielle Koordinierung*"), and Kaminsky (President of the State Bank), in which the period of time in which the GDR had any financial room for manoeuvre, until it would have to declare the necessity for rescheduling its debts, was set at about one year. See: B-interview with Dr Grabley dated 1st April 1993. The level of foreign debt was quantified for Modrow on 16th November 1989 as US $ 20.6 billion; a second assessment in February 1990 set the sum, including the accounts of "*Kommerzielle Koordinierung*", at $ 18.5 billion. See: written information from Dr Grabley dated 10th April 1993.

21 The establishment of the Working Group was initiated by Modrow after he had been recommended by the Central Committee of the SED to the *Volkskammer* as the new Minister-President.

22 As late as 20th January 1990, resolutions were still being passed in the Economic Cabinet "On Meeting the Demand for Ranges of 1,000 Small Items" with the aim of "defining final consumer prices", and on 22nd January the Economic Cabinet decided "to prepare a programme for the production and supply of ice-cream". *Bundesarchiv, Abt. Potsdam*, C-20 (Council of Ministers of the GDR) 11378/2.

23 As late as December 1989, the French President Mitterand, the SPD politician Egon Bahr, and leading representatives of West German companies were still holding talks with the GDR government.

in mid-December to prepare "basic requirements for a strategic concept for the structure of the economy of the GDR" with the optimistic title of "A Structural Concept for the Economy of the GDR until 2010".[24] And at its meeting on 14th December 1989, the Council of Ministers passed resolutions for the "Proposals for the Draft 1990 Plan". The plan itself was based on a basic agreement with the Soviet Union set to run until 1995; it had been verified and revised in contractual form for 1990. However, it turned out that the Soviet Union was not willing, or perhaps not able, to adhere to this agreement.[25] In December 1989 even the Council of Ministers had discovered that the 1990 financial deficit could not be covered by GDR reserves.[26] No help could be expected from the COMECON countries; on the contrary, with the planned change-over to invoicing in transferable roubles, and with fixed prices moving in the direction of world prices and into convertible currencies, the collapse of exports to the COMECON countries was already in sight.[27] It was thus only from the West that any help could be expected. The demand for a "sharing of the load" had been raised by Modrow as early as 19th December 1989 on the occasion of Chancellor Kohl's visit to Dresden, when Modrow mentioned the opening of the border for West Germans to visit the GDR. Kohl took up the idea, and labelled it a "contribution to solidarity". On the occasion of his state visit to Bonn on 13th February 1990, Modrow finally named a figure of between DM 10 and 15 billion. This demand was to be regarded not only against the background of the latest difficulties, but also in light of the looming total state bankruptcy.[28]

The only planning work with any political relevance was being done by the Working Group on Economic Reform. Straight away in November it had been requested to work up immediate proposals for a "freer planned economy" which would permit reactions to the "signals from the market" and provide "room for manoeuvre in setting prices".[29] This working group asserted a market economy was necessary but that it should not be based on private ownership. Nevertheless, the government announced that cautious steps were to be taken in the direction of privatisation in order to make the economy more flexible. The many small companies which had been "semi-nationalised" in the 1972 wave of "socialisation" were to be reprivatised. In reality, the government merely lifted some administrative inconveniences from few private companies, and permitted foreigners to hold up to 49 % of the equity.

Some of the ministers wanted to go further than Modrow was willing to. Gerhard Beil and Lothar de Maizière suggested to the Council of Ministers on 8th January that general privatisation should be initiated, starting with housing, and that in the end the whole GDR economy

24 Point 5 of the "Service consultation with the Deputy Chairman of the Council of the Ministers for the Economiy on 11th December 1989"; minutes, signed by Ms Luft on 12th December 1989, *Bundesarchiv, Abt. Potsdam*, C-20 (Council of Ministers of the GDR) 13878/1.

25 B-interview with Dr Grabley on 1st April 1993.

26 B-interview with Lothar de Maizière on 27th January 1993.

27 At the COMECON conference in Sofia, in January 1990, the resolution approving the transition was formally proposed and moved. The "transfer-Rouble" was to retain its validity until the end of 1990. However, it had been known "a long time ahead" that this transition was to take place. See: telephone B-interview with Christa Luft on 5th March 1993.

28 The GDR justified this sum on the grounds of the difference in prices between the two states. After travel restrictions had been lifted, this way was intended to compensate for subsidised goods such as foodstuffs purchased in the GDR by West Germans.

29 B-interview with Wolfram Krause on 26th January 1993.

should be under "trustee administration".[30] This initiative can be regarded as the first attempt to establish a trustee institution;[31] it was made a good month before the suggestions brought up in the Round Table meeting of 12th February. However, at this point in time the proposal did not meet with any consent from the Council of Ministers. Meanwhile, the time pressure was growing. In January 1990, Krause's Working Group had been asked to present the Economic Cabinet with basic ideas for economic reform within four days, and to present a complete draft within another ten days.[32] It kept to this deadline, and on 1st February 1990 the Council of Ministers accepted the submission: "Aims, basic strategy, stages, and immediate action on economic reform". Its aims were the stabilisation of the economy and, based on the government declaration,[33] the implementation of the achievement principle. However, in terms of content there was no concealing the break with the government declaration, which had merely intended to mend the planned economy. "This basic set of aims requires a radical and rapid transition from a command economy with central direct planning to a socially and ecologically oriented market economy."[34] The economy of a GDR which was to continue to exist was thus to be converted into a market economy, the old "plan" would be abolished, and a new "democratic state based on the rule of law" would set only the general conditions for a new political order. Until such time, however, work as usual was to be continued, "because we bore responsibility for ensuring that people were fed, clothed, and housed."[35]

Those involved were well aware that private property is the institutional core of a free market economy, and this question was therefore accorded plenty of space in the Working Group's paper.[36] In the very first section of the document one reads: "The decisive steps in the transition to a social and ecologically oriented market economy are: the immediate opening up of room for manoeuvre to entrepreneurs in all forms of ownership and organisation."[37] However, this "opening up" process came to a halt after taking its first steps. Private entrepreneurship was to be concentrated in small businesses, particularly in the crafts trades and services, and the "state ownership of companies, *Kombinate* (vertically or horizontally integrated groupings of state-owned companies), and economic associations" was to remain as it was, as was other property then owned by the central or local governments. Also, co-operatives were to be allowed. A

30 B-interview with de Maizière on 27th January 1993, confirmed by Beil's account on 27th February 1993.

31 Also confirmed by de Maizière in a B-interview on 27th January 1993.

32 Various minutes in the *Bundesarchiv, Abt. Potsdam*, C-20 (Council of Ministers of the GDR) 13878/1.

33 The brochure printed in February 1990 bears the title "Aims, Basic Strategy, Stages, and Immediate Action on Economic Reforms" (Zielstellung, Grundrichtung, Etappen und unmittelbare Maßnahmen der Wirtschaftsreform) but with the addendum "as further implementation of the Government Declaration of 17th November 1989". This additional justification reflects the government's feeling of uncertainty, as it was itself already in the process of winding down. See: Interview with Christa Luft in *Neues Deutschland*, 3rd/4th February 1990.

34 Page 1: a copy was made available by Wolfram Krause.

35 B-interview with Dr Modrow on 26th January 1993. Based on this attitude, planning continued down to the tiniest detail. It was typical of this time that "strategic and everyday work was mixed together". See: telephone B-interview with Christa Luft on 5th March 1993.

36 It is therefore hard to understand Christa Luft's version, that there was "no reason to rethink state ownership". See: Interview with Ms Luft by Stefan Kapferer on 4th August 1992.

37 Zielstellungen, page 2.

period of three years was proposed for the conversion process, so that "from 1993 onwards a socially and ecologically oriented market economy operating under state-controlled general regulations" would be "in full effect". This would in particular create the conditions for the convertibility of the East German Mark.[38] The general regulations were to be set tightly, in Ms Luft's opinion: "The market economy as we understand it must be based in its key areas on common ownership. We need this as a foundation to keep the legally enforceable right to employment intact."[39] The hope of finding a "third route" had not yet officially been abandoned.

Once the Council of Ministers had approved the economic reform programme, the Round Table set to work on it, adding the imprimatur of its economic committee and commending the paper "as a basis for the further necessary decisions for implementing economic reform".[40] This was astonishing; in February 1990 the document could no longer be regarded as in tune with the times, because political developments had already made far more progress in the direction of unification.

The collapse in the government's power proceeded apace. Before the end of January it was finally aware of its character as a transitional government.[41] Modrow was now prepared, and said so, to retain only the "key industries" in the state's hands and to dissolve the locally managed *Kombinate*.[42] Wolfram Krause also knew that the proposals made by his working group were in actual fact obsolete before they were submitted.

No further steps of any significance could have been implemented without the agreement of the Round Table. Modrow therefore suggested on 28th January 1990 that a "Government of National Responsibility" should be formed, with the inclusion of the main opposition forces, to cover the period until the elections on 6th May. A supplementary suggestion to bring the elections forward to 18th March came immediately from the SPD and was supported by the SED or the PDS (Party of Democratic Socialism, or PDS, which became the successor party to the SED). The other parties, however, had difficulty in bringing themselves to give their consent.[43] On 1st February, Dr Modrow gave a speech which invoked the slogan widely used in demonstrations mounted by the opposition, *Deutschland, einig Vaterland* – "Germany, our united Fatherland", itself a quotation from the East German national anthem – and changed the official political course to one steering towards unification.[44] The outward and inward signs of the collapse of the GDR regime had become everyday events; for instance, on 21st January pieces of the Berlin Wall started to be sold off to the public, and at the end of January the Council of Ministers changed the form of address for SED-PDS members from "Comrade" to "Colleague". The government itself knew it would only exist until the elections on 18th March. It intended to do its duty until then, but the dream of a "third route" was over.

38 op. cit., page 17.

39 Interview in *Neues Deutschland* of 3rd/4th February 1990.

40 Zielstellungen, introduction.

41 B-interview with Dr Modrow on 26th January 1993.

42 op. cit.

43 Letter from Dr Modrow to the authors dated 6th April 1993.

44 *Für Deutschland, einig Vaterland – Konzeption für den Weg zu einem einheitlichen Deutschland.*

3. Western reform proposals

In the first half of 1990, West German experts were also working on various different models for economic reform in East Germany, one main reason being that West Germany's Federal Ministry for German-German Affairs did not produce any all-embracing strategy. In these proposals, issues concerning the separation and privatisation of state-owned property were mainly secondary to such topics as the currency and legal system.[45] A few examples can be discussed which are typical of the many suggestions which might well have had some effect in the GDR on the creation of the Treuhand, as they were published in January and February of 1990. It cannot be proved that there was any direct influence from Bonn on the decisions of the East German government; on the other hand these proposals were taken up in general discussions at the time, especially by the citizens' movement.

The Council of Economic Advisors, in its Special Assessment of 20th January 1990, suggested to split the *Kombinate* up into smaller units and to privatise them.[46] East German citizens would acquire "workers' shares" under preferential conditions or common shares at a preferential issue price.[47] Peter Bofinger, a member of the economics department of the *Landeszentralbank* (State Central Bank) of Baden-Württemberg, proposed on 5th February 1990 that a holding company for joint stock corporations should be founded which should take over the entire productive capital of the GDR for the purpose of privatisation. This holding company would be required to split up all the major corporations within five years and transfer their shares to the stock exchange. Local employees would be able to acquire shares on preferential terms.[48] Count Matuschka (head of a management consultancy company specialising in mergers and acquisitions) recommended the rapid privatisation of the companies and, at the same time, the issue of "People's Shares" to cover in total 49 % of state-owned property.[49] The Federal Minister of Finance, Dr Theo Waigel, also took up the idea of "People's Shares" in February.[50]

This discussion shows that at this point in time experts in West Germany were still assuming that the state-owned assets of East Germany had a significant value, and they concentrated on questions concerning how these assets were to be handled. The various different positions held until the Treuhand Act was passed on 17th June 1990 had already been worked out in detail in January and February, even if they were later changed in certain individual cases. The urgent need for such an institute was emphasised on all sides, and differences only arose in defining its objectives and field of responsibility.

---

45 See: Lösch and Plötz, *Soziale Marktwirtschaft – Jetzt*; Willgerodt, *Vorteile der wirtschaftlichen Einheit Deutschlands.*

46 (Council of Economic Advisors) Sachverständigenrat zur Begutachtung der gesamtwirtschaftlichen Entwicklung, *Zur Unterstützung der Wirtschaftsreform der DDR*, Article 27, page 21 et seq.

47 op. cit., Articles 28 and 29, pages 22 et seq.

48 Peter Bofinger, *Konzentration der DDR-Wirtschaft auf eine Holding mit Privatisierungszweck*, in: *Handelsblatt* (the daily business newspaper) of 5th February 1990.

49 The shares were to be supplied with 300 coupons each made out to individual companies and tradable separately. 51% was to be offered to investors from the West. Matuschka, *Zehn Schritte zu einer attraktiven DDR.*

50 It "could be worth thinking about issuing People's Shares" – Dr Waigel in the Bundestag debate on 7th February 1990; Deutscher Bundestag (editor), *Auf dem Weg zur Deutschen Einheit*, page 468.

III. The establishment of the Original-Treuhandanstalt

Anyone looking at the creation of the Treuhand needs to make a distinction between two organisations which arose on the basis of two different legal steps, one of them an ordinance and the other an act of parliament. Although the second Treuhand evolved from the first one, there were such enormous differences in their aims that it makes sense to define them separately and in detail. Various different authors created a number of different descriptions, most of them relating to specific people's names (e. g. the Modrow-THA). Because the first initiative for founding a Treuhandanstalt did not come from Modrow, and because various different people exerted influence on the formulation of the Treuhand Ordinance of March and the Treuhand Act of June 1990, the following text uses the neutral adjective "original" to describe the first Treuhand.

Wolfgang Ullmann's proposal to the Round Table on 12th February 1990 was picked up by all political forces at the same time. The Economic Reform Working Group had already set to work on planning such an institute between 5th and 15th February 1990.[51] The "Democratic Renewal" party and the "New Forum" citizens' movement were likewise working on a form of organisation for economic reform.[52] The SPD presented a draft bill to the Round Table on 26th February for a "trustee bank", which was to be more independent, and particularly independent of the state, than that proposed by Ullmann.[53] Why was this such a burning question at this point in time for so many different people and groups?

The first aim of the citizens' movement – keeping the government leaders from influencing developments – had already been attained for the most part and hence played no great role in the discussion from then on. This fact made them all the more eager to bring the idea of "people's property" more powerfully into discussions. Assets were to be transferred into a legal entity under civil law, and at the same time kept out of the hands of outsiders. Two aims were pursued here; one was to keep the old elite cadre of the GDR from becoming rich through their knowledge and contacts, the other was to prevent the widely feared possibility that East Germany would be "sold off cheaply", mainly to West Germans. (This fear was heightened by the fact that the black-market exchange rate in West Berlin at that time was at times as high as 1 West German mark to 18 East German marks.) Everyone in the East, from the left to the right, agreed that both of these possibilities should be prevented, but arguments arose over the demands from the Round Table that state-owned assets should be distributed to the citizens of East Germany. "Democracy Now" proposed that one quarter of the assets should be issued to the people free of charge; the SPD advocated the same policy for three quarters of the assets.[54] According to estimates made by Horst Schneider and Martin Wolf (both SPD), the value of all of the assets in question totalled about 1,400 billion (East German) marks. "After deducting losses to cover restructuring (and bankruptcies) of about 30 %, the total comes out to about 40,000 marks per

51 B-interview with Wolfram Krause on 26th January 1993.

52 Briefly described in an article: *Wir fragten nach Wirtschaftskonzepten*, in: *Die Wirtschaft* (business magazine), 2/1990, page 6 et seq.

53 *Wirtschaftliches Programm der SPD*, page 8; Herles and Rose (editors), *Vom Runden Tisch zum Parlament*, pages 223 et seq.

54 Herles and Rose (editors), *Vom Runden Tisch zum Parlament*, page 233.

inhabitant" in East Germany.[55] The Scientific Advisory Council of the West German Federal Ministry of Finance calculated the total state assets to be several hundred billion deutschmarks.[56]

At the government's request, Wolfram Krause produced a draft ordinance within two weeks which outlined a kind of trustee institute, and this was presented to the Round Table at its meeting on 26th February 1990. It was based on the publicly expressed view that the Council of Ministers was merely a transitional government, and the ordinance was supposed to remain a draft until a new government was in place. This "Ordinance for the conversion of state-owned *Kombinate*, companies, and other organisations into joint-stock companies" stated its aim to be the transfer of the entirety of the state's assets into the West German company forms of "GmbH" (roughly equivalent to a limited liability company, or "Ltd.") and "AG" (a joint stock or public limited company, or "plc"). The funds for this purpose were to be supplied by an "institute for the trustee administration of state property (Treuhandanstalt)", to which title over all property was to be transferred. The Treuhand would have the right to sell shares, but such sales would have to be confirmed by the people's representatives if the "controlling relationships"[57] were thus changed. The fact that the ministers delegated by the Round Table approved this draft requires some explanation, as the major demands of the opposition groups were only addressed to a limited extent.

Delegates from every group represented at the Round Table had entered the Modrow government on 5th February as ministers without portfolio in order to remove the incipient contradictions between the two centres of power; some latent mistrust did, however, remain on both sides. In the view of Frank Bogisch of the SPD, the government's failure to supply full information hindered the work of the opposition groups and the Round Table.[58] The Self-Organisation group even talked of deliberate delays caused to the Round Table by diverting it to "subsidiary questions" such as the problems of justification likely to crop up in the distribution of shares, before this matter had even been decided.[59] These arguments should not be dismissed out of hand; one case in point is the following instructions which were issued at a "service consultation" with the Deputy Chairwoman of the Council of Ministers for Economics, Christa Luft, on 22nd December 1989: "Responsible for preparing and influencing the meeting of the Round Table on 3rd January 1990 and for drafting an independent list of problems for the future meetings of the Round Table: Comrade Krause. Deadline: immediately".[60] This attempt at exerting influence was not, according to Krause, aimed at sabotaging the Round Table, but at sensitising the mem-

55 Horst Schneider and Martin Wolf, *Grundlagen zur Privatisierung des produktiven Volkseigentums zugunsten der Bürger der DDR*, dated 3rd February 1990, expanded and augmented on 14th March 1990, Table 4 (a copy was given by Frank Bogisch).

56 Description by Professor Werner Ehrlicher, member of the Advisory Council, in his presentation to the Society for Economic and Social History in Bamberg on 16th April 1993. Although it considered the estimates of DM 1,000 billion which had been given in the debate in the *Volkskammer* to be exaggerated, it regarded a figure of about DM 350 billion to be "not improbable".

57 This was intended to mean the voting majority on the Supervisory Board.

58 Information provided on the telephone by Frank Bogisch on 16th March 1993.

59 B-interview with Dr Artzt on 30th October 1992.

60 Minutes and record dated 27th December 1989, *Bundesarchiv, Abt. Potsdam*, C-20 (Council of Ministers of the GDR) 11378/1.

bers of the various groups at the Round Table, whose orientation was highly political, to economic problems as well as emphasising the issues concerning stabilisation of the economy and economic reform.[61]

Minister Ullmann was not immediately in agreement with Krause's proposals for a Treuhandanstalt, and he passed it on to the Self-Organisation group for more detailed examination. This group had concerned itself more intensively with economic policy than Ullmann had. The group raised the objection that the draft did not contain their central demand for vouchers, and was defective in other respects as well. The group was then entrusted by the two ministers, Ms Luft and Professor Ullmann, with the task of working up a detailed critique; the job was taken on by Artzt and Gebhardt. The critique and an alternative version were handed to Ms Luft on 28th February 1990 and jointly discussed.[62] The main points of criticism were: firstly, the absence of any privatisation; secondly, a voucher system ("Why should ordinary people be sold those assets which already belong to them?"); thirdly, the centralism of the Treuhand; and fourthly, the supervision of the Treuhand by the government instead of by parliament. With the exception of privatisation, these were also the issues which later played a central role in the debate on the Treuhand Act under the de Maizière government. For the moment, however, the main question at hand was the creation of the Original-Treuhand with the aid of a government ordinance.

The alternative draft, which Ullmann presented, bore the revealing title: "Law on the transfer of nationalised state property into private and other forms of ownership." Under the supervision of the various state parliaments (East Germany was shortly to be re-organised as five states – *Länder* – for incorporation into the Federal Republic), a number of institutes were to be set up at the state level (§ 1) which would not be the owners but "brokers between state owners and new owners" (§ 4). Nevertheless, the states were to offer equity holdings by tender, so that the "capital stock" could be "retained and enlarged by foreign investments" (§ 5). This was not the only contradiction in the draft, which under pressure of time had to be written in one single all-night session.[63] It is plausible that it was not adopted on account of various defects, some of them purely formal. At the same time, however, privatisation as an overall aim was no longer under discussion, and the Council of Ministers approved the government document without amendment on 1st March 1990.[64] Even Ullmann, who had prepared the alternative draft, and who

61 Information provided on the telephone by Wolfram Krause on 10th June 1993.

62 These documents were made available to us by Günter Nooke together with hand-written marginal notes.

63 According to § 5, persons acquiring shares would have to have "their place of residence within the territory" of East Germany, which would have stopped the flight of capital altogether. According to § 1, "real estate in particular is to be transferred to private, co-operative ownership", whereas § 7 laid down: "State-owned land shall only be transferred into the ownership of local communities, municipalities, state, or federal governments." Unfair treatment would also have arisen during the distribution of shares because this would have been carried out on the basis of (different) state laws and under state administration. Finally, confrontations would have been inevitable because supervision was to have been placed in the hands both of the relevant state parliament (§§ 2 and 5) and of "select committees of companies and citizens".

64 B-interview with Wolfram Krause on 26th January 1993. The ordinance co-incided with the "Resolution on the establishment of an institute for the trustee administration of state property (Treuhandanstalt) dated 1st March 1990", which took effect on 8th March 1990.

represented Alliance (*Bündnis*) 90 (an electoral alliance formed at the beginning of February by the New Forum, Democracy Now, and the Initiative for Freedom and Human Rights), gave his approval "with misgivings"; however, he did not elaborate on what his misgivings were.[65]

The general public reacted quite differently. The establishment of the Original-THA was met with massive criticism, although this has to be evaluated against the background of the closing phases of the election campaign. The representatives of Democracy Now had already criticised what they called an intention to "steal the people's property" before this discussion was public.[66] The SPD even raised legal action, through its member Wolf, against the ordinance before the County Court of Berlin-Mitte, although this was later rejected by the court. For Heinz Suhr of the Green Party, the establishment of the THA was "Modrow's last coup – the Comrades' Treuhand".[67] The fact that the recommendations on the issuing of vouchers were not taken up may really have been due to the lack of any practicable proposal which could have accommodated the necessary influx of new capital.[68]

It is even possible to imagine that the Modrow government was trying to keep as much of the existing structure as possible intact (i. e., avoiding privatisation and decentralisation) as part of a speculation that this would facilitate a return to socialism some day in the distant future. However, Hans Modrow himself denies this emphatically. His government, he asserts, was mainly concerned with keeping the economy functioning until such time as new structures were in place.[69] This representation is plausible, as Modrow's government had given up all expectations about its future and illusions about itself by January at the latest. Having started as a "government of transformation", it had long since been reduced to a "transitional government" with no ability to transform anything.[70] From January onwards, Modrow says his government was really only concerned with preventing bloodshed, starvation and freezing in the GDR until elections could be held in March. This was in fact a real achievement of the Modrow government. Although de Maizière's accusation hits home – he claims valuable time was wasted over the Original-Treuhand which could have been saved had there been a privatisation model in place –[71] it could hardly be expected that a government which had originally come into power with the intent of creating a better socialist system would relinquish the very basis of its own model of society. Although it had *de facto* created the instrument of transformation, actually starting the reform was a task reserved for the subsequent, freely elected government.

65 Interview by Stefan Kapferer with Ms Luft on 4th August 1992. Ullmann did not show any different attitude when speaking to the press either, see: *Neues Deutschland* of 2nd March 1990, page 1. Ullmann was very largely convinced by the criticism voiced on the alternative draft, but dismissed his remaining misgivings with the thought: "This law is better than none at all". See: description by Professor Ullmann to Dr Artzt and the information provided by the latter on 21st April 1993.

66 See footnote 65.

67 Suhr, *Der Treuhandskandal*, page 44.

68 op. cit.; Stefan Kapferer's interview with Christa Luft on 4th August 1992.

69 B-interview with Dr Modrow on 26th January 1993.

70 op. cit.

71 B-interview with de Maizière on 27th January 1993.

IV. The Original-THA until June 1990

Nearly all sides were dissatisfied with the work of the Original-THA. In fact the mildest criticism came from Christa Luft, who pointed a finger at "the laggard formation of joint-stock companies and the step-by-tiny-step reprivatisation of companies seized by the state in 1972".[72] In the *Volkskammer*, Dr Steinecke described its achievements as "unsatisfactory" (in German this term is used by schoolteachers to describe the poorest work a pupil can submit). Suhr even accused the "Comrades' Treuhand" of "embezzlement".[73] Modrow, on the other hand, displayed pride in its work, even with regard to privatisation: "Let the present-day Treuhand try to copy that!"[74] The Original-Treuhand was thus under cross-fire from the very start; how is its performance be judged generally?

The Original-Treuhand was formed immediately after its statutes had been approved, on 15th March 1990, with a central office in Berlin and 15 external offices in the *Bezirke* (districts, each of which comprised several counties). Its chairman was Dr Peter Moreth of the LDPD (one of the old East German political parties), who was a former minister in Modrow's cabinet. Wolfram Krause was named deputy chairman.[75] Its beginnings were modest. The work was done in Moreth's office at first, and later in the defunct Ministry of Foreign Trade. It sorely lacked proper equipment; in April, a staff of 91 shared only ten typewriters, three photocopy machines, and nine motor vehicles.[76] The organisational plan valid until July 1990 provided for a staff of 143, and they were supposed to take about 8,000 *Kombinate* and companies, split some of them up, and turn them all into joint-stock companies – all before the date set for monetary union, meaning within three months. The whole task was impossible from the start.[77] The staff came mainly from the former ministries, including the Ministry of Finance. They were nearly all from the ranks of the "old cadre", and the suspicion of disloyalty was hard to suppress. However, the Original-Treuhand was unable to obtain any staff with the proper professional training. For this reason, and because the volume of work was so great and the time so limited, de Maizière did not make a clean sweep of Treuhand staff when he was elected Minister-President, but only dismissed its chairman, Dr Moreth. One important factor in this was political pressure from outside. Deputy chairman Krause then headed up the Treuhand until handing over office to Rainer Maria Gohlke, who came from the Executive Board of German Federal Railways. Krause then continued working in a senior position. There was no dispensing with his professional competence and willingness to co-operate.[78]

---

72 Luft, *Treuhandreport*, page 55.

73 Steinecke, in: *Volkskammer der DDR, Protokolle*, volume 28, 14th session on 15th June 1990, page 480: "With the blessing of the Modrow Treuhandanstalt, the people's property is being embezzled and handed over to party and *Stasi* bosses". Suhr, *Der Treuhandskandal*, page 59.

74 B-interview with Dr Modrow on 26th January 1993.

75 Moreth was Deputy Chairman of the Council of Ministers for local organs of state.

76 Information on the work of the Institute for Trustee Administration of state property for the period from 15th March to 18th April 1990 (signed by Dr Moreth), pages 10 et seq.

77 By the end of June, the Institute had 133 employees in its central office and about 30 in each of the 14 external offices: Situation report to the Administrative Council of the Treuhand (on the work of the Treuhand up to 15th July 1990), signed by W. Krause, page 11. The external office in Berlin is not mentioned.

78 This is referred to a number of times by de Maizière and Holzwarth (for details see footnote 114): B-interview with de Maizière on 26th January 1993, B-interview with Dr Holzwarth on 24th February 1993.

The Original-Treuhand saw as its task primarily the conversion and splitting up of *Kombinate* and individual companies, the prevention of "illegal sales", and the utilisation of its assets "as a prime source for the mobilisation of funds for restructuring the national budget and providing start-up capital, as well as providing our contribution in general terms to monetary union".[79] Its work started with detailed but brief discussions with more than 4,000 companies concerning this conversion. It produced sample articles of association for GmbH-type (Ltd.) companies and statutes for the AG-type (joint stock). With the aim of generating "several competitors with equal rights in the market", it split up some companies and simultaneously merged others in order to give "less competitive companies an opportunity to develop".[80] However, it was the conversion into joint-stock companies that occupied the focal point. Thousands of contracts had to be supervised for this purpose. The few notaries with chambers in East Berlin could not handle all of the certification work; consequently recourse was made from May onwards to their counterparts in West Berlin.

The conversion work started in April, but for the first 150 cases the Original-Treuhand needed about six weeks – a shortfall in performance which the Treuhand admitted in its second progress report.[81] In collaboration with the Ministry of Finance, it therefore drew up guidelines for the valuation of companies and of land and property.

An initial estimate of the competitiveness of East German companies was produced by the Original-Treuhand in the middle of April 1990, according to which 30 % of the companies would be able to stand up to competition after monetary union. 50 % would "be able to reach this aim after a longer phase of thorough restructuring, and 20 % are faced by almost inevitable bankruptcy".[82] Two months later, however, the estimates produced by the companies themselves were far more extreme in both directions: 40 % considered themselves capable of competing, 30 % felt they were "worth restructuring", but no fewer than 30 % thought they were in danger of bankruptcy. Companies in this last group had on the average the largest numbers of employees.[83] The writing was already on the wall for the East German economy in the early summer of 1990.

By the time monetary union came about, the Original-Treuhand had converted 3,600 companies into joint-stock companies, and the remaining 4,400 were converted by law into "joint-stock companies being formed". 2,800 companies, most of them small in size, had been reprivatised or were on their way as joint ventures.[84] In the end, the work of the Original-Treuhand appeared "inadequate" because its task of conversion had not been completed, but accusing the institute of "sleeping on the job" is unfair; in quantitative terms alone it had handled an enor-

79 Report on the work of the Institute for Trustee Administration of state property for the period from 15th March to 15th May 1990, pages 2 and 16.

80 Report on the work of the Institute ... from 15th March to 18th April 1990 (signed by Dr Moreth), page 4.

81 Report on the work of the Institute ... from 15th March to 15th May 1990, page 9.

82 Report on the work of the Institute ... from 15th March to 18th April 1990 (signed by Dr Moreth), page 5.

83 Situation report to the Administrative Council ... on the work of the Institute up to 15th July 1990 (signed by W. Krause), page 4 et seq.

84 This is the point Modrow was referring to when speaking of the respectable performance of the Original-THA: B-interview with Hans Modrow on 26th January 1993.

mous work-load.[85] The Treuhand had not been able to make full use of its approved organisational plan because the various obstacles in the way of its work lay outside its own ranks.[86] The performance of the original institute must be assessed as very respectable against the background of these technical and personnel bottle-necks.[87]

V. The wording of the Treuhand Act of 17th June 1990

The CDU won the *Volkskammer* elections on 18th March and appointed Lothar de Maizière Minister-President. The government was elected on 12th April, and contained no members of the left-wing citizens' movement. The coalition agreement went into detail on the problems of the Treuhand. In its section on "proposed legislation for economic reform", it mentioned a new "legislative regulation of the tasks and working methods" of the Treuhand, meaning a re-orientation of its work and organisation. In fact this point on its own determined that land and property were to be privatised. Section 1.4 stated that the new THA would continue with the Original-Treuhand's task, breaking *Kombinate* up and converting them into suitable legal entities. The prime aim was to convert state property into "the property of private persons, and in particularly well justified cases into the property of regional authorities". In addition to this, the procedures were defined for valuating companies undergoing privatisation and dealing with the complexities of their shares was to be handled. The national budget was to benefit only from fees and taxes, and not from the proceeds of sales. The expectation still dominated that the sale of companies would bring in significant sums of money.

A dispute broke out almost at once between the Minister of Finance, Romberg (SPD), and the Minister for Economic Affairs, Pohl (CDU), as to which of them the Treuhand should report to. De Maizière settled the matter by incorporating the Treuhand into the Minister-President's Office, and because of this the new act was drawn up there as well. According to de Maizière, deliberations on this began as soon as he had formed his government.

However, even more urgent than the Treuhand Act was the need to draw up the treaty between East and West Germany which was to be signed by the two countries' finance ministers on 18th May, a month after the formation of the government.[88] This laid down a number of important parameters for the future Treuhand Act: for instance, that state assets should be used primarily to restructure the economy and balance the national budget, and only secondarily to benefit the holders of savings.[89] The treaty was based on a cautious estimate of the situation. It took privatisation for granted.

---

85 The *Frankfurter Allgemeine Zeitung* (an authoritative West German daily newspaper) accused the Treuhand in its 8th June 1990 edition of "sleeping on the job and even deliberately delaying the reorganisation and privatisation of the economy".

86 The bottle-necks listed were: 1. the (tiny) number of notaries, 2. the (equally small) number of lawyers with the relevant training, 3. the restricted office accommodation, and 4. the "turf" battles between the Minister of Finance and the Minister for Economic Affairs. Information provided by W. Krause on 22nd March 1993.

87 "I do not agree at all with criticism of the (Original-) THA's work": information by telephone from Dr Herbert B. Schmidt on 22nd May 1993; for details about Schmidt see page 32.

88 Treaty creating the monetary, economic, and social union; see: Summary of legislation on page XVI et seq.

89 Article 10 section 6 and Article 26 section 4 of the Treaty.

Unlike the public at large, those insiders who had been concerned with the state of the East German economy and had made international comparisons did not expect that privatisation would yield any great proceeds. For Dr Steinecke, the chairman of the *Volkskammer* Economic Committee, the idea of vouchers was "nothing but a dream – it was the debts we should have been distributing".[90] The members of the former Planning Commission were aware that the level of foreign debt had been out of control for years.[91] Even worse, the Modrow government had already discussed the urgency of obtaining massive funds from abroad several times because the budget for 1990 could not even approach a balanced number without foreign input. Immediately after forming his government, de Maizière called in Minister of Finance Romberg and the Vice-President of the State Bank, Stoll, to discuss the financial situation. The discovery that the dreaded national bankruptcy could be upon them before the year was out if re-unification was not achieved[92] acted as a catalyst for quick negotiations. They did not want the country's imminent disaster to be made apparent to the outside world.[93] At the same time, a swift conclusion of negotiations was in line with the aims of the governments of Kohl and de Maizière, both of whom wanted to achieve unification as quickly as possible.

A number of drafts for the new Treuhand Act were produced during this time. The versions most worth mentioning are the so-called Bonn plan and the Bielefeld plan. The proposals from the Economic Association of the Saxon Alliance (CDU, DSU, DA) can be taken here as typical examples, but all these initiatives had the aim of exerting influence on the very first draft, and not on later versions debated in the *Volkskammer*.

The Saxon Alliance started at a very early stage with its attempts to influence the government. The chairman of this organisation and of the Economic Association of the CDU in Bonn, was Dr Herbert B. Schmidt, who had gone to East Germany to assist with the election campaign and who founded the Saxon Alliance after the elections. The conversion of the Original-Treuhand was a strategic goal for him, and he went to work on it at once.[94] The first submission dated from March 1990; it adhered very largely to the regulations still in force, and was primarily directed against the persons who were still in office in operational company management positions.[95] In addition to this, on 8th April there were specific proposals for the coalition negotiations: there should be a broadscale privatisation, and the proceeds should go via vouchers to "the people" and not to "the state". The co-determination rights of employees on the supervisory board of the new trustee institute were to be reduced to one-third; even the problem area of former owners was touched

90 B-interview with Dr Steinecke on 28th August 1992.

91 "To me it was clear that things could not go on in this way. From the mid-1980's onwards. Foreign debt was out of control, it was out of control even then, absolutely definitely." A-interview with Professor-Dr Götz Jordan on 8th September 1992. This estimate tallies with that of the "top secret" matter of 31st October 1989; see: page 20 and footnote 15.

92 B-interview with de Maizière on 26th January 1993.

93 A further vital factor was that the Soviet Union was not allowing itself to be used as a trump card. Its Minister of Foreign Affairs, Ryshkov, had made clear to de Maizière in no uncertain terms, during the latter's visit to Moscow in April, that his country had no interest in the GDR. B-interview on 1st April 1993 with Dr Grabley, who took part in the negotiations.

94 A-interview with Dr Schmidt on 31st July 1992.

95 Detailed draft dated 26th March 1990: Dr Schmidt's private files.

upon. Thus, this first paper addressed almost every point which was to dominate discussions over the coming weeks.[96]

The extent to which the Economic Association of the Saxon Alliance managed to gain any influence is still disputable. According to Dr Holzwarth, its initiatives "did not have the slightest influence",[97] whereas Dr Schmidt insists that the Economic Association succeeded in having an effect on the draft bill via the Council of Experts under Minister for Economic Affairs Pohl. One version of the story says that the task of privatisation was only moved up to a prominent position in the preamble at the suggestion of Dr Ollig, a member of the Council of Experts.[98] The question as to who managed to push which proposal through and when is now virtually impossible to answer. The pressure of time under which this work was done did not permit complete documentation. Various groups gave their views, orally or in writing, on economic reform and on the Treuhand, but the extent to which written or spoken ideas, suggestions, or bits of each found their way into the final discussions leading up to the wording of the act is now impossible to ascertain.

On 17th May, the Federal Chancellor's Office and the Federal Ministry for Economic Affairs presented the "Bonn plan" for a Treuhand Act. They wanted to create three different organisations, one each for commercial assets, residential property, and agriculture. The legal form envisaged was an *Aktiengesellschaft* (*AG*, or a joint stock company); implicit in the western AG structure were rules about making decisions and bearing responsibility, definitions of co-determination with equal representation from both sides of industry, and a clear separation of business and government. AG's were considered to be more flexible and more able to take actions than institutions under public law.

Competing with this, and arriving only three days later, came the "Bielefeld plan", prepared by the two Professors, Hommelhoff (University of Bielefeld) and Krebs (University of Münster), the lawyer and banker Dr Annecke, and the Federal Business Manager of the Economic Council of the CDU, Rüdiger von Voss. They pressed for a status under public law for the new Treuhand, because it had to take over state functions: "The task consists essentially of distributing and allocating the opportunities of freedom and competition".[99] The Treuhand was to be given a combination of centralised and decentralised organisational structures, and was to report to government and parliament equally. Co-determination would be provided with equal representation from both employers and employees.

There are many different claims concerning the extent to which the various plans found their way into the draft bill. Some authors and politicians attribute the most crucial influence to Bonn. De Maizière says that various plans were presented to him, but the answer was always "OK, so that's your version, now let us get on with ours";[100] he claims that any attempt to exert influence on the bill was fended off. According to Steinecke, the Chairman of the *Volkskammer* Economic

96 Submission of the Saxon CDU delegates of the *Volkskammer* to the party chairman on 8th April 1990: Dr Schmidt's private files.

97 Information from Dr Holzwarth dated 4th March 1993.

98 Information from Dr Schmidt on 22nd May 1993. The Council of Experts at the Ministry of Finance included Dr Martin Bangemann, Professor Kurt Biedenkopf, Dr Ollig, and Dr Herbert B. Schmidt.

99 "*Bielefelder Konzept*" of 20th May 1990 on the organisation of the THA in East Germany, Section II.1, in: Hommelhoff and Krebs (editors), *Treuhandanstalt und Treuhandgesetz*.

100 B-interview with de Maizière on 26th January 1993.

Committee, "there were a few consultants from (the West) in the Ministry for Economic Affairs and they had an enormous finger in the Treuhand Act pie."[101]

The draft bill was not drawn up by the staffs of the Ministries for Economic Affairs or of Finance, but by the Minister-President's Office. Some suggestions made by Gunter Halm from the Ministry for Economic Affairs were however incorporated. De Maizière had appointed a six-man working group representing legal, financial, economic, and political spheres.[102] Two members, Dr Holzwarth and Dr Thomas de Maizière, came from West Germany. Various strategies and individual suggestions were presented to this working group, with some fruitful ideas coming from the Ministry of Finance in Bonn.[103] It was not the Bonn plan from the Chancellor's Office and the Ministry for Economic Affairs which served as the basis for discussion at this stage, but rather the Bielefeld plan. The de Maizière government placed great value on working out the draft bill without too much outside help, so it regarded the Bielefeld version not as a basic document but merely as an aid. Although it had "consulted" western sources, it worked out the details, including "all wordings and explanations" entirely on its own.[104]

The cabinet's desire was to establish a single, all-embracing institute under public law. In this manner the problem of co-determination (workers' participation in company management), which had been proposed in all of the other plans, would be avoided. The cabinet had a basic mistrust of co-determination and feared it would delay and complicate the decision-making process. The idea of using vouchers was dropped; the Treuhand was to answer only to the government.

The draft bill from the Minister-President's Office was discussed and agreed, as a second step, with the Ministries for Economic Affairs, of Finance, and of Justice. The Council of Ministers also discussed it, mentioning the intention not to permit co-determination at the topmost level of the Treuhand. There were still no contacts with parliamentary representatives at this stage.[105] The cabinet approved the draft bill only fourteen days after the state treaty for a monetary, economic and social union between the two Germanys had been signed, and passed it to the *Volkskammer* for debate. It remained to be seen whether the delegates in the *Volkskammer* could keep up this break-neck pace.

Klaus Reichenbach, the minister in the Minister-President's Office, presented and justified the draft bill to the *Volkskammer* on 7th June 1990. The session was a lively one, because on the one hand this was a bill which would have decisive effect on the future, and on the other hand the government had put the parliamentary parties under considerable pressure by setting such a brisk working pace for itself. The Economic Committee had only been constituted three weeks earlier. For its meeting on 6th June, for instance, it was given a proposal for the interpretation of the state treaty and a defintion of its effect on the Treuhand. The Economic Committee had also decided on 30th May, in response to a motion from the SPD and the coalition Alliance 90/The Greens, to form a special committee to oversee the Original-Treuhand. These initiatives were now obsolete, as the government had a complete draft bill for a new Treuhand on the table by

---

101 Stefan Kapferer's interview with Dr Steinecke on 28th August 1992.

102 Professor Penich (chairman), Dr Thomas de Maizière, Dr Holzwarth, Professor Günther Krause, Wolfram Krause, and Professor Supranowitz.

103 B-interview with Dr Holzwarth on 24th February 1993.

104 Information from Wolfram Krause dated 21st May 1993.

105 Stefan Kapferer's interview with Dr Steinecke on 28th August 1992.

then, whereas the delegates of the *Volkskammer* were still busy with the detail work on the existing treaty. The bad temper perceptible in the Economic Committee is understandable; the committee complained that parliamentary bodies were not even being consulted in the detailed preparation of the draft bill.[106]

Opposition representatives repeated all the arguments which had originally been brought up against the Original-Treuhand. One delegate, Dr Meyer-Bodemann (DBD/DFD), pleaded that time pressure should not cause the quality of the bill to suffer, he said, " this bill will set the course for the efficient use of assets totalling around one trillion marks, meaning the lion's share of all state assets previously floating in no-man's land". He particularly missed the "idea of the people's share".[107] Günter Nooke (Alliance 90/The Greens) found the draft "unacceptable" and even "scandalous" in many respects. He foresaw civil unrest if decisions determining the "well-being and suffering in this part of Germany" were made in this way. It was clear to him "that *we alone* will have to pay the price for German unity", and he described the bill as a "expropriation of the people's property on an unprecedented scale". The point at stake was the several hundred billion deutschmarks which he felt belonged to East Germans who had elected the *Volkskammer* delegates. He considered that these assets had to be "disposed of and administered in the best possible manner", adding loudly: "Our plans for the Treuhand are quite different". He wanted to know how much of the people's property could be "privatised into the hands of East German citizens". The question of ownership had not yet been solved politically. "This is no way to treat the huge volume of people's property." However, he received a short, blunt rejoinder from another delegate, Horst Schulz (CDU/DA): "This government has inherited the responsibility of a bankruptcy caused by 40 years of a GDR regime, and a bankruptcy administrator does not have assets at his disposal, he has debts to pay off."

After this debate, the *Volkskammer* passed the draft bill on to the Economics Committee, which added various demands to the second reading of the bill. One change brought East German holders of savings in a better position should funds be left over after structural changes had been made and the budget brought somewhere near a balance. Although this was not going far enough for the adherents of the voucher solution, it did take up the proposal from the Economic Association of the Saxon Alliance. The rights of regional and local authorities were to be supported, not in case-by-case decisions but across the board. The *Volkskammer* should be given the right to confirm their statutes. The Economic Committee thus did not give in to the demand to transfer supervision of the Treuhand from the government to the parliament. All the same, it weakened the access both of the Minister-President and of the government by, on the one hand, not leaving the decisions as suggested with the head of government alone, but having the cabinet take them, and on the other hand having the members of the Treuhand Executive Board not appointed by the government but by the THA's Administrative Board. Two members of the Administrative Board were, moreover, to be appointed by the *Volkskammer*. Finally, it

---

106 "Criticism of the government was voiced to the effect that it would have been more to the point, in the interest of gaining as much time as possible and in view of the significance of the bill, if the parliament had been involved in drafting it." Report by a delegate, Dr Steinecke, Chairman of the *Volkskammer* Economic Committee, on Printed Document No. 55 as presented, "Act for privatisation ... ", page 1.

107 This quotations and those that follow: *Volkskammer der DDR, Protokolle*, 10th elective period, 11th session, 7th June 1990, pages 354 et seq., documented in: Hommelhoff and Krebs, *Treuhandanstalt und Treuhandgesetz*, Clause 2.8.

demanded that all agricultural co-operatives were to be excluded from the Treuhand.[108] With these few amendments, the Economic Committee recommended the acceptance of the bill. Its draft was presented to the *Volkskammer* at its second reading as Printed Document No. 55a. The debate was once again adversarial, but the recommendations of the Committee were passed by a majority vote.[109]

These rather hostile arguments were caused by a gross overestimation of the value of the state property, and by an underestimation of the seriousness of ecological contamination in the GDR.[110] Only a few people doubted the estimates, and most of them only did so secretly.[111] The possibility of cashing in vouchers, the question of the central or state-level organisation of the Treuhand and its parliamentary control, which the *Volkskammer* delegates mainly debated, were intended to prevent the Federal (West German) Ministry of Finance from making a transfer from East to West, i. e., strengthening the financial position in Bonn rather than those of the emerging "new *Länder*" (the five states comprising the former GDR territory). The decentralised organisation of the Treuhand, which de Maizière had originally preferred, was dropped because the state governments did not yet exist and because his government was afraid that any transfer of funds to the benefit of economically weaker states would thus be blocked.[112]

The Committee had only one day in which to revise the bill for its third reading. The amendments therefore had to be kept fairly minimal, apart from the point about agricultural co-operatives being excluded.[113] At its 15th Session, on 17th June 1990, the *Volkskammer* passed the Treuhand Act by a huge majority, and approved the Treuhand's statutes only a few days later.

VI. Conclusions

The question remains as to who played the largest role in shaping the current Treuhandanstalt. The outlines of the Bielefeld plan are recognisable still today, the attractions of which were possibly strengthened by the personal relationship between its authors and de Maizière's advisor on fundamental economic questions, Dr Holzwarth.[114] However, the bill was drafted by the working group in the Minister-President's Office, which maintained constant discussion with de Maizière. Dr Steinecke's assessment of the group of which he was a member ("there we were, insisting on getting it even 'more right' than the consultants could, because, if we were going to

108 The exceptions to this were state-owned farms and forests, which were to remain with the THA. The co-operatives were not allocated to the THA until 1991.

109 Minutes of the East German *Volkskammer*, volume 28, pages 480 et seq.

110 Minister-President Modrow had quantified the "net asset value" of the GDR as DM 1.4 trillion, Christa Luft in May 1990 mentioned DM 0.9 trillion. Detlev Rohwedder, in a speech in Vienna in August, was still estimating the value of THA assets at DM 600 billion.

111 Lothar de Maizière and Wolfram Krause both pointed out to this widening divergence, and both considered the estimates stated in public to be too high, but did not voice their views publicly: B-interviews on 26th and 27th January 1993.

112 B-interview with de Maizière on 26th January 1993.

113 Minutes of the East German *Volkskammer*, volume 28, pages 557 et seq.

114 Dr Holzwarth was the manager of the Economic Policy department in Konrad-Adenauer-Haus (CDU party headquarters in Bonn). According to Holzwarth, he and the Bielefeld group worked closely together on this topic. Information from 4th March 1993.

adopt the West German system, we wanted to do it without the slightest hitch") could apply not only to the *Volkskammer* but also to the government itself, which for instance shifted the co-determination proposed for the Treuhand by advisors from West Germany to the next level within its *AG* companies. While the *Volkskammer* was working on the bill, the Chairman of the Economics Committee, Dr Steinecke, "did not have one single visitor from Bonn".[115] The Treuhand Act therefore cannot be described as a *diktat* from Bonn, even though the difference between the western concept and the final Treuhand Act is small and mainly consists of the absence of co-determination and the separation of agriculture from the Treuhand's sphere of responsibility.

The initiators of the act have emphasised that their draft bill was approved without any significant amendments. Given the enormously wide impact of the act, this is indeed remarkable. Ms Luft attributes this primarily to the general mood of the time, but also gives four other reasons: "1. precipitous obedience with the aim of building a career, for example Günther Krause; 2. incompetence, shown in the principle of restitution before compensation, for instance Walter Romberg;" 3. attitudes made crazy by the frenzied anticipation of the deutschmark; 4. pressure from the "Chancellor of Unity" Helmut Kohl. After all, she says, 1990 was "the year of the politicians, not of the economists."[116]

This last sentence is definitely true. However, it should first and foremost be pointed out that various basic convictions on which the Treuhand Act was based have since been accepted by most of the political spectrum in eastern Germany, including the PDS. There was no dispute over the necessity of bringing the economic system of East Germany into that of West Germany or the need to privatise a majority of the companies. On the issues concerning the sale or leasing of land and the use to which the proceeds of sales were to be put, differences of opinion came to light but no-one started digging trenches. Even tensions which were inevitable under time pressure – such as the rift between the forces in favour of privatisation and those preferring restructuring first – were regarded as an unavoidable evil. In addition to this there are a number of factors worth mentioning: the existence of the Grand Coalition placed such a brake on the willingness of the SPD to criticise that the part this party – and the trade unions – played was quite minimal, although people within the party talked of "expropriation"[117]. Monetary union, imminent at that time, prevented anyone from taking the long-term view of the ramifications of the Treuhand Act. The time pressure under which the act was passed also prevented any broadscale mobilisation of interest groups. The discussion climate in the *Volkskammer*, despite a number of sometimes heated debates, was a constructive one, and apologies were expressed for even the smallest of slip-ups. The most hostile resistance came not from the PDS but from the Alliance 90/ The Greens, and was personified in one of the delegates, Günter Nooke. However, even he acknowledged a number of economic necessities, even if in the debates he continued to call for a

115 Stefan Kapferer's interview with Dr Steinecke on 28th August 1992.

116 Stefan Kapferer's interview with Christa Luft on 4th August 1992; Luft, *Treuhandreport*, page 9.

117 "The transfer authorised in this Article (25 of the Treaty of Union) of trustee ship to the Federal Finance Minister violates the rights of the East German states and means for all practical purposes that their property is being sequestrated and their own, independent economic policy is being intolerably cut back to nothing." Undated minority submission of the SPD members in the *Volkskammer* Economics Committee.

voucher system.[118] In his submission to the Economics Committee of 6th June, Nooke discussed "budget deficits" and even suggested that the necessity of "restructuring most companies should be placed from the state's hands in the private hands of entrepreneurial citizens, who are more prepared to take risks and to take on this job."[119] The proposal was aimed at promoting local small and medium-sized businesses. He called for "a complete and tidy clarification of the question of ownership", and finally warned against the "deterioration of the Treuhand into a state corporate group", saying bureaucratisation had deleterious effects and crippling consequences in the market economy as well ("like in Austria, for instance"). The most important opposition representative in the Treuhand question thus also took up positions which can be perfectly well described as liberal. But in doing so he differentiated his position in many questions only marginally from that of the government or of western advisors. One of these advisors, Count Matuschka, presented his proposals to the Treuhand for the distribution of vouchers even after the elections in March/April.[120]

In addition to the quality of the submission, there was thus also a whole bundle of political, structural, short-term, and personal reasons which prevented any greater amendments to the government's draft bill. Whereas the organisational structure of the Treuhand, during the course of time, wandered further and further away from the guidelines approved by the parliament, its overall systematic and political task stayed intact as the *Volkskammer* had approved them. With the Treuhand Act, the de Maizière government completed an important step in advancing the integration of East Germany into West Germany, and it thus started the economic transformation into a market economy system based on private ownership.

VII. Literature

Artzt, Matthias, Gerd *Gebhardt*, H. *Lehmann*, R. *Schönfelder*, and J. *Wolf*: Zukunft durch Selbstorganisation, Erneuerung der DDR: Aus der Erstarrung verwalteter Objekte im Subjektmonopolismus zur Selbstorganisation in Subjektpluralität (Thesen). In: *Deutsche Zeitschrift für Philosophie* 38 (1990), pages 422 to 435.

Bogisch, Frank, and Lothar *Pawliczak* (editors): Denkmodelle zur künftigen Wirtschafts-, Umwelt- und Sozialpolitik der Sozialdemokratischen Partei der DDR. In: *Querschnitt* (closing deadline 10th January 1990).

Deutscher Bundestag (editor): *Auf dem Weg zur Deutschen Einheit: Deutschlandpolitische Debatten im Deutschen Bundestag.* Bonn 1990.

Erklärung der Arbeitsgruppe Wirtschaft des Runden Tisches. In: *Die Wirtschaft* 39 (1st February 1990), page 10.

Wirtschaftspolitische Grundsätze der SPD. In: *Die Wirtschaft* 39 (1st February 1990), pages 2 and 3.

118 Nooke had not been involved in preparing the hasty and inconclusive alternative proposal for the establishment of the Original-THA, see page 27 et seq.

119 Submission to the Alliance 90/The Greens at its 6th meeting on 6th June 1990.

120 Information on the work of the THA . . . for the period from 15th March to 18th April 1990 (signed by Dr Moreth), page 10.

Gutmann, Gernot, and Werner *Klein*: *Skizzen zu Reformen des Wirtschaftssystems in der DDR*. Königswinter 1990.

Herles, Helmut, and Ewald *Rose* (editors): *Vom Runden Tisch zum Parlament*. Bonn 1990.

Hommelhoff, Peter, and Walter *Krebs* (editors): *Treuhandanstalt und Treuhandgesetz*. Cologne 1990.

Lösch, Dieter, and Peter *Plötz*: Soziale Marktwirtschaft – Jetzt: Ein Konzept für die Systemtransformation in der DDR. *HWWA Report* No. 82, Hamburg 1990.

Luft, Christa: Antrittsrede. In: *Wissenschaftliche Zeitschrift*. Bruno Leuschner Academy of Economics Berlin. 34 (1989), Number 1, pages 12 to 17.

ditto: *Treuhandreport. Werden und Vergehen einer deutschen Behörde*. Berlin and Weimar 1992.

Matuschka, Albrecht Count: Zehn Schritte zu einer attraktiven DDR. In: *Forbes Essay*, no. 3, 1990.

Mitter, Armin, and Stefan *Wolle* (editors): *Ich liebe euch doch alle! Befehle und Lageberichte des MfS, Januar – November 1989*. Berlin 1990.

Neues Forum (editor): *Wirtschaftsreform der DDR: Internationale Wirtschaftskonferenz des Neuen Forums am 25. und 26.11.1989*. Berlin 1990.

Wirtschaftliches Programm der Sozialdemokratischen Partei Deutschlands (1st March 1990).

Sachverständigenrat zur Begutachtung der gesamtwirtschaftlichen Entwicklung: *Zur Unterstützung der Wirtschaftsreform in der DDR, Voraussetzungen und Möglichkeiten*. Wiesbaden, 20th January 1990.

Schürer, Gerhard, Gerhard *Beil*, Alexander *Schalck*, et al: *Geheime Verschlußsache b5 1158/89*. Document for submission to the Central Committee of the SED, 30th October 1989. Reprinted in: *Deutschland Archiv* 10 (1992), pages 1112 to 1120.

Suhr, Heinz: *Der Treuhandskandal – Wie Ostdeutschland geschlachtet wurde*. Frankfurt am Main 1991.

Willgerodt, Hans: *Vorteile der wirtschaftlichen Einheit Deutschlands (erstellt im Auftrage des Bundeskanzleramtes)*. Untersuchungen zur Wirtschaftspolitik 84. Cologne 1990.

Zielstellung, Grundrichtung, Etappen und unmittelbare Maßnahmen der Wirtschaftsreform in weiterer Verwirklichung der Regierungserklärung vom 17.11.1989. February 1990.

The Treuhandanstalt under public law

by Michael Kloepfer, with the assistance of Jobst-Friedrich von Unger

I. Legal form

Since the Original-THA[1] was established on 1st March 1990 its legal basis and its whole legal environment has changed many times, but its legal form has remained unchanged throughout.

1. Original-THA

The Original-THA existed from March to June 1990 on the basis of decisions made by the Modrow government. The legislative foundation stone was laid by the East German Council of Ministers on 1st March 1990,[2] when it passed a resolution to establish the *Anstalt zur treuhänderischen Verwaltung des Volkseigentums*, the "Institute for the Trustee Administration of State Property" ("Original-THA Establishment Resolution"). This was supplemented on 15th March 1990 by the Statutes of the Institute for the Trustee Administration of State Property[3] (the "Original-THA Statutes").

Both legal sources describe the legal status of the Original-THA by using the term *Anstalt öffentlichen Rechts*, "institute under public law".[4] This choice is surprising, as an institute under public law had up to then been unknown in the GDR as an instrument of state action.[5] The transfer of its responsibilities out of the immediate sphere of state administration into an organisationally separate administrative body contradicted the so-called principle of democratic centralism and the postulation derived from it of unified, central management which had always dominated East German law on administrative organisation.[6] The Modrow government had however followed the idea of decentralisation of the decision-making structures in the economic field since February 1990.[7] The establishment of an institute under public law on West German lines, and – going hand in hand with this – the internal administrative independence in the economic and administrative tasks entrusted to it,[8] was a step in this direction.

1 For the definition of the "Original-THA", see the article by Fischer and Schröter in this volume.

2 *Gesetzblatt der DDR* 1990 I, page 107.

3 *Gesetzblatt der DDR* 1990 I, page 167.

4 Clause 1 sentence 3 of the Original-THA Resolution of Establishment; § 1 section 1 sentence 1 of the Original-THA Statutes.

5 Rother, *Die Errichtung der Treuhandanstalt*, marginal note 2; Busche, *Gesetz zur Privatisierung und Reorganisation des volkseigenen Vermögens* (commentary), § 2, marginal note 1.

6 Schulze, *Die gesellschaftliche Funktion und Gegenstand des Verwaltungsrechts der DDR*, pages 25 et seq.

7 See: article by Fischer and Schröter in this volume.

8 See: Berg, *Die öffentlichrechtliche Anstalt*, page 2299; Krebs, *Die öffentlichrechtliche Anstalt*, page 615; Rüfner, *Zur Lehre von der öffentlichen Anstalt*, page 609.

The SPD in East Germany had proposed an even greater degree of independence for an institute to be entrusted with the work of transformation in the draft bill it submitted to the 14th session of the Round Table on 26th February 1990 for creating a "Trustee Bank".[9] In contrast to a legal entity under private law, the institute under public law known in West Germany is characterised by a closer link to the political leadership. The sovereign character of the tasks of the Original-THA[10] and its political dimension thus argued in favour of the legal form chosen.

2. Treuhand Act

The Act for the Privatisation and Reorganisation of State Property (the *Treuhandgesetz*, abbreviated in German to THG)[11] of 17th June 1990 dissolved the legal basis described above[12] with effect from 1st July 1990, and thus paved the way for the disappearance of the Original-THA. The successor organisation which was set up at the same time, the THA proper, was likewise given the status of an institute under public law.[13] Once again, the intention was to copy the West German example. This demonstrated that the THG was following a West German suggestion regarding the question of legal status, the "Bielefeld plan"[14] of 20th May 1990 for organising the THA in East Germany.[15] This proposed reform favoured an institute under public law of the West German type because of its "responsibilities being genuinely those of the state".

3. Treaty of Unification

The treaty between the Federal Republic of Germany and the German Democratic Republic on the Creation of the Unity of Germany (the Treaty of Unification, *Einigungsvertrag*) of 31st August 1990[16] turned the THA into a legally competent institute under public law directly subordinate to the Federal government.[17] It is thus an organisationally separate part of the Federal administration within the meaning of Article 86 and Article 87 section 3 sentence 1 of the German Constitution, the *Grundgesetz.*

II. Internal organisation

Legislation also exists to cover legal aspects of the THA's internal organisation, such as its executive and administrative boards, its branches and offices, and the THA companies.

9 Herles and Rose (editors): *Vom Runden Tisch zum Parlament*, pages 223 et seq.
10 See III.1 below.
11 *Gesetzblatt der DDR* 1990 I, page 300.
12 § 24 section 3 of the THG.
13 § 2 section 1 sentence 1 of the THG.
14 Reproduced in: Hommelhoff and Krebs, *Treuhandanstalt und Treuhandgesetz*, section II.2.6.
15 See: article by Fischer and Schröter in this volume.
16 *Bundesgesetzblatt* 1990 II, page 889; *Gesetzblatt der DDR* 1990 I, page 1629.
17 Article 25 section 1 sentence 2 of the Treaty of Unification.

1. Executive Board

The Original-THA was headed up by a "*Direktorium*".[18] Its five[19] members were to be appointed by the Administrative Board (*Verwaltungsrat*) for a five-year period of office.[20] In actual fact, this directorate was appointed by the Council of Ministers because the Administrative Board was not yet in existence at the time.[21] Their appointment could be cancelled at any time should there be a serious reason for so doing.[22]

The directorate was charged with the independent[23] management[24] in the sense of overall management responsibility,[25] representing the Original-THA in legal transactions,[26] and reporting to the Administrative Board.[27] The members of the directorate were subject to personal legal liability towards the Original-THA in the event of any violation of their obligations .[28]

The THA is managed by the Executive Board (*Vorstand*).[29] It is made up of the President and at least four other members,[30] appointed by the Administrative Board for four years; they likewise can be dismissed prematurely if there is a serious reason.[31]

The Executive Board manages the business of the THA, and is not bound to instructions given to it.[32] Its members represent the THA in legal transactions.[33] Instead of overall and joint management responsibility as basically foreseen in the Statutes,[34] each individual member of the Executive Board manages the division of the business allocated to him or her in accordance with the rules of procedure (referred to by their German abbreviation GO-THA) issued by the Administrative Board,[35] which first required confirmation by the Council of Ministers,[36] and does so on his or her own responsibility.[37] According to the ramifications of the measures to be

18 §§ 7 and 8 of the Original-THA Statutes.

19 § 7 section 1 of the Original-THA Statutes.

20 § 7 section 2 sentence 1 of the Original-THA Statutes.

21 See: Article by Seibel in this volume; Rosener and Roitzsch, *Die Umwandlung von volkseigenen Betrieben in Kapitalgesellschaften*, page 39.

22 § 7 section 2 sentence 2 of the Original-THA Statutes.

23 Derived from: § 8 section 1 of the Original-THA Statutes.

24 Derived from: § 7 section 2 sentence 2 of the Original-THA Statutes (inability to conduct proper business operations as grounds for cancellation of the appointment).

25 Derived from: § 8 section 2 sentence 2 of the Original-THA Statutes.

26 § 8 section 2 sentence 1 of the Original-THA Statutes.

27 § 8 section 3 of the Original-THA Statutes.

28 § 7 section 3 sentence 1 of the Original-THA Statutes.

29 § 3 section 1 (1st half-sentence) of the THG; § 12 section 1 sentence 1 of the THA Statutes.

30 § 3 section 2 sentence 1 of the THG; § 11 section 2 sentence 1 of the THA Statutes.

31 § 3 section 2 sentence 2 of the THG; § 11 section 2 sentence 2 of the THA Statutes.

32 § 12 section 1 sentence 1 of the THA Statutes.

33 § 3 section 1 (2nd half-sentence) of the THG; § 11 section 4 of the THA Statutes.

34 § 12 section 1 of the THA Statutes.

35 Treuhandanstalt, *Organisationshandbuch*, Guideline 03/91, *Geschäftsordnung der Treuhandanstalt*, serial no. 1.2.3, version valid as of 1st January 1993.

36 § 12 section 1 sentence 1 of the THA Statutes.

37 § 9 section 1 sentence 1 GO-THA in the version dated 9th December 1992.

taken, a decision by two members of the Executive Board[38] or of the whole Board[39] could be necessary. In addition to the general duties of the management of the THA, the Executive Board is also particularly charged with the execution of the resolutions of the Administrative Board,[40] with reporting to the Administrative Board,[41] and the preparation of the Annual Report and Accounts.[42] § 93 of the *Aktiengesetz* (West German Companies Act covering *Aktiengesellschaften*) applies as relevant to the legal liability borne by members of the Executive Board.[43]

By laying down these regulations, legislation created an Executive Board following the example of a West German *Aktiengesellschaft* even more closely than had been the case for the directorate of the Original-THA.[44]

2. Administrative Board

The Administrative Board exercises supervision over the activities of the THA.[45] A similar body had been foreseen for the Original-THA[46] but was never constituted.[47]

The position of the Administrative Board towards the THA was made similar to that of a Supervisory Board towards an *Aktiengesellschaft*.[48] Its main responsibilities are to appoint and dismiss members of the Executive Board[49] and to supervise their conduct of the business.[50] It is granted the right to scrutinise and investigate in accordance with § 111 section 2 of the *Aktiengesetz*.[51] In addition to this, the Executive Board is required to report regularly to the Administrative Board in accordance with § 90 of the *Aktiengesetz*.[52] This takes the form of monthly meetings of the Administrative Board, which is presented with a written monthly report containing compendious statistical material. In addition to this, the members on the Executive Board give oral reports on the activities of their own Divisions. Over and above this general duty to report on the business, the President of the THA has to inform the Chairman of the Administrative Board without delay about all important business matters.[53]

---

38 § 10 GO-THA in the version dated 9th December 1992.

39 § 9 section 1 and § 11 GO-THA in the version dated 9th December 1992.

40 § 12 section 1 sentence 2 (2nd half-sentence) of the THA Statutes.

41 § 3 section 3 of the THG.

42 § 16 section 1 sentence 1 of the THA Statutes.

43 § 12 section 2 of the THA Statutes.

44 On the Original-THA, see: Hoffmann and Völter, *Die Umwandlung von volkseigenen Betrieben in Kapitalgesellschaften*, page 19.

45 § 4 section 1 of the THG; § 8 section 1 of the THA Statutes.

46 §§ 9 to 11 of the Original-THA Statutes.

47 See: article by Seibel in this volume.

48 Spoerr, *Treuhandanstalt und Treuhandunternehmen*, page 9.

49 § 3 section 2 sentence 2 of the THG; § 11 section 2 of the THA Statutes.

50 § 4 section 1 sentence 1 of the THG; § 8 section 2 sentence 2 of the THA Statutes.

51 § 8 section 2 sentence 1 of the THA Statutes; § 14 section 4 GO-THA in the version dated 9th Dec. 1992.

52 § 4 section 1 sentence 2 of the THG; § 8 section 2 sentence 1 of the THA Statutes; § 14 section 2 GO-THA in the version dated 9th December 1992.

53 § 4 section 1 sentence 3 of the THG; § 8 section 3 of the THA Statutes; § 14 section 3 GO-THA in the version dated 9th December 1992.

Decisions of particular significance made by the Executive Board require the assent of the Administrative Board, on the general lines of § 111 section 4 sentence 2 of the *Aktiengesetz*.[54] This includes, among other things, the preparation of the business plan, the drawing of funds from the capital market, the establishment of companies, and the privatisation, restructuring, and close-down of companies of more than a given size.[55]

In addition to this supervisory function, the Administrative Board is also required to support the Executive Board in its work by means of consultation and other suitable forms of collaboration on all fundamental questions.[56] The issuing of basic principles of business policy[57] is to be regarded as an expression of the supervisory duty with which the Administrative Board guides the THA in the fulfilment of its statutory obligations.

3. Branches and offices

Taking its line from the structure of the economic administration,[58] the Modrow government had provided for internal territorial differentiation in the Original-THA.[59] This led to the setting up of external offices (*Außenstellen*), which were not legally independent entities, in Berlin and the 14 East German cities which were the administrative centres of the *Bezirke*, or Districts, with territorial responsibility for the Region in which each was located.[60]

No such internal territorial differentiation was statutorily provided for in the case of the (present-day) THA, but the external offices were retained as branches (*Niederlassungen*)[61] and authorised to carry wide-ranging decision-making responsibility for small and medium-sized companies.[62] So-called *Beiräte*, advisory boards with a purely consultative function, helped the branches to maintain contact with the political, business, and social forces in their surrounding areas.[63] As soon as the privatisation tasks assigned to the branches have been completed, they

---

54 § 4 section 1 sentence 5 of the THG; § 8 section 4 of the THA Statutes; § 16 GO-THA in the version dated 9th December 1992.

55 § 16 GO-THA in the version of 9th December 1992.

56 § 4 section 1 sentence 1 and § 4 of the THG; § 8 section 1 and section 2 sentence 2 of the THA Statutes; § 15 GO-THA in the version of 9th December 1992.

57 Treuhandanstalt, *Organisationshandbuch*, Guideline 2/90, *Leitlinien der Geschäftspolitik*, serial no. 1.2.2, version valid as of October 1991.

58 See: article by Seibel in this volume.

59 Clause 1 sentence 3 of the Resolution establishing the Original-THA; § 1 section 1 sentence 2 (2nd half-sentence) of the Original-THA Statutes.

60 Bleckmann and Erberich, *Die Treuhandanstalt und ihre Unternehmen*, marginal note 4; Spoerr, *Treuhandanstalt und Treuhandunternehmen*, page 10; Rother, *Die Errichtung der Treuhandanstalt*, marginal note 4.

61 Detlev Rohwedder, speech before the *Volkskammer* on 13th September 1990, shorthand record of the Volkskammer session on that day, page 1681; Busche, *Gesetz zur Privatisierung und Reorganisation des volkseigenen Vermögens* (commentary), § 2, marginal note 15.

62 Treuhandanstalt, *Organisationshandbuch*, Organisation Order no. 8, *Berufung von Beiräten bei den Niederlassungen*, version valid as of November 1990.

63 Treuhandanstalt, *Organisationshandbuch*, Organisation Order no. 01/90, *Leitlinie zur Berufung und Arbeit von Beiräten bei den Niederlassungen*, serial no. 2.9.1, version valid as of October 1991; Weimar, *Entscheidungspraxis der Treuhandanstalt*, page 494.

will remain as so-called branch offices (*Geschäftsstellen*) with a reduced level of authority to carry out any tasks remaining.[64]

In terms of organisational law, the branches are subordinate and dependent parts of the institute under public law,[65] and are thus not a lower-tier authority, the creation of which would have been impermissible under Article 87 section 3 sentence 1 of the German constitution.[66] Although the individual branches have attained a certain degree of independence, to the extent that the THA Executive Board has assigned certain tasks to them to carry out on their own responsibility, this internal arrangement has not led to any hierarchically constructed civil-service organisation. For instance, there is no possibility to contest decisions made by branches in a formal series of administrative actions at the central office of the THA.[67] Such decisions have instead to be attributed directly to the central office.

Retaining the branches as decentralised business divisions represents an internal organisational decision by the THA Executive Board which was made possible by having recourse to the internal organisational power of the Executive Board and its authority to issue orders.[68]

4. Treuhand-Aktiengesellschaften

In creating the THA, legislation provided mandatorily for an internal differentiation by sector of the economy rather than by geographical area,[69] by setting up four so-called *Treuhand-Aktiengesellschaften* (THA AG-companies)[70] as 100 % subsidiaries[71] of the THA.[72]

Detlev K. Rohwedder, as the President of the THA, despite having earlier voiced other views,[73] decided against the setting up of THA AG-companies, so the THA Executive Board

64 Treuhandanstalt, *Organisationshandbuch*, Circular 07/92, *Umgestaltung der Niederlassungen in Geschäftsstellen* (Phase II), serial no. 2.9.2, version valid as of October 1992.

65 County Court of Chemnitz City, Ruling of 29th July 1991, in: DB 1992, page 132; County Court of Gera, Ruling of 14th October 1991, in: VIZ 1992, page 115 et seq.; County Court of Dresden, Ruling of 28th April 1992, in: VIZ 1992, page 332; Regional Court of Cottbus, Judgement of 20th February 1992, in: VIZ 1992, page 322.

66 Maunz, Article 87 of the Constitution (commentary), marginal note 84; Broß, Article 87 of the Constitution (commentary), marginal note 26; for a different view see: Schmidt-Bleibtreu, Article 87 of the Constitution (commentary), marginal note 9.

67 See: Federal Constitutional Court, Judgement of 14th July 1959, in: BVerGE 10, page 20 (48), in a case relating to the Stiftung Preußischer Kulturbesitz (Foundation of Prussian Cultural Assets).

68 Busche, *Gesetz zur Privatisierung und Reorganisation des volkseigenen Vermögens* (commentary) § 2, marginal note 14; Schmidt-Räntsch, *Anmerkung zum Beschluß des Kreisg Gera*, page 116; Spoerr, *Treuhandanstalt und Treuhandunternehmen*, pages 10 et seq.; Weimar, *Treuhandanstalt und Privatisierung*, page 374; ditto, *Entscheidungspraxis der Treuhandanstalt*, page 494; for critical comments: Lipps, *Gesetzgebungs- und Anwendungsfehler im Treuhandrecht*, page 4.

69 § 7 sections 1 and 2 of the THG (old version); § 5 sections 1 and 2 of the THA Statutes.

70 Appendix to THA Statutes.

71 § 7 section 2 of the THG (old version); § 5 sections 3 and 4 of the THA Statutes.

72 See on this point: Lachmann, *Das Treuhandgesetz*, page 239 et seq.; Messerschmidt, *Unternehmensrecht und Unternehmenskauf in den neuen Bundesländern*, marginal note 43.

73 Rohwedder on 24th August 1990, as quoted in *Berliner Zeitung* of 5th July 1990.

failed in this respect to carry out an order given by law.[74] The decisive factor here was the conviction gained in the meantime that the establishment of THA AG-companies would have hindered the THA in doing its real job for a long time to come because of the problems of demarcation and co-ordination that this would have entailed, and because of the difficulties involved in staffing the THA quickly with properly qualified people.[75] The government and parliament of the still existing GDR approved this attitude to some extent,[76] but otherwise accepted it without comment.[77] Legislation later put this violation of the law to rights (although not retroactively) and amended the mandatory instruction to a measure which the THA "can" carry out.[78]

III. Tasks and duties

The requirements and expectations placed on the THA have changed constantly, depending on the overall political and economic conditions obtaining from time to time. The description of the THA's functions and tasks, conditioned as ever by its status under public law, has nevertheless only been changed once, namely in connection with the replacement of the Original-THA with the "new" THA.

1. Original-THA

The tasks and duties of the Original-THA result from its Resolution of Establishment and its statutes, mainly supplemented by the Ordinance converting state-owned *Kombinate*, companies, and other organisations into joint-stock companies dated 1st March 1990[79] (the "Conversion Ordinance") and by the Act on the establishment and activities of private companies and company equity holdings dated 7th March 1990[80] ("Companies Act").

---

74 Rohwedder on 24th August 1990, as quoted in the *Handelsblatt* of 27th August 1990, page 5; see, on this point: Balz, *Rechtseinheit – Wirtschaftseinheit*, page 42 et seq.; Horn, *Gesellschaftsrechtliche Probleme der Umwandlung der DDR-Unternehmen*, page 203; Lipps, *Gesetzgebungs- und Anwendungsfehler im Treuhandrecht*, page 4; Weimar, *Entscheidungspraxis der Treuhandanstalt*, page 493.

75 Rohwedder, speech before the *Volkskammer* on 13th September 1990, shorthand record of the Volkskammer session on that day, page 1680; Balz, *Rechtseinheit – Wirtschaftseinheit*, page 42 et seq.

76 Shorthand record of the Volkskammer session on 13th September 1990, page 1680: "Applause from CDU/DA and DSU".

77 See: article by Seibel in this volume; Lipps, *Gesetzgebungs- und Anwendungsfehler im Treuhandrecht*, page 4.

78 Article 9 no. 1 letter a) of the Act for the Removal of Obstacles to the Privatisation of Companies and for Promoting Investment of 22nd March 1991, *Bundesgesetzblatt* I, page 766; see on this point also: Weimar, *Entscheidungspraxis der Treuhandanstalt*, page 494.

79 *Gesetzblatt der DDR* 1990 I, page 107.

80 *Gesetzblatt der DDR* 1990 I, page 141.

a) *Safeguarding and administering state property*

The task of the Original-THA was to exercise *Treuhandschaft* (trusteeship) over public property,[81] i.e., to administer them in the public interest[82] with the aim of safeguarding the people's property.[83] Turning its back on the previous East German practice of central control of the economy, however, the GDR did not intend that the Original-THA should exercise any function in guiding the economy.[84] In formal terms, as to West German criteria, this was only a trustee relationship in a rather broad sense, as the Original-THA did not become the owner of the property entrusted to it.[85] State property was *de jure* not the property of the state[86] but of the people[87] and thus attributable to society as a whole.[88] The state as the instrument of the people[89] exercised the highest sovereign power of the people over the people's assets,[90] and was thus the holder of the people's rights of ownership of the means of production.[91] By using the term "holder of the legal rights of ownership", the terminology of the GDR described a form of asset categorisation characterised by the granting of operative administrative authority with rights similar to those of ownership, without conferring ownership as such.[92] As the assets administered by the Original-THA remained the property of the people,[93] they could not be property of the Original-THA.

---

81 Clause 2 sentence 1 of the Original-THA Resolution of Establishment; § 2 section 1 sentence 1 of the Original-THA Statutes.

82 § 2 section 3 of the Original-THA Statutes; Hannemann and Bergmann, *Zur Gesetzgebung in der DDR*, page 185.

83 Clause 1 sentence 1 of the Original-THA Resolution of Establishment.

84 Clause 5 sentence 2 of the Original-THA Resolution of Establishment.

85 For a different point of view, see: Rother, *Die Errichtung der Treuhandanstalt*, marginal note 5; Busche, *Gesetz zur Privatisierung und Reorganisation des volkseigenen Vermögens* (commentary), § 1, marginal note 18.

86 Lipps, *Die Zuordnung des ehemals volkseigenen Vermögens*, page 14.

87 Article 10 section 1 (1st amendment) of the GDR Constitution.

88 Mampel, *Die sozialistische Verfassung der Deutschen Demokratischen Republik*, Article 10, marginal note 13; Egler and Schüßler, *Gegenstand und gesellschaftliche Funktion des Staatsrechts der DDR*, page 21; for a different view, see: Moschütz, *Die ökonomischen Grundlagen*, page 132; for a less clear view, see: Seiffert, *Wirtschaftsrecht der DDR*, page 9.

89 Egler and Schüßler, *Gegenstand und gesellschaftliche Funktion des Staatsrechts der DDR*, page 21.

90 Mampel, *Die sozialistische Verfassung der Deutschen Demokratischen Republik*, Article 10, marginal note 13.

91 Egler and Schüßler, *Gegenstand und gesellschaftliche Funktion des Staatsrechts der DDR*, page 21; Seiffert, *Wirtschaftsrecht der DDR*, page 9; Weimar, *Treuhandanstalt und Privatisierung*, page 373.

92 Busche, *Gesetz zur Privatisierung und Reorganisation des volkseigenen Vermögens* (commentary), preliminary note before § 1, marginal note 8; Reblin, *Volkseigentum – Konzeption und rechtliche Ausgestaltung*, marginal note 5; Seiffert, *Wirtschaftsrecht der DDR*, page 15.

93 See, for economic units prior to their conversion into joint-stock companies: Clause 2 sentence 1 of the Original-THA Resolution of Establishment and § 2 section 1 sentence 1 of the Original-THA Statutes; for joint-stock companies, see: § 2 section 2 of the Original-THA Statutes as well as Knüpfer, *Wandlungen der Eigentumsverhältnisse*, page 7; for land and property see: § 5 section 2 sentence 1 of the Original-THA Statutes.

These theoretical refinements, however, had no practical significance at all, as the people's assets were treated as the state's property anyway.[94]

b) Conversion of economic units into joint-stock companies

The Original-THA, in taking on the administration of state-owned assets, took on the task which previous had been that of the state administration directly. Its most urgent task was to collaborate on the conversion of state-owned economic units into joint-stock companies,[95] in order then to take over the administration of the company shares which were about to be created – and which were the property of the people.[96]

c) Privatisation

Even if the Original-THA did serve the purpose of retaining the people's property as a central institution of the communist economic system, it was nevertheless also authorised to undertake privatisation to a limited extent. Interested parties from within East Germany[97] were able to acquire shares, buildings, or machinery from state-owned companies via the Original-THA for the purpose of establishing or enlarging a private company of *Mittelstand* character (small to medium-sized, and usually family-owned and managed).[98] In addition to this, the Original-THA had to collaborate supportively on the reprivatisation of the companies and production co-operatives transferred into state ownership on the basis of the Resolution of the Presidium of the Council of Ministers of 9th February 1972 and thus in connection with existing regulations,[99] for instance with the "unbundling" (division of large companies into smaller units) necessary for this purpose.[100] Another step in the direction of privatisation was the establishment of joint ventures involving the economic units and the joint-stock companies of the

94 Knüpfer, *Wandlungen der Eigentumsverhältnisse*, page 3; Reblin, *Volkseigentum – Konzeption und rechtliche Ausgestaltung*, marginal note 1; Lipps, *Gesetzgebungs- und Anwendungsfehler im Treuhandrecht*, page 1; Mampel, *Die sozialistische Verfassung der Deutschen Demokratischen Republik*, Article 10, marginal note 13; Seiffert, *Wirtschaftsrecht der DDR*, page 15.

95 § 2 section 2 sentence 1 and § 4 section 1 of the Conversion Ordinance; § 4 sentence 1 of the Original-THA Statutes; Hoffmann and Völter, *Die Umwandlung von volkseigenen Betrieben der DDR in Kapitalgesellschaften*, page 19; Rother, *Die Umwandlung von Wirtschaftseinheiten der DDR nach der Umwandlungsverordnung*, marginal notes 9 and 13; Rosener and Roitzsch, *Die Umwandlung von volkseigenen Betrieben in Kapitalgesellschaften*, page 40; Messerschmidt, *Unternehmensrecht und Unternehmenskauf in den neuen Bundesländern*, marginal note 22; Thietz-Bartram and Pfeifer, *Privatisierung von Volkseigentum*, page 5 et seq.

96 § 3 section 1 of the Conversion Ordinance; § 2 section 2 of the Original-THA Statutes.

97 Reverse conclusion from § 1 section 4 of the Companies Act in the version of 7th April 1990.

98 § 5 section 1 sentence 1 in conjunction with § 2 sentence 1 of the Companies Act; Thietz-Bartram and Pfeifer, *Privatisierung von Volkseigentum*, page 15; Zieger and Schönemann, *Neue Bestimmungen zur Förderung privater Unternehmen in der DDR*, page 98.

99 §§ 77 et seq. of the Companies Act.

100 § 5 of the First Implementation Ordinance to the Companies Act of 8th March 1990, *Gesetzblatt der DDR I*, page 144.

Original-THA and legal entities or natural persons from West Germany or farther afield on the basis of the Ordinance on the Establishment and Activities of Companies with Foreign Shareholdings in East Germany dated 25th January 1990[101] ("Joint Venture Ordinance").[102]

2. The THA

The THG removed the validity of the Resolution of Establishment and the Statutes of the Original-THA.[103] This also abolished, with effect from 1st July 1990,[104] the existing description of the purpose and responsibilities of the THA. In its place, the THG and the five Implementation Ordinances supplementing it[105] principally formulated new responsibilities for the THA. The Statutes of the THA dated 18th July 1990[106] and its Rules of Procedure dated 18th September 1990[107] supplement and expand on these regulations.

a) Privatisation

At a prominent point, namely the first sub-clause of the Preamble and in § 1 section 1 sentence 1 of the THG, the legislation states its commitment to privatisation. The task of carrying out the necessary measures is placed on the THA by § 1 section 3 of the THG and by Article 25 section 1 sentence 1 of the Treaty of Unification. The transfer of public assets entrusted to the THA to private legal entities or natural persons is to be carried out as swiftly as possible and to the greatest possible extent[108] by selling them.[109] It was thus not totally prohibited for the THA to grant usufruct rights or easements without also transferring ownership, but this was only permissible as an interim measure until proper privatisation was possible.

The privatisation mandate of the THA does not cover the creation of private ownership through restitution.[110] Likewise, the transfer of tangible assets by the THA to other bearers of

---

101 *Gesetzblatt der DDR 1990 I*, page 16.

102 Maskow and Hoffmann, *Rechtsfragen der Privatisierung in den ostdeutschen Bundesländern*, page 3 et seq.; Messerschmidt, *Unternehmensrecht und Unternehmenskauf in den neuen Bundesländern*, marginal note 21.

103 § 24 section 3 of the THG.

104 § 24 section 2 of the THG.

105 1st Implementation Ordinance to the THG of 15th August 1990, *Gesetzblatt der DDR* I, page 1076; 2nd Implementation Ordinance to the THG of 22nd August 1990, *Gesetzblatt der DDR* I, page 1260; 3rd Implementation Ordinance to the THG of 29th August 1990, *Gesetzblatt der DDR* I, page 1333; 4th Implementation Ordinance to the THG of 12th September 1990, *Gesetzblatt der DDR* I, page 1465; 5th Implementation Ordinance to the THG of 12th September 1990, *Gesetzblatt der DDR* I, page 1466.

106 *Gesetzblatt der DDR* 1990 I, page 809.

107 Treuhandanstalt, *Organisationshandbuch*, Guideline 03/91, *Geschäftsordnung der Treuhandanstalt*, serial no. 1.2.3, version valid as of 9th December 1992.

108 Preamble (first sub-clause) of the THG.

109 § 8 section 1 (1st sub-clause) of the THG; § 3 (1st sub-clause) of the THA Statutes; § 3 section 2 sentences 1 and 2 of the 2nd Implementation Ordinance to the THG.

110 For the definition of the distinction between these terms, see: Rother, *Privatisierung in den neuen Bundesländern – Begriffsbestimmung*, marginal note 7.

public powers, particularly State governments and municipal authorities, is also excluded from the definition of privatisation.

b) Restructuring

The THA's second task consists of implementing measures serving the purpose of (re-)creating the viability of the companies in which it held equity.[111] This includes financial measures,[112] such as the re-organisation of a company's structure,[113] namely "unbundling".[114] Legislation occasionally summarises this with the simple term "restructuring"[115] and thus gives a wide base to this term in economic science.[116]

The THA's restructuring mandate relates only to those companies which are in need of and at the same time are capable of being restructured.[117] This means that only those companies can be taken into consideration for which the expenditure necessary for making them competitive is not disproportionately high.

One apparent, but not actually genuine, exception from the principle that measures for ensuring the survival of companies should only benefit those capable of being restructured is contained in Article 25 section 7 of the Treaty of Unification, according to which the THA is under an obligation to bear temporarily the costs of interest charges on loans taken out prior to 30th June 1990 (monetary union) by companies with registered offices in East Germany, so-called old loans,[118] until an opening balance sheet denominated in Deutschmarks could be drawn up.[119] A final decision has to be made in connection with the relief of old loans,[120] and this in turn can only be taken if the competitiveness of the company will thereby be enhanced.[121] This, however, assumes that the company is capable of being effectively restructured.[122]

111 Preamble (2nd sub-clause) of the THG; § 2 section 6 sentences 1 and 2 of the THG; § 8 section 1 (2nd sub-clause) of the THG; § 9 section 1 of the THG; § 1 section 2 sentence 2 of the 1st Implementation Ordinance to the THG; § 2 sentence 2 (1st sub-clause) of the THA Statutes.

112 Article 25 section 5 of the Treaty of Unification; § 9 section 4 of the THG; § 4 section 1 (3rd sub-clause) of the THA Statutes.

113 § 1 sections 2 and 6 of the THG; § 2 section 6 sentence 2 of the THG; § 9 section 1 of the THG; § 2 (2nd and 3rd sub-clauses) of the THA Statutes.

114 § 2 section 6 sentence 2 of the THG.

115 § 2 section 6 sentence 1 of the THG; § 2 section 7 of the THG; § 9 sections 3 and 4 of the THG; § 2 (2nd sub-clause) of the THA Statutes; § 3 (3rd sub-clause) of the THA Statutes; § 1 section 2 sentence 2 of the 1st Implementation Ordinance to the THG.

116 Kolbeck, definition of "*Finanzierung III: Vorgänge*", page 76.

117 § 2 section 6 sentence 1 of the THG; § 8 section 1 (3rd sub-clause) of the THG; § 3 (5th sub-clause) of the THA Statutes.

118 § 2 section 2 of the Ordinance on measures to relieve previously state-owned companies from the debt burden of old loans (Debt Relief Ordinance) of 5th September 1990, *Gesetzblatt der DDR* I, page 1435.

119 § 4 section 2 sentence 2 of the Debt Relief Ordinance.

120 § 4 section 2 sentence 3 of the Debt Relief Ordinance.

121 § 2 section 2 sentence 1 of the Debt Relief Ordinance.

122 For the initial liquidity adequacy on the "principle of indiscriminate all-around distribution", see: Homann, *Treuhandanstalt – Zwischenbilanz, Perspektiven*, page 1277.

c) Close-down

If the company is not capable of being restructured, the THA has the task of closing it down.[123] The company's operating assets have to be realised,[124] i. e. properly sold off. Such a realisation can be carried out as part of a so-called silent liquidation, but also under the heading of formal liquidation or bankruptcy proceedings (*Gesamtvollstreckung*).

d) Structural adaptation to the economy

The THA is entrusted with the task of creating functioning, i. e. intensively competitive, market structures.[125] This is, however, not linked with any general economic mandate, and particularly not with one of pursuing any regional economic policy.[126]

e) Preserving and creating jobs

The intent of legislation is that the THA should preserve existing jobs and create new ones.[127]

f) Reprivatisation

The decision on claims for the restitution of property or other assets is basically the task of the Property Offices (*Vermögensämter*).[128] The THA collaborates in carrying through reprivatisation to the extent to which the assets entrusted to it are affected. After the justification of the claims at the competent Property Offices is established, the THA is concerned particularly with arriving at an amicable settlement with the beneficiaries in order to clarify their claim.[129]

g) Communalisation

Until the Treaty of Unification came into force, it was in certain cases the duty of the President of the THA to conduct proceedings, in response to applications from municipalities, with the

---

123 § 8 section 1 (3rd sub-clause) of the THG; § 3 (5th sub-clause) of the THA Statutes.

124 § 8 section 1 (3rd sub-clause) of the THG.

125 § 2 section 6 sentences 1 and 2 of the THG.

126 See: Busche, *Gesetz zur Privatisierung und Reorganisation des volkseigenen Vermögens* (commentary), preliminary note before § 1, marginal note 47; Wild, *Die Treuhandanstalt ein Jahr nach Inkrafttreten des Treuhandgesetzes*, page 12; Schlecht, *Politische Entscheidungen und wirtschaftspolitischer Handlungsbedarf*, page 60.

127 Preamble (2nd sub-clause) of the THG; § 2 page 2 (1st sub-clause) of the THA Statutes.

128 § 34 of the Act to regulate unsettled property questions (Property Act), in the version of 3rd August 1992, *Bundesgesetzblatt* I, page 1446; Liebs and Preu, *Probleme der Rückgabe enteigneter Unternehmen in der früheren DDR*, page 149 et seq.; Messerschmidt, *Aktuelle Probleme der Unternehmensrückgabe in den neuen Bundesländern*, pages 2 and 4; for an unclear view, see: Balz, *Rechtseinheit – Wirtschaftseinheit*, page 45; van Scherpenberg and Hornuf, *Die Rückübertragung von enteigneten Unternehmen in den neuen Bundesländern*, page 16.

129 Van Scherpenberg and Hornuf, *Die Rückübertragung von enteigneten Unternehmen in den neuen Bundesländern*, page 16; Wellhöfer, *Struktur und System der Unternehmensrückgabe-Vorschriften*, page 87.

aim of granting parish, town, city, and rural county authorities the ownership of previously state-owned assets used for the purposes of municipal work and services.[130]

The regulations contained in Article 21 section 2 and Article 22 section 1 sentence 1 of the Treaty of Unification initiated, with effect from 3rd October 1990 (unification day), a statutory transfer of the ownership of previously state or communally owned property indirectly serving communal tasks, services, and other purposes.[131] However, this still does not mean that all those tangible assets and property have now come into the possession of the local communities which legislation decrees to be administrative or financial property,[132] and for this reason the President of the THA will continue to be required to bring the relevant property into the possession of the local communities by means of constitutive transfer acts.[133]

h) Property assignment

A further responsibility for the President of the THA consists of establishing, but with only declamatory effect,[134] the statutory transfer of property under Articles 21 and 22 of the Treaty of Unification, the Communal Property Act, or the THA Act, in those cases in which the THA has been assigned the property or the administration thereof.[135] In the same way, the President of the THA has to establish that the statutory assignment of basic property to joint-stock companies has been carried out[136] by means of an administrative act.[137]

i) Issuing investment priority notices

Under § 3a of the Property Act, which was inserted by the Act for the Removal of Obstacles in the Privatisation of Companies and Property and for the Promotion of Investment (Removal of Obstacles Act) of 22nd March 1991,[138] the THA decides by means of an administrative

130 § 1 section 1 sentence 3 of the THG in conjunction with § 1 sentence 1 and § 7 of the Act on the Property of Municipalities, Towns, and Rural Counties (Communal Property Act) of 25th July 1990, *Gesetzblatt der DDR* I, page 781.

131 Schmidt and Leitschuh, *Vertrag zwischen der Bundesrepublik Deutschland und der Deutschen Demokratischen Republik*, Article 21, marginal note 12, and Article 22, marginal note 13.

132 See: article by König in this volume.

133 § 7a of the Act for establishing the assignment of formerly state-owned property (Property Assignment Act) of 22nd March 1991 (*Bundesgesetzblatt* I, pages 766 and 784), in the version of 3rd August 1992 (*Bundesgesetzblatt* I, page 1464); Article 21 section 3 of the Treaty of Unification in conjunction with § 1 section 1 of the Property Assignment Act.

134 Schmidt and Leitschuh, *Vertrag zwischen der Bundesrepublik Deutschland und der Deutschen Demokratischen Republik*, Article 21, marginal note 12, and Article 22, marginal note 13.

135 § 1 section 1 no. 1 of the Property Assignment Act; Schmidt-Räntsch, *Das Vermögenszuordnungsgesetz*, page 976; ditto, *Zum sogenannten Enthemmungsgesetz*, page 172 et seq.

136 § 11 section 2 of the THG in conjunction with § 23 of the THG; § 2 of the 5th Implementation Ordinance to the THG.

137 § 4 of the Property Assignment Act; Schmidt-Räntsch, *Das Vermögenszuordnungsgesetz*, pages 974 et seq.; ditto, *Zum sogenannten Enthemmungsgesetz*, pages 172 et seq.

138 *Bundesgesetzblatt* 1991 I, page 766.

act[139] on the sale, letting, or leasing of land, buildings, or companies encumbered by claims for restitution over which it was entitled to dispose or which was in the possession of one of its equity shareholding companies.[140] Since the Act on Priority for Investments in Restitution Claims under the Property Act (Investment Priority Act) came into effect on 14th July 1992,[141] it has been the THA's responsibility to carry out an investment priority procedure, including the issuing of an Investment Priority Notice in those cases which concern its authority to dispose over the company shares directly or indirectly assigned to its ownership or entrusted to its administration, and any other tangible assets in the possession or the administration of the THA or any of its equity holding companies.[142]

j) Granting of real estate transaction licences

Under § 7 sentence 2 of the Real Estate Trading Ordinance,[143] the President of the THA is responsible for the granting of real estate transaction licences, to the extent that the THA or a THA company is authorised to dispose of the real estate which is to be sold or on which a heritable building right is to be settled.[144] The requirement for a real estate transaction licence serves the purpose of securing claims under property law.[145] The licence can therefore only be granted if there are no restitution claims opposing disposal.[146]

k) Administration of special assets

The trustee administration of the assets of political parties and their affiliated organisations, legal entities, and the mass organisations of the GDR which existed on 7th October 1989 or subsequently took the place of these assets is likewise assigned to the THA.[147] Under the Treaty of

---

139 Derived from § 3a section 4 of the Property Act; Messerschmidt, *Unternehmensrecht und Unternehmenskauf in den neuen Bundesländern*, marginal note 231; Uechtritz, *Das Zweite Vermögensrechtsänderungsgesetz*, page 1654.

140 Balz, *Rechtseinheit – Wirtschaftseinheit*, page 46; Keil, *Ungeklärte Eigentumsverhältnisse*, pages 123 et seq.; Rodegra and Gogrewe, *Zum Unternehmenskauf in den neuen Bundesländern*, page 355; Hübner, *Das Gesetz über besondere Investitionen in der DDR und seine Novellierung*, pages 163 et seq.; Schmidt-Räntsch, *Zum sogenannten Enthemmungsgesetz*, page 171 et seq.; Wittmann, *Öffentlichrechtliche Fragen zum Gesetz über besondere Investitionen im Bereich der neuen Bundesländer*, page 179.

141 *Bundesgesetzblatt* 1992 I, page 1268.

142 §§ 4 to 7 and 25 of the Investment Priority Act in conjunction with § 2 section 3 of the Property Act.

143 Dated 15th December 1977, *Gesetzblatt der DDR* I, page 73, in the version promulgated on 3rd August 1992, *Bundesgesetzblatt* I, page 1477.

144 § 2 section 1 of the Real Estate Trading Ordinance.

145 Von Craushaar, *Grundstückseigentum in den neuen Bundesländern*, page 361; Cremer, *Immobiliengeschäfte in den neuen Bundesländern*, page 33 et seq.; Etzbach, *Grundstücks- und Immobilienrecht*, marginal note 177.

146 § 1 section 2 of the Real Estate Trading Ordinance.

147 Appendix II Chapter II Specialist field A Section III letter d of the Treaty of Unification in conjunction with § 20b sections 2 and 3 of the East German Parties Act; Rein, *Die Parteivermögenskommissionsverordnung*, page 291; Bärwaldt, *Die Treuhandanstalt nach dem Inkrafttreten des Einigungsvertrages*, page 347 et seq.; Volkens, *Kompetenzfragen bei der Rückführung von DDR-Parteivermögen*, page 145 et seq.

Unification, these assets are to be returned to their previous and rightful owners, or otherwise, if they were properly acquired under the criteria applicable in a state under the rule of law, to be returned to the parties and mass organisations, or if not, to be applied to use in the public interest.

Since the Act Amending the Property Act and other regulations came into force in 1992,[148] the Federal Office for the Regulation of Unsettled Property Questions is responsible under § 29 section 2 of the Property Act for the restitution of property and other assets. The other tasks are the responsibility of the THA, which has to act in conjunction with the Independent Commission for Investigating the Assets of the East German Political Parties and Mass Organisations; this Commission is entrusted with investigating the organisations concerned and their assets.[149]

l) Financing of the Loan winding-up Fund and the State Insurance of East Germany (in liquidation)

One last task of the THA consists of bearing part of the costs of the "Loan winding-up Fund"[150] and all of the costs arising in connection with the administration and winding-up of the East German state insurance scheme.[151]

m) Granting of certificated savers' share rights

In pursuance of the regulation contained in Article 10 section 6 of the State Treaty, Article 25 section 6 of the Treaty of Unification, the Preamble (4th sub-clause) and § 5 section 2 of the THG, as well as § 4 section 2 of the THA Statutes, provide for savers in the former GDR to be granted a certificated share right over state-owned assets at a later point in time to compensate for the reduced amount produced by the currency change-over. This is based on the notion that was contained in the proposal submitted as long ago as 12th February 1990 by Alliance 90 to the Round Table which first discussed the setting up of a kind of trustee institution.[152] The so-called people's property was now indeed to become the property of the people in East Germany.[153] Similar considerations had occupied the GDR government at the beginning of 1990.[154] However, it is not possible to perceive any specific allocation of responsibility to the THA from the legislation mentioned. It is more a call upon the legislator, once the structural adaptation of the economy and the restructuring of the budget of the former GDR has been completed, to find a legal basis for distributing ownership of any remaining part of the formerly state-owned assets.

---

148 Second Property Law Amendment Act of 14th July 1992, *Bundesgesetzblatt* I, page 1257.

149 § 10 section 1 of the Ordinance on the Organisation and Procedures of the Independent Commission (Party Assets Commission Ordinance) of 14th June 1991, *Bundesgesetzblatt* I, page 1243.

150 Article 23 sections 3 and 4 of the Treaty of Unification in conjunction with § 6 of the Loan Winding-up Fund Act; Bärwaldt, *Die Treuhandanstalt nach dem Inkrafttreten des Einigungsvertrages*, page 348.

151 § 9 of the Act for the Establishment of the East German State Insurance Scheme in Liquidation; Bärwaldt, *Die Treuhandanstalt nach dem Inkrafttreten des Einigungsvertrages*, page 348.

152 Süß, *Eine Behörde verkauft die ostdeutsche Volkswirtschaft*, page 13.

153 Busche, *Gesetz zur Privatisierung und Reorganisation des volkseigenen Vermögens* (commentary), preliminary note before § 1, marginal note 51.

154 Resolution of the Council of Ministers of 1st February 1990, in: Arbeitsgruppe Wirtschaftsreform beim Ministerrat der DDR (editor): *Regierungskonzept zur Wirtschaftsreform in der DDR*, page 19.

3. Conflicts of aims and ranking order of the tasks

From the above explanations it is clear that both the Original-THA and the THA proper were allocated a large number of tasks. The danger of a conflict of aims in this respect leads to the question of a hierarchical order of tasks.

a) *Original-THA*

As indicated, the Original-THA was given the job of safeguarding state assets. The task of collaborating in converting state-owned economic units was not at odds with this, as the newly created joint-stock companies were themselves the people's property.[155]

However, the activities described of the Original-THA with a privatising character were a different matter, as they shattered the principle of the inviolability of people's property.[156] The conclusion has to be drawn from this that the Original-THA was called upon to safeguard not the stock of capital it found itself with but only the institution of people's ownership. This was in line with the Modrow government's economic policy strategy of the time, which was to stabilise the economy by providing more scope for private ownership but at the same time to retain people's ownership as a form of property ownership.[157]

b) *THA*

The focal point of the tasks entrusted to the THA proper were the handling of the assets allocated to it, or, to be more specific, the privatisation, restructuring, and closing down of companies and the creation of more efficient economic structures. The latter represents the higher mission, which privatisation and restructuring, but also the closing down of companies have to serve.[158] As the top priority, the THA was required to privatise the tangible assets entrusted to it.[159] This is not only revealed by the emphasis on the privatisation task in the THG, in particular the categorical wording in § 1 section 1 sentence 1 of the THG, but also follows from § 2 sentence 2 of the THA Statutes, in consequence of which the restructuring measures have to be carried out for the purpose of privatisation.

There are two different consequences to be drawn from the final interlinking of the privatisation and the restructuring responsibility. Restructuring measures are only allowed to be carried out on those companies (the ones capable of being effectively restructured) where there is a chance of their being privatised. They can only be carried on to the extent that, and for so long

155 For a different point of view, see: Rosener and Roitzsch, *Die Umwandlung von volkseigenen Betrieben in Kapitalgesellschaften*, page 40.

156 Voss, *Veräußerung von volkseigenen Liegenschaften durch DDR-Ministerien zu gewerblicher Nutzung*, page 7.

157 Arbeitsgruppe Wirtschaftsreform beim Ministerrat der DDR (editor): *Regierungskonzept zur Wirtschaftsreform in der DDR*, pages 1 and 18 et seq.; Luft, *Die Treuhandanstalt*, page 1271; Süß, *Bilanz einer Gratwanderung*, page 600.

158 § 2 section 6 sentence 1 of the THG.

159 Keil, *Investitionsvorrang in der Praxis*, page 89; ditto, *Ungeklärte Eigentumsverhältnisse*, page 121; see: Schlecht, *Politische Entscheidungen und wirtschaftspolitischer Handlungsbedarf*, pages 58 et seq.

as, it is necessary to create the conditions which permit privatisation. As soon as it is possible to privatise a company (without any further restructuring), the task of restructuring finishes.[160]

The conflict of aims between restructuring firms and privatising them on the one hand, and closing them down on the other, is resolved by applying the criteria of whether they are capable of being restructured. A company is only to be closed down when there is no prospect of its being restructured; otherwise it is – where necessary – to be restructured and privatised.

One imperative task of the THA, that of securing existing jobs and creating new ones, would run at cross-purposes to the task of restructuring[161] because the adaptation of employment is one of the most urgent restructuring tasks in the THA companies.[162] Closures would also be impossible, and privatisation almost impossible to realise if measures to adapt the numbers employed were not carried out at the same time. As can be seen from the wording of the relevant regulations[163] however, legislation did not give the THA the job of producing its own independent employment policy, but only stated an intended effect of the restructuring of companies which it is required to carry out. As the goal of maintaining employment is subordinated to that of restructuring, it follows that the THA is by no means forbidden to carry out restructuring programmes which lead to a reduction in the numbers employed. On the other hand, the THA does have to endeavour to produce the most labour-intensive solutions it can within the confines of fulfilling its other duties. In the case of companies which are not capable of being restructured, and thus not immediately capable of being privatised either, the retention of jobs by the THA exceeds the limitations of the possible when seen in terms of liquidating assets and cannot be considered apart from intermediate solutions for providing a social safety-net for those declared redundant. Any further area of responsibility for labour market policy on the part of the THA cannot be justified, neither by invoking the German constitution's principle of the "social state"[164] nor by pointing to the THA's over-riding economic responsibility under the Stability Act, in which the aim of full employment[165] is anchored.[166]

The above-mentioned activities of the THA take second place to those tasks under which the THA executes legislative decisions on the assignment of assets. This includes communalisation and the execution of property assignment and investment priority proceedings. The outcome of these proceedings determines whether the THA can take any steps of the type mentioned above

---

160 For a different point of view, see: Weimar, *Entscheidungspraxis der Treuhandanstalt*, page 494.

161 Busche, *Gesetz zur Privatisierung und Reorganisation des volkseigenen Vermögens* (commentary), preliminary note before § 1, marginal note 45.

162 See: Deutsches Institut für Wirtschaftsforschung, *Wochenbericht* 13/93 of 1st April 1993, page 132; Deutsche Bundesbank, *Monatsbericht* for June 1993, page 11; Biehl, *Lösungsvorschläge für Sonderprobleme der ostdeutschen Industrie*, page 33.

163 Preamble (2nd sub-clause) of the THG; § 2 sentence 2 (1st sub-clause) of the THA Statutes.

164 Article 1 section 1, Article 20 section 2, and Article 28 section 1 of the Grundgesetz, the (West) German Constitution.

165 Article 104a and Article 109 section 2 of the Grundgesetz; Article 11 section 1 sentence 2 of the State Treaty; § 1 and § 13 section 3 of the Stability Act.

166 Busche, *Gesetz zur Privatisierung und Reorganisation des volkseigenen Vermögens* (commentary), preliminary note before § 1 of the THG, marginal note 47; see also: Schlecht, *Politische Entscheidungen und wirtschaftspolitischer Handlungsbedarf*, page 60; for a different view, see: Bleckmann and Erberich, *Die Treuhandanstalt und ihre Unternehmen*, marginal note 31.

in the first place. The same applies to the granting of real estate transaction licences, which represent a prerequisite for the disposal of plots of land.

In light of the THA's financial position, the task of providing financial contributions to the Loan Winding-up Fund and the East German State Insurance in Liquidation seriously conflicts with the very costly task of restructuring. Legislation has given precedence to the latter.[167]

IV. Financing

When the Original-THA was set up, the opinion predominated that it would generate for itself the funds that it needed for its activities, principally, so it was thought, from the earnings of THA assets (dividends from companies, revenues from property usufruct contracts and tenancies) and from the proceeds of the privatisation and liquidation of companies entrusted to the Original-THA.[168]

In implementing Article 27 section 1 sentence 2 of the Treaty for the Creation of a Monetary, Economic, and Social Union[169] of 18th May 1990 (the State Treaty), GDR legislation produced the THG and the THA Statutes, which for the first time permitted loans to be taken out and debentures to be issued by the THA.[170] According to these regulations, the THA was authorised to enter into debts totalling DM 17 billion in the period 1990 to 1991. In the Treaty of Unification, the credit limit for 1990 and 1991 was raised to DM 25 billion, and at the same time means were provided for this level of debt to be paid off by 31st December 1995.[171] The Federal Minister of Finance was given authority to prolong the period of the loans and, as already provided for under the State Treaty,[172] permit the credit limit to be exceeded in the event of a major change in general conditions.[173]

During the period that followed, the financial requirements of the THA became increasingly evident.[174] Legislation therefore created, in the Act for the Regulation of the Acceptance of Credit Commitments by the THA[175] of 3rd July 1992 (THA Credit Act), regulations for 1992 to 1994 linked to those of the Treaty of Unification but greatly increasing the THA's room for manoeuvre. It has now been granted a credit limit of DM 30 billion for each financial year,[176] and an additional DM 8 billion could if necessary be taken up with the specific consent of the Federal Minister of Finance.[177]

---

167 § 5 section 1 sentence 1 of the THG; see also: Schäuble, *Der Vertrag*, page 178.

168 § 13 section 1 letters a-d of the Original-THA Statutes.

169 *Bundesgesetzblatt* 1990 II, page 537; *Gesetzblatt der DDR* 1990 I, page 332.

170 § 2 section 7 of the THG; § 4 section 1 of the THA Statutes.

171 Article 25 section 4 sentences 1 and 2 of the Treaty of Unification.

172 Article 27 section 1 sentence 3 of the State Treaty.

173 Article 25 section 4 sentence 3 of the Treaty of Unification.

174 See: Pilz and Ortwein, *Das vereinte Deutschland*, page 166; Siebert, *Das Wagnis der Einheit*, pages 108 et seq.

175 *Bundesgesetzblatt* I 1992, page 1190.

176 § 1 section 1 sentence 1 of the THA Credit Act.

177 § 3 section 2 of the THA Credit Act.

The THA Credit Act made it easier for the THA to raise credit on the capital market by freeing it from the necessity of publishing a prospect prior to selling its securities,[178] and permitting it to issue debentures on German stock exchanges for official trading on the regulated market but without any preceding audit.[179] The THA is therefore considered in financial terms to be a special asset of the Federal government.[180]

Unlike special assets, however, the Federal government bears legal liability for the obligations of the THA. This is due, according to majority opinion, to its position as the body responsible for an institute formed under public law and subordinate directly to the Federal government, which thus bears the onus and obligation of supporting the THA financially.[181] However, this basic principle of the law regarding such institutions is not uncontested,[182] and has anyway so far mainly been developed for savings banks.[183] It is for this reason that § 4 of the THA Credit Act makes the Federal government's legal liability for the debts of the THA unambiguously clear.

V. Supervision

One decisive factor in choosing the legal status of the THA was the fact that as an institute under public law it would stand in a definite context of responsibility dominated by public law.[184] In actual fact, the THA is not only subject to the supervision of its own Administrative Board,[185] but is also integrated in to a many-layered system of external supervision, augmented by the internal control mechanisms of the THA for which the various specialist departments are responsible (Controlling, Finance, Legal, Internal Audit, etc.), and by the various layers of managers and the full normal requirements for counter-signatures and approval. These "internal" control mechanisms are thus similar to those within a company in the private sector, and are not dealt with further in the argumentation set out below.

1. Executive supervision

As an institute under public law, the THA is directly integrated into the hierarchy of public administration and subject to supervision by its superior executive hierarchical levels.

178 § 1 of the Offering Prospectus of Securities Act of 13th December 1990, *Bundesgesetzblatt* I, page 2749.

179 § 5 of the THA Credit Act.

180 Busche, *Gesetz zur Privatisierung und Reorganisation des volkseigenen Vermögens* (commentary), § 2, marginal note 66; Weimar, *Das Treuhandkreditaufnahmegesetz*, page 318.

181 Weimar, *Das Treuhandkreditaufnahmegesetz*, page 318.

182 For an example of an opposing view, see: Oebbecke, *Die Anstaltslast – Rechtspflicht oder politische Maxime?*, page 965; Ehlers, *Verwaltung in Privatrechtsform*, page 321, footnote 156.

183 Berg, *Die öffentlichrechtliche Anstalt*, page 2299 and passim, with further proofs in footnote 51.

184 Schuppert, *Öffentlich-rechtliche Vorgaben für die Treuhandanstalt*, page 457.

185 See above, page 43 et seq.

a) Original-THA

The Original-THA "reported" to the government.[186] The concept of such a reporting relationship was a familiar one in GDR economic administrative law, and indicated a relationship in which the superior executive organ had to maintain a watching brief over the adherence of the economic administrative unit below it with regard to its fulfilment of its duties and to legal discipline, but without the lower unit losing any of its independence – *de jure*, at least.[187]

b) THA prior to 3rd October 1990

When the THG was issued, supervision by the Minister-President[188] took the place of subordination to the government. The Executive Board of the THA had to report regularly to the Council of Ministers on whose behalf the THA was acting,[189] particularly on the progress of privatisation.[190]

It was incumbent upon the Minister-President, as the member of government maintaining supervision, to maintain control under budget law over the financial behaviour of the THA.[191] He had in particular to ensure that companies were only privatised with his approval,[192] and he was only allowed to grant this after the assent of the Minister of Finance had been given.[193] Further budgetary law powers of the Minister-President were connected with the THA's Annual Report and Accounts,[194] but because East Germany joined the Federal Republic of Germany on 3rd October 1990 this was never put into effect. The Minister-President also never completely took over the power of executive supervision over the THA. It was planned that the preparation of the THA's business plan would require the consent of the complete Council of Ministers.[195]

One remarkable point which can only really be understood in its historical context is that, even before the unification of the two German states, authority had been given to the Federal (West German) Minister of Finance to supervise the financial behaviour of the THA. Whether or

---

186 Clause 1 sentence 2 of the Original-THA Resolution of Establishment.

187 See: § 4 section 2 of the Ordinance on the state-owned *Kombinate*, the companies within them, and the state-owned companies dated 8th November 1979, *Gesetzblatt der DDR* I, page 355.

188 § 2 section 2 of the THG; § 1 section 2 of the THA Statutes.

189 § 1 sections 2 and 3 of the THG.

190 § 3 section 3 of the THG.

191 § 96 section 2 sentence 1 of the Act on the budgeting system of the Republic (HO-DDR) dated 15th June 1990, *Gesetzblatt der DDR*, page 313, in conjunction with § 2 section 5 of the THG.

192 § 57 section 3 sentence 1 of the HO-DDR in conjunction with § 96 section 2 sentence 1 of the HO-DDR; § 2 section 5 of the THG.

193 § 57 section 3 sentence 2 of the HO-DDR in conjunction with § 96 section 2 sentence 1 of the HO-DDR, § 2 section 5 of the THG.

194 § 58 section 1 of the HO-DDR in conjunction with § 96 section 2 sentence 1 of the HO-DDR, § 2 section 5 of the THG; § 50 section 1 of the Act on the basic principles of the Republic's budgetary law and of the States of the German Democratic Republic of 15th June 1990 (HGrG-DDR), *Gesetzblatt der DDR* I, page 306, in conjunction with § 59 section 1 of the HO-DDR, § 96 section 2 sentence 1 of the HO-DDR, § 2 section 5 of the THG.

195 § 15 of the THA Statutes.

not the THA was allowed to exceed its uppermost credit limit depended, as defined in the State Treaty of 18th May 1990,[196] on his consent, which would only be given if basic conditions changed fundamentally.[197] The creation of the monetary union on 1st July 1990 had made the granting of sovereign powers to the Federal Republic of Germany over the area of the GDR necessary in order for the Federal government and the Bundesbank to control financial and monetary policy.

c) THA after 3rd October 1990

Since the Treaty of Unification came into force, the Federal Minister of Finance has been exercising executive and legal supervision of the THA, with the executive aspect being exercised under mutual agreement with the Minister for Economic Affairs and the other relevant Federal ministers responsible.[198] The duty to report correlates with the authority to supervise,[199] and is met by the Executive Board submitting a written monthly report ("*Monatsinformation der THA*").[200]

Unlimited executive and legal supervision is unusual in the field of indirect state administration, but not unique, as can be seen from the example of the *Bundesanstalt für landwirtschaftliche Marktordnung* (Federal Institute agricultural Market Regime).[201] Although the usual characteristic of an institute, corporation, or foundation under public law is that it is not subject to the (full) executive and directive power of their superior ministries,[202] legislation can at any time provide specifically for a greater degree of executive supervision in individual cases.[203] Even in the case of unlimited executive supervision, legal entities under public law are entitled to a certain amount of essential independence compared with authorities belonging directly to state administration.[204]

At the same time as being responsible for legal and executive supervision, the Federal Minister of Finance has supervisory duties under budgetary law towards the THA as governed by § 65 section 1 nos. 3 and 4, and sections 2 and 3, and under § 4, § 68 section 1, and § 69 of

196 Article 27 section 1 sentence 2 of the State Treaty (creating a Monetary, Economic and Social Union); sea above also, page 57.

197 Article 27 section 1 sentence 3 of the State Treaty in conjunction with § 2 section 7 of the THG; § 4 section 1 of the THA Statutes.

198 Article 25 section 1 sentence 3 of the Treaty of Unification.

199 § 3 section 3 of the THG as relevant.

200 See above, page 43.

201 § 8 section 3 of the Act for the Re-organisation of the Market Regime Departments of 23rd June 1976, *Bundesgesetzblatt* I, page 1608.

202 Bull, Article 87 of the German Constitution (commentary), marginal note 44; Krebs, *Verwaltungsorganisation*, page 600 et seq.; Maunz, *Article 87 of the German Constitution* (commentary), marginal note 66.

203 Dittmann, *Bundesverwaltung*, page 271; Maunz, *Article 87 of the German Constitution* (commentary), marginal note 66; Lerche, *Article 86 of the German Constitution* (commentary), marginal note 84, footnote 10; Rüfner, *Die Lehre von der öffentlichen Anstalt*, page 609; Spoerr, *Treuhandanstalt und Treuhandunternehmen*, page 89.

204 Maunz, *Article 87 of the German Constitution* (commentary), marginal note 66; Spoerr, *Treuhandanstalt und Treuhandunternehmen*, page 89 et seq.

the Federal Budget Ordinance, as the THA is a "company" within the meaning of § 112 section 2 sentence 1 of the Ordinance.[205] These regulations are supplemented by § 55 and § 53 Section 2 of the Budget Principles Act.

In order to ensure that executive and budgetary law supervision is exercised properly, the Federal Minister of Finance has ordered the THA, in exercising his powers of command under executive supervisory law, only to privatise companies with his consent. A comparable reservation can be derived from the Treaty of Unification itself for the granting of financial assistance and the assumption of other guarantees by the THA.[206] Based on § 65 section 4 of the Federal Budget Ordinance, a simplified procedure applies in the sense that not all the THA's cases of privatisation and financial assistance require approval, but only those above a certain level of significance. Whether any specific case comes under this regulation is determined on the basis of prescribed criteria. The privatisation of a company would, for example, require approval as soon as the numbers employed, its balance sheet total, or its turnover exceeded certain figures laid down by the Federal Minister of Finance.[207] These upper limits have been changed during the course of time, mainly downwards. The Federal Minister of Finance, taking his limited personnel capacity into account, is thus pursuing the goal of checking a constant number of only the most important cases. The THA likewise has to obtain the assent of the Federal Minister of Finance when drawing up its business plan.[208]

The requirement of his prior consent to the prolongation of maturity dates and the exceeding of upper limits in connection with loans extended by the THA under the Treaty of Unification served the purpose of preventive supervision of the THA's financial conduct in 1990 and 1991 by the Federal Minister of Finance.[209] Under the regulations subsequent to the THA Credit Act, his consent is also necessary not only to the exceeding of the upper credit limit[210] but also for the transfer of any part of the credit line not used in any one year into the next financial year.[211]

If so requested by the Federal Minister of Finance, a more extensive version of the auditing and reporting system can be implemented at the THA.[212] As a supplement to the provisions of company law on the auditing of annual accounts, the correct and proper management of the THA's business also has to be examined in accordance with § 93 section 1 sentence 1 of the *Aktiengesetz* or § 43 section 1 of the *GmbH-Gesetz*[213] (the Companies Acts for AG or GmbH-type companies).[214]

---

205 Piduch, *Bundeshaushaltsrecht*, § 112 of the Ordinance, marginal note 3; Busche, *Gesetz zur Privatisierung und Reorganisation des volkseigenen Vermögens* (commentary), § 2, marginal note 24.

206 Article 25 section 5 of the Treaty of Unification.

207 Treuhandanstalt, *Organisationshandbuch*, Organisation Order No. 20/91, *Genehmigungserfordernisse der Treuhandanstalt*, serial no. 1.7, version valid as of 23rd July 1991.

208 § 15 of the THA Statutes in conjunction with Article 25 section 1 sentence 3 of the Treaty of Unification; Spoerr, *Treuhandanstalt und Treuhandunternehmen*, page 14.

209 Article 25 section 4 sentence 3 of the Treaty of Unification.

210 § 3 sentence 2 of the THA Credit Act.

211 § 3 sentence 1 of the THA Credit Act.

212 § 55 section 2 of the Act on the Basic Principles of Budgetary Law in conjunction with § 53 section 1 of the same Act.

213 Basic principles for the auditing of companies in accordance with § 53 of the Budgetary Principles Act, in: MinBlFin 1978, pages 338 et seq.

214 § 53 section 1 no. 1 of the Budgetary Principles Act.

2. Parliament

The THA has been subject, ever since the Original-THA was founded, to parliamentary supervision, which can be divided into control and monitoring functions.

a) Regulation

Parliamentary control primarily takes the form of legislation.[215] It is based on the integration of the executive into sovereign acts of this kind by the people's representatives. This is laid down in the constitution of the Federal Republic of Germany.[216] The legislative acts of the East German *Volkskammer* were also entitled to this kind of binding effect – at least in principal.[217] In addition to the large number of special Acts passed by the *Volkskammer* and the *Bundestag* to guide the Original-THA and the THA proper, budgetary law can be cited as a classical parliamentary control instrument.[218] The *Volkskammer* passed the economic plans and that annual state budget plan in the form of Acts of Parliament,[219] and the Federal government's budget plan is likewise incorporated into an Act by the Bundestag.[220] It should be noted that the *Volkskammer* was initially only formally responsible for legislation. The substance of legislation was dictated by the SED for as long as it represented the supreme political leadership organisation of the GDR. The function of the *Volkskammer* was limited to transforming this political power into state power.[221]

The *Bundestag*, in the course of passing the THA Credit Act, also took on additional powers for guiding the THA by making the possibility of using the 1993 and 1994[222] credit lines and of exceeding the upper credit limit[223] dependent on the approval of its Budget Committee.

b) Monitoring

The monitoring of the Original-THA by the *Volkskammer* was mainly based on the obligation of the Original-THA to account for its activities to the *Volkskammer*.[224] The Council of Ministers was likewise accountable to the *Volkskammer*,[225] and this provided a route for the indirect moni-

---

215 Busch, *Parlamentarische Kontrolle*, page 33.

216 Article 20 section 3, Article 80 in conjunction with Article 77 of the Grundgesetz.

217 Article 49 section 1 of the East German Constitution; § 1 section 2 sentence 1 of the Statutes of the Original-THA.

218 Busch, *Parlamentarische Kontrolle*, page 70.

219 § 3 section 2 of the Act for ordering the GDR state budget dated 13th December 1968, *Gesetzblatt der DDR* I, page 383.

220 Article 100 section 2 of the Grundgesetz; Ellwein, *Das Regierungssystem der Bundesrepublik Deutschland*, pages 141 et seq.

221 Mampel, *Die sozialistische Verfassung der Deutschen Demokratischen Republik*, Article 48, marginal note 6; Jesse, *Die Verfassung der DDR*, page 1821 et seq.

222 § 1 section 2 of the THA Credit Act.

223 § 3 sentence 2 of the THA Credit Act.

224 § 1 section 2 sentence 2 of the Statutes of the Original-THA; see also: § 5 section 2 sentence 2 of the Companies Act in its old version (footnote 97).

225 Article 76 section 1 sentence 3 of the East German Constitution.

toring of the Original-THA. This accountability, anchored in Article 88 of the East German Constitution, meant submitting a comprehensive account of all areas and aspects of the subordinate executive organ.[226]

The THG did not directly take over this accountability obligation towards the government, but the Council of Ministers' duty of accountability under Article 76 section 1 sentence 3 of the East German Constitution was retained, and even strengthened by § 1 section 2 (2nd half-sentence) of the THG.

The work of the *Volkskammer* had to a large extent been transferred to its parliamentary Committees.[227] No special Committee was formed for the Original-THA, so that the 15 standing Committees of the *Volkskammer*[228] were responsible to the extent of their normal areas of responsibility[229] for the affairs of the (Original-)THA. For the execution of their responsibilities the Committees had the right (which is typical of parliamentary systems) to call in and question members of the government and other state and economic administration officials, linked with rights to be given information.[230] It should be added that the *Volkskammer* gave just as little importance *de facto* to its monitoring function as to powers of control so long as the SED retained its dominant position over all state and social organisations, also over the Council of Ministers and the Original-THA.

The monitoring powers of the *Bundestag* are covered primarily by Article 43 section 1 of the German Constitution. The right anchored there to summon members of the government, with which according to ruling opinion an obligation is linked to summon them to answer delegates' questions,[231] is one of which the parliament has made extraordinarily rare use,[232] and none whatever so far in questions affecting the THA.

The monitoring instruments of the formal Parliamentary Question,[233] *Aktuelle Stunde*[234] (roughly equivalent to an "early-day" motion), and informal requests for information[235] are not actually mentioned in the German Constitution, but intensive use[236] is made of them in the Bundestag. It can be proved from the printed papers and plenary session minutes of the *Bundes-*

226 Schulze, *Grundsätze und Mittel zur Durchführung von Entscheidungen der Organe des Staatsapparates*, page 146.

227 Roggemann, *DDR-Verfassungen*, page 225.

228 § 28 section 1 of the Rules of Procedure for the Volkskammer (GO-V), dated 7th October 1974, *Gesetzblatt der DDR* I, page 469.

229 Roggemann, *DDR-Verfassungen*, page 371 et seq.

230 Article 61 section 2 of the East German Constitution; §§ 33 and 34 of GO-V.

231 Achterberg, *Parlamentsrecht*, page 462 et seq.; Busch, *Parlamentarische Kontrolle*, page 117; Magiera, *Rechte des Bundestages*, page 1423 et seq.; Steffani, *Formen und Wirkung der Parlamentarischen Kontrolle*, page 1332; Vonderbeck, *Parlamentarische Informations- und Redebefugnisse*, pages 20 et seq.

232 Achterberg, *Parlamentsrecht*, page 464; Busch, *Parlamentarische Kontrolle*, page 118; Magiera, *Rechte des Bundestages*, page 1424; Vonderbeck, *Parlamentarische Informations- und Redebefugnisse*, page 10.

233 Major parliamentary question, § 76 sections 1, 100–103 of the Bundestag Rules of Procedure; Minor parliamentary question, § 75 sections 3, 104 of the same Rules; Oral questions, 105 of the Rules.

234 *Richtlinien für Aussprachen zu Themen von allgemeinem aktuellem Interesse*, Appendix 5 to the Bundestag Rules of Procedure.

235 Troßmann, *Parlamentsrecht und Praxis des Deutschen Bundestages*, page 14.

236 Busch, *Parlamentarische Kontrolle*, page 118; Vonderbeck, *Parlamentarische Informations- und Redebefugnisse*, page 23.

tag that, up to and including March 1993, the *Bundestag* dealt with five major questions, 37 minor questions, and 12 early-day motions concerning the THA. In addition to this, delegates directed more than 300 (informal) written and oral requests concerning the THA to the Federal Government.

One further source of information for the Bundestag on the THA is the annual report of the Federal Court of Audit (*Bundesrechnungshof*),[237] which includes the findings of the THA's audit.[238] Also, it is possible at any time for the Federal Court of Audit to report immediately to the *Bundestag* on any matters of particular significance.[239]

The discussions and decisions of the *Bundestag* are regularly prepared in its parliamentary Committees.[240] After East Germany joined the Federal Republic of Germany, the various standing Committees concerned themselves with the THA's work within the parameters of the responsibilities allocated to them. The Budget Committee additionally set up a THA sub-committee in accordance with § 55 of its Rules of Procedure which was constituted very quickly, on 24th October 1990, and started work immediately after the first all-German parliamentary elections on 2nd December 1990.[241] Its 13 members were recruited exclusively from ordinary members of the Budget Committee.[242]

The setting up of the THA sub-committee under the Budget Committee correlated with the far-reaching responsibility of the Federal Minister of Finance for the THA within the Federal government.[243] Consideration of the THA principally from the budgetary point of view incurred increasing criticism from the public and from parliament.[244] The *Bundestag* therefore decided on 22nd January 1993 to set up an independent THA Committee to replace the sub-committee, and it started work on 10th April 1993. Amongst its 24 members there are budget experts, as before, but now also delegates with particular competence in other specialist areas such as economics or agriculture.[245]

The work of the newly created parliamentary Committee stands on broader foundations, but in its substance it is continuing the work of the preceding sub-committee, which stretches from collaborating on draft legislation affecting the THA and critical supervision of the THA's ongoing work to the handling of petitions.[246] In order to make the best possible use of the information available to the *Bundestag*, concentrate various different kinds of expert knowledge, and avoid duplication of effort, the THA Committee co-operates closely with other committees such

237 Article 114 section 2 sentence 2 of the Grundgesetz; § 97 of the Federal Budget Ordinance.

238 § 111 section 1 and § 112 section 2 sentence 1 of the Federal Budget Ordinance; § 55 section 1 of the Budget Principles Act; see Section V.3 below for details on the audit carried out on the THA by the Federal Court of Audit.

239 § 99 of the Federal Budget Ordinance.

240 § 54 section 1 of the Bundestag Rules of Procedure; see: Achterberg, *Parlamentsrecht*, pages 678 et seq.; Troßmann, *Parlamentsrecht des Deutschen Bundestages*, § 60, marginal note 4.

241 Cloes, *Die parlamentarische Kontrolle der Treuhandanstalt*, page 292.

242 Article 55 section 1 sentence 1 of the Grundgesetz.

243 See above, pages 60 et seq.

244 For instance: Motion for setting up a THA Committee, Bundestag printed paper 12/433 of 26th April 1991.

245 See: Kriedner, Speech during the Bundestag debate on the setting up of a THA committee on 22nd January 1993, PlPr 12, 11737 (11738).

246 Cloes, *Die parlamentarische Kontrolle der Treuhandanstalt*, page 292.

as those for food, agriculture, and forestry, or the Committee of Enquiry investigating the business activities of the East German group of companies "*Kommerzielle Koordinierung*".

Of the various different instruments for parliamentary monitoring work, one available to the Committees is its power to summon officials for questioning.[247] This right has no relevance in practice, but the THA Committee does make intensive use of the facility for obtaining information on a subject under discussion by arranging so-called "hearings"[248] with experts, representatives of interest groups, and others able to supply information. Such information can come not only from the Federal government and the THA but also from State governments.

Bundestag delegates, particularly those in the SPD, have voiced dissatisfaction over the information provided by the THA and the Federal government to the THA Committee, and have even linked this with the demand for a Committee of Enquiry to be set up.[249] They are concerned by individual cases in which parties acquiring companies from the THA are accused of irregularities in the way they then handled these companies.[250]

According to Article 44 section 1 sentence 1 of the German Constitution, the Bundestag has the right and, if one quarter of its members make an application, the duty to set up a Committee of Enquiry, the work of which can then basically relate to executive bodies subordinate to the government, such as the THA, but only within the parameters of a tightly defined area of investigation. Continual monitoring of the administration is no part of the task of a Committee of Enquiry.[251] To clear up special events and suspected abuses a Committee of Enquiry gathers evidence, the criminal procedures are applied analogously.[252] Witnesses and experts can be placed under oath and penalties can be imposed to enforce or prevent action.[253]

The use of a Committee of Enquiry thus gives parliament very far-reaching powers to investigate the specific individual cases on which its investigations are centred. The existing THA Committee has neither the special legal resources at its disposal, nor, because of the wide scope of matters under discussion, enough time to explore specific individual matters intensively. However, looking at the matter from the opposite point of view, a Committee of Enquiry would not be any substitute for the existing THA Committee in its on-going monitoring of the THA because it is being necessarily limited to a specific brief.

3. Courts of Audit *(Rechnungshöfe)*

The financial behaviour of the THA is subject to a special, external supervision. For the Original-THA, this financial control was the responsibility of the State Finance Audit.[254] From

247 Article 43 section 1 of the Grundgesetz; § 68 of the Bundestag Rules of Procedure.

248 § 70 of the Bundestag Rules of Procedure.

249 *Frankfurter Allgemeine Zeitung* of 3rd June 1993, page 15.

250 Hinrich Kuessner, a SPD delegate, as quoted in *Der Tagesspiegel* of 17th June 1993, page 23.

251 Achterberg, *Parlamentsrecht*, page 449.

252 Article 44 section 2 sentence 1 of the Grundgesetz.

253 Achterberg, *Parlamentsrecht*, page 700; Schröder, *Untersuchungsausschüsse*, pages 1254 et seq.

254 § 13 section 4 of the Statutes of the Original-THA; also: Brunner, *Kontrolle in Deutschland*, page 407.

1st July to 2nd October 1990, the newly created East German Court of Audit[255] was responsible for supervising it.[256] Once the Treaty of Unification came into force the Federal Court of Audit took on this responsibility.[257]

The two first-named institutions in actual fact had no opportunity of making an appearance because of the short time available and the particular situation surrounding the creation of the Original-THA, then of the THA proper, on the one hand, and of the East German Court of Audit on the other.

The only point of practical relevance is therefore the public financial control exerted by the Federal Court of Audit (*Bundesrechnungshof*). The subject of its audit is the economic management of the THA,[258] i. e. all measures decided upon or against which could potentially have financial effects.[259] The criteria applied to this audit are those of correct and proper financial behaviour and its economic aspects.[260] The definition of "correct and proper" relates to the legal suitability of asset management in a very broad sense.[261] "Economic" management means the optimal relationship between costs and benefits,[262] with the principal of "economy" in the sense of thrift[263] being applied to mean that the resources used to fulfil the task in hand are limited to the minimum absolutely necessary.[264] This applies in particular to staff costs and the organisational structure.[265]

The Federal Court of Audit is granted wide scope for its unlimited discretion in selecting the audit project, the demarcation of the audit material, and defining the depth of audit[266] and the type of audit.[267] At the start of its auditing work on the THA, the Federal Court of Audit carried out so-called orientation audits,[268] in order to gain an insight into certain of the THA's working areas such as the handling of the problem of environmental pollution caused by East

255 § 8 sections 1 and 3 of the Act on the East German Court of Audit of 15th June 1990, *Gesetzblatt der DDR* I, page 325.

256 § 95 section 1 in conjunction with § 96 section 2 of HO-DDR, § 2 section 5 of the THG; § 17 of the THA Statutes.

257 § 111 section 1 in conjunction with § 112 section 2 sentence 1 of the Federal Budget Ordinance and § 2 section 5 of the THG where relevant; § 17 of the THA Statutes where relevant; § 55 section 1 of the Federal Budget Principles Act.

258 Piduch, *Bundeshaushaltsrecht*, § 111 of the Federal Budget Ordinance, marginal note 3; Heuer, *Parts IV to IX of the Federal Budget Ordinance*, § 112, marginal note 14.

259 § 89 section 1 no. 2 in conjunction with § 111 section 1 sentence 2 of the Federal Budget Ordinance.

260 Article 114 section 2 sentence 1 of the Grundgesetz; § 90 in conjunction with § 111 section 1 sentence 2 of the Federal Budget Ordinance.

261 § 90 (1st half-sentence) in conjunction with § 111 section 1 sentence 2 of the Federal Budget Ordinance.

262 Provisional administrative regulations on § 7 of the Federal Budget Ordinance, Clause 1.1.

263 § 90 section 3 in conjunction with § 111 section 1 sentence 2 of the Federal Budget Ordinance.

264 Provisional administrative regulations on § 7 of the Federal Budget Ordinance, Clause 1.1.

265 § 90 section 4 in conjunction with § 111 section 1 sentence 2 of the Federal Budget Ordinance.

266 § 89 section 2 in conjunction with § 111 section 1 sentence 2 of the Federal Budget Ordinance.

267 § 94 (1st half-sentence) in conjunction with § 111 section 1 sentence 2 of the Federal Budget Ordinance.

268 Provisional guidelines for work planning in the Federal Court of Audit, Clause 2.7.

German companies. After that, with regard to number of important audit subjects, or where a particularly high susceptibility to mistakes was found, so-called priority audits emerged and are still continuing to emerge.[269] In addition to this, the Federal Court of Audit now carries out an increased number of so-called system audits, in which it is the suitability for its purpose of a procedure prescribed for or created by the THA which is subjected to close scrutiny.[270]

The THA is subject to a wide range of obligations to provide information and reports to the Federal Court of Audit. These form the necessary correlation to the authority of the Federal Court of Audit to maintain complete financial control. The focal point is the THA's obligation to submit all such documents and provide all such information as the Federal Court of Audit considers necessary for fulfilling its tasks.[271] The Federal Court of Audit's right to demand the submission of documents includes the allowance to look at existing documents as well as obtaining supplementary items of information. In addition to this, the Federal Court of Audit can request documents which do not already exist to be presented and submitted if they ought to be available should the business be conducted and the filing maintained in a correct and proper manner.[272]

The authority of the Federal Court of Audit to obtain information from the THA is limited to the appropriate level.[273] The Federal Court of Audit has to take sufficient account of the particular circumstances under which the THA started its work; in the start-up phase in particular the THA had neither the appropriate set of regulations nor sufficient experience or time at its disposal to be able to produce and file documentation to the extent that an auditor would consider ideal. The work of the Federal Court of Audit is also not permitted to restrict the THA's working capacity excessively.

Regardless of the duty to supply information outlined above, the THA has to provide the Federal Court of Audit with certain documents without waiting to be asked; these include the Annual Report and Accounts.[274] In the same way, the THA has to inform the Federal Court of Audit of all measures relevant to the national budget.[275] This in particular includes the privatisation of the companies in which it holds equity if the approval of the Federal Minister of Finance is required.[276]

In actual fact, with regard to all these duties to supply information, the extensive practicability agreements in force between the Federal Court of Audit, the Federal Minister of Finance, and the THA effectively relieve the THA of the burden of work in that the Federal Court of Audit is regularly kept informed by the Federal Minister of Finance, who has the necessary information

269 op. cit., Clause 2.4.

270 op. cit., Clause 2.6.

271 § 95 in conjunction with § 111 section 1 sentence 2 of the Federal Budget Ordinance.

272 Federal Court of Audit, letter of 9th October 1989, I. 1-206011, reprinted in KHR, Part VIII, No. 22.

273 See: Heuer, Parts IV to IX of the Federal Budget Ordinance, § 95, marginal note 3, which applies the principle of commensurate action here.

274 § 69 sentence 1 in conjunction with § 112 section 2 sentence 1 of the Federal Budget Ordinance.

275 §§ 102 and 103 in conjunction with § 111 section 1 sentence 2 and § 112 section 2 sentence 1 of the Federal Budget Ordinance.

276 § 65 section 3 in conjunction with § 102 section 1 no. 3 of the Federal Budget Ordinance.

available to him.[277] This practice gives no rise to legal objections so long as the Federal Court of Audit is kept informed to the same extent and with no significant delay.

The end of the audit procedure as such is marked by an audit memorandum containing the findings of the audit including any consequences or recommendations to be derived from them.[278] The recipient of this memorandum is regularly the THA, which can discuss the finding with the Federal Court of Audit and has to express its view on the memorandum. In addition to this, the audit findings are passed on to the Federal Minister of Finance and to the Administrative Board of the THA.[279] It is possible for the *Bundestag* and the *Bundesrat* (the Upper House of the German parliament) to be informed of matters of particular importance at any time,[280] and otherwise as part of the annual reporting procedure.[281]

4. The *"Länder"* (Federal States)

Since the East German States joined the Federal Republic they have been entitled to fundamental and direct legal rights of control and supervision as part of the work of the *Bundesrat*.[282] In addition to this, the five eastern States (and the whole of Berlin) exert in direct influence by law-making insofar it sets a legal and economic framework for the work of the THA.

In particular, the eastern German states can exert influence over the THA through their representatives on the Administrative Board[283] and the Advisory Boards of the branches.[284] The so-called THA Economic Cabinets (*Treuhand-Wirtschaftskabinette*) are of greater political relevance; they were formed at the various State governments during the course of 1991 on the basis of an agreement dated 14th March 1991 between the eastern German states and Berlin, the THA, and the Federal government.[285] They normally meet monthly, and representatives of the THA take part. The function of these Cabinets is to co-ordinate the work of the THA and the relevant State government particularly with regard to actions relevant to the labour market.[286] The THA Economic Cabinets thus serve to synchronise the responsibilities of the THA with those of the States.[287] The work of the THA is of the greatest possible relevance to employment policy,[288] but

277 For the Federal Minister of Finance's supervision of the THA see above, pages 60 et seq.

278 Provisional guidelines for the treatment of audit findings and for concluding the audit procedure, No. 10.10, reprinted in: KHR, Part VIII, no. 9.

279 § 96 section 1 sentence 1 in conjunction with § 111 section 1 sentence 2 of the Federal Budget Ordinance.

280 § 99 sentence 1 of the Federal Budget Ordinance.

281 § 114 section 2 sentence 2 of the Grundgesetz; §§ 97 and 114 of the Federal Budget Ordinance.

282 Articles 76 and 77 of the Grundgesetz.

283 Article 25 section 2 sentence 2 of the Treaty of Unification.

284 For the status and work of Administrative Board see above, pages 43 et seq.; for the status and work of the Advisory Boards see above, page 44 et seq.

285 *Grundsätze Aufschwung Ost*, extracts reprinted in ZIP 1991, A 43.

286 op. cit., 2nd and 3rd sub-clauses.

287 Spoerr, *Treuhandanstalt und Treuhandunternehmen*, page 12 et seq.; R. Schmidt, *Aufgaben und Struktur der Treuhandanstalt*, page 34.

288 R. Schmidt, *Aufgaben und Struktur der Treuhandanstalt*, page 30.

it has no mandate to make any kind of employment policy itself.[289] It is the States who are primarily responsible here,[290] for instance by taking measures to improve the structure of the region.

5. Commission of the European Communities

When the East German States joined the Federal Republic on 3rd October 1990, this led to a geographical expansion of the European Community,[291] and since then the area of validity of Community law has also covered the eastern German states and thus also the THA.[292] The THA is thus bound by the law on subsidies of the Community[293] in granting financial help. The Commission of the European Communities (Commission) exercises the relevant control over this. In light of the huge number of matters potentially relevant to the provision of aid and subsidies connected with the work of the THA, the Commission took a fundamental decision on 18th September 1991[294] to dispense with the notification of a large number of individual cases by the Federal government,[295] and to reserve the right to examine individual cases mainly when the companies concerned are in the so-called sensitive industries: steel, shipbuilding, motor vehicle manufacturing, fishing, and chemical fibres, as well as certain areas of agriculture.

In order nonetheless to fulfil its supervisory duty, the Commission has imposed the obligation on the Federal government to report in detail every six months on the activities of the THA.

6. Courts

Decisions made by the THA are subject to the supervision of the Courts if the possibility of appeal against them exists. The position of the THA in the field of tension between private and public law[296] leads to the question as to whether in any given case the court of competent jurisdiction is a civil or an administrative court. So long as legislation provides no explicit answer to this question, this will depend on whether the dispute is of a private-law or a public-law nature.[297] The essential point here will be whether the redress being sought is directed towards the norms of private law, which apply to every citizen, or to the principles of public law, i. e. a special law for the state which impinges upon general law in the interests of fulfilling public duties.[298]

---

289 op. cit., page 34.

290 Article 91a section 1, 104a of the Grundgesetz.

291 Rengeling, *Das vereinte Deutschland*, page 1308.

292 Article 10 section 1 of the Treaty of Unification; Rengeling, *Das vereinte Deutschland*, page 1308.

293 In particular, Articles 92 et seq. of the EEC Treaty and Articles 4 and 54 of the EC Coal and Steel Treaty.

294 For details, see: Schütterle, *Treuhandanstalt und EG-Beihilfenkontrolle*, pages 16 et seq.

295 Article 293 section 3 of the EEC Treaty.

296 Weimar, *Handlungsformen und Handlungsfelder der Treuhandanstalt*, page 813; ditto, *Die Treuhandanstalt im Verwaltungsprivatrecht*, page 1; Schuppert, *Öffentlich-rechtliche Vorgaben für die Treuhandanstalt*, page 455.

297 § 13 of the Courts Constitution Act, § 40 section 1 sentence 1 of the Administrative Courts Ordinance.

298 General Senate of the Supreme Federal Courts, in NJW 1988, page 2295 (2296); Kopp, *Verwaltungsgerichtsordnung*, § 40, marginal note 11.

Parties affected by the THA's decisions on investment priority[299] or the assignment of property[300] can, according to the law, make recourse to administrative law. In addition to this, a negative ruling from an administrative court against interim legal protection against an investment priority notice has already been successfully opposed by a constitutional complaint and an interim order applied for in accordance with § 32 of the Federal Constitutional Court Act.[301]

The road must also be taken to the administrative courts in the case of disputes between the THA and a political party or mass organisation affected by asset administration under § 20b section 3 of the GDR Parties Act concerning THA decisions connected with administration of this type of asset.[302] This arises from the fact that the parties concerned are linked to one another in a relationship of sovereign subordination dominated by particular legal regulations which give the state power and place it under obligations.[303] The same applies to the granting of real estate transaction licences.

On the other hand, it is still a matter of debate which courts are competent to examine the THA's privatisation decisions. Before the two German states united, the Commercial Divisions of Berlin-Mitte's City District Court (*Stadtbezirksgericht Berlin-Mitte, Kammern für Handelssachen*) took the decisions in proceedings in which interim orders were being applied to prohibit a planned sale by the THA.[304] The fact that courts and their subdivisions were competent to that extent is not very surprising since there was no independent administrative jurisdiction in the GDR.[305]

---

299 Administrative Court of Berlin, Ruling of 24th August 1992, in Neue Justiz, 1992, pages 514 et seq.; § 12 of the Investment Priority Act; § 3a section 4 of the Property Act in the version dated 18th April 1991; Hübner, *Das Gesetz über besondere Investitionen in der DDR und seine Novellierung*, page 167; Uechtritz, *Das Zweite Vermögensrechtsänderungsgesetz*, page 1657.

300 § 8 of the Property Assignment Act; Federal Administrative Court, Ruling of 19th February 1993, VIZ 1993, page 205; Kittke, *Anmerkung zu dem Beschluß des OVG Berlin*, page 14; Lipps, *Die Zuordnung ehemals volkseigenen Vermögens*, page 15; for a different view with regard to assignment decisions in connection with the 5th Implementation Ordinance to the THG: Wächter, *Übertragungsansprüche nach der 5. Durchführungsverordnung*, page 8.

301 Federal Constitutional Court, Ruling of 12th January 1993, in VIZ 1993, page 111; rejecting at that time: Federal Constitutional Court, Ruling of 3rd December 1991, VIZ 1992, page 64; see also: Uechtritz, *"Gebremste Vorfahrt"?*, pages 142 et seq.

302 Higher Administrative Court of Berlin, Ruling of 8th October 1991, DVBl. 1992, page 280; Administrative Court of Berlin, Judgement of 24th August 1992, in VIZ 1993, page 82 (83); Administrative Court of Berlin, Ruling of 28th September 1992, VIZ 1993, page 171 (172); Constitutional Court of Berlin, Ruling of 11th September 1991, ZOV 1991, page 101 (104); Administrative Court of Berlin, Ruling of 5th June 1991, NJW 1991, page 1970; Administrative Court of Berlin, Judgement of 6th June 1991, NJW 1991, page 1969 (1970); Weides, *Rechtsweg bei Streitigkeiten*, page 820; Stein, *Die Treuhandanstalt im einstweiligen Verfügungsverfahren*, page 895.

303 § 20b of the East German Parties Act, Article 9 section 2 in conjunction with Appendix II Chapter II Special field A Section III No. 1 letter d of the Treaty of Unification.

304 Central Berlin City District Court, Ruling of 8th August 1990, DtZ 1990, page 286; Central Berlin City District Court, Ruling of 16th August 1990, DtZ 1990, page 288.

305 Christoph, *Erweiterung der Zuständigkeit der Gerichte*, page 179; Sendler, *Verwaltungsgerichtsbarkeit in der DDR*, page 166; Stelkens, *Die Einführung der Verwaltungsgerichtsbarkeit*, page 306.

Once the East German states had joined the Federal Republic, there was initially a negative conflict of competence between civil and administrative jurisdiction.[306] The Chamber Court of Berlin (*Kammergericht*) did not find the civil courts but the administrative courts competent – in a case in which an applicant for restitution had been trying to prevent the sale of shares of which he was demanding the return.[307] The Chamber Court agreed that the dispute was one under public law and pointed out the public-law nature both of the claim under property law and of the THA's privatisation responsibility.

The Administrative Court of Berlin (*Verwaltungsgericht*), ruling in a similar case, referred to the *Zwei-Stufen-Theorie* (two-stage theory) and found that the administrative court was the competent one in another case as well.[308] In the appeal proceedings that followed, however, the Higher Administrative Court of Berlin (*Oberverwaltungsgericht*) sent the case to the civil courts.[309] The appeal court found that the outwardly directed behaviour of the THA to which this petition related, i. e. the disposal of assets or the decision not to dispose of them, was designed by legislation under civil law, whereas the assumption that it was preceded by an investigative or decision-making step under public law was pure fiction. The "two-stage theory" did not apply in view of the active legal status endowed up on the THA by legislation.

This legal opinion of the Higher Administrative Court of Berlin has been widely supported in other court decisions.[310]

However, there is still a degree of uncertainty regarding the transfer of mining property.[311]

The ruling opinion in legal literature is, however, that appeals against decisions of the THA relating to the process of privatisation should be taken to the administrative courts.[312] In the

306 Kittke, *Anmerkung zu dem Beschluß des OVG Berlin*, page 13.

307 Regional Court of Berlin, Ruling of 5th December 1990, in BHEI, 8323.

308 Administrative Court of Berlin, Ruling of 19th December 1990, in BHEI, 8324.

309 Higher Administrative Court of Berlin, Ruling of 22nd January 1991, in BHEI, 8325.

310 Administrative Court of Berlin, Ruling of 24th January 1991, RGV, I 16; Administrative Court of Berlin, Ruling of 6th June 1991, RGV, D V 1; County Court of Erfurt, Judgement of 29th July 1991, in BHEI, 8321; Regional Court of Dresden, Ruling of 29th November 1991, DtZ 1992, page 220; Chamber Court, Judgement of 3rd March 1992, ZIP 1992, page 955; however, for a divergent view see: Chamber Court, Judgement of 25th November 1991, ZIP 1992, page 211 (212).

311 Competence of civil courts: Administrative Court of Berlin, 8th April 1991, RGV, I 20; competence of administrative courts: State Court of Berlin, Judgement of 15th August 1991, DtZ 1992, page 159.

312 Horn, *Das Zivil- und Wirtschaftsrecht im neuen Bundesgebiet*, page 386; Spoerr, *Treuhandanstalt und Treuhandunternehmen*, page 208; Krebs, *Rechtsschutzprobleme bei Entscheidungen der Treuhandanstalt*, page 1515; Hohmeister, *Handlungsbefugnisse der Treuhandanstalt*, page 288; Weimar, *Handlungsformen und Handlungsfelder der Treuhandanstalt*, page 822; ditto, *Die Treuhandanstalt im Verwaltungsprivatrecht*, page 14; ditto, *Treuhandanstalt und Treuhandgesetz*, page 13; Bleckmann and Erberich, *Die Treuhandanstalt und ihre Unternehmen*, marginal note 87; Busche, *Gesetz zur Privatisierung und Reorganisation des volkseigenen Vermögens* (Commentary), § 2, marginal notes 7–8; Kerber and Stechow, *Das Treuhandaußenrecht*, page 113; for a different view see: Scheifele, *Praktische Erfahrungen beim Unternehmenskauf*, page 560; ditto, *Zur Anwendung des § 3a Vermögensgesetz*, page 1353; Stein, *Die Treuhandanstalt im einstweiligen Verfügungsverfahren*, page 895; Weides, *Rechtsweg bei Streitigkeiten*, page 820.

majority of cases the "two-stage theory" is invoked here;[313] it was developed for the field of service-providing administration,[314] and it is as a consequence of this that the decision is made on whether the conditions have been met for an allocation under public law by means of an administrative act while the implementation of this decision can, at choice, take a public law or a private law course.[315] Although other authors categorise THA decisions on the sale of their assets under private law, because of the special public-law ramifications under which the THA has to work as a public authority, they find in favour of the administrative court competence.[316]

Another part of the literature, which likewise categorise THA privatisation decisions under private law, finds in agreement with the ruling opinion described here that existing court decisions indicate the competence of the civil courts.[317]

The last-mentioned opinion deserves to be given preference. Privatisations by the THA cannot be regarded as active administration because no assets are being distributed in favour of the party being allowed to make the purchase. The THA is in such cases pursuing responsibilities which are genuinely those of the state in re-ordering the economic structure by disposing of formerly state-owned assets. Privatisation decisions by the THA therefore do not fall within the area of application of the "two-stage theory", and should instead be categorised as single-stage proceedings under private law.[318] Actions seeking to overturn THA privatisation decisions are in fact seeking to enforce or prohibit actions under private law, and the route to civil law is provided for petitions for legal protection in such matters. The fact that the THA is subject in its decisions to particular public-law regulations is not determining the legal route, but it has to be taken into account by the civil court.[319]

---

313 Fahrenbach, *Das Privatisierungsverfahren nach dem Treuhandgesetz*, page 269; Hohmeister, *Handlungsbefugnisse der Treuhandanstalt*, page 288; Kerber and Stechow, *Die Treuhandanstalt im Spannungsverhältnis*, page 51; ditto, *Das Treuhandaußenrecht*, page 107 et seq.; Wolter, *Rechtswegprobleme bei Treuhandentscheidungen*, page 305; Kohler, *Verwaltungs- oder zivilrechtliche Sicherung*, page 132; R. Schmidt, *Aufgaben und Struktur der Treuhandanstalt*, page 22; Horn, *Privatisierung und Reprivatisierung von Unternehmen*, page 155; ditto, *Das Zivil- und Wirtschaftsrecht im neuen Bundesgebiet*, page 385; Busche, *Gesetz zur Privatisierung und Reorganisation des volkseigenen Vermögens* (commentary), § 2, marginal note 7; Spoerr, *Treuhandanstalt und Treuhandunternehmen*, page 208; Bleckmann and Erberich, *Die Treuhandanstalt und ihre Unternehmen*, marginal note 87.

314 Zuleeg, *Die Zweistufenlehre*, page 279.

315 Weimar, *Handlungsformen und Handlungsfelder der Treuhandanstalt*, page 816.

316 Krebs, *Rechtsschutzprobleme bei Entscheidungen der Treuhandanstalt*, pages 1520 et seq.; Weimar, *Handlungsformen und Handlungsfelder der Treuhandanstalt*, pages 816 et seq.; ditto, *Die Treuhandanstalt im Verwaltungsprivatrecht*, pages 7 et seq. and page 14.

317 Kittke, *Anmerkung zu dem Beschluß des OVG Berlin*, page 14; Scheifele, *Praktische Erfahrungen beim Unternehmenskauf*, page 560; ditto, *Zur Anwendung des § 3a Vermögensgesetz*, page 1353; Stein, *Die Treuhandanstalt im einstweiligen Verfügungsverfahren*, page 895; Weides, *Rechtsweg bei Streitigkeiten*, page 819.

318 Weides, *Rechtsweg bei Streitigkeiten*, page 819; Weimar, *Handlungsformen und Handlungsfelder der Treuhandanstalt*, page 816; ditto, *Die Treuhandanstalt im Verwaltungsprivatrecht*, page 7.

319 Higher Administrative Court of Berlin, Ruling of 22nd January 1991, BHEI, 8325, page 4 et seq.; Kittke, *Anmerkung zu dem Beschluß des OVG Berlin*, page 14; Scheifele, *Praktische Erfahrungen beim Unternehmenskauf*, page 560; ditto, *Zur Anwendung des § 3a Vermögensgesetz*, page 1353; Stein, *Die - Treuhandanstalt im einstweiligen Verfügungsverfahren*, page 896; Weides, *Rechtsweg bei Streitigkeiten*, page 821.

Agreement reigns in court decisions and in the legal literature on the fact that a contract between the THA and a purchaser for the privatisation of THA assets is to be categorised as existing under civil law, and that the civil courts are therefore competent to adjudicate on actions against the THA arising out of this legal relationship.[320] This also applies to the obligation taken on by the purchaser under § 3c of the Property Act to tolerate the reverse conveyance of the property to the beneficiary.[321]

Decisions by the THA on restructuring activities, particularly those involving relief from old debts, the granting of compensatory claims to payment, and the taking on of sureties and guarantees is in some literature given the character of private law, so that the route to the civil courts would be open in the event of a dispute.[322] This view is based on the notion that the THA is simply acting in these cases as the sole shareholder of its subsidiary companies.

In most cases, THA restructuring activities are allocated to public law, so that they can be revised by the administrative courts.[323] The argument in favour of this view is that the acceptance of the old debts and the settlement of compensatory claims for payment represent in any case financial measures based on special legal grounds[324] and on conditions which a private businessman would not accept. This is in fact state financial aid for boosting the economy, taking account of the special circumstances of the companies affected in connection with the transfer from a planned to a free market economy. The same applies to guarantees and loans by the THA made because of the weak credit ratings of these companies.[325] Disputes over all these activities therefore belong in the administrative courts, being disputes about subsidies. When the THA provides financial assistance on terms customary in the market, the situation of a subsidy cannot be stated to exist, and in these cases, in which the THA is merely pursuing its interests as

---

320 Chamber Court, Ruling of 30th May 1991, RGV, I 23; Chamber Court, Judgement of 3rd March 1992, ZIP 1992, page 955; Horn, *Das Zivil- und Wirtschaftsrecht im neuen Bundesgebiet*, page 386; Krebs, *Rechtsschutzprobleme bei Entscheidungen der Treuhandanstalt*, page 1520; Spoerr, *Treuhandanstalt und Treuhandunternehmen*, page 208; Stein, *Die Treuhandanstalt im einstweiligen Verfügungsverfahren*, page 895; Weimar, *Treuhandanstalt und Treuhandgesetz*, Page 13; Busche, *Gesetz zur Privatisierung und Reorganisation des volkseigenen Vermögens* (commentary), § 2, marginal note 8; Bleckmann and Erberich, *Die Treuhandanstalt und ihre Unternehmen*, marginal note 87.

321 Weimar and Simon, *Offene Fragen zum § 3c Vermögensgesetz*, page 100.

322 Kerber and Stechow, *Das Treuhandaußenrecht*, page 115; Busche, *Gesetz zur Privatisierung und Reorganisation des volkseigenen Vermögens* (commentary), § 2, marginal note 5.

323 Bleckmann and Erberich, *Die Treuhandanstalt und ihre Unternehmen*, marginal note 88; Hohmeister, *Handlungsbefugnisse der Treuhandanstalt*, page 289; Krebs, *Rechtsschutzprobleme bei Entscheidungen der Treuhandanstalt*, page 1514 and pages 1518 et seq.; Timm, *Die Sanierung der sogenannten "Treuhandunternehmen"*, page 424; Weimar, *Treuhandanstalt und Treuhandgesetz*, page 13; ditto, *Handlungsformen und Handlungsfelder der Treuhandanstalt*, page 822; ditto, *Die Treuhandanstalt im Verwaltungsprivatrecht*, pages 9 et seq.

324 § 2 of the Debt Relief Ordinance, § 24 of the Deutschmark Balance Sheet Act.

325 Bleckmann and Erberich, *Die Treuhandanstalt und ihre Unternehmen*, marginal note 88; Hohmeister, *Handlungsbefugnisse der Treuhandanstalt*, page 289; Krebs, *Rechtsschutzprobleme bei Entscheidungen der Treuhandanstalt*, page 1514 and pages 1520 et seq.; Timm, *Die Sanierung der sogenannten "Treuhandunternehmen"*, page 424; Weimar, *Treuhandanstalt und Treuhandgesetz*, page 13; ditto, *Handlungsformen und Handlungsfelder der Treuhandanstalt*, page 822; ditto, *Die Treuhandanstalt im Verwaltungsprivatrecht*, page 9 et seq.; see also: Schütterle, *Treuhandanstalt und EG-Beihilfenkontrolle*, page 17, on the point of view of the EU Commission.

the sole shareholder, it is acting under private law,[326] which means that the civil courts are competent.

It is a matter of some debate whether companies whose shares are directly or indirectly in the hands of the THA would be entitled to raise an action against the THA before the administrative courts. They would be so entitled if the relevant decision of the THA in connection with the restructuring of the company, particularly if it was a decision not to undertake some given restructuring activity, was able to damage the personal rights of the company affected.[327] To this extent, opinion is unanimous that the only claim that could be entertained would be one for equal treatment under Article 3 section 1 of the German Constitution in conjunction with the principles of the administration's self-commitment, as special legal principles[328] do not help to define the legal position.[329] The majority of authors who discuss this problem consider, however, that any claim of this kind from the companies affected would have to be rejected.[330] The companies involved are subject to the privatisation intentions of the state, and do not hold any rights or fulfil any function that can be separated from the area of responsibility of the THA.[331] They are therefore not to be categorised under the private sphere under constitutional protection but to the state function sphere, which offers no such protection.

To the extent that the THA exercises co-determination and supervisory powers over the companies in which it holds equity, it is acting on the basis of the provisions of civil law.[332] The same applies to the unbundling and closure of companies.[333] For actions in this connection one have to apply to the civil courts.[334]

326 Busche, *Gesetz zur Privatisierung und Reorganisation des volkseigenen Vermögens* (commentary), § 2, marginal note 5; on this subject in general, see: Weimar, *Zum Wirkungsbereich der Treuhandanstalt*, page 107; ditto, *Die Treuhandanstalt im Verwaltungsprivatrecht*, page 10.

327 § 42 section 2 of the Administrative Courts Ordinance.

328 In particular §§ 24 and 26 of the Deutschmark Balance Sheet Act, § 2 of the Debt Relief Ordinance, and Article 25 section 5 of the Treaty of Unification.

329 Timm, *Die Sanierung der sogenannten "Treuhandunternehmen"*, page 424 et seq.; Horn, *Das Zivil- und Wirtschaftsrecht im neuen Bundesgebiet*, page 388 et seq.; Krebs, *Rechtsschutzprobleme bei Entscheidungen der Treuhandanstalt*, page 1517.

330 Timm, *Die Sanierung der sogenannten "Treuhandunternehmen"*, page 424 et seq.; Horn, *Das Zivil- und Wirtschaftsrecht im neuen Bundesgebiet*, page 388 et seq.; Müller, *§ 24 of the Deutschmark Balance Sheet Act*, marginal note 12; see also: Administrative Court of Berlin, Ruling of 19th December 1990, BHEI, 8324, pages 7 et seq. on the right of a company to raise an action against its privatisation.

331 For a different view see: Krebs, *Rechtsschutzprobleme bei Entscheidungen der Treuhandanstalt*, page 1517.

332 Weimar, *Die Treuhandanstalt im Verwaltungsprivatrecht*, page 10.

333 Busche, *Gesetz zur Privatisierung und Reorganisation des volkseigenen Vermögens* (commentary), § 2, marginal note 5; Kerber and Stechow, *Das Treuhandaußenrecht*, page 51; Weimar, *Die Treuhandanstalt im Verwaltungsprivatrecht*, pages 9 and 11, referring to administrative private law.

334 For a different view see: Weimar, *Die Treuhandanstalt im Verwaltungsprivatrecht*, page 14, who regards the administrative court route as the correct one for disputes under administrative private law.

VI. Legal liability

The position of the THA in the field of tension between private and public law leads to the further question as to whether it would have to bear liability towards an injured third party under the public law regulations on the legal liability of the state or an official department for the actions of any employee that gave rise to an action for damages. If this is not the case, the THA would bear liability for improper behaviour by its employees only under the special conditions of the general civil law regulations on the imputation of liability (§§ 31, 89, 278, and 831 of the Civil Code).[335]

One approach that could be considered would be government liability under the terms of Article 34 sentence 1 of the German Constitution. Although the East German State Liability Act of 12th May 1969,[336] which provides for direct state liability independent of the question of culpability for the harmful consequences of illegal sovereign behaviour,[337] remained in force in a modified form even after the unification of the two states,[338] it has gained no significance for administration at the Federal level; as state law, it merely impinges upon state and lower-tier government in the eastern German States.[339]

Government liability under Article 34 sentence 1 of the German Constitution only takes effect if a government employee (who does not have to be a *Beamter* or professional civil servant with security of tenure as defined in German law[340]) behaves improperly in a manner that gives rise to a claim for damages – under the provisions of ordinary law, in particular § 839 of the Civil Code –[341] from a third party.[342] Liability is transferred to the THA, which at the same time releases its employees from liability for damages,[343] if the employee concerned has been acting

335 Bender, *Staatshaftungsrecht*, marginal notes 401 et seq.; Dagtoglou, *Article 34 of the German Constitution* (Commentary), marginal note 86; Papier, *Article 34 of the German Constitution* (Commentary), marginal notes 89 and 106; Rüfner, *Das Recht der öffentlich-rechtlichen Schadensersatz- und Entschädigungsleistungen*, § 51, marginal note 33.

336 *Gesetzblatt der DDR* 1969 I, page 34, amended by the Act of 14th December 1988, *Gesetzblatt der DDR* I, page 329.

337 § 1 section 1 of the GDR State Liability Act; see: Amtliche Erläuterung zu Anlage II Kapitel II Sachgebiet B Abschnitt II Nr. 1 of the Treaty of Unification, *Bundestag printed paper* 11/7817, of 10th September 1990, page 63; Maurer, *Allgemeines Verwaltungsrecht*, § 28, marginal note 39; Ossenbühl, *Staatshaftungsrecht*, page 394.

338 Article 9 section 1 sentence 1 and section 2 in conjunction with Appendix II Chapter III Specialist field B Section III No. 1 of the Treaty of Unification; for a critical view, see: Ossenbühl, *Staatshaftungsrecht*, page 392.

339 Maurer, *Allgemeines Verwaltungsrecht*, § 28, marginal note 42; Rüfner, *Das Recht der öffentlich-rechtlichen Schadensersatz- und Entschädigungsleistungen*, § 50, marginal note 11.

340 For a general view, see: Bender, *Staatshaftungsrecht*, marginal note 423.

341 Papier, *Article 34 of the German Constitution* (Commentary), marginal note 87.

342 Meyer, *Article 34 of the German Constitution* (Commentary), marginal note 31; Scholz, *Staatshaftungs- und Entschädigungsrecht*, page 17.

343 Bender, *Staatshaftungsrecht*, marginal note 389; Papier, *Article 34 of the German Constitution* (Commentary), marginal note 87; Rüfner, *Das Recht der öffentlich-rechtlichen Schadensersatz- und Entschädigungsleistungen*, § 51, marginal note 5; Scholz, *Staatshaftungs- und Entschädigungsrecht*, page 38.

"in the exercise of the public office entrusted to him or her" (Article 34 sentence 1 of the German Constitution). This is incontestably the case if the behaviour under discussion is attributable to public law.[344] In the context of investment priority, property assignment, and real estate transaction approval proceedings, the employees of the THA are acting with sovereign authority.[345] The same applies to the THA's administration of special assets[346] and to the first stage of the procedure for granting subsidies.[347] Accordingly, it is possible for the THA to be sued under the law on government liability if the events concerned fall within these fields.[348]

It is questionable whether it is correct to refer to the exercise of official office within the meaning of Article 34 of the German Constitution in the field of administrative private law as well, with respect to those cases in which the THA employee is fulfilling public administrative functions under private law.[349] According to the legal opinion taken in this article,[350] the THA is acting here purely under private law, even if it is at the same time fulfilling the state's task of rearranging the economic structure in the eastern German states.[351] One legal opinion (which was the ruling one in the beginning) held that the area of application of the rules on government liability was defined strictly according to the legal form of the administrative action concerned and was thus limited to the field of public activities.[352] Justification for this view is based on the history of the origination of Article 34,[353] and leads to the conclusion that Article 131 of the Weimar Constitution as interpreted by decisions handed down by the Weimarian courts should be absorbed into the present-day German Constitution in Article 34.[354] Taking this view, any

---

344 Bender, *Staatshaftungsrecht*, marginal notes 400 et seq.; Papier, *Article 34 of the German Constitution* (Commentary), marginal notes 88 and 108; Maurer, *Allgemeines Verwaltungsrecht*, § 25, marginal note 12; Ossenbühl, *Staatshaftungsrecht*, pages 25 et seq. and 38; Meyer, *Article 34 of the German Constitution* (Commentary), marginal note 39.

345 See above, pages 69 et seq.

346 See above, pages 70.

347 See above, pages 73 et seq.

348 For government liability at the first level within the meaning of the "two-stage theory", see: Bender, *Staatshaftungsrecht*, marginal note 409; Dagtoglou, *Article 34 of the German Constitution* (Commentary), marginal notes 87 and 418.

349 Bender, *Staatshaftungsrecht*, marginal note 442; Maurer, *Allgemeines Verwaltungsrecht*, § 25, marginal note 56.

350 See above, page 72 et seq.

351 See above, page 51; Scheifele, *Praktische Erfahrungen beim Unternehmenskauf*, page 560; Weimar, *Die Treuhandanstalt im Verwaltungsprivatrecht*, page 13.

352 Bender, *Staatshaftungsrecht*, marginal note 408; Papier, *§ 839 of the Civil Code* (Commentary), marginal notes 124 et seq.; ditto, *Article 34 of the German Constitution* (Commentary), marginal notes 88 and 111; Maurer, *Allgemeines Verwaltungsrecht*, § 25, marginal note 56; Jarass, *Article 34 of the German Constitution* (Commentary), marginal note 6; Rittstieg, *Article 34 of the German Constitution* (Commentary), marginal note 14; Klein, *Article 34 of the German Constitution* (Commentary), marginal note 5.

353 Described in detail in: Dagtoglou, *Article 34 of the German Constitution* (Commentary), origins and history.

354 Dagtoglou, *Article 34 of the German Constitution* (Commentary), marginal note 86; Papier, *Article 34 of the German Constitution* (Commentary), marginal notes 107 et seq.

(and every) sovereign action could lead to government liability.[355] However, this line of argument tends to overlook the fact that administration under private law, and the problems that arise in its wake, have only recently started to be discussed by legal scholars.[356] Legislation still had the picture in mind of an administrative body acting regularly with public power in exercising its office.[357] Legislation relating to Article 34 of the German Constitution has therefore not yet taken up any definite stand on the question of government liability in cases when official duty is being performed under private law.

If the executive makes use of forms of action under private law in fulfilling its responsibilities, it cannot thus absolve itself of the specific terms of public law.[358] For example, one of the THA's most important duties is to be consistent in tendering proceedings and to treat all participants equally.[359] These requirements of public law are official obligations which also exist under private law and which can give rise to claims under government liability if not properly observed.[360] This is ignored by those authors who think that government liability principals can be applied across the board to administrative private law.[361]

VII. Summary

Even the Original-THA was set up as an institution under public law and on the basis of West German models, and the THA proper has retained this legal status. Legislation has given it a constitution which includes an Executive and an Administrative Board and is thus similar to an *Aktiengesellschaft* (the German equivalent of a joint-stock company). Internal differentiation in the form of external offices was provided for in legislation relating to the Original-THA, but this did not apply to its successor. The THA's power to decide on its own organisation made it possible to maintain them as branches. The decision not to form THA *Aktiengesellschaften*, on the other hand, was taken regardless of legislative instructions but with political approval.

Whilst it was the main task of the Original-THA to retain the core of public ownership, the main and focal task of the present-day THA is to create a new structure for the economy in the

---

355 Bender, *Staatshaftungsrecht*, marginal note 406; Dagtoglou, *Article 34 of the German Constitution* (Commentary), marginal note 86; Papier, *Article 34 of the German Constitution* (Commentary), marginal note 107.

356 Achterberg, *Allgemeines Verwaltungsrecht*, § 12, marginal note 1; Ehlers, *Verwaltung in Privatrechtsform*, page 532.

357 Achterberg, *Allgemeines Verwaltungsrecht*, § 12, marginal note 1; Bender, *Staatshaftungsrecht*, marginal note 406

358 Bender, *Staatshaftungsrecht*, marginal note 405; Ehlers, *Verwaltung in Privatrechtsform*, pages 212 et seq.

359 Dagtoglou, *Article 34 of the German Constitution* (Commentary), marginal notes 88 and 420 et seq.

360 op. cit., marginal note 88; Meyer, *Article 34 of the German Constitution* (Commentary), marginal note 44.

361 Ossenbühl, *Staatshaftung*, page 25 et seq.; Ehlers, *Verwaltung in Privatrechtsform*, pages 532 et seq.; Böhme, *Die Beschränkung der Amtshaftung auf die Hohheitsverwaltung*, pages 158 et seq.; for the THA specifically, see: Scheifele, *Praktische Erfahrungen beim Unternehmenskauf*, page 560; and: Weimar, *Die Treuhandanstalt im Verwaltungsprivatrecht*, page 13.

eastern German states by taking the privatisation route. The restructuring of companies thus has to take its line from the first priority of privatising them. Preserving existing jobs and creating new ones has not been laid down as a prime task of the THA but merely has to be taken into account in the fulfilment of its other duties.

Contrary to first assumptions, enormous amounts of outside capital are necessary for the THA to finance its activities; the THA can take on this debt on relatively soft terms, but still only within limitations laid down by law.

As an institute under public law, the THA is subject to control by the government, parliament, the Federal Court of Audit, the various States, and the European Commission. The civil courts are responsible for examining the THA's privatisation decisions, as well as – under company law – the dealings in its companies in which it holds equity, but restructuring programmes would mainly come under the administrative courts because of their subsidy-like character. The same applies to the field in which the THA acts with public power.

Government liability under Article 34 of the German Constitution in the event of improper behaviour by its employees applies only if it has been acting with public power or at least violating specific public law requirements in the case of private law actions. Otherwise, the THA bears legal liability under general civil law.

VIII. Literature

Achterberg, Norbert: *Parlamentsrecht*. Tübingen 1984.

ditto: *Allgemeines Verwaltungsrecht*. Heidelberg [2]1986.

Arbeitsgruppe Wirtschaftsreform beim Ministerrat der DDR (editor): *Regierungskonzept zur Wirtschaftsreform in der DDR*. Berlin 1990.

Bärwaldt, Roman: Die Treuhandanstalt nach dem Inkrafttreten des Einigungsvertrages. In: *Deutsch-Deutsche Rechts-Zeitschrift* 1990, pages 347 and 348.

Balz, Manfred: Rechtseinheit – Wirtschaftseinheit: Die Rolle der Treuhandanstalt. In: *Zeitschrift für Vermögens- und Investitionsrecht* 1992, pages 41 to 47.

Bender, Bernd: *Staatshaftungsrecht – Schadensersatz-, Entschädigungs- und Folgenbeseitigungspflichten aus hoheitlichem Unrecht*. Karlsruhe [2]1974.

Berg, Wilfried: Die öffentlichrechtliche Anstalt. In: *Neue Juristische Wochenschrift 1985*, pages 2294 to 2301.

Biehl, Helmold: *Lösungsvorschläge für Sonderprobleme der ostdeutschen Industrie*. In: Ludwig-Erhard-Stiftung (editor): *Wirtschaftliche und soziale Ausgestaltung der deutschen Einheit*. Krefeld 1993, pages 33 to 37.

Bleckmann, Albert and *Erberich*: *Die Treuhandanstalt und ihre Unternehmen*. In: Albert J. *Rädler*, Arndt *Raupach*, and Gerold *Bezzenberger* (editors): *Vermögen in der ehemaligen DDR*, Part 2 C. Herne and Berlin (version of January 1993).

Böhme, Rolf: *Die Beschränkung der Amtshaftung auf die Hoheitsverwaltung*. Freiburg 1969.

Broß, Siegfried: Article 87 of the German Constitution (Commentary). In: Ingo *von Münch* (editor): *Grundgesetz-Kommentar*, Volume III. Munich 1978.

Brunner, Georg: *Kontrolle in Deutschland*. Cologne 1972.

Bull, Hans Peter: Article 87 of the German Constitution (Commentary). In: Rudolf *Wassermann* (editor): *Kommentar zum Grundgesetz für die Bundesrepublik Deutschland* (Reihe Alternativkommentare), Volume II. Neuwied and Darmstadt 1984.

Busch, Eckart: *Parlamentarische Kontrolle. Ausgestaltung und Wirkung*. Heidelberg 1985.

Busche, Jan: *Gesetz zur Privatisierung und Reorganisation des volkseigenen Vermögens (Commentary)*. In: Georg *Brunner*, Hermann *Clemm*, Ernst *Etzbach* et al (editors): *Rechtshandbuch Vermögen und Investitionen in der ehemaligen DDR*, Volume I, Second Section, Part B, Serial No. 200. Munich (March 1993 version).

Christoph, Karl-Heinz: Erweiterung der Zuständigkeit der Gerichte der DDR auf dem Gebiet des Verwaltungsrechts. In: *Deutsch-Deutsche Rechts-Zeitschrift* 1990, pages 175 to 179.

Cloes, Roger: Die parlamentarische Kontrolle der Treuhandanstalt. In: *Deutsch-Deutsche Rechts-Zeitschrift* 1991, pages 291 and 292.

Craushaar, Götz von: Grundstückseigentum in den neuen Bundesländern. In: *Deutsch-Deutsche Rechts-Zeitschrift* 1991, pages 359 to 363.

Cremer, Matthias: *Immobiliengeschäfte in den neuen Bundesländern*. Cologne 1992.

Dagtoglou, Prodromos: *Article 34 of the German Constitution* (Commentary). In: Rudolf *Dolzer* (editor): *Bonner Kommentar zum Grundgesetz*. Heidelberg (October 1992 version).

Deutsche Bundesbank: *Monatsbericht*. June 1993.

Deutsches Institut für Wirtschaftsforschung: *Wochenbericht* 13/93 of 1st April 1993.

Dittmann, Armin: *Die Bundesverwaltung*. Tübingen 1983.

Egler, Gert, and Gerhard *Schüßler*: *Gegenstand und gesellschaftliche Funktion des Staatsrechts der DDR*. In: Akademie für Staats- und Rechtswissenschaft der DDR (editor): *Staatsrecht der DDR*. Textbook. Berlin [2]1984, pages 17 to 44.

Ehlers, Dirk: *Verwaltung in Privatrechtsform*. Berlin 1984.

Ellwein, Thomas. *Das Regierungssystem der Bundesrepublik Deutschland*. Cologne and Opladen 1963.

Etzbach, Ernst: *Grundstücks- und Immobilienrecht*. In: Georg *Brunner*, Hermann *Clemm*, Ernst *Etzbach* et al (editors): *Rechtshandbuch Vermögen und Investitionen in der ehemaligen DDR*, Volume I, First Section V. Munich (March 1993 version).

Fahrenbach, Ralf-Friedrich: Das Privatisierungsverfahren nach dem Treuhandgesetz. In: *Deutsch-Deutsche Rechts-Zeitschrift* 1990, pages 268 to 270.

Hannemann, Karl-Heinz, and Siegfried *Bergmann*: Zur Gesetzgebung in der DDR nach dem 18.3.1990. In: *Deutsch-Deutsche Rechts-Zeitschrift* 1990, pages 183 to 188.

Herles, Helmut, and Ewald *Rose* (editors): *Vom Runden Tisch zum Parlament*. Bonn 1990.

Heuer, Ernst: *Teil IV-IX BHO*. In: Ernst *Heuer* (editor): *Kommentar zum Haushaltsrecht*, Volume I. Neuwied etc. (December 1992 version).

Hoffmann, Jutta, and Jochen *Völter*: Die Umwandlung von volkseigenen Betrieben der DDR in Kapitalgesellschaften und die Rolle der Treuhandanstalt zur Verwaltung des Volkseigentums. In: *Wertpapier-Mitteilungen* 1990, special supplement 4, pages 17 to 22.

Hohmeister, Frank-Udo: Handlungsbefugnisse der Treuhandanstalt und Rechtsschutzmöglichkeiten Betroffener. In: *Betriebs-Berater* 1992, pages 285 to 290.

Homann, Fritz: Treuhandanstalt – Zwischenbilanz, Perspektiven. In: *Deutschland Archiv* 1991, pages 1277 to 1287.

Hommelhoff, Peter, and Walter *Krebs*: *Treuhandanstalt und Treuhandgesetz*. Cologne 1990.

Horn, Norbert: *Privatisierung und Reprivatisierung von Unternehmen. Eigentumsschutz und Investitionsförderung im Lichte der neuesten Gesetzgebung*. In: Peter *Hommelhoff* (editor): *Treuhandunternehmen im Umbruch*. Cologne 1991, pages 133 to 172.

ditto: *Gesellschaftsrechtliche Probleme der Umwandlung der DDR-Unternehmen*. In: Reinhard *Goerdeler*, Peter *Hommelhoff*, Marcus *Lutter* et al (editors): *Festschrift für Alfred Kellermann*.

Berlin and New York 1991, pages 201 et seq.
ditto: *Das Zivil- und Wirtschaftsrecht im neuen Bundesgebiet*. Cologne 1991.
Hübner, Jürgen: Das Gesetz über besondere Investitionen in der DDR und seine Novellierung. In: *Deutsch-Deutsche Rechts-Zeitschrift* 1991, pages 161 to 169.
Jarass, Hans D.: *Article 34 of the German Constitution* (Commentary). In: Hans D. *Jarass* and Bodo *Pieroth* (editors): *Grundgesetz für die Bundesrepublik Deutschland*. Munich ²1992.
Jesse, Eckhard: *Die Volkskammer der DDR – Befugnisse und Verfahren nach Verfassung und politischer Praxis*. In: Hans-Peter *Schneider* and Wolfgang *Zeh* (editors): *Parlamentsrecht und Parlamentspraxis*. Berlin 1989, pages 1821 to 1844.
Keil, Martin: Ungeklärte Eigentumsverhältnisse als praktische Probleme bei der Privatisierung von Treuhandunternehmen. In: *Zeitschrift für Vermögens- und Investitionsrecht* 1992, pages 121 to 125.
ditto: Investitionsvorrang in der Praxis. In: *Zeitschrift für Vermögens- und Investitionsrecht* 1993, pages 89 to 96.
Kerber, Markus C., and Wilfried *Stechow*: Die Treuhandanstalt im Spannungsverhältnis zwischen öffentlichem und privatem Recht. In: *Deutsche Zeitschrift für Wirtschaftsrecht* 1991, pages 49 to 52.
ditto: Das Treuhandaußenrecht. In: *Deutsche Zeitschrift für Wirtschaftsrecht* 1991, pages 105 to 115.
Kittke, Horst-Dieter: *Anmerkung zu dem Beschluß des OVG Berlin vom 22.1.1991 – 8 S 6/91*. In: Adelhaid *Brandt* and Horst-Dieter *Kittke* (editors): *Rechtsprechung und Gesetzgebung zur Regelung offener Vermögensfragen*, Part I Serial No. 3 (November 1992 version), pages 13 and 14.
Klein, Franz: Article 34 of the German Constitution (Commentary). In: Bruno *Schmidt-Bleibtreu* and Franz *Klein* (editors): *Kommentar zum Grundgesetz*. Neuwied and Frankfurt am Main ⁷1990.
Knüpfer, Werner: Wandlungen der Eigentumsverhältnisse durch die neue Wirtschaftsgesetzgebung in der DDR. In: *Betriebs-Berater* 1990, appendix 20 to issue 15, pages 1 to 9.
Kohler, Jürgen: Verwaltungs- oder zivilrechtliche Sicherung der Rückerstattung von Grundstücken in den neuen Bundesländern. In: *Zeitschrift für Vermögens- und Investitionsrecht* 1992, pages 130 to 133.
Kolbeck, Rosemarie: "*Finanzierung III: Vorgänge*". In: Willi *Albers*, Karl Erich *Born*, Ernst *Dürr* et al (editors): *Handwörterbuch der Wirtschaftswissenschaften*, Volume 3. Stuttgart etc. 1981, pages 59 to 83.
Kopp, Ferdinand O.: *Verwaltungsgerichtsordnung*. Munich ⁹1992.
Krebs, Walter: Die öffentlich-rechtliche Anstalt. In: *Neue Zeitschrift für Verwaltungsrecht* 1985, pages 609 to 616.
ditto: Rechtsschutzprobleme bei Entscheidungen der Treuhandanstalt. In: *Zeitschrift für Wirtschaftsrecht* 1990, pages 1513 to 1523.
ditto: *Verwaltungsorganisation*. In: Josef *Isensee* and Paul *Kirchhof*: *Handbuch des Staatsrechts der Bundesrepublik Deutschland*, Volume III. Heidelberg 1988, pages 567 to 622.
Lachmann, Jens-Peter: Das Treuhandgesetz. In: *Deutsch-Deutsche Rechts-Zeitschrift* 1990, pages 238 to 240.
Lerche, Peter: *Article 86 of the German Constitution* (Commentary). In: Theodor *Maunz*, Günter *Dürig*, Roman *Herzog* et al (editors): *Grundgesetz Kommentar*, Volume III. Munich (September 1991 version).

Liebs, Rüdiger, and Peter *Preu*: Probleme der Rückgabe enteigneter Unternehmen in der früheren DDR. In: *Der Betrieb* 1991, pages 145 to 153.

Lipps, Wolfgang: Gesetzgebungs- und Anwendungsfehler im Treuhandrecht der ehemals volkseigenen Wirtschaft. In: *Betriebs-Berater* 1991, appendix 9 to issue 12, pages 1 to 6.

ditto: Die Zuordnung ehemals volkseigenen Vermögens. In: *Zeitschrift für Vermögens- und Investitionsrecht* 1992, pages 14 to 16.

Luft, Hans: Die Treuhandanstalt. Deutsche Erfahrungen und Probleme bei der Transformation von Wirtschaftsordnungen. In: *Deutschland Archiv* 1991, pages 1270 to 1276.

Magiera, Siegfried: *Rechte des Bundestages und seiner Mitglieder gegenüber der Regierung*. In: Hans-Peter *Schneider* and Wolfgang *Zeh* (editors): *Parlamentsrecht und Parlamentspraxis*. Berlin 1989, pages 1421 to 1446.

Mampel, Siegfried: *Die sozialistische Verfassung der Deutschen Demokratischen Republik*. Frankfurt am Main ²1982.

Maskow, Dietrich and Jutta *Hoffmann*: Rechtsfragen der Privatisierung in den ostdeutschen Bundesländern. In: *Betriebs-Berater* 1990, appendix 40 to issue 35/36, pages 1 to 10.

Maunz, Theodor: *Article 87 of the German Constitution* (Commentary). In: Theodor *Maunz*, Günter *Dürig*, Roman *Herzog* et al (editors): *Grundgesetz Kommentar*, Volume III. Munich (September 1991 version).

Maurer, Hartmut: *Allgemeines Verwaltungsrecht*. Munich ⁸1992.

Messerschmidt, Burkhard: Aktuelle Probleme der Unternehmensrückgabe in den neuen Bundesländern. In: *Zeitschrift für Vermögens- und Investitionsrecht* 1992, pages 1 to 6.

ditto: *Unternehmensrecht und Unternehmenskauf in den neuen Bundesländern*. In: Georg *Brunner*, Hermann *Clemm*, Ernst *Etzbach* et al (editors): *Rechtshandbuch Vermögen und Investitionen in der ehemaligen DDR*, Volume I, First Section II. Munich (March 1993 version).

Meyer, Wolfgang: *Article 34 of the German Constitution* (Commentary). In: Ingo *von Münch* (editor): *Grundgesetz-Kommentar*, Volume II. Munich 1976.

Moschütz, Hans Dietrich: *Die ökonomischen Grundlagen*. In: Akademie für Staats- und Rechtswissenschaft der DDR (editor): *Staatsrecht der DDR*. Textbook. Berlin ²1984, pages 130 to 142.

Müller, Hans-Peter: *Article 24 of the Deutschmark Balance Sheet Act* (Commentary). In: Wolfgang Dieter *Budde* and Karl Heinz *Forster* (editors): *D-Markbilanzgesetz 1990*. Munich 1991.

Oebbecke, Janbernd: Die Anstaltslast – Rechtspflicht oder politische Maxime? In: *Deutsches Verwaltungsblatt* 1981, pages 960 to 965.

Ossenbühl, Fritz: *Staatshaftungsrecht*. Munich ⁴1991.

Papier, Hans-Jürgen: *Article 34 of the German Constitution* (Commentary). In: Theodor *Maunz*, Günter *Dürig*, Roman *Herzog* et al (editors): *Grundgesetz Kommentar*, Volume II. Munich (September 1991 version).

ditto: *§ 839 of the Civil Code* (Commentary). In: Kurt *Rebmann* and Franz Jürgen *Säcker* (editors): *Münchener Kommentar zum Bürgerlichen Gesetzbuch*, Volume III, 2nd half-volume. Munich 1986.

Piduch, Erwin Adolf: *Bundeshaushaltsrecht*. Stuttgart etc. (January 1993 version).

Pilz, Frank, and Heike *Ortwein*: *Das vereinte Deutschland. Wirtschaftliche, soziale und finanzielle Folgeprobleme und die Konsequenzen für die Politik*. Stuttgart and Jena 1992.

Reblin, Ulrich: *Volkseigentum – Konzeption und rechtliche Ausgestaltung*. In: Thomas *Kaligin* and Klaus *Goutier* (editors): *Beratungshandbuch Eigentum und Investitionen in den neuen Bundesländern,* Fach 1211. Heidelberg (December 1992 version).

Rein, Detlev B.: *Die Parteivermögenskommissionsverordnung*. In: *Deutsch-Deutsche Rechts-Zeitschrift* 1991, pages 290 to 291.

Rengeling, Hans-Werner: *Das vereinte Deutschland in der Europäischen Gemeinschaft. Grundlagen zur Geltung des Gemeinschaftsrechts*. In: *Deutsches Verwaltungsblatt* 1990, pages 1307 to 1314.

Rittstieg, Helmut: *Article 34 of the German Constitution* (Commentary). In: Rudolf *Wassermann* (editor): *Kommentar zum Grundgesetz für die Bundesrepublik Deutschland* (Reihe Alternativkommentare), Volume I. Neuwied 1989.

Rodegra, Jürgen, and Martin *Gogrewe*: Zum Unternehmenskauf in den neuen Bundesländern – Ein Überblick nach den jüngsten Gesetzesänderungen. In: *Deutsch-Deutsche Rechts-Zeitschrift* 1991, pages 353 to 359.

Roggemann, Herwig: *Die DDR-Verfassungen. Einführung in das Verfassungsrecht der DDR*. Berlin [4]1989.

Rosener, Wolfgang, and Frank *Roitzsch*: Die Umwandlung von volkseigenen Betrieben in Kapitalgesellschaften. In: *Deutsch-Deutsche Rechts-Zeitschrift* 1990, pages 38 to 42.

Rother, Christopher: *Die Errichtung der Treuhandanstalt*. In: Thomas *Kaligin* and Klaus *Goutier* (editors): *Beratungshandbuch Eigentum und Investitionen in den neuen Bundesländern,* Fach 4210. Heidelberg (December 1992 version).

ditto: *Privatisierung in den neuen Bundesländern – Begriffsbestimmung*. In: Thomas *Kaligin* and Klaus *Goutier* (editors): *Beratungshandbuch Eigentum und Investitionen in den neuen Bundesländern,* Fach 4010. Heidelberg (December 1992 version).

ditto: *Umwandlung von Wirtschaftseinheiten der DDR nach der Umwandlungsverordnung*. In: Thomas *Kaligin* and Klaus *Goutier* (editors): *Beratungshandbuch Eigentum und Investitionen in den neuen Bundesländern,* Fach 4110. Heidelberg (December 1992 version).

Rüfner, Wolfgang: *Das Recht der öffentlich-rechtlichen Schadensersatz- und Entschädigungsleistungen*. In: Hans-Uwe *Erichsen* and Wolfgang *Martens* (editors): *Allgemeines Verwaltungsrecht*. Berlin [9]1992, pages 575 to 679.

ditto: Zur Lehre von der öffentlichen Anstalt. In: *Die Öffentliche Verwaltung* 1985, pages 605 to 610.

Schäuble, Wolfgang: *Der Vertrag*. Aktualisierte Taschenbuchausgabe. Munich 1993.

Scheifele, Bernd: Praktische Erfahrungen beim Unternehmenskauf in den neuen Bundesländern (Erster Teil). In: *Betriebs-Berater* 1991, pages 557 to 566.

ditto: Zur Anwendung des § 3a Vermögensgesetz durch die Treuhandanstalt. In: *Betriebs-Berater* 1991, pages 1350 to 1356.

Scherpenberg, Norman van, and Reiner *Hornuf*: Die Rückübertragung von enteigneten Unternehmen in den neuen Bundesländern. In: *Informationsdienst für Lastenausgleich, BVFG, und anderes Kriegsfolgenrecht, Vermögensrückgabe und Entschädigung nach dem Einigungsvertrag* 1992, pages 13 to 17.

Schlecht, Otto, *Politische Entscheidungen und wirtschaftspolitischer Handlungsbedarf*. In: Ludwig-Erhard-Stiftung (editor): *Vom Zentralplan zur Sozialen Marktwirtschaft. Erfahrungen der Deutschen beim Systemwechsel*. Stuttgart etc. 1992, pages 49 to 71.

Schmidt, Manfred, and Thomas *Leitschuh*: *Vertrag zwischen der Bundesrepublik Deutschland und der Deutschen Demokratischen Republik über die Herstellung der Einheit Deutschlands – Einigungsvertrag (Kommentierung zu Artikel 21 und 22)*. In: Georg *Brunner*, Hermann

Clemm, Ernst *Etzbach* et al (editors): *Rechtshandbuch Vermögen und Investitionen in der ehemaligen DDR*, Volume I, Second Section, Part B, Serial no. 20. Munich (March 1993 version).

Schmidt, Reiner: *Aufgaben und Struktur der Treuhandanstalt im Wandel der Wirtschaftslage*. In: Peter *Hommelhoff* (editor): *Treuhandunternehmen im Umbruch*. Cologne 1991, pages 17 to 38.

Schmidt-Bleibtreu, Bruno: *Article 87 of the German Constitution* (Commentary). In: Bruno *Schmidt-Bleibtreu* and Franz *Klein* (editors): *Kommentar zum Grundgesetz*. Neuwied and Frankfurt am Main [7]1990.

Schmidt-Räntsch, Jürgen: Anmerkung zu dem Beschluß des Kreisg Gera vom 14.10.1991 – 2 D 249/91. In: *Zeitschrift für Vermögens- und Investitionsrecht* 1992, page 116.

ditto: Das Vermögenszuordnungsgesetz. In: Zeitschrift für Wirtschaftsrecht 1991, pages 973 to 980.

ditto: Zum sogenannten Enthemmungsgesetz. In: *Deutsch-Deutsche Rechts-Zeitschrift* 1991, pages 169 to 174.

Scholz, Georg: *Staatshaftungs- und Entschädigungsrecht*. Munich [2]1978.

Schröder, Meinhard: *Untersuchungsausschüsse*. In: Hans-Peter *Schneider* and Wolfgang *Zeh* (editors): *Parlamentsrecht und Parlamentspraxis*. Berlin 1989, pages 1245 to 1259.

Schütterle, Peter: Treuhandanstalt und EG-Beihilfenkontrolle. In: *Zeitschrift für Vermögens- und Investitionsrech*t 1992, pages 16 to 18.

Schulze, Gerhard: *Die gesellschaftliche Funktion und Gegenstand des Verwaltungsrechts der DDR*. In: Akademie für Staats- und Rechtswissenschaft der DDR (editor): *Verwaltungsrecht*. Textbook. Berlin [2]1988, pages 19 to 49.

ditto: *Grundsätze und Mittel zur Durchführung von Entscheidungen der Organe des Staatsapparats*. In: Akademie für Staats- und Rechtswissenschaft der DDR (editor): *Verwaltungsrecht*. Textbook. Berlin [2]1988, pages 142 to 146.

Schuppert, Gunnar Folke: Öffentlich-rechtliche Vorgaben für die Treuhandanstalt bei der Leitung der Treuhandunternehmen. In: *Zeitschrift für Unternehmens- und Gesellschaftsrecht* 1992, pages 454 to 476.

Seiffert, Wolfgang: *Wirtschaftsrecht der DDR*. Berlin 1982.

Sendler, Horst: Verwaltungsgerichtsbarkeit in der DDR – Wie können wir helfen? In: *Deutsch-Deutsche Rechts-Zeitschrift* 1990, pages 166 to 175.

Siebert, Horst: *Das Wagnis der Einheit. Eine wirtschaftspolitische Therapie*. Stuttgart 1992.

Spoerr, Wolfgang: *Treuhandanstalt und Treuhandunternehmen zwischen Verfassungs-, Verwaltungs- und Gesellschaftsrecht*. Cologne 1993.

Steffani, Winfried: *Formen, Verfahren und Wirkung der parlamentarischen Kontrolle*. In: Hans-Peter *Schneider* and Wolfgang *Zeh* (editors): *Parlamentsrecht und Parlamentspraxis*. Berlin 1989, pages 1325 to 1367.

Stein, Günther: Die Treuhandanstalt im einstweiligen Verfügungsverfahren, Rechtswegbestimmung und Interessenabwägung. In: *Zeitschrift für Wirtschaftsrecht* 1992, pages 893 to 902.

Stelkens, Paul: Die Einführung der Verwaltungsgerichtsbarkeit im Gebiet der früheren DDR – eine Wende? In: *Deutsch-Deutsche Rechts-Zeitschrift* 1990, pages 305 to 308.

Süß, Walter: Eine Behörde verkauft die ostdeutsche Volkswirtschaft. In: *Das Parlament*, 20th March 1992, page 13.

ditto: Bilanz einer Gratwanderung – Die kurze Amtszeit des Hans Modrow. In: *Deutschland Archiv* 1991, pages 596 to 608.

Thietz-Bartram, Joachim, and Axel *Pfeifer*: Privatisierung von Volkseigentum. In: *Wertpapier-Mitteilungen* 1990, special supplement 4, pages 3 to 17.

Timm, Wolfram: Die Sanierung der sogenannten "Treuhandunternehmen" zwischen Marktkonformität und Insolvenzrecht. In: *Zeitschrift für Wirtschaftsrecht* 1991, pages 413 to 425.

Troßmann, Hans: *Parlamentsrecht des Deutschen Bundestages*. Munich 1977.

ditto: *Parlamentsrecht und Praxis des Deutschen Bundestages*. Bonn 1967.

Uechtritz, Michael: "Gebremste Vorfahrt"? – Der Investitionsvorrang und der vorläufige Rechtsschutz vor dem Bundesverfassungsgericht. In: *Zeitschrift für Vermögens- und Investitionsrecht* 1993, pages 142 to 145.

ditto: Das Zweite Vermögensrechtsänderungsgesetz. Zu den Neuregelungen für Restitution und Investitionsvorrang. In: *Betriebs-Berater* 1992, pages 1649 to 1661.

Volkens, Sönke: Kompetenzfragen bei der Rückführung von DDR-Parteivermögen. In: *Zeitschrift für Vermögens- und Investitionsrecht* 1993, pages 145 to 147.

Vonderbeck, Hans-Josef: *Parlamentarische Informations- und Redebefugnisse*. Berlin 1981.

Voss, Karl Ulrich: Veräußerung von volkseigenen Liegenschaften durch DDR-Ministerien zu gewerblicher Verwendung. In: *Deutsch-Deutsche Rechts-Zeitschrift* 1992, pages 6 to 10.

Wächter, Gerd H.: Übertragungsansprüche nach der 5. Durchführungsverordunung zum Treuhandgesetz und nach dem Kommunalvermögensgesetz. In: *Betriebs-Berater* 1991, appendix 9, pages 6 to 11.

Weides, Peter: Rechtsweg bei Streitigkeiten über die Veräußerung von Geschäftsanteilen einer GmbH durch die Treuhandanstalt – OVG Berlin, NJW 1991, page 715 et seq., and VG Berlin, NJW 1991, page 1969 et seq. In: *Juristische Schulung* 1991, pages 818 to 821.

Weimar, Robert: Entscheidungspraxis der Treuhandanstalt zwischen unternehmerischer Freiheit und verwaltungsrechtlichem Ermessen. In: *Deutsche Zeitschrift für Wirtschaftsrecht* 1992, pages 493 to 500.

ditto: Handlungsformen und Handlungsfelder der Treuhandanstalt – öffentlich-rechtlich oder privatrechtlich? In: *Die Öffentliche Verwaltung* 1991, pages 813 to 823.

ditto: Treuhandanstalt und Privatisierung. In: *Der Betrieb* 1991, pages 373 to 375.

ditto: Treuhandanstalt und Treuhandgesetz. In: *Betriebs-Berater* 1990, appendix 40, pages 10 to 15.

ditto: Die Treuhandanstalt im Verwaltungsprivatrecht. In: *Zeitschrift für Wirtschaftsrecht* 1993, pages 1 to 14.

ditto: Das Treuhandkreditaufnahmegesetz. In: *Deutsch-Deutsche Rechts-Zeitschrift* 1992, pages 117 and 118.

ditto: Zum Wirkungsbereich der Treuhandanstalt gegenüber ihren Gesellschaften. In: *Deutsch-Deutsche Rechts-Zeitschrift* 1991, pages 105 to 108.

Weimar, Robert, and Erika *Simon*: Offene Fragen zu § 3c Vermögensgesetz. In: *Zeitschrift für Vermögens- und Investitionsrecht* 1992, pages 96 to 101.

Wellhöfer, Werner: Struktur und System der Unternehmensrückgabe-Vorschriften. In: *Zeitschrift für Vermögens- und Investitionsrecht* 1992, pages 85 to 91.

Wild, Klaus-Peter: *Die Treuhandanstalt ein Jahr nach Inkrafttreten des Treuhandgesetzes – eine aktuelle Zwischenbilanz*. In: Peter *Hommelhoff* (editor): *Treuhandunternehmen im Umbruch*. Cologne 1991, pages 1 to 15.

Wittmann, Eckart: Öffentlichrechtliche Fragen zum Gesetz über besondere Investitionen im Bereich der neuen Bundesländer. In: *Deutsch-Deutsche Rechts-Zeitschrift* 1991, pages 174 to 179.

Wolter, Henner: Rechtswegprobleme bei Treuhandentscheidungen. Nachrichten aus dem "rechtlichen Bermuda-Dreieck". In: *Wirtschaftsrecht* 1991, pages 302 to 309.

Zieger, Klaus, and Günter *Schönemann*: Neue Bestimmungen zur Förderung privater Unternehmen in der DDR. In: *Deutsch-Deutsche Rechts-Zeitschrift* 1990, pages 97 to 101.

Zuleeg, Manfred: *Die Zweistufenlehre. Ausgestaltung, Abwandlung, Alternativen.* In: Peter *Oberndorfer* and Herbert *Schambeck* (editors): *Verwaltung im Dienste von Wirtschaft und Gesellschaft, Festschrift für Ludwig Fröhler zum 60. Geburtstag.* Berlin 1980, pages 275 to 296.

The legal framework and its changes

by Harm Peter Westermann[1]

I. On the individual questions: the contribution made by private law to the history of the THA

In its present form as an institute under public law, and under the general principles of administrative law,[2] the THA is fully endowed with all the powers of a legal entity under private and public law. It is first and foremost an independent body with its own budget responsibility, separate from the next superior body, i. e. the Federal government, which is responsible for approving its budget.[3] Nevertheless, in addition to supervision by ministerial technical and legal departments, there is a certain level of parliamentary control with different responsibilities for the Ministries for Economic Affairs and of Finance.[4] Thus the THA's work can definitely be categorised as belonging to the field of responsibility of the German Federal Government; in particular, it does not come under the aegis of the States, not even of the eastern States, although their economic and political interests are crucially affected, especially in regional and structural policy, by the THA's decisions and the eastern States (*Länder*) can exert influence through the THA's Administrative Board under Article 25 section 2 sentence 2 of the Treaty of Unification. In these circumstances it is not immediately obvious why an article dealing with private law should be included as part of an assessment of the THA's function.

On the other hand, the sovereign nature of the tasks of the THA as generally accepted[5] does not make a difference to the actions it takes in privatising former state property, some at least of which are clad in the garments of private law.[6] It is thus possible to examine the THA from the point of view of private law with the aim of seeing whether the parameters of its autonomous decision-making processes as laid down in the *Treuhandgesetz* or THG – the Public Trustee Act which established it – and the further legal regulations facilitate the best possible fulfilment of the tasks entrusted to it and whether, as has often been asserted in relation to the field of com-

---

1 Mr Matthias Hink, of Berlin, assisted in the preparation of this article by helping to collect material and giving pointers on the treatment of the legal questions.

2 Spoerr, *Treuhandanstalt und Treuhandunternehmen,* pages 5 et seq. and 12 et seq.

3 For THA finances, see: Kerber, *Unternehmenssanierung durch die Treuhand*, pages 221 to 227.

4 For more details see the article by Kloepfer in this volume, pages 40 et seq.

5 Higher Administrative Court of Berlin, ZIP 1991, pages 198 and 199; Krebs, *Rechtsschutzprobleme*, pages 1512 to 1523; Kerber and Stechow, *Die Treuhandanstalt im Spannungsverhältnis*, pages 49 to 51; Horn, *Das Zivil- und Wirtschaftsrecht*, pages 385 et seq.

6 The so-called "two-stage theory" (*Zweistufenlehre*) is often invoked in this context: Fahrenbach, *Das Privatisierungsverfahren nach dem Treuhandgesetz*, pages 268 to 270; Kerber and Stechow, *Die Treuhandanstalt im Spannungsverhältnis*; Schmidt, *Aufgaben und Struktur der Treuhandanstalt*, pages 17 to 22; Busche, *Kommentar zum Treuhandgesetz*, § 2, marginal notes 6 et seq.; Horn, *Das Zivil- und Wirtschaftsrecht*, pages 385 et seq.; detailed discussion in Weides, *Rechtsweg bei Streitigkeiten*, pages 818 to 822; Spoerr, *Treuhandanstalt und Treuhandunternehmen*, pages 177 et seq.

pany and commercial law,[7] the overall judgement on the work of the THA and the value of its legal basis in practice suffer from the possibility of substantial legal claims under private law against it, its successor, or the organisation behind it. In other matters, such as the decisions made under the (amended) *Vermögensgesetz* or Property Act on the priority to be accorded to an investment project, the THA operates by issuing "administrative acts" (rulings based exactly on administrative law).[8] The THA has to be brought in to proceedings at the Property Offices (*Vermögensämter*) on the restitution of companies (to their former rightful owners) and, in the reverse situation, a mutual exchange of information is required between the THA and the Property Offices in all cases of privatisation projects.[9] The consequences of this concatenation for the legal protection of those entitled to dispose over property, or to its restitution, are not to be dealt with in this article, but, in evaluating the fulfilment of statutory possibilities, it is important always to bear in mind the context of the measures in public law if a decision is made as the result of either "limited" or conscientious free discretion.[10]

If one breaks the question down into its component parts it can be seen to relate for one thing to the matter of whether the legal regulations which require the THA to carry out the privatisation of the ownership of property and therefore provide for a division of responsibility and for a collaboration with various government authorities such as Property Offices have led to such a clear legal situation as would be desirable with regard to the successful execution of the task of privatisation from the point of view of general policy. This then applies particularly with regard to the privatisation of THA companies, which belongs to the THA's central area of responsibility and which has so often been a source of complaint for making progress too slowly on account of many areas of insufficient clarity surrounding the allocation of the land used by the companies in question. The inherent contradiction between restitution and fresh privatisation has also arisen in connection with complete companies. One particular set of problems resulted from potential collisions between the categorisation of formerly state-occupied property for transfer to local authorities and regional corporations and the claims made on such property by companies (mainly those up for privatisation). Finally, a proper legal basis had to be created for the administration by the THA of the companies which had fallen to it *ex lege*, for the "unbundling" or dismemberment of them (in order better to facilitate privatisation), for their restructuring, and if necessary also for their liquidation. All this is covered by the THG and by the Treaty of Unification, but in many cases the rulings are unclear or even contradictory.[11] Later laws, particularly those that shifted the relationship between the restitution of property used by a company and the fresh privatisation of it (through the sale to a previously outside purchaser or, indeed, the

---

7 For more details see Weimar, *Nachprivatisierungsprobleme*, especially pages 78 et seq.

8 Horn, *Privatisierung und Reprivatisierung von Unternehmen*, pages 133 to 135; Liebs, *Diskussionsbeitrag* in: Hommelhoff (editor), *Treuhandunternehmen im Umbruch*, page 174; Leo, *§ 3a VermG*, pages 1505 to 1510. For the decisions under § 2 of the Investment Priority Act see also: Weimar, *Entscheidungspraxis der Treuhandanstalt*, pages 493 to 497.

9 Overlack, *Diskussionsbeitrag* in Hommelhoff (editor), *Treuhandunternehmen im Umbruch*, pages 180 and 181.

10 For more detail see Weimar, *Nachprivatisierungsprobleme*, page 94.

11 See: Horn, *Das Zivil- und Wirtschaftsrecht*, pages 370 et seq.; Schmidt, *Aufgaben und Struktur der Treuhandanstalt*, pages 17 et seq.; Spoerr, *Treuhandanstalt und Treuhandunternehmen*, pages 493 to 497.

previous directors), always with the aim of making fresh privatisation easier, have resulted in the original concept being to some extent lost or even abandoned.

Admittedly, it does appear doubtful whether the description of the legal basis of the THA's work will in the last analysis contribute anything crucial to an assessment of the route chosen in Germany for converting a planned economy into a market economy, in view of the room for manoeuvre in action and judgement (for instance with regard to the competitive structure and the possibility of restructuring the companies) which positive law granted the THA, as indeed it probably had to. Even the controversy raging in economic science circles as to whether the originally desired precedence for reprivatisation programmes was correct, or whether it was right to push it into the background, cannot be answered from the point of view of private law alone but only, and at best, in terms of constitutional law.[12]

II. The responsibilities of the THA

1. Divergent responsibilities for a new market structure

Amongst all the responsibilities imposed on the THA, § 1 section 1 of the THG places the privatisation of state property firmly at centre-stage, as does the Preamble to the Act. This is reinforced by the fact that these regulations, unlike the preceding Conversion Ordinance of 1st March 1990 which they replaced,[13] implement the idea of an automatic conversion into joint-stock companies *ex vi legis* of state-owned economic units (both the *Volkseigene Betriebe*, the individual state-owned companies, and the *Kombinate*, or industrial groupings of companies) held (in trust) under company law by the THA and is connected with an equally automatic transfer of the operating assets of the economic units into the possession of the newly created joint-stock companies. This all arises out of § 1 section 4 and § 11 sections 1 and 2 of the THG.[14]

This definition of the significance of the task of privatisation is important because this task can run into a conflict of aims with the other tasks incumbent on the THA, for which reason

---

12 For reports on earlier requests by the first President of the THA to be allowed to take privatisation decisions regardless of constitutional and political aspects and regardless of the question of previous rightful ownership, see: Balz, *Rechtseinheit als Grundlage*, pages 43 to 54. For the validity under constitutional law of the sequestrations carried out between 1945 and 1949 on the basis of the law of the occupying power and their effect on restitution, see: Federal Constitutional Court, ZIP 1991, page 614, and a brief commentary by Albrecht Tintelnot in EWiR on Article 14 of the German Constitution 1/91. The Constitutional Court has nonetheless demanded equal treatment for all claimants to compensation and damages; see: Niederleithinger, *Drei Jahre Vermögensrecht*, pages 2 et seq.

13 § 24 section 3 of the THG does not expressly mention the Conversion Ordinance as one of the regulations specifically superseded by the THG, but the Ordinance is not one of those laws kept in force in the Treaty of Unification (Appendix II Chapter IV, *Bundesgesetzblatt* 1990 II, page 1194), which means it is one of those that lost its validity on 2nd July 1990: see Horn, *Das Zivil- und Wirtschaftsrecht*, page 321. The Ordinance therefore remains in force for the companies already converted by 1st July 1990.

14 This regulation is transferred by § 23 of the THG to the companies converted under the Conversion Ordinance. However, there is dispute over its extension to those economic units which had already existed as joint-stock companies in the former GDR; on this point, see: Regional Court of Erfurt, ZIP 1993, page 876; for a different view, see: Neye, *Anmerkung zu BezG Erfurt*, page 878.

some legal scholars have accused the THG of a lack of clarity in weighting its various functions.[15] It is after all possible to define the term "privatisation", which has never really be canonised in law, as basically meaning the creation of an organisation under private law as it will exist in future with a sufficient amount of capital behind it before the company is sold to a private investor.[16] Nevertheless, § 2 section 6 of the THG expressly mentions the THA's responsibility for exerting influence on the development of companies capable of being effectively restructured to make them competitive, and this presupposes a judgement on whether this can be achieved. The THA, according to § 2 section 6 sentence 2 of the THG, is required to work in the direction of "forming companies capable of surviving in the market by means of the expedient dismemberment of company structures, and thus creating an efficient economic structure". A similar form of words is used in Article 25 section 1 of the Treaty of Unification. Although it can be observed that the language used is somewhat more "narrative" than the normative and ordering style of such texts, it is certainly not stretching interpretation too far to suggest that this is a requirement for the restructuring of those companies likely to survive such a process, and indeed for them to be endowed with the necessary assets in terms of equipment, buildings and personnel, and with a business strategy on the basis of which the company, once in the hands of a private purchaser, will be able to hold its own in the market, and do so without co-ordinating its efforts with those of other previously state-owned companies.[17] Thus parameters of industrial and regional policy are principally excluded from the start in any assessment of efficiency.

Similar to "privatisation", "restructuring" is the result of a complex series of events not solely covered by the THG, particularly if one considers the close connection with the creation of a competitive structure. § 2 section 6 of the THG, for instance, directly mentions dismemberment, and under § 2 section 7 of the THG the THA can take out loans and issue debentures "in anticipation of the future proceeds of privatisation". Under Article 25 section 5 of the Treaty of Unification it can also stand guarantees and sureties on behalf of its companies. Thus the THA had a set of tools at its disposal right from the start which were not to be used in any cast-iron sequence laid down by law as soon as any given set of circumstances appeared; instead, the THA was granted room for manoeuvre and scope for judgement with regard to actual business conditions.[18] This applies primarily to the restructurability of companies, to the creation of structures favourable to competition, and, as far as privatisation proper is concerned, to the achievement of the best possible realisation.[19] It should be borne in mind at this point that the capability of a company to be restructured does not merely depend on its own economic position but also on the resources available for restructuring it and the people responsible for doing this. The THA, admittedly, does not absolutely have to carry out restructuring programmes whenever it considers restructuring to be possible, but can also decide for itself to hand the task of restruc-

---

15 Schmidt, *Aufgaben und Struktur der Treuhandanstalt*, page 25; this view is followed by: Spoerr, *Treuhandanstalt und Treuhandunternehmen*, page 71 (lack of leadership).

16 According to: Horn, *Das Zivil- und Wirtschaftsrecht*, page 319.

17 Spoerr, *Treuhandanstalt und Treuhandunternehmen*, page 72 et seq.

18 For comments on this, following the differentiation under administrative law between discretionary action and scope for judgement (which has, admittedly, been contested recently), see: Weimar, *Entscheidungspraxis der Treuhandanstalt*, pages 499 et seq.

19 See the combination of goals given in: Horn, *Das Zivil- und Wirtschaftsrecht*, page 499 et seq.; for the permitted use of resources see: Spoerr, *Treuhandanstalt und Treuhandunternehmen*, page 79.

turing over to the purchaser taking over the company, on condition it makes quite sure that the purchaser really does restructure the company and does not merely indulge in asset-stripping.

With the task to judge the suitability of a company for restructuring, which includes taking a decision on the market capability of individual companies,[20] it is also part of the THA's job to decide to liquidate companies not capable of being restructured. This is not expressly stated anywhere, but is the inevitable conclusion to be drawn from the application of the prerequisites for the restructuring instruments.[21] If one agrees that restructuring can only be carried out in light of the future ability of a company to hold its own in the market, one must also agree that this does not depend on the mere asset situation of the company in question but solely on a forecast regarding the future profitability of the specific company for a future investor under the relevant market conditions. This observation is important with regard to the aims laid down in the preamble to the THG of securing existing jobs and creating new ones.

2. Priority order of the tasks?

a) The aim of preserving jobs must not be regarded in isolation, but bears a relation to the creation of competitive-minded company structures and, depending on that, the restructurability of the individual companies. This demonstrates particularly clearly that legislation does not give the THA any responsibilities for regional or structural policy. It must therefore estimate a company's ability to be restructured and to compete effectively in light of its present state and the resources available for preserving it. Regardless of the problems whether such aims are litigable or not, which arise from the cardinal political significance of such decisions, it is fair to sum up at this point that the THA's tasks were not so precisely defined as to prevent data on the economic situation in general coming to the fore when the assessment was being made. These include, for instance, the amount of the proceeds that could be achieved from the sale of the company and, on the other side of the equation, the amount of the tax resources available, the interest of outside investors for starting up business activities in the newly-joined eastern States, including the traditional selling markets for these companies, the changes in the costs of production and marketing, and finally the appearance of competitors from East and West. Thus the aims set for the THA by legislation were extremely complex[22] and this appears to be an explanation for the fact that implementing them in the field of tension between the public responsibility for privatisation and the restitution of property to its former rightful owners was always going to be full of problems.

However, some motives which could perfectly well have played a part in the THA's decisions, and which keep on cropping up in public discussion, can be eliminated from the start.

b) Companies not capable of being restructured are not allowed to be kept alive for reasons of employment policy, and it is also forbidden under the THG to preserve jobs by means of measures designed to divide up markets between companies not capable in their own right of being

20 This view appears to be supported by Möschel, *Treuhandanstalt und Neuordnung der früheren DDR-Wirtschaft*, pages 175 to 182; Spoerr, *Treuhandanstalt und Treuhandunternehmen*, page 79.

21 Horn, *Das Zivil- und Wirtschaftsrecht*, page 381.

22 For the "prioritisation" of the tasks see the earlier article in this volume by Kloepfer, pages 55 et seq.

competitive. Close-down is prescribed mandatorily under the conditions mentioned in § 8 of the THG, with no scope for free discretion.[23]

One problem, the relevance of which has only emerged as the THA's work proceeded, cannot be solved at this point: companies capable of restructuring and kept alive by the THA for a length of time under certain circumstances cannot be privatised through sale because of the currently unfavourable economic development of the industrialised western nations, a point not taken into account when the THG and the Treaty of Unification were being drawn up.[24] It must also be understood that restructuring can sometimes be a process taking a very long time and has to involve not only just keeping companies alive but can also demand the provision of funds for investment and development projects needed to safeguard the future. Therefore it is not impossible that there will be companies which have been restructured but which cannot be privatised, at least for a longer period of time, and the simple formula[25] that the THA should privatise that which can be privatised and close down that which cannot is not one that can be justified by any clause in the THG. One solution which has already been initiated but cannot be visualised to its conclusion for the numbers of the THA companies affected involves bringing companies that can be restructured but not yet privatised under the control of "Management-KG" companies.[26]

c) A partial new orientation can be seen from the "Principles for a Boom in the East" (*Grundsätze Aufschwung Ost*).[27] These provide for additional co-operation between the THA and the State governments outside the Administrative Board of the Central Office and the Advisory Boards of the THA regional branches with the aim of allowing the consequences of closures on social, regional, and structural policy to affect the THA's decisions. It is permissible to doubt whether the priority position of the eastern as against the western German States is justified in this connection in light of the economic impact on the latter in the form of the *Länderfinanzausgleich* (the complicated mechanism by which financially stronger States subsidise the weaker ones).[28] But in any case it is impossible to see in the "Principles for a Boom in the East", which in legal terms is nothing more than a "gentlemen's agreement", any binding effect on the THA's decisions or any limitation on its free discretion, where it has any at all.[29]

d) Despite certain obligations contained by statutory regulations on the tasks of the THA and the preconditions affecting its individual activities, the law has accorded it a very wide range of

---

23 For a convincing set of conclusions derived from the situation as a whole see: Spoerr, *Treuhandanstalt und Treuhandunternehmen*, pages 81 et seq., for a rejection of any tasks relating to regional policy see in particular: Wild, *Die Treuhandanstalt ein Jahr nach Inkrafttreten des Treuhandgesetzes*, page 12; on the absence of any scope for free discretion, see in particular: Weimar, *Entscheidungspraxis der Treuhandanstalt*, page 498.

24 For the reasons underlying this wrong estimate of the possible rate at which the THA would fulfil its responsibilities, see: Wild, *Die Treuhandanstalt ein Jahr nach Inkrafttreten des Treuhandgesetzes*, pages 7 et seq.

25 op. cit., page 9.

26 On this point, and for the ATLAS model developed by the Free State of Saxony, see the articles in this volume by Schwalbach and by Kern and Sabel, pages 206 et seq., 481 et seq., and 492 et seq.

27 *Grundsätze Aufschwung Ost*, presented in ZIP 1991, number 6, page XIII; for a legal assessment, see: Schmidt, *Aufgaben und Struktur der Treuhandanstalt*, pages 34 et seq.

28 See: op. cit., page 36.

29 For the same conclusion see: op. cit., page 37.

individual responsibility. By making the THA companies report directly to the THA itself,[30] and by allocating the tangible assets to the newly created companies using them, the THA has also been placed close enough to the matters relating to its task and for making decisions which sometimes has to be done in a great hurry. The question does remain, however, as to whether perhaps the obligations left to the THA alone, and in some cases its interconnected task of the restitution of sequestrated or coldly-sequestrated companies and land (other tangible assets have apparently not played any part in this) have handicapped it in fulfilling its obligations, or might later give rise to claims against the THA or its successors in law. The huge number and the rapid sequence of the legislative measures regulating these problems permit the conclusion that coping with these problems will have a crucial influence on the judgement of history as to whether the basic idea which was pursued with the THA in the political sphere was successful.

III. The role of the THA in the transformation of state-owned into privately owned property

1. The relevant laws

The questions to be discussed here cannot be fully presented solely on the basis of the THG and the five Implementation Ordinances,[31] but must be split down into a number of sections in the same sequence as the two major amendments of the Act for Regulating Unsettled Property Questions (the Property Act) and looked at separately. The results have been included in the Property Act as most recently amended and have altered its appearance considerably.

Accordingly, a distinction needs to be made between the Property Act in the form in which it was included in the Treaty of Unification, on which the Federal Government presented its explanations,[32] the amendment to the Property Act made by the Removal of Obstacles Act of 22nd March 1991,[33] and finally the amendment and revision of both Acts by the Second Property Law Amendment Act of 14th July 1992.[34] All in all, therefore, the Property Act in the version of 14th July 1992, that has been in force since 22nd July 1992, is the one that matters. This Act has been in force since the Treaty of Unification became valid on 3rd October 1990 in the States making up the former GDR and in Berlin (East) as Federal law. The Removal of Obstacles Act as an

30 The concept of "mediatisation" of influence at the highest level over the THA companies, which was never put into effect (see: Horn, *Das Zivil- und Wirtschaftsrecht*, pages 326 et seq.), has not been considered here.

31 1st Implementation Ordinance to the THG of 15th August 1990, *Gesetzblatt der DDR* I, page 1076; 2nd Implementation Ordinance to the THG of 22nd August 1990, *Gesetzblatt der DDR* I, page 1260; 3rd Implementation Ordinance to the THG of 29th August 1990, *Gesetzblatt der DDR* I, page 1333; 4th Implementation Ordinance to the THG of 12th September 1990, *Gesetzblatt der DDR* I, page 1465, amended by the Agreement of 18th September 1990, *Bundesgesetzblatt* II, page 1239; 5th Implementation Ordinance to the THG of 12th September 1990, *Gesetzblatt der DDR* I, page 1466.

32 Bundestag printed paper 11/7831; Act in *Bundesgesetzblatt* II 1990, pages 889 and 1159.

33 Bundestag printed paper 12/103 with written justification for the draft bill; Act in *Bundesgesetzblatt* I 1991, page 766.

34 *Bundesgesetzblatt* I, page 1268, with justification dated 3rd April 1992, Bundestag printed paper 227/92.

article act was not restricted to the amendments of the Property Act but also contained the Act on the definition of the assignment of formerly state-owned property, otherwise known as the Property Assignment Act, which applies today in the version promulgated on 3rd August 1992.[35]

There was a similar development in the field of investment promotion. Originally, the Act on special investments in the German Democratic Republic applied in the version included in the Treaty of Unification. The Act was likewise amended[36] by the Removal of Obstacles Act of 22nd March 1991, and is in force today, via the Second Property Law Amendment Act,[37] as an Act on the priority of investments in claims for restitution under the Property Act (usually called the Investment Priority Act). Another regulation to be taken into account in this connection is the Ordinance on the registration of claims under property law of 11th July 1990,[38] which has likewise been applicable in the form in force since 22nd July 1992.[39]

A final regulation to consider is the Ordinance on the Property Act relating to the restitution of companies (the Restitution Ordinance) of 13th July 1991,[40] issued by the Federal Minister of Justice on the basis of § 6 section 9 of the Property Act. It is not possible however to give any more detailed explanation here of the Act of 6th July 1990 on the Property of the Municipalities, Towns, and Rural Counties (Communal Property Act).[41] The THG itself has not been significantly amended, but was basically only adapted by the Removal of Obstacles Act which deleted the THA AG-companies originally provided for in § 7 of the THG. Of far greater importance is the Act for the splitting of companies in the THA's administration (Splitting Act), of 5th April 1991,[42] by which the THA was given the possibility, not previously all that familiar in West German law, for unbundling the joint-stock companies in which it held the shares, with the aim of making them easier to privatise and of creating companies of a size more appropriate to the demands of the market.

The steps taken by East and by West German legislation[43] summarised here, which have now grown to a complex mass which is a little hard to comprehend, and which in some cases came about in something less than the best of circumstances, often arose out of the political necessity of the day, as can be seen just from the rapid sequence in which they appeared. They were not all dealt with in detail by the relevant parliament, but were produced by members of a ministerial bureaucracy who were personally fully familiar with the complex material and in some

---

35 *Bundesgesetzblatt* I, page 1464.

36 Original version: *Bundesgesetzblatt* 1990 II, page 1157. For explanations by the Federal Government see Bundestag printed paper 11/7817. The government's justification of the amendment can be found in Bundestag printed paper 12/103.

37 Government justification in Bundestag printed paper 227/92.

38 *Gesetzblatt der DDR* I, page 718.

39 *Bundesgesetzblatt* I, page 1257.

40 *Bundesgesetzblatt* I, page 1542.

41 *Gesetzblatt der DDR* I, page 660, last amended by § 9 of the Property Assignment Act of 22nd March 1991 (*Bundesgesetzblatt* I, page 786).

42 *Bundesgesetzblatt* I, page 854; Government justification in Bundestag printed paper 12/105; for more details see: Welter, *Spaltung von Treuhandunternehmen*, pages 265 to 273.

43 For some of their characteristics see comments by: Liebs, *Diskussionsbeitrag* in: Hommelhoff (editor), *Treuhandunternehmen im Umbruch*, page 173; also: Horn, *Privatisierung und Reprivatisierung von Unternehmen*, page 134.

cases were involved exclusively with these issues. Therefore, in addition to the official government justifications, the views expressed by high-ranking ministerial civil servants[44] concerned with these laws should also be accorded attention. By now there are also commentaries available on individual Acts affecting such areas of interest here as the Treaty of Unification, the Property Act in version of 18th April 1991 (partly), the Company Restitution Ordinance, the Ordinance on the registration of claims under property law, the THG itself, and the Splitting Act.[45]

The attempt must now be made to present the key elements in the field of tension between the privatisation of companies capable of being restructured and the restitution of assets to their rightful owners, which are the most important issues for assigning the THA's tasks and the problems involved in fulfilling them their place in contemporary history. Taken in detail, the following aspects of a first phase could be of interest: the types of sequestration measures capable of being annulled; the fate of the rights to dispose at the point in time when the GDR came to an end or when the THG came into force; the consequences of the measures taken by claimants; and finally the whole complex question of the assignment and allocation of property.

2. Tangible assets to be privatised

The Property Act, complying with the Joint Declaration of the West and the East German governments on 15th June 1990, does not cover the sequestration of property rights based on the laws of the Occupying Power (§ 8 section 8 letter a). These are the measures taken during the course of "land reform" (*Bodenreform*) and the sequestration and nationalisation of industrial assets.[46] In this respect, it was intended to provide statutorily in even more detail for compensation payments. Where sequestrations took place during the lifetime of the GDR which were contrary to the rule of law, and where German citizens suffered them who had, under the laws in force at the time, fled the country illegally, the solution was to be restitution. This was extended to cover the numerous cases in which property was transferred "voluntarily" into state ownership by procedures known as "cold sequestration": under the pressure of confiscatory taxes, charges imposed on private businesses, or the withdrawal of trading licences.

In the GDR there were further losses of property by forced state partnerships and by forced collectivisations of independent peasants into the agricultural productive cooperatives (*Landwirtschaftliche Produktionsgenossenschaften*).

---

44 For instance, see: Schmidt-Räntsch: *Zum sogenannten Enthemmungsgesetz*, pages 169 to 174; ditto, *Das Vermögenszuordnungsgesetz*, pages 973 to 980; Niederleithinger, *Beseitigung von Hemmnissen*, pages 205 to 216.

45 Commentaries (in the sequence in which the Acts are named in the text) from Wasmuth and Wellhöfer, Wasmuth, Busch, and Haritz, all in: Brunner et al (editors), *Rechtshandbuch Vermögen und Investitionen*, Part B.

46 For a more detailed treatment see: Brunner, *Rechtshandbuch Vermögen und Investitionen, Abschnitt: Systematische Darstellungen I*, pages 2 et seq.; on the assessment under constitutional law, see footnote 11; for the enlarged area of application for the special regulation see: Administrative Court of Berlin, ZIP 1993, page 1979 (Wertheim); Papier, *Rechtsfragen des Restitutionsausschlusses*, pages 806 to 812.

In terms of their numbers, the cases of sequestration without compensation never added up to any great total, with the exception of the assets of refugees and migrants from East to West Germany and foreigners.[47] It is therefore understandable that § 1 of the Property Act comprehensively covers cases of sequestration without compensation, the sale to third parties by state administrators or any other authorised person, and the transfer to public ownership (in the 1972 campaign), and places them on the same footing as the waiving of ownership rights, donation or hereditary entailment because of over-indebtedness caused by a rent which did not cover costs. The same applied to the nationalisation of assets brought about by misuse of office, corruption, and similar. Cases also subject to restitution include state trustee administration of the property of refugees who had "escaped from the Republic" (absconded from East Germany without permission), and foreigners.

Powerful forces had arisen from the start in the political sphere which sought to influence all considerations for regulating "unsettled property questions" which aimed to give preference to "*status quo* interests".[48] This has led to the protection of *bona fide* purchasers, an instrument, although discredited by some spectacular cases, which was thought for pacification. It has also led to a few individual exceptions regulated casuistically in which sequestration during the GDR period was exempted from the obligation of restitution and subjected to a mere obligation to pay compensation. The main points[49] worth mentioning are cases of sequestration for the purpose of rebuilding urban districts destroyed by warfare, and for public construction projects, particularly those involving defence or frontier security.[50] Such sequestration was legal under GDR law if compensation was paid, but in many instances it appeared that no compensation has been paid, and it is for this reason that § 1 sections 1a and 1b of the Property Act also provide for restitution if any compensation had been paid that was less than that provided for under GDR law. Otherwise, however, the introduction of the new law also had to lead to the validity of the basic principles of a legal and social state for all German people.

3. The first phase of privatisation

The actual privatisation of state property was basically to involve two major stages; firstly the transfer of assets into trustee administration, and then their sale to the private sector by the trustee administrator.

a) Responsibility for the first stage, as far as the companies were concerned, fell to the Original-THA and the Conversion Ordinance of 1st March 1990,[51] which provided for the transfer of communist economic units into organisational structures under private law and had

47 See likewise: Brunner, *Vermögen und Investitionen*, marginal note 9. The rule explained below taken from § 1 section 2 is considered "extensive" by: Niederleithinger, *Drei Jahre Vermögensrecht.*

48 Brunner, *Vermögen und Investitionen*, marginal note 11; see data in footnote 11.

49 For a survey with sources see: Brunner, *Vermögen und Investitionen*, marginal notes 26 to 34.

50 The Administrative Court of Berlin turned down claims for restitution by former owners of land in the area of the Berlin Wall – Ruling of 25th June 1992, dossier no. VG 25 A 593/91.

51 Ordinance for the conversion of state-owned *Kombinate* and other organisations into joint-stock companies, *Gesetzblatt der DDR* I no. 14, amended by § 12 No. 9 of the Ordinance dated 28 June 1990, *Gesetzblatt der DDR* I no. 38, page 509; for further details see footnote 13.

already to be implemented by the THA.[52] Following a declaration of conversion made by the company in question and the THA, and the entering of the conversion in a register, the THA became the owner of all the shares, whilst the company acquired ownership of the operating assets, which had previously been held by it under a form of collective possession called *Fondsinhaberschaft*. This did not cover the land, which was publicly-owned and over which the company only had a so-called legal right of organisation (*Rechtsträgerschaft*). Despite the apparently considerable number of companies which arose in this way and in some cases were even reprivatised, doubt has often been expressed as to the willingness to follow this route and to create really new structures, particularly when this involved restitution to previous owners or a transfer to new, private investors.[53]

b) As described at the beginning, § 11 section 1 of the THG and § 2 section 2 of the Property Act take a different approach, and regard the joint-stock companies converted under this Act and allocated to the THA as sole shareholder as being "authorised to dispose", and thus in possession of the formal status of owners.[54] This applies even though the terms "ownership" and "authorisation to dispose" do not match up exactly with one another.[55] Authorisation to dispose over assets applies far more closely to the companies' operating assets previously held in *Fondsinhaberschaft*, but under § 11 section 2 sentence 2 of the THG, unlike the Conversion Ordinance, even the assets and even land held under foreign *Rechtsträgerschaft*, the simple legal right of organisation, and used by the companies for operational purposes under an indefinite contract of usage or easement.[56] The owner of a company's shares is entitled to the "power to dispose" over the company. In those cases in which the objects had been sequestrated, and principally have to be returned, § 2 of the Property Act places the person "authorised to dispose" face to face with the "authorised user", who under §§ 2 and 3 of the Property Act can demand the return of sequestrated property and under § 11 can also demand the cessation of state administration over sequestrated property. The person "authorised" to dispose is thus the debtor facing a claim for restitution, and so the problem arose from the outset that those companies which had come into being during the lifetime of the GDR and had now been converted were in economic terms rarely identical with the companies that had been sequestrated.[57]

This, taken together with the obvious fact that with an organisation under the laws of a joint-stock company it is possible to dispose over "the company" – the real-life economic unit – both by selling off its physical operating assets and by selling the shares in it, the regulation inserted by the Removal of Obstacles Act into § 2 section 3 of the Property Act made it compulsory to

52 For more details on how this was done, see: Elsner, *Die Umwandlung der volkseigenen Betriebe*, pages 3024 to 3028; Roitzsch and Rosener, *Die Umwandlung von volkseigenen Betrieben*, pages 38 to 42; Targan, *Die Rechtsnachfolge bei Umwandlung der volkseigenen Betriebe*, pages 3060 to 3061; Horn, *Das Zivil- und Wirtschaftsrecht*, page 358 et seq.

53 See, for instance: G. and U. Dornberger, *Das Gesetz zur Privatisierung*, pages 3042 to 3045; for a similar view to theirs: Horn, *Das Zivil- und Wirtschaftsrecht*, page 321.

54 op. cit., page 240.

55 Wasmuth, *Gesetz zur Regelung offener Vermögensfragen*, § 2, marginal note 86.

56 Horn, *Privatisierung und Reprivatisierung von Unternehmen*, page 136. Details arise in this respect from the 2nd Implementation Ordinance to the THG (see footnote 31); see also: Horn, *Das Zivil- und Wirtschaftsrecht*, pages 352 et seq.

57 Wasmuth, *Gesetz zur Regelung offener Vermögensfragen*, marginal note 88.

appoint as the parties authorised to dispose both, those who have possession of or control over the sequestrated company and the direct or indirect owners of the shares. This means double authorisation for the companies allotted to the THA,[58] but § 2 section 3 sentence 3 of the Property Act lays down that the THA, if it is entitled to "share rights over parties with authorisation to dispose", will "represent" them exclusively. Finally, the state administrator also has this authority.

c) The transformation of state property into "authorisation to dispose" gave rise to a number of practical problems, some of which were clarified by new legislative regulations. One of these was the possibility provided by the Property Assignment Act to resolve doubts concerning the authorisation to dispose over assets which had been allocated by Articles 21 and 22 of the Treaty of Unification (relating to administrative and financial property), by the Communal Property Act, and by the THG and its implementation ordinances. This regulation in § 1 of the Property Assignment Act, which related chiefly to disputes between territorial authorities, extends § 4 of the Act to cover disputes relating to the allocation of land to the converted joint-stock companies. The 5th Implementation Ordinance to the THG had already given the THA the job of arbitrating over differences of opinion between legal entities and companies holding the rights of use or mediation.[59] The companies allocated in this way to a communal organisation are to continue in operation in the future as companies owned by the municipalities themselves. Allocation of property is still possible even after privatisation; before this was introduced, companies had to be sold with a mere guarantee that all relevant land belonged to them, but in actual fact such exact allocation was still questionable. In order to rule out guarantee claims under the Civil Code, retroactive proceedings under the Property Assignment Act can still have the character of arbitration. If the parties involved are in agreement, the notice issued by the THA under § 2 section 1 sentence 2 of the Property Assignment Act will become final and absolute at once, so that in this way a clear situation can be created on which the companies affected can rely.

It can also be disputed whether the THA, which certainly has authorisation to dispose over the shares in the companies allocated to it, can also dispose over individual assets in its possession.[60] One argument against this view of direct authorisation, which in joint-stock company law is unusual anyway, by some other party than the executive organs of the company is the fact that the statutory power of the THA to represent the company, previously provided for under § 3a of the Property Act, was cancelled with respect to the THA companies by the Second Property Law Amendment Act.[61] However, the THA, in its capacity as sole shareholder, can normally impose its thinking on the board of management of any of its companies when assets which are no longer needed as a result of unbundling have to be sold off.[62]

58 op. cit., marginal note 89.

59 For more details on this see: Horn, *Das Zivil- und Wirtschaftsrecht*, page 354.

60 On this point, see: Leo, § 3a VermG, page 1551 et seq.; G. and U. Dornberger, *Zur Änderung des Gesetzes über offene Vermögensfragen*, pages 897 and 898; for a different opinion see: Messerschmidt, § 3a VermG, pages 2 to 4; Wente, *Die Bedeutung des Begriffs des "Verfügungsberechtigten"*, pages 125 to 127; Wasmuth, *Gesetz zur Regelung offener Vermögensfragen*, § 2, marginal note 92.

61 The differing view given in: Horn, *Privatisierung und Reprivatisierung von Unternehmen*, page 140, is actually based expressly on § 3a of the Property Act.

62 op. cit. for a supporting view.

This THA process known as unbundling or dismemberment will when necessary be one of those taken prior to the actual privatisation. One possibility in this direction was already provided in § 12 section 3 of the original version of the THG, which placed an AG-type company hived off from a *Kombinat* under the obligation of offering shares in a GmbH-type company held by the AG to the THA (for a suitable consideration) if the executive board of the GmbH so requested. Admittedly, the willingness to submit such applications on the part of companies attempting to break away from the AG-type group does not appear to have taken on any great proportions.[63] In any case, the hiving off of companies from AG-groups was made far easier by the Splitting Act for joint-stock companies, whose shares are all in the THA's hands, and, although this has to be prepared in detail by the executive board of the departing company, the final decision lies solely with the shareholder,[64] so that in this instance as well the THA can take the initiative. One final point worth emphasising is that companies split off or converted prior to 1st July 1990, which in doing so often ignored the provisions of the Conversion Ordinance, can be put back on the rails by means of registration under § 12 section 1 sentence 1 of the Splitting Act.[65] As with companies that have already been privatised, it is also possible in these instances as well for property to be allocated under the Property Assignment Act.

4. The significance of property assignment

The basic outlines have now been sketched in of the first phase of the privatisation of state property, which can be described as the transformation of ownership. Before the second phase can be dealt with, in which the main factor is the demarcation of areas of interest between former owners entitled to restitution and of new investors, the work involved in the categorisation and allocation of property must be analysed in more detail and submitted to an initial evaluation because of the practical importance of this work of the THA for the success of the transformation process.

a) The sharing out of formerly state-owned property displays certain dynamic characteristics. On the one hand, companies were in this way equipped with operating assets and the basis of collateral for loans, and this proved very important in light of the reorientation made necessary by the collapse of the markets in which they previously sold. On the other hand, the intention was really to set the companies on their own two feet, an intention certainly quite unique when compared internationally with those countries which previously had a centrally planned economy. Also, considerable difficulties arose in the creation of the kind of legal security in the field of real estate which banks require as collateral for loans. The central point of contention was the sharing out of state-owned property which up to then had been held in *Fondsinhaberschaft*, a kind of operative administration of company assets with rights similar to that of ownership,[66] or *Rechtsträgerschaft*, possession of and authorisation to dispose over land and property.[67] The latter was supposed to be entered in the Land Register under § 2 section 1c of the Land

63 See: op. cit., page 138, and: Balz, *Rechtseinheit als Grundlage*, page 46.
64 Haritz, Commentary on the Splitting Act, § 7, marginal note 1 (see footnote 45).
65 For more details see: Horn, *Privatisierung und Reprivatisierung von Unternehmen*, page 139.
66 Busche, *Kommentar zum Treuhandgesetz*, § 1, marginal note 20.
67 op. cit.

Documentation Ordinance of 6th November 1975,[68] but because of a lax approach to such matters this appears to have been done only rarely.[69]

Thus the situation was not always clear from the start, at the moment when the new law came into force, but at least claims could be raised which contested the authorisation of companies to dispose over their property, including particularly those companies which had been given the plot of land as being necessary for their operations but without the *Rechtsträgerschaft* to go with it. If this use was not just of a temporary nature, and affected "most of" the plot of land, § 2 of the 5th Implementation Ordinance to the THG placed the party entitled to use it on the same footing as if it had always had *Rechtsträgerschaft*. This then meant at least the possibility of a claim for transfer against the legal entity (*Rechtsträger*), and possibly also, despite certain misgivings based on constitutional law, a direct transfer of ownership to the company authorised to use the land under § 11 section 2 of the THG.[70] The situation proved to be particularly complex when the *Rechtsträgerschaft* party and the party with authorisation to use the plot of land were both making active use of it; one possibility considered in the case of buildings was to divide the object by means of two entries in the Land Register while at the same time creating imagined co-ownership rights over the building as a whole.[71]

In all such cases, the THA takes the decision in formal administrative proceedings and applies to the Land Registry for the appropriate entry to be made under § 38 of the Land Register Ordinance. The property allocation notice can be contested before the Administrative Court of Berlin. The Land Registry offices were instructed not to make any entry without such a notice, but this can lead to delays in achieving final clarification in simple cases of property allocation.

b) The crucial factor in the allocation of former state-owned property to corporations under public law was the issue of which body had been responsible on 1st October 1989 for specific administrative operations to carry out with the land (see Articles 21 and 22 of the Treaty of Unification for more details).[72] Restitution claims by corporations under public law can be raised against companies which regarded land as belonging to them even before the Treaty of Unification came into force, for instance under § 11 section 2 of the THG. The dimensions of this problem are considerable, because many facilities such as polyclinics or crèches, which in West Germany would have been a municipal responsibility, were in East Germany organised within companies (§ 6 of the Communal Property Act). The transfer prescribed by this Act to the competent local authority was submitted to a limitation by the Second Property Law Amendment Act as far as facilities necessary for the company's operations were concerned, if these were integrated into a company unit which could not be transferred to the local authority without seriously affecting the company (§ 7a sentence 4 of the Property Assignment Act).

---

68 *Gesetzblatt der DDR* I, page 697.

69 For the first registration as the legal organisation, or for transfers from one organisation to another, this regulation of 7th July 1969 (*Gesetzblatt der DDR* II no. 68, page 433) prescribed a procedure for the *Rechtsträgerschaft* of publicly-owned property which, however, merely ended with a declaratory entry, so that there was no great necessity to ensure punctilious registration.

70 For more details on the 5th Implementation Ordinance to the THG see: Bärwaldt, *Probleme des Eigentumsübergangs*, pages 133 to 135; Lipps, *Fragwürdiger gesetzlicher Eigentumserwerb*, pages 14 to 16; Graf Lambsdorff, *Vermögensübergang bei ehemals volkseigenen Betrieben*, pages 102 to 105.

71 Graf Lambsdorff, *Vermögensübergang bei ehemals volkseigenen Betrieben*, page 105.

72 On this point see: Lange, *Wem gehört das ehemalige Volkseigentum?*, pages 329 to 336.

c) A distinction needs to be made with respect to the competence regarding this allocation procedure.[73] If the THA is the owner or the trustee administrator, meaning, in the case of companies converted from state into private ownership, land and forests used by agricultural productive cooperatives, former military property, and communal facilities formerly owned by the state and scheduled for communalisation, the President of the THA is responsible and makes the decision in his capacity as a Federal authority. For other cases of transfer of ownership the responsibility lies with the president of the local *Oberfinanzdirektion*, in effect the Regional Inspector of Taxes. One decision is sure to be the most important one for privatisation: which joint-stock company is entitled to a given building or plot of land; and § 4 of the Property Assignment Act leaves this responsibility with the President of the THA. He can decide merely to allocate a building, which then has to be entered on the appropriate page of the Land Register, and this can lead to difficulties if the company is using only a building which it acquired or built on a state-owned plot of land. With a firm eye on the practical aspects, the THA will as a rule endeavour to apply uniform treatment, although § 4 of the Property Assignment Act would not prevent the legal separation of the building from the land.

d) It can already be seen at this point that the laws covering details of these procedures are in many cases merely so-called process laws, which can give only a relatively uncertain statement about the requirements for action under substantive law or for decisions on disputes (for instance by such requirements as the use of a plot of land that is necessary for a company's business operation, covers most or all of the land, and is not merely of a temporary nature), and otherwise provides for participation rights in a process in which the THA makes the final and definitive decision, not as a disinterested and neutral party but as the sole shareholder with a very real interest in the outcome. Under the circumstances currently obtaining, characterised among other things by the urgent need to clarify the property ownership situation, such regulations force the parties involved to come to an agreement with one another which is legally only of limited determining power and gives the THA scope for its creative purposes – which can of course be motivated by considerations of economic and even general policy. The danger is even acknowledged in the literature[74] that decisions may be made one-sidedly in the interplay between the government departments and the private investor behind the backs of the party claiming restitution.

IV. The role of the THA in restitution to former owners and fresh privatisation

In order to be able to provide a general view of the possibilities and difficulties involved in the fulfilment of the THA's tasks it is necessary to describe (1) the holder and the substance of claims to restitution, (2) the regulations governing the priority given to investment, and (3) the assessment of a rival investment project by a former owner, and finally (4) the claimants or former owners entitled to compensation or damages.

---

73 For more details on the following points see: 2nd, 4th, and 5th Implementation Ordinances to the THG (referred to in footnote 31).

74 Niederleithinger, *Drei Jahre Vermögensrecht*.

1. The claimant or the substance of a restitution claim

When sequestration is to be cancelled, the property concerned is to be restored to its "rightful owners" upon their application. The basic principle is established in §§ 2 and 3 of the Property Act, and the return of companies in §§ 6 to 6b. The application by the claimant normally has to be preceded by registration under the Registration Ordinance.[75] The period of time during which claims to restitution or for compensation could be registered was fixed for 31st December 1992 by the Second Property Law Amendment Act, which also abolishes the facility for registering claims even after the set period has expired. The decision, which originally lay exclusively with the Property Offices, is widened in the Removal of Obstacles Act by the possibility of taking the decision to a court of arbitration; provision is also made for mutual agreement between the claimant and the current authorised user, and this has now even become the normal procedure, as can be seen from § 30 section 1 sentence 2 of the Property Act. It precedes any decision by the Property Office.[76]

There is no way of simplifying the identification of the legitimate claimants; this is made more difficult by problems in establishing facts and clarifying the legal situation, one main factor being that frequently a long period of time has elapsed since the official or the "cold" sequestration. In many cases the limited companies or partnerships which lost their business operation have long since disappeared, although a partnership can continue in existence as a "company in liquidation" under civil law, and can under West German law return to life even after liquidation if they possess assets in the form of a claim to restitution, and thus become claimants within the meaning of § 2 section 1 sentence 1 of the Property Act as introduced by the Removal of Obstacles Act.[77] This regulation does not apply to the return of companies; this is covered solely by § 6 of the Property Act, and has the particular characteristic that, in the case of companies which had been sequestrated, more than half of the shareholders or their successors in law now have to register their claim. The former shareholders in a joint-stock company are only indirectly injured parties, and as such are not entitled to restitution within the meaning of § 6a of the Property Act.[78] Therefore, the old companies have to be resurrected under the company names which appeared in the trade registers prior to confiscation, liquidators have to be appointed, and the deletion notices in the trade registers must themselves be deleted. The ironical term used for this state of affairs, "Lazarus companies",[79] symbolises one part of the practical difficulties which restitution has to overcome.

Natural persons who suffered sequestration are in many cases no longer alive, so that the problem arises of their legal successors establishing their claims. If it was a community of co-heirs that suffered sequestration, any person authorised to act on behalf of all the co-heirs can

75 For more details on the procedure see: Horn, *Das Zivil- und Wirtschaftsrecht*, pages 242 et seq.

76 On this point see: Horn, *Privatisierung und Reprivatisierung von Unternehmen*, page 142.

77 Wasmuth, *Gesetz zur Regelung offener Vermögensfragen*, § 2, marginal note 60.

78 Niederleithinger, *Beseitigung von Hemmnissen*, pages 205 to 208; Wasmuth, *Gesetz zur Regelung offener Vermögensfragen*, § 2, marginal note 20.

79 See: Liebs and Preu, *Ein Gesetz zur Beseitigung der restlichen Investitionsmöglichkeiten*, pages 216 to 220; and for the practical difficulties see: Horn, *Privatisierung und Reprivatisierung von Unternehmen*, page 158 et seq.

raise the claim.[80] Nevertheless, companies have been returned in such large numbers, and certainly not only, but presumably initially, to persons still living in East Germany,[81] and so it would certainly not be fair to say that former owners only had an eye on compensation. With regard to the substance of restitution claims, a distinction needs to be made between the return of real estates and of companies. Instead of a claim for the return of land under § 3 of the Property Act, the claimant (or, if this is in fact a number of joint claimants, all of them acting unanimously) can select compensation (§ 8 of the Act). This does not apply if land was taken into state ownership by waiver of ownership, by donation, or by renunciation of an inheritance (§ 8 section 1 sentence 2 of the Property Act), meaning that these cases of "cold" sequestration were not put on the same footing, when the basic restitution claim was established .

A restitution claim is categorised under public law,[82] but is very close to private law because it is a claim directed towards the transfer of private property against a likewise authorised private user. In the Removal of Obstacles Act, the claim can be made transferable (§ 3 section 1 sentence 2 of the Property Act) in order to enable claimants to transfer their claims to investors. However, there are practical barriers in the way of this if the claim is weakened by a counterclaim for investment priority (see also IV.2).

The special regulations for the return of a company had to take the fact into account that the complex of assets of many different kinds, relationships, opportunities, and risks, regardless of the legal status of the originally sequestrated company, rarely if ever still exists in the same shape and context (and probably would not even if it had not been sequestrated). In addition to this, the sequestrated companies have often been integrated into larger company units, which were partly organic, but partly conglomerate. The practical difficulties arising from doubts over the identity of the company and sometimes from the necessary unbundling were among the objections generally raised against the principle of "restitution before compensation".[83] The attempt is made in § 6 of the Property Act to grapple with this highly complex situation; § 6a of the Removal of Obstacles Act added a regulation on the temporary installation of the claimant at his old company, and § 6b added one on unbundling. It should also be noted the Restitution of Companies Ordinance. Under § 3 section 1 sentence 3 of the Property Act the claimant cannot limit his claim to restitution to individual assets used by the company, but has to decide in favour of the restitution of the company as a whole, unless the business operations have been discontinued and cannot be started up again (§ 4 section 1 sentence 2 of the Property Act). In this last instance there is a right to claim the return of individual assets if they were present in the company at the time of sequestration or have since been acquired to replace them (§ 6 section 6a sentence 1 of the Act).

Even greater uncertainty can arise in connection with the requirement in § 6 section 1 of the Property Act for the company to be returned to be comparable with the one originally se-

80 Wasmuth, *Gesetz zur Regelung offener Vermögensfragen*, marginal note 12.

81 See figures given in the article in this volume by Willgerodt, pages 251 et seq.

82 See: Horn, *Privatisierung und Reprivatisierung*, page 161; Brunner, *Vermögen und Investitionen. Systematische Darstellung*, marginal note 62.

83 For a discussion of this point see: Horn, *Das Zivil- und Wirtschaftsrecht*, pages 20 et seq. and 34 et seq.; Balz, *Rechtseinheit als Grundlage*, page 50.

questrated.[84] The mere merger of the sequestrated company with one or several others is no barrier to the comparability (§ 6 section 1 sentence 4). A further problem thus arises consequently from the idea of restitution, namely the necessity of compensation for the increase or decrease in value of the company which has to be handed back. The various laws attempt to regulate this by taking the approach of balance-sheet law to cover the compensation claims and liabilities of the companies if the creditor or debtor is the company to which the shares are to be transferred free of charge for the purpose of the privatisation and re-organisation of the state-owned property (§ 24 section 3 and § 25 section 2 of the Deutschmark Balance Sheet Act). It is still not possible to pass any judgement on this extraordinarily complicated set of regulations, which is, in many practical respects, difficult to carry out.[85] On the other hand, however, even these elements of the legal situation can only at best be individual items within the overall framework of mutually agreed solutions between the various parties involved.

2. The questions arising from investment priority

a) Since the THA took up its work, the regulations on the relationship between restitution to former owners and fresh privatisation have been changed many times in the name of "investment priority", awoke considerable public interest from the outset, and probably they will become the trouble spot in the historical assessment of the THA concept. The many complaints raised at the unsatisfactory speed of privatisation have been justified, among other things, by the claims which have been registered by former company owners for the return of ownership to them, that these claimshad prevented or at least held up the sale of the shares to outside investors, and that by the lack of clarity on whether land used for operational purposes would have to be given back to its rightful owners. This has discouraged potential purchasers of companies and prevented quick decisions. The same applies in practice, of course, to unclear situations regarding property assignment, the treatment of which was covered in III.2 and 3.

b) Admittedly, not all restitution claims have become significant obstacles to privatisation. The characteristic already mentioned, comparability of the company for which restitution is claimed with the company originally sequestrated, as part of the basis of a claim, certainly favours the continuation of elaborate company structures to the disadvantage of the previous owners, who have to accept that it is not possible to turn "the wheel of history" back to any required point in time. The exemption under § 5 of the Property Act, originally created to apply to land and buildings but also applicable to companies,[86] is apparently similar in many respects. It forbids restitution if the property has been altered at considerable expense in terms of its use and purpose, and if there is public interest in this use being continued, and similar rules apply if the property has been devoted to common use through the integration into a complex scheme of habitations and settlements, or, finally, if it has been integrated into a business unit and cannot

84 See also: Horn, *Das Zivil- und Wirtschaftsrecht*, page 68; for a comparison of companies see the detailed description by Wellhöfer in: Brunner et al (editors), *Rechtshandbuch Vermögen und Investitionen*, Part B, Commentary on § 6 of the Property Act, marginal notes 30 to 42.

85 A view supported by: Horn, *Das Zivil- und Wirtschaftsrecht*, page 169.

86 op. cit., page 164, but with the additional instructions that unbundling measures have to be examined.

be extricated from it without causing it considerable damage. Accordingly, the point is not merely to ensure the *status quo* of the company, but the property must have been allocated by sequestration or legal sale for its first operational use; the former owner can avoid exemption if he declares his willingness to permit continuation of the hitherto existing use by concluding a tenancy or leasehold agreement.[87]

The conditions under which § 5 of the Property Act will apply are relatively narrowly drawn, but these laws do not initially acknowledge any general priority for investment in the interests of preserving or creating a company and a number of jobs. One exception was made by Article 41 section 2 of the Treaty of Unification for land and buildings which do not have to be given back if the property "is needed for urgent investment purposes yet to be defined in detail, in particular for the setting up of commercial operations, and the implementation of the investment decision is valuable in general economic terms, particularly if it creates or preserves jobs." In respect to the return of companies neither the Treaty of Unification nor the Investment Act contains any such general decision on priority for outsiders' investment, and this led to misgivings in relation to constitutional law with regard to the basic principle of equal treatment for all;[88] as a basic principle this has not been upheld against the demands of real life and political necessity.

The history of the regulations covering priority for investment was full of variety; whilst the amendment by the Removal of Obstacles Act initially provided in § 3a of the Property Act for a particularly wide-ranging priority for investment up to the end of 1992, which was then to be replaced by the end of 1993 by a less wholesale regulation (changing from "super-priority" to "simple priority"), but then led to a general regulation of the Investment Act without any special reference to companies. Legislation then intervened with the Second Property Law Amendment Act and bundled up the priority regulations, which had actually been intended to apply for a limited period of time, in the Investment Priority Act. The main criteria and scope for making decisions thus remained principally with the THA;[89] this can be attributed to the fact that the hopes enshrined in the Removal of Obstacles Act that restitution and privatisation, and with them all the most difficult cases of conflict, could be wound up by the end of 1992 or in 1993 at the latest, did not all come true. The following basic features of the regulations should be emphasised in detail.

According to the basic principle stated in § 1 of the Investment Priority Act, plots of land, buildings, and whole companies to which restitution claims have been or could be made under the Property Act can be used partly or entirely for investment purposes, and the claimant will receive compensation under the terms of the Investment Priority Act. The new regulations have not changed the rule, that the THA itself, so long as it continues to be the authorised user, is not permitted to issue the investment priority notice, with the exception of those proceedings relating to land, buildings, and individual parts of THA companies covered by § 25 section 2 of the Investment Priority Act. It are only private persons who require this notice from the Rural County or County Borough in which the asset in question is located (§§ 4 section 2), so the THA can act quickly although it does have to keep to the procedure laid down in §§ 4 to 7 and to inform the authority which is dealing with the restitution claim and inform the claimant that the

87 Explanations by the Federal government on the Property Act in the version of the Treaty of Unification, § 5d.

88 See: Horn, *Privatisierung und Reprivatisierung von Unternehmen*, page 145.

89 Horn, *Das zweite Vermögensrechtsänderungsgesetz*, pages 309 to 316.

asset is required for investment purposes. Pending restitution proceedings are then suspended. The investment priority notice at the same time replaces the property transaction licence and other official approvals which are necessary to dispose over assets of the state sector (§ 11 section 1). The intention which becomes evident at this point of accelerating new investments as much as possible can be seen in the fact that the possibilities open to the claimant under § 12 section 2 to raise an objection or a counter-claim are by law not permitted to have any suspensory effect. However, this does not prohibit recourse to the administrative courts, which can make use of § 80 section 5 of the Administrative Courts Ordinance to bring about a suspensory effect . It is said[90] that ample use is being made of this in practice.

It is of course crucial in the practical handling of investment priority to see how "investment purposes" of prime importance are defined in § 3 of the Investment Priority Act. The foremost position is taken by the preservation or creation of jobs, particularly by the setting up or continuation of a commercial operation, the building of homes, and the creation of infrastructure necessary for investments or otherwise covered by them. In the case of companies, investment purposes can also include "investments for securing competitiveness" and the possibility of forestalling the liquidation of a company on account of insolvency or over-indebtedness. In this context, legislation has recently stuck to the principle[91] that the use of an asset for investment purposes is to be placed on the same footing as a situation in which "the authorised user gives no guarantee that he will keep the company in existence or restructure it". The assumption that it is always better to sell the asset rather than hand it back to a previous owner whose intention to keep the business in existence is in doubt throws an elucidating light on the general assessment of restitution claimants.

3. Rival investment projects

It cannot be denied that these various laws turned the THA and the restitution claimants to a certain extent into antagonists. If the THA intends to devote capital to the company which the claimant is claiming, or to privatise it by transferring its shares or selling its assets, the provisions of § 3 sections 3 to 5 of the Property Act will not be applicable, which otherwise forbid economically irreversible measures being taken by the authorised user prior to restitution; that is to say, the THA cannot be prevented from carrying out individual measures contrary to the claimant's plans. However, it is perfectly possible for the THA and the restitution claimant to reach agreement by these means on the transfer of the asset for a suitable consideration and to make the payment of the agreed purchase price dependent upon the outcome of restitution proceedings.[92]

Apart from this, the claimant can in many respects go over to the attack. As soon as he is informed of the intention of using the assets for investment purposes he can announce (if he does so within a remarkably short period of time) that, as the registered claimant under § 5 section 3 of the Investment Priority Act, he too intends to sign an undertaking to make investments. However, he must also submit his own investment plan very quickly, and it must be capable of

90 Horn, *Privatisierung und Reprivatisierung von Unternehmen*, page 155 et seq.; see also the case of the sale of a series of regional newspapers reported in: Balz, *Rechtseinheit als Grundlage*.

91 Misgivings in: Horn, *Privatisierung und Reprivatisierung von Unternehmen*, page 146.

92 On this point see also: op. cit., page 147 (the "greyhound" procedure).

being assessed in comparison with that of the authorised user. Although there was no guarantee under the Removal of Obstacles Act that the previous owner would be given preference,[93] § 21 of the Second Property Law Amendment Act imposes an obligation on the authorised user to grant the claimant's project an investment priority notice if the claim is plausible and the claimant is in a position, personally and financially, to provide a guarantee that he will carry out his investment project and that he will undertake to make the same or roughly the same investments as the other would-be investor. Finally, the possibility is still open to the claimant of being provisionally introduced to the claimed company under § 6a of the Property Act, this being a decision for the Office for the Regulation of Unsettled Property Questions to make. All the same, the claim must be "substantiable" and not merely plausible, and this test will often be failed in the case of companies where a long period of time has elapsed since the sequestration, the companies have been restructured several times, and now a number of previous owners have registered claims. The claimants then only have the possibility of applying for unbundling under § 6b of the Property Act.

The THA can use the pressure which the restitution claimant is under to bring about agreement on the partial or complete return or on a waiver of the relevant rights. This will then specifically come up for consideration as soon as the amount of the sale proceeds from fresh privatisation can be discerned, as the claimant can then decide whether to demand payment of a share of the proceeds attributable to his share of the assets being claimed (§ 16 of the Investment Priority Act). The claimant can, as a matter of choice, also be eligible for damages awardable under other regulations (§ 17). It is also no rare occurrence, and seems to be a practical solution, for the claimant to transfer his restitution claim to an investor and for the price to be paid by the investor to be taken into account in calculating the purchase price.[94] The point is once again noticeable that the legal basis for the THA's work tends in the direction of reaching agreement between the new investors and the former owners; accordingly, attention is drawn in meetings between the parties that investment priority proceedings often do not need to be carried through to the bitter end.

4. Questions of damages

The interpretation of the provisions for the cancellation of restitution claims on account of legal and proper acquisition by a third party under § 4 of the Property Act,[95] which has given rise to controversy in the discussion on legal policy and, specifically, to its very problematic effect on the application of general private-law norms does not need to be covered in any more detail in

---

93 For a critical view see: op. cit., page 148.

94 Overlack, *Diskussionsbeitrag* in Hommelhoff (editor), *Treuhandunternehmen im Umbruch*, page 182.

95 For more details see: Horn, *Privatisierung und Reprivatisierung von Unternehmen*, page 164 et seq.; for a critical view advocating strengthening the possibility of acquisition in *bona fides* under the Second Property Law Amendment Act, see: Horn, *Das Zweite Vermögensrechtsänderungsgesetz*, page 310; on the compensation regulations so far as they can currently be forecast, see: Niederleithinger, *Drei Jahre Vermögensrecht*, page 310; for the misgivings under constitutional law see the report on the hearing of the Financial and Legal Committee of the German Bundestag in the *Frankfurter Allgemeine Zeitung* of 16th September 1993.

this article, because although the THA's work is indirectly affected by any such exclusion of the claim for restitution, its own activities in the one or the other direction are not required. The same applies, or has done up to now, to damages due to former owners in the cases envisaged in § 4 of the Property Act, whereas § 9 section 1 of the Act does not in any way define the nature of the damages to be awarded anyway. Although the system of compensation assets and liabilities does, as already described, under certain circumstances also cover the obligation to pay compensation for any major worsening of a company that is being handed back, and although this compensation is anchored in the Property Act, it is only comprehensible within the context of the requirements and measures under balance sheet law which the THA companies have to carry out for restructuring[96] and, in parallel with this process, which the THA has to fulfil to integrate the formerly state-owned companies into the social and economic legal systems of West Germany. The point has already been mentioned that the previous owners could have a claim to a share of the sale proceeds, which they might possibly prefer to a claim for compensation in view of the complete confusion as to the amount they might one day be offered as compensation for a sequestration which cannot be reversed.

V. Conclusion

1. Summary

The preceding pages have presented a view of the legal basis for the THA's work in order to show whether it enabled the THA to fulfil the tasks it has been set, tasks which for historic reasons were highly unusual if not indeed unique. This applies particularly with regard to the fact that interference of this kind in the rights of private persons requires a legal basis the application of which, in view of the provisions of Article 14 of the German Constitution, can be reasonably accepted by the holders of the relevant private property rights in light of the constitutional rank of their position. This is one of the tenets of the supervision and legitimisation system which the THA has to satisfy.[97] The observation of these rules definitely does not suffice, as the other aims of the THA, which are likewise related to the public interest (see above, II.1), have to be located sufficiently firmly at the level under the constitution so that its decisions in resolving conflicts of aims and its considerations in weighing the relative interests of former owners and the public, wishing as it does to see new investments made, can be supported as soon as possible by a secure legal framework. It is clear, from the legal point of view, and has been submitted in detail above, that only a few of the THA's decisions and actions preceding the selection of a private purchaser for formerly state-owned assets, meaning mainly companies, are and can be left to the free discretion of those responsible.

There is a distinction that needs to be made in the question of assessing the value of the statutory basis of the THA's work. The achievements of the THG, the Property Act, and other more or less supporting legislation, in coping with highly complex legalistic problems deserve recognition, and the success achieved by the THA in its privatisation work was to a large extent only

96 See a detailed account in: Spoerr, *Treuhandanstalt und Treuhandunternehmen*, pages 290 et seq.

97 The main reference here is: op. cit., pages 113 et seq. and 139 et seq.

possible as a result of this. Admittedly, legislation imposed in many respects sacrifices and deprivations on the interests of restitution claimants which are considerable and hard to tolerate in a legal system which feels itself under an obligation to subjective law and private autonomy. The legislative means with which the legislative bodies had operated here, perhaps without even being aware of them, were a procedure with a relative indeterminate basis for making decisions but with a very firm set of participation rights of private persons and public interest groups. The expectation can thus be raised that the THA, standing at the focal point of these interwoven interests, could succeed in acting to some extent as a clearing house and in reconciling the interests of many different dimensions. The procedural steps and creative instruments described in sections III and IV of this article apparently did not function properly at first and, as was also to be shown, had to be adapted quickly to fit the actual circumstances of the privatisation business as they came to light over time. It would probably be fair to say that the cost of this was very largely borne by the restitution claimants and former rightful owners, but another result has been, perhaps resulting largely in the Second Property Law Amendment Act, an increased sensitivity in many respects to the safeguarding of the position of the applicants for a restitution claim.

2. Prospects

The legal history of the THA does not come to an end with a statement of this kind; perhaps it has not yet even started on the decisive phase of its existence. The possibility cannot be ruled out, and it might even be assumed, that the legal basis for the THA's work will be examined in legal actions on totally different matters and for its durability in the face of the many, various, and controversial, decisions it has to make. It could thus happen that decisions made under the Property Assignment and the Investment Priority Acts could give rise to actions for damages.[98] In respect to the choice of one out of a number of potential purchasers for a THA company, the dispute over the legal character is already pending before the courts.[99] The purchase contracts already concluded by the THA could possibly harbour risks from the point of view of commercial guarantee liability, and the measures taken during the course of the THA's work on contract control could reach the outer limits of contract law but still be justified basically under the convincing argument, which has anyway to be worked out in detail[100] under re-unification law, of the absence and disappearance of the business basis.

One particularly broad field is opened up in this respect by the company law of THA companies. The question might possibly come up for decision as to whether the retrospective creation of the necessary conditions for the establishment of the THA joint-stock companies that had been created *ex vi legis* perhaps runs the risk that the THA, as their sole shareholder, could find itself in a position of founder's responsibility – the personal liability borne by shareholders immediately prior to the establishment of a limited-liability company – which could have prac-

98 On this point see: Weimar, *Nachprivatisierungsprobleme*, pages 39 et seq.

99 For the decision in the Salzwedel sugar factory case, see: Administrative Court of Berlin, NJW 1991, page 376; Higher Administrative Court of Berlin, NJW 1991, page 715; and Spoerr, *Treuhandanstalt und Treuhandunternehmen*, pages 174 et seq.

100 On this point see: Horn, *Die heutige Auslegung des DDR-Rechts*, pages 44 to 52; most recently, Federal Court of Justice, WM 1993, page 1041 with further references.

tical consequences in the all too frequent cases of insolvency.[101] § 28a of the Introductory Act to the *Aktiengesetz*, which is supposed to prevent this sort of occurrence, has been subjected to doubts under constitutional law.[102] The financial assistance of the THA for those of its companies in financial difficulties could become relevant from the point of view of fonds placed in lieu of share capital and, in particularly serious cases, postponement of bankruptcy to the detriment of the creditors.[103] The much-discussed possibility of the THA's liability as the ultimate holding company at the head of a so-called *de facto* group made up of all the THA companies, and possibly also liability on the basis of a qualified *de facto* grouping, on which one County Court has already issued a judgement,[104] may end up as nothing more than a false alarm, but such a possibility is not so far away that it must be mentioned in a presentation of the THA's history leading up to the future.

This historical account, for which the time is perhaps not yet ripe, will at the most contain a small contribution by lawyers specialising in private law. From this point of view it can at the moment only be stated that the legal norms created *ad hoc* were perhaps not the best imaginable in their auxiliary function in assisting the THA's overall economic aims, but that they did prove satisfactory and began to fulfil the function of a rolling transition into the role of controlling criteria for the THA's fulfilment of its tasks.

VI. Literature

Bärwaldt, Roman: Probleme des Eigentumsübergangs nach dem TreuhandG und seiner 5. DurchführungsVO. In: *Zeitschrift für Vermögens- und Investitionsrecht* 1992, pages 133 to 135.

Balz, Manfred: Rechtseinheit als Grundlage für die soziale und wirtschaftliche Einheit – rechtliche Hindernisse bei der Bewältigung der Treuhandaufgaben. In: *Bitburger Gespräche*, Jahrbuch 1991/92, pages 43 to 54.

Brunner, Georg (editor): *Rechtshandbuch Vermögen und Investitionen in der ehemaligen DDR, Kommentar THG*. Loose-leaf collection as of October 1992.

---

101 See: Ulmer, *Gläubigerschutz bei Treuhandunternehmen*, pages 39 and 43 et seq.; and Weimar, *Nachprivatisierungsprobleme*, pages 143 et seq.

102 The Local Court of Halle/Saalekreis passed on the exclusion of the THA's group liability under § 28 of this Introductory Act and § 56e of the Deutschmark Balance Sheet Act to the Federal Constitutional Court in its Ruling of 10th December 1992, dossier no. 50 N 21/92.

103 For the duties of the THA in connection with its task of liquidation see: Spoerr, *Treuhandanstalt und Treuhandunternehmen*, pages 349 et seq.; for postponement of bankruptcy to the detriment of creditors as grounds for the application of § 826 see: Erman – Schiemann, *BGB-Handkommentar*, § 826, marginal notes 31 et seq.

104 The most recent comment here is the detailed summary in: Weimar, *Nachprivatisierungsprobleme*, pages 96 et seq.; see also: Spoerr, *Treuhandanstalt und Treuhandunternehmen*, pages 369 et seq.; the judgement handed down by the County Court of Erfurt (ZIP 1991, page 1233), condemning the THA in its capacity as ultimate holding company at the head of a company group on account of its management activities in agreeing to defray the losses of a THA company undergoing compulsory liquidation, ended in the withdrawal of the action after the THA had indemnified the plaintiff employees.

Busche, Ian: *Kommentar zum THG*. In: Georg *Brunner* (editor): *Rechtshandbuch Vermögen und Investitionen in der ehemaligen DDR*.

Dornberger, Ute, and Gerhard *Dornberger*: Das Gesetz zur Privatisierung und Reorganisation des volkseigenen Vermögens (Treuhandgesetz). In: *Der Betrieb*, DDR-Report 1990, pages 3042 to 3045.

ditto: Zur Änderung des Gesetzes über offene Vermögensfragen und das Gesetz über besondere Investitionen. In: *Der Betrieb* 1991, pages 897 and 898.

Elsner, Joachim: Die Umwandlung der volkseigenen Betriebe in Kapitalgesellschaften. In: *Der Betrieb*, DDR-Report 1990, pages 3024 to 3028.

Erman, Walter: *BGB-Handkommentar in zwei Bänden*. Münster [9]1993.

Fahrenbach, Ralf-Friedrich: Das Privatisierungsverfahren nach dem Treuhandgesetz. In: *Deutsch-Deutsche Rechts-Zeitschrift* 1990, pages 268 to 270.

Hommelhoff, Peter (editor): *Treuhandunternehmen im Umbruch. Recht und Rechtswirklichkeit beim Übergang in die Marktwirtschaft*. Cologne 1991.

Horn, Norbert: Die heutige Auslegung des DDR-Rechts und die Anwendung des § 242 BGB auf DDR-Altverträge. In: *Deutsche Zeitschrift für Wirtschaftsrecht* 1992, pages 44 to 52.

ditto: *Privatisierung und Reprivatisierung von Unternehmen. Eigentumsschutz und Investitionsförderung im Lichte der neuesten Gesetzgebung*. In: Peter *Hommelhoff* (editor): *Treuhandunternehmen im Umbruch*, pages 133 to 172.

ditto: Das Zweite Vermögensrechtsänderungsgesetz und die Verfügbarkeit von Grundeigentum im neuen Bundesgebiet. In: *Deutsche Zeitschrift für Wirtschaftsrecht* 1992, pages 309 to 316.

ditto: *Das Zivil- und Wirtschaftsrecht im neuen Bundesgebiet*. Cologne 1991.

Kerber, Marcus C.: Unternehmenssanierung durch die Treuhand. In: *Deutsche Zeitschrift für Wirtschaftsrecht* 1993, pages 221 to 227.

Kerber, Markus C., and Wilfried *Stechow*: Die Treuhandanstalt im Spannungsverhältnis zwischen öffentlichem und privatem Recht. In: *Deutsche Zeitschrift für Wirtschaftsrecht* 1991, pages 49 to 51.

Krebs, Walter: Rechtsschutzprobleme bei Entscheidungen der Treuhandanstalt. In: *Zeitschrift für Wirtschaftsrecht und Insolvenzpraxis* 1990, pages 1513 to 1523.

Lambsdorff, Konstantin Graf: Vermögensübergang bei ehemals volkseigenen Betrieben. In: *Deutsch-Deutsche Rechts-Zeitschrift* 1992, pages 102 to 105.

Lange, Manfred: Wem gehört das ehemalige Volkseigentum? Grundfragen zu den Art. 21 und 22 EV. In: *Deutsch-Deutsche Rechts-Zeitschrift* 1991, pages 329 to 336.

Leo, Ian: § 3a VermG – Vorfahrt für Investitionen. In: *Der Betrieb* 1991, pages 1505 to 1510.

Liebs, Rüdiger: *Diskussionsbeitrag* in: Peter *Hommelhoff* (editor): *Treuhandunternehmen im Umbruch*, pages 174 to 184.

Liebs, Rüdiger, and Peter *Preu*: Ein Gesetz zur Beseitigung der restlichen Investitionsmöglichkeiten in der früheren DDR? In: *Zeitschrift für Wirtschaftsrecht und Insolvenzpraxis* 1991, pages 216 to 220.

Lipps, Wolfgang: Fragwürdiger gesetzlicher Eigentumserwerb durch Grundstücksnutzer. In: *Zeitschrift für Wirtschaftsrecht und Insolvenzpraxis* 1991, pages 14 to 16.

Messerschmidt, Burkhard: § 3a VermG – Investitionsvorfahrt oder Investitionsbremse? In: *Zeitschrift für Wirtschaftsrecht und Insolvenzpraxis* 1991, pages 2 to 4.

Möschel, Wernhard: Treuhandanstalt und Neuordnung der früheren DDR-Wirtschaft. In: *Zeitschrift für Unternehmens- und Gesellschaftsrecht* 1991, pages 175 to 182.

Neye, Hans-Werner: Anmerkung zu BezG Erfurt. In: *Zeitschrift für Wirtschaftsrecht und Insolvenzpraxis* 1991, page 878.

Niederleithinger, Ernst: Beseitigung von Hemmnissen bei der Privatisierung und Förderung von Investitionen in den neuen Bundesländern. In: *Zeitschrift für Wirtschaftsrecht und Insolvenzpraxis* 1991, pages 205 to 216.

ditto: Drei Jahre Vermögensrecht – Versuch einer Zwischenbilanz. In: *OV-Spezial* no. 9/1993, dated 6th May 1993, pages 2 et seq.

Overlack, Arndt: *Diskussionsbeitrag* in: Peter *Hommelhoff* (editor): *Treuhandunternehmen im Umbruch*, pages 180 and 181.

Papier, Hans-Jürgen: Rechtsfragen des Restitutionsausschlusses bei besatzungrechtlichen Enteignungen. In: *Zeitschrift für Wirtschaftsrecht und Insolvenzpraxis* 1993, pages 806 to 812.

Roitzsch, Frank, and Wolfgang *Rosener*: Die Umwandlung von volkseigenen Betrieben in Kapitalgesellschaften. In: *Deutsch-Deutsche Rechts-Zeitschrift* 1990, pages 38 to 42.

Schmidt, Reiner: Aufgaben und Struktur der Treuhandanstalt im Wandel der Wirtschaftslage. In: Peter *Hommelhoff* (editor): *Treuhandunternehmen im Umbruch*, pages 17 to 22.

Schmidt-Räntsch, Jürgen: Zum sogenannten Enthemmungsgesetz. In: *Deutsch-Deutsche Rechts-Zeitschrift* 1991, pages 169 to 174.

ditto: Das Vermögenszuordnungsgesetz. In: *Zeitschrift für Wirtschaftsrecht* 1991, pages 973 to 980.

Spoerr, Wolfgang: *Treuhandanstalt und Treuhandunternehmen zwischen Verfassungs-, Verwaltungs- und Gesellschaftsrecht*. Cologne 1993.

Targan, Norbert: Die Rechtsnachfolge bei Umwandlungen der volkseigenen Betriebe in Kapitalgesellschaften. In: *Der Betrieb*, DDR-Report 1990, pages 3060 and 3061.

Ulmer, Peter: Gläubigerschutz bei Treuhandunternehmen. In: Peter *Hommelhoff* (editor): *Treuhandunternehmen im Umbruch*, pages 39 to 59.

Wasmuth, Johannes: *Gesetz zur Regelung offener Vermögensfragen – Kommentierung*. In: Georg *Brunner* (editor): *Rechtshandbuch Vermögen und Investitionen in der ehemaligen DDR*.

Weides, Peter: Rechtsweg bei Streitigkeiten über die Veräußerung von Geschäftsanteilen einer GmbH durch die Treuhandanstalt. In: *Juristische Schulung* 1991, pages 818 to 822.

Weimar, Robert: Entscheidungspraxis der Treuhandanstalt zwischen unternehmerischer Freiheit und verwaltungsrechtlichem Ermessen. In: *Deutsche Zeitschrift für Wirtschaftsrecht* 1992, pages 493 to 497.

ditto: *Nachprivatisierungsprobleme – Rechte und Haftungsrisiken für die Beteiligten nach Erwerb eines Treuhandunternehmens*. Cologne 1992.

Welter, Reinhard: Spaltung von Treuhandunternehmen. In: *Deutsche Zeitschrift für Wirtschaftsrecht* 1992, pages 265 to 273.

Wente, Jürgen: Die Bedeutung des Begriffs des "Verfügungsberechtigten" für die Anwendung des VermG. In: *Zeitschrift für Vermögens- und Investitionsrecht* 1992, pages 125 to 127.

Wild, Klaus-Peter: *Die Treuhandanstalt ein Jahr nach Inkrafttreten des Treuhandgesetzes – eine aktuelle Zwischenbilanz*. In: Peter *Hommelhoff* (editor): *Treuhandunternehmen im Umbruch*, pages 12 to 19.

The organisational development of the THA[1]

by Wolfgang Seibel, with the assistance of Stefan Kapferer

I. The THA as the institutional legacy of the GDR

The THA is a product of 1990, the year of German re-unification and "a year for the politicians, not for the economists".[2] No general guideline could be laid down for the design of an institutional framework for the economic process of transformation in East Germany. The position and the tasks of the THA did not, apparently, play any disputed or otherwise significant role in the preparation, by the lead negotiators of West and East Germany, of the Treaty of Unification, signed on 31st August 1990.[3]

By the same token, the conversion of the THA into an institution of the re-united Germany had to be covered in the Treaty of Unification. Discussions were held on the basic outline of this change over in July and August 1990 between the Chairman of the Administrative Board, Dr Detlev Rohwedder, and leading officials from the Federal Ministries for Economic Affairs and of Finance.[4] This resulted in Article 25 of the Treaty of Unification which decreed that the (East German) *Treuhandgesetz* or THG, the Act establishing the THA, should remain in force with several additional measures. These included the THA's conversion to a legally competent institute under public law (*Anstalt öffentlichen Rechts*) reporting directly to the Federal government, attached to the Federal Ministry of Finance ("who shall exercise expert supervision in agreement with the Federal Ministry for Economic Affairs and the relevant responsible Federal Minister"), an adjustment in the number of Administrative Board members and the increase in its credit limit to DM 25 (previously 17) billion ("which should under normal circumstances be paid back by 31st December 1995").

The individual provisions had been worked out in detail by officials of the Bonn Ministries of Finance and for Economic Affairs in early August 1990. There was no repetition of the squabbles over areas of responsibility as there had been during the preparation of the THG of 17th June 1990 between the coalition partners and the Ministers involved from the de Maizière

---

1 The author wishes to thank Roland Czada for helpful comments on the original draft of this article, and in particular to the members of the Clearing Office of the "THA 1990–1993" research project. One member deserves mention by name: Ms Jutta Wietog, who headed up the Office. Without her energetic but patient assistance the empirical work forming the foundation of this treatise could never have been carried out. Another is Dr Hartmut Maaßen, head of the department P GU, for his knowledgeable guidance and support which he accorded the author.

2 B-interview (Kapferer) with Professor Christa Luft on 4th August 1992; see also: article by Fischer and Schröter in this volume and its footnote 116.

3 See: Schäuble, *Der Vertrag*, in which neither the THA nor its leading representatives are even mentioned.

4 B-interview with Wolf Schöde on 15th March 1993.

government.[5] Following the initial clarification with the Chairman of the Administrative Board just mentioned, agreement had been reached between the West German Federal Ministers for Economic Affairs and of Finance that the THA should come under the jurisdiction of the latter's Ministry. This impulse had come from leading officials of the Federal Ministry for Economic Affairs,[6] in which deliberations of practicality and, at least indirectly, of coalition politics played a part. Everyone in the Ministry for Economic Affairs was well aware that the restructuring of the eastern German economy would inevitably generate an enormous demand for financial resources, and could still visualise the structural changes that had already taken place in West Germany's crisis regions. It was obvious that these financial resources could not be produced, if only for technical reasons, in the short term from the proceeds of the sale of THA assets, which it was hoped at this stage could still be realised. It therefore seemed a better idea to allocate the THA to the Minister of Finance from the start.

Once the THA had been attached to the Federal Ministry of Finance instead of the Ministry for Economic Affairs, it was among another things spared the need to co-ordinate its work between two different Ministries, which was all the more welcome since the two Ministers came from different parties in the government coalition. The foreseeable financial requirements of a THA reporting to the Minister for Economic Affairs might have meant that this co-ordination was fraught with tension which would then have affected the government and the coalition. Allocating the THA to the Minister of Finance also gave it a certain prospect of being de-politicised from a technical point of view, as the Ministry for Economic Affairs might have found it more difficult to defend itself under the necessity of justifying itself politically for the actual impact on economic policy of the THA's work. Also, it was plausible from the point of view of technical supervision to allocate the THA to the relevant department, Dept. VIII of the Ministry of Finance, which is responsible for state-owned industry.

The decision on the organisation of Federal supervision over the THA was thus made at a level below that of the political leadership during the course of the preparation of the Treaty of Unification.[7] No consideration was given to any basic change in the organisational structure of the THA, and certainly none to its being wound up. West Germany thus took over an institutional legacy of the late days of East Germany; interesting to note at this point is that West Germany was apparently nothing like as actively involved in the preparation of the THG of 17th June 1990 as some people later tended to assume.[8] The "institute" status (*Anstaltsstatus*) which

5 See: article by Fischer and Schröter in this volume.

6 B-interview with Wolf Schöde on 15th March 1993.

7 The political leadership of the Federal Ministry for Economic Affairs nevertheless later and repeatedly claimed the right to be responsible for the THA. *Die Zeit* reported at the end of August 1990 of demands made by Mr Haussmann, the Federal Minister for Economic Affairs of the day, that the THA should be converted after the first pan-German elections into a public-law authority directly under the Federal government and subject to the technical and legal supervision of the Ministry for Economic Affairs (*Die Zeit*, 24th August 1990, page 19). The new Economics Minster, Mr Möllemann, was still demanding in February 1991 that the THA should come under his ministry (*Frankfurter Rundschau*, 25th February 1991, page 15; *Die Welt*, same date, page 11). The decisions of the leading officials and the opinions voiced by the political leadership in the Federal Ministry for Economic Affairs had apparently not been co-ordinated. All in all, the obvious inference is that neither of the two ministers, Mr Haussmann or Mr Möllemann, possessed a sufficient measure of technical knowledge and control over their own ministries such as would have given their statements the character of opinions which needed taking seriously.

8 See: article by Fischer and Schröter in this volume, with further references.

had been in force since the Statutes of the Original-THA were passed on 15th March 1990[9] remained in existence. Under West German public law, this meant a self-administration structure and the renunciation of being directly integrated into the Ministry of Finance.

An alternative form of organisation, which would indeed have had great affinity with the federal principle underlying the West German constitution, would have been the decentralisation of the THA to Institutes of the States (*Länderanstalten*), but in the summer of 1990 the political and practical conditions were entirely against it, although there had been considerations along these lines in the East German *Volkskammer* (parliament).[10]

Nevertheless, the practical problems of any State-level concept were obvious enough. The East German States did not yet even exist, and it was easy to forecast that they would need much time to develop into functioning administrative structures. It was not to be expected that the West German States would advocate a State-level THA out of any federalist ethos; their policy during the negotiations over the Treaty of Unification had been far more a defensive guardianship over their own possessions.[11] And one important reason was that possession of the THA by the Federal government was generally perceived at that time as being rock-solid collateral with which it could take out credit during the process of unification.

It was in this way that the THA took on the institutional halfway-house position that was to be characteristic of its later work. On the one hand it took its place in the institutional continuity of the Original-THA, and became as such a central administrative authority with the largest industrial holdings of any western industrial nation.[12] On the other hand it was meant to be largely independent of any instructions from the state, and to carry out its task of the privatisation of the eastern German economy under state supervision but otherwise on its own responsibility. Finally, however, it was intended to remain as an organisation within the Federal government after unification even though its tasks fell *de facto* in the state domain of regional economic policy.

---

9 For sources of laws and legislation see Summary of Laws on pages XVI et seq.

10 A decentralised State structure for the THA was called for during the discussion of the THG and the THA Statutes by the opposition delegates Steinitz (PDS) and Nooke (Alliance 90/The Greens) in the Volkskammer debate (10th legislature period, 15th session, 17th June 1990, shorthand record page 559; 26th session, 20th July 1990, shorthand record page 1124). In connection with the *Treuhand-Aktiengesellschaften* provided for in the THG (§§ 7 and 8), they apparently came up for discussion in the East German CDU, according to the *Volkskammer* delegates Mr Zocher (CDU/Democratic Renewal) and Dr Steinecke (Liberal) in the *Volkskammer* session on 20th July 1990; both of these delegates themselves opposed any State-level solution. Later, according to them there was discussion in the CDU of a territorial division of the THA AG-type companies under which each of the East German States would have become the owner of one THA AG company. See: Volkskammer der Deutschen Demokratischen Republik, 10th legislature period, 26th session, 20th July 1990, shorthand record pages 1125 and 1127.

11 Schäuble, *Der Vertrag*, pages 168 to 184.

12 On the key date of 1st July 1990, the THA held about 8,000 companies in its possession. It is not possible to put any exact figure on the number of companies. The THA itself did not have a complete set of standard company files until March 1991, so it was only then that it had a reasonably reliable overview of its company portfolio: A-interview with Dr Rolf Goldschmidt on 10th July 1992.

II. The THA as a "virtual" organisation

The THG of June 17th 1990 came into force on July 1st 1990, and according to the latest information[13] at that time the THA had 123 employees. The situation report of the last provisional head of the Original-THA, Wolfram Krause, who had now become a member of the Executive Board of the THA proper (and remained on it until 26th June 1992) to the Administrative Board meeting on 15th July 1990 gave a figure of 133, but probably meant only the Berlin Central Office.[14] These people, and the 400 or so employees in the 14 external offices (*Außenstellen*), were managing about 8,000 companies and their 4 million or so employees.[15] Under these circumstances any "operational business", i. e. the implementation of the THA's statutory responsibilities, was out of question. Following the currency conversion of 1st July 1990, the THA's prime concern was to ensure the liquidity of its companies.[16] Apart from that, it had to make a start on finding out how many and what kind of companies it had in its portfolio,[17] and on creating at least a rudimentary organisational structure, starting with the one required of it directly by law. This included appointing members to its Administrative and Executive Boards and forming the *Treuhand-Aktiengesellschaften* (THA AG-type companies) provided for in the THG.

Under the THG of June 17th 1990, the bodies of the THA were to be its Administrative and Executive Boards (*Verwaltungsrat* and *Vorstand*). The Original-THA had already had both bodies; the predecessor of the Executive Board has been the *Direktorium* of the Original-THA as provided for in the Statutes of 15th March 1990, but the Administration Board was in the end never formed. The THA's Administrative Board originally consisted of 16 members, raised to 23 when the Treaty of Unification came into effect on 3rd October 1990. Under § 4 section 2 of the THG, seven of these and the Chairman of the Administrative Board were to be appointed by the Council of Ministers, two members were to be elected directly by the *Volkskammer* (one of them being proposed by the opposition), and seven further members were to be appointed by the *Volkskammer* after being proposed by the Minister-President.

In the *Volkskammer* session of 5th July 1990, Minister-President de Maizière issued the names of the Administrative Board members appointed by the Council of Ministers: Rohwedder (Chairman), Piltz, Niethammer, Pastuszek, Leysen, Henkel, Köhler, and Gellert; and the seven members to be elected by the *Volkskammer* in response to the Minister-President's proposals: van Tilburg, Döring, Mäder, Tausch-Marton, Grimm, Modes, Wulf.[18] All of the Administrative Board members appointed by the Council of Ministers were managers from Western companies (one of them, Leysen, was Belgian). The members proposed for election by the *Volkskammer* were elected by acclamation after a short debate in which one delegate, Ms Hildebrandt

---

13 THA, PE T1/B2/Ve/lh: Personnel development of the THA from 1990 to 1993, 25th February 1993. 112 of these employees came from the East, 11 from the West.

14 Situation report (with the hand-written addition "to the THA Administrative Board") – on the work of the Treuhand up to 15th July 1990, author not named (Wolfram Krause). See also: article by Fischer and Schröter in this volume (footnote 77).

15 See footnote 12 on the problems surrounding these figures. The Berlin External Office is not included.

16 B-interviews with Wolfram Krause and Dr Wolf Klinz on 24th February 1993.

17 A-interview with Dr Rolf Goldschmidt on 10th July 1992.

18 Volkskammer der Deutschen Demokratischen Republik, 10th legislature period, 21st session, 5th July 1990, shorthand record page 858.

(Alliance 90/The Greens) asked about the political past of the candidates.[19] The election of one of the two directly elected Administrative Board members (Steinecke, Liberal) also went without a hitch, whereas the delegate proposed by the opposition, Mr Nooke (Alliance 90/The Greens) was not elected until the third round of voting, in the *Volkskammer* session on 13th July 1990.

The newly elected Administrative Board held its constitutive meeting on 3rd July 1990 and on 15th July 1990 appointed a basic Executive Board of only four members (Gohlke, Krause, Halm, and Schirner). Of these, it was only Krause who had been on the Executive Board of the Original-THA.[20] They were joined in September 1990 by the Board members Breuel, Klinz, and Wild, and in November by Krämer.

One obvious question is the role which any proportional system based on party or association membership played in the appointments to the Executive Board. There was in any case no openly visible system of supply patronage as otherwise happens with public utilities and services in West Germany. The first appointment that might have given rise to any such assumption was that of Ms Birgit Breuel, who had lost her position as State Minister of Finance in April 1990 as a result of the defeat of the CDU in the Lower Saxony State elections, but the personal qualities of Ms Breuel made clear the logical process by which places on the Executive Board were presumably being filled;[21] technical competence was in any case to play the crucial role, with any proportional system acknowledging membership of a political party or an association being kept in mind at a subordinate level. It is possible that this subordinate role was one factor in the appointments of Ms Breuel or of Mr Wild, an Executive Board member who came from the Bavarian ministerial administration, and just possibly of Mr Halm (NDPD/FDP), who was later followed by a highly political figure, Mr Rexrodt (FDP – later Federal Minister for Economic Affairs). The same might be said of the appointment of Dr Rohwedder (SPD) as Chairman of the Administrative Board. One exceptional case was the appointment of Wolfram Krause, with no party affiliation, to the Executive Board; he had been Deputy Chairman of the Directorate of the Original-THA, and had temporarily headed it up from April until 15th June 1990. As a former SED member, unlike Halm, he was exempted from the outset from any protection of a proportional representation system, and his retention on the new Executive Board was purely for reasons connected with his technical competence.[22]

1. The short reign of President Gohlke

The Chairman of the Executive Board of the THA, officially called its President, was Dr Rainer Maria Gohlke, who up to then had been Chairman of the Executive Board of German Federal Railways. As the President responsible for strategic business policy, he was confronted in a particularly brutal manner in the summer of 1990 with a dilemma which was to haunt the THA for a long time to come: if the organisation was to be built up into a proper, functioning form as tra-

19 op. cit., page 859. The Minister-President replied: "I have not allowed myself to be influenced by checking the party affiliation [of each candidate], and therefore cannot make any definite statement on this point, but I assume they were mostly in the SED."

20 See: article by Fischer and Schröter in this volume.

21 B-interviews with Wolf Schöde on 15th March 1993 and with Dr Hartmut Maaßen on 2nd April 1993.

22 See: article by Fischer and Schröter in this volume and its footnote 78.

ditionally required, this could only mean that the implementation of its statutory task would be delayed, but if on the other hand the statutory task was to be carried out briskly it would be necessary to accept major organisational shortcomings and possibly also wrong decisions in the operational business. Gohlke's failure was no doubt due to the fact that he was unable to decide in favour of either alternative.[23]

Every manager in the THA as it existed at that time was to a certain extent compelled to adopt a dynamic, "get-things-done" working style, such as was also attributed to Gohlke.[24] The THA President was faced with the necessity of pushing the privatisation business ahead, all the more so since criticism was being publicly voiced that the organisation was sitting on its hands.[25] It seems very questionable whether the THA had any possibility at all at this stage of carrying out even some important "show" privatisations without running risks. The THA President's problem was apparently that he achieved neither this nor any visible organisational consolidation of the THA, and also that his way of working and his style of leadership did not arouse any confidence that he would succeed in either of these tasks in the immediate future.

Any active business policy was, at this point in time, regardless of the leadership of the decision-maker responsible, confronted with the acute asymmetry between, on one hand, the East German company management's and West German investors' ability to take action and on the other, the THA's. The THA was at this stage, in July and August of 1990, to a large extent only a "virtual" organisation, because neither the statutory company structure of "THA-*Aktiengesellschaften*"[26] nor a properly functioning central organisation existed. It was therefore also incapable of imposing any professional control over the resolute actions of western investors and experienced East German works managers.

This became clear in a spectacular manner in the case of the privatisation of the East German high-class state hotel chain Interhotel, which had been converted in the spring of 1990 into Interhotel AG. In a single-handed effort and together with the West German luxury hotel chain Steigenberger GmbH the Chairman of the Interhotel AG's Executive Board had founded a joint holding company. This in turn had concluded leasing contracts in July 1990 with the 34 Interhotels in East Germany on terms which were highly unfavourable to the owner, the THA.[27] The blame in this case was later placed on the doorstep of the THA President,[28] Mr Gohlke, by the press, even though their better informed reporting makes it thoroughly discernible that the President, the Executive Board, and even the Administrative Board were all victims of the organisational shortcomings of the THA Central Office.[29] Nevertheless, the Interhotel/Steigenberger deal certainly showed up the limitations of activistic "muddling-through" as a strategy of action.[30]

---

23 B-interviews with Wolfram Krause on 24th February and 19th March 1993.

24 *Handelsblatt* of 22nd August 1990, page 3.

25 *Handelsblatt* of 5th June 1990, page 2, and 21st August 1990, page 2.

26 See below, pages 118 et seq.

27 Documented in *Die Zeit*, 31st August 1990, pages 23 and 24.

28 See: *Die Zeit*, 24th August 1990, page 19.

29 *Handelsblatt*, 22nd August 1990, pages 1 and 3; *Die Zeit*, 31st August 1990, pages 23 and 24.

30 See: *Handelsblatt*, 21st August 1990, page 2, and 22nd August 1990, pages 1 and 3; and *Die Zeit* of 24th August 1990, page 19.

There was indeed a considerable amount of tension between the President, Gohlke, and the Chairman of the Administrative Board, Dr Rohwedder, which were due as much to their different personalities as to differences in their view of the priorities in business policy.[31] The implacable logic of the supervisory construction led to Gohlke's resignation on 20th August 1990.[32] Gohlke himself may have been under an illusion as to the actual state of the THA companies and of the East German economy in the whole. But he admitted that the task of privatisation was "more difficult than he had imagined"[33] and the East German economy was in any case a "chaos".[34]

2. The decision not to form the Treuhand-Aktiengesellschaften

Dr Gohlke's successor was the previous Chairman of the Administrative Board, Dr Detlev Karsten Rohwedder. Chairmanship of the Administrative Board was taken over by Jens Odewald, Chairman of the Executive Board of a major department store chain, Kaufhof Holding AG. Immediately after taking office, Rohwedder made it clear in a number of interviews that there was going to be a clear change both in management style and in business policy. He himself would be devoting himself to the basic guidelines of business policy, and not to the details.[35]

Rohwedder principally set the tone of organisational policy in a spectacular manner. The new President made organisational policy as such, one of the priorities of business policy. Unlike his predecessor, he accepted as a priority task making the organisation, as such, capable of working efficiently. He therefore concentrated special efforts on designing the structure of the organisation. In the seven months of his presidency, from the end of August 1990 to the end of March 1991, the organisational profile of the THA was shaped into the form it is to retain until 31st December 1994. Several times the President intervened directly and forcefully in this matter. The first and most prominent victims of the President's organisational initiative were the THA AG-companies, which were to have been the cornerstones of its corporate organisation, but which never grew beyond the point of a "virtual" structure.

The THG of 17th June 1990, the Statutes of the THA approved by the *Volkskammer* on 18th July 1990, and the 1st Implementation Ordinance to the THG of 15th August 1990 provided for "THA AG-companies" at the next level below the two Boards (§§ 7 and 8 of the THG and §§ 5 and 6 of the Statutes). These THA AG-companies were designed to be temporary state-owned companies formed for the purpose of privatisation, a task they were to carry out "on commercial

---

31 B-interview with Wolfram Krause of 19th March 1993.

32 Announced in a 14-line press release from the THA on 20th August 1990 with the terse justification: "Dr Gohlke's request to be released from his duties springs from differences between him and the members of the Administrative Board as to the fulfilment of the THA's responsibilities and the co-operation between the Executive and the Administrative Boards." There was not any reference to words of thanks from the Minister-President.

33 *Frankfurter Allgemeine Zeitung*, 21st August 1990, page 11.

34 op. cit.; see also: *Archiv der Gegenwart*, 3rd October 1990, page 34920.

35 Rohwedder enjoyed using colourful language and impressive sound-bites. This sentence was therefore frequently quoted: "I regard myself as the captain of a ship which is crewed by a large number of strong men, and not as the man in the engine-room shovelling coal into the boiler all by myself." *Frankfurter Allgemeine Zeitung*, 22nd August 1990, page 13.

lines and with a very largely decentralised organisation" (§ 8 section 1 of the THG). They were "to be organised and to work in accordance with commercial principles and to carry out the privatisation and realisation of the assets entrusted to them quickly and comprehensively" (§ 6 section 1 of the Statutes). The sentence added to this was remarkable: "The THA can make use of all possibilities available to it under company law towards the THA AG-companies in the fulfilment of their tasks" (§ 6 section 2 of the Statutes). The THA and its AG-companies thus without doubt formed a qualified *de facto* "*Konzern*", or consolidated group of companies, although the consequences of this may not have been given much consideration.

The plan provided for four AG-companies covering the fields of heavy industry, the capital goods industry, the consumer goods industry, and services.[36] The AG-companies were to be structured "to cover a number of industries at once" (§ 5 section 2 of the Statutes), and each was to have had a portfolio of up to 2,500 companies. The organisational structure of the THA was thus less linked than that of the Original-THA to the structure of the *Kombinate*, each of which was restricted to its own industry, and distinguished from them by the fact that the previous *Kombinate*, VEB's (state-owned companies), and LPG's (agricultural productive co-operatives) had been centrally managed. Therefore the THA external offices holding in trust the *Kombinate* and VEB's which had been previously managed by the *Bezirke*, or Districts, were not compatible with the AG-structure of the THA as based on the Act of 17th June 1990.

The THA AG-companies were a parliamentary product from the time of the Original-THA and, also, of the preparation of the new Act. The Administrative Board elected or confirmed to office by the *Volkskammer* on 5th and 6th July, and the Executive Board appointed on 15th July 1990, inherited this construction and regarded the THA AG-companies as an "unwanted child"; this in particular was the view of Rohwedder as Chairman of the Administrative Board.[37] The overriding impression was that the construction of THA AG-companies owed more to the commandments of political compromise than to any business or economic logic.[38]

All the same, as Chairman of the Administrative Board Rohwedder had initially made no attempt to block the incipient formation of the THA AG-companies. The main tasks of the THA and in particular of its Administrative Board were to form Supervisory Boards of the THA companies. However, when the search started for suitably qualified managers for the positions on the Supervisory Boards, for the THA the private-law form of an AG as such was definitely more attractive, and also more plausible as a means to the privatisation of a centrally planned economy, than anything that looked like a government authority (which the THA was then *de facto* to become).[39] Apart from this, it is possible that some people hoped for synergy effects here if, in the course of recruiting members to the Supervisory Board, the leading personalities approached allowed themselves to become closely associated under other organisational conditions with the THA – as indeed happened in a good number of cases.

---

36 Appendix to the THA Statutes of 18th July 1990: organisation of the THA AG-companies to be established by the THA.

37 B-interview with Wolfram Krause on 24th February 1993.

38 Günter Nooke (Alliance 90/The Greens) elected by the *Volkskammer* to the THA Administrative Board as a representative of the opposition, spoke in the *Volkskammer* debate on the draft Statutes of the THA of a "reasonable compromise between conserving the old structures of the Industry Ministries and a centralised mammoth concern". See: Volkskammer der Deutschen Demokratischen Republik, 10th legislature period, 26th session, 20th July 1990, shorthand record, page 1124.

39 B-interview with Wolfram Krause on 24th February 1993.

To this extent, Rohwedder as Chairman of the Administrative Board had the pragmatic attitude of "let things carry on as they are" – all the more so since, at this stage (July 1990) there was no conceptual alternative available.[40] The Act had anyway also provided for the THA to establish the AG-companies "without delay, and no later than within two months of this Act coming into force" (§ 8 section 2 sentence 1 of the THG). The formation of the Supervisory Boards of the THA AG-companies started (admittedly only on paper, but with every definite intention) with initial agreements being made with the future Chairmen of the THA AG-companies, the locations of the head offices being defined (e. g. Magdeburg for the heavy industry company, Berlin for the services company, and Leipzig for the basic commodities company), and possible office accommodation being looked at.[41]

However, the essential design fault of the THA AG-companies soon came to light. The very process of allocating companies to the multi-industry THA AG's[42] became difficult and time-consuming. The question of the right to dispose over the funds realised from privatisation (should it be the THA or the relevant AG?) would probably have kept creating tension for ever, and would also have hindered the distribution and application of the funds for restructuring purposes. Serious problems also emerged in connection with the question of legal liability under the *Aktiengesetz* (AG-company law). Primarily, however, it could be forecast that the AG-companies would have represented only a fictitious decentralisation.[43] The subsidiary companies of each one would have been scattered all over the whole East German territory, which in turn would have given them a considerable similarity with the old East German industrial administration of industry ministries and *Kombinate*; and the effect of this on the management and control structures would have been even more serious as this superficial comparison would lead one to believe. Because of their economic importance and territorial scatter, the THA AG-companies would not have been compatible with any political or administrative structures of any kind. In practice, they would have been built up in a vacuum of control.

The Administrative and Executive Boards of the THA apparently gained their first inkling of these problems during the preliminary discussions with the leading business figures they wanted to recruit onto the Supervisory Boards of the four THA AG's, in particular the chairmen. The THA would have been left with the thankless, but statutory task of damping down political conflicts without exerting any real influence on the causes of these conflicts, the privatisation business of the AG's. This impression was re-inforced by the fact that some of the would-be Supervisory Board recruits appeared so self-confident that it did not appear at all certain that they and the THA-AG's really would "work themselves out of a job" as quickly as the law pro-

40 op. cit.

41 op. cit.

42 A structure to cover several industries at a time was essential to the THA AG-company concept because this differentiated absolutely clearly from the structure of the East German Industry Ministries. On this point, see: statements by Mr Nooke, a *Volkskammer* delegate (Alliance 90/The Greens) in footnote 38. The necessity of categorising companies under the THA AG's had been turned into a virtue: "Demarcation has been deliberately kept vague in order to retain freedom in allocation" (Nooke, op. cit.). At the same *Volkskammer* session another delegate, Mr Zocher (CDU/DA), made a similar point. See: Volkskammer der Deutschen Demokratischen Republik, 10th legislature period, 26th session, 20th July 1990, shorthand record page 1124.

43 The section on the THA AG-companies in the THA Statutes (§§ 5 and 6) bore the heading "Decentralised organisational structure".

vided for.[44] However, another factor was that the THA AG's would have come under the Co-Determination Act of 1976, which gave rise to the fear of crippling dissent between the employer and the employee sides on the Supervisory Boards – less, perhaps, with regard to privatisation, but certainly in questions of restructuring companies or closing them down.[45] This might possibly have led to delay in the making of necessarily rapid decisions. In addition to this, there was also a danger that the THA AG's would be regarded as the core of future state holding companies.[46]

There was therefore a risk that power centres would arise in the AG's which could avoid the THA's execution of its privatisation task. Thus a process of rethinking at least started in the THA Administrative Board, and specifically in the head of its Chairman, some time early in August 1990[47] (whilst the THA President showed no sign of grasping the initiative in organisational policy with regard to this problem). The preparations for winding up the THA external offices was stopped on the orders of the Chairman of the Administrative Board.[48] The management consultancy company of Roland Berger was commissioned to develop a new organisational structure with the following tasks: genuine decentralisation with a clear separation between "above" and "below"; regional structure, and division of the THA companies by size between Central Office and the decentralised units.[49]

On 24th August 1990, immediately after taking office as President of the THA, Rohwedder announced the decision not to set up the THA AG-companies to a meeting of THA Directors (the management level immediately below the Executive Board).[50] Rohwedder went on to outline the key features of the future organisational structure: a "broadly based lower organisation", a strengthening of the external offices (later turned into branches), and a division of responsibilities between the central and the external offices, with the Central Office looking after the biggest firms and the external offices the medium-sized and small ones. The external offices, said Rohwedder, were to be given "a spring-clean" and a change of personnel. Referring to the fact that he was thus departing from the provisions of the THG, the President used the usual proverb: "Where there is no plaintiff there is no judge".[51]

This casual attitude on the part of the President to a violation of the law cannot disguise the fact that such a serious contempt for the legislative will was only possible in the unusual situation of the death-throes of the GDR, and that Rohwedder was clearly well aware of it. It was a gesture of reparation that Rohwedder attended the *Volkskammer* on 13th September 1990 and

---

44 B-interview with Wolfram Krause on 24th February 1993.

45 B-interview with Dr Wolf Klinz on 24th February 1993.

46 op. cit.

47 B-interview with Wolfram Krause on 24th February 1993.

48 op. cit.

49 op. cit.

50 *Handelsblatt*, 27th August 1990, page 5. The 5th Implementation Ordinance, dealing exclusively with the THA AG-companies, had been published on 15th August 1990, only nine days before Rohwedder made this speech. According to Appendix II Chapter IV Section I No. 6 of the Treaty of Unification, the 1st Implementation Ordinance remained in force, together with the THG itself, as Federal law. As far as can be seen, at the moment the Treaty of Unification was signed on 31st August 1990, no-one took any notice of the fact that the President of the THA had already pulled off the rug from under this ordinance.

51 *Handelsblatt*, 27th August 1990, page 5.

submitted a report on the work to date of the THA. As reasons for not establishing the AG-companies,[52] Rohwedder listed "demarcation difficulties", "co-ordination difficulties", and the problem of recruiting suitably qualified staff quickly, which would have diverted the work of the THA for months from its "proper job". Rohwedder used a traditional proverb on this occasion as well: "Real life comes before the letter of the law".[53]

The President also explained the basic concept of decentralisation through powerful external offices ("or branches, as we prefer to say, borrowing a term from banking jargon"), which were intended to "look after carefully, expand, clean out thoroughly ... look at, check over, and re-staff". Rohwedder emphasised the wide range of powers which the "branches" would have, and interestingly enough indicated that they would also have important responsibilities for structural policy: collaboration "on the design and initiation of local and regional economic promotion programmes" and in the "strategies for attracting industry".[54]

III. Basic decisions on organisational strategy: centralisation and decentralisation, divisional and functional structure

At the time of Rohwedder's report to the *Volkskammer*, in the middle of September 1990, the THA was still anything but a fully functioning organisation. Some 250 people were at this stage working in the Central Office, and because of the uncertain future of the external offices there had been no real change in the numbers employed there since July of that year. From September 1990 onwards, more and more western German managers joined the THA who had mainly been carefully recruited by the members of the Executive Board or by personnel consultants. They entered an organisation, at that time the THA Central Office in eastern Berlin's famous Alexanderplatz, which must have seemed to them to embody the quintessence of total chaos. Nearly every account and report relating to this period of time makes this clear, although they do contain a certain touch of nostalgia for the pioneering spirit and gung-ho daring.[55]

The outward manifestations of this chaos included overcrowded offices, unclear and constantly changing lines of responsibility, no proper internal telephone directories or organisational charts, and no secretaries or other assistants. The most serious problems were caused by the totally inadequate state of technical communications. The telephone and fax connections were such that it was only possible to use them with great patience, and good fortune by day, or else outside normal office hours. The unreliability of the technical equipment increased the physical presence both of would-be purchasers and of delegations from the East German firms in the

52 Rohwedder put it in a somewhat roundabout way, at once barefaced and cautious: "Putting it roughly, ladies and gentlemen: I introduced the thought that we should refrain, at least for the moment, from establishing these THA AG-companies because it had become clear to me that developments in the GDR had gone beyond that point." Volkskammer der Deutschen Demokratischen Republik, 10th legislature period, 35th session, 13th September 1990, shorthand report page 1680.

53 op. cit.; the record adds: "Applause from CDU/DA and DSU".

54 op. cit., page 1681.

55 A-interviews with Dr Wolfgang Vehse on 5th August 1992; Dr Manfred Balz on 10th September 1992; Peter Gemählich on 22nd December 1992; Conrad Friebel on 25th January 1993; and Christoph Urban on 19th May 1993.

corridors of the THA Central Office, and also in the external offices/branches. Sales discussions went on in every corner of every larger room. Company decisions of wide-ranging importance were made on the landing. Meetings which at all cost had to be conducted in peace and quiet, as well as in confidence, took place after 11.00 at night or even after midnight. The atmosphere was topped off in every respect by the shabby interior of the former "House of the Electrical Industry" in the Alexanderplatz.

The decision not to set up the THA AG-companies was the first significant action of independent organisational policy taken by the THA, and one which at the same time made the strategic problems of the organisational design apparent, namely the allocation of authority and responsibility and, in a word, power. By making this decision, the THA had turned itself into the central administrative authority for a gigantic industrial complex, and was thus confronted, apart from the absolutely different aims with regard to the political order of the economy for which it was founded, by exactly the same problems as in any centrally planned economy, and particularly by the problem of information and management capacity. However, unlike a central administration authority set up with the aim of lasting, it was faced by the further dilemma that it was on the one hand required to "work itself out of a job" and on the other to consolidate its own organisation, meaning first and foremost making it more "intelligent" and more capable of managing but without letting it degenerate into a hidebound control machine.

The organisational reform carried out by Rohwedder in the first weeks of his period of office attempted initially to solve these problems by conventional means, namely by reducing the range of responsibility and authority of the Central Office. The branches were designed and equipped in a manner which systematically implemented the principle of regional decentralisation. Unlike the originally planned AG-companies, this construction had on principal the advantage at least of sharing out the work clearly both horizontally and vertically. The branches had more or less clearly defined lines of responsibility both in territorial terms and in terms of the size of their companies.

1. Construction of the THA branches

In territorial terms, the branches were based on the 14 *Bezirke* or Districts of the GDR, and in institutional terms on the economic administration of the former regionally managed *Kombinate*, *VEB*'s, and agricultural co-operatives, the direct successors of what would have been the THA "external offices". The branches were therefore all located in the relevant District capital, plus a regional office in Berlin, making a total of 15: Berlin, Chemnitz, Cottbus, Dresden, Erfurt, Frankfurt/Oder, Gera, Halle, Leipzig, Magdeburg, Neubrandenburg, Potsdam, Rostock, Schwerin, and Suhl. In theory, all THA companies with fewer than 1,500 employees were to be allocated to the branches, a rule that was not formalised until the end of November 1990[56] and which took until well into 1991 to put into effect.[57]

The division of work according to territorial and size-category criteria was an organisational compromise. It was meant on the one hand to take some of the work-load off THA Central Office but at the same time to leave it with a sizeable proportion of the operational business, par-

56 Treuhandanstalt, *Organisationshandbuch*, Guideline No. R-11/91, 30th November 1990.

57 A-interview with Richard Graf zu Eulenburg on 30th July 1992.

ticularly those parts of it that covered several regions at once, and to facilitate the co-ordination of the branches via a hierarchical integration. One member of the Executive Board was responsible for the branches. Whether any of the work-load was shed, and the division of labour worked properly, was therefore crucially dependent upon the design of this organisational framework. This was the organisational policy task which the Executive Board member responsible had to cope with; from 18th September 1990 this was Birgit Breuel.

The branches were designed to be powerful units operating independently to the largest possible extent.[58] The branch managers (*Niederlassungsleiter*) were thus accorded a key position. They were all new appointees, the former external office managers having been dismissed wholesale. They were predominantly cast in the western German businessman mould,[59] and in practice "mainly came from the smaller parts of industry or medium-sized firms",[60] with the relevant experience as company managers; most of them were in their fifties.

The recruitment, inauguration, and taking up duty of the branch managers was carried out under equally semi-chaotic conditions.[61] Some of them were recruited only a few days before they were due to start work, often only on the basis of an oral agreement and a brief meeting, followed by only a short time to think it over, but all 15 of them started work on the same day, 4th October 1990. Before starting they were introduced to the public at a press conference by Executive Board member, Birgit Breuel. It was in this way that in the branches, or former external offices the actual THA era began.

The branch managers had "enormous power"[62] during their initial period in office. In formal terms, this was expressed in their financial freedom of decision, with an upper limit of DM 30 million.[63] However, it was the factual relationships that caused those of them who were later questioned to describe their position in the metaphors of oriental feudalism: "miniature kings",[64] "gurus",[65] or "oriental potentate"[66]. The branch managers first had to dismiss their own predecessors, or demote them two or three ranks, gain the confidence of their staff – almost without exception eastern Germans – and also try to gain some notion of the portfolio of companies held by their branches, build up the organisation, and still manage to hold sales negotiations. The technical communication problems were enormous here as well; as a result use had to be made of the telephone networks formerly used by the East German armed forces or Ministry of State Security (the dreaded *Stasi*). Many of the regional offices were housed in the former *Stasi* buildings.[67]

---

58 op. cit., and A-interviews with Helmuth Ofterdinger on 13th October 1992, Dr Dirk Wefelscheid on 25th November 1992, and Helmuth Coqui on 7th January 1993.

59 A-interviews with Helmuth Ofterdinger on 13th October 1992 and Helmuth Coqui on 7th January 1993.

60 A-interview with Helmuth Coqui on 7th January 1993.

61 A-interviews with Richard Graf zu Eulenburg on 30th July 1992, Dr Dirk Wefelscheid on 25th November 1992, and Helmuth Coqui on 7th January 1993.

62 A-interview with Richard Graf zu Eulenburg on 30th July 1992.

63 op. cit.

64 A-interview with Dr Dirk Wefelscheid on 25th November 1992.

65 op. cit.

66 A-interview with Helmuth Coqui on 7th January 1993.

67 A-interviews with Helmuth Ofterdinger on 13th October 1992 and Dr Dirk Wefelscheid on 25th November 1992.

This manner of managing the branches was only possible because the choice of capable and qualified branch managers proved to be serendipitously successful and because Birgit Breuel, as the Executive Board member responsible, and the relevant Director (van Scherpenberg), acted as guardian angels to protect the branches.[68] Ironically enough, the hallowed position of the branches during this initial phase was further re-inforced by the terrible telecommunication situation.[69]

The allocation of companies by size-category was only to a limited extent compatible with the geographical decentralisation in the form of the branches. Understandably enough, the branch managers were not very pleased when especially important companies "outside their own front doors" were looked after from distant Berlin, particularly as the local staff considered that they as the local THA representatives knew these companies far better than their colleagues at Central Office ever could.[70]

The main source of friction, however, came from the practical workings of the allocation of companies. For one thing it took until 11th March 1991 until the databank containing all information on companies within the THA's portfolio was ready on the sole basis of which the allocation was to be carried out.[71] For another, the Allocation Guideline[72] which came into force on 30th November 1990 provided for no fewer than 14 categories of exception. Regardless of the numbers employed by the individual units, the subsidiaries of company groups or holding companies, and the subsidiaries of the subsidiaries, were thus automatically allocated to the Central Office if their total number of employees exceeded 1,500, as were foreign trading companies, banks, printers, newspaper and magazine publishers, travel agents, hotel chains, former DEFA (*Deutsche Film AG*) companies, scientific organisations and circuses, transport companies, those in the energy and petroleum business, and those involved in water or waste water – the latter only if being already in the hands of the Central Office when the Allocation Guideline was issued.[73]

The implementation of the Allocation Guideline was therefore "not welcomed everywhere with open arms",[74] and it took more than six weeks before the process of allocation had been completed "in a tortuous process"[75] involving in the Central Office the various Industry Directorates (*Branchendirektorate*) and the branches[76] and in which a sensible allocation of individual companies could give rise to a dispute at any time.[77] Until this allocation was complete, about the end of April 1991, there was nothing but confusion in the branches, and in the Central

68 A-interview with Helmuth Coqui on 7th January 1993; later it appears that tensions arose between the branch managers and those Executive Board members who had not properly understood the philosophy behind the special position of the branch managers; A-interview with Richard Graf zu Eulenburg on 30th July 1992.

69 A-interview with Helmuth Ofterdinger on 13th October 1992.

70 B-interview with Helmut Wotte on 17th March 1993.

71 A-interview with Dr Rolf Goldschmidt on 10th July 1992.

72 Treuhandanstalt, *Organisationshandbuch*, Guideline no. R-11/91, 30th November 1990.

73 Treuhandanstalt, *Organisationshandbuch*, Guideline no. R-11/91, 30th November 1990, page 2.

74 A-interview with Dr Rolf Goldschmidt on 10th July 1992.

75 op. cit.

76 op. cit., and A-interview with Richard Graf zu Eulenburg on 30th July 1992.

77 A-interview with Richard Graf zu Eulenburg on 30th July 1992.

Office Industry Directorates as they existed from 1st January 1991 onwards, as to the actual portfolio of companies for which each was responsible. Finally, on the cut-off date of 1st January 1991, a total of 3,826 companies were being looked after by Central Office and 6,718 by the branches.[78] Despite the exceptions mentioned above, the branches were thus totally swamped by the number of companies for which they had portfolio responsibility. One portfolio officer in each branch had to look after anything from 20 to 40 companies, or in extreme cases 60 to 70, so that it was pure fiction from the start to imagine that any of them could manage so many companies competently.[79] As a rule, all that the staff in the branches learned about the relevant companies was often what potential purchasers told them.[80]

Nevertheless, the branches started work on the privatisation business in the autumn of 1990. In view of the unclear allocation of companies there was no avoiding cases in which companies during this period of time were sold twice: once by Central Office and once by the regionally responsible branch. The unclear categorisation was particularly awkward for AG-companies or GmbH-companies with subsidiaries when it was unclear who was allowed to sell the parent company and who the subsidiaries.[81] Sales also went ahead without any reliable company information (and the contracts were correspondingly short).[82] This was no obstacle to trade, as there was a clear surplus of demand over supply at this time.[83] It seems that no serious disasters occurred as a result of the terms of any contract.[84] Later, however, the Audit Directorate produced many significant retroactive reproofs which the branch managers, referring to the circumstances ruling in 1990 and 1991, did not always regard as fair.[85]

The jumbled confusion of the situation on the one hand, and the specifically intended independence and delight in decision-making of the branch managers on the other, required at the very least a clarification of the liability question. This was provided by the President at the beginning of December 1990 with a statement of exemption from liability.[86] A later and more detailed regulation contained exemption from liability even in cases of gross negligence for contracts concluded up to and including 30th June 1991, and in cases of minor negligence for later contracts up to and including 30th June 1992.[87]

Task Forces, as they were called even in German, were set up with the intention of reducing the severe problems of information and control which dominated the branches, and Central

---

78 *Treuhandanstalt Informationen* 6 (October 1991), page 6.

79 A-interview with Richard Graf zu Eulenburg on 30th July 1992.

80 B-interview with Dieter Zochol (Roland Berger, Dresden) on 17th March 1993.

81 A-interview with Richard Graf zu Eulenburg on 30th July 1992.

82 A-interview with Dr Dirk Wefelscheid on 25th November 1992.

83 B-interview with Dieter Zochol (Roland Berger, Dresden) on 17th March 1993. One branch manager said: "The investors smashed the door in to get at us." A-interview with Dr Dirk Wefelscheid on 25th November 1992.

84 A fact registered with astonished delight by some branch managers. See: A-interviews with Helmuth Ofterdinger on 13th October 1992, Dr Dirk Wefelscheid on 25th November 1992, and Helmuth Coqui on 7th January 1993.

85 A-interviews with Richard Graf zu Eulenburg on 30th July 1992 and Helmuth Ofterdinger on 13th October 1992.

86 A-interview with Helmuth Coqui on 7th January 1993.

87 A-interview with Richard Graf zu Eulenburg on 30th July 1992.

Office as well, until well into 1991. The formation of these Task Forces reflected once again a further characteristic feature of the THA's organisational development, namely the excessive use made of external consultants. The Task Forces of the branches were formed from the autumn of 1990 onwards from employees of management consultant firms and were not ready to start work until the first Quarter of 1991. It was their task to collect the most important company data in the area of each branch, categorise the companies according to whether they were capable of being privatised or restructured, and to do the groundwork for the preparation of an Deutschmark opening balance-sheet.[88]

In view of the fundamental nature of these tasks, the Task Forces took on a key role in the implementation of operational business in the branches. It proved possible to improve the information and control facilities with the aid of Task Forces deployed from the Central Office and managed by a Steering Committee. This can also be seen as a contribution toward the maintenance of the extensive independence of the branches. However, in some cases the Task Forces were apparently never more than "foreign bodies" in the branches,[89] because in the initial phase at least the Task Forces had a clear head-start over the staff in the branches not only in terms of information but also, as teams from western German management consultant firms, in terms of professional qualifications as well. It was thus very much in the branches' interest if a kind of symbiosis developed over time between them and the Task Forces, and many Task Force people for their part developed a kind of THA identity instead of a consultant identity.[90]

These Task Forces are a part of the whole camp-follower scene of external consultants, whose numbers in some cases accounted for a third or more of the staff of the branches.[91] Without this huge number of external consultants, the THA would apparently never have been able get started with its operational business as early and as quickly as it did, particularly in 1991. At the same time, the symbiotic relationship between the consultants and the permanent organisation as was in the case of the Task Forces and the branches showed that there was a risk of "rent-seeking".[92] The firm relationships between the consultancy industry and the THA, which at times reached the point where it was no longer possible to differentiate in day-to-day work between the consultants, engaged for long periods but at a daily fee rate,[93] and the permanent staff, led not only to excessively high personnel costs for the THA as a whole[94] but apparently also to the consultancy firms becoming accustomed to these lucrative conditions and being unwilling to give them up.[95]

---

88 B-interview with Dieter Zochol (Roland Berger, Dresden) on 17th March 1993.

89 op. cit.

90 B-interviews with Michael Blatz and Dieter Zochol (Roland Berger, Dresden) on 17th March 1993.

91 A-interview with Dr Dirk Wefelscheid on 25th November 1992.

92 Buchanan, Tollison, and Tullock (editors): *Toward a Theory of the Rent Seeking Society*.

93 Daily fees lie between DM 800 and 4,500; A-interview with Richard Graf zu Eulenburg on 30th July 1992.

94 The annual costs to the THA for about 1,000 consultants exceed the costs of employing its permanent staff of 4,000, which is about DM 350 million. A monitorium was therefore issued in the autumn of 1992 by the Federal Court of Audit, on which the (German) television magazine programme *Monitor* reported on 3rd June 1993. The Federal Court of Audit put a figure of DM 450 million on the annual fee costs of the consultants.

95 A-interview with Richard Graf zu Eulenburg on 30th July 1992.

2. The re-organisation of the THA Central Office

With the full manning of the Executive Board in sight by September 1990 (with the arrivals of Breuel, Klinz, and Wild, followed in October by Koch and in November by Krämer), the distribution of divisions could be nearly completed. Like its predecessor the Original-THA, the THA proper intended at this stage to divide the organisation into functional areas rather than by industry.[96] The Executive Board was divided into eight Divisions (or nine, from November onwards), entitled: President (Rohwedder), Equity Holdings (Klinz), Privatisation (Schirner), Restructuring/Winding-up (Wild), Special Assets/Administration (Halm), Refinance/Real Estate (Krämer, from November 1990 onwards), Branches (Breuel), Finance (Krause), and Personnel (Koch, from October 1990 onwards).[97] One motive for avoiding a divisional organisation based on industries was the endeavour to permit as little similarity as possible with the former industry administration structure of the GDR.[98] Instead of this, the organisational construction of the THA clearly emphasised its statutory tasks, meaning specifically privatisation and restructuring, each of which represented a Division of its own. It was also expected the privatisation know-how would thus accumulate more quickly and generate a "learning curve".

These advantages of a functional organisation structure were, however, counterbalanced by serious disadvantages. The functional organisation made the THA opaque from the start, particularly for its main customers, the investors, because it provided no plausible criterion for the allocation of companies. The main category in which a company was placed – equity holdings, privatisation, restructuring/winding-up – was very difficult for the outsider to guess at. On top of this, sizeable internal co-ordination problems started to appear. The separation of "equity holdings" (companies managed by the THA) and "privatisation" into two separate Board-level Divisions would have created an advanced need for co-ordination and agreement because companies were constantly being transferred from "equity holdings" to "privatisation". Strictly speaking, the organisational separation of the management of equity holdings from the task of restructuring was senseless as it could be forecast that restructuring was going to be the main priority for the companies under THA management.

In addition to this, the decision not to divide up the organisation at Executive Board level by industry was bound to create unmanageable capacity bottle-necks. If the structures at least of the Equity Holdings, Privatisation, and Restructuring/Winding-up Divisions were to be made compatible with one another, each of these Divisions would have to be a mirror-image of the industrial structure of the East German economy. And this is exactly what initially happened,[99] but the implementation of a parallel structure corresponding to the industries would have led to interface problems and duplication of work, proportionately higher personnel costs, and during the privatisation a greater inward and outward movement of personnel on account of the shift in the

96 For the organisation of the Original-THA see: Trausch, *Organisatorischer Wandel am Beispiel der Treuhandanstalt,* page 60. The Original-THA had Executive Board members in charge of: External Offices, Economics, Finance, and Law. The work of the Economics division was apparently restricted to implementing the Conversion Ordinance of 1st March 1990; op. cit.

97 Treuhandanstalt, Organisation chart, 15th November 1990.

98 B-interview with Dr Wolf Klinz on 24th February 1993.

99 The organisation chart of 15th November 1990 even displays this kind of parallel arrangement by industry, and was thus an early attempt at a better co-ordination structure; B-interview with Dr Wolf Klinz on 24th February 1993.

volume of work between the various Executive Board Divisions. Each of the Divisions for Equity Holdings, Privatisation, and Restructuring/Winding-up would have had the enormous complexity which comes from a range of responsibilities covering a number of different industries.

In addition to all this, the clear reflection of the THA's statutory tasks in its organisational structure also had its disadvantages. The political implications of the alternative of "privatisation" versus "restructuring", and the conflicts which could be expected to arise from them, could be transferred straight into an organisational structure which made exactly this alternative clearly visible at Board level.

This functional organisation structure was still mainly only a "virtual" one until well into the autumn of 1990, and was certainly a long way away from being effective. To this extent it was still initially possible to cope with its discrepancies. Pressure built up for a decision to be made when a meeting of the Supervisory Boards of all the THA companies was arranged for 25th November 1990, and clarity had to be achieved prior to that meeting on the future organisational structure of the Central Office.[100] At the preceding Executive Board meeting on 22nd November a new organisational structure for the Central Office, produced by a central "Organisation Project THA" staff team, was discussed and decided upon,[101] and duly put into effect on 1st January 1991.

This new organisational structure, which is basically still in force today, was internally described as a "matrix" organisation even though it is dominated by the divisional principle, meaning organisation by industries. The term *Branche*, meaning an industry, is avoided in the terminology of the organisational hand-book,[102] but the new, divisional organisation is similar to the industry-based administrative structure of the GDR from which the previous, functional organisation was actually supposed to differentiate itself. In fact, the allocation of industries under the various Executive Board Divisions did not follow any logical system but came about more or less spontaneously during the relevant Executive Board meeting[103] – each member shouted for the industry he wanted to have.

The core of the divisional organisation was now to be five *Unternehmensbereiche* or "Corporate Divisions" (U1 to U5 – initially designated "Corporate Groups",[104] a nomenclature later transferred to the directorates for the various industries). In addition to this there was the President's Division and one Division each for Branches, Personnel, and Finance, thus making a total of nine: President (Rohwedder), U1 (Schirner), U2 (Wild), U3 (Halm), U4 (Klinz), U5 (Krämer), Branches and States Affairs (Breuel), Personnel (Koch), and Finance (Krause).

This organisational structure greatly improved clarity, and brought technical knowledge and competence together effectively, as far as the industries were concerned. For these corporate groups, the whole responsibility for privatisation, management of holdings, and corporate finance now lay in one pair of hands.

On the other hand, the functional responsibilities had been made a little more opaque by this organisational structure. The classical cross-sectional functions of personnel and finance were

---

100 B-interview with Dr Wolf Klinz on 24th February 1993.

101 A-interview with Christoph Urban on 19th May 1993; B-interview with Dr Wolf Klinz on 24th February 1993. The originator of the new organisational concept and manager of the "Organisation Project THA" was the Siemens manager Christoph Urban, initially as a THA consultant and later as a THA Director responsible for administration.

102 Treuhandanstalt, Organisationshandbuch, serial no. 2.3.1, of 31st January 1991.

103 B-interview with Dr Wolf Klinz on 24th February 1993. The basic categorisation was very roughly that used by the Federal Office of Statistics.

104 Organisation Project THA: organisation chart dated 19th December 1990.

each as before Executive Board Divisions in their own right, and responsibility for the branches also remained as a Division. Other cross-sectional functions remained unchanged under the President's responsibility: fundamental questions, communications/media, management committee, organisation/EDP, and law, plus the only corporate group in the President's Division, Energy Industry. However, the areas of responsibility of the previous functional Executive Board Divisions had to be redefined and in some cases redistributed between the Divisions. Thus the number of Directorates with central or cross-sectional functions grew. Of the 46 Directorates (as of 1st February 1993), only 15 are Industry Directorates.

There was inevitably, now a division within the Divisions into the fields of "business responsibility" and "functional responsibility": each Corporate Division took on cross-sectional functions for all the other Divisions, such as U1 (Schirner) initially taking on the function of "privatisation", still a cross-sectional function, and U2 (Wild) taking on "restructuring" and "winding up".

The new matrix structure on a divisional basis came into force on 1st January 1991. The organisational structure in Central Office now deviated from the uniform organisational structure of the branches. These were still organised functionally, with directorates for "privatisation", "equity holdings", "finance" and "personnel". The branches were later to suffer exactly the co-ordination problems between the privatisation business and the management of equity holdings which had been avoided at an early stage in Central Office by introducing the industry-based organisation. So-called Industry Teams were formed at the level below the Directorates, according to the size of the branch, which were intended to compensate for the disadvantages of the division of labour between management of equity holdings and privatisation.[105]

THA Central Office started moving house on 10th March 1991, from the Alexanderplatz to the Leipziger Straße, into a building originally built to house Göring's Air Ministry in the days of the Third Reich, and which was later the House of the Ministries of the GDR. This building, with its gigantic dimensions and 2,200 offices, had been the property of the Federal Government since 3rd October 1990. Half of the offices were to be placed at the disposal of the THA.[106] Everyone concerned was probably well aware that this was not a fortunate choice, bearing in mind the history surrounding the building. Not only had Hitler's vassal, Göring, resided here, it had also been the offices for most the GDR industry ministries. In the eyes of most eastern German companies, Leipziger Straße was therefore not regarded as "a posh address". The alteration to the building, started in December 1990, was completed within four months at a cost believed to be well over DM 20 million.[107] The removal of the members of the Executive Board started on 20th April 1990.

105 B-interview with Dieter Zochol (Roland Berger, Dresden) on 17th March 1993.

106 A-interview with Conrad Friebel on 25th January 1993; A-interview with Christoph Urban on 19th May 1993.

107 The building was on the property register of the Federal Ministry of Finance, and it was initially planned to provide the THA with 1,100 of its offices. This figure was later raised to about 1,500. A interview with Conrad Friebel on 25th January 1993. A figure of DM 20,000 for fitting out each office was given in the press: *Der Morgen* of 8th February 1991, page 2. Specific criticism was also voiced of the "garage sale" of the former contents: *Wirtschaftswoche*, 7/1991. The press spokesman of the THA pointed to an expert assessment from the Federal Court of Audit, according to which the accommodation in the Leipziger Straße "was at the lower limit": *Berliner Zeitung*, 9th February 1991, page 18. However, there appear to have been fraudulent irregularities in the carrying out of the alteration work: A-interview with Christoph Urban on 19th May 1993.

IV. Organisational consolidation

By January 1991 the organisational shape of the THA had taken on the form that it was to retain for the whole duration of "THA 1", i. e. until the privatisation work was finished. Also the continuity of the THA organisation since the end of 1990 and beginning of 1991 faced a number of challenges. On the one hand, the political pressure had to be resisted which was created by the social costs of privatisation and the discrimination of investors. On the other hand, the privatisation process had to be accelerated, or at least not slowed down by political interference. Finally, the enormous dynamic forces created by the organisation development[108] had to be absorbed, and a feeling of identification achieved by at last 4,000 THA employees with their difficult and controversial task.

1. Improvements in political integration

In February 1991, the THA's existence under the wind-shadow of politics came to an abrupt end. Neither in the campaign for the election to the first all-German Bundestag on 2nd December 1990 nor in the negotiations leading up to the Treaty of Unification it had played any special role. The phenomenon, THA, was for the requirements of catchy election campaign slogans too insignificant and perhaps even too obscure. German Unification Day, 3rd October 1990, was likewise of no great organisational or practical significance except for the enlargement of the Administrative Board and the appointment of the branch managers. Initially, everything was totally overshadowed by the spectacular foreign policy events which led up to the Gulf War in January 1991, but after the Unification Year of 1990 and the Bundestag election campaign this changed into a definitely more sober attitude towards the prospects opened up by the unification process. One first indicator of this was the massive pressure exerted by the Minister-Presidents of the eastern German States for action to correct the worst of the structural deficits in their financial resources. Account was very largely taken of this in the Minister-Presidents' Resolution at the end of February and the "Joint Project for the Boom in the East" (*Gemeinschaftswerk Aufschwung Ost*) of 8th March 1991.[109]

The THA had now become the target of public criticism, principally on account of the slow pace of privatisation and the mass unemployment which was beginning to emerge at the same time, and above all, of course, from the eastern German States. There was no sign of the boom in sales and investments in eastern Germany which everyone had been hoping for, and by 31st March 1991 the THA had allegedly not sold more than 1,261, or about 15 %, of its companies for total proceeds of DM 5.5 billion.[110] At the same time, in the first half of 1991 the gross domestic product of eastern Germany had sunk to about 55 % of its level in the first half of

---

108 The number of permanent staff in the THA (Central Office and branches) grew in 1990 and 1991 as follows: 123 as of 30th June 1990; 1,140 as of 31st December 1990; 2,722 as of 30th June 1991; 3,604 as of 31st December 1991: *Personalentwicklung der THA von 1990–1993*, THA, PE T1/B2/Ve/lh, 25th February 1993.

109 Federal Press and Information Office, Bulletin, 12th March 1991, pages 177 to 182.

110 See, among other sources: Treuhandanstalt, *Auftrag, Zwischenbilanz, Grundsätze*.

1990, and the unemployment rate had risen to 11.7 %. Hidden unemployment, made up of "short-time working at the rate of zero", participation in job creation schemes, advanced vocational training, and early retirement, added up to an additional 13 %, so the effective unemployment rate was heading for something like a quarter of the whole working population.[111] Towards the end of the first half of 1991, the numbers employed in all the THA companies had been reduced by privatisation, resignations, and redundancies to 2.1 million, or a little more than half the figure of a year earlier in the same companies.[112] As part of the privatisation process, the investors had agreed to secure 512,000 jobs and in addition to this they had taken over further employees.[113]

In February 1991, spontaneous protests had broken out in many THA companies against the threat of redundancies, some of them accompanied by almost riot-like scenes (on 27th February 1991, mutinous shipyard workers forced their way into the *Landtag* – State Parliament – in Schwerin).[114] The political pressure brought to bear on the various State governments was passed straight on to the THA, and demands arose from eastern German States for the central THA to be broken up and converted into State-THA's.[115]

In view of massive political pressure of this kind, induced regionally but re-inforced all across the country, it could soon be seen that the political conflict-suppression mechanisms provided for up to then were insufficient. In consequence, they were developed in various different directions through improved co-opting, intensive use of loose coupling with the government and administrative system, and more skilful political rhetoric.

The THA's policy on co-opting helpers was refined on the basis of the "Basic principles of co-operation between the Federal Government, the eastern German States, and the THA to produce the Boom in the East" dated 14th March 1991,[116] with the creation of "THA Economic Cabinets"[117] (*Treuhand-Wirtschaftskabinette*) together with the eastern German State governments, and the work of the THA sub-committee of the Budget Committee. An "early warning system" was introduced in the autumn of 1991, with the aid of which the State governments could be informed of forthcoming winding-up plans for THA companies.[118] In the context of this improvement in the THA's political integration, it is also worth mentioning the "Joint Declaration" of the German Federation of Trade Unions (*DGB*), the German Trade Union of Employees (*DAG*), and the THA dated 13th April 1991 (with guidelines for the "social plans"

111 Institut für Weltwirtschaft Kiel, *Gesamtwirtschaftliche und unternehmerische Anpassungsprozesse in Ostdeutschland*, page 5.

112 Beschäftigungsobservatorium Ostdeutschland No. 5, November 1992.

113 *Treuhandanstalt Informationen* 3/4 (July/August 1991), page 6; no definite figures are available for this period of time on the actual number of employees taken over permanently by the investors.

114 *Frankfurter Allgemeine Zeitung*, 28th February 1991, page 5.

115 *Leipziger Volkszeitung*, 14th February 1991, page 1; *Magdeburger Allgemeine Zeitung*, 6th March 1992, page 4.

116 Bundespresse- und Informationsamt, *Bulletin*, 15th March 1991, reprinted in: Treuhandanstalt, *Organisationshandbuch*, RS-1/91, serial no. 2.10.1.1.

117 THA, Submission for the Administrative Board Meeting on 3rd May 1991.

118 First presented at a meeting between the Executive Board of the THA and the eastern German Minister-Presidents on 30th October 1991; note by the THA department responsible for the State of Thuringia dated 31st October 1991.

which have to accompany mass redundancies) and, finally, an outline agreement on the societies for the promotion of labour, employment, and structural development of 17th July 1991.[119]

The basic construction of the THA as an "institute" was an important prerequisite for its being able to suffer the slings and arrows of outraged politicians. A mechanism called "loose coupling"[120] had been established between the THA and its parent body, the Federal government, which offered major advantages for both sides, the Federal Government and the THA, in comparison with direct state management. On the one hand, the effect really achieved was that the THA, and not the Federal government, became the symbol of the state-prescribed and painful economic conversion processes in eastern Germany.[121] Like Winkelried drawing the enemy's spears, the THA took all the flak which would otherwise have spattered the Federal government. On the other hand, one of the main danger zones for the THA itself was thus stabilised. However much it was necessary from the fiscal point of view first to disappoint the Federal Government and then to make massive claims on it, it was nevertheless clear to all that a valuable service was being performed in return. Because the Federal government and the parties in it presumably knew all along what the THA really means to them, none of the attempts to force a fundamental change of course onto it or even to question its organisational and legal status bore fruit.

The rhetoric with which the THA explained its position deserves special attention in relation to the THA's stability. The language used by the THA to the outside world always endeavoured to be unpolitical and, first and foremost, unpolemical.[122] This could only be implemented because the THA press spokesman, Wolf Schöde, and his deputy, Dr Franz Wauschkuhn, held the monopoly on public announcements.[123] Not all new arrivals in the THA accepted this unconditionally, and some, particularly at the Director level, had to have this "house style" made very clear to them, both with regard to areas of authority and to the tone of voice to be used.[124] This, at any rate, was part of the "Winkelried" function of the THA: it had to put up with everything and never hit back.[125] The THA could only carry out its political task if it remained unpolitical. This is a psychological achievement which should not be undervalued, because neither the outside world's criticism of the THA was allowed to undermine the motivation of its staff nor was the staff permitted to compensate the criticism with a "draw the covered wagons round into a circle" mentality.[126]

Even if the assertion was conscientiously rejected by the press department staff that there were "language regulations" in force,[127] there is still no mistaking the fact that the internal terminology of the THA, and the one it used for public announcements, particularly those outside

---

119 On this point, and the subject in general of political integration and co-operation relationships of the THA, see: article by Czada in this volume.

120 See: Glassman, *Persistence and Loose Coupling in Living Systems*, pages 83 to 98; Aldrich, *Organizations and Environments*, pages 83 to 84, Orton and Weick, *Loosely coupled systems*, pages 203 to 223.

121 See also: article by Kepplinger in this volume.

122 B-interview with Dr Franz Wauschkuhn on 7th May 1993.

123 op. cit.

124 op. cit.

125 A-interview with Wolf Schöde on 4th February 1993.

126 See under "THA culture", below.

127 B-interview with Dr Kristian Dorenberg on 25th February 1993.

the regular media links, had been carefully tuned to harmonise with political requirements. This principally applies to the avoidance of any undesirable associations or hopes. Terminology reminiscent of the old GDR was undesirable, as were forms of words which permitted any such associative links to be made. Thus the Executive Board Divisions orientated towards the various industries were called "corporate divisions" and not "industrial divisions" (*Unternehmensbereiche*), thus suppressing any mental association with the GDR industrial ministries; these Divisions were their *de facto* successors, in the functional sense, not in any institutional sense. Terms were also step by step suppressed which could have emphasised the potential conflict of aims or indicated any actively commercial restructuring activity by the THA. As already mentioned, these were for instance the advantage of changing over from the functional organisation with the Divisions for "privatisation" and "restructuring/winding-up" to the divisional organisation of the Central Office. During the course of this re-organisation in the late autumn of 1990, the department for "Regional and Sectoral Structures" was separated out from the "Restructuring/Winding-up" Division and brought into the "Branches" Division, where it was converted into a Directorate with the harmless title of "States Questions".[128]

The potentially irritating words "structural policy" and "restructuring" were thus pushed into the background. As a further example the "Guideline on the Evaluation and Examination of Corporate Concepts" approved by the Executive Board in March 1991 had originally been called the "Restructuring Guideline".[129]

The "Easter Letter" from the President, Dr Rohwedder, to the staff of the THA, dated 27th March 1991,[130] which had been carefully discussed and agreed with Birgit Breuel,[131] picked up on the statements made two weeks earlier in the "Basic principles of co-operation between the Federal Government, eastern German States, and the THA" and turned them into a language which the THA staff would find plausible and effective. The letter bore the title which later became a proverb: "Rapid privatisation – Resolute restructuring – Considerate closure". The core sentence within it, which was later much quoted, was: "Privatisation is the most effective form of restructuring".

The triple phrase: Privatisation – Restructuring – Closure contained in the heading later became an independent maxim, which might have been a rhetorical way of diverting attention from the fact that the THA itself had struggled for months[132] with setting its priorities, but that with the publication of this letter from Rohwedder, if not before, had at last achieved clarity on the point that the sale of the THA companies was being achieved in order to permit the restructuring by the private owners, and not the restructuring in order to permit the sale. In fact, the "Easter Letter", which as a result of the assassination of the THA President on Easter Monday 1991 became a kind of testimony,[133] did damp down internal discussion within the THA on the ques-

128 B-interview with Wolf Schöde on 25th February 1993.

129 B-interview with Dr Norman van Scherpenberg on 24th February 1993.

130 Dr Detlev Rohwedder: To all THA employees: the THA is fulfilling its task: Rapid privatisation – Resolute restructuring – Considerate closure. 27th March 1991.

131 A-interview with Wolf Schöde on 4th February 1993.

132 op. cit.; B-interview with Dr Norman van Scherpenberg on 24th February 1993.

133 A-interview with Wolf Schöde on 4th February 1993; on this point see also commentary on a reprint of the letter in: *Frankfurter Allgemeine Zeitung*, 3rd April 1991, page 13.

tion of aims,[134] and, in the estimate of senior employees, the business policy line of the THA was at least sufficiently accepted amongst the main political and business elites.[135]

2. The assassination of Dr Detlev Rohwedder, THA President, and the resultant reorganisation of the Executive Board

In the evening of 1st April 1991, Easter Monday, the President of the THA, Dr Detlev Rohwedder, was killed in the study of his Düsseldorf home by a shot fired from the plot of ground opposite. When his wife rushed to his help, she was injured by two further shots.

This murder set of a wave of outrage and dismay not only in the public at large but also, obviously, within the THA itself, which was clearly expressed in the opinions gathered from employees.[136] The murderer is still unknown.[137]

Rohwedder's successor was Birgit Breuel, until that date Executive Board member in charge of the "Branches" Division. Speculation had spread through the public of a possible repetition of the line of succession of the summer of 1990, thus bringing the Chairman of the Supervisory Board, Jens Odewald, into the office of President.[138] However, Odewald let it be known straight away on 3rd April that he was not available for this position.[139]

With all respect for the personal qualities of Ms Breuel, which were later to be rewarded by the almost unconditional loyalty of her subordinates at all levels,[140] it was quite clear that a man of Rohwedder's personality could not be replaced. Detlev Karsten Rohwedder, who had worked since the early 1960's initially as a commercial lawyer in an auditing company, in the civil service as Secretary of State in the Federal Ministry for Economic Affairs with the rank of a civil servant, and finally, from 1978 onwards, as Deputy Chairman and shortly afterwards as Chairman, of the Executive Board of Hoesch Werke AG,[141] came with a biographical background which predestined him as virtually no other in the western German industrial elite to take over the central authority in charge of the gigantic economic revolution in eastern Germany. The rapid integration of the THA into both the economic and the political decision-making networks, a process controlled basically by the selection of personnel and personalities, could hardly have been achieved so quickly and effectively without Rohwedder's experience and wealth of contacts and influence.

---

134 B-interview with Dr Norman van Scherpenberg on 24th February 1993.

135 A-interview with Wolf Schöde on 4th February 1993.

136 A-interviews with Wolf Schöde on 4th February 1993, Dr Wolfgang Vehse on 5th August 1992, and Helmuth Coqui on 7th January 1993.

137 The ultimate head of the THA, Federal Minister of Finance Theo Waigel, requested that the murder investigation should also cover possible connections between the *Rote Armee Fraktion* ("RAF"), former members of the GDR Ministry of State Security (the *Stasi*), and the SED's successor organisation the PDS: *Frankfurter Allgemeine Zeitung*, 4th April 1991, page 1.

138 *Frankfurter Allgemeine Zeitung*, 3rd April 1991, page 13; *Wirtschaftswoche*, 16/91 (12th April 1991), pages 16 to 23.

139 *Frankfurter Allgemeine Zeitung*, 4th April 1991, pages 1 and 15.

140 A-interview with Helmuth Coqui on 7th January 1993; B-interview with Dr Hartmut Maaßen on 2nd March 1993.

141 Munzinger Archiv/International Biographical Archive 20/ 91, P 012540–7 Ro-ME.

It was very hard indeed to find a successor with Rohwedder's practical industrial background, a failing which was applied to Ms Breuel and even to the Administrative Board Chairman Odewald, despite his being a veritable big-company manager as Chairman of the Executive Board of Kaufhof AG, who in addition to this apparently enjoyed a close and confidential relationship with the Federal Chancellor.[142] However, there were three important reasons which must have favoured Birgit Breuel as the new President. One was that she had become incontestably the "No. 2" on the Executive Board after having been a member of it for a good six months and in light of her technical and management competence.[143] The second was the political experience she had to offer after having been Minister for Economic Affairs and Minister of Finance of the State of Lower Saxony for many years. But thirdly, although Ms Breuel had no actual industrial experience, she enjoyed an enormous amount of "confidence capital" with western German business, and of course a wide range of contacts with top-manager circles in western German industry. In terms of the political order of the economy she was regarded as an ordo-liberal "hard-liner" with a clear option of privatisation as the one and only means of economic reconstruction, which enabled the SPD to describe her appointment to the presidency of the THA as "the wrong political signal".[144]

The change in the president's office provided the impetus for a "reshuffle" in the Executive Board in May 1991. Mr Halm and Mr Schirner left the Board, so including the Division vacated by Ms Breuel there were now three Divisions waiting for new Executive Board members to head them. In the following weeks, these were taken up by Hero Brahms (U1, previously headed by Schirner), Dr Günter Rexrodt (U3, previously Halm), and Dr Klaus Schucht, who took on the newly created U6 (municipal assets/water management, energy industry, chemicals, textiles/clothing/leather, potash and ore mining/stone/earth), whilst Ms Breuel's former Division (Branches and States Questions) was dissolved and split between U4 (Dr Klinz, who now personally took on responsibility for co-ordinating the branches) and the President's Division to which the Directorate of "State Questions" was added.

The composition of the new Executive Board was once again characterised by technical and potentially political aspects. Mr Brahms and Mr Schucht were two experienced managers from the Ruhr industrial area who now joined the Board. Brahms had previously been a member of the Executive Board of Hoesch AG, where he had first worked under and later closely alongside Rohwedder as Chairman of the Executive Board, and, as had been reported, had been under consideration for a position on the THA Executive Board for a long time on account of this personal connection.[145] Schucht had formerly been Chairman of the Executive Board of Ruhrkohle AG,

---

142 On this point, see the tributes paid to Odewald on the occasion of his resignation from the chairmanship of the Administrative Board in April 1993, e. g.: *Frankfurter Allgemeine Zeitung*, 15th April 1993, pages 13 and 17; *Die Welt*, 16th April 1993, page 1.

143 A-interview with Helmuth Coqui on 7th January 1993.

144 On this point, see: *Munzinger Archiv*/International Biographical Archive 40/ 92, P 014884–7 Br-ME, page 3. Here, just as in many other interpretations of Ms Breuel's THA policy, the proverb "Privatisation is the best kind of restructuring" is quoted in a way that arouses the impression that it was Ms Breuel who coined the phrase. However this might have been when Dr Rohwedder was preparing his "Easter Letter", the phrase itself is to be found for the first time, as far as anyone can see, in his letter of 27th March 1991.

145 B-interview with Wolf Schöde on 15th March 1993.

so both brought with them the advantage Rohwedder had had, industrial experience from a region suffering economic crises and restructuring; in this respect they made good any shortcomings in the new President. A new political balance also came about, without any tensions: Schucht belonged to the SPD, the new President to the CDU, and Halm's successor, Rexrodt (Federal Minister for Economic Affairs from January 1993 onwards) was, like Halm, in the FDP.

The position of Vice-President of the THA was created when Hero Brahms joined. He was 50 years of age in 1991, and gave up a very successful industrial career for the sake of the THA.[146] The corporate division he took over, U1, was now given a number of strategic and cross-sectional functions: one was the staff function, "Examination of corporate concepts" (U1 U, *Prüfung von Unternehmenskonzepten*), a term which internally concealed the so-called "Management Committee" (*Leitungsausschuß*). This committee consisted at times of up to 80 external auditors and management consultants organised into a number of industry teams (up to eight) with the task of continually making an inventory of about 1,800 THA companies and placing them on a 6-point scale (12 including sub-categories) from "1" = "company is operating profitably" to "6" = "company cannot be restructured".[147] Until the Executive Board reshuffle in May 1991 the Management Committee, having been constituted as a consensus body, had been organised under the President.[148] Another cross-sectional function created for U1 was the Directorate for "Central Equity Holdings Financial Control/Consultancy" (U1 BC), a directorate in which the management reporting data of all the THA companies are collected and recorded and turned into the appropriate top-level reports. It also monitors basic contract principles for uniformity and the fulfilment of contracts. Bearing in mind that U1 also has business responsibility for the whole engineering industry, it can be seen that it is a key Division which is put together according to the abilities of the Vice-President.

The appointment of Brahms as Vice-President and the bundling up of strategic areas of responsibility into his Division meant at the same time that stress was being laid on organisational policy as a THA priority at the operational level. One could expect from a man like Brahms that market-orientated privatisation and indeed restructuring policies would be pursued consistently. Unlike the President of the THA, Ms Breuel, Brahms on account of his age and previous biography would inevitably have had a great personal interest in the success of this policy. It was obvious that the Vice-President, as a former top manager in industry, would hardly want to acquire status as the deputy head of an industrial administration authority, but would have to build an image as a future head of a competitive successful state concern, regardless of whether he saw his future career options in the state or the private sector. It was just this route that started to open up towards the end of 1991 with the idea of the "Management-KG" companies.[149]

Under its new President Ms Breuel the top management layer had been strengthened by bringing the Directorates for Federal and State Affairs into the President's Division and by re-

---

146 Munzinger Archiv/International Biographical Archive 42/91, P 019921 -1 Br-ME.

147 THA: *Aufgabenspektrum und Lösungswege* (Hand-book, March 1993), Section 22 *Prüfung von Unternehmenskonzepten.*

148 From July 1990 it was headed up by Horst Plaschna, later the managing director of one of the two "Management-KG" companies founded in 1992 (see below), and from March 1992 onwards by Reinhold Fries.

149 See: article by Kern and Sabel in this volume.

lieving this Division of responsibility for specific industries (under Rohwedder it had been responsible for the energy industry). Another newly created position was *Generalbevollmächtigter* or General Manager of the THA (initially Dr Wolfgang Müller-Stöfen and from 21st April 1992 onwards Dr Norman van Scherpenberg). All in all, this was a more strongly team-orientated management structure than it had been when Rohwedder was President, and the THA practically came to be headed by a *troika* (President, Vice-President, and General Manager). In addition to the reasons relating to the personal qualities of the new President, namely her lack of industrial experience, this structure also took the increasing complexity of the operational business into account and the resultant need for delegation.

3. Particular features of the personnel structure and "THA culture"

The organisational consolidation of the THA which started to take effect in the spring of 1991 was exposed to three particularly disadvantageous factors. One was that it had to come to grips with the extraordinary dynamic forces of its own growth. The numbers employed by the THA, just in the Central Office, rose between 1st July 1990 and 30th June 1991 from 114 to 1,678 (plus, on 30th June 1991, 1,044 staff in the branches).[150] Another was the need to work on the THA's operational business, which was likewise orientated towards high growth rates. And finally, the THA was under continuous political pressure, from the start or at the very latest from the crisis in the spring of 1991 onwards; indeed, as described above, it was part of the very essence of its function to draw this pressure onto itself and absorb it.

Burdens of this kind have a direct effect on the members of an organisation and therefore make particular integration efforts necessary. If all goes well, the sense of identification with the organisation and its tasks consolidates into a team spirit which in the relevant context can be given the label of "corporate identity". The top management of the THA started taking this need for mental integration more and more into account during 1991; President Rohwedder's "Easter Letter" was one early and striking example.

As the extraordinary character of THA work could be forecast,[151] the personnel structure itself reflected a selection with characteristic features. This included, in the view at least of the senior THA employees, the atypical age structure of THA employees, dominated by young university graduates and "established people"; the point most often stressed is the smooth, often mutually stimulating, co-operation between the younger members and the older ones, the latter being sometimes in their sixties.[152] This perception of the age structure is at least in part an optical illusion resulting from the hierarchical pyramid, because there were obviously more young executives (*Referenten*) than senior directors and departmental heads. An opinion poll conducted

150 *Personalentwicklung der THA von 1990 bis 1993*, THA PE T1/B2/Ve/lh, 25th February 1993.

151 President Rohwedder is attributed with the description of the THA as a galley with volunteer slaves: they might come on board voluntarily, but they ought to agree to being chained up voluntarily. B-interview with Wolf Schöde on 15th March 1993.

152 A-interviews with Richard Graf zu Eulenburg on 30th July 1992 and with Christoph Urban on 19th May 1993; B-interview with Jürgen Allert on 26th February 1993.

by the present author in March and April 1993 on directors, departmental heads, and executives[153] revealed the picture given below.

The average age (rounded arithmetical mean) of the executives was about 38, but this average is of little use as it conceals huge deviations from the average between the western and eastern German executives. Whilst the average for those from western Germany (including western Berlin) was 32, the average for those from the east was 46. It is thus only for the western German executives that the stereotype can be made to fit of the young, dynamic, infinitely hard-working employee, whilst the eastern Germans were practically a different generation and of course had totally different experience behind them.[154]

The average age of the departmental heads questioned, on the other hand, was 43, and thus well under that of the eastern German executives (eastern Germans accounted for 17 % of the departmental heads questioned). In a typical instance, therefore, an eastern German executive would thus be working under a much younger western German departmental head. Co-operation between eastern and western Germans in the THA is described unanimously as very good and free of friction.[155]

Finally, the average age of the directors questioned was 53, so it would be fair to speak of a clear generation gap between the executives and departmental heads on the one side and the directors on the other, which is in line with the observer's immediate perception.

Both with regard to the seniority and to their formal hierarchical position and professional backgrounds, the directors were similar to the branch managers (as of 1st February 1993 the Central Office had 45 directorates in comparison with 15 branches and branch offices). 61.5 % of the directors questioned, but all the industry directors and all the branch managers questioned, came from the private sector of the economy, and only 27 % from the civil service; of the remaining three directors, one came from an association and one from abroad, and the third had been already in retirement before he was appointed. Amongst the departmental heads as well, most (54 %) came from western German private industry, 19 % from western German or western Berlin civil service, and 12 % (or 70 % of the eastern German departmental heads) from the for-

---

153 The questionnaire was sent to all 57 directors or holders of equal positions and all 172 heads of departments and similar in the THA Central Office, and a random sample of 170 executives. The response rate was 45.6 % for the directors, 34.3 % for the heads of departments, and 61.7 % for the executives.

154 Because of the lack of disaggregated data, no statement can be made as to the overall distribution of western German and eastern German THA employees by hierarchical level. Overall the eastern German employees are far and away in the majority (as of 30th June 1993: 2,764, or 69 % from the east, 1,260 or 31 % from the west). However, the proportion of eastern German employees drops off sharply in the upper hierarchical levels. Amongst the executives who replied to the questionnaire, 41 % (43 out of 105) were eastern Germans, of the heads of departments 19 % (11 out of 57), and none of the directors. However, these figures should only be regarded as approximations which may if anything exaggerate the proportion of eastern German executives and heads of departments as the response rate can be assumed to have been higher amongst the eastern German respondents. This view is supported by the fact that questionnaires were on average sent back more promptly by the eastern Germans than by the western Germans.

155 A-interviews with Richard Graf zu Eulenburg on 30th July 1992; Dr Manfred Balz on 10th September 1992; Dr Volker Charbonnier/Götz von Borries on 1st October 1992; Helmuth Ofterdinger on 13th October 1992; Dr Dirk Wefelscheid on 25th November 1992, all of them, however, western Germans.

mer GDR civil service. Amongst the executives questioned, 25 % were just starting their careers (in 1989, 37 % of those questioned, exclusively western Germans, had still been trainees); of the others, 42 % came from the private sector of the western German or western Berlin economy, 20 % (or 37 % of the eastern German executives) from the GDR civil service, 12 % (or 21 % of the eastern German executives) from a GDR business company, and only 6 % from the western German civil service. 5 % had been unemployed before joining the THA, and the remaining 15 % came from associations or had been self-employed or else gave no information.

Women were heavily under-represented in the THA, even at the middle-management level. Of the executives questioned, 71 % were male and 29 % female. The interesting point is, however that the numbers of either sex were more or less equal amongst the eastern German executives (51 % male, 49 % female), which means, looked at the other way, that amongst the executives coming from western Germany or western Berlin only 16 % (10 out of 62) were women. At the departmental head level, the THA organisational plan can be taken as the basis; as of 1st July 1992, out of these 166 departmental heads, only 13 (8 %) were women. And all the 46 directors were men.[156]

The stress to which the entire THA organisation was subject was shown by this inquiry to have had its greatest effect in the middle and upper echelons.[157] Respondents' own estimates of their average working week was 58 hours for the directors questioned, 55.5 for the departmental heads, and 51 hours for the executives. One remarkable point is that while only 23 % of the directors questioned, 58 % of the departmental heads questioned responded that they had advanced their careers by joining the THA. Answering the more precise question, "In what respect did your career improve or worsen when you joined the THA?", however, 73 % of the directors and also 73 % of the departmental heads said it had worsened in terms of the general work-load, and 84 % of the directors and 66 % of the departmental heads in terms of the disadvantages to family life. Career and personal situations had their effects on the external circumstances of their lives; 73 % of all the directors, but only 29 % of the departmental heads, are "week-end commuters". 54 % of even the overworked group of directors however stated that they had advanced their careers by transferring to the THA in terms of the attractiveness of the work.

A number of conclusions can be drawn concerning the motivation situation of the THA employees from these figures, and thus on its integrational power. The top level, the directors and branch managers – a group of only 60 people, definitely the management elite of the THA, was apparently recruited from a professionally successful management elite in business and public administration. Their motivation for joining the THA lay not so much in enhanced career prospects but the attraction of taking on a major challenge once again in probably the closing phase of their careers (the average age of the directors questioned was 53).[158] Just as great a pro-

156 Geschäftsverteilungsplan der Treuhandanstalt, *Organisationshandbuch*, serial no. 1.5.1, organisational instruction no. 0–01/92, as of July 1992.

157 Specifically on this aspect, see: A-interview with Günther Himstedt on 5th February 1993.

158 On this point, see also: A-interviews with Dr Eberhard Sinnecker on 27th July 1992; Horst Bräuhäuser on 28th July 1992; Richard Graf zu Eulenburg on 30th July 1992; Dr Ken-Peter Paulin on 30th July 1992; Hans-Jürgen Rohr on 15th September 1992; Helmuth Ofterdinger on 13th October 1992; Dr Dirk Wefelscheid on 25th November 1992; Helmuth Coqui on 7th January 1993; and the very revealing report by Dr Albrecht Krieger, *Begegnung mit der politischen Vergangenheit im Osten Deutschlands*.

portion of this group, but mainly those directors over 60 and mainly working in consultancy or staff positions, could also add patriotic reasons in the best sense of the word.[159] For the young executives, meaning typically the young western Germans, there are no primary statements available but it can be assumed that the attraction in joining the THA and the motivation to the commitment was the high level of responsibility in relation to their age and the pioneering aspect of the THA's work which they probably regarded as enhancing their careers.

This structure of age and motivation proved to be problematic in two respects. For departmental heads in particular, who can be counted as the middle management level in terms of their age and career seniority, the future career is all in all more critical than for directors or for executives. Except where these departmental heads were, as employees or civil servants in the western German state sector or employees in private sector companies, allowed a leave of absence for a predetermined period of time, can it later prove difficult to reappoint them to their former job.[160]

For the young executives, on the other hand, there is often an asymmetrical relationship between the level of responsibility and professional or general experience. Many an eastern German works manager must have felt heavily put down when he had to explain his carefully prepared corporate strategy to a few "yuppies" in the THA Central Office who sometimes tried to disguise their embarrassment with arrogance.[161] The resultant negative impression given to eastern German managers and employees was very well noted by the THA Executive Board and taken as a reason to issue the necessary warnings.[162]

As far as the career background is concerned, the THA mixes civil service and industrial careers, although in purely quantitative terms with a clear dominance by the private sector of the economy.[163] This situation, which reflects the THA's hermaphroditic institutional position between the market and the state, did not as far as anyone can see lead to any significant frictions. Branch managers and industry directors tended to regard the auditors, who likewise came from the private sector, specifically from auditing and consultancy firms, as far more of a pedantic nuisance than the ministerial civil servants, most of whom would have been lawyers by training.[164] There have even been occasional expressions of some surprise at the skilful way in which experienced "bureaucrats" deal with the political environment of the THA, which is of course less familiar to the THA managers who came from the private economy.[165] Tensions and rivalries amongst managers are often reduced by the mere fact that the THA's lifetime is limited and its character as a "temporary organisation" which has been emphasised more and more since the second half of 1991.[166] As the managers' opportunities for advancement within the THA itself are extremely limited, competitive battles are simply not worthwhile.[167]

---

159 For instance: A-interview with Horst Bräuhäuser on 28th July 1992; Krieger, *Begegnung mit der politischen Vergangenheit im Osten Deutschlands*.

160 B-interview with Henning Birkholz on 15th March 1993.

161 B-interview with Gerd Schwarze (managing director of Pactec, Dresden) on 17th March 1993; see also: A-interview with Richard Graf zu Eulenburg on 30th July 1992.

162 A-interview with Richard Graf zu Eulenburg on 30th July 1992.

163 See above.

164 A-interviews with Richard Graf zu Eulenburg on 30th July 1992 and with Helmuth Ofterdinger on 13th October 1992.

165 A-interview with Dr Volker Charbonnier/Götz von Borries on 1st October 1992.

166 See below.

167 A-interview with Hansjörg Schaal on 11th January 1993.

Is there a "THA culture" with any practical effect? The statements made by those affected and other interested parties are very varied. In the early phase of the THA, the metaphor of a "melting pot" might have been appropriate as was used by the press spokesman. The work of the THA was having a powerful homogenising effect on the action orientation and institutional identity of the staff.[168] On the other hand, attention is often drawn to the very different kinds of experience and working styles, particularly of the industrial directors who came from the private sector on the one hand and the senior managers schooled in public administration on the other.[169]

In most of the interviews an explicit or implicit reference is made to the unique and historic nature of the THA and the fascination and working motivation that arises from it. It can be seen that there is a certain "comradeship of the trenches" at work, a pride in being able to say "I was there".

At the same time, it is not possible to prove that there is any clear-cut identification with the THA as an institution. In reply to the question, "In what respect did your career improve or worsen when you joined the THA?", only 29 % of the executives questioned by the present author, 24 % of the departmental heads, and, an even bigger gap, only 11.5 % of the directors mentioned "institutional prestige" as one of the ways in which their careers had "on the whole improved" when they joined the THA. There is, however, a clear difference between eastern and western Germans amongst the executives, the only middle-management level with a high proportion of eastern Germans. 37 % of the western Germans but only 23 % of the eastern Germans said that their careers had "on the whole improved" in terms of institutional prestige. On the other side, 29 % of the executives, 34 % of the departmental heads (37.5 % of the western German but only 18 % of eastern German ones), and 34 % of the directors stated that in terms of institutional prestige their careers had "on the whole worsened".

When questions are asked expressly about "THA culture" or *esprit de corps*, the overall picture only changes slightly. 27 % of the directors, 37 % of the departmental heads, and 25 % of the executives answered that they had "on the whole improved" their position in this respect by joining the THA (with no significant differences between eastern and western German executives). Likewise, 27 % of the directors, 20 % of the departmental heads, and 23 % of the executives stated that their positions had "on the whole worsened" in this respect. In this instance again there is a remarkable difference between western and eastern Germans, this time at the departmental head level. None of the eastern German departmental heads questioned considered that his position had worsened with regard to "THA culture" or *esprit de corps*, but this view was stated by 25 % of the western German departmental heads.

In contrast to these generally negative figures for the staff's own estimate of prestige and THA culture at the middle and senior management levels, very positive figures appear regarding the attractiveness of the work. In reply to the question, "In what respect did your career improve or worsen when you joined the THA?", and to the category "attractiveness of the work", 54 % of the directors, 62 % of the departmental heads, and 52 % of the executives stated that in this respect their position had "on the whole improved". Only 16 % of the executives, a mere 5 % of the departmental heads, and 4 % of the directors stated that in this respect their position had "on the whole worsened".

---

168 B-interview with Wolf Schöde on 25th February 1993.

169 B-interview with Dr Wolfgang Vehse on 26th February 1993.

As the attractiveness of the work at the middle and upper management levels is relatively high, but institutional prestige and THA culture and *esprit de corps* is rated fairly low, it is possible to draw the conclusion that it is less the demands of internal control and loyalty as the external justification and its reciprocal effect on motivation that characterise the identity problem of the THA. The THA's daily communication work takes this into account. The extract of press reports on the THA, which in comparable authorities or major companies is more a status symbol reserved for management, is printed and circulated in 1,000 copies and thus in practice available to all THA employees. This gives them a realistic picture of the external perception of the THA, and a mixture of feed-back and a feeling of importance.

Special efforts were concentrated in the autumn of 1991 on communicating the general business policy line and strengthening the team spirit of THA employees. A closed meeting of the Executive Board on 18th/19th October 1991 approved "Project Everyone Together" (*Projekt Miteinander* = "with one another", often regarded as the opposite of "against one another"). Its focal point was two meetings, one for middle and upper management ("Management meeting"), which was held on 9th November 1991, and two "Staff Meetings", one of them the first plenary meeting of all THA staff (which, however, because of the sheer numbers involved had to take place on two separate days, 23rd and 30th November). In addition to this, a "family day" was arranged in the THA Central Office in September 1992.

At the major meetings for management and staff (referred to by insiders as "Drumhead Service"), the President gave a key-note speech with the title "Everybody together – working for the social market economy".[170] Although her speech contained an appeal for more team spirit (explicitly referred to as such: *Wir-Gefühl*, the feeling that "we" all belong together), it was basically a call to improve and refine the operational business,[171] and centred on the small amount of time available.[172] The THA, she said, would have to complete its work "in two, three, or four years" and is only "a temporary organisation". Everyone was heading "at full speed down the final straight". This was followed by the announcement of individual incentives based on agreed targets for "maintaining the pace of privatisation".

The strategy and the myth of the THA were thus dramatically welded together in this speech. The aspect of the shortage of time and thus the priority for speed in privatisation was very clearly emphasised.[173] The factor of time had undergone a fundamental change of assessment

---

170 Birgit Breuel, *Miteinander – Arbeiten für die Soziale Marktwirtschaft: Grundsatzreferat*, given at the staff meetings on 23rd and 30th November 1991, Berlin Wuhlheide.

171 This included agreeing targets for the working units in the industrial directorates and branches, and "incentives" in the form of a cash bonus scheme for departmental heads and directors. The feed-back on the detailed definition of the business policy line and new management measures were summarised in two reports by the staff department for corporate planning: THA, P GU, *Projekt Miteinander, Zusammenfassung der Feedbacks aus den Mitarbeiter-Tagungen*, March 1992 (I) and April 1992 (II).

172 "Time is certainly the scarcest resource available to us. Or, to put it more exactly: not usually available to us. We are therefore compelled to use factual knowledge, intelligence, idealism, motivation, and dynamism at record speed." Breuel, *Miteinander – Arbeiten für die Soziale Marktwirtschaft*, page 15 (see: footnote 170).

173 "There are nevertheless voices to be heard, even in the THA, which claim that the pace of privatisation which has been attained cannot be maintained much longer. But we oppose that view with our action essentials which help to determine the pace of privatisation." op. cit., page 9.

within one year. In the late summer of 1990 the first President, Rohwedder, had described the shortage of time rather than of money as the major obstacle to restructuring,[174] but it was already clear in the spring of 1991, at the time of the "Easter Letter" ("Privatisation is the best form of restructuring"), that it was no longer possible even to conceive of a restructuring programme for all eastern Germany under the aegis of the THA, if only because of the gigantic financial sums that would be required. The problem of the shortage of time was thus turned on its head: the THA companies should be managed in the THA's possession not for as long as was financially affordable, but for the shortest time humanly possible.

The President's key-note speech of November 1991 re-inforced this knowledge and drew further organisational policy consequences out of it. Unlike in Rohwedder's "Easter Letter" of that same year, the target dimensions (privatisation, restructuring, closure) no longer played any central role in the repertoire of convictions expressed in this speech. Instead, she emphasised the route to the goal, the living process of achieving targets. From the necessity of goal definition a virtue was made of finite time and thus an *élan vital* produced for the organisation.[175] This "vitalism" in the organisational policy[176] can be deemed to be the actual THA myth. If a guiding myth is to be durable it must be just as functional as it is capable of arousing identification.[177] This vitalism as the guiding myth of the organisation is one with which the pioneers of the "age of chaos" can identify themselves with just as much as the young "yuppie" executives and the eastern German employees, who can see in it a radical rejection of the bureaucratic attitudes of GDR economic administration. It is presumably this vitalism and the view, now turned round to appear positive, of the impossibility of coping with the task under conventional criteria of diligence and the rational deployment of resources which determine the essential integrational force of the organisation.[178]

V. Prospects for the THA and its gradual liquidation

The organisational policy of "vitalism", and the emphasis on the finite amount of time available, had the intended effect of mobilising the THA staff and at the same time of throwing them into anxiety. In February 1992, the Executive Board member responsible for personnel, Alexander

---

174 "Wir kaufen Zeit", in *Wirtschaftswoche*, 7th October 1990, pages 189 to 194.

175 "Only in this way (by retaining the rapid pace of the operational business) can we prevent the pendulum of free creativity swinging back into total bureaucratisation. Bureaucratic structures are characterised by intolerance and safety-mindedness." Breuel, *Miteinander – Arbeiten für die Soziale Marktwirtschaft*, page 15 (see: footnote 170). This addressed among other things the negative associations which the eastern German THA employees would inevitably have connected with the term "bureaucratic structures".

176 Derived from the sociological vitalism of George Sorel. See his *Les illusions du progrès*, pages 287 to 336

177 See: Brunsson, *The Irrationality of Action and Action Rationality*, pages 29 to 44.

178 "It would in fact be true to say that everything that is being done in the THA was impossible from the start and has to be done all the same, meaning that the basic contradiction of this institution is that it has to do something which actually cannot be done – and, at the same time, meet the strict demands of rationality and pragmatism. And that in Germany, where we have no tradition of rational pragmatism." A-interview with Wolf Schöde on 4th February 1993.

Koch, in presenting the new bonus system for directors and departmental heads, referred to a "tendency for the THA to liquidate itself",[179] which appeared in the press as a "redundancy plan"[180] or under the headline "The THA is running out of work".[181] The unique situation the THA staff found themselves consisted of "doing such good work that they are making themselves redundant and committing ,functional suicide'."[182]

Such wording was not designed to arouse confidence amongst the THA employees, and must have had a certain counterproductive effect on the accelerated pace of the operational business which the THA could not tolerate.[183] Objectively, however, the pressure increased to develop an operational strategy for the future of the THA which would give all involved an orientation both for its work and for their own personal career planning.

This was first done for the THA branches, whose portfolios of small and medium-sized businesses was perceptibly diminishing more quickly than that of the Central Office. The strategy for "Phase II" of the branches was presented at a directors' conference on 27th July 1992,[184] under which the branches as such would be closed down once the work of selling off the companies had been completed and converted into "Branch offices of the THA and the TLG" (the latter being the real estate holding organisation). They would be run jointly by a THA and a TLG managing director and under this plan the THA business would come under corporate group U2 and the TLG business under U5. The THA and TLG branch offices would maintain joint accommodation and also a joint legal department. The numbers employed in all the branches would be reduced from 1,769 employees and 317 consultants (as of 30th June 1992) to 998 employees and 99 consultants (as of 1st January 1994). Pilot models of the new organisation were formed in the branches in Halle and Cottbus.

All the branches were to be converted between the second half of 1992 and the end of 1993 into THA/TLG branch offices of this kind as soon as each one's privatisation business had been completed. Delays occurred here as well; the branches in Schwerin, Cottbus, Halle, Rostock, Suhl, and Neubrandenburg were originally to have been converted to branch offices before the end of 1992,[185] but in none of these cases was this possible before February or even May 1993.[186]

The conversion of the branches into branch offices entailed considerable changes in areas of responsibility and in working style. The entrepreneurial and dynamic phase of the branches came to an end, and the residual business of reprivatisation, winding up, contract management,

---

179 *Handelsblatt* 28th/29th February 1992, page 1.

180 *Neue Zeit*, 28th February 1992, page 9.

181 *Leipziger Volkszeitung*, 28th February 1992, page 1.

182 *Mitteldeutsche Zeitung*, 28th February 1992, page 2.

183 A little later a new Executive Board member for the Personnel Division was appointed: *Neue Zeit*, 19th March 1992, page 11. Dr Horst Föhr, formally an Executive Board member of Aral AG, joined the THA as successor to Dr Alexander Koch, "who had already given notice several months ago that he was leaving" (op. cit.). On 31st July 1992 the Director in charge of the Personnel Directorate, Mr Bellwied, also left: THA press release, 21st July 1992.

184 Information zur Phase II der Niederlassungen, meeting of the directors on Monday, 27th July 1992, no author mentioned (THA Koordination Niederlassungen).

185 op. cit.

186 Treuhandanstalt, *Aufgabenspektrum und Lösungswege* (Handbook, March 1993), Section 5: Aufgaben der Niederlassungen und Geschäftsstellen.

controlling and personnel management became more formalised, standardised, and bureaucratic, and at least had different operational priorities than the branches' business of managing the equity holdings and privatisation.[187] All the branch managers, who were nearly all "business manager" types, left, and were replaced by branch office managers. The old co-ordination problems between the core branch business and the TLG business, however, were not solved by the new organisational model; if anything, they were made more acute. Little hope of success is held out for a model involving joint business management in joint office accommodation, because of differences of substance but also simply for reasons of space.[188] It will not be long before the previous dominance of the THA business over the real estate business of the TLG in the branch offices will be reversed, as the TLG business will continue to be an extensive and operational demanding activity for many years to come.

The concept for the THA's successor presented to the staff for the first time in March 1993 provides for a total of 2,800 people to be employed on the remaining work during 1995. The organisations behind the THA real estate business, the TLG and the BVVG, responsible for the land administration and realisation, were already in place for the administration and sale of THA property, including its residential property and agricultural and forestry land. The forecast here was a requirement of 800 employees for the TLG and the transfer of 140 employees to the BVVG. According to this forecast, some 480 employees would remain in the successor organisation to the THA, the name of which has not yet been decided. The responsibilities of this successor organisation are to consist of maintaining the debtor and creditor function and the function of the party to legal actions and the documentation and servicing of terminating business such as closed down nuclear power stations. In addition to this it will have such functions as property assignment, communalisation, investment priority proceedings, property transaction licences, and the administration of special assets, as well as certain service functions such as EDP which will be designed as independent companies and privatised. The THA consultancy company for Eastern Europe, TOB or *Treuhand-Osteuropa Beratungsgesellschaft*, will remain in existence to promote know-how transfer to the countries of central and eastern Europe.

The supervision of the Management-KG companies (there will be "up to ten" of them, it is said), the financing of the successor organisation, and the management of "a few major corporations representing exceptional solutions" will be allotted to the Federal Ministry of Finance. A total of 260 persons will be required for this.

Finally, some 880 employees will be needed for monitoring contracts, regional winding-up work, reprivatisation, and the handling of historic environmental pollution under "Contract Management Companies". No details have been released on the status of these "Contract Management Companies" – it is apparently not even known whether there will be several or only one – or on the organisation to be responsible.

The internal announcement of the THA's plans for its own future should be looked at against the background of the future orientation of its staff. For this reason, the concept is of course a provisional one, but it does lay emphasis on points which will become guiding principles for the re-organisation of the THA in 1994. Furthermore, there is a pragmatic justification for replacing THA responsibilities by State responsibilities, as indeed the eastern German States were calling

187 A-interview with Richard Graf zu Eulenburg on 30th July 1992.
188 B-interview with Hans-Günter Bolten (TLG) on 7th May 1993.

for at an earlier stage, before they were even in a position to shoulder them. Admittedly, a special structure would have to be created for the privatisation cases which affect several States at once and which can only be handled directly or indirectly at Federal level. This would lead to another division of responsibilities between major projects and mass business.

Another question is whether the prospect of the eastern German States being able to build up a large part of the East German economic planning apparatus for their regional structural policy by taking over contract management for the mass business and thus obtaining a huge stock of data on individual businesses would be effectively counterbalanced by the risk of state-economy relationship in the eastern part of Germany being stamped for many years to come with the imprint of the planned economy, all according to the use made by each State of this instrument. Developments in 1994 will contribute substantially to this and will show the extent to which the structural levelling off of state-economy relationships in re-unified Germany will take only a few years or several decades.

VI. Literature

Aldrich, Howard E.: *Organizations and Environments*. Englewood Cliffs 1979.

Beschäftigungsobservatorium Ostdeutschland No. 5, November 1992.

Brunsson, Nils: The Irrationality of Action and Action Rationality – Decisions, Ideologies, and Organizational Actions. In: *Journal of Management Studies* 19 (1982), pages 29 to 44.

Buchanan, James M., Robert D. *Tollison*, and Gordon *Tullock* (editors): *Toward a Theory of the Rent Seeking Society*. College Station (Tex.) 1980.

Glassman, Robert B.: Persistence and Loose Coupling in Living Systems. In: *Behavioral Science* 18 (1973), pages 83 to 98.

Institut für Weltwirtschaft, Kiel: *Gesamtwirtschaftliche und unternehmerische Anpassungsprozesse in Ostdeutschland*. Third report, Kiel 1991.

Krieger, Albrecht: *Begegnungen mit der politischen Vergangenheit im Osten Deutschlands. Als Vertrauensbevollmächtigter beim Vorstand der Treuhandanstalt*. In: Marcus *Bierich*, Peter *Hommelhoff*, and Bruno *Kropff* (editors): *Unternehmen und Unternehmensführung im Recht, Festschrift für Johannes Semler zum 70. Geburtstag am 28. April 1993*. Berlin and New York 1993, pages 19 to 66.

Orton, Douglas J., and Karl E. *Weick*: Loosely coupled systems: a reconceptualisation. In: *Academy of Management Review* 15 (1990), pages 203 to 223.

Schäuble, Wolfgang: *Der Vertrag – Wie ich über die deutsche Einheit verhandelte*. Edited by and with a foreword from Dirk Koch and Klaus Wirtgen. Stuttgart 1991.

Sorel, George: *Les illusions du progrès*. Paris 1921.

Trausch, Eiko: *Organisatorischer Wandel am Beispiel der Treuhandanstalt*. Unpublished diploma thesis to a business management degree, Augsburg 1991.

Treuhandanstalt: *Auftrag, Zwischenbilanz, Grundsätze*. Berlin, July 1991

Treuhandanstalt: *Treuhandanstalt Informationen*, various issues.

The THA in its environment of politics and interest groups

by Roland Czada

The development of the market economy in eastern Germany is a course of events with a high number of preconditions and involving numerous protagonists from the world of politics and business. The THA stands at the centre of this historical process. It acts as the anchor for the task of organising and legitimising a complete change in the economic system. This gives the THA extensive authority and scope for influencing events. However, it also makes it the recipient of contradictory demands. Political parties, parliaments and governments, interest groups, companies, local authorities, former owners of property and businesses, the Federal Cartel Office, the Federal Court of Audit, and other interested parties (such as the Commission of the European Union) are constantly attempting to gain influence over the whole organisation or over individual decisions, and to exercise rights of disposal and supervision.

It is not possible to cover the entire gamut of the external political relationships of the THA within the scope of this article, therefore the principal problem areas have been brought to the fore: the THA's process of growing into the political interconnection between Federal and State governments, into the network of relationships between the state and the private sector, and into the system of industrial relations.

I. Dependencies and networks

"It passes judgement on the life and death of entire regions and branches of the economy and, finally, on the fate of 16 million people in the eastern States of Germany."[1] The THA was accredited at times in this or similar language with a scope for independent action which it never had. On the contrary, it was dependent to a very particular extent on external co-operation and support. For instance, it was usually only able to obtain information vital to its decisions during the transformation process, stamped as it was by conditions of uncertainty, by carefully maintaining intensive and constant mutual relationships with all concerned. In addition to the need to discuss and agree so many points in political quarters, there was a demand for external consultancy services, mainly from legal and management advisors.[2] In addition to this, the THA depended on the supply of material resources of an incomparable order of magnitude if one takes debts adding

1 *Neues Deutschland* (formerly the East German Party newspaper), 22nd March 1991.

2 In 1992, the THA employed a permanent staff of 4,000 plus 1,000 consultants at daily fee rates between DM 800 and 4,500: A-interview with Richard Graf zu Eulenburg on 30th July 1992.

up to more than DM 250 billion in only a few years as a measure.[3] The organisation was neither able to finance itself from the proceeds of privatisation nor to make recourse to the productivity of an established organisation structure. Instead, in the shortest possible time it was compelled to obtain liquidity loans for the companies in which it held equity and to recruit a large number of managers and public administration experts who should be of the best possible quality but on engagements limited in time. These resource problems could likewise only be solved by close co-operation with state authorities, associations, organisations on the capital markets, and consultancy companies.

The transformation process is coming out in an extensive organisational network characterised by specific constellations of interests. The number of organisations involved has grown constantly. The governments of the five new States, numerous Federal authorities, associations representing interests groups from all realms of society, and organisations from the world of finance stepped one after the other onto the stage of economic transformation policy on which the THA, after having been founded in East Germany by a decision of the GDR Council of Ministers in March 1990, had been the first actor. The accelerated growth of the THA organisation following German unification in October 1990, and the increase in the number of protagonists active in the transformation process, generated an extraordinary political dynamism which intensified the economically caused confusion of the situation and the anxieties of all involved.

The THA countered the rapid increase in the complexity of its political surroundings by setting up departments designed to serve as "bridge-heads" to the outside world. This included Directorates for "States Questions", "Relationships with Federal and foreign governments", "Communications / Media", and "Investor Services", and separate departments for wage policy, labour market and social affairs, and a Bonn office as a contact-point to the *Bundestag*. It was in this way that the development of the organisation interacted with the outward system of networks. An organisational form developed characterised by "privatisation managers" in the industry directorates (the U-departments) and "interface managers" in the presidential departments (P-departments). The great dependency on this organisational environment, which was mobile and involved many interrelationships, caused at the same time co-ordination problems in the internal organisation by intensifying the internal division of the THA.[4]

In addition to liaison offices and formal lines of contact, a wide variety of *informal* relationships developed between the THA and its environment. This arose from the fact that it took on a staff of more than 4,000 within a very short time, many of whom retained their professional contacts with their previous firms, administrative bodies, States, and circles of friends. At management level, such contacts were even decisive in the selection of personnel. Industrial managers and ministerial officials from west and east were supposed to contribute not only their knowledge but also their personal contacts to enable them to keep their knowledge up to date

---

3 This includes DM 70 billion of old loans to the THA companies which have to be serviced by the THA: B-interview with Dr Paul Hadrys on 6th April 1993; see: Pilz and Ortwein, *Das vereinte Deutschland*, page 166.

4 From the point of view of organisation theory, the THA is living in the worst of all possible worlds: its environment is not static but turbulent, not simple but complex, not predictable but uncertain. Bureaucratic forms and principles are thus condemned to failure from the outset. The chances of success for the formation of a consistent, pro-active strategy are just as slim. All that remains is a reactive process of adaptation to the environment in order to retain its own goals as far as possible; see: article on organisational development by Wolfgang Seibel in this volume.

and contribute to smooth external co-ordination. For instance, it was an obvious choice to man the Labour Market Policy department with the personal assistant of the President of the Federal Institute of Labour, and the department for Federal relations with officials from Federal and State ministries, and to assign the task of the restitution of municipalities' property to someone from the *Deutscher Städtetag* (the national standing conference of town and city representatives) and responsibility for the Agriculture and Forestry Corporate Group to the legal advisor of the Schleswig-Holstein Farmers' Association.[5]

An extensive "THA-complex" has built up in German politics through the formation of formal and informal networks which throws up a large number of practical and political-science questions. Of particular interest appear the problems of compatibility and adaptation of a centralist THA construction coming from the GDR government to the Federal system and to the traditional state-association relationships of West Germany. The THA's work has made the political accommodation between the Federal and the State levels even more complicated, and it has subjected the "neo-corporatist" integration of the economic interest-group associations into the political process of the Federal Republic to a severe test.

II. Intermediary between Federal and State levels

The Federal structure of the German State has always been characterised by overlapping responsibilities between the Federal and the State levels, such as in regional structure policy, and thus exposed to a severe political compulsion to negotiate between governments formed by rival political parties. Because of its complicated internal allocation of powers, the Federal Republic has been described, as a "semi-sovereign state"[7] – an often laborious political mechanism, which even in the post-war period brought forth efficient compromise techniques and decision-making patterns. Whether it would prove a match for the challenges of the unification process was one of the questions which was being met with increasing scepticism.[8]

In the run-up to German unification, during the negotiations on the Treaty of Unification, the Electricity Contracts, the *Treuhandgesetz* or THG (the East German Act setting up the THA), and the legislation on municipalities' property, the German federal negotiating system was temporarily switched off, one reason being that the States themselves kept out of things.[9] It was not

---

5 These examples all involve secondments, after which the persons involved were to return to their original appointments. The THA is composed as follows, in terms of the origins of their operative staff (directors, branch managers, departmental heads, and executives): out of 155 persons questioned, 48 % said they came from private-sector companies in the west, 9 % from eastern German companies, 14 % from the public sector in western Germany and 17 % from the eastern, 3 % from the world of western German industrial associations and 2 % from eastern German social organisations. These figures are based on a partial evaluation of an extensive written survey carried out within the THA (evaluation as of 20th May 1993).

6 See: Scharpf, *Versuch über Demokratie im verhandelnden Staat*, page 35.

7 Katzenstein, *Politics and Policy in West Germany*, pages 371 et seq.

8 H. Schmidt, *Handeln für Deutschland*, pages 105 et seq.; Hankel, *Die sieben Todsünden der Vereinigung*, page 179 et seq.; Lehmbruch, *Die deutsche Vereinigung*, page 592 et seq.; M. Schmidt, *Die politische Verarbeitung*, page 448.

9 Lehmbruch, *Die deutsche Vereinigung*, page 586 et seq.

until the new eastern German States entered the scene and their need for resources became urgent that the question arose as to the shape which the federal structure in the united Germany should take in future. This question revolved around both the political and fiscal position of the Federal authorities towards the States, of which there were now 16, and the horizontal *Finanzausgleich* (the virement, by which economically stronger states subsidise weaker ones) as it would operate between the western and the eastern German States. The THA, which reports directly to the Federal government, played a crucial role here because it took on responsibilities which should actually have been within the realm of authority of the eastern German States. At that point in time, this applied primarily to the consequences for structural policy of the THA's works. The situation in 1990 initially, if one pursued the centralist intentions of the THG and then thought about the fiscal problems of the new eastern German States, gave rise to fears of a big shift in the direction of centralisation in the relationship between the Federal and the State levels.[10]

The first test case for the relationship between the Federal and State governments in the unification process came with the quarrels about the rights and co-ordination ways of the eastern German States in their dealings with the THA. Even before taking office in October 1990, the Minister-President of Saxony, Kurt Biedenkopf, had demanded that the tasks of privatisation and restructuring of THA companies should be transferred to the State level. The President of the THA at that time, Rohwedder, and other members of its Executive Board, acting in consort with the Federal government, were able to fend off attempts at liquidating the THA into State-THA's. Even the THA sub-committee of the *Bundestag* acknowledged demonstratively only two months after German unification that the management bodies of the THA had "done outstanding work in the organisational and personnel areas"; any decentralisation that went beyond strengthening the staff in the various branches would not be appropriate.[11]

The rejection of the States' demands had to be purchased at the price of concrete concessions and institutional integration. The THA already had its own directorate for "Federal Relations" in the autumn of 1990, which from 15th October onwards was managed by a ministerial official with experience in financial and foreign business from Bavaria, Dr Wolfgang Vehse. Criticism from eastern Germany was countered mainly with pragmatic arguments and a readiness to negotiate. Greater difficulties arose from dealings with the western German States which had perceived in the THA concept a centralist line of attack hostile to the free market.[12] Whilst the eastern German States went straight to the THA with their demands, the western German States operated through the Conference of Ministers for Economic Affairs and submissions to the Federal government, as well as via individual consultants who had been posted to eastern Germany.[13] Thus the Bavarian Minister for Economic Affairs and Chairman of the Conference of Ministers for Economic Affairs, Dr August Lang, objected strongly to the surreptitious trans-

10 Seibel, *Necessary Illusions*, page 194; M. Schmidt, *Die politische Verarbeitung*, page 453.

11 Declaration by the THA sub-committee of the Budget Committee of the German Bundestag of 12th November 1990 in Berlin; for the position taken up by Christian Neuling (CDU), the Committee Chairman, and his deputy Helmut Esters (SPD), see: *Süddeutsche Zeitung*, 13th November 1990, page 25.

12 A-interview with Dr Wolfgang Vehse on 5th August 1992.

13 op. cit.

fer of regional and structural responsibilities to a Federal institution. One line of attack adopted by the THA aimed to make the consequences clear which the State governments' budgets would suffer if they took on the THA's responsibilities. Another aim was to win over the eastern German States for co-operation in regional, structural, and labour market political questions without the THA having to give up the last word in decisions, but also "without absolving politicians from their political responsibilities".[14]

The President of the THA, Detlev Rohwedder, on the day before the first joint conference of the Minister-Presidents of the eastern German States on 1st December 1990 in Potsdam, had promised regular and comprehensive information, and a willingness to make concessions in controversial questions, to the host, Manfred Stolpe of Brandenburg.[15] Only a few weeks later, on 19th December 1990, Rohwedder explained the THA's course to the Conference of Ministers for Economic Affairs and Senators of the western and eastern German States in Berlin. On this occasion, remaining regional and structural political conflicts of authority were cleared up to such an extent that Rohwedder was able to announce that the THA had won "new allies".[16] Even in advance of this, the THA Executive Board had called on the Federal government to support its work with additional measures to promote trade and industry in eastern Germany. The later political network was already beginning to become apparent in which the THA would be taking up an intermediary role between the Federal and State levels. This arrangement generally benefited its autonomy. It operated in those areas where important decisions were not already preempted politically with a changing choice of allies.

Rohwedder, the President of the THA who was later to be assassinated, no doubt foresaw this political development when he indicated to the States that he was prepared to make concessions and at the same time demanded autonomous room to manoeuvre in negotiations with the Federal government. This is also the context of the plan to set up a permanent presence in Bonn. The THA Bonn office was set up in April 1991 to plead for the THA's interests in the parliamentary area. It is thus fully comparable with the offices of the various associations and major companies based in Bonn. In its first two years it dealt with some 2,000 enquiries, most of them from Bundestag delegates, and organised more than 30 information events.[17] Except for the Tennessee Valley Authority's Congress Office in Washington, the THA Bonn Office is probably the only lobby organisation of a federal administrative agency at the seat of parliament and government.

1. States co-ordination institutions

The position of the States towards the THA is made particularly clear in the "Basic principles for co-operation between the Federal government, the eastern German States, and the THA for the economic boom in the east" of 14th March 1991,[18] which says: "The complete change in the system in eastern Germany requires unusual measures in a concerted collaboration between the

14 op. cit.; B-interview with Dr Wolfgang Vehse on 26th February 1993.

15 *Handelsblatt*, 17th/18th November 1990, page 20; *Süddeutsche Zeitung*, 3rd December 1990, page 5.

16 *Süddeutsche Zeitung*, 20th December 1990, page 27.

17 THA Bonn Office, *Zwei Jahre Büro Bonn der Treuhandanstalt,* manuscript of 28th April 1993.

18 *Treuhandanstalt Informationen* no. 1 (May 1991), page 11; *Zeitschrift für Wirtschaftsrecht* 6/1991, page 13; see also: R. Schmitdt, *Aufgaben und Struktur,* pages 31 et seq.

Federal government, the eastern German States, and the THA." The role of the THA is also prescribed as a "service supplier" to the States in the construction of socially acceptable regional economic structures, and it undertakes to provide the States with all important information in the event of closures and redundancies: a schedule of all planned measures (demolition, recycling, landscape restoration and restructuring), lists of redundant employees broken down by age and qualifications etc., list of possible contributions from the THA for job creation schemes, and information on land and property being supplied to the State departments concerned in each case. In addition, the Minister-Presidents themselves occupied the seats on the Administrative Board provided for the States in the Treaty of Unification (Article 25 section 2) and were thus informed anyway about organisational development, the overall concept, and any large or difficult decisions.

The "Basic principles for the economic boom in the east" quotes other organisational interfaces to the eastern German States in addition to the Administrative Board: THA Economic Cabinets (*Treuhand-Wirtschaftskabinette*), Advisory Boards for the branches, and direct contacts for government and administrative departments with the corporate divisions responsible for privatisation. The *THA Economic Cabinets* were constituted on the basis of the Section 8 of the "Principles" in April 1991 at the State governments of all the eastern German States and included – taking as an example the 6th session of the THA Economic Cabinet for Saxony in Dresden on 30th May 1991 – the THA State department for Saxony, representatives of the THA corporate divisions affected by items on the agenda, the THA branches in Saxony (Chemnitz, Leipzig, and Dresden) and, for the State, a number of departments from the Ministries for Economic Affairs, of Finance, and of Agriculture, the manager of the Office for the Regulation of Unsettled Property Questions, the Deputy Chairman of the Economic Committee of the *Landtag* (State parliament), and representatives of the parliamentary parties in the *Landtag*. The composition varied according to the State and the items on the agenda; Saxony was mostly represented by Secretaries of State, Brandenburg often by its Minister-President and the various departmental Ministers.

Closely related to the Economic Cabinets were the monthly meetings (*Monatsgespräche*) between the Ministers for economic affairs of the States and representatives of the THA corporate divisions, as well as industry meetings and restructuring meetings. Some times they met immediately after the Economic Cabinets, or else separately and with a different composition. The industry meetings mostly followed a uniform pattern: 1. information on companies, initial and latest situation, assessment by the Management Committee of the THA (*Leitungsausschuß*); 2. status of privatisation, interested parties; 3. investment projects; 4. possibilities for stimulation schemes; 5. other agreed action.[19] Industry meetings also included discussions with parliamentary delegates and *Landtag* committees from the eastern German States. By giving information in advance to the members of parliaments the State departments of the THA tried to keep the number of parliamentary enquiries as small as possible to which the State governments requested answers from them.[20] The State governments were regularly the first to be informed of

19 See: Report by Department P L3 on *Schwerpunktaufgaben der Länderabteilung Sachsen-Anhalt* dated 27th January 1992.

20 On the treatment of enquiries: P L3, *Benennung von Einzelfällen und Schwerpunktthemen im ersten Halbjahr 1992,* dated 14th August 1992.

the liquidation of companies and mass redundancies as part of a confidential "early warning system" which was likewise the product of the outline agreement made in the spring of 1991.

In its co-operation with the State governments, the promotion of THA companies by the States came increasingly to the fore. They mainly attempted to use funds from the "GA" (*Gemeinschaftsaufgabe*) regional economic promotion scheme and various other special schemes to counter the number of jobs being lost. Agreements with individual States indicate that the THA had a completely positive attitude to this way of taking some of the burden off it. For instance, in the Breuel-Schommer agreement of 23rd April 1992 the Saxony government undertook "to support regionally important companies which it will define with all the facilities at its disposal, particularly GA funds and guarantees ... to promote the necessary public infrastructure measures, and to provide it with the appropriate instruments of labour market policy."[21] In return, the THA wanted the companies promoted by the State to be given "the necessary room for manoeuvre in entrepreneurial and financial terms", and this should even take place "if the agreed concept would require a modernisation process for several years".[22] Co-operation with the States gave birth to various schemes for defining and jointly promoting regionally important companies, the best known of which was Saxony's ATLAS project, under which the industry meetings were held with Saxony from May 1992 onwards. The ATLAS list contained about 200 "selected THA companies in the State registered for restructuring" (which can be abbreviated to ATLAS in German).

2. The THA as a "second eastern German government"?

Ex-Chancellor Helmut Schmidt called the THA a "very powerful second government for all six eastern German State governments".[23] This underlines its significance for these States, but at the same time implies that it was an institution that mainly followed *political* calculations and *managed* the process of economic conversion in close co-ordination with the Federal government. This statement very well represents the assessment made in academic, journalistic, and political circles of the THA's position in the transformation process.[24] However, the extent to which its work, particularly when divided down into departments, can be categorised under the headings of economics, politics, state administration, or intermediary institutions is an open question. It was at any rate conceived in the THG of 17th June 1990 (§§ 7 to 10) as a conglomeration of AG-type companies under the supervision of an Administration Board, and was even referred to occasionally as the "world's biggest company".[25] The question is also open as

21 Named after the President of the THA, Birgit Breuel, and the Minister for Economic Affairs of Saxony Kajo Schommer, quoted in the letter from the THA President to the Minister-President of Saxony, Kurt Biedenkopf, on 27th April 1992 on "Co-operation between the THA and the Free State of Saxony".

22 op. cit.

23 H. Schmidt, *Handeln für Deutschland,* pages 110 and 32.

24 Schuppert, *Die Treuhandanstalt,* page 190; Lehmbruch, *Die deutsche Vereinigung*, page 597; Marissal, *Der politische Handlungsrahmen der Treuhandanstalt.*

25 This term was used by the Federal Minister for Economic Affairs of the day, Jürgen Möllemann, who would have preferred to see the THA subordinated to his ministry than to the Federal Ministry of Finance.

to how much autonomy of action it was given in its specific fields of responsibility towards the Federal government, the State governments, the European Commission, and the major interest-group associations.

Legally the THA was not a company and for all practical purposes it was not a state authority.[26] Its responsibilities and the practical aspects of its work place it much more at the interface between state and economy.[27] It operated as an "agent" of the state for the development of the private sector of the economy. To this extent it is reminiscent, as is its legal form, of the *Kreditanstalt für Wiederaufbau* (Credit Institution for Reconstruction) set up to administer funds under the Marshall Plan after the Second World War. Both represent a special Federal asset and are controlled by an Administrative Board made up preponderantly of representatives of the economic sector. One major difference lies in the fact that the THA itself is the owner of the firms and finances them until they are privatised or closed down. The final point of difference is the extent of the financial and organisational commitment and the physical complexity or, in a word, the sheer *size* of the THA's task, the extraordinary economically caused *pressure* on it to solve its problems and a politically mediated coercion to *succeed*, as well as, resulting from that, its central political and social *significance*.

The THA was first conceived as a government authority, and its first 150 employees came from East German ministries. Later, when the THG was passed on 17th June 1990, its business character came to the fore, but at this stage no-one could have foreseen the political role into which this "enterprise" was to grow. The extent of its political "involvement" can be seen from the enormous responsibility which the THA bears for the development of employment and for the social safety-net underneath the structural change in eastern Germany. This responsibility accrued to the THA partly from factual necessity, partly for political reasons; but the THG made no provision for this task. The course was definitively set in June 1991, when it started to participate in the promotion of employment. This brought the THA's scope of duties a step nearer that of the Federal Labour Institute, likewise an institute under public law and the supervision of a Federal Minister (of Labour), but self-administered by a board of labour, state, and employers' representatives. The other organisation with which the THA is sometimes compared, the *Kreditanstalt für Wiederaufbau* (or *KfW*), has on the other hand always been a capital market institution depending on the German major banks but operating independently of politics. The THA maintains close links with both bodies, mainly on account of their joint financing or organisation of projects connected with employment policy or the use of *KfW* funds for THA companies.

---

26 Its legal status as an institute under public law reporting directly to the Federal government hardly permits any conclusions to be drawn as to its actual position in the political system of the Federal Republic of Germany.

27 Schuppert places it, for reasons of legal theory, as an "organisation in the overlap area between two spheres of law" where its task under public law coincides with its practical work under civil law: Schuppert, *Die Treuhandanstalt,* page 186.

Table 1:
External influences on the THA's work (in %)

Compared with public administration:

	less	same	greater	
1991	46.2	25.2	28.6	(N=119)
1992	21.4	31.3	47.3	(N=131)

Compared with private companies:

	less	same	greater	
1991	42.0	22.3	35.7	(N=143)
1992	18.5	15.3	66.2	(N=157)

Note: Partial evaluation of a survey conducted on THA officials (as of 22nd July 1993). The question asked was: "To what extent would you say, looking back, and comparing the THA with other organisations, that the following statements are correct: "External factors limit the flexibility with which the THA does its work". The five possible responses were: much less often, less often, about the same, more often, far more often. For the sake of simplification the two upper and the two lower categories have been added together. The difference in the total number of replies is due to the fact that comparative statements called for differing experience in respondents' past experience in public administration or private companies, and some respondents, who did not join the THA until 1992, were unable to answer the question in respect of 1991.

It is also possible to measure the degree of the THA's autonomy by comparing it with the German *Bundesbank*, which is also a legally independent institution under public law reporting directly to the Federal government. Under Article 88 of the German Constitution it likewise bears responsibility for an extremely important aspect of economic policy. In its highest decision-making body, the Central Bank Council, the States have the opportunity to exert influence just as they do in the THA's Administration Board. The form, variety, and breadth of impact of the THA's work give rise to the impression that, like the *Bundesbank*, it represents a third level in the federal system and for a limited period of time is bearing responsibilities which are, like that for monetary policy, not entrusted to the Federal or the State government. Admittedly, the Bundesbank is granted autonomy under its establishing legislation, the *Bundesbankgesetz*, whilst the THA has increasingly had to share its decision-making authority with other sources of political decisions. In response to a question on the external restrictions on the THA's work, a survey carried out on THA officials showed that 58.8 % considered these were increasing, 31.5 % that they were remaining unchanged, and 9.7 % that they were declining.[28] Questions were also asked concerning external restrictions on day-to-day work in comparison with public administration and with private companies in 1991 and 1992 (see Table 1).

It can be seen from Table 1 that the THA has lost some of its autonomous room for manoeuvre to an extent which most of its employees notice. This came about in connection with the increasing diversity of the work, the growing need to co-ordinate with the States, and tougher

28 These data are based on the partial evaluation of a questionnaire sent to all directors, branch managers, and departmental heads, and a random sample of executives (evaluation date 18th June 1993, n = 165). The question referred to outside influence in 1992 compared with 1991.

controls imposed by Cartel Office, Court of Audit, *Bundestag*, and Federal ministries. In 1993 it was estimated that 1,000 man-days were required in the "Winding-Up" Directorate alone (the one responsible for closures) to answer enquiries from ministries, the Court of Audit, the *Bundestag*, and the various State parliaments.[29]

3. Management Committee, "Ludewig group", Bundestag

Ignoring the requirement for various decisions on finances and conceptions to be submitted for approval, and informal day-to-day discussions with Bonn ministries, particularly the Ministry of Finance, there are two institutions of particular interest here: the THA Management Committee and the so-called "Ludewig group", named after Johannes Ludewig, the *Ministerialdirektor* (head of a ministerial department) in the Chancellery appointed by the Federal Chancellor to handle questions concerning the reconstruction of eastern Germany.

The Management Committee came into being as a result of the situation surrounding monetary reform (the replacement of the East-Mark by western Deutschmarks), when the first groups of auditors were dispatched by the Federal Ministry of Finance to Berlin to supervise the application of funds.[30] When monetary union started on 1st July 1990, 8,000 companies were allowed to register their requirements with the THA for working capital in Deutschmarks, broken down into wages, social insurance contributions, order-processing, investments, etc. As the THA was not at that point directly subordinate to the Federal government, but was financed by it, the point at issue was to examine these applications more under business accounting than under legal criteria. Auditors and management consultants were therefore appointed who were later, after German unification, to form the THA Management Committee under Horst Plaschna. It was on the basis of their assessments that the Federal government decided to grant only 41 % of the working capital applied for – an early piece of discouragement which many managing directors of East German companies blamed on the THA.[31] The Management Committee – an independent consultative body of the Federal Ministry of Finance working within the THA but not integrated into it – from then on checked all corporate strategies and plans submitted to the Central Office and issued recommendations as to how they should be treated.

One high-ranking political co-ordination body came into being with the formation of the "Ludewig group", which met for the first time on 13th May 1991 and then at intervals of several weeks, or sometimes more often, mainly at the Berlin office of the Federal Chancellery. Its task was to attend and probably to supervise mutually the implementation of decisions concerning the reconstruction of the East which had been taken in the first months of 1991. From the beginning of 1992 onwards, these meetings also served for the preparation of meetings between the Federal Chancellor and the Minister-Presidents of the eastern German States plus the Governing Mayor of Berlin.

29 Ludwig Tränkner, "Winding-Up" Director in the THA, in *Süddeutsche Zeitung*, 22nd July 1993, page 17.
30 A-interview with Detlef Scheunert on 6th October 1992.
31 op. cit.

Those taking part in the "Ludewig group" meetings were the THA General Manager, the heads of the State Chancelleries of the eastern German States, and the Federal Chancellery represented by *Ministerialdirektor* Johannes Ludewig and the head of the Berlin Office of the Federal Chancellery. The main items on the agenda were the financial requirement of the eastern German States, topical economic questions, initiatives relating to the reconstruction of the East, administrative aids, trade with East European countries and Hermes export credit insurance (Hermes is the government-owned export loan and credit insurance company), job creation projects, and the urgent questions of the day such as the transfer of Federal land and property to the States or the activities of the criminal investigation authorities in the THA.

In comparison with other co-ordinating bodies with participation of the THA, the Ludewig group was characterised by its multilateral composition, the highly binding nature of its utterances, and the regularity and frequency with which it made personal meetings possible. It linked all the political nerve-centres on one working level below that of the heads of governments and of the presidium of the THA. Unlike the Bonn "Chancellor's Round for Reconstruction in the East", which met less often and more informally, this group brought political executives together into relatively small meetings and without any interference from social interest groups. Unlike bilateral States relationships, these mainly covered general, multi-State questions and politically urgent questions relating to the transformation of the economic system. In those cases where the meetings had to be co-ordinated with the conferences of the Federal Chancellor and the Minister-Presidents of the eastern German States, the definitive criteria for granting guarantees under "Hermes" export credit insurance and the Property Law Amendment Act were prepared. This gave the THA the opportunity of participating in the design of legislation, as it also had in its direct contacts with the Bundestag and individual Federal ministries.[32]

Parliament supervision of the THA was initially vested in a sub-committee of the *Bundestag* Budget Committee. In comparison with Federal and State governments, this was of only minor significance in monitoring and controlling the THA. The reason for this is, firstly, that the usual control mechanisms and the approval reservations of parliamentary budget law are not applicable to the THA as a legally independent institute under public law.[33] Another was that during the first six months after unification the majority of the committee members tended to take an affirmative attitude, which could be connected with the fact that Bundestag delegates of the "Alliance 90/The Greens" group started at a very early stage to issue statements, submit questions, and propose motions exerting massive criticism, and in June 1991 even tried to introduce a draft Bill to amend the THG. The Committee did not want to give any backing to their demands for organisational reform, more parliamentary control, cancellation of historic debts, and restructuring of THA companies, all the more so since, in view of its weak legal position, it was dependent on achieving mutual agreement with the THA.

The THA Credit Act, passed on 3rd July 1992, limited the borrowing powers of the THA to DM 30 billion in each financial year and required the approval of the Budget Committee if they

---

32 It was the THA which gave the initial impetus, for instance, on individual regulations later contained in the Property Assignment Act and the Investment Priority Act: B-interview with Martin Keil on 23rd February 1993; on the amendment to the Labour Promotion Act: B-interviews with Werner Bayreuther on 24th February 1993 and Peter Gemählich on 5th April 1993; on the THA Credit Act: B-interview with Dr Paul Hadrys on 6th April 1993.

33 Spoerr, *Treuhandanstalt und Treuhandunternehmen*, page 15.

were fully utilised in 1993 and 1994. Although parliamentary control over new borrowing did not give it any preventive influence, the THA then broadened the information it supplied to the Committee, to the point of setting up frequent meetings in Berlin or at industrial centres in eastern Germany. Then, in February 1993, a separate Bundestag THA Committee was formed which now covered the whole spectrum of the THA's work. The THA kept it regularly informed on the operational business, contract supervision, restructuring concepts, new privatisation initiatives, and the trends in its expenditure. On 16th June 1993 the THA informed the THA Committee that it intended to exceed the credit limit laid down for it and borrow a further DM 8 billion on the capital market, for which it required the approval of the Budget Committee via the Federal Ministry of Finance. The amount had already been negotiated and agreed between the Federal and State governments in connection with the Federal Consolidation Programme, the solidarity pact for reconstruction in the east, and was mainly intended to safeguard and renew industrial core areas. The *Bundestag* Budget Committee then only gave its approval for DM 7 billion, whereupon the THA announced that it was restricting its participation in "employment companies" (*Beschäftigungsgesellschaften*, created to absorb and retrain redundant workers) in the field of the metal-working and electrical industries. The background to this announcement was connected with wage bargaining politics; it was meant to compel IG Metall, the metal-workers' trade union, to apply a hardship clause agreed in a collective wage agreement to THA companies.[34] The hardship clause had provided wage cuts, but the union had previously refused to agree to the reduction in wage rates in ailing THA companies because these companies were anyway being kept alive with public funds. In this situation, the Committee's decisions could be taken as a signal that THA companies and trade unions could not prevent the use of the hardship clause at the taxpayer's expense without themselves having to bear the consequences – plants closures and unemployment. This now brings us to wage and employment policy; for the THA, too, this became a major problem area of the transformation process in 1993.

III. Interest associations and administrative bodies in the THA complex

The THA's privatisation work is something like a high-wire act; it has to balance as far as possible investment and employment targets, the acceptance of historic debts, participation in the disposal of historic environmental pollution, and the proceeds of privatisation in the right relationship with one another so as to take into account all the different interests of the Federal and State departments, employers' associations, and trade unions. But this is impossible to meet ideally. Whilst the Federal and the State governments only occasionally appear as representatives of special interests, as amongst other things they are under pressure to reconcile opposing interests because of election tactics, questions relating to the preservation of jobs and the encouragement of investment run into clear, sometimes vital, but conflicting interests with trade unions and employers' associations. For the representatives of the employers' side, who form the majority on the THA Administrative Board (Table 2), it is also of some significance to see what kind of investment aids the THA is giving to their potential competitors in eastern Germany and what kind of industrial structure is being created by the THA's work. Thus, for instance, the President

---

34 *Frankfurter Allgemeine Zeitung*, 3rd July 1993, page 12.

of the German engineering industry association VDMA, Berthold Leibinger, keeps a critical eye open at Administrative Board meetings on plans which favour eastern German engineering companies which used to be part of the mammoth state concerns.

Table 2:
Distribution of seats on the THA Administrative Board

Employers	8
States	6
Trade unions	4
Federal government	2

Source: Treuhandanstalt, Organisationshandbuch, serial no. 1.1.1.1, as of May 1993.

Representatives of the employers' side were at times the resolutest opponents on the Administrative Board of any active entrepreneurial policy of the THA. They criticised central marketing activities for THA companies (e. g. the THA "Made in Germany" Leipzig Fair) and voiced the fear that state subsidies to the East could endanger companies in the West, particularly in view of the precarious economic situation of the engineering industry at that time.[35] On the other side, the States and the trade unions sometimes supported highly risky modernisation strategies mainly for regional and social reasons.

Major privatisation plans had to be approved by the Administrative Board,[36] as must specific Executive Board decisions on organisation, privatisation guidelines, financing activities, the annual business plan, etc. Most of its decisions were taken unanimously following detailed discussions in advance of the meetings, but subject to the further consent of the Minister of Finance and the European Commission.[37] The Administrative Board was originally not meant to serve the purpose of representing interest groups. The THG (§ 4) mentions neither employers' associations representatives nor any participation by the States, and makes the only criterion of appointment expertise in economics. It was not until the Treaty of Unification (Article 25 section 2) that the representation of the States was formalised by creating additional seats. Representation of the trade unions is attributable solely to the appointment practice of the Federal Government.

Initially, the supervisory board forming the upper tier of directors of an *Aktiengesellschaft* (roughly, a joint-stock company) served as the model for the THA Administrative Board. Its function in representing the THA to the outside world did not arise until later, and was less fully formalised. This function is a sign of the politicisation of the THA, and in real-life practice reflects "a mixture of elements such as is customary on the supervisory boards of public broadcasting or public-owned industrial companies".[38] During the process of providing the States, social groups, and local authorities with greater accessibility to the THA, Advisory Boards of

35 B-interview with Dieter Schulte (union representative on the THA Administrative Board) on 27th January 1993.

36 According to the THA Rules of Procedure (§ 16), as of January 1993, consent has to be obtained (from the Administrative Board) if one of the following criteria is met: balance-sheet total over DM 150 million, turnover more than DM 150 million, or more than 1,500 employees.

37 B-interview with Dieter Schulte on 27th January 1993, see footnote 35.

38 Spoerr, *Treuhandanstalt und Treuhandunternehmen,* page 9.

the branches were also formed in March 1991 on the orders of the THA Central Office.[39] They served the purpose of "ensuring harmonisation between the political, business, and social forces in their regions".[40]

Table 3:
Advisory Boards of the branches: Distribution of seats in the 15 branch Advisory Boards (Status in March 1991, Berlin branch in June 1991)

	Number	%
Employers' associations, professional Chambers, etc.	45	33
Rural counties, municipalities	28	20
Trade unions	18	13
State governments	14	10
Churches	14	10
Agricultural interest groups	9	7
Citizens' movements	9	7
Total	137	100

Source: Appendix to report on "Kooperation zwischen Ländern, Bund und THA" dated 28th November 1991, prepared by the THA Bonn Office. Data on Berlin: minutes of the constituting meeting of the THA Berlin Branch Advisory Board on 11th June 1991.

The composition of the Advisory Boards varied considerably from one branch to another. The employers' associations were particularly strongly represented in Chemnitz, Cottbus, Dresden, Berlin, and Halle, the trade unions in Frankfurt/Oder, Leipzig, and Rostock, the churches in Erfurt and Frankfurt/Oder, the municipalities in Gera, and the citizens' movements in Neubrandenburg (see Table 3).

The THA served not only as a focal organisation for the relationships between the Federal and the State levels in the unification process. Through its participation also the expression of associations' interests developed. The initial exclusion of the neo-corporatist systems of consultation and negotiation which had been so influential in the post-war period had the approval of employers' associations and trade unions. Although some managers had voiced the view at the first Chancellor's Meeting on all-German policy, in February 1990, that in relation to the planned currency union "East Germany would never be able to stick such an operation out",[41] the leading role of politics preceding business "was approved by all participants at the Chancellor's Meeting". At later Chancellor's Meetings it was mainly the THA and leading men in politics, business, and trade unions that took part. In addition to these meetings, the system of integrating national federations of employers' associations and trade unions was not re-activated until June 1991, and this was during the course of negotiations over the institutional structure and the role of the THA in eastern German employment policy.

39 Treuhandanstalt, *Organisationshandbuch*, serial no. 2.9.1, organisational instruction no. 8, dated 14th November 1990, as of October 1991.

40 op. cit., page 2.

41 *Handelsblatt*, 23rd February 1990.

1. Labour market and industrial relations

In the "Basic principles for the economic boom in the east", the establishment and financing of companies to organise and carry out job creation schemes (*ABM-Trägergesellschaften*) was left exclusively to the States and to the Federal Institute of Labour.[43] This plan was problematic from the start, simply because such companies could only be accommodated on the business premises of THA companies, made demands on the companies for assistance in establishment, and in some cases carried out renovation and restructuring work for these companies, and because anyway the THA could set off these activities at any time with its redundancy plans. By the middle of 1991, the political conflict between the Federal government, the THA, the State governments, the trade unions, and the employers' associations over the employment companies had reached such a pitch that the THA approved a compromise agreed upon in basic outline on 1st July 1991 at the offices of the Federal association of employers' associations in Cologne between itself and the both sides of industry.[44] This compromise then led to a formal outline agreement between the trade unions, the employers' associations, and the THA which was signed on 17th July 1991 and was to form the basis in particular of the "Companies for promoting work, employment, and structural development" (*Gesellschaften zur Arbeitsförderung, Beschäftigung und Strukturentwicklung*, known by their German abbreviation as ABS companies).

The THA had made its participation on job securing measures dependent from the start on its privatisation work not being thereby jeopardised. It therefore insisted, together with the employers' associations, on the termination of employment in the THA companies and the establishment of "a new kind of contractual basis" for the employees of employment companies.[45] This lightened the THA's burden as an employer. Employment companies also made it easier to release workers. The THA declared itself willing to pay for managing directors, via the companies in which it held equity, for the ABS companies for up to six months (or a whole year in exceptional cases) and to provide consultancy and management assistance. The same applied to initial assistance with administrative work such as wages and salary administration, social-security insurance, etc. Finally, the THA advanced money to cover the cost of numerous ABS companies, with the result that it has sums running into millions outstanding from the States, which are in turn demanding a heavier financial involvement from the Federal government or the Federal Institute of Labour.

A completely new view of the problem resulted from the insertion of § 249h into the *Arbeitsförderungsgesetz* or AFG, the Labour Promotion Act. This new regulation had been urged by the THA; for five years it facilitated the payment of grants towards wage costs by the Federal Institute of Labour to companies in eastern Germany designed to serve such purposes as improving the environment, the social services, or youth welfare. On this basis, and in an agreement with IG Chemie, the trade union for the chemical industry, the THA undertook to endow a retraining scheme called "Qualification programme for the chemical industry" (*Qualifizierungswerk Chemie*)

---

42 op. cit.

43 *Grundsätze für den Aufschwung Ost* in: *Treuhandanstalt Informationen* No. 1 (May 1991), page 11, section 5.

44 Declaration of 1st July 1991 following the "Discussion between the social-contract parties and the Treuhandanstalt on 1st July 1991 in Cologne".

45 op. cit.: Outline agreement between the trade union for the chemicals, paper, and ceramics industries and the THA of 29th March 1993.

with DM 75 million and to administer it "in close collaboration with IG Chemie". This programme works as follows: the THA first provides ear-marked funds with which the employment companies can buy the necessary equipment. Then, the compensation (social) plans (*Sozialpläne*, particularly redundancy payments) of those THA companies which come under the organisational area of IG Chemie must provide that for employees allocated under § 249h of the Labour Promotion Act to a reconstruction company promoted by the labour administration should be paid compensation in the form of wages. Together with grants from the Federal Institute of Labour, each allocated worker thus attains a gross income which has to be less than that paid under a collective wage agreement by a company not benefiting from § 249h of the Act.

These allocated workers come under a collective wage agreement concluded by the IG Chemie and an employers' association founded by the THA. Under the provisions of the Labour Promotion Act, the agreed wages are 90 % of the corresponding wage paid under the collective agreement for the chemical industry. The worker is then retrained during part of his working hours on the basis of the retraining (or continued training) components included in the company plans to carry out environmental restructuring work, such as is urgently needed in the "chemical triangle" around Halle, Leipzig, and Bitterfeld for the dismantling of elderly factories and will be for a long time to come. These measures improve the chemical companies' hopes of being privatised because they reduce the number of jobs in them and release the THA from the problems of historic environmental pollution.

The THA has signed a similar outline agreement with the trade union for mining and energy, under which miners from the potash and brown coal areas shall be taken on by restructuring companies, retrained as landscape gardeners, and set to work on large-scale clean-up projects. The two schemes together provide up to 40,000 jobs, which shows the THA's willingness to support job creation schemes if they are mainly of an investment character, make the privatisation of its companies easier, and do not hamper the workers from returning later to normal employment. In total, the THA provided DM 1.2 billion for measures under § 249h of the AFG in the second half of 1993 alone.

Policy on employers' associations and collective agreements is a further field in which the involvement of the THA in economic and social matters becomes very clear. Right from the start, the THA found it difficult to prevent the managers in charge of the THA companies from making concessions to their workers. Only a few months after unification it discovered that works dismissal-protection agreements and compensation plans were being made with the aid of western German consultants with compensation payments which sometimes verged on the breathtaking. In one instance, the full salary was to be paid until the worker reached retirement age, in another compensation was to be paid to every dismissed worker of DM 156,000 - always in the blissful expectation that THA Central Office would foot the bill.[46] A uniform regulation for reconciling interests in cases of dismissal was only reached with the first outline agreement between the THA, the German Federation of Trade Unions (*DGB*), and the German Trade Union of Employees (*DAG*) of 13th April 1991. However, this had only become possible after the Federal Ministry of Finance had agreed to finance redundancy compensation plans to the tune of DM 10 billion.

---

46 *Frankfurter Allgemeine Zeitung*, 29th January 1991; B-interviews with Hermann Wagner on 22nd March 1993 and Werner Bayreuther on 24th February 1993; on the practical course taken to reconcile interests over redundancies see: article by Hanau in this volume.

THA guidelines on works wage agreements and on THA companies becoming members of employers' associations aimed, given the situation at the time, at cutting back on the wild overgrowth of works agreements. The guidelines state: "The THA has an interest in its companies being organised into employers' associations which are able, together with the trade unions, to produce an effective social consensus ... If the THA takes a cautious stance towards factory wage or supplementary settlements, and is above all restrictive in this regard, this is primarily because of its existing preference for industry-wide collective wage agreements".[47]

Membership of employers' associations was almost compulsory for THA companies, all the more since in some of them, e. g. in the fields of steel or ship-building, the works councils were able to secure this membership contractually on the urgings of the metal-workers' or the chemical workers' unions. THA companies have promoted the growth of employers' associations in eastern Germany to the extent that they, unlike some privatised companies, pay their membership fees punctually and made no claim to any right of involvement in the association's affairs. The THA, working in consort with the unions, also strove to ensure that foreign investors maintained the employers' association membership of private companies and avoided making separate factory wage settlements with their own employees.[48]

As 1992 gave way to 1993, the THA instructed its companies to include a 9 % increase in the collective wage agreement for 1993. The graduated wage agreement for the metal-working industry, which together with the chemical and energy industries represented the great majority of workers in THA companies, had meanwhile provided for wage increases of 26 % in that year. The metal-workers' union therefore demanded, in a letter to the Minister of Finance, that he instruct the Executive Board of the THA to take a neutral position proper to a Federal institution in questions of wage policy.[49] The employers' association for the metal-working industry had already, in November 1992, brought the offer of a 9 % wage increase into discussion to compensate for inflation by invoking the audit clause in the step-by-step agreement. It was not only the THA which was focusing its attention on this figure; both sides of the chemical and of the construction industries later agreed on wage increases at this level. In the metal-working industry, however, a two-week strike broke out which mainly affected THA companies. Some wanted, even before that, to comply with the wage agreement which their employers' association had already terminated. They were thereupon virtually ordered by THA Central Office to follow the instructions of the employers' association with a reference to the "Guideline on works agreements and factory wage settlements".[50]

A further conflict between the THA and the metal-workers' union arose over the application of the hardship clause agreed in the collective agreement to permit individual firms to adjust the collective wage-rate downwards. In this case also THA Central Office instructed the managements of its companies to "refrain from doing anything which could prevent the application of the hardship clause",[51] and instead of this to exploit every possibility provided by the procedure agreed with the metal-working employers' association for reducing collective wage rates; the

---

47 Treuhandanstalt, *Richtlinie für Betriebsvereinbarungen und Haustarifverträge vom 1. September 1992*, page 3.

48 B-interview with Dieter Schulte on 27th January 1993 (see footnote 35).

49 op. cit.

50 Treuhandanstalt, *Richtlinie für Betriebsvereinbarungen und Haustarifverträge vom 1. September 1992.*

51 *Süddeutsche Zeitung*, 28th May 1993, page 23.

union rejected this course of action with the argument that wage payments were covered, rightly, by public funds because no-one should ask the poorly paid eastern German workers to meet the entirety of the cost of preserving their industrial locations.[52]

However, the conflict over collective wage agreements in the metal-working industry cannot disguise the fact that the unions have a central position with their very close consultative relationships with some of the State governments, particularly in Saxony[53] and Brandenburg, and through the Chancellor's Meeting in Bonn in partial networks of transformation policy. This has further increased their scope for influencing the policies of the THA.

2. Municipalities, former owners, and investment priority

It has always been the aim of the THA Executive Board to present itself as the Group Board of a major business corporation. The fact that it is still a state-owned "company" becomes clear not only through its diverse external relationships and the way it reconciles conflicting political interests but also from the fact that legislation has given it sovereign responsibilities. This applies primarily to the restitution of municipal assets and for defining investment priorities, procedures which have been completed with the issue of an administrative notice. They came under the "Law" Directorate of the President's Division, and under the "Municipal Assets/Water Management" Directorate of this corporate division, in which responsibility for reprivatisation was also anchored.[54] The THA's function as a government authority created totally different relationship structures than those germane to the political President's Division departments and Corporate Divisions.

The Municipal Assets Directorate had its own separate sections for the various States, separate from the President's level, and a contact office for the national associations representing the municipalities. Its Director was seconded to the THA from the *Deutsche Städtetag* and maintained close contacts with it and with the associations representing rural counties and urban and smaller districts.[55] In addition to this there were direct links with departments in Federal and State Ministries of the Interior and of Justice whose administrative regulations cover the work of this department. One important link is called *Infodienst Kommunal*, published by the Federal Minister of the Interior and also serving as a guideline for the other administrative bodies in the eastern German States.

The "Municipal Assets" Directorate was also integrated into a network of relationships with parliaments and public administration. Enquiries were frequently booked in from the *Bundestag* THA Committee, phone calls came every day from the various departments of the Federal Ministry of Finance, and there were "constant requests for information and suggestions from

---

52 op. cit.; see: Handelsblatt, 16th February 1993.

53 The "district secretary" of the metal-workers' union and the Minister-President of Saxony are now collaborating with one another on industrial policy "like Siamese twins": B-interview with Dieter Schulte on 27th January 1993 - see footnote 35.

54 In the THA, reprivatisation came under a Directorate in Corporate Division U2, which among other things is responsible for policy on small and medium-sized companies and the co-ordination of branches and branch offices.

55 B-interview with Michael Schöneich on 23rd February 1993.

individual *Bundestag* delegates on behalf of their constituency and from the working groups of the Federal and State parliamentary parties responsible for communal policies".[56] In addition to this, the Directorate together with other THA departments and the regional tax offices (*Oberfinanzdirektionen*) which are responsible under the Property Assignment Act had frequently attended local authority conferences organised by the Federal Ministry of Finance and the Federal Ministry of the Interior alternately for county and city chief executives from eastern Germany. The Directorate itself also held such local authority conferences at the level of the old GDR *Bezirke*, or Districts, in order to report on the process and latest state of restitution. One important point here is the theoretical basis of municipal planning for the future in eastern Germany. Through this interface, the THA was also involved in building up municipal and State administration in eastern Germany.

The department of the THA most usually approached by the former, disappropriated owners of property or assets, and parties representing their interests,[57] and by municipalities, is the one covering public law, the Investment Priority Act and lawsuits, and § 3a of the Property Act. It is about the suspension of limitations or bans imposed by the THA on the sale of land and property, or companies, to which the former owners are laying claim. The Property Act, as originally passed on 23rd September 1990, proved to be a brake on investment, so the THA demanded, at hearings on the Removal of Obstacles Act, that it would have to get the facility for refusing a reprivatisation if the former owner is only interested in getting his hands on the property and is unwilling or unable to take over the management of the business. As a result of the insertion of § 3a into the Property Act, the THA was enabled as early as March 1991 to define investment priorities. The claim for restitution was thus converted into a claim for compensation. The start of investment priority proceedings by the THA interrupted the proceedings for restitution before the competent state office for the regulation of unsettled property questions (*Landesamt zur Regelung offener Vermögensfragen*).

In the running dispute between the THA's interests in investment, employment, and reconstruction and the establishment of restitution claims by the Property Offices, a kind of administrative race broke out known colloquially as "greyhound races".[58] The thrill was taken out of them by joint working meetings between the THA and the Property Offices. Nevertheless, there had been Property Offices which "regard the THA as their worst enemy".[59] Others, some of which share office accommodation with the THA, were more open-minded towards investment priority, all the more since they were dependent on the working contribution from the THA departments, mostly those responsible for restitution, reprivatisation and for property assignment to the former owners.[60] Despite legal and other less formal precautions, restitution notices

---

56 op. cit.

57 Basically the *Bund der Mitteldeutschen,* a federation for all those with interests in eastern Germany, and the *Organisation der Besitzer von Berliner Mauergrundstücken,* for those owning land on which the Berlin Wall was built. Others involved are the *Deutscher Industrie- und Handelstag,* the national standing conference of Chambers of Commerce and Industry, and other industry associations.

58 B-interview with Martin Keil on 23rd February 1993.

59 op. cit.

60 Under the successor concept for the THA, the reprivatisation work still unfinished in 1994 and the supervision of adherence to requirements imposed in investment priority notices will be handed over to a more tightly defined successor organisation.

sometimes counteract the THA's work. It usually sued the Property Office for its notice if this is getting in the way of an existing privatisation plan, and particularly if former owners were trying to bring major projects to a halt in order to obtain a greater amount of compensation under civil law than that already on offer under the Property Act.

The legal departments which many Directorates have created for themselves are primarily occupied with the private law side of privatisation work. On the other hand, the Legal Directorate itself acts in cases before the administrative courts as legal counsel and representative of the THA. Among other things it represented the THA in the action before the Constitutional Court over the validity and implementation of the Electricity Contract. The Directorate was also involved in out-of-court arbitration proceedings with the association of municipal enterprises.

The Legal Directorate was also the home of the staff department for "Special Tasks", a THA organisational unit equipped with the authority of a public prosecutor's investigatory office. It mainly employed public prosecutors and detective officers on secondment from Federal and State offices and police forces. Four departments, working in close collaboration with criminal investigation authorities and auditors, investigate cases of fraudulent business management, illegal asset-stripping, subsidy fraud, criminal actions exploiting the opportunities created by unification, corruption, breach of secrecy, libel, and crimes against the environment.[61] They also have links with the internal auditing departments of the THA, and accept information from THA employees and from outsiders. Swift investigatory action enabled 90 % of the DM 3 billion in fraudulently converted funds investigated up to December 1992 to be secured. The largest part of this had been in the hands of outsiders.

3. Refinancing the THA

The THA is not only dependent on external information. This degree of dependency could be easily reduced by observation of its organisational environment and making appropriate use of opportunities for exchange. The "tough" restrictions on its actions result from political pressure, external demands for control rights, and, as an important cause, dependence on material resources.

In September 1990 the THA had to obtain DM 2.5 billion at short notice in order to be able to service the first quarterly DM-denominated interest on the historic loans to its companies. At that time, while the GDR was still in existence, the question of taking on responsibility for historic debt was not clarified. The German banks approached the THA's request to make this volume of credit available with considerable caution. It was not until unification had been achieved that the Federal government directly shouldered the THA's charges and thus opened the way to the THA to raise money directly on the money and capital markets. Thereafter it took care for itself with revolving money-market instruments which permitted the best possible credit and cash management. This means that a certain credit system was built up out of short-term liabilities permitting loans due for repayment to be matched daily against incoming payments, both

61 B-interview with the public prosecutor in charge of the staff department, Daniel Noa, on 23rd February 1993.

regular and unforeseen. It was thus mainly possible to avoid expensive losses on intermediate deposits. This concept, together with the relevant computer program, was contributed rapidly by the Finance Director, Dr Paul Hadrys, from Deutsche Airbus GmbH, Munich, where it had been developed and tried out over a period of ten years. In addition to this, the THA was the first public-sector body to introduce a "commercial paper" programme. Through its early and comprehensive commitment it even helped the DM Commercial Paper, a form of short-term debenture on a discount basis introduced in Germany not before 1991, to make its first decisive breakthrough.

The funds mobilised by these means were insufficient, however, at the end of 1991; the THA had to go to the capital market with its own bond, and to offer it without prospectus, because in this special case it was not possible to submit the three consecutive and sound balance sheets which stock exchange law requires. Negotiations with the Frankfurt Securities Exchange failed to produce the exceptional regulation the THA had been aiming for. It was not until the THA Credit Act came into force on 3rd July 1992, placing the THA as a debtor on the same footing as the Federal Government, that it became possible to issue securities without a prospectus. However, it intended to spare the German capital markets any excessive burden and to place its future bonds abroad, whenever possible with major institutional investors, so the financial department applied for inclusion in the credit-rating lists of the international rating agencies. It was given the highest possible rating, Triple-A. On this basis, it prepared the national and international market for the issuing of medium and long-term bonds and debentures. The President of the THA, Birgit Breuel, presented the "company" in the autumn of 1992 to the main international financial centres with such success that THA bonds could be placed abroad at about 40 % and with a rising trend. The emission of loans and debentures with the help of the Federal Bond Consortium brought the THA financial department into daily contact both with the relevant departments of the Federal Ministry of Finance and with the *Bundesbank*.[62] The financial directorate enjoyed a high and constant degree of independence both within the THA and in its external relations. Whilst an opinion survey showed that 63.5 % of THA employees complained about growing external restrictions on their work, in the financial directorate the figure was only 28.5 %.

The liabilities are supposed to be merged together with those of the Credit winding-up fund and the historic debts of the municipal housing authorities by 1st January 1995 into a "historic debt repayment fund" (*Erblastentilgungsfonds*) to be set up as a special asset of the Federal government.[63] In the case of the THA, the fund will merely be the co-debtor of the liabilities accumulating up to 31st December 1994, so that the THA remains on the capital market as the debtor. The successor organisation of the THA was named "Federal Institution for Special Tasks resulting from Unification". It will be established on January 1st 1995, and will continue to undertake sovereign functions (property assignment, communalisation, investment priority proceedings, property transaction licences, administration of special assets) and corporate functions (as party to court actions and supervising companies which are being wound down). Financing will be a responsibility of the Federal budget. The remaining THA-companies will be brought

62 B-interview with Dr Paul Hadrys on 6th April 1993.

63 Implementation of historic debt repayment fund Act of 23rd June 1993, published in *Bundesgesetzblatt* I, page 984.

together into so-called "Management-KG" companies. In addition to direct administrative costs, it can be expected that the new institution will take on responsibilities for losses secured under contract from privatised THA companies, provide capital to companies in which THA-II holds equity, and in some cases take companies back that have once been privatised. In addition to this there will be costs arising from supervising shut-down nuclear power stations and responsibilities relating to employment policy.

IV. Conclusion: Politics in a network-like decision-making structure

The politics of unification and the transformation into a market economy revealed a rapid and mainly institutional adaptation to the functional requirements and traditional solutions of German federalism. Witness to this is the development of the THA from a central economic agency into a part of the complex political system of West Germany. Installed between the Federal government and the eastern German States, it operated *de facto* as a "third layer" of co-operation in the federal system. It was not only within its Administrative Board but also in numerous co-ordination bodies that both the Federal and the State governments were represented, as were also the representatives of both sides of industry. This was the framework in which the THA's rooms for manoeuvre and the pre-conditions for its success developed. Earlier assumptions that "in eastern Germany the power of the centralist state will be strengthened by its economic role"[64] therefore need to be qualified; although the state proportion of the eastern German GNP has reached 80 %, the centralist state is only one of a number of authorities able to decide on the use of funds destined to promote the construction of a market economy.

What effect has the THA's intermediary position in the competitive relationships of the federal system and political interests had on its success? It is not easy to answer this question because a distinction needs to be made here between institutional and practical restrictions on its actions. Otherwise it would prove impossible to achieve the impossible, it was the political institutions which could in the end be held responsible. It has to be assumed that many of the THA's problems are caused solely by the diversity and contradictory nature of its responsibilities. This is the prime cause of the "infinitely excessive demands" made on it (Birgit Breuel).[65] The very real conflicts of aims and overall economic conditions running counter to success in transformation politics existed regardless of the institutional configuration of the organisations behind them. Developments in foreign economies were a large part of the cause, such as the collapse of the markets in Eastern Europe and the global economic recession with all the consequences this had for incomes, employment, and public budgets. The pressure of problems, shortage of time, and the vital necessity to achieve success all grew, while at the same time the room for manoeuvre to react diminished. The question ought therefore have been the following: Will the "excessive demands placed on the THA which exist anyway be further increased because of the large number of bodies exerting them and which are officially allowed to interfere with the THA?"[66]

---

64 Seibel, *Necessary Illusions*, page 194.

65 Quoted by Helmut Schmidt, *Handeln für Deutschland,* page 108.

66 This is Helmut Schmidt's opinion, op. cit.

or did the external network of connections proffer rather more of a chance of countering this excessive burden of responsibilities?

First of all, the inclusion of decision-makers into the network of the transformation has taken some of the load off the THA to legitimate its decisions. It achieved this effect with its co-opting strategy, by opening itself up to the politicians and the associations, and did so deliberately.[67] In addition to this, the co-opting of external protagonists contributed to a better co-ordination of aims in the transformation process. Without it, there would have been enormous waste in expended energy and one side would always have ended up blocking the other. The "THA-complex" is a fine example of how fixed battle-fronts between proponents in the worlds of politics and associations who are dependent on one another can crystallise out into an extensive network of co-ordination and control. In the last analysis it was the THA which itself knitted major parts of this network of transformation policy together. Because of its legal status, and because of its systematically pursued co-option strategy, it was in a position to bring in powerful proponents on its side and at the same time to create joint room for manoeuvre. Where it entered into mutual relationships with its political and association environment, be it on the basis of the "economic boom in the east" programme, numerous outline agreements with the unions, internal guidelines, or in the co-ordination bodies, many of which it created itself, it pinned its hopes on the common interests of all involved on the success of economic conversion and called for support for its course of action - but not without indicating a willingness to compromise in those situations which would otherwise have deteriorated into a blockade.

The precarious position of the THA in its role as an employer confronted with demands to design a structure and promote employment and with requirements in social policies harboured the constant danger of priorities being set unilaterally and political conflicts escalating. The THA had hardly any other choice but to face up to this challenge in any different way than through willingness to compromise. Otherwise it would have become involved in a political power struggle between the Federal and the State governments, employers' associations, and trade unions, and torn to piece before the eyes of a critical public. In a constantly threatening and confusing situation mutual adaptation, even if it looked from outside like "muddling through", was the only solution for keeping the organisation in being which promised any kind of success. The THA's flexible approach to solving problems has been interpreted as a consequence of its need to learn as it went along.[68] Learning as the ability to recognise mistakes and correct them, however, is only possible if the problem situation remains the same, or at least fairly similar, so that the knowledge acquired can then be put to use. If the problem situations and their solutions change continually, as in the case of the THA,[69] the only attempt that remains to be tried is to construct learning effects through situation analyses, analogous conclusions, and external consultation and to bring these into the next round of concepts – a rationalist variant of coping with problems. A second possibility would appear to exist in retaining solutions which

---

67 Its attitude here is similar to that generally observable in other organisations enmeshed in politics and acting in a crisis; see: Rosenthal and Pijnenburg (editors), *Crisis Management and Decision Making*; Selznick, *TVA and the Grassroots*, pages 74 and 219 et seq.

68 Seibel, *Lernen unter Unsicherheit*, page 367.

69 The THA had to keep reacting to rapidly changing problem situations: the collapse of the markets in Eastern Europe, the recession, uncertainties in wage policy, etc.

have proved to work even though the problem situations change – a variant which one often encounters in organisations which used to be successful but have become bureaucratic and set in their ways. None of these two approaches seems to apply to the actions and development of the young THA, operating in turbulent environments and under conditions of extreme uncertainty. The THA's main strategic variant would seem instead to consist of adapting itself to changing preferences in a new sphere of protagonists and thus safeguarding its own interests to the greatest possible extent. This could be assumed from the very low priority accorded to comprehensive problem analysis, the success of which, in light of the complex and dynamic sequence of events, must anyway have seemed very dubious. As every change in the protagonists called forth different results, the network of unification policy was presumably better able to bring the problem structure to light than any central co-ordinating authority, all the more so since the prerequisites – articulative ability, great density of interaction, and a wide participation of interests – had been constantly improving.

The THA's pragmatic, "muddling through" attitude[70] was the appropriate reaction to the dynamic problem development, but at the same time a foreseeable consequence of the institutionalised complexity of the German government system. A greater degree of control would have been hard to achieve in this system, even if the problem situations had been simpler. All the same, programmatic coherence and predictable behaviour remain the aim of every rational problem solution, all the more so in the internal area of large organisations. The THA as a "business enterprise", however, viewed with disfavour from all sides the demands to "make its mainly shapeless procedures more objective".[71] The political networks, complex problem situations, and the need for flexibility in its dealings with investors were not the only reasons for a lack of procedural control. This was also caused by the expectation that the standardised treatment of tasks required a thoroughly thought-out concept, or perhaps even a plan, which was the last thing the THA wanted.[72]

The task of the THA was subject to one essential special condition, which in addition to the actual and institutional complexity ran counter to a rationally calculated and routine method of coping with problems. It was the conviction of almost everyone involved that the route from the planned to the market economy was not itself capable of being planned. Against this background, the THA, and with it the Federal government, had relied totally, on the self-healing power of the market. A simple framework of organisational policy and administrative matters ought to suffice to bring about the "second German economic miracle". Therefore it must have been all the more painful to notice that this was more than the market and the state administration, including the THA, could handle - despite a maximum deployment of funds. Where the market and a hierarchy are not yet working, or as a control mechanism cannot guarantee any satisfactory solutions to problems, it is only the political compromise principle of interwoven decision-making structures that remains.

---

70 Lindblom, *The Science of "Muddling Through"*.

71 H. Schmidt, *Handeln für Deutschland,* page 109.

72 "Management by Chaos" was the main action principle mentioned in many interviews and principally evaluated positively.

73 On the institutional and economic substantiation of this thesis see: Powell, *Neither Market Nor Hierarchy;* Ouchi, *Markets, Bureaucracies, and Clans;* on the political science aspects see: Scharpf, *Versuch über Demokratie,* pages 25 et seq.

If it is right to say that the route to the market cannot be planned, the Federal Republic was better placed to face the risks of the system transformation that any hierarchically ordered unitary state. Its political institutions are designed for negotiations and the reconciliation of conflicting political interests. They do not represent any hierarchically interactive system of cogs and levers, but are capable to cope with the constantly and mutually changing shapes of various problems. For such a system the THA of the GDR government was "an inappropriate design" (Helmut Schmidt), and had first to separate itself painfully from its rigid "plan targets" in order to find its place in the negotiating democracy of western Germany. Now that it has set itself up there, its remaining tasks will be allocated to successor organisations newly to create or by Federal or State authorities. It cannot be ruled out that with this measure again the incalculable residual risks of reconstruction in the East will increase, because the THA always operated, if almost as an afterthought, as a safety net to the government apparatus, capable of absorbing the shattering blows of the unification process, making the extent of the economic problem clear, and helping to mark out the political and monetary limits of the whole operation. Of all the tasks which it accumulated during the course of the unification process, this was one the THA really mastered: that of casually stripping governments, interest groups, and the entire public of their illusions.

V. Literature

Hankel, Wilhelm: *Die sieben Todsünden der Vereinigung*. Berlin 1993.

Katzenstein, Peter: *Politics and Policy in West Germany. The Growth of a Semisovereign State*. Philadelphia 1987.

Lawrence, Paul R., and Jay W. *Lorsch*: *Organization and Environment: Managing Differentiation and Integration*. Homewood, Il. 1967.

Lehmbruch, Gerhard: Die deutsche Vereinigung. Strukturen und Strategien. In: *Politische Vierteljahresschrift* 32 (1991), pages 585 to 604.

Lindblom, Charles E.: The Science of "Muddling Through". In: *Public Administration Review* 13 (1959), pages 79 to 88.

Marissal, Matthias J.: *Der politische Handlungsrahmen der Treuhandanstalt.* Bern and Frankfurt am Main 1993.

Pilz, Frank, and Heike *Ortwein*: *Das vereinte Deutschland. Wirtschaftliche, soziale und finanzielle Folgeprobleme und die Konsequenzen für die Politik*. Stuttgart and Jena 1992.

Ouchi, William G.: Markets, Bureaucracies, and Clans. In: *Administrative Science Quarterly* 25 (1980), pages 129 to 141.

Powell, Walter W.: Neither Market nor Hierarchy: network forms of organisation. In: *Research and Organizational Behavior* 12 (1990), pages 295 to 336.

Rosenthal, Uriel, and Bert *Pijnenburg* (editors): *Crisis Management and Decision Making*. Dordrecht and London 1991.

Scharpf, Fritz W.: *Versuch über Demokratie im verhandelnden Staat.* In: Roland *Czada* and Manfred G. *Schmidt* (editors): *Verhandlungsdemokratie, Interessenvermittlung, Regierbarkeit.* Opladen 1993, pages 25 to 50.

Schmidt, Helmut: *Handeln für Deutschland - Wege aus der Krise.* Berlin 1993.

Schmidt, Manfred G.: *Die politische Verarbeitung der deutschen Vereinigung im Bund-Länder-Verhältnis.* In: Wolfgang *Seibel*, Arthur *Benz* and Heinrich *Mäding* (editors): *Verwaltungs-*

reform und Verwaltungspolitik im Prozeß der deutschen Einigung. Baden-Baden 1993, pages 448 to 453.

Schmidt, Reiner: *Aufgaben und Struktur der Treuhandanstalt im Wandel der Wirtschaftslage*. In: Peter *Hommelhoff* (editor): *Treuhandunternehmen im Umbruch. Recht und Rechtswirklichkeit beim Übergang in die Marktwirtschaft*. Cologne 1991, pages 17 to 38.

Schuppert, Gunnar Folke: Die Treuhandanstalt - Zum Leben einer Organisation im Überschneidungsbereich zweier Rechtskreise. In: *Staatswissenschaften und Staatspraxis* 3 (1992), pages 186 to 210.

Seibel, Wolfgang: Necessary Illusions - The Transformation of Governance Structures in the New Germany. In: *The Tocqueville Review* 13 (1992), pages 177 to 197.

ditto: *Lernen unter Unsicherheit - Hypothesen zur Entwicklung der Treuhandanstalt und der Staat-Wirtschaft-Beziehungen in den neuen Bundesländern*. In: Wolfgang *Seibel*, Arthur *Benz*, and Heinrich *Mäding* (editors): *Verwaltungsreform and Verwaltungspolitik im Prozeß der deutschen Einigung*. Baden-Baden 1993, pages 359 to 370.

Selznick, Philip: *TVA and the Grassroots. A Study in the Sociology of Formal Organization*. Berkeley 1949.

Spoerr, Wolfgang: *Treuhandanstalt und Treuhandunternehmen zwischen Verfassungs-, Verwaltungs- und Gesellschaftsrecht*. Cologne 1993.

Treuhandanstalt Informationen, various issues.

Treuhandanstalt: *Richtlinie für Betriebsvereinbarungen und Haustarifverträge vom 1. September 1992*. Berlin 1992.

Zeitschrift für Wirtschaftsrecht 6/1991.

Part B

The Treuhand's working priorities

Supporting companies capable of being restructured on their way to privatisation

by Joachim Schwalbach, with the assistance of Sven-E. Gless[1]

I. Introduction

When the *Treuhandgesetz* or THG (the Act setting up the THA) came into force and the formerly state-owned *Kombinate* (industrial combines), companies, organisations, and other legally independent economic units were converted into joint-stock companies, the THA became the owner[2] of some 8,000 to 9,000 companies operating at more than 45,000 sites.[3] Under the terms of § 2 section 6 of the THG, the THA was required to aim at "creating companies capable of operating in the market by appropriately dismantling corporate structures and producing an efficient economic structure". Also, "the THA is required to promote the structural adaptation of the economy to meet the needs of the market, in particular by influencing the development of firms capable of being restructured into competitive companies and their privatisation."[4] It was thus a statutory responsibility of the THA to promote restructuring, and this was reflected accordingly in Detlev Rohwedder's summing up of the THA's tasks: "Rapid privatisation – resolute restructuring – considerate closure."[5]

In practice, however, priority was given to privatisation because the THA was convinced that this was the most effective route to restructuring. When privatisation started to lag in 1991, particularly with regard to companies in manufacturing industry, the economic problems of eastern Germany not only nudged restructuring into the forefront of public discussion but also made it an increasingly significant task for the THA. In 1991 alone, the THA made DM 77.5 billion available to its companies for restructuring by write-off of debts, liquidation guarantees, loans, and investment finance.[6] The entire stock of 6,500 companies still on the THA's books in October 1991 were categorised as needing restructuring, and 70 % of them as capable of being restructured.[7]

It is the aim of this article to investigate the possibilities open to the THA for restructuring its companies and comparing them with the way it actually went about the task. In the second section of this thesis, basic questions of company restructuring will be discussed and, in the third,

---

1 We would like to express our thanks for assistance in the preparation of this article to Ms Wietog and her staff in the Clearing Office, Dr Maaßen of the THA, and Ms Erlinghagen and Ms Köller. Our special thanks are due to Mr Salleck. The unabridged version of this article appeared as Research Report No. 93/1 of the Institute for Management at the Humboldt University of Berlin.

2 See § 1 section 4 sentence 1 of the THG.

3 See: Nolte, *Privatisierung und Sanierung*, page 556.

4 § 2 section 6 of the THG.

5 Detlev Rohwedder, letter to all THA employees of 27th March 1991.

6 See detailed reports in *Zwischenbericht für den Verwaltungsrat vom 28. April* in: *Treuhandanstalt Informationen* 13 (1992), page 1.

7 See: *Treuhandanstalt Informationen* 6 (1991), page 1.

the THA's methods for investigating whether a company could be restructured or was worth restructuring. Part 4 will investigate the question of which persons and organisations were principally able to plan, implement, and check on its aims, strategies, and crisis management measures. These points can in the last analysis only be evaluated on the basis of the typical problem areas of eastern German companies, as is shown in Part 5, which also features a case-study of a successful company restructuring programme reflecting the subjects discussed in the preceding sections. Part 6 explains the form and amount of the financial support given to the companies and evaluates it in terms of the restructuring policy of the THA. Finally, samples of the way restructuring was supervised will be presented.

II. Fundamental questions of company restructuring[8]

1. The process of restructuring

A company crisis is the emergency suffered by a company as the result of an involuntary process during the course of which profitability and the net assets and/or liquidity of a company have changed so unfavourably that its economic survival is seriously jeopardised.[9] If the crisis cannot be overcome by restructuring it will end with the company, or the organisation backing it, going into liquidation.[10]

Restructuring is the sum total of all financial, technical, and organisational or legal measures taken in order to make a company work efficiently and achieve the profitability needed to ensure survival.[11] Restructuring always applies the unit which produces and sells, and not the organisation legally responsible for it.[12]

Restructuring is a complex process, made up of the phases shown in Fig. 1. In examining the restructuring process a strict chronology is less important than a physical categorisation of the tasks to be carried out;[13] the various phases can overlap one another or can be repeated several times.[14]

2. Restructuring concept

An analysis of a company and its environment permits conclusions to be drawn as to the prospects for its restructuring. A comparison of the company's actual situation and the present situation and the future development of its environment make it possible to assess the opportunities and risks affecting its further existence. The areas to be covered in this examination of the company and its environment are shown in Fig. 2.

8 The full version of this article (see footnote 1) goes into detail on these fundamental questions.

9 See: Gross, *Grundsatzfragen der Unternehmenssanierung*, page 1572; Müller, *Krisenmanagement*, page 15.

10 See: Dörner, *Sanierungsprüfung*, page 208.

11 See: Krystek, *Reorganisationsplanung*, page 584; Böckenförde, *Unternehmenssanierung*, page 7.

12 See: Hax and Marschdorf, *Insolvenzrecht*, page 112.

13 See: Müller, *Krisenmanagement*, page 317.

14 op. cit.; Hess and Fechner, *Sanierungshandbuch*, page 48; Krystek, *Unternehmenskrisen*, page 91.

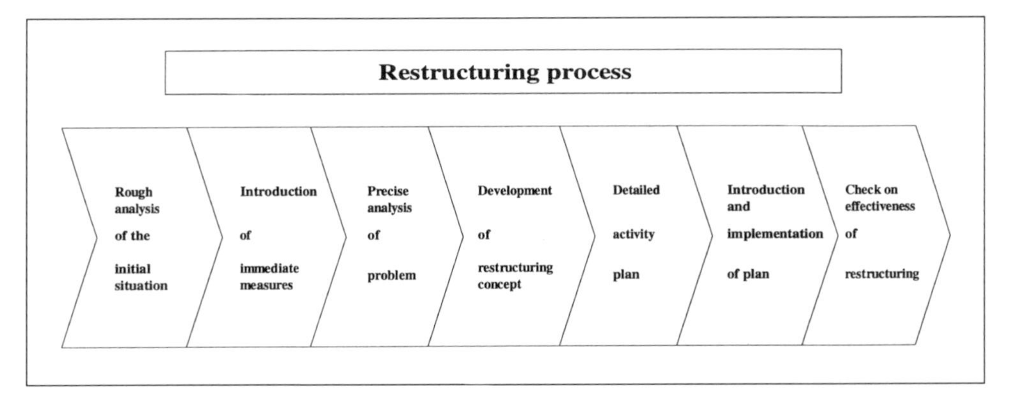

Figure 1 Phases in the restructuring process

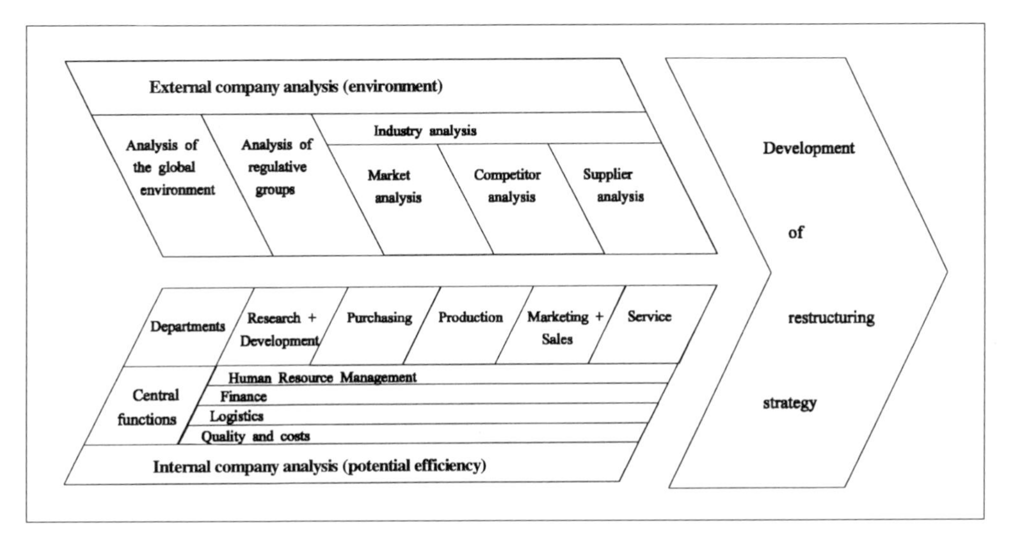

Figure 2 Company and environment analysis

The results of the company and environment analysis provide the basis for developing a restructuring concept designed to recreate the company's efficiency and ensure its survival.[15] The aim is not to abolish loss-making activities instantly but to generate an appropriate and sustainable level of profit.[16]

The main component of a restructuring concept is the development of a route leading out of the crisis. A distinction needs to be made between answering fundamental strategic questions and deriving from them operational action plans. Whilst the strategy determines the

15 See: Böckenförde, *Unternehmenssanierung*, page 80.

16 See: Krystek, *Unternehmenskrisen*, page 232; see, too: Böckenförde, *Unternehmenssanierung*, page 80.

product/market combination to be worked on in future and the competitive advantage that needs to be striven for, the operational action plans aim to define restructuring activities which can be carried through in the short to medium term and achieve corporate goals that coincide with the long-term strategy.

The restructuring concept serves as the basis for assessing whether the company is capable of being restructured, and is worth restructuring. Whilst the determination of the company's ability to survive restructuring is based entirely on criteria related to business management, the evaluation of whether it is worth restructuring also takes into account the interests, and the willingness to take risks, of those affected by restructuring respectively of those enfranchised interest groups entitled to influence the decision to take this option.[17]

The economic examination of the company's capability of being restructured is based on a comparison between its continuation value and its break-up value.[18]

This examination cannot be entirely insulated from subjective factors because the information available is never complete and any business management indicators of future profitability are often ambiguous.[19] These subjective factors relate to the evaluation of competitors, the future trends in the market, the effectiveness of operational action plans, and so on. Factors affecting the assessment of whether it is worthwhile restructuring a company, on the other hand, are different because they also bring non-economic criteria into play. The decision as to whether a company is worth restructuring is dependent on the interests of those involved in the restructuring.

III. The THA's examination of a company's ability to be restructured

1. Necessity of developing restructuring concepts

The structure and size of the gigantic *Kombinate* and the companies within them was not in conformity with the demands of the market and this meant that dismantling, or "unbundling", them was a precondition for the privatisation and restructuring of the individual companies. This is why the THA worked on the restructuring of its companies right from the start of its operations in March 1990.[20]

The process of unbundling the THA companies involved two phases. The aim of the first phase was to convert formerly state-owned companies into legally independent enterprises. According to the THG, with effect from 1st July 1990 the state-owned Kombinate were converted into AG-type companies, and the companies within them, as well as the independent ones, into GmbH-type companies (see § 11 of the THG). This conversion was in the last analysis a

17 See: Schmiedel, *Die Prüfung der Sanierungswürdigkeit*, page 761.

18 The continuation value is calculated on the basis of the present cash value of all the profits generated in the productive area before deduction of payments to the provider of capital. The break-up value, on the other hand, is calculated from the sum total of the proceeds of the sale of all the individual assets. If the continuation value is greater than the break-up value, the owner(s) would find it advantageous to continue its existence; if the situation is the other way round, the company ought to be broken up. This decision is unrelated to the company's degree of indebtedness. See: Hax and Marschdorf, *Insolvenzrecht*, page 116.

19 See: Kayser, *Sanierungsfähigkeitsprüfung*, page 415.

20 See: Treuhandanstalt, *Entschlossen Sanieren*, page 4.

purely formal, legal action. Any economic aspects aiming to create companies of a size and structure capable of surviving were almost entirely ignored. No other situation was possible at this point in time, as the THA was only sparsely informed about its portfolio of companies, and had no adequate analysis of any of them available to it.

Unbundling to meet economic criteria was only possible in the second phase, starting on 1st July 1990 and continuing to the present day. Its main features were the interests of investors in context of privatisation and the efforts of the companies to create "lean" structures and make themselves competitive. The legal basis was the so-called Splitting Act, created specially for this purpose to simplify the transfer of assets to the newly established joint-stock companies (splitting up and splitting off).[21] By breaking up excessively large economic units under the Splitting Act, and with the aid of a new legal institution to contain a succession of special rights covered by it, it was possible to circumvent the complicated and expensive one by one transfer of assets and liabilities.[22]

The Splitting Act was thus an important legal requirement for the unbundling of the *Kombinat* structures in order to create more efficient company units. The basis for the decisions involved could however only be the restructuring concepts developed by the organisation responsible for the restructuring or those submitted by potential investors. Irrespective of its nature and size nearly every company was obliged to prepare a company concept to identify possible deficits resulting from the system transformation and, if necessary, to counteract them.

If the concepts were necessary for the companies for economic reasons, they were needed by the THA to fulfil its statutory responsibility. Privatisation negotiations are only possible on the basis of a realistic corporate strategy which reveals the potential of the company and thus helps to determine the terms of its sale. Also, § 19 section 2 of the Deutschmark Balance Sheet Act indirectly contains an obligation to prepare a restructuring plan by requiring all planned measures to be described "which have been decided on or planned for the time after 30th June 1990 in order to adapt the company to changing circumstances".[23]

The THA had to make the granting of loans, the take-over of guarantees, the acknowledgement of settlement demands, and the acceptance of historic debt dependent on the company's ability to be restructured. The companies were therefore required to draw up a restructuring concept on the basis of "guidelines" from the THA.

2. Guidelines for preparing restructuring concepts

In a letter dated 15th July 1990, the THA called on the directors of all the various companies in which it held the equity to submit their restructuring strategies no later than 31st October 1990 in order "to prepare for the distribution of loans and the take-over of guarantee liabilities by the

---

21 See: § 1 of the Splitting Act, and: Priester, *Gesellschaftsrechtliche Zweifelsfragen*, pages 2373 et seq.

22 See: Ganske, *Spaltung der Treuhandunternehmen*, page 791. The process of splitting up or off made the shareholder in the previous company (the THA) also the shareholder of the newly created companies. In addition to these two kinds of splitting there was also the possibility of „hiving off", which gave the previous company the position of shareholder of the newly created one. See op. cit., page 791, and: Weimar, *Entflechtungen*, page 772.

23 § 19 section 2 of the Deutschmark Balance Sheet Act; see also: Kurtkowiak, *Sanierungen*, pages 7 et seq.

THA".[24] Attached to this letter was a copy of the "THA Guidelines for the Design of Restructuring Concepts" which laid down the overall structure and substance of these strategies.[25]

These guidelines consist of three parts. Part A requires general information to provide an overview of the company and include information about the industry, the company's product and service groups, its legal form and organisation, parent and subsidiary companies, management, main groups of customers, number of operating locations and employees, age of machinery and buildings, use of EDP, obligations under contracts with COMECON countries, risks caused by historic environmental pollution, and the nature and number of any co-operation agreements.

Part B is called the restructuring concept proper, and is made up of strategies for products, production, and staffing.

In the product strategy, which had to be prepared by the Executive or Management Board, the company's products and/or services had to be grouped into business divisions and the attractiveness of the relevant market estimated in terms of size and growth. Also the relevant competition and the competitive situation (strength and weakness) should be identified. Working from this basis, it was then required to show the possibilities for improving the competitive situation, particularly by means of product innovation and the creation of a sales organisation, in order to arrive at a realistic estimate of market share. The final result had to include the business divisions that would have to be closed down and those which would continue in operation.

The production strategy had to start with an analysis of the technological situation of the production facilities and processes in comparison with western German competitors, followed by the definition of the manufacturing locations on which the company would in future concentrate. In the case of action plans for reducing costs or increasing productivity, a distinction had to be made between those which would involve investment and those which would not. Examples of measures not involving investment were a reduction in numbers employed, the selection of new materials suppliers, the buying-in of components (to reduce the depth of manufacturing), improvements in logistics, and greater motivation for the staff. In the case of investment plans, the priority and the impact over time of each investment had also to be shown, together with the internal sources of finance (e. g. sale of assets not required for operations) and the external financing facilities. The opportunities and risks entailed in contract manufacturing were to be discussed as an alternative to in-house manufacture.

The staffing strategy had to discuss the possibilities of reducing the numbers employed to a level which would produce the turnover per employee customary in the industry. Any reduction necessary was to be achieved as far as possible by natural wastage, early retirement, splitting off and privatisation, short-time working, the creation of operating companies, and release from duty. The companies had to produce plans covering the period up to the end of 1993 which also included plans for improving the training and qualifications of their workforces.

The quantitative impacts of the action plans developed in Part B had to be brought together into a corporate plan which made up Part C. This included a forecast of corporate profits for 1990 to 1993 on the basis of a turnover forecast and detailed forecasts of costs. Capital requirements were to be calculated on the basis of a cash flow forecast. The aim of these requirements

24 THA letter dated 15th July 1990 to all Executive Boards and Directors of the companies where it held equity.

25 On the following points, see: von Keller, *Sanierungsrichtlinie*, pages 171 to 175; Kurtkowiak, *Sanierungen*, pages 7 to 12.

was a cost-benefit analysis of the planned corporate restructuring. The opening DM balance sheet was to be appended to the restructuring strategy in order to clarify the asset situation.

As laid down in the THA "Guidelines for the Preparation and Treatment of Corporate Concepts", approved in an Executive Board resolution of 6th December 1990, a workable corporate strategy had normally to be made up of privatisation, restructuring, and financing plans. These strategies had to be drawn up by the board or directors of each company on their own responsibility and confirmed by an independent assessment by an expert. The privatisation strategy had to show the activities that had been undertaken in order to be able to examine the seriousness of the efforts behind them. Also, the prospects for privatisation had to be shown which formed the background for the planned restructuring measures.[26]

In summary, it is possible to identify two goals in these restructuring guidelines. One was to provide management with assistance in drawing up restructuring strategies, and the other was to assess more easily, by means of standardised strategy documents, which companies were capable of being restructured and which ones were worth the effort.[27] The restructuring guidelines took on considerable practical significance on account of their use in the companies and by the THA itself.

3. Sequence of treatment and bodies giving approval

The lines of responsibility within the THA for the various companies were first of all organised on the basis of the general division of responsibilities for companies looked after by Central Office and by the branches. Accordingly, companies with fewer than 1,500 employees[28] came under the branches and larger ones were the responsibility of THA Central Office.[29] However, the Central Office had the right to take over responsibility for any company.[30]

The subsidiary companies run from Central Office were allocated to the various Industry Directorates which were responsible for looking after and privatising them. If the total liabilities were no more than DM 10 million, the concepts were examined, evaluated, and if possible approved by the Industry Directorate itself; if the total liabilities were greater, the case went before the Management Committee (*Leitungsausschuß*).[31] The Management Committee is an independent, neutral body and no subject to directives; it acts in an advisory capacity to the Executive Board or the Industry Directors and branch managers of the THA. It is appointed by

26 See: Treuhandanstalt, *Organisationshandbuch, Richtlinie zur Erstellung und Behandlung von Unternehmenskonzepten*, 6th December 1990, serial no. 3.2.2, pages 3 et seq.

27 See: von Keller, *Sanierungsrichtlinie*, page 173.

28 Categorisation was based on an initial survey of company data as of 31st December 1990; see: Treuhandanstalt working book *Richtlinie zur Erstellung und Behandlung von Unternehmenskonzepten* dated 20th August 1991, section 4, page 3.

29 See: Nolte, *Privatisierung und Sanierung*, page 556. For exceptions, see article by Seibel in this volume, page 125.

30 See: Treuhandanstalt working book *Richtlinie zur Erstellung und Behandlung von Unternehmenskonzepten* dated 20th August 1991, section 10, page 9.

31 op. cit., section 1.2.2, page 1.

the Federal Ministry of Finance, and its staff[32] evaluate the suitability of companies for restructuring and recommend appropriate action to the executive body responsible for the relevant decision.[33]

Approval for restructuring decisions was laid down in the "Guidelines for the Preparation and Treatment of Corporate Strategies" and the relevant working book dated 20th August 1991 as being dependent on the total financial commitment involved. The various layers of approval are shown in Table 1.[34]

Table 1:
Levels of responsibility for corporate concepts/restructuring assistance

Maximum level in DM million

Loans, sureties, guarantees (Special regulations apply to liquidity loans)	Acknowledgement of settlement claims, freeing of debt	Financial aid (export assistance, increase in company capital, loans, preferential interest rates) to lower-tier companies	Maximum permissible commitment (This total applies when a number of different financial instruments are being used; the limit must not be exceeded by any one alone.)	Approval by:
10	30	10	30	Signature by branch manager or Executive Board member and Director
30	50	30	50	Signature by Financial Executive Board director and one other
100	100	100	100	Resolution by entire THA Executive Board
>100	>100	>100	100	Resolution by THA Administrative Board and approval by Restructuring Committee

32 The Management Committee comprised for a time eight (later four) industry teams staffed up to 80 auditors, management consultants, and industry experts in peak periods. See: Treuhandanstalt, *Handbuch Aufgabenspektrum und Lösungswege*, 1993, section 22, page 1.

33 op. cit.

34 The regulations have since then been modified but the basic principles have remained the same.

Table 1:

Maximum level in DM million

Loans, sureties, guarantees (Special regulations apply to liquidity loans)	Acknowledgement of settlement claims, freeing of debt	Financial aid (export assistance, increase in company capital, loans, preferential interest rates) to lower-tier companies	Maximum permissible commitment (This total applies when a number of different financial instruments are being used; the limit must not be exceeded by any one alone.)	Approval by:
>100	–	>100	–	Approval by Federal Ministry of Finance/for Economic Affairs

Tolerance regulation: Increases to be made within restructuring strategies, loans, and guarantees already approved: 10 % of the originally approved total volume, subject to a maximum of 50 % of the limit of each level of approval.

Source: Working book on "Guidelines for the Preparation and Treatment of Corporate Strategies"

While restructuring strategies and the financial support applied for are being approved, the entire financial plan of the company was subjected to a detailed examination by the Finance Department. Continual monitoring of the restructuring process was in the hands of the relevant Industrial Directorate. In addition to permanent progress communication, quarterly and annual reports were used for control purposes. The examination followed the same system as when the strategy was originally presented, with the Annual Report containing the certified annual accounts and with the auditors' report serving as additional sources of information.[35]

4. Categorisation of suitability for restructuring

The examination of a company's (suit)ability for restructuring was carried out on the basis of a check list. The outline of the examination can be seen below in Fig. 3.

In addition to the formal assessment of the corporate strategy with regard to completeness, correctness, and basic assumptions, the privatisation strategy was also scrutinised. The new strategic possibilities were of particular interest both for privatisation and for restructuring, as only those company units which were capable of being effectively restructured stood any chance of being privatised. The basic programme for creating units capable of survival had been the dismemberment of the *Kombinate* and the separating out of the individual companies, but with the

35 See: Treuhandanstalt working book *Richtlinie zur Erstellung und Behandlung von Unternehmenskonzepten* dated 20th August 1991, section 1.2.2, page 2 et seq.

examination of each strategy the problem of unbundling had to be discussed again as only the elaborated restructuring concept could answer the question on whether useful synergies would be terminated, whether parts of the company individually capable of survival could be splitted off, or still other parts existed which would have a negative effect on restructuring plans. There was thus a mutual and interactive relationship between the privatisation and the restructuring strategies.

The areas of the restructuring strategy examined were basically in line with the requirements laid down for the companies in the Guidelines. It comes as a surprise, however, to find that the delimitation of terms and the substantial structuring differ from one another. Whilst the structure used by the Management Committee was in line with the normal procedure described in the literature and used in practice, the Guidelines are divided up into product, production, and staffing strategies. There are no discernible advantages in this.

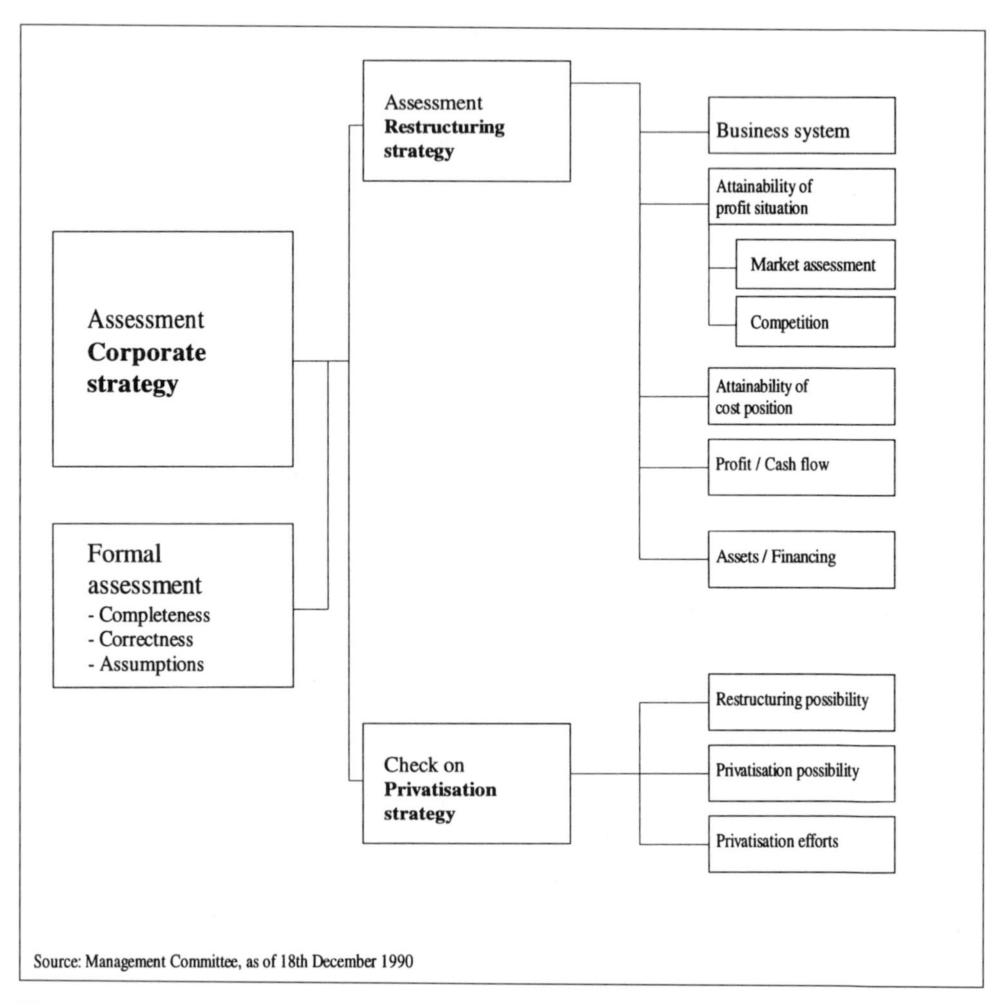

Figure 3 Areas examined by the Management Committee regarding suitability for restructuring

It has already been shown, in Section II. 2, that the preparation of a catalogue of unambiguous indicators related to business management for determining a company's suitability for restructuring would have been almost impossible. The calculation of the amortisation period or of equity profitability as the finally decisive criterion was not possible because of the enormous extent of the restructuring activities necessary and the difficulty of assessing their effects. The THA therefore, according to information it supplied itself,[36] brought qualitative aspects of the examination of suitability for restructuring to the fore, and did not attempt to set up a catalogue of criteria. It was and is crucial to answer the question as to whether the balance sheet and profit structure normal in that particular industry could be reached within three to five years. As of the areas of uncertainty in the examination of suitability for restructuring, and the awareness of responsibility for the economy as a whole, the THA tended to evaluate the crisis situations with a positive slant. A purely business management examination would no doubt in many cases have led to a different result. The THA took account of the various different prospects for restructuring by applying a detailed system of categorisation (see Table 2).

Table 2:
THA company categorisation

1.	Company is operating profitably. No further need for restructuring. Press ahead quickly with privatisation.
2.	Company expected to enter profitability in 19xx. Virtually no further need for restructuring. Press ahead quickly with privatisation.
3.	Corporate strategy appears successful.
3.1	Definite take-over purchaser must be identified, otherwise demote to Group 5 or 6.
3.1.1	Small liquidity requirement. Purchaser must be found within a definite period of time.
3.1.2	Large liquidity requirement. Identification of purchaser necessary within a short period of time.
3.2	Corporate strategy is successful even without purchaser. Press ahead quickly with privatisation regardless of this.
4.	Company appears capable of being effectively restructured, strategy not yet sufficient; alternative strategies need to be developed.
4.1	It would appear possible to rescue the entire company.
4.2	It is forecast that substantial parts of the company can be rescued.
5.	Capability of restructuring appears dubious. Detailed examination necessary.
6.	Company is not capable of being restructured. Decision must be taken whether to liquidate or declare bankrupt.
6.1	Liquidation.
6.2	Bankruptcy.

Source: Working book on "Guidelines for the Preparation and Treatment of Corporate Strategies"

36 Information by telephone from Dr Maaßen on 11th May 1993.

A summary of the categorisation made by the Management Committee and the Industry Directorates is shown in Table 3, but it should be noted that this is only an extract. The categorisation made by the branches has not been analysed. Also, the number of companies categorised relates to the net portfolio on the THA's books on the date given. It shows that the vast majority of companies fell into Groups 3 and 4; the relative increase in those categorised into Group 4 could be the result of the successful privatisation of those in Group 3.

Table 3:
Categorisation by the Management Committee and the Industry Directorates of THA companies capable of being restructured

Effective date Groups	30th June 1991	31st Dec. 1991	30th June 1992	31st Dec. 1992
1	26 (2.3 %)	29 (1.9 %)	33 (2.1 %)	13 (1.3 %)
2	82 (7.1 %)	109 (7.1 %)	83 (5.2 %)	46 (4.6 %)
3	206 (17.8 %)	431 (28.1 %)	348 (22.1 %)	120 (12 %)
3.1	200 (17.3 %)	212 (13.8 %)	323 (20.5 %)	263 (26.3 %)
4	295 (25.6 %)	380 (24.7 %)	458 (29 %)	415 (41.6 %)
5	162 (14 %)	96 (6.2 %)	55 (3.5 %)	30 (3 %)
6	184 (15.9 %)	279 (18.2 %)	277 (17.6 %)	112 (11.2 %)
Total no. of THA companies categorised	1,155 (100 %)	1,536 (100 %)	1,577 (100 %)	999 (100 %)
No. privatised by that date including privatised parts of companies	2,583	5,210	8,175	11,043
No. of liquidation/bankruptcy proceedings opened	529	983	1,589	2,249
Total no. of THA companies	10,334	6,128	4,340	2,575

Source: Own processing of THA figures. Further analysis is available in the unabridged version of this article which appeared as Research Report No. 93/1 of the Institute for Management at the Humboldt University of Berlin.

IV. Persons and organisations responsible for the management of restructuring

The persons and organisations responsible for the management of the restructuring process are those that plan, implement, and monitor the aims, strategies, and measures for crisis management and thus take over the management of the company during the restructuring process.[37] The extraordinary extent and breadth of impact of the processes of adaptation[38] in the eastern German companies placed particularly severe demands on those responsible for carrying out the restructuring.

The following pages will consider the institutions of relevance to the THA companies prior to discussing the limits to the THA's ability to monitor restructuring.

Restructuring management can be made up of institutions, persons, or groups of persons both internal and external to the company.[39] In the case of THA companies, the parties that can be considered responsible internally for restructuring are the management and controlling bodies of the company itself and the staff and departments of the THA as the owner of the capital. The work of restructuring has to be handled on site, i. e. within the company, by the Executive Board or the top management, the Supervisory Board or, if there is one, the Advisory Board, and by middle and junior management. External bodies responsible for restructuring can be primarily banks and management consultancy companies. The tasks to be carried out as part of crisis management have to be distributed across these institutions or bodies stated in such a way that the best possible results are assured given the relevant management competence and capacity.

1. Internal groups

a) Executive Board/managing directors

Coping with a corporate crisis is one of the most basic tasks of the company's Executive Board (of a joint-stock company) or of the managing directors (of a limited liability company); they can both be referred here as "the Board".[40] This is not easy when mismanagement by the Board was the cause of the crisis in the first place. Complete replacement of all the Board members is then unavoidable.[41]

Although the present management of the THA companies could not be made directly responsible for the crisis, it could be seen that the overall social conditions, the in-house socialisation and the organisation of the "planned" economy had produced managers of a different profile in East Germany from those in the West.[42] A survey of 219 THA companies[43] showed that just

37 Krystek, *Unternehmenskrisen*, page 97.

38 See: Donges, *Konservierende Industriepolitik*, page 69.

39 See: Böckenförde, *Unternehmenssanierung*, page 96.

40 See: Müller, *Krisenmanagement*, page 431.

41 See: Böckenförde, *Unternehmenssanierung*, page 98.

42 See: Münch, *Innovation oder Anpassung*, page 826.

43 See: Myritz, *Mangel an Kompetenz*, page 16, where the companies were analysed that came under the control of the 15 THA branches in the fields of construction, services, trade, food, metal and metal-working, textiles, etc. As the only companies examined were those with fewer than 3,000 employees, it is only possible to a limited extent to generalise from the results obtained.

under half of all the managers at the top level and just below it had an adequate professional qualification,[44] and that about 40 % could only be rated as barely suitable or even unsuitable for their positions. Only 12.3 % displayed a high level of competence.[45] Shortages of technical ability were most apparent in the fields of marketing and sales, financial management and controlling, materials management and logistics, and in personnel and law.[46]

This shortfall in management ability would have caused problems enough in a "healthy" company. In companies whose very survival is in jeopardy and which need a highly qualified and experienced management team this shortfall makes the situation nearly desperate. The THA therefore had to try to find experts with which to replace a large proportion of the management in its companies. Although recruiting highly qualified managers is no easy job, it proved possible to bring in several thousand experienced people.[47] A period of grace for introducing new people to their working and making up for management deficiencies had to be granted both to the new and to the old managers when the latter were deemed basically suitable for their positions.

b) Supervisory/Advisory Boards

In addition to the Executive Board or the managing directors who manage a company, the body which supervises them can also be drawn into the job of restructuring management. The Supervisory Board of the joint-stock companies or the Advisory Board of limited liability companies basically has no authority to issue orders to the managers of the company, but by designing the Articles of Association, e. g. to require their approval for important transactions, they can still control the restructuring process.[48]

The THA set up more than 500 Supervisory Boards within a space of months in order not only to delegate the control function but also to provide active support from the Supervisory Boards for the restructuring process. The THA attempted to obtain experienced managers from western Germany for seats on the Supervisory Boards, and particularly as chairmen (and occasionally chairwomen). The THA as the owner appointed the chairman and let him appoint the other members in its name as representatives of the shareholder's side; at the same time, members were appointed to represent the employees' interests in accordance with the regulations under the Co-determination Act.[49]

Many people were appointed to the chair of Supervisory Boards who had been former top managers in western Germany and were now in retirement; most of them had many years of experience in the relevant industry behind them. Because of their experience and their motivation to help in reconstruction, a joint spirit of endeavour soon developed between them to master the crisis together with their management Boards. The formal separation of fields of responsibility became blurred. In many cases, the ability and experience of the Supervisory Board chairmen actively involved in the business was of great assistance in compensating, briefly or perma-

---

44 This emerged from an evaluation of the technical, management, reporting, and financial qualifications and ability and from the managers' „social skills".

45 See: Myritz, *Mangel an Kompetenz*, page 16. The survey was probably carried out at the end of 1991.

46 See: Treuhandanstalt, *Entschlossen Sanieren*, page 7, and: Treuhandanstalt, *Handbuch Aufgabenspektrum und Lösungswege*, 1993, Part 24, page 5.

47 See: Treuhandanstalt, *Entschlossen Sanieren*, page 7. It was not possible to obtain exact figures.

48 See: Krystek, *Unternehmenskrisen*, page 98 et seq.

49 See: Treuhandanstalt, *Handbuch Aufgabenspektrum und Lösungswege*, 1993, Part 24, page 5.

nently, for the shortcomings in the eastern German management teams, inexperienced as they were in the ways of the market economy.[50] The appointment of former politicians to the chairs of Supervisory Boards was only defensible if the company already had an experienced top management team and the Supervisory Board was only required to perform the duties prescribed to it by law.

c) Middle and junior management

Depending on the size of the company, the hierarchical levels immediately below the Board also consists of managers of the middle and junior levels. These were, for instance, managers in charge of production locations and spheres of function, production departments, staff departments, and other departments in the central administration.[51]

As to the preparation of the restructuring strategy and its implementation the managers of these levels represented a decisive factor of success, because they were familiar with the specific problems, had to submit recommendations for solving them, and also had to implement the operational plan of action developed in collaboration with the Board. Shortcomings of the people at this level thus represented a hindrance to the preparation and implementation of corporate strategies. Even if the managers responsible at Supervisory or Executive Board levels were qualified and experienced in restructuring work, they could not directly compensate the consequences of lack of experience at the middle and junior management levels. A longer time-scale is required to develop the existing potential by means of programmes of continued training or "learning by doing". But in the midst of a crisis a company could hardly afford the time required and the costs of the mistakes that were made.

d) THA

The THA had principally three routes open to it for improving restructuring management:

1. replace and improve the local management
2. provide direct assistance with THA staff
3. engage management consultancy companies.

The limits to which the THA could itself pursue active restructuring management, i. e. send its own staff to take on management functions in planning, implementing, and monitoring restructuring processes, have already been mentioned. These limits were largely set as a consequence of the great complexity of company restructuring and by the relationship of the number of staff at the THA experienced in carrying through company restructuring to the number of THA companies in need of a turnaround. This relationship had developed more favourably, and had been underpinned by the growing experience of everyone involved, but the possibility for carrying out company restructuring programmes have still been subject to very severe limits.

The numbers employed by the THA rose from 1,231 in December 1990 to 3,929 in December 1992. Against this, the number of companies in the THA's portfolio fell from its original figure

50 Through privatisation, the number of companies required to have a Supervisory Board fell from the original 455 in 1991 to 241 in 1992. When necessary, competent Supervisory Board members who had proven their worth through competence and collaboration were re-appointed in order to improve the management know-how of the companies encumbered with serious problems. See: op. cit., Part 24, page 2.

51 See: Böckenförde, *Unternehmenssanierung*, page 103.

of 12,795 in 1990 to 1,871 in May 1993. The number of staff employed in the Industry Directorates rose from 425 in December 1990 to 1,146 in December 1992. Looking at the structure of the directorates one can clearly see that only a few of the staff could have been considered for involvement in restructuring management. Taking into account also that the main task of the Industry Directorates is the privatisation of companies, the limits of the THA's ability to become actively involved in restructuring its companies become all the more apparent. It can also be assumed that only a few of these employees had or could have had experience in company restructuring.

In personnel deployment terms the THA therefore concentrated on supporting restructuring and did not take on the main responsibility for the restructuring processes going on within its companies. Direct personnel support by the THA mainly covered "initiation, examination, discussion, collaboration on planning, and approval of the corporate strategy, and pursuing the implementation, with any necessary later auditing work".[52] The instruments used included the "THA Guidelines for the Design of Restructuring Concepts" and the required quarterly reports. The intensity with which a company needed to be supported was affected by its size, the specific crisis position it was in, the influence being exerted by politicians, and even the personal relationships between the persons involved.

In addition to this, the companies received assistance in special fields such as protecting foreign trade, communalisation, reprivatisation, splitting/hiving off, compensation plans, etc. There were programmes for sales promotion such as "Setting up Contacts with western Customers, Purchasing Campaign East, Marketing to Government Authorities, Trading initiatives East ... specialist publications campaigns, involvement in trade fairs and exhibitions ... THA Tours eastern Germany".[53]

2. External groups

a) Management consultancy companies

The shortcomings in management knowledge and capacity were an obstacle to the rapid preparation and implementation of restructuring plans. To fill this gap already the THG itself (in § 9 section 3) created the possibility to engage external consultants to improve the profit position of companies and to carry out restructuring programmes. The use of management consultancy companies was arranged on the initiative and at the expense of both the companies and the THA.

The use of management consultants in company crises made quickly available the necessary management capacity and enlargement of know-how. Because of their varied experience, consultants are able to apply systematic methods to analyse complex problems.[54] Both the diagnosis of the problem and the preparation of a restructuring strategy are often carried out by mixed teams made up of consultants and managers of the highest hierarchical level (this is called participative consultancy on the work-shop principle).[55] Implementation remains the task of com-

52 Treuhandanstalt, *Handbuch Aufgabenspektrum und Lösungswege*, 1993, Part 2, page 2.

53 op. cit.

54 See: Böckenförde, *Unternehmenssanierung*, page 107.

55 op. cit., page 454.

pany management. For this reason, consultancy work which does not involve the integration of the company's staff has to be criticised.

Inadequate knowledge on the consultant's side of the specific situation in an industry or a company can also have a negative effect on the results of his consultancy work. The considerable time pressure arising from the generally high demand for consultancy work often led to a less diligent analysis of the industry. However, taking the possible difficulties into account, it can be stated that the extensive use of well known management consultancy companies proved to be an effective aid in assisting the reconstruction processes in the THA companies.

b) Banks

In western Germany banks are often actively involved in the restructuring of companies. This is based on the higher level of exposure, in relationship to other creditors, the better level of information, and the greater know-how in examining corporate strategies. The very survival of the company is usually dependent on their consent to the restructuring strategy and to the granting of additional credit to facilitate the restructuring. It is therefore often in a bank's interest to collaborate from the start on the development of restructuring strategies.

In the case of the THA companies, the banks' level of interest and the necessity for taking part in the restructuring process was that much less because their liquidity and investment loans were covered by global and individual guarantees from the THA. In addition to this, the banks did not have enough qualified personnel to assess the risk involved in loans for restructuring.

Of the loans outstanding from THA companies at the end of March 1992, 92 % were backed by state guarantees. At the end of 1990 about DM 13.5 billion had been advanced, by the end of 1991 about 20.6 billion, and by the end of March 1992 19.7 billion.[56] The reduction in the absolute volume of loans advanced can be attributed, amongst other factors, to the debts taken over or paid off by private investors as part of the privatisation process, or by the previous owners as part of the reprivatisation process, the paying off of debts or conversion of them into shareholders' loans as part of the winding-up process, and, to a lesser extent, to the paying off of debt by the companies themselves.

V. Coping with the crisis in eastern German companies

The difficulties encountered by individual companies in coping with the transformation process depended mainly on the industry to which each company belonged. Whilst, for instance, companies in the services or trade sector had relatively minor problems during the change-over to the market economy, companies involved in manufacturing industry which sold nation-wide soon found themselves faced with a threatening company crisis. The individual situation of the company depended on the market segment in which it operated, and was only of secondary importance in determining the adaptation measures necessary. The following pages describe typical approaches to the restructuring of eastern German companies which must apply to manufacturing companies selling to nation-wide markets. This is followed by a case-study showing the problems which determined the restructuring process for a gas appliances manufacturer, Dessauer Gasgeräte GmbH.

---

56 See: Bundesverband deutscher Banken, *Aktivitäten der privaten Banken*, page 357.

1. Problem areas in restructuring

a) Strategy

The restructuring of eastern German companies was not intended to be restricted to (instant) action designed to cut costs and raise profits. All measures, whether short, medium or long term, had to be derived from a strategically orientated overall plan[57] defining the products or product groups to be produced in the future, and the competitive advantages to be striven for (product features, service, costs). This decision determines the way how to work the market (whole market, specific segment, niche market), the definition of sales areas, and finally adaptation within a company's business system.[58]

b) Product

The main problem for eastern German companies was creating competitiveness for their goods and services. Depending on whether the products fell into the high, medium, or low technology categories, there were various different initial situations and adaptation difficulties. The products had to be adapted with regard both to technical standards and visual design.[59] According to the THA's estimates, in 1990 only about one third of the products produced in its companies met the demands of the international market, one-third were to a limited extent capable of being sold, and the rest had to be categorised as unsellable.[60] As in the last analysis all the shortcomings of a company (R&D, manufacturing processes, employee motivation, etc.) cumulatively come home to roost in its product output, many companies were simply unable to achieve any short-term improvements. For many, the only route out of this situation was licence production and contract manufacturing.[61]

c) Company structure

One of the consequences of the planned economy system was an enormous depth of manufacturing and inefficient company structures, which had to be rearranged in order to create any kind of competitiveness. To this end it was necessary to look at the value-creation chain to analyse the core areas and to take "make-or-buy" decisions. The disintegration and re-integration of the value-creation structures, sometimes to the extent of 80 or 90 %, could be achieved easily by splitting off the ancillary units not essential for core operations (e. g. carpentry shops, holiday homes, a dry-cleaning plant in an engineering works, etc.). Decisions on splitting off parts of the manufacturing process, on the other hand, were rather more difficult.[62]

---

57 See Section II and: Schoppen, *Restrukturierung eines Kombinats*, page 14.

58 See: Becker, *Marketing-Konzeption*, page 122.

59 See: von Keller, *Sanierungsrichtlinie*, page 172.

60 See: Zanger, *Unternehmenskrise und Produktentwicklung*, page 982.

61 See: Gross, *Sanierungsberatung in der ehemaligen DDR*, page 231.

62 See: Kröger, *Restrukturierung zur Privatisierung*, page 101, and: Gross, *Sanierungsberatung in der ehemaligen DDR*, page 233.

d) Production

Production in eastern German companies was generally speaking typified by:
- elderly/obsolete plants
- high scrap/reject rates
- excessive depth of manufacturing
- inefficient work flow, all leading to
- overmanning.[63]

Depending on the type of production organisation (workshop, group, or line production) and the specific circumstances, there was a varying need for restructuring and investment. Concentration on core activities made it possible to reduce manning levels and avoid investment by hiving departments off (thus reducing fixed costs). Also, in many cases it proved possible to improve rapidly the cost effectiveness of the manufactured goods because the bought-in parts and components usually offered better quality at lower prices. Reducing the manufacturing depth and introducing rationalisation measures, whether needing investment or not, had substantial effects on the structure and organisation of core and auxiliary activities.[64]

e) Purchasing

Opening markets also to the purchasing side and buying in a larger proportion of components placed new demands on the purchasing and internal logistics managers. By re-orientating themselves to western suppliers, companies were able to reduce the prices of bought-in goods by 50 or 60 %.[65] In addition to this, it was also possible to reduce the costs of keeping very high stocks necessitated by the short supply economy. Whilst competition opened up opportunities on the purchasing side, it led to adaptation difficulties on the selling side.

f) Sales/marketing

Companies operating in the planned economy had never had any problem with selling. Because everything was in short supply, demand was nearly always ahead of supply and sales always constituted 100 % of output.

The opening of the domestic market, and the collapse of the COMECON markets, led to substantial drops in turnover of companies which were in national and international competition. The rule was that turnover fell off between 1990 and 1992 by 50 to 80 %,[66] attributable to the arrival on the market of western competitors and changes in purchasing behaviour particularly in the field of consumer goods. On the eastern European markets, the change-over to world-market prices, invoicing in convertible currencies, and inadequate cover from "Hermes" guarantees were also partly responsible for the fall-off.[67] The proportion of exports to the East had been greatest in heavy engineering (40 %), the armaments industry (29.5 %), in machine tools (28.1 %),

---

63 See: Gross, *Sanierungsberatung in der ehemaligen DDR*, page 232 et seq.; the assessments mentioned above applied not only to the production centres but also to the whole companies.

64 See: case-study on Dessauer Gasgeräte GmbH, page 64 (cf. footnote 78).

65 See: Kröger, *Restrukturierung zur Privatisierung*, page 100 et seq.

66 Own investigations; see also: *Treuhandanstalt Informationen* 16 (1992), page 8.

67 See: article by Hedtkamp and Clement in this volume, page 503 and 517 et seq.

and in motor vehicles (24.4 %). In total, however, the degree of the THA companies' dependency was 10.4 % of turnover – not as great as had often been expected.[68]

Even holding market share in eastern Germany and trying to open up markets in western Europe proved virtually impossible on account of the usual absence of products of any competitive value. Even products that were capable of generating sales were hard to market because there was no proper marketing or sales know-how, and because of the old "GDR" image.[69] Companies which under the planned economy had had no direct contact with their customers either at home or abroad had first to set up an efficient sales organisation.[70] This was particularly difficult in industries where sales go through specific sales chains; for instance, producers of food products or clothing and textiles had problems getting their products included into the range of the various all-German retail chains.[71] The sales and service networks specific to each industry thus determined the course of action.

Investigations have shown that restructuring strategies were very often based on over-optimistic sales forecasts, so that the normal procedure came to be a revolving restructuring plan with a series of modified forecasts. Corresponding to this the original sales expectations of the THA companies were to be reduced from the original DM 200 billion to about DM 130 billion, accompanied by losses of DM 15 to 20 billion.[72] This drop in turnover called for drastic reductions in capacity, and thus also in numbers employed, in order to bring the costs structure into line. By the end of the first half of 1991, the numbers employed in THA companies had been reduced, through privatisation and redundancies, by almost half from the previous year's figure to 2.1 million. As private investors had signed undertakings to employ only 512,000, this means that within one year the THA companies had shed 1.4 million jobs.[73]

g) Management/administration

The excessive overhead burden caused by over-administration had to be reduced. Cost reductions in the areas of planning, co-ordination, and supervisory levels of 80 to 90 % were by no means an exception.[74]

In order to identify a company's exact situation, draw up a restructuring strategy, and finally keep control of the restructuring process, it was first necessary to implement a suitable accounting system and a functional book-keeping department. Introducing cash management or calculating net contribution often represented tasks which companies could not even begin to carry out.[75]

---

68 op. cit., page 508; see also: *Treuhandanstalt Informationen 2* (1991), page 4.

69 See: Schoppen, *Restrukturierung eines Kombinats*, pages 10 and 15 et seq.

70 This had previously been operated in other countries via the authorised foreign-trading companies. Within East Germany, sales of consumer goods had been made via the *Handelsorganisation*, the trading organisation which operated all the main supermarkets and other retailers, and of capital goods via the *VEB Maschinenhandel*; see: von Keller, *Sanierungsrichtlinie*, page 172.

71 See: Gross, *Sanierungsberatung in der ehemaligen DDR*, page 232.

72 See: Treuhandanstalt, *Entschlossen Sanieren*, page 36.

73 See: article by Seibel in this volume, page 131 et seq, and *Treuhandanstalt Informationen* 3/4 (1991), page 6.

74 See: Kröger, *Restrukturierung zur Privatisierung*, page 101.

75 op. cit., and: Schoppen, *Restrukturierung eines Kombinats*, page 10.

h) Company profits

As a result of the shortcomings listed above, productivity was about 30 to 40 % of western German levels. The products were produced at a cost level which exceeded western reference prices by anything from 20 to 100 %[76] or even more. This led to losses at a level often close to total turnover and which in some cases even exceeded it. Table 4 shows examples of typical trends in numbers employed, turnover, and annual profits collected in the authors' own survey. The companies concerned are not named, only the industry in which each operated.

Table 4:
Typical individual examples drawn from six different industries

Industry from which example is taken[1]	Year	Employees[2]	Turnover DM '000	Pre-tax profit DM '000	Return on turnover in %
Textiles and clothing	1990, 2nd half	2,741	35,312	–14,824	–41,98
	1991	1,226	23,569	–25,114	–106,56
	1992	529	25,010	–13,009	–52,02
Food and allied industries	1990, 2nd half	258	10,400	–294	–2,83
	1991	182	24,200	–1,784	–7,37
	1992	123	30,600	-335	–1,09
Electrical engineering and electronics	1990, 2nd half	1,058	53,728	–27,302	–50,82
	1991	782	57,420	–18,050	–31,44
	1992	473	54,252	–22,285	–41,08
Glass, ceramics	1990, 2nd half	725	17,314	–12,203	–70,48
	1991	524	34,862	–17,149	–49,19
	1992	344	25,635	–12,137	–47,35
Engineering	1990, 2nd half	3,914	119,503	–45,951	–38,45
	1991	2,658	106,159	–122,225	–115,13
	1992	1,342	55,369	–49,063	–88,61
Chemicals, cosmetics	1990, 2nd half	869	29,948	–134	–0,45
	1991	561	13,023	–18,935	–145,39
	1992	294	6,245	–12,651	–202,58

[1] Portfolio as of early 1993; [2] average number of employees over the year

The general situation of the THA companies can be illustrated by those 2,913 companies which were still in the THA portfolio on 30th November 1992. In the third quarter of 1992 their cumulated operating results reached DM -1,734 million. With a total turnover of about DM 8.25 billion the average return on turnover amounted -21% in the third quarter. The return on turnover varied from industry to industry between +42% (wood and paper) and –90% (special engineering).

Numbers employed were reduced during the period from 1st January to 30th November 1992 by 254,000, to 507,000. Employees were declared redundant in all industries with the sole exception of services. The rate of reduction lay in the range from 24.41% (motor vehicles), 46.74% (special purpose machines), 66.24% (textile and leather), to 72.54% (agriculture/forestry).[77]

76 See: von Keller, *Sanierungsrichtlinie*, page 172.
77 See: Treuhandanstalt, *Vorstandsinformation* No. 7, November 1992.

2. Example of restructuring: Dessauer Gasgeräte GmbH[78]

Any description of the acute problem areas in eastern German companies reveals the great complexity of the restructuring needed. As a result of this complexity and of the enormous pressure for action, the degree of difficulty in restructuring a company in eastern Germany is many times greater than that in any free-market system. However, it is possible to cope even with extreme crisis situation, as the example of the restructuring of Dessauer Gasgeräte GmbH (DGG) will show. Its main features are the great speed at which the crisis was overcome after it had reached its climax in the middle of 1990 and was brought under control during the course of 1992. The case was selected mainly because it can be presented a finished case of restructuring.

This company was founded by Hugo Junkers in 1892 and underwent a colourful history. During the lifetime of the GDR it produced gas cookers and gas continuous-flow water-heaters, and as a state-owned VEB company came under the *Kombinat* for household appliances (which used the brand name "Foron"). In 1989, the *Kombinat* consisted of 28 VEB companies with a total of 34 factories. With effect from 1st July 1990, the former *VEB Gas- und Elektrogeräte Dessau* was transformed into *Dessauer Gasgeräte GmbH* (DGG), a limited liability company.

With a turnover of DM 50 million and losses of DM 18.1 million in the second half of 1990, the company found itself in a full-blown success and liquidity crisis. A detailed analysis of the company and its business environment showed that its profit potential was badly disturbed, and that the company was therefore also in a strategic crisis. The causes were, on the one hand, the poorer quality of its products compared with those of the competitors, and on the other hand the high costs which could not be covered by prices achieved in the market. The company had no competitive strengths, and its survival was in acute jeopardy. The profit situation was thus basically similar to all those quoted as examples in the preceding section.

Immediate action was taken even before the end of 1990 to increase turnover and cut costs, but without reducing the room for manoeuvre in making strategic choices. The long-term company strategy was to be developed with the help of a management consultancy company which had been working for the company since the beginning of 1990. Because of a poorly prepared company and environment analysis, a false assessment of the initial crisis resulting from it, and a lack of creativity in the search for alternatives, the action recommendations by the consultants had to be regarded as inadequate. A retrospective analysis shows that it was not until early 1991, when a west German manager with experience in the industry was appointed Chairman of the Supervisory Board that the company was provided with a new orientation and strategic direction. This Board, together with an executive board made up of eastern German managers, agreed on a strategy on the basis of which operative restructuring measures could be introduced and implemented in nearly all departments (see Table 5). These are basically comparable with the restructuring areas dealt with in the preceding sections.

The restructuring measures were already showing their effects in 1991 and produced the first positive annual results in 1992, in which year the company had a turnover of DM 162 million and a profit of DM 4.7 million. The survival crisis had been overcome. By repositioning itself strategically in the medium segment, the company had also developed into Germany's biggest producer of gas cookers.

78 The unabridged version of this case study was published as Research Report No. 93/2 by the Institute for Management at the Humboldt University of Berlin.

The search for factors affecting the success of a restructuring programme and the discussion over their effects on the trends in turnover and costs showed that this success was dependent on a large number of factors and that these were in turn highly interdependent on one another. The main activities can be summarised as follows:

- The prime requirement for success in restructuring was the development and production of a competitively effective product. R&D efforts and substantial changes to the production process and methods were necessary to achieve this.
- A major factor was the reduction in the depth of manufacturing in all functional departments of the company, particularly in the production area. Concentrating on the core activities made it possible to reduce numbers employed and avoid investments with a large element of fixed costs. The value-for-money element of the products being produced was improved rapidly, as the bought-in parts and components generally offered better quality at lower costs. Reducing the depth of manufacturing, accompanied by rationalisation activities requiring more or less investments, had a major impact on the structure and organisation of the core and auxiliary areas.

Table 5:
Example of restructuring: Dessauer Gasgeräte GmbH

Management Committee Category: 4

Initial situation, mid-1990

Turnover in 2nd half of 1990:	DM 50 million
Operation result in 2nd half of 1990:	– DM 18.1 million
Numbers employed as of 1st July:	1,790
Gas cookers produced:	12,906 per month
Gas heaters produced:	6,640 per month

Result of company and business environment analysis:

Non-competitive products [Design (-), utility (-), safety (-), service (-), ⇒ value for money (-)]; cost/price ratio: cookers DM 570/450, gas heaters DM 470/335; inadequate cost structure, shortcomings in almost all departments.

Strategic crisis/Profit and liquidity crisis

Restructuring process/crisis management

Immediate action:	Results of measures introduced:
– Introduction of immediately effective measures to improve visual design and raise quality of workmanship (→ increase turnover) – redundancies (→ cost reduction) – application for liquidity guarantees (securities, sureties) of the THA in 1990 Strategic goal: – Positioning in medium quality and price segment and concentration on eastern Germany. Operational action: – Improve all departments. Special effects were achieved by: – setting up sales system – hiving off ancillary activities (226 redundancies) – market-orientated R&D	– Product innovation: No. of products less than 3 years old: 1990: 20% 1992: 81% – Reduction of average production time per unit Cookers: from 3.9 to 2.3 hours Heaters: from 2.3 to 1.9 hours – Reduction in depth of manufacturing 1990: approx. 80% 1992: approx. 50% – Productivity increase by 275%

Table 5:

Restructuring process/crisis management:	
Operational action: – hiding off of production departments (499 redundancies) – introduction of co-ordinated purchasing policy (reduction of costs, improvement of quality) – rationalisation of production process – investments (DM 4.4 million in 1990, DM 3.9 million in 1991, DM 9.6 million in 1992) – cut-down in administrative staff (322 redundancies) Restructuring carried out by: – Chairman of Supervisory Board appointed by THA – Local management board Financial support from THA: – bank guarantee upper limits: 1990: DM 17.1 million 1991: DM 32 million 1992: DM 28.2 million	Results of measures introduced: – Positive net contribution levels from the product groups: gas cookers, gas water-heaters, and adapters and fittings Cancellation of historic debts: approx. DM 37 million.

Last categorisation by Management Committee: 3.2

Development up to end of 1992:

	Year	Turnover DM/million	Profit DM/million	Employees
2nd half	1990	50	–18.1	1790
	1991	106	– 3	1032
	1992	162	4.7	770
1992:	Cookers produced:		approx. 14,200 per month	
	Heaters produced:		approx. 8,800 per month	

Germany's largest manufacturer of gas cookers
48% share of gas cooker market in eastern Germany (next largest: Seppelfricke, 16%)
60% share of gas water-heater market in eastern Germany (next largest: Junkers, 20%)

- Raising the proportion of bought-in parts made new demands on the purchasing department and on internal logistics. This was taken into account by setting up a new short-term ordering centre.
- The decision on sales activities took account of the company's strengths and weaknesses. A good product image, a complete service network, and a high market share in eastern Germany, combined with high barriers to entry in western German market, led to marketing efforts being concentrated in the east.
- Extensive restructuring was also carried out in the administrative and management areas as well.

Despite this successful restructuring process, it had still not proved possible to privatise DGG by the middle of 1993. One reason for this was that the process of selling a company even after it has been largely restructured takes a considerable amount of time (one aspect being the problem of valuing it); another is that the privatisation effort was characterised by intensifying rivalry between the investors. Whether privatisation, as discussed at the beginning of 1993, in a pool of other companies which are hardly capable of being restructured is the right approach seems open to doubt. After all, just as with the decision on restructuring, the decision on privatisation has to depend on the market opportunities open to the investor.

VI. Financial contributions by the THA

A prime requirement for the effective restructuring and re-organisation of THA companies was always an entirely new capital and asset structure. The "Deutschmark Balance Sheet Act" of 23rd September 1990 formed the basis for this. It required companies, among other things, to draw up an opening balance sheet and define their registered capital as of 1st July 1990. The valuation of assets and debts was to be carried out on the basis of the principles of a market economy, valuation of the individual assets, prudential considerations, and with the company regarded as a going concern. In addition to various other special regulations, debit and credit accounts had to be evaluated at the conversion rate of 2 East Mark = 1 Deutschmark. Effective equity is calculated as the balance of assets against liabilities. If this resulted in a minus figure, special regulations applied to formerly state-owned companies. Under § 24 of the Deutschmark Balance Sheet Act, companies are entitled to an interest-bearing claim against the shareholder to settle any balance deficit in the opening balance sheet. However, the THA as the shareholder needed to approve the Deutschmark balance sheet and to accept the claims for compensation only if the company was capable of being restructured.[79]

Companies whose opening balance sheets had been approved were normally granted the equity base backing normal for their industries. If necessary, reserves were formed equal to the expected initial losses. The cancellation of historic debt[80] was an important instrument for producing an adequate debt-equity ratio. The THA believes that, of the DM 104 billion of historic debt stated in the balance sheets of 1st July 1990, it had to take over about DM 70 billion.[81] The following were the basic alternatives: conversion into equity, conversion into shareholders' loans, liquidation of settlement claims, and redemption of outstanding capital contributions. The THA also assumed responsibility for the regular interest payments on these loans in order to relieve the companies of the financial load.

Until the THA had taken the necessary balance sheet action retroactively as of 1st July 1990 by approving the opening DM balance sheet or taking over the historic debt, it had to support the credit rating of its companies by different means in order to ensure their solvency and the continuation of their business operations.

---

79 See: Göllert and Ringling, *DM-Eröffnungsbilanz*, pages 20 et seq. The opening balance sheet and the appendix had to be approved by the shareholder (the THA) before the end of the twelfth month (or for smaller companies the fifteenth month) after the effective balance sheet date (1st July 1990 – § 35 of the Act). However, in practice these deadlines were not always met.

80 These are debts incurred by the legal predecessor of the THA at the (East German) Deutsche Staatsbank. See: Treuhandanstalt, *Entschlossen Sanieren*, page 36.

81 op. cit., page 37.

Table 6:
THA's financial support for restructuring and re-organisation

All figures in DM millions	1991	1992 (up to Dec.)
Expenditure		
Financial assistance/loans from THA	6,442	5,288
Contributions to compensation plans	3,391	1,684
Interest charges on historic debt	9,252	5,644
Redemption of liquidity loans covered by global guarantees	3,380	*8,473
TOTAL	22,465	21,089
Contingency liabilities**		
Individual guarantees	4,020	11,336
Global guarantees	26,200	15,183
TOTAL	30,220	26,519

* Including DM 4,542 million categorised under closures
** As of 31st December of the relevant year

Balance sheet measures in the opening DM balance sheet as of 1st July 1990	
Historic debt taken over in opening DM balance sheets	38,493
Acknowledgement of settlement claims in THA companies' opening DM balance sheets	14,546
TOTAL	53,039

Source: Treuhandanstalt, Vorstandsinformation 12/92, page 2.1.

The financial collapse of the former state-owned VEB companies was initially staved off by means of global guarantees. At the latest by the second Quarter of 1991, the individual applications had been processed and individual guarantees were issued. As a maximum, "guarantees were given for a loan volume of DM 30 billion and for 7,331 companies placed with about 100 different banks."[82] In addition to securing loans and freeing from debt, the THA also supported its companies with direct contributions. This included contributions to the compensation plans, the redemption of liquidity loans covered by global guarantees, shareholder loans, and the above-mentioned payment of the interest charges on historic debt.

Table 6 shows the total amount of the THA's[83] financial contributions to restructuring and reorganising its companies.[84] These include not only expenditure but also balance sheet measures and guarantees.

82 Treuhandanstalt, *Handbuch Aufgabenspektrum und Lösungswege,* 1993, Part 25, pages 2 et seq.
83 See: Treuhandanstalt, *Entschlossen Sanieren*, page 10.
84 Source of data: THA, Zentrales Controlling 1992, page 2.1. The THA was not able to provide any further data.

To assess these various forms of support for company it is necessary to make precise distinctions. There were basically three routes open for financing the restructuring activities of the THA companies:

1. financing from its own cash flow,
2. financing from the capital market, and
3. financial support from the THA.

Financing restructuring programmes from the companies' own turnover was in most companies quite impossible because of the collapse of their turnover and their unsatisfactory cost structures. Financing them by disposing of assets, particularly the capital assets not required for business operations, might have been effective in some cases, but this kind of activity was generally speaking quite inadequate for balancing out losses and financing investment. The THA companies were therefore forced to resort to the financial support of their shareholder or of third parties.

Important prerequisites for obtaining finance on the open market are profitability and an acceptable balance sheet structure. But the eastern German companies had temporarily taken over their historic debts, which thus imposed an enormous debt burden on them, with in most cases no assets to compensate which might have generated any real profits. The THA therefore had to make decisions of balance sheet policy and implement them regarding the amount of the necessary equity, the offsetting of settlement claims against historic debts, balancing the special losses account or raising it further in accordance with § 17 section 4 of the Deutschmark Balance Sheet Act, freeing from historic debt, and paying in the remaining equity.[85] The balance sheet activities which did not affect liquidity, and which by 31st December 1992 had however grown to a total of about DM 57,216 million were still insufficient, on account of the poor revenue situation, to restore the credit-worthiness of the companies. As shown in detail in Section IV.2.b, external finance was in most cases only possible with THA guarantees.

The companies were therefore dependent on the support of the THA both to finance investment and to cover their losses. According to information from the THA, it spent a total of DM 14.944 billion in 1992 (including DM 4.041 billion in connection with privatisation), and DM 14.006 billion in 1991 (including DM 792 million in connection with privatisation), on restructuring its companies. It should be noted here that the money spent in 1992 covered a far smaller portfolio of companies and a smaller number of employees.[86] DM 10.903 billion was spent in 1992 on restructuring the THA portfolio companies, consisting of:

1. expenditure on restructuring, particularly in the form of shareholder loans and payments to cover losses (DM 4.515 billion),
2. expenditure to redeem short-term loans covered by global guarantees (DM 3.391 billion),
3. contributions to compensation plans, also in connection with privatisation (DM 1.684 billion),
4. expenditure to re-imburse revenue from the sale of assets (DM 756 million),
5. interest on or redemption of settlement claims (DM 15 million), and
6. expenditure to remove historic environmental pollution (DM 2 million).

85 See: Lohse and Sonnemann, *Entschuldung und Kapitalneufestsetzung*, page 38.

86 See: THA, *Finanzbericht 1992,* page 8.

Restructuring expenditure per employee rose from about DM 5,700 in 1991 to about DM 12,100 in 1992.[87]

However, the crucial question in assessing financial support is how much was made available to finance investments, with the focus of attention resting on the purpose for which guarantees were given and loans made by the THA. Of all the guarantees in force on 31st March 1993, which had been issued to a total of 2,080 companies, only just under 13% were used for investment purposes. Two-thirds of the guarantees were issued to cover losses and secure liquidity. As of 31st March 1993, out of a total of about DM 8.3 billion in loans paid out, almost 65% were used to redeem guarantees and thus had no direct effect on the companies' liquidity. About 14% of the total amount was used to secure liquidity, whilst only 2% was spent on financing of investment.[88]

Without being able to determine the optimum level of investment for restructuring the companies, the figures reflect the cautious investment policy of the THA. This is in line with official THA policy, which had been stated in detail in the "Guidelines on Business Policy" (*Leitlinien der Geschäftspolitik*) issued in October 1990 and which gave privatisation priority over the restructuring of companies or parts of companies. "The THA is convinced that privatisation is the best form of restructuring."[89] The THA was confirmed in this attitude by the Council of Economic Advisors in its 1990/91 annual assessment, in which it took the view that the THA would have been hopelessly overburdened if it had taken on responsibility for restructuring and came to the conclusion that "privatisation is the road that leads to restructuring, and not *vice versa*".[90]

The THA therefore concentrated, as has been shown, on supporting the management task of restructuring without itself attempting to play any major role.[91] This assistance could however only be gradually intensified on account of the following developments:

- improved information on the situation and strategies of its companies,
- improved local management and installation of monitoring bodies,
- reduction through privatisation of the number of companies needing assistance,
- development of the THA's own organisation (increased staff, division of authority and responsibility, procedural regulations, etc.), and
- accumulation of experience by all concerned.

Even if the THA laid no claim to any major role in the restructuring of its companies, by categorising them according to their suitability for restructuring and, as a result, by approving or tur-

87 These calculations relate to the average numbers employed by THA companies, which was about 2.3 million in 1991 and about 0.9 million in 1992. Source: THA, *Finanzbericht 1992,* page 9.

88 See: Report dated 27th April 1993 (pages not numbered) by Department F P2, Financial Controlling. The THA was unable to give figures on the financing proportion of investments with the aid of guarantees and loans which had been withdrawn, paid back, or converted by 31st March 1993. It is however assumed that these proportions were higher, as in particular in 1990 urgently necessary investments were made.

89 Treuhandanstalt, *Fragen und Antworten zur Privatisierung*, page 4.

90 Sachverständigenrat zur Begutachtung der gesamtwirtschaftlichen Entwicklung (Council of Economic Advisors), Jahresgutachten 1991/92, clauses 516 and 517, page 230.

91 „The THA has at no time laid claim to taking over the industrial management of its companies." Treuhandanstalt, *Entschlossen Sanieren*, page 7.

ning down their applications for financial funds it retained a decisive influence on their restructuring programmes. The accusation that the THA invested too little too late in restructuring is hard to understand, as it was not until a relatively late stage that the THA was able to assess the state of its companies, and in any case, in addition to this, its primary task was to privatise and not to restructure. In addition to the inevitable risk attending restructuring investment, that it might be money well wasted, there was also the danger that future investors, although interested in the company, would have other aims for its restructuring and would not be prepared to pay the THA back for the investments it had financed.

The difficulties surrounding privatisation, particularly for manufacturing companies, were already becoming apparent by the middle of 1991. This situation even applied to the companies which had been by and large categorised as capable of restructuring. As the failure or delay suffered in the privatisation efforts did not lead directly to the conclusion that lack of capability to restructure was the root cause,[92] the THA was faced by the question (and still is) as to how long privatisation endeavours should be continued.[93] The THA, if only on account of its responsibility as sole shareholder, was compelled to let companies survive if they were capable of being restructured and to support them in a constructive manner.[94] The problems of the labour market and the economic structure in eastern Germany, however, increased the political pressure on the THA to involve itself more actively in restructuring.[95] As a consequence, new models were designed in 1992 for providing organisational and financial support to the process of "on-site restructuring". At the end of 1992, the THA also started a programme for accelerating the pace of investment in its companies.[96]

VII. Models for continuing the restructuring of THA companies

The difficulties which became more and more apparent towards the end of 1991 and during the course of 1992 in privatising many THA companies led to increased public and political pressure on the THA to pursue a policy of actively restructuring its companies. These demands were based on the view that the THA had up to then not pursued any consistent restructuring policy but was well able to do so. However, the situation and events described above show clearly that the THA's scope for shouldering full responsibility for restructuring in any serious manner had been very limited indeed.

---

92 This failure or delay initially only shows that there is no demand for ownership of companies or production facilities in general or of that particular kind. The causes, apart from those related to the specific situation of one company, can also be traced back to the general characteristics of company ownership: large capital investment, high investment risk, plus risks from „moral hazard", low fungibility, valuation difficulties, etc. This greatly reduced the number of possible investors.

93 See: Heise and Ziegler, *Struktur- und Industriepolitik*, page 551.

94 See: Gemählich, *Politik der Treuhandanstalt*, page 57.

95 See: Nolte, *Privatisierung und Sanierung*, page 559.

96 To this end the THA developed a guideline to enable it to apply uniform methods to assessing whether investment projects are qualified for assistance.

1. Management-KG companies

The model of a "Management KG" was developed in the early part of 1992. (A KG, or *Kommanditgesellschaft*, is a private partnership in which at least one partner bears unlimited personal liability and the liability of at least one partner or of the other partners is limited to their initial capital contribution.) The THA's aim was first to privatise the management and thus the restructuring (and privatising) task itself, so that the companies held within could be privatised in a later step after the restructuring process had been completed or at least effectively started. The basis for this model in company law was to form a holding company as a "*GmbH & Co KG*", a KG-company in which a management-GmbH becomes the active partner with unlimited liability (towards the KG's creditors – as a GmbH its liability towards the KG itself is automatically limited). The active partners of the GmbH are managers with the qualifications and experience to carry out restructuring work. The sole limited partner in the KG is the THA, which provides a portfolio of companies it owns as an initial capital contribution in kind to the holding company, plus liability capital which can, if the company's financial situation requires, be contributed in cash. The portfolios are intended to consist of companies which are basically capable of being restructured, have at least 200 employees each, and appear capable of being privatised in the medium term. The basic concept provides for a turnover level of between DM 0.5 and 1.0 billion for the individual portfolios.[97]

Success in restructuring is meant to be brought about basically by the participation of the partners of the full partner GmbH in the proceeds of the later sale of the company. This is intended to provide the managers with an incentive for restructuring their companies quickly and privatising them remuneratively.[98]

Based on this model, two Management-KG's were founded in 1992 and three more in early 1993. In the early months of 1993 they contained 69 companies in various different industries which employed a total of about 32,000 people.[99]

Problems in implementing these models arose from the extensive body of contracts needed to establish a Management-KG. The danger exists that the room for manoeuvre granted to the management team responsible for restructuring is not thereby widened and that those of them best able to handle restructuring become bogged down in administrative work resulting from the co-determination rights and approval processes of the THA. These stretch from corporate planning and reporting at the level of the GmbH[100] and of the KG[101] through to THA approval for a defined number of business operations requiring the shareholder's assent (under Article 3 of the management agreement).[102] But the argument that this "wasted effort" would be compensated

97 Treuhandanstalt, *Handbuch Aufgabenspektrum und Lösungswege*, 1993, Part 2, pages 6 et seq.

98 op. cit., page 6.

99 See: THA press release dated 17th February 1993, *Gründung weiterer Management-Kommanditgesellschaften*, page 1; *Handelsblatt*, 18th February 1993: „*Management-KG*".

100 Article 6 of the GFV (*Geschäftsführungsvereinbarung* or management agreement) covers the GmbH's budget and the related half-yearly reports.

101 Article 2 of the same agreement covers the restructuring plan, on the basis of which an annual plan has to be drawn up and monitored with quarterly and even monthly reports.

102 See: THA, *Informationen des Zentralen Beteiligungscontrolling*, Dr Hendrickx, 24th September 1992, pages 4 to 20.

for in full, or even more than that, by the improved incentive scheme is irrelevant because it can be assumed that these highly paid top managers have a built-in motivation of their own. This means that the directors of the Management-KG's who like their subordinates had had a position in the THA anyway, would have been able to carry out the restructuring work, so to speak, from their desks in THA Central Office.

It is also necessary to find an explanation for the fact that between 9 and 21 companies are being brought in to the individual holding companies[103] to be restructured by restructuring teams of up to 10 managers.[104] This relationship makes the local task of managing the restructuring, as the THA has always advocated, quite impossible. Moreover, the planning horizon of three years, after which the companies are to have been restructured and privatised,[105] is unrealistic in light of the poor situation from which these companies are starting.[106]

2. The ATLAS model

There are other approaches, apart from that embodied by the Management-KG's, for preserving and restructuring THA companies. The "ATLAS" model developed by the State of Saxony has gained considerable attention in public discussion. This is the German acronym for "selected THA companies registered by the State for restructuring" (***A**usgewählte **T**reuhandunternehmen vom **L**and **a**ngemeldet zur **S**anierung). The plan is that individual States identify companies of regional significance for inclusion in the project. If in the THA's view they are capable of being restructured, a joint restructuring programme is set up by the THA and the State, and if not the State can keep the company in existence at its own expense; but the aim is later privatisation in both instances.[107]

The top-priority element in this concept is the opening up of the financial aid instruments of the States (including funds from the Joint Project and guarantees) for the benefit of the THA companies involved which would not otherwise qualify for assistance.[108] Another declared aim

103 See: *Handelsblatt*, 16th March 1993, page 23.

104 See: *Handelsblatt, „Solidarpakt à la Breuel"*.

105 See: Treuhandanstalt, *Handbuch Aufgabenspektrum und Lösungswege*, 1993, Part 2, page 6.

106 See: *Wirtschaftswoche* No. 43, 16th October 1992, pages 140 et seq.; *Handelsblatt, „Management-KG"*, 18th February 1993.

107 See: Donges, *Konservierende Industriepolitik*, page 68; also: BMWi-Tagesnachrichten (Federal Ministry of Economic Affairs daily bulletin) no. 9960, 15th December 1992; *Handelsblatt, „Solidarpakt à la Breuel"*. At the time this article was written, plans for the Saxony trust fund were the most advanced. By 24th March 1993, 147 companies had been registered by Saxony and out of them 55 already confirmed by the THA. They included two machine-tool companies, Heckert-Chemnitzer Werkzeugmaschinenbau GmbH and Mikrosa Werkzeugmaschinenbau GmbH, and a textile engineering company, Spinnereimaschinenbau GmbH). Other models are, for instance, the „B-9" Model in Berlin and the „Anker" model in Mecklenburg/West-Pomerania. For all these models see articles in *Handelsblatt* on 2nd/3rd May, 19th/20th September, and 23rd December 1992, and 17th January, and 8th and 14th April 1993, and also in *Tagesspiegel*, 30th January 1993, page 33.

108 See: Kajo Schommer, as quoted in *Handelsblatt*, 2nd/3rd May 1992: *Sanierung von Betrieben.*

is the strengthening of the management team responsible for restructuring, but how this aim is to be attained is not readily apparent.[109]

As the THA is required by the Treuhand Act, the THG, to support companies capable of restructuring even without outside help (this is the interpretation of § 2 section 6 of the THG), and in the official descriptions of the model criteria of regional policy are brought to the fore, the assumption can easily be made that the companies involved are not so much those deemed capable but those deemed worthy of restructuring that are involved. Political reasons are therefore taking precedence ahead of the criteria of economic efficiency.[110]

VIII. Conclusion

The crisis in the THA companies caught up in the transformation process is more serious than originally assumed. Crisis management methods familiar from the market-economy system attained only limited success when transferred to eastern German companies because the initial situation to which they were applied was totally different. Numerous pointers indicate that some companies are coping successfully with the crisis, but the period of time which it is possible to consider in this article is too short to be able to state the probability of success in achieving a complete turnaround.

More crucial is the experience gathered over the last three years in restructuring eastern German companies to bring the remainder of them into profit. The THA and its successor organisation will be coming under increasing political pressure to develop and implement strategies for the organisation of restructuring management. The danger exists here that the assessment of whether a company is worth restructuring will be considered from the political and not from the economic point of view. Political measures can only be justified if they contribute, on the basis of market-economy principles, to securing an effective and long-term competitive position for the companies.

The principles need to be adhered to rigidly that privatisation is the form of restructuring that offers the best prospects, and that the THA should restrict itself to support restructuring. The restructuring work itself should be carried out by organisations which have the advantages of experience. The models practised so far represent feasible routes, but in future far more imagination and greater resolve will be necessary for the development of alternatives.

IX. Literature

Becker, Jochen: *Marketing-Konzeption.* Munich ^{3}1990.

Böckenförde, Björn: *Unternehmenssanierung.* Stuttgart 1991.

Bundesverband deutscher Banken: Aktivitäten der privaten Banken in den neuen Bundesländern. In: *Die Bank* 6/1992, pages 357 to 361.

109 According to information from the Clearing Office referred to by Mr Darkow there is no clearly formulated overall strategy. Inquiries with the relevant State governments have confirmed this statement.

110 See: Donges, *Konservierende Industriepolitik*, page 68.

Donges, Jürgen B.: Konservierende Industriepolitik – unwirksam, kontraproduktiv, teuer. In: *Wirtschaftsdienst* 1993/II, pages 67 to 69.

Dörner, Dietrich: *Sanierungsprüfung*. In: Wirtschaftsprüfer-Handbuch 1992, Bd II. Düsseldorf 1992, pages 207 to 332.

Ganske, Joachim: Spaltung der Treuhandunternehmen. In: *Der Betrieb* 15/1991, pages 791 to 797.

Gemählich, Peter: *Erfahrungen und Politik der Treuhandanstalt*. In: Dirk *Ipsen* and Egbert *Nickel* (editors): *Probleme der Einheit – Ökonomische und rechtliche Konsequenzen der deutschen Vereinigung*. Marburg 1992, pages 55 to 64.

Göllert, Kurt, and Wilfried *Ringling*: Analyse der DM-Eröffnungsbilanz. In: *Die Bank* 1/1991, pages 20 to 25.

Gross, Paul J.: Grundsatzfragen der Unternehmenssanierung. In: *Deutsches Steuerrecht* No. 47 (1991), pages 1572 to 1576.

ditto: *Sanierungsberatung in der ehemaligen DDR*. In: *Bericht über die Fachtagung ... des Instituts der Wirtschaftsprüfer in Deutschland e.V.* Düsseldorf 1991, pages 217 to 236.

Hax, Herbert, and Hans-Joachim *Marschdorf*: Anforderungen an ein Insolvenzrecht aus betriebswirtschaftlicher Sicht. In: *BFuP* 2/1983, pages 112 to 130.

Heise, Arne, and Astrid *Ziegler*: Struktur- und Industriepolitik in ostdeutschen Bundesländern. In: *WSI Mitteilungen* 9/1992, pages 545 to 555.

Hess, Harald, and Dietrich *Fechner*: *Sanierungshandbuch*. Neuwied [2]1991.

Kayser, Georg: Sanierungsfähigkeitsprüfung insolvenzbedrohter Unternehmen. In: *Betriebs-Berater* No. 7/1983, pages 415 to 421.

Keller, Eugen von: Sanierungsrichtlinie. In: *WPK-Mitteilungen*, special issue, September 1990, pages 171 to 175.

Kröger, Fritz: Restrukturierung zur Privatisierung. In: *Zeitschrift für Betriebswirtschaft*, supplementary issue 1/1993, pages 97 to 107.

Krystek, Ulrich: Reorganisationsplanung. In: *Zeitschrift für Betriebswirtschaft*, 1985, pages 583 to 612.

ditto: *Unternehmenskrisen*. Wiesbaden 1987.

Kurtkowiak, Klaus: Sanierungen in der ehemaligen DDR. In: *Buchführung, Bilanz, und Kostenrechnung* No. 1, 3rd January 1991, pages 7 to 12.

Lohse, Dieter, and Erik *Sonnemann*: Entschuldung und Kapitalneufestsetzung im Zuge der DM-Eröffnungsbilanz. In: *Die Bank* 1/1992, pages 37 to 41.

Müller, Rainer: *Krisenmanagement in der Unternehmung*. Frankfurt am Main [2]1986.

Münch, Reinhard: Innovation oder Anpassung – Besonderheiten der Unternehmensführung in Ostdeutschland. In: *Deutschland Archiv* 25 (1992), pages 820 to 828.

Myritz, Reinhard: Mangel an Kompetenz – Manager in Treuhand-Beteiligungsunternehmen. In: *Unternehmen und Gesellschaft* 26 (1992), No. 5, pages 16 to 19.

Nolte, Dirk: Zwischen Privatisierung und Sanierung. In: *WSI Mitteilungen* 9/1992, pages 552 to 563.

Priester, Hans-Joachim: Gesellschaftsrechtliche Zweifelsfragen beim Umgang mit Treuhandunternehmen. In: *Der Betrieb* 1991, pages 2373 to 2378.

Sachverständigenrat zur Begutachtung der gesamtwirtschaftlichen Entwicklung: *Jahresgutachten 1990/91, "Auf dem Weg zur wirtschaftlichen Einheit Deutschlands"*. Stuttgart 1990.

ditto: *Jahresgutachten 1991/921, "Die wirtschaftliche Integration in Deutschland. Perspektive – Wege – Risiken*". Stuttgart 1991.

Schmiedel, Ekkehard: Die Prüfung der Sanierungswürdigkeit unter betriebswirtschaftlichen Gesichtspunkten. In: *Zeitschrift für Betriebswirtschaft* 54 (1984), pages 761 to 772.

Schoppen, Willi: Restrukturierung eines Kombinats. In: *Zeitschrift für Betriebswirtschaft*, supplementary issue 1/1993, pages 9 to 17.

Treuhandanstalt Informationen, various issues.

Treuhandanstalt: *Entschlossen Sanieren. Die Rolle der Treuhandanstalt beim Umstrukturierungsprozeß in den neuen Ländern.* April 1992.

ditto: *Fragen und Antworten zur Privatisierung ehemaligen Volksvermögens in den neuen Bundesländern.*

Weimar, Robert: Die Entflechtung von Treuhandunternehmen. In: *Zeitschrift für Wirtschaftsrecht,* June 1991, pages 769 to 777.

Zanger, Cornelia: Unternehmenskrise und Produktentwicklung. In: *Zeitschrift für Betriebswirtschaft* 61 (1991), pages 981 to 1006.

Privatisation strategies

by Klaus-Dieter Schmidt, with the assistance of Uwe Siegmund

I. Introduction

The THA was given a key role in the transformation of the East German planned economy into a free market economy. It became temporarily the owner of some 8,000 companies with more than 45,000 operational sites, 33,000 shops, hotels, cafés and restaurants, dispensing chemist outlets, cinemas, book-shops, considerable real estate which had once belonged to the main political parties, party mass organisations, and the Ministry for State Security (the Stasi), not to mention 3.9 million hectares (15,000 square miles) of agricultural and forestry land; and all this together with the task of "making them competitively by restructuring and privatising ... in accordance with the provisions of the Treuhandgesetz" (or THG).[1] Siebert logically describes this task as "the core of the transformation process".[2]

The THA has now very largely completed its work, so that it can begin to contemplate an early end to its "operative business" (Table 1). This is a very respectable achievement, and one which hardly anyone would have believed possible when it started.[3] Nevertheless, the large number of completed privatisations is no indicator of whether the THA acted efficiently and in accordance with the aims laid down for it. The results it has achieved depend almost entirely on the quality of its decision-making, because for every privatisation decision there was always at least one alternative: the THA could have sold the company to another bidder, could have continued running it a while longer, or could have liquidated it straight away. Its work can thus only be evaluated on the basis of a comprehensive analysis, and one which has to cover all facets of its privatisation work: its aims, the possible courses of action open to it, the decision-making processes, and the results achieved.

---

1 The Act setting up the THA. The quotation is from Article 25 of the Treaty of Unification; for the sources of the other Acts see pages XVI et seq.

2 Siebert, *Das Wagnis der Einheit*, page 84.

3 Of the numerous articles critical of the THA during the course of its work, it is sufficient to mention: Sachverständigenrat, *Jahresgutachten 1990/91* and *1991/92*; Cox, *Entflechtung, Perspektiven und Vermögenspolitik*; Luft, *Treuhandreport*; Maurer, Sander and Schmidt, *Privatisierung in Ostdeutschland*; Mörschel, *Treuhandanstalt und Neuordnung*; Smith, *Privatization Programs*; Hax, *Privatization Agencies*; Naujoks, Sander and Schmidt, *Von der Privatisierung zur Sanierung*.

Table 1:
Companies in which the THA held equity (as of 30th June 1993)

Total number of companies	12,993
including:	
Privatisation	5,831
complete	5,370
majority	461
Reprivatisation	1,360
Communalisation	259
Preliminary assignment	70
Liquidation	2,857
in hand	2,800
completed	57
Mergers and split-offs	297
Others[1]	651
Awaiting privatisation	1,668
for information: privatised parts of companies	6,364

1 Mine ownership (rights), THA assets (including forestry operations), THA equity under examination, and others.
Source: THA, *Monatsinformation*, as of 30th June 1993.

The following article will attempt to do this as concisely as possible, by covering the following in detail:

- defining the task of privatisation against the background of complex and often contradictory aims,
- discussing the strategic options open to the THA and instruments available to it,
- outlining the route taken in practice to arrive at decisions, and
- evaluating the results achieved so far by privatisation.

This article cannot describe the broad spectrum of privatisation work in full detail. "Privatisation is more than just selling ... Privatisation means finding commercially active business owners quickly" – this was the THA's definition of its core task as stated in a set of internal working instructions.[4] To this end it developed a number of very different strategies over the course of time, each tailor-made for the market and the competitive conditions in each given industry. There is no "THA model". In the following pages it will only be possible to analyse the main lines of its privatisation work. How it conducted its privatisation business in real-life will be shown in the appendix with three brief case-studies.

4 Treuhandanstalt, *Handbuch Privatisierung*, section 1.1, page 1, as of March 1992.

II. Aims of privatisation

Looked at from the business economist's point of view, the task of privatisation can be defined as a decision-making problem for which specific aims have been laid down and in which privatisation itself is one of these aims. Economic decision theory[5] provides clear criteria to show the actions to be taken in the sale of a company. However, the THA also has a highly political task, as Schuppert[6] so rightly emphasises. This arises directly from the task as defined by legislation, as understood by the public, and finally as interpreted by the THA itself. A review must first be made of all these definitions.

1. Task defined by legislation

As stated in the Preamble to the THG of 17th June 1990, the THA is required "not only to reduce the entrepreneurial activity of the state as quickly and as widely as possible through privatisation", but also "to create in as many companies as possible the ability to compete, thus securing existing jobs and creating new ones". This requirement is stated in more detail in § 2 section 6 of the THG: "The THA shall promote the structural adaptation of the economy to the demands of the market, in particular by influencing the development and privatisation of those companies capable of being restructured into firms capable of competing. It works towards creating companies capable of operating in the market by appropriately dismantling corporate structures and producing an efficient economic structure." This task thus covers far more than the privatisation of the companies in its possession; legislation intends that it should also:

- restructure the companies and parts of companies, i. e. create units capable of being privatised by splitting, hiving off (and closing), or selling off (including "sale and lease back"); and
- start work on restructuring them, i.e. taking appropriate measures such as developing workable corporate strategies, reducing numbers employed, freeing from debt, exempting them from payments for historic environmental pollution, or regulating lines of authority (allocation of assets, issue of investment certificates), in order to make them ready for sale.

In all this, the THA was supposed to carry out privatisation as quickly as possible, instigate investment, and preserve or create jobs, as well as realise suitable proceeds from the sale of companies and other assets. It was also required to ensure that privatisation achieved the planned degree of success by installing a system of contract management and contract control for the period following privatisation. Furthermore the THA had to observe several rules set by competitive policy. It thus had a very complex bundle of tasks on its hands, which caused problems for a number of reasons:

- The aims are very vague. Legislation gave the THA plenty of room for manoeuvre. Schuppert describes the statutory aims as a cross between conditional and final programming in which neither the task nor the procedure is properly defined. "The relationship between ... the aims one against another is somewhat unclear, we are told nothing of the decision-making process,

5 Sieben and Schildbach, *Betriebswirtschaftliche Entscheidungstheorie*.

6 Schuppert, *Die Treuhandanstalt*.

and we search in vain for any criteria or guidelines for practising the process."[7] This may cause misgivings when looked at with a lawyer's eye, but there were good reasons for legislation having been formulated in this way: it gave the THA plenty of scope for manoeuvre, and it needed this to carry out its task.

- The various aims are not entirely consistent with each other. Thus the THA can decide that the best thing is to liquidate a company straight away, and yet it can regard itself as being compelled "for over-riding reasons" to ensure its survival. It must then itself attempt to minimise such conflicts of aims. In such cases, legislation gives the THA a virtually free hand, well aware that it is easier to resolve such conflicts at the administrative level rather than the political.
- There is no hierarchical relationship between the aims. The THA is required to privatise the companies "as quickly and as widely as possible" but at the same time "to maximise the proceeds from the sale as far as the fulfilment of its other aims allows".[8] It is rarely possible to achieve both at once. Some companies could perhaps only have been sold (as a complete unit) after a long search for investors and lengthy negotiations. Whilst the more attractive parts of the company would find a buyer quickly, the remaining parts could only be sold at an indefensibly high cost if at all. In such an instance, the THA must itself decide which aim is to be given priority.

The THA is aware of this problem, and has therefore not sought to define priorities even in its internal working instructions. In its guidelines for the Privatisation Directorates, only very vague rules are given under the heading of "Decision Principles", which state that "in addition to achieving an appropriate net cash result, ... the following criteria have to be taken into account: undertakings to preserve existing profitable jobs and create new ones as part of the continuation of business operations, undertakings to make investments, security (e. g. contractual penalties) to cover these undertakings, bearing at least part of the cost of limiting and removing historic environmental pollution, the bidder's credit rating, the investor's position as a *Mittelstand* company [a small or medium-sized company managed by its owner] ... These criteria will be subjected to a relative weighting for each case separately, depending on the economic position, the regional business environment, the regional labour market, and the reactions of potential investors on the basis of the competition between bidders."[9] It is far from clear what this was to mean in individual cases, and another passage in the same hand-book only says succinctly: "The THA has broad scope to use its judgement ... in weighting the aims and the solution to the conflicts of aims in individual cases."[10]

The THA has however to observe a large number of statutory regulations in carrying out its task; these limit its scope, but without tying it up in knots. The main ones are:

- public-sector budget law, which binds it to the principle of the economic and thrifty use of public funds in concluding privatisation contracts;
- the ban anchored in constitutional law against public servants acting arbitrarily, which means that the THA cannot exclude any bidder without good reason;

---

7 op. cit., page 193.

8 Treuhandanstalt, *Handbuch Privatisierung*, section 2, appendix 1, page 3, as of January 1993.

9 op. cit., section 6.1, page 1, as of March 1992.

10 op. cit., section 2, appendix 1, page 3, as of January 1993.

– the laws of the European Community (now the European Union), which mean that the THA has to observe the European law on subsidies.

However, the THA can basically decide freely, under the rules of private (civil) law, which company or other asset it wishes to sell when, how, and to whom.

2. The public's expectations

The THA operates autonomously on the principles of private law even though its task is defined under public law, and is expected to act not only with business acumen but also with political skill. Its decisions affect millions of people, either directly as employees or investors or indirectly as tax-payers. The THA is thus under the constant pressure of having to justify itself towards the public. It stands to reason that it can never be right in everybody's eyes at once.

In this respect the main scope for free action which legislation grants to the THA thus proves to be a disadvantage. It is almost totally exposed to the consolidated demands of private and political interest groups, and sometimes finds it very hard to escape this pressure, especially when it has to close down major companies or to declare large numbers of workers redundant. The attitude is widely held that the THA decides arbitrarily over the fate of its companies and is even capable – if it really wants – of breathing health back into companies that are in fact in their death-throes. This often leads to the demand that restructuring should be given priority over privatisation, or that privatisation should even be postponed.[11]

The THA is not subject to directives and does not need to submit to political pressure. Nevertheless, it has no way of getting round the fact that it has to take aspects of structural, regional, labour, and social policy into account in its work; if it did not, many privatisation decisions would have been taken differently. The long arms of the State governments, the political parties, and the trade unions reach far down into the THA.[12]

3. The THA's point of view

The THA has made rapid privatisation its core task. This places it in harmony with the vast majority of theoretical economists, who see privatisation as the form of restructuring which offers the best prospects for the future.[13] "Restructuring for Competition" by dismantling the giant industrial groupings is only a first step, although an important one, on the way to privatisa-

11 The wording was extreme but the mental attitude was fully in accord with that of a broad swathe of the population in eastern Germany when the German Federation of Trade Unions in the summer of 1992 called for a programme of immediate industrial policy action, saying: "Lop-sided privatisation is finishing eastern Germany off as an industrial location. It is necessary to give the THA a completely new orientation. Although the THA has given itself the motto ‚Rapid privatisation, resolute restructuring, considerate closure' it is in fact concentrating almost entirely on privatisation – an irresponsible policy". Deutscher Gewerkschaftsbund (German Federation of Trade Unions), *Industriepolitisches Sofortprogramm*, page 2.

12 See: articles by Hanau, Czada, and Seibel in this volume.

13 See: Sachverständigenrat, *Jahresgutachten 1990/91* and *1991/92*; Kronberger Kreis, *Wirtschaftspolitik für das geeinte Deutschland.*

tion.[14] It endeavoured to hold to this maxim consistently, even though with increasing difficulty and decreasing success in recent times.[15]

However, the THA has made the task of privatisation subject to conditions, derived them from its statutory task. The internal regulations which the Privatisation Directorates have to adhere to explicitly contain the following criteria:[16]

- Speed of privatisation: priority is given to a privatisation that can be carried out quickly. It is even recommended in cases when other aims could be better attained if the THA were prepared to wait for a buyer.
- Complete privatisation: the endeavour must be made to sell the company off as a whole, and partial privatisation only aimed at if it is the only possible route.
- Preserving and creating jobs: negotiations must aim to ensure guarantees of jobs and/or investment, and to use contractual penalties, as adequate as possible, to ensure their implementation.
- Creation of efficient economic structures: privatisation should help to create markets with a high degree of competitiveness, and preference should be given to *Mittelstand* companies.
- Realisation of proceeds: within the confines imposed by the attainment of other goals, formerly state-owned property is to be sold off in a manner which realises the maximum proceeds.

General promotion of the economy or the relevant region, on the other hand, is not on the list, and therefore the THA does not regard this as its job.

The basic line for privatisation is to preserve a company as far as possible. The THA therefore requires potential investors to produce a strategy in which they can demonstrate convincingly that they can continue the business operation of the company with a reasonable hope of success. The term "continuation" is interpreted very narrowly to mean retaining the main emphasis of the business and its location. This greatly restricts the range of possibilities for privatisation. A potential investor will generally speaking not be successful if he intends to turn the company to some other use or re-sell it. The THA thus assumes (not always on any firm basis) that the investor will carry out his project somewhere else if he is turned down.[17] It is without any doubt

14 The internal Guidelines on the privatisation of companies dated 23rd October 1990 make this point: "Privatisation has priority over restructuring. Restructuring should only be provided for if this is demonstrably necessary in order to prepare the company for potential purchasers". See: Treuhandanstalt, *Organisationshandbuch*, serial no. 3.1.1, page 1, as of February 1991; in the 1993 "Principles of Privatisation" it says: "Privatisation is more than selling off. Privatisation is the most effective form of restructuring... Restructuring should whenever possible be initiated by the investor. On the way toward privatisation, the THA will support companies on condition they have a workable corporate strategy for financial and organisational restructuring"; Treuhandanstalt, *Organisationshandbuch*, serial no. 2.4.1, page 2, as of March 1992.

15 Naujoks, Sander and Schmidt: *Von der Privatisierung zur Sanierung*.

16 Treuhandanstalt, *Handbuch Privatisierung*, section 2, Appendix 1, pages 2 et seq., as of January 1993.

17 The minutes of a meeting of the Privatisation Directors on 23rd August 1991, page 2, contain the following: "If two investors are bidding for a company, both with similar strategies, preference should be given to the interested party who intends to keep the company in being and/or at the same location. Competing bidders who are planning on the basis of a completely different strategy, and only need the property on which to establish their project, should be given assistance in putting their plan into effect in the open country site. With regard to job guarantees it is possible under certain circumstances, in the inter-

difficult to justify this fixation with the preservation of companies and production locations on any economic grounds. As the THA itself concedes, it can be that an investor offering a better strategy is turned down. As two experts with inside knowledge have written, "The Treuhand's motivation for requiring business continuation clauses is ... to realize its social goals. ... In one extreme case ... the Treuhand faced the choice of permitting the company to go bankrupt and then selling its parts – or trying to find a buyer for the entire business, 'gold doorknobs' and all. If the company had gone bankrupt, the Treuhand would have further weakened an already economically weak area."[18]

The issue may be put this way: The THA is pursuing a privatisation strategy which focuses not only on the goal itself but on the route leading to it. In the words of its lady President, its strategy is not selling but buying. "We are purchasing: ... we give preference to a buyer if he is contributing sales channels, if he can close the innovation and technology gap ... as quickly as possible and thus enable the company to survive."[19] The THA is thus attempting to prevent privatisation leading to *cracks and faults*, which could result in serious regional employment problems, and is therefore prepared to make concessions against its final aims if it can thereby more readily attain its intermediate ones. The consequence of this is that it is not pursuing privatisation in accordance with any rigid set of rules, but is keeping its options open.

III. Privatisation procedures

Two basic models can be used when companies or parts of them are being sold: the auction model, and the bargaining model. Each procedure used in practice can be attributed to one of these two:

- Using the auction model, the company is sold to the highest bidder in either a public or a limited tender or auction. The criteria for the decision can be chosen freely: the highest offer price, the offer that promises the largest number of jobs, the most convincing corporate strategy, or a combination of all of them. The auction model has some advantages, and is therefore favoured by many theoretical economists.[20] It guarantees relatively rapid privatisation, and principally it ensures transparency, but it does require sufficiently intensive competition between bidders and a relatively simple tendering process. The auction model is therefore particularly suitable for mass privatisation (e. g. shops, hotels, plots of land), but is not much use for the privatisation of more complex companies, and of little use at all if the company is in a critical economic situation.
- Using the bargaining model, although the company can be offered under a restricted tender, potential buyers are mainly addressed directly. Bilateral discussions and negotiations then decide which buyer is to be successful. This procedure has the advantage that both sides get

---

est of retaining workable structures, to make concessions to the bidder who intends to retain the production location, because if an existing production location is abandoned it does not as a rule lead to a new one being created in eastern Germany": THA, Directorate for the co-ordination of the branches, minutes of meeting of the Privatisation Directors on 23rd August 1991, page 2.

18 Dodds and Wächter, *Privatization contracts*, pages 78 et seq.

19 Breuel, *Die Rolle der Treuhandanstalt*, page 33.

20 Smith, *Privatization Programs*.

the chance to realise their often differing conceptions. The negotiations parties enjoy – in contrast to the auction – additional degrees of freedom in designing the contract. The procedure is always to be recommended when only a small number of bidders appear or can be considered as suitable buyers. Its weaknesses are that it provides little transparency and is usually time consuming.

Each of the two basic models has, admittedly, further advantages and disadvantages which have to be weighed up. For instance, the question should be asked as to which will lead to the best possible valuation of the company and thus to a good selling price; which will be most likely to ensure the continuation of the business, and which will most quickly enable the company to obtain good management. The auction model is thus superior to the bargaining model in fixing the price, on the condition that competition between the bidders is sufficiently lively and is not manipulated by collusions.

The THA, which is principally free in its choice of privatisation instruments, has decided in favour of a flexible approach, referring to this as "industry-orientated marketing": "The means and methods necessary to achieve success vary from one industry or size of company to another. A combination of instruments will often be necessary – there simply is no 'miracle' method for privatising an entire national economy."[21] However, this means that the THA is demanding a great deal of itself. In order to be able to use the right instruments for a sale, it needs not only to know its own companies very well but also the markets in which they operate.[22] It does not always achieve both at once. The THA often enters into negotiations with a party which is in a stronger position because it has a better knowledge of the market and can better assess the company it wishes to acquire, than the THA itself. At the beginning this was indeed usual, as the example of the privatisation of the Interhotel chain shows.[23] In addition to this, the choice of instrument is determined by the aims the THA is striving to attain, as its interest is not to find "any" buyer but the "right" buyer, one who is willing and able to restructure a run-down company and continue its operations.

The THA first makes a distinction between five different sales procedures, which can be attributed to the two basic sales models and in some cases are only differentiated by shades of emphasis: free sale, bidding, limited tender, open tender, and public auction.[24]

1. Free sale, negotiating with interested parties without following any formal procedure, has attained a varying level of significance. It only played a certain role in the initial stages in the sale of companies organised by THA Central Office, as at that time many of the giant *Kombinate* or industrial groupings and the smaller companies had already signed up co-operation agreements with western companies with a view to later take-over. The THA was thus often faced with a *fait accompli* which it was no longer able to overturn. However, when the sale was organised by one of the branches, this procedure appears to have been used in

21 Wild, *Privatization marketing*, page 212.

22 Kl. Müller, *Industry-specific privatization marketing*, page 213.

23 See: article by Seibel in this volume, page 117.

24 Treuhandanstalt, *Handbuch Privatisierung*, section 4.4, pages 18 to 20, as of March 1992. In May 1992, a sixth process was added, the "simplified procedure for the sale of small businesses". A benchmark price is set by the THA branch manager or Industry Director in order to accelerate negotiations; op. cit., section 4.4.6, page 20, and appendix 4, page 3, as of December 1992.

later stages as well. This informal selling process has its advantages and disadvantages; on the one hand a company can be privatised fairly quickly this way, but on the other hand the danger exists that the seller, meaning the THA, can "be taken to the cleaners".

2. Bidding is the procedure which the THA uses the most often, and uses a very special variant: the direct approach. Investors, mainly companies already in the industry to which the company on offer belongs, are requested by the THA to submit an offer. It has made particularly frequent use of this procedure for privatising large, complex companies, mainly those in processing industry: chemicals, petroleum, paper, iron and steel, as the number of serious interested parties is very small in these industries. The THA sees the advantage of this procedure in the fact that all the stages of privatisation – unbundling, initial restructuring, contract drafting, and finally the sale – can be argued out quickly and efficiently. The disadvantage is the lack of transparency in the decision-making process; also, it does not guarantee equality of opportunity – any potential investor who has not been approached has hardly any chance of being allowed to tender.
3. The limited tender process is the one which the THA prefers to use if the company is of a small or medium size and simple in structure. Thus nearly all the companies in the textile and clothing industry, or in wood-working and furniture that were capable of privatising were put out to tender internationally. The limited tender is a largely formalised procedure in which the THA lays down a large number of conditions but still leaves them open to negotiation. As with the bidding procedure, it is usually only a predetermined group of potential investors that is called upon to make an offer. In putting 54 companies in the wood-working and furniture industry out to tender, for instance, the THA sent out a total of 2,000 company profiles and received 43 offers. The advantages which the THA sees in this procedure are that a precise selection of possible investors can be approached directly, the decision-making process is transparent and can be followed and comprehended even by outsiders, the sale can be carried out quickly, and it is easier to optimise the sale price. The THA itself determines the group of potential buyers in limited tenders; this may be an advantage from the THA's point of view, as it can for instance exclude from the start any bidders who might only be interested in the real estate, but the disadvantage is that it might "overlook" perfectly good bidders and thus fail to attain the best possible result.[25]
4. Public tender, a standardised bidding procedure, has been used twice by the THA, once for the mass privatisation of more than 30,000 retail shops in January 1991, and the second time when larger items came up for sale later. On those occasions, anybody could bid, but the chances of success were not uniformly distributed because the THA made certain demands on the bidders. "The criteria for selecting of purchasers were personal competence, the business plan and indeed the origins of the applicants ... it was generally tried to ensure that the retail outlets were taken over by their own employees." "This was intended to minimize the risk that the shops were not used for the agreed purpose. The Treuhandanstalt pursues the policy that a grocery should be in the future where a grocery had been in the past." The main aim in the mass privatisation of retail outlets was to create a broad swathe of medium-sized business

25 In this case the interest was not particularly lively. On average, only two or three offers are sent in for each company on offer. See: Kl. Müller, *Industry-specific privatization marketing*, page 218.

all in one sweep, and it was very largely attained. 90% of the smaller shops and just over 50% of the larger ones went to eastern German bidders.[26]

5. Public auction, which is likewise a public bidding procedure, but one in which normally all the terms of sale are known except the purchase price and every bidder knows what all the others are offering, is not used by the THA. The objections which the THA brings up against this instrument, namely that it considers the purchase price as only one of a number of criteria (and not even the most important one), are not very convincing. Even an assorted bundle of aims can be optimised by means of a public auction; for instance, a minimum purchase price can be stated and the property sold to the bidder who guarantees the highest investment sum or the largest number of jobs.

The floating of shares can be regarded as a special form of auction, but the THA has not used this method either – this time, for good reason,[27] as there was hardly one single company that would have been suitable for privatisation via the stock exchange. It would have been necessary to create a simplified route to the stock exchange for them, and even then the prospects of success would have been very uncertain. Up to now, only one eastern German company (the dairy products company Sachsenmilch) has dared to take the perilous route to the stock exchange, and then only after a quoted western German company (Südmilch AG) had taken it over and restructured it.[28]

It must be pointed out in this context that the THA is exempt from the requirement of carrying out a public tender procedure prior to a privatisation such as the Federal Budget Ordinance normally requires in similar circumstances. It is only required to observe the ban imposed by constitutional law against acting arbitrarily, and must not favour one bidder over the others, or discriminate against one, without good reason. Apart from this it is free to choose which procedure it follows.

In deciding in favour of one procedure or another, the THA basically observes two criteria: the chances of success, and the time needed. The aim is to privatise quickly and successfully. If it cannot achieve both at once, it places greater weight on the criterion of success, and this explains why in most cases it selects the negotiation route, even if under certain circumstances this means losing time.

IV. Privatisation in practice

Privatisation can be broken down into three phases: preparation, execution, and monitoring the success. Each phase is of great importance for the THA. In the preparation phase, the items on the agenda are: the creation of sellable units by unbundling or merging companies, the valuation

26 Dierk, *The schematic procedure*, pages 246 and 245.

27 In the central and eastern European countries undergoing economic reform, on the other hand, this procedure, used in one form or another, has taken on great significance, such as privatisation by voucher. See: Frydman, Rapaczynski, and Earle (editors): *Privatization Process in Central Europe*.

28 Nevertheless, Sachsenmilch had to declare itself bankrupt in July 1993, and Südmilch entered insolvency proceedings shortly after. See *Börsenzeitung*, 24th July 1993, page 5, and *Süddeutsche Zeitung*, 29th July 1993, page 20. Trading on the regulated market for ordinary bearer shares was suspended on 13th September 1993. See *KWD-Neue Bundesländer* No. 177, 14th September 1993.

of assets and liabilities, the assessment of the company's suitability for restructuring, the initiation of marketing activities, and finally the preliminary discussions with potential investors. It is in this phase that the foundation stone will already be laid for the success or failure of the privatisation. In the execution phase the focal point is the actual sale negotiations. The THA first checks the bidders' credit ratings and the viability of their corporate strategies, and only then does it negotiate in detail with the individual bidders: on planned investments, and numbers of jobs, planned environmental protection measures, and even the purchase price. The third phase, after privatisation, includes contract supervision and, if necessary, subsequent negotiations. As the former owner the THA regards itself as being continuously responsible for the companies, and under certain conditions will even take a company back if an investor fails.

It should be noted that the THA only very gradually came round to using a systematic and probably efficient procedure for privatisation. In the initial months, from the summer of 1990 to the early part of 1991, when the THA was still in the process of organising itself, a large number of activities were carried out in a totally haphazard manner.[29] It is thus possible to discern a learning process characterised by three main phases:

- the transition from reactive to active privatisation
- the development of standardised privatisation procedures on the "modular" principle, and
- the preparation of network solutions.

Thus the THA needed a certain amount of time before it could set up an efficient privatisation marketing organisation. When it started its actual work in the summer of 1990, its Central Office and its 14 or 15 external offices only had about 550 employees (most of them East Germans).[30] It started by selling those assets in which the investors themselves were interested; in these cases, the purchaser was usually better informed than the privatiser, and it took time until the THA had managed to catch up on the other side's insider knowledge. By the time it had finished building up its organisation, in the summer of 1991, the number of staff had risen to 2,700, and it was not until then that it could set about its work systematically and concentrate properly on the privatisation of individual companies and whole industries. Any description of privatisation in practice must bear in mind the individual phases of development which the THA passed through.

1. Preparation

a) Splitting and hiving off for closure

Although the process of unbundling the *Kombinate* and state-owned VEB companies started only just after the fall of the East German communist regime, with the THA taking over some 8,500 legally independent companies, many units were clearly incapable of being privatised on account of their size and general structure. "For the purpose of promoting privatisation and creating structures orientated towards the free market economy", an internal set of instructions for THA staff involved in privatisation stated, "it is necessary to examine the idea of unbundling

---

29 See in place of other sources: A-interview with Dr Eberhard Sinnecker on 27th July 1992.

30 See: article by Seibel in this volume, page 115.

these companies."[31] Unbundling is taken as meaning not only the splitting up of companies and the hiving off of parts of them, but also the individual sale of parts not needed for operations, particularly real estate. By separating out assets not needed for the business the THA is pursuing two aims: making the company "leaner", in order to make it possible for investors to buy them who cannot raise infinite amounts of capital, and it is preventing investors from acquiring companies in order merely to speculate with the real estate without any interest in continuing their operation.

In order to make the unbundling process easier, a legal instrument known as the "splitting" of corporations (*Kapitalgesellschaften*) was created specially for the THA; German company law prior to that was only familiar with *Ausgründung*, hiving off a part of a company. Under the *Spaltungsgesetz* or Splitting Act of 5th April 1991 it is possible to split a corporation into separate parts or to split parts away from it. In comparison with the hiving off the splitting provides a number of advantages for the THA, particularly in making the process easier to handle in technical terms.

Above all the THA principally uses the instrument of splitting when it has to find a "tailor-made" solution for one particular investor, for instance if he is only interested in certain parts of a company or cannot raise the purchase price for the whole of the company. The THA is then admittedly running the risk that the other parts of the company then have to go into liquidation, but it regards this risk as the lesser of two evils.

b) Classification

In order to be able to sell its companies, the THA not only has to restructure them but must also value them in terms of their prospects to survive restructuring. To this end it can fall back on an independent group of consultants, the so-called Management Committee (*Leitungsausschuß*). "The Management Committee works on behalf of the Federal Ministry of Finance as an independent body in a consultancy function for the Executive Board and the Directorates."[32] For some time eight (but in summer 1993 only four) industry teams were allocated to it, in the busiest times manned with anything up to 80 experts (auditors, management consultants, other specialists) and charged with the job of classifying each of their companies in terms of its overall situation. As a basis for this the Committee took the corporate strategies submitted to it and the DM opening balance sheet. The result of the Management Committee's evaluation was to place each company into one of the following categories: (1) Company is operating profitably, (2) Company expected to enter profitability soon, (3) Corporate strategy appears successful, (4) Company appears capable of being effectively restructured, strategy not yet sufficient, alternative concepts should be drawn up, (5) Restructuring capability appears dubious, (6) Company is not capable of being restructured.[33] On average, the Management Committee's judgement placed about two-third of the companies in the category of being capable for privatisation, although usually not until they had been restructured, and one third were to be liquidated and

31 Treuhandanstalt, *Handbuch Privatisierung*, section 3.1, page 1, as of January 1993.

32 Treuhandanstalt, *Organisationshandbuch*, serial no. 1.5.3.1, *Beurteilung und Verfolgung der eingestuften Unternehmenskonzepte durch die Beratergruppe U1 U*, page 1, as of July 1992.

33 See: Treuhandanstalt, *Informationskongreß*, 7th May 1992: *Aufgabe und Tätigkeit des Leitungsausschusses*, page 3.

wound up. However, the THA is not bound to act in accordance with these evaluations; the Executive Board and the Directorates can take their own autonomous decisions on the fate of a company. In actual fact, only about half the companies placed in Groups 1 to 4, and a good third of those in Groups 5 and 6, were privatised by the end of 1992 (Table 2). The question must remain open as to whether the Management Committee made mistakes in classifying the companies or whether the Executive Board of the THA ignored its recommendations.

Table 2:
THA companies examined and classified as suitable for and worthy of being restructured (as of November 1992)

Classification		Total		of which: fully or partially privatised	
		No.	%	No.	%
Total		1.438	100.0	722	50.2
1.	Company is operating profitably	25	1.7	16	64.0
2.	Company expects to enter profitability soon	102	7.1	76	74.5
3.	Corporate strategy appears successful	593	41.2	340	57.3
4.	Company appears capable of being effectively restructured, strategy not yet sufficient	347	24.1	163	47.0
5.	Restructuring capability appears dubious	70	4.9	34	48.6
6.	Company is not capable of being restructured, alternative concept should be drawn up	301	21.0	93	30.9

Source: THA, U1 BC4: Central reporting

c) Initial restructuring

In the opinion of the THA, many companies classified as capable for privatisation could not be sold off as they stood, but first needed to be prepared for the market. These preparations included unbundling, dismissing redundant staff, freeing from historic debt and liability for historic environmental pollution, and injecting fresh capital. The THA refers to these cases as "initial restructuring" (*Ansanierung*) as a preliminary stage in privatisation. However, it frequently goes far beyond the initial level by providing management assistance, financing investment, or covering losses from the operational business; this is then referred to as "supported restructuring". The "Guideline for the preparation and treatment of corporate strategies" dated 6th December 1990 states: "If it has not yet proved possible to conclude privatisation despite the relevant activities, the THA is prepared to assist in and supervise the continuation of the necessary measures on the basis of the corporate strategy, provided this has been examined and classified as workable."[34]

34 Treuhandanstalt, *Organisationshandbuch*, serial no. 3.2.2, *Richtlinie zur Erstellung und Behandlung von Unternehmenskonzepten vom 6. 12. 1990*, page 8.

The THA only ever wanted supported restructuring to be regarded as a preliminary stage in privatisation. The pre-requisite for its financial commitment was always a workable corporate strategy, one which made not only the restructuring but also the later privatisation look as if it had reasonable prospects of success. Increasingly, however, it has been difficult for the THA to maintain this stance consistently. In its annual economic report for 1993, the Federal Government laid down a different strategic direction for the THA by saying clearly: "For a manageable number of large companies capable of being effectively restructured but for which the completion of privatisation is not yet in sight, the THA will pursue individual restructuring programmes on a case-by-case basis." "The THA will not permit the implementation of the agreed corporate strategies of those of its companies which are classified as capable of being restructured to fail for lack of finance." And: "The companies will be given the necessary time, to be defined for each one individually, but as a rule at least one year. Endeavours at privatisation must continue to be made even within this period *provided the goal of restructuring is not thereby put in doubt*."[35] Applying such conditions to privatisation only makes sense if the THA has to strive for a set restructuring goal. Normally, an investor will be wanting to restructure a company for himself once he has bought it, but not necessarily in the way the THA has in mind.

d) Privatisation marketing

In order to improve the chances of privatising its companies, the THA operates a well directed privatisation marketing operation, partly through its own internal organisation (Central Office, branches, and offices in other countries) or through its subsidiaries (such as the successor companies of the *Gesellschaft zur Privatisierung des Handels*, the corporation responsible for privatising wholesale and retail trade, the real estate holding corporation or *Liegenschaftsgesellschaft der Treuhandanstalt*, and the forestry corporation, the *Forstbetriebs GmbH*), or else through third parties such as investment banks or consultancy firms. The main aim here is to awake the interest of certain investors in acquiring a certain company. The main activities are:

- offering the company in the press,
- approaching selected potential investors by sending them company profiles,
- holding branch oriented meetings,
- commissioning brokers and investment banks to find investors,
- arranging or taking part in trade fairs and exhibitions,
- approaching industrial associations, chambers of commerce, and other organisations,
- arranging information events, and
- other special sales campaigns such as *Mittelstandsexpress, Arbeitsprogramm MBO*, and *Aktion Kleinunternehmen*.

For the kind of marketing activities which it uses, and which it terms the creation of primary contacts, the THA has laid down a number of fixed rules. The nature and scope of the activities are related to the size of the company and the particular characteristics of the industry. How, when, where, and to whom the companies are offered is decided on the basis of market studies.

The THA lays particular importance on the assistance of third parties. It hopes thereby to accelerate the privatisation process and to intensify the competition between bidders. The sup-

35 *Jahreswirtschaftsbericht 1993*, pages 50 and 49; emphasis added by the present author.

plier of the marketing service is given exclusive rights to market the property for a fixed period of time, prepares the negotiations, and supports and advises the process until the contract is signed. This procedure can be called "privatising privatisation".

2. Execution

a) Selling procedure

The THA works with an eye on its goals and using the instruments at its disposal, employing a large number of privatisation procedures which cannot be adequately described and evaluated within the limited scope of this article. Apart from the mass privatisation in the retail and catering trades, and of some hotels, where fixed procedures have been used (based particularly on standardised evaluation regulations for calculating their value), the THA nearly always regards the sale of a company as a unique event. In individual cases it ties up a "package" and endeavours to privatise more than one company at a time in each tender. It has used the tendering process in some problem industries (steel, chemicals, ship-building, micro-electronics) where the crucial point was the preservation of industrial networks, and here it has included companies in the same package of which some were fully capable of privatisation and some would otherwise have had only a slender chance of being sold.

Unless it delegates the job to a third party, the THA conducts most of its privatisation negotiations via its 15 branches (although by June 1993 nine of these had completed their privatisation work and had been converted into branch offices), and only a small proportion via Central Office. Responsibility is decided mainly on the basis of the size of the company: those with fewer than 1,500 employees basically come under the responsibility of the branches, but there are exceptions.[36] At the Central Office, negotiations are generally in the hands of the respective Division, which are divided by industries and where there are special privatisation teams who conduct the negotiations with the investors.

aa) Normal method

For average cases, the THA recommends its privatisation teams to keep to the following procedure, although they frequently digress from it:

- The interested party should first submit an offer in very general terms, stating the industry, location, and size of the company he is looking for and the investment and employment undertakings he is prepared to make.
- If his offer is of interest to the THA, he can select a company on the basis of the offer documentation (e. g. THA catalogue of companies or tenders).
- If the conditions are suitable for privatisation (e. g. no claims pending for restitution) he can inspect the company for himself.
- He then has to submit a detailed corporate strategy, without which sale negotiations cannot even start.

---

36 See: article by Seibel in this volume, page 125.

- During these negotiations, the THA attempts to lay down as many details as possible in the contract, even including those which within the context of a normal company acquisition are not even discussed. This includes particularly the securement of investment and employment undertakings by means of penalty clauses. This can make negotiations a long drawn-out affair.

The THA has developed minimum criteria for the privatisation process, containing among others the following steps: offer registration, calculation of value, sales negotiations, sale decision, contract formulation and contract carrying out. There is also a privatisation check-list with further compulsory points for clarification. Apart from this, however, the privatisation teams are given plenty of free scope in their negotiations and decisions. Normally they decide for themselves whether a given bidder is to be selected as the buyer or not.[37] This is seen by many as a shortcoming since this takes a major proportion of the decision-making process out of the range of public supervision. The THA is of a different opinion, and attributes at least part of its success in privatisation to this regulation.

bb) Special methods

As early as the autumn of 1990, when the THA issued its "Guidelines for Business Policy", it had already taken the stance that it intended to promote the formation of *Mittelstand* companies through its privatisation programme – small to medium-sized companies, often of family character, managed by the sole or principal shareholder.[38] To this end it later formulated a number of basic principles which it then implemented in a programme called *Treuhand-Initiative Mittelstand*.[39] The following groupings were to be included: former senior managers and employees of the companies, managers from outside the company intending to set up in business, and western German owners of small and medium-sized businesses. Bidders from such groupings who presented a strategy of equal value to that from competitive bidders were to be given preference. In order to create companies suitable for such groups to take over (with up to 50 employees), the THA has been unbundling larger companies in order to have a "stock in trade"; at times (middle of 1992) it had about 2,500 on offer for MBO (management buy-out) or MBI (management buy-in).

---

37 In the privatisation of companies from a certain order of magnitude upwards, however, the approval of the Executive Board and the Administrative Board, and the assent of the Federal Ministry of Finance, are necessary. This is the case with companies which meet any two of these three criteria: 2,000 or more employees, DM 100 million or more as their balance-sheet total, DM 300 million or more turnover. In other instances, other approval procedures come into force. Treuhandanstalt, *Handbuch Finanzen/ Rechnungswesen*, section 1.4, *Genehmigungserfordernisse der THA*, page 3, as of July 1992. Slightly modified approval procedures have been in force since March 1993; approval must be obtained from the entire Executive Board when the company has more than 1,000 employees, DM 100 million turnover, or a balance-sheet total of more than DM 150 million. The Administrative Board and the Federal Ministry of Finance have to be consulted when a company has more than 1,500 employees, DM 150 million turnover or a balance-sheet total of more than DM 150 million. Treuhandanstalt, *Organisationshandbuch*, serial no. 1.7, page 4, as of March 1993.

38 Treuhandanstalt, *Organisationshandbuch*, serial no. 1.2.2, *Leitlinien der Geschäftspolitik*, page 1, as of October 1991. "The Treuhandanstalt is anxious to revive this structure of small to medium-sized enterprises and uses for this purpose the instruments of management byout (MBO), management byin (MBI) and a combination of both approaches." See Klinz, *Venture capital companies*, page 263.

39 Treuhandanstalt, *Initiative Mittelstand*.

However, the THA will only consider companies for MBO/MBI if they have reasonably sound prospects for the future. These companies must:
- „possess a cash-flow generating product range based on competitive advantages,
- operate in stable, often regional, markets,
- be subject to relatively small fluctuations in profit level,
- have the possibility of providing an adequate amount of equity."[40]

Privatisation then follows a special procedure. The benchmark price is first defined on the basis of an assessment by independent auditors. A bidders' auction is then held and the company is sold to the bidder presenting the best strategy. Payment of the purchase price can be deferred, or reduced by leasing the company's site. Grants and subsidies can be claimed to assist in financing. If a restitution claim has been lodged, the THA can open investment priority proceedings under § 3a of the Property Act or under the Investment Priority Act.[41]

The "*Initiative Mittelstand*" proved very successful, even though not every campaign produced the results the THA had been hoping for.[42] By the end of February 1993 almost 2,000 firms or parts of firms had been sold as MBO's, totalling about 17% of all privatisations. MBO was far and away the most popular of all the various special programmes, but the THA has now discerned its weaknesses. Many of the MBO companies are having difficulties because the new owners are often short of the necessary knowledge and experience and because the equity resources are too small to carry the firms through the difficult start-up phase.[43] For some time the THA has therefore been keeping a watching brief on these sold companies and provides or arranges for help as soon as it notices that problems are coming to the surface. It primarily attempts to find western German partners for MBO companies who might be able to make their know-how and their financial strength available by means of an MBI.

In contrast to its *Mittelstand* campaigns, the Treuhandanstalt was rather less successful in its attempts at interesting institutional investors in a commitment to an eastern German company. By the end of 1992, German and foreign investment funds and capital investment companies had only invested a sum total of DM 400 million in take-overs. In addition to this, until the summer of 1993 there was however made an unknown total of investments in newly established companies.[44] All in all, the amounts invested by institutional investors are very small in comparison with the sum total of investment undertakings obtained by the THA; buyers of eastern German companies have promised to invest a total of more than DM 150 million. The THA makes no secret of its disappointment at the low level of interest shown by investment compa-

---

40 Treuhandanstalt, *Organisationshandbuch*, serial no. 3.1.11, *Orientierungsrahmen der Treuhandanstalt zur Veräußerung von Beteiligungsunternehmen an deren leitende Mitarbeiter (MBO)*, page 4, as of January 1991.

41 See also: Removal of Obstacles Act and the Investment Priority Act.

42 The campaign started in 1991, *Mittelstandsexpress*, with the aim of accelerating the privatisation of hotels, boarding houses, and holiday homes, made only slow progress because of unsettled questions of ownership and uncertainty as to the application of the investment priority rule.

43 The Privatisation Directors of the branches were already voicing critical remarks on the "success" of the MBO campaigns in the summer of 1991 that at the moment nobody can make any reliable forecast as to the state these MBO's will be in after another three to five years. See: Treuhandanstalt, Directorate for the co-ordination of the branches, minutes of meeting of the Privatisation Directors on 23rd August 1991, page 5.

44 Naujoks, Sander, and Schmidt: *Von der Privatisierung zur Sanierung*, pages 433 et seq.

nies and funds, and considers that the problem lies in their conservative investment policies:[45] their sole interest is to minimise risk, and a commitment to a THA company is usually only considered when it is already on a rock-solid path to making a profit. There are however further reasons: most capital investment companies are subsidiaries of major banks, and their parents are often committed with loans. These closely interlinked banks and investment companies often find it difficult to take equity in a company when they already hold most of its debt. Also, many of the owners of the smaller eastern German companies are unhappy with the idea of an "outside" shareholder, and fear that he or it will exert too much influence on business policy. Nevertheless, the THA still continues to court institutional investors because they are most able to bring the equity into the privatisation process which most of the smaller, recently privatised companies lack. The THA has therefore created a special "Investor Services" department to operate as the central co-ordination point between the companies needing equity and the institutional investors seeking investment opportunities.

The prospects of success for the Management-KG's (precisely Management GmbH & Co. KG, an institution designed for the privatisation of companies which have undergone some previous restructuring) are also uncertain. This form of company is a THA "invention" and each contains a dozen or so companies from various industries, as a rule ones which are hard to privatise in the short term but which are assessed as capable of restructuring and therefore of privatisation in the longer term. The first two Management-KG's were formed in May 1992, and three more have since been added. Their particular characteristic is that for each KG-member company a manager is inserted as an "intermediate owner" with the right to a proportion of the proceeds of privatisation. The amounts they stand to receive are usually set on a series of sliding scales, and are correspondingly higher if the company is sold more quickly and if the purchaser undertakes to make more investments or to preserve and create more jobs. The THA is hoping that by these means it will be able to make good the shortage of qualified managers in its companies. However, the model had serious initial weaknesses, as Härtel et al have pointed out:[46] the demands made on the managers running a complicated industrial conglomerate are extremely high; also, their capacity for work is absorbed by the parent company and is not be available to the individual GmbH-companies.[47]

Companies which the THA cannot privatise and cannot even restructure must be "wound up". It endeavours to save as many jobs as possible in the process, and is achieving a certain level of success in this. The approach of "privatising via winding-up" has proved to be a quite successful method of privatisation. In principal, the THA is faced by a choice between opening bankruptcy proceedings against its own company or liquidating the company under the rules of company law. If it comes to the conclusion that the continued operation of individual parts of the business is possible and financially tenable it will decide in favour of liquidation, and in such an instance will attempt to find a buyer for the rump of the business, often via its "Investor Services" department or the TLG (the THA real estate holding corporation), by writing to interested parties of which it is already aware or by publishing an open offer to tender.

---

45 See, among other sources: Klöttschen, *Capital investment companies*, page 271; Klinz, *Venture Capital*, page 268.

46 Härtel, Krüger, Seeler, and Weinhold: *Unternehmenssanierung*, pages 26 et seq.

47 With regard to the companies the three newly established Management-KG's possess a far more homogeneous character than their two predecessors.

b) "Sensitive" areas

In selecting the privatisation procedure, the THA enjoys a certain degree of freedom, but not an infinite amount. The decision to use any special procedure, and the privatisation decision itself, depends on the goals laid down, but these are not determined exclusively by the THA itself. In any instance in which a large number of jobs are at stake there is always massive intervention from third parties: State governments, trade unions, and political parties. In such cases privatisation is preceded by long drawn-out and complicated negotiations with one or a number of interested parties, the outcome of which is highly uncertain. The privatisation of the eastern German shipyards dragged on for more than two years, and in other significant industries such as chemicals or engineering the end is still not yet in sight (Table 3).

Table 3:
Privatisation status of eastern German branches of industry, as of July 1993

Industry	Total number of companies (gross)		% of these:[1]		
				owned by THA	
	No.	%	fully privatised	in liquidation	awaiting privatisation
TOTAL	5,996	100	41.6	29.0	12.3
including:					
Chemical industry	255	4.3	45.5	25.5	14.1
Plastic, rubber, and asbestos processing	179	3.0	38.5	31.3	6.7
Minerals, fine ceramics, glass	462	7.7	56.7	16.0	12.1
Ferrous and non-ferrous metals, foundries, steel products	245	4.1	41.6	24.1	21.6
Steel and light metal structures	203	3.4	39.9	16.3	18.7
Engineering	1,102	18.4	46.2	24.0	17.5
Automotive industry	363	6.1	55.4	20.4	11.8
Electrical and electronic industry	491	8.2	38.3	36.7	8.8
Precision and optical engineering	80	1.3	38.8	32.5	10.0
Iron, metal, sheet metal goods, musical instruments, sports equipment, toys and games, jewellery	323	5.4	30.3	35.6	10.5
Wood-working and timber	505	8.4	32.9	31.9	8.5

Table 3:

Industry	Total number of companies (gross)		% of these:[1]		
				owned by THA	
	No.	%	fully privatised	in liquidation	awaiting privatisation
TOTAL	5,996	100	41.6	29.0	12.3
including:					
Paper and printing industries	244	4.1	50.8	27.0	8.2
Leather and shoe-making industries	169	2.8	18.3	54.4	11.8
Textile and clothing industries	519	8.7	19.5	45.3	16.8
Food and allied industries	856	14.3	48.7	28.2	5.8

[1] Difference: already liquidated, reprivatised, communalised, partially privatised
Source: THA, documentation department

The reader must continually be reminded that the THA is not just selling the "jam", not even mainly the "jam", but is mainly selling "bread-and-butter" companies, many of them stale and mouldy enough to be candidates for bankruptcy. The latter type ought, if the normal criteria were applied, to be liquidated on the spot, but the THA is not always free to do this. For instance, its original intention with the eastern German micro-electronics industry was to send them off wholesale into liquidation (as, probably, the Management Committee proposed on two separate occasions), but it has given up this idea after the State governments most affected (Saxony, Thuringia, and Brandenburg) had strongly intervened and tried to privatise them first all together and later bit by bit.

Whenever politics become involved in privatisation negotiations the THA finds itself playing a weak hand. It then falls between two stools, and this makes its handling of the negotiations decidedly problematic:

- It has no weapon in its hands to defend itself from political pressures. It is not a government authority with cut-and-dried lines of responsibility. Its actions (and this may be the only grounds on which it can defend itself) are "technically-managerially orientated" (Mörschel). It can only exert its influence by other means, such as by trying to persuade the State government to commit itself financially.[48]
- It is also in a weak position when facing potential purchasers. Normally there is a limit to the concessions either side can make in bargaining, defined by the liquidation value of the company on offer. As soon as word gets round that a company is not allowed to be liquidated, the interested parties will try to force the price downwards. Privatisation can provide enough examples of this from practical experience.[49]

48 See: article by Czada in this volume, page 154.

49 In connection with the privatisation of the shipyards the press started referring generally to a "Kvaerner" effect (after one of the firms proposed as a rescuer).

It is not possible within the confines of this chapter to describe in detail how the THA tackles its job in these circumstances. In the appendix, the privatisation process is outlined as it affected three industries, including ship-building and micro-electronics, and these case studies show that politics help to determine the THA's strategic direction.

3. On-going supervision and monitoring success

The THA's work does not finish with the privatisation of a company, as most sales contracts contain clauses in which the investor undertakes to provide jobs and investment. The THA therefore has to make sure that these undertakings, some of which were purchased with considerable concessions regarding the purchase price, are actually met. It is currently in the process of setting up a Contract Control system; this is not a simple matter, because in the early stages there was rarely any obligation on the part of the purchaser to submit proof of adherence. It is also an open question as to what the THA will actually do if the investors cannot adhere to their undertakings for economic reasons. Its reactions so far have been varied: in some cases it accepted taking up negotiations afresh, in others it refused to assent. The THA is thus in a quandary: if it accedes to the situation it creates a precedence and could set off an avalanche of petitions for renegotiation, but if it takes a tough stance it may force the companies into bankruptcy, thus jeopardising its privatisation aim.

The THA will also have to expect that numerous privatised companies which fall into difficulties will sooner or later insist on amendments to their contracts. It can be assumed that the need for renegotiation will arise with about a fifth of the 10,000 or so privatised companies. The THA is admittedly under no obligation to re-work its contracts, and certainly under no obligation to take the companies back, but it is prepared to help in difficult cases, as can be seen from a number of recent examples (*Plauener Spitzen*, a lace factory in Plauen, *Märkische Faser*, a fibres factory in north-east Brandenburg). There are in any case clauses in some contracts that permit amendment if the company's financial position worsens, and in some cases purchasers have only undertaken a purely management role in the running of the business or individual parts of it because the risk of further financial involvement seemed to be too great. The THA is thus also "in the boat" and under an obligation to man the pumps if there is a danger of its sinking.

V. Evaluation of privatisation

The THA has now coped with the largest part of its main task, the reorganisation and privatisation of the former *Kombinate* and state-owned VEB companies. By the end of June 1993 it only had some 1,668 companies still on offer. This enormous achievement deserves acknowledgement, even if it should later emerge that no purchasers can be found for some of the remaining companies. In some cases these are companies that should really have been sent off into liquidation but which cannot be abandoned "for over-riding reasons".

The THA is required to privatise not only quickly but also successfully. Its success in privatisation must therefore be measured by the extent to which it has:
- found owners for its companies who can lead them to a better future,
- excluded arbitrary decisions from its privatisation work, and
- minimised the costs of privatisation within the limits imposed by its other responsibilities.

For the time being it is only possible to give provisional answers to these questions.

1. Effectiveness

The privatisation of a company does not guarantee its survival. Like any other company, it can still fail if its new owners are not up to the job. It will therefore only be possible after a few years to say whether the THA's work was successful in this respect.

The THA has a clear preference for taking its line from the investor's corporate strategy when reaching privatisation decisions; the purchase price is a comparatively secondary matter. This is a weak-point in its approach; a corporate strategy is not an objective basis for making decisions, and gives broad scope for subjective judgement to the party doing the privatising. If a number of bidders submit different strategies, the choice often becomes very difficult, and all the more so since due to pressure of time the examination of them can often only be superficial. The purchase price is a different matter; an investor who offers a higher price than the other bidders usually has the superior corporate strategy, as he will only risk good money if he can expect an appropriate return on it.

The preservation and continuation of each company is the central goal of the THA, one which it pursues even when there might have been better alternatives in terms of the price to be realised or of other goals such as the number of jobs secured under the contract. The onus of proof here is on the THA, and it cannot easily wash its hands of the matter if the purchaser to whom it has given preference later fails.

2. Transparency

The THA reaches most of its decisions behind closed doors, and it is hard to check up on them. It is often only the THA that knows why one particular bidder was given preference over the others. It is therefore surprising that rejected bidders do not complain noisily to the THA about its privatisation practices. On the other hand, protests would not do much good because there is no legal recourse to contest privatisation decisions. The THA decides at its own discretion, and does not need to state any reason for rejecting competitive bids. It is only liable for damages in exceptional cases, and even then the onus of proof lies generally with the party raising the complaint.

The lack of transparency in the way decisions are reached results from the practical methods used in privatisation: the THA makes far greater use of the negotiation model than the auction model. As a rule it negotiates with a number of applicants but without informing each about the discussions it is having with the others. This strengthens its negotiating position but makes it virtually impossible for any outsider to track the decision process retrospectively.

3. Costs

As often as possible the THA is meant to realise a positive amount as the proceeds of its privatisation sales, but it is also allowed to sell at a loss if privatisation is thus achieved more quickly and successfully. Its own statement of its total proceeds, up to 31st December 1992, was DM 40.6 billion, but this figure has to be set against the expenditure incurred during the course of privatisation which was considerably higher than the proceeds.

It is not possible adequately to quantify the amounts the THA is spending to find investors for its companies. The budget for 1992 totals DM 41.2 billion and includes expenditure on privatisation activities of DM 4.6 billion and revenues of DM 11.6 billion. Part of the expenditure on privatisation, however, is also contained under other headings, such as restructuring (DM 10.9 billion) and company closures (DM 7.5 billion).[50] In addition to this, the opening balance sheet of the THA as of 30th June 1990 includes on the asset side a large amount for tangible asset writeoffs, and sizeable reserves on the liability side for the restructuring of the companies in which it holds shares. The deficit in the opening balance sheet totals all in all DM 209.3 billion.[51]

The blame for the fact that the campaign to privatise companies ended up with a huge deficit cannot be laid at the THA's door, not even the major part of it. The deficit has to be traced back mainly to the mismanagement of the old system, which drained the companies of their financial lifeblood. However, the question does need to be asked as to whether the deficit shown in the balance sheet and in the profit-and-loss account might not have been smaller if the THA had pursued its privatisation task exclusively, and had not also had to fulfil obligations under structural and social policy as well. In actual fact, the size of these deficits results from the THA placing far greater emphasis in its negotiations on other goals, in particular the preservation of jobs, rather than maximisation of the proceeds. This puts it into a weaker position faced with potential investors; all they see is the public purse, held wide open,[52] and they are obviously happy to dive in.

VI. Appendix: Privatisation in three branches of the economy

1. Manufacture of food, beverage, and tobacco

The food and drink industries used to play a subordinate role in the GDR. 579 companies were under the heading of the food industry at the end of 1989, employing a total of 275,000 people. Although they were scattered widely across the country, they were mainly organised into *Kombinate*,[53] and produced almost exclusively for the home market. Most of them were in a poor way, with worn-out production machinery; industry experts estimated that their production technology was 20 years behind the times.

Nevertheless, the interest shown by western investors in eastern German food companies was high from the start. When the THA started work on privatisation, numerous co-operation agreements were already in place. There were various reasons for this:

- As soon as the western German grocery retailing chains had established a foot-hold on the eastern German market, western German manufacturers had to follow suit especially because they were already operating at full capacity.
- Although the consumer initially tended not to accept products manufactured in eastern Germany, foodstuffs and food products were soon able to re-establish their position in the market, particularly if they enjoyed well known brand names (e. g. in such fields as beer, laundry products, and cigarettes).

50 Treuhandanstalt, *Finanzbericht 1992*, page 29.
51 Treuhandanstalt, *DM-Eröffnungsbilanz*, page 14.
52 Dodds and Wächter, *Privatization Contracts*, page 69.
53 *Statistisches Jahrbuch '90 der DDR*, page 158.

– Finally, the acquisition of eastern German companies brought scarce production quotas for regulated agricultural products with it, such as sugar and milk.

It is therefore not surprising that the privatisation process in the eastern German foodstuffs and food products industry went ahead energetically, even though it was not entirely free of problems.[54]

When the THA started work, it took over some 300 major food companies; this shows that there had been relatively little change in the old structures. Only the legal status of the *Kombinate* altered which were formerly managed either by central ministries or by the 15 regional district councils. The unbundling process only made any great progress in the brewing industry and in bakery, meat, and dairy products; the latter had been mainly organised on a co-operative basis and had split off at an early stage from the *Kombinate* and gone their own ways.

The continued existence of the *Kombinat* structures had consequences. Interest groups soon formed consisting of the western German market leaders who pleaded powerfully for the one piece take-over of the companies which had succeeded the old *Kombinate*. A number of sugar companies: *Südzucker AG*, *Zuckerverband Nord AG*, *Zucker AG Ülzen*, and *Pfeifer & Langen KG* wanted to acquire the whole of *Ostzucker AG Halle*, the successor to the former *Kombinat Zucker*. Philip Morris already even had an option on the purchase of the former *Kombinat Tabak* in Dresden. The Federal Cartel Office however put a stop to most of these take-over projects. A decentralised solution was found for sugar: three western German companies took over the sugar markets immediately adjoining their own areas, and the fourth one, together with the Danish firm Danisco, took over the two markets which did not adjoin the West. There were however in total far more than just these five bidders, and some of them came from France and Italy. As for cigarettes, only the Dresden factory (Vezifa) went to Philip Morris. The western German company Reemtsma took over the Nordhausen works (*Nortak*), and Reynolds the brand name *Club* from the *Berliner Zigarettenfabrik*, which had been sold in April 1993 to *Lübecker Zigarettenfabrik GmbH*. In the beer market, likewise, the major western German brewers had had a head-start and quickly carved up the market between them. The THA was not able to do much about it, except to conduct tough negotiations and obtain relatively favourable contractual conditions. The majority of eastern German breweries are now in the hands of the five largest western German brewery groups: *Oetker*, *Gebrüder März AG*, *Brau und Brunnen AG*, *Holsten*, and *Becks*.

The THA operated at something of a disadvantage in the privatisation of the food industry. It is assumed that the Federal Ministry of Food, Agriculture, and Forestry and the Federal Cartel Office affected the privatisation of companies at the first stage of manufacture (sugar, grain, eggs, milk, meat) and determined their economic structure. The THA has been obviously reacting more than acting, basically restricting its role to implementing the decisions made by the principal protagonists.

The THA did not run into lively purchasing interest in all fields. There were, and still are, problems in the fields of meat and vegetable processing. Most of these very dilapidated companies are only hard to restructure, and it is often more remunerative to put up new factories at different locations. The THA even had to close down almost all eastern Germany's flour-milling capacity.

The THA has now attained a high level of privatisation. Out of the 860 companies which it either took over originally or created through splitting, only 50 were still on its books at the end

54 See: Th. Müller, *Wege von der Planwirtschaft zur Marktwirtschaft*.

of June 1993. 440 had been partially or completely privatised, 108 reprivatised, and 241 were liquidated or heading that way.

2. The micro-electronic industry

Micro-electronics had been a very young industry in the GDR, having been created only in the 1980's. This has been done to correct an unequal division of labour in the COMECON countries. Although the government made this industry into a status symbol and invested huge sums in it, success was not forthcoming. Experts consider that it was anything from three to eight years behind the West in research and technical productions, and eight to twelve years behind in applications. It was in the end concentrated into one of East Germany's biggest industrial companies, *Kombinat Mikroelektronik* in Erfurt, which contained 25 companies at various levels and employed some 60,000 people. A small proportion, employing about 1,000 people, belonged to another *Kombinat*, *Carl Zeiss Jena*, and was solely concerned with research work.

After the fall of the communist regime the *Kombinat Mikroelektronik* was converted into a number of legally independent companies under a holding company, *PTC electronic AG* of Erfurt, which also took on a semi-conductor firm, *Halbleiterwerk Frankfurt/Oder*, with 8,000 employees. Another unit was formed by *Zentrum Mikroelektronik Dresden GmbH* (ZMD), which was hived off from *Carl Zeiss Jena*.

Western investors' interest in eastern German companies was very limited. Although *PTC electronic* held some discussions with a few international producers (*LSI Logic Corporation*, *Siemens*, and *Samsung*), these did not immediately lead to any tangible results. It is said that the THA Management Committee urged the Executive Board to liquidate the micro-electronics industry in its entirety, but the Executive Board apparently did not follow this recommendation and decided initially to wait and see. It had requested an expert assessment from two consultancy companies, F. Hayek Engineering and Arthur D. Little, and this was submitted in January 1991. They came to the conclusion that the core of the eastern German micro-electronic industry could be rescued and recommended drastic restructuring: the merger of the activities in Erfurt and Dresden, and a dramatic reduction in numbers employed to no more than 5,000. News also arrived in March 1991 of a study carried out by the Federal Ministry for Economic Affairs which also gave a positive rating to certain parts of the holding company's empire, such as software production. In the end the THA decided on restructuring, but with an even more drastic slimming-down than the experts had recommended, to no more than 2,500 employees. In May 1991, the production capacity in Erfurt and Dresden was merged together into *Mikroelektronik und Technologie GmbH* (MTG) of Erfurt, and in July 1991 the new company entered into a "master collaboration agreement" with *LSI Logic* with the long-term aim of the latter taking a (minority) holding. The American company had already signed a co-operation agreement in the summer of 1990 with *ERMIC GmbH* of Erfurt, a subsidiary of *PTC*, which provided for a concentration of activities at the Erfurt and Frankfurt/Oder locations. However, resistance sprang up against this plan, led by the State government of Saxony, where it was suspected that ZMD, the *Zentrum Mikroelektronik Dresden*, was likely to vanish as a victim of asset stripping.[55] The

55 This suspicion arose when another bidder appeared, VLSI Technology, one of LSI Logic's main competitors. VLSI only showed interest in ZMD.

Minister for Economic Affairs of Saxony, Kajo Schommer, called for ZMD to be hived off from MTG. In October 1991 the THA denied that it intended to close down ZMD, and stated that agreement had been reached with the States concerned to the effect that the core of the existing locations would have to be retained in order to provide close access for users to micro-electronic industry. It promised to give financial support to the restructuring of the companies.

However, as for economic reasons MTG was in the considered opinion of the Management Committee not capable of being restructured, ways out of the crisis were negotiated with the States concerned, as they had determinedly taken up arms for reasons of structural policy to ensure the retention of "their" locations. Although the solution which the THA preferred on economic grounds – complete privatisation covering a number of locations at once – could not be realised because of the interests of the individual States, the following individual solutions have now been found for the various individual locations:

- *Erfurt*: The Erfurt part of MTG was turned into *Thesys GmbH* of which 19.8% were taken over by LSI Logic and 80.2% by the *Hessisch-Thüringische Landesbank* (the central bank covering the States of Hesse and Thuringia). LSI Logic has an option which it can exercise until the end of 1994 to take over Thesys GmbH completely. However, the Landesbank can sell its shares meanwhile, but only with the consent of LSI Logic. 480 jobs shall be preserved, though only 400 of them are guaranteed under contract. As start-up finance, the THA made DM 125 million available.
- *Dresden*: 19.8% of ZMD was to go to *VLSI Technology* and the remaining shares to banks, with the support of the Free State of Saxony. However, VLSI backed out in September 1992 after its subsequent financial demands had been rejected. The State of Saxony managed to arrange for two major German banks, *Commerzbank* and *Dresdner Bank*, to take over half of the shares of ZMD each in trust. Siemens committed itself by granting licences and placing orders, and also by providing management assistance, but is not bearing any part of the commercial risk. 580 jobs shall be preserved, all covered by contract. As start-up finance, the THA made DM 125 million available.
- *Frankfurt an der Oder*: MTG went into liquidation in September 1992. In February 1993 the THA gave its assent to a partial privatisation of the core business to be bought from the liquidator under the leadership of Synergy Semiconductor Inc., which will take on 19.8% of the shares with an option for its partners to increase this to 49%. The State of Brandenburg has provided a guarantee to back this. The remaining 51% is being administered by a trustee. In the former semi-conductor works, 630 jobs shall be preserved, 550 secured by contractual penalties.
- *Neuhaus*: A private investor, Zetex of Great Britain, was found for the Neuhaus location and a contract signed in July 1993 under which about 100 jobs will be preserved.

3. Ship-building

In terms of capacity, the ship-building industry in East Germany ended up almost the same size as that in West Germany. It did not start to develop until after the Second World War, prior to which the *Neptun* yard in Rostock had been the only one in existence; this yard even built ocean-going vessels. The *Warnow* yard in Rostock and the *Mathias-Thesen* yard in Wismar were opened in 1946, followed by the *Volkswerft* in Stralsund in 1948. East German shipbuilding was soon promoted to the position of "shipbuilders by appointment" to the Soviet Union, and initially had to deliver ships as part of post-war reparations; later it had to contribute to financing East Germany's raw materials imports. However, it was also designed to be a source of hard currency. The yards and their suppliers were organised into the *Kombinat Schiffbau Rostock*, which by the end of 1989 employed some 54,000 people.[56]

This *Kombinat* was converted legally in June 1990 into *Deutsche Maschinen- und Schiffbau AG* (DMS), a holding company for all 24 shipyards and suppliers. The new executive board (which was identical with the old one) wanted to keep this industrial group in being, and to restructure it "under its own steam". Superficially, the state of the East German ship-building industry appeared to be quite good in comparison with other branches of the economy. The yards had an established presence on the world market, and had been able to fill their order books very well prior to economic, monetary, and social union. It emerged later, however, that the prices at which these orders had been booked did not cover costs. In the autumn of 1990 the executive board submitted its first corporate strategy; this contained almost no measures for adapting the company to changed conditions and made no mention of reducing capacity. On the contrary, it assumed that it would be able to hold its position in its established markets, principally the Soviet Union, and that the THA would take over responsibility for historic debts totalling DM 6.6 billion, including DM 4.3 billion for orders executed at a loss. The strategy did not exclude the possibility of the company later being taken over by one or several western German shipyards, which had already expressed interest. Of these, the best position was held by *Bremer Vulkan AG*, which signed a wide-range co-operation agreement with DMS in August 1990.

In December 1990, the old executive board of DMS was dismissed. The new board submitted a revised strategy in February 1991 which likewise aimed at retaining an independent eastern German ship-building concern. Only the Neptun yard would have to give up ship-building (as opposed to refitting and repair), and merge with the Warnow yard. However, capacity and numbers employed would have to be cut by more than half. The THA gave its consent to this strategy and declared its willingness to support it financially, but did not state clearly whether privatisation or restructuring was to have priority. The management of DMS probably thought it was creating a state-owned concern which would at least remain in existence until restructuring was complete. The answer was not long in coming. A month previously, five other western German shipyards (*Blohm & Voss*, *HDW*, *Thyssen Nordseewerke*, *Mayer and Brand*) had already presented an "Anti-Vulkan" document to the THA demanding that the eastern German yards be privatised separately. They proposed, as an alternative to Bremer Vulkan taking over DMS, that three medium-sized firms should be formed from the yards which were independent of DMS, but left the question open as to whether they themselves would want to participate in them. In essence, these ship-building companies were concerned to prevent the creation of a mammoth eastern German ship-yard company which they would have been bound to regard as a dangerous competitor.

The DMS strategy did not fail because of the attitude of the THA, nor of the trade unions, but because of resistance from the western German yards and differences of opinion between the politicians in the State concerned, Mecklenburg/West-Pomerania. Of all the parties which were opposed to the plan, the western German yards were the only ones which knew what they wanted – or rather, did not want: a powerful group of companies being towed along in the wake of Bremer Vulkan. The State government and the parties making up the governing coalition had no

56 See: Heseler and Löser, *Ostdeutscher Schiffbau*, pages 2 to 4, table. 3.1.

one common opinion between them; Mr Gomolka, the Minister-President, and Mr Lehment, the State Minister for Economic Affairs, tended to favour separate privatisation, whilst the CDU parliamentary party under the guidance of Mr Krause, at this time Federal Minister of Transport, wanted to form a group of ship-yards. The local works councils and the heads of the regional trade unions, on the other hand, supported the idea of a unified concern headed by Bremer Vulkan.

It was already clear to the THA by the autumn of 1991 that restructuring would only offer any hope of success if it went hand in hand with privatisation, and appeared to tend in favour of a group of shipyards, preferably headed by Bremer Vulkan. However, the State government at that time was demanding a "private, pluralistic ship-yard structure" in order to prevent the big Bremen ship-builder from "seizing power". The joker in the pack, which the Minister of Economics Affairs played, was the Norwegian *Kvaerner* concern, and thus the following constellation of interest groups began to emerge:

- Bremer Vulkan and the Thyssen-Bornemisza group showed interest in taking a majority holding in the Mathias-Thesen and the Neptun-Warnow yard, and a further company, *Dieselmotorenwerk Rostock*.
- The Kvaerner group intended initially to take over the Mathias-Thesen yard and later the Warnow yard (but without Neptun).
- The *Hegemann* group was considering taking over the Peene yard in Wolgast.
- *M.A.N.* (*Maschinenfabrik Augsburg*) had expressed interest in Dieselmotorenwerk Rostock.
- Finally, the *Meyer-Werft* in Papenburg, was planning to build a new yard in the region, on the island of Rügen. This would have affected the distribution of ship-building capacity.

The main western German competitors of Bremer Vulkan, who had started by noisily demanding privatisation of the various companies separately, were not amongst the bidders.

When in January 1992 the THA called for specific offers, violent political arguments broke out; the most prominent political victim was the Minister-President of Mecklenburg/West-Pomerania, Mr Gomolka. His resignation finally opened the way to privatisation negotiations. In March 1992, the THA decided to sell the Mathias-Thesen yard and the Dieselmotorenwerk to Bremer Vulkan, and the Warnow yard to the Kvaerner group. Further negotiations were to be conducted with the Kvaerner group concerning the Neptun yard, but Kvaerner announced in April 1992 that it was not going to take over Neptun and made additional financial demands. It was not until October 1992 that contracts were ready for signature – and without Neptun. Two offers were on the table for Neptun: one from Bremer Vulkan (combined with an MBO), the other from the *Peter Rothe* group (together with Blohm & Voss). The yard went to Bremer Vulkan. In return, the THA sold the main eastern German shipping line, *Deutsche Seereederei Rostock* (DSR), to a medium-sized company, *Rahe-Schües*, and not to Bremer Vulkan, which had bid for it and then even increased its bid.

A solution has now been found for the remaining major shipyards. The Peene yard was bought by the Hegemann group, Volkswerft Stralsund by a consortium made up of Bremer Vulkan, the Hegemann group, the city of Stralsund, and the *Lürssen* yard. An inland waterways yard, *Elbewerft Boizenburg*, went to a medium-sized western German steel structures firm.

In total, of the original 40,000 jobs in eastern German yards (excluding their suppliers), there will be in the end at most 7,000 left; at least this is the number which the new owners guaranteed by contract. In return, the THA has absolved them of virtually every business risk for a longer time to come; the yards will be receiving investment aids, compensatory payments for restructuring measures, and equity, totalling DM 3.2 billion – about DM 500,000 for each job saved. A similarly large figure is foreseen to take care of the liabilities incurred in the past (losses on preliminary orders, historic debt, environmental pollution). Various grants and subsidies have been left out of these figures, particularly the subsidies available on contracts for new ships.

VII. Literature

Breuel, Birgit: *Die Rolle der Treuhandanstalt beim Umstrukturierungsprozeß in den neuen Ländern.* In: Treuhandanstalt: *Entschlossen Sanieren. Die Rolle der Treuhandanstalt im Umstrukturierungsprozeß in den neuen Ländern.* May 1992.

Cox, Helmut: *Entflechtung, Perspektiven, und Vermögenspolitik – Perspektiven des Umstrukturierungsprozesses in den neuen Bundesländern.* In: Uwe *Jens* (editor): *Der Umbau – von der Kommandowirtschaft zur öko-sozialen Marktwirtschaft.* Baden-Baden 1991, pages 113 to 130.

Deutscher Gewerkschaftsbund (DGB): Stabilisieren statt zerstören – ein industriepolitisches Sofortprogramm mit arbeitsmarktpolitischer Flankierung für die neuen Bundesländer. *Informationen zur Wirtschafts- und Strukturpolitik* 4/1992, 3rd June 1992.

Dierk, Günther: *The schematic procedure in privatizing the trade.* In: Treuhandanstalt et al (editors): *Privatization – Together into the social market economy.* Cologne 1992, pages 244 to 246.

Dodds, Paul, and Gerd *Wächter*: Privatization Contracts with the German Treuhandanstalt – an insider's guide. In: *The International Lawyer* 27 (1993), pages 65 to 90.

Frydman, Roman, Andrzej *Rapaczynski*, and John S. *Earle* (editors): *The Privatization Process in Central Europe*, vol. 1. Budapest 1993.

Härtel, Hans-Hagen, Reinhold *Krüger*, Joachim *Seeler*, and Marisa *Weinhold*: Unternehmenssanierung und Wettbewerb in den neuen Bundesländern. *HWWA Report* No. 103. Hamburg 1992.

Hax, Herbert: *Privatization Agencies – the Treuhand approach.* In: Horst *Siebert* (editor), *Privatization-Symposium in Honor of Herbert Giersch.* Tübingen 1992, pages 143 to 155.

Heseler, Heiner, and Heike *Löser*: *Die Transformation des ostdeutschen Schiffbaus – Restrukturierung, Privatisierung, Arbeitsmarktfolgen, 1990–1992.* Rostock, November 1992.

Statistisches Jahrbuch '90 der Deutschen Demokratischen Republik 35 (1990). Edited by Statistisches Amt der DDR.

Jahreswirtschaftsbericht 1993 der Bundesregierung. Bonn 1993.

Klinz, Wolf: *Venture Capital Companies, MBO/MBI, Funds. Introduction.* In: Treuhandanstalt et al (editors): *Privatization – Together into the social market economy.* Cologne 1992, pages 263 to 270.

Klöttschen, Karlhermann: *Capital investment companies and funds.* In: Treuhandanstalt et al (editors): *Privatization – Together into the social market economy.* Cologne 1992, pages 270 to 272.

Kronberger Kreis: *Wirtschaftspolitik für das geeinte Deutschland.* Frankfurter Institut für wirtschaftspolitische Forschung, documents volume 22. Bad Homburg, December 1990.

Luft, Christa: *Treuhandreport.* Berlin and Weimar 1992.

Maurer, Rainer, Birgit *Sander*, and Klaus-Dieter *Schmidt*: Privatisierung in Ostdeutschland. Zur Arbeit der Treuhandanstalt. In: *Die Weltwirtschaft* 1991, volume 1, pages 45 to 66.

Mörschel, Werner: Treuhandanstalt und Neuordnung der früheren DDR-Wirtschaft. In: *Zeitschrift für Unternehmens- und Gesellschaftsrecht* 20 (1991), volume 1, pages 175 to 188.

Müller, Klaus: *Industry-specific privatization marketing*. In: Treuhandanstalt et al (editors): *Privatization – Together into the social market economy*. Cologne 1992, pages 213 to 222.

Müller, Thomas: *Wege von der Planwirtschaft zur Marktwirtschaft in der Nahrungsmittelindustrie: Das Beispiel Ostdeutschland*. Konstanz 1993.

Naujoks, Petra, Birgit *Sander*, and Klaus-Dieter *Schmidt*: Von der Privatisierung zur Sanierung – Kursänderung bei der Treuhandanstalt. In: *Die Weltwirtschaft* 1992, volume 4, pages 425 to 451.

Sachverständigenrat zur Begutachtung der gesamtwirtschaftlichen Entwicklung: *Jahresgutachten 1990/91, "Auf dem Weg zur wirtschaftlichen Einheit Deutschlands"*. Stuttgart 1990.

ditto: *Jahresgutachten 1991/921, "Die wirtschaftliche Integration in Deutschland. Perspektive – Wege – Risiken*". Stuttgart 1991.

Schuppert, Gunnar Folke: Die Treuhandanstalt – Zum Leben einer Organisation im Überschneidungsbereich zweier Rechtskreise. In: *Staatswissenschaft und Staatspraxis* 3 (1992), volume 2, pages 186 to 210.

Sieben, Günter, and B. *Schildbach*: *Betriebswirtschaftliche Entscheidungstheorie*. Düsseldorf [3]1990.

Siebert, Horst: *Das Wagnis der Einheit – eine wirtschaftspolitische Therapie*. Stuttgart 1992.

Smith, Roy C.: Privatization Programs of the 1980s: Lessons for the Treuhandanstalt. *Kieler Vorträge*, N.F. 119. Kiel 1991.

Treuhandanstalt: *DM-Eröffnungsbilanz zum 1. Juli 1990*. Berlin, October 1992.

ditto: *Treuhand-Initiative Mittelstand*. Berlin, September 1992.

Wild, Klaus-Peter: *Privatization marketing/The search for capital and investors. Introduction.* In: Treuhandanstalt et al (editors): *Privatization – Together into the social market economy*. Cologne 1992, pages 210 to 212.

Restitution of property to the previous owners (reprivatisation)

by Hans Willgerodt[1]

I. Privatisation as the THA's responsibility

Private property in the former German Democratic Republic (GDR) had been very largely replaced by collectivisation, but 41% of residential property was still legally in private hands in 1989[2] as was 71% of usable agricultural land in the middle of 1990.[3] Admittedly, in the GDR it was only possible to make such use of land as was in accord with state planning. The residual private property would have been able to resume its free-market function in agriculture and the housing industry when Germany was united if these areas had been subject to the free-market system, but as this was not the case the possible initiation of reform was lacking. A number of far-reaching measures had to be taken concerning the ownership of agricultural land, in order to separate private property from the Agricultural Production Co-operatives or LPG's (*Landwirtschaftliche Produktionsgenossenschaften*).[4] The principal form of ownership for commercial property had been "ownership by the people as the whole of society" (Article 10 of the East German constitution), but for craft enterprises there was also "co-operative common ownership" and also, finally, a certain residue of private ownership. If an efficient market economy was to be introduced in the eastern German States, private ownership would have to be restored as the dominating form of ownership of the means of production as well.[5]

For this reason, the Treuhand Act (*Treuhandgesetz* or THG) of 17th June 1990 which set up the Treuhandanstalt or THA required it to privatise the so-called "people's property" if it was not state property in the wider sense (including communities and other public institutions). In the case of companies, the THA was given authority on the strength of § 1 section 4 of the THG having made it the owner of the shares in the corporations which had been formed from the previously state-owned companies; its authority in other cases was created by the various Implementation Ordinances to the THG and by instructions from the Federal Minister of Finance. Privatisation could take one of two forms: (1) sale of the assets to private purchasers ("fresh" privatisation), or (2) restitution of the assets to their previous, rightful owners (reprivatisation).

The two German governments had agreed on the restitution of ownership rights in those instances in which it was possible, initially in the "Joint Declaration" of 15th June 1990 and

---

1 I would like to thank Ms Simone Spengler for her helpful criticism and legal advice.

2 Buck and Reuter, *Das Scheitern des SED-Wohnungsbauprogramms*, page 112.

3 *Agrarbericht* 1991, page 140.

4 See: *Landwirtschaftsanpassungsgesetz* of 3rd July 1991, as amended on 14th July 1992: rights of usership over land on which a person owns a building remain initially in place under Article 233 section 4 of the EGBGB, the Introductory Act to the Civil Code, other ownership rights of house-owners over land are provisionally secured under Article 233 section 2a of the same Act only until 31st December 1994; the Federal Minister of Justice can grant one extension to this transitional period.

5 See: Eucken, *Grundsätze*, pages 134 et seq. and 270 et seq.

later in the Act for the Regulation of Unsettled Property Questions (§ 3 section 1 of the Property Act), which became a component part of the Treaty of Unification. Property was excluded from restitution if it had been expropriated under "the legal regulations of the occupying powers or on the basis of the sovereignty of occupation" (i. e. between 1945, when the Third Reich was overthrown, and 1949, when the East German republic was founded) and also if they had been honestly and properly acquired by East German citizens. Reprivatisation was then further limited by the Investment Act, passed at the same time and later replaced and widened by the Investment Priority Act. Under the Investment Act the Chief Executive of a county (*Landkreis*) or town which is an administrative district in its own right (*kreisfreie Stadt*) could issue a certificate confirming a given investment purpose if the project included the preservation or creation of jobs, the construction of urgently needed housing with the creation of the necessary infrastructure. The Investment Act related to land and buildings which could even then be sold to an investor with the backing of an investment certificate if claims to restitution had been lodged; any appeal to the courts however would then postpone the effect of the certificate. On the other hand, compulsory administration by the state was to be suspended, initially by placing an application under § 11 section 1 of the Property Act.

It is hard to establish the relative importance of privatisation and reprivatisation for the one initial reason that not all restitution applications have so far been processed.[6] Property over which there are virtually no restitution claims pending[7] included those items expropriated straight away in 1945 by the Soviet occupying power,[8] and the agricultural enterprises expropriated by "Land ownership reform" up to 1949.[9] These measures covered all the larger industrial companies and agricultural enterprises and many smaller ones as well. In 1948, about 40% of industrial production had been transferred to state ownership, and state-owned companies accounted for 49.2% of "net product" in 1950.[10] Not all the companies existing at the moment of

6 See: page 253 et seq. below and footnote 38.

7 With the exception of earlier expropriations, made between 30th January 1933 and 8th May 1945 (i. e. during Nazi rule) for racist, political, religious, or other ideological reasons (§ 1 section 6 of the Property Act) which can count as being entitled to restitution even if expropriated all over again by the (Soviet) occupying power. The same applies in general terms in cases of the reversal of other decisions made contrary to the law of a law-abiding state, under the pretext of criminal, quasi-criminal, or administrative law (§ 1 section 7 of the Property Act). Under § 1 section 8a of the Property Act, claims under sections 6 and 7 (by victims of Nazism and other illegal measures) remain unaffected.

8 Some 9,870 commercial businesses of all kinds were expropriated under Orders 124 and 126 of the „SMAD" (the Soviet military administration in Germany) on 30th October 1945; see: Ehrenforth, *Bodenreform und Enteignungsentschädigung*, page 490. According to Hamel, *Bundesrepublik Deutschland – DDR*, page 62, more than 10,000 firms were confiscated, of which 9,281 were nationalised; 3,843 of them were industrial companies.

9 11,390 agricultural and forestry enterprises covering 2,628,600 hectares (6.5 million acres), and including 4,278 enterprises of less than 100 hectares (247 acres). At the same time, 2,167,602 hectares (over 5 million acres) were handed out to small farmers as private property, but later collectivised in the Agricultural Production Co-operatives and subjected to limitations on free use even though still formally in private hands; see: Bundesministerium für gesamtdeutsche Fragen, *SBZ von A-Z*, page 33.

10 See: *Statistisches Jahrbuch '90 der DDR*, page 105. The calculation of "net product" was based on plan figures which were wrong from the economist's point of view, so the above statements can only be taken as a general trend.

German re-unification were the product of expropriation. Many new companies had by then been created over which restitution claims could at most be lodged if, for instance, the land they stood on had been taken away from its rightful owners without compensation. Apart from this, expropriations and other transfer into state ownership continued after 1950, with the illegal expropriation of industrial companies in 1972 making a striking feature. Where property was expropriated after 1949, the course of action to be considered is restitution. Nevertheless, the THA's job of "fresh" privatisation is particularly large in the commercial sector. As part of "land ownership reform", land with limited rights which had been handed out to small farmers and retained by them, has become their private property. This has somewhat reduced the job of "fresh" privatisation, but for the THA's work it held quantitatively the top position. This was all the more the case since reprivatisation was described in public and expert discussion as being of subordinate importance and even harmful. Influential representatives of the THA shared this majority opinion, and supported it to the Federal government. As a result the general trend was reinforced, through an appropriate amendment to the Property Act, for reprivatisation to be pushed a few rungs lower still.[11]

Reprivatisation has been strengthening slightly for some time in the Central Office and the branches of the THA, either because there has been a shift in opinion, or because "fresh" privatisation has now been largely completed, or else because, in the residual stock of the problem cases, it is running into more and more difficulties. As early as 21st May 1991, anyway, Reprivatisation Officers were appointed at THA Central Office, at the branches, and at the TLG (the THA real estate holding corporation) with the job of helping with decisions on restitution. The reason for this had less to do with accelerating restitution by institutionalising the arrangements and more with being able to react to the growing number of restitution notices being sent in by the competent Property Offices. Apart from the job of the THA to collaborate on the practical implementation of these notices, it wanted also had to exploit all available possibilities for lodging appeals.[12]

The sale of the THA's real estate other than agricultural and forestry land is the job of the TLG, and this means very largely but not exclusively the real estate of the THA companies which is not essential for business operations. The problem of reprivatisation has taken on considerable significance for this property, as well as for agricultural and forestry property, because

11 See: Wissenschaftlicher Beirat beim Bundesministerium für Wirtschaft (Scientific Advisory Council to the Federal Ministry for Economic Affairs), Gutachten v. 16. Februar 1991; Möschel, *Strukturwandel in den fünf neuen Bundesländern*, pages 489 to 493, with a few items of information in footnote 9; G. and H.-W. Sinn, *Kaltstart*, pages 85 et seq.; Siebert, *Das Wagnis der Einheit*, pages 56 to 64; Sievert, *Probleme des Übergangs*, page 214; A-interview with Dr Manfred Balz on 10th September 1992; ditto, considered statements of position of 13th November 1990 and 20th February and 3rd March 1991; for a differing view, see: Hansjörg Schaal, A-interview on 11th January 1993; also, part of the THA staff concerned with privatisation; also, on general principles: Willgerodt, *Ökonomische und soziale Folgen*, pages 154 et seq.

12 THA, press release of 11th July 1991: Government departments take precedence in these cases against each other. This is intended to safeguard the interests of the THA companies involved and to avoid legal mistakes. When property is being allocated under the Property Assignment Act, the scope for an appeal is limited (see § 8 of the Act) and there is no possibility for the Land Registry Offices to re-examine the case legally (§ 3 section 2). This seems to assume that government departments responsible for assignment make fewer mistakes than Property Offices do.

most of the restitution applications relate to real estate;[13] restitution of the property itself, however, seems to occur less often than a sale of the property on the basis of mutual agreement.[14]

A large number of cases can be expected to go through the *Bodenverwertungs- und -verwaltungsgesellschaft mbH* or BVVG, the land sale and administration company of the THA set up on 23rd April 1992 to administer and sell state-owned agricultural and forestry land on behalf and for the account of the THA. Reprivatisation can, however, only be considered with regard to expropriations made after 1949, and there were far fewer of these than the irreversible expropriations made from 1945 to 1949.[15]

Despite the dominance of privatisations, and despite the obstacles that stand in the way of reprivatisation, cases of restitution are by no means insignificant, all the more so since the THA departments involved in reprivatisation have been endeavouring to reach pragmatic and mutually acceptable solutions. Of the 9,916 companies shed from the THA's books up to 30th June 1993, 1,360 were reprivatised, or 13.7%. The number of companies wound up or communalised has to be deducted from this total to show the total number of concluded privatisations, which were 6,730, and based on this total reprivatisations accounted for 20.2%.[16] The proportion of the original portfolio of the THA lies between 9 and 10%. In the case of real estate, about 24% of all applications for restitution have been dealt with by the Property Offices, and of these no less than 31.2% ended with a restitution notice (requiring the property to be handed back).[17]

II. Is restitution an obstacle to investment and reconstruction?

Unsettled ownership matters are regarded as one of the main obstacles to the reconstruction of eastern Germany, and are blamed on the principle of restitution. Anyone who wishes to understand the reasons for this needs to look at the administrative sequence of events. For every item of state-owned assets there is a person or legal entity having the right of disposal of it (whom we can call the "authorised" party); usually this is the THA or one of its companies. Once a claim

13 2,111,375 applications had been entered for the restitution of real estate as of 30th June 1993, but only 130,378for companies. The number of applications relating to property is lower than the number of pieces of property because one application can cover several properties; the number of companies affected is lower, on the other hand, than the number of applications, because several people can raise claims to the same company; see: Bundesamt zur Regelung offener Vermögensfragen (BAROV, Federal Office for the Regulation of Unsettled Property Questions), statistical summary as of 30th June 1993.

14 Discussion of Jutta Wietog with the TLG Reprivatisation Officer, Mr Bischoff, on 10th March 1993. The TLG only looks after a proportion of the plots of land over which restitution claims have been raised, mostly on behalf of the THA companies. As of 30th June 1993, 11,346 properties had been sold for a total of DM 10.15 billion: Treuhandanstalt, *Monatsinformation der THA* for 30th June 1993, page 17; it was not possible to discover how much of these proceeds were paid to the former owners.

15 A total has been calculated of 0.3 million hectares, whereas up to 1949 a total of 2,628,600 hectares were expropriated; see: Schrader, *Anpassungsprozesse in der ostdeutschen Landwirtschaft*, page 17.

16 Calculated by Treuhandanstalt, *Monatsbericht*, June 1993, page 1.3.

17 Calculated by BAROV, statistical summary as of 30th July 1993, page 9. Taken together with the termination of state administration, which were even statutorily prescribed up to the end of 1992 and therefore increased by leaps and bounds, 58.4% were decided in favour of the former owners, but the figure rises to 88% of valid applications if rejections and withdrawals are deducted.

for restitution has been made, this party is allowed to make physical use of the asset, or to use it under a long-term contract, but only with the consent of the "beneficiary" (of restitution) or in such cases where legal obligations and the maintenance of the asset's value make it necessary (§ 3 section 3 of the Property Act). How much of a hindrance this regulation really was depended on its application in practice; the 1990 version of the Property Act contained too narrow a definition with regard to legal transactions being allowed ("absolutely necessary"), although an appropriate interpretation might have made it practicable. The Removal of Obstacles Act of 22nd March 1991 widened this formulation to the point where there was no legal barrier in the way of normal commercial business management. However, it was clear enough to everybody that if former owners had laid claim to a company the "allowed party" would not demonstrate the same commercial commitment as if they were preparing the company for privatisation and sale. The conclusion would thus have been obvious; restitution would have to be accelerated. The Removal of Obstacles Act had created the possibility, by inserting a new § 6a into the Property Act, of restoring possession of a company temporarily to its previous owner, if he was willing to run the company, and this was in fact frequently done.

Numerous examples show that reprivatisation never needed to have taken more time than "fresh" privatisation, but it could have been an administrative obstacle to "fresh" privatisation and this represented the THA's main priority. Before a sale can even take place, the relevant Office or State Office for the Regulation of Unsettled Property Questions (AROV or LAROV, *Amt* or *Landesamt zur Regelung offener Vermögensfragen*), as the recipient of the registration of any claim for restitution, has to issue a certificate to confirm that none has been received (negative attestation). If these offices are overloaded with work, inefficient, or ill-equipped, the issuing of such information takes longer and privatisation is delayed. Negative attestation is necessary for real property and for companies, but the registration is listed by the Property Offices under the name of the applicant, and their work in producing a separate list by property leaves much to be desired. The applicants often refer to the property or the company by its old name, which could have changed, particularly if it was assigned to some other user. Nevertheless, the problem could have been solved. For instance, after the end of the Second World War the West German administration, even though working under very difficult circumstances, managed to handle the problems caused as a result of the war in a shorter time even though the order of magnitude was incomparably greater and even though they did not have any of the modern means of communication available today even in eastern Germany. Today, the labour and social administration system in the eastern German States has coped with a comparable, or perhaps even larger, volume of work despite some inadequacies.

Even without general reprivatisation, however, there would have been no way of dispensing with negative attestation if, for instance, the victims of Nazism were to be given the right of restitution. Also, a similar information system would have had to be kept if the States and municipal authorities had claims to restitution of the assets which had once belonged to them as promised in Articles 21 and 22 of the Treaty of Unification. Although negative attestation is not prescribed mandatorily as a defence against restitution claims by the public sector, internal administrative instructions shall ensure that no property is sold without such claims having been clarified. Apart from this, the departments responsible under the Property Assignment Act for assignment are supposed to solve the problem by accelerating restitution just as much as the Property Offices are supposed to do this for former private owners. The introduction of a reservation of restitution clause in contracts of purchase is extraordinarily unpractical, and may expose the purchaser to an excessive risk. The appropriate documentation demonstrating ownership have also to be produced in cases of restitution to the public sector, but they run into the same administrative obstacles as proof of former private ownership, even though a more generous practice and statutory facilitation is provided for in the restitution of former communal assets.[18]

Restitution claims from private claimants had to be registered by 13th October 1990. On this date set for private claimants, the limitations imposed on the "authorised" party also ceased to apply, but could be re-imposed if late registrations were received up to the end of 1992, or for movable property up to 30th June 1993. For the public sector, on the other hand, initially no deadline was set for the registration of restitution claims although legal uncertainty was spread around when delays occurred here just as with private claims. It has now been laid down, by § 9 section 3 of the Property Assignment Act, that 30th June 1994 is to be the deadline; compared with the treatment of private persons, this is a very considerable prolongation. By the end of June 1993 the Property Offices had received 1,215,382 applications containing 2,631,700 individual claims.[19] However, only 130,378 of these related to companies, and only about half of them to commercial enterprises. In the State of Saxony, 47% of the applications relating to companies have been settled in June 1993, so the problem is capable of being solved.[20] Compared with the annual number of normal administrative matters and similar once-off cases which were to be administered after 1945 in consequence of war and as a result of the financial compensation paid for losses suffered during it, the number of restitution claims is relatively small[21] and the work required to deal with them is not, on average, more complicated than other administrative tasks. The task of equipping the Property Offices adequately was therefore just as manageable as the one taken on earlier by offices responsible for the financial compensation of war losses and now by the THA.

With regard to the compensation, the same facts should have been established as for restitution with at worst a certain delay for the beneficiaries' disadvantage. The complete replacement of restitution by "fresh" privatisation would have saved neither time nor administrative work, because complicated inspection and selection proceedings and negotiations with purchasers would have taken the place of negotiations with those entitled to restitution. With privatisation by selling the items, buyers have a large number of alternatives open to them which applicants for restitution do not; the bargaining position of the THA is correspondingly weaker with "fresh" privatisation. The recourse to appeal which the former owner can make use of is only a slight compensation for this, and has been pushed down by legislation into a subordinate position for reasons of minimising legal actions and encouragement of investment by the new purchasers.[22]

---

18 "Finally, notarised affidavits are accepted from the Lord Mayors, Mayors, and County Chief Executives to substantiate the communal status of the assets over which the claims are being raised": Treuhandanstalt, *Fragen und Antworten zur Übertragung von Vermögenswerten*, page 17.

19 BAROV, press release, 11th August 1993.

20 BAROV, statistical summary as of 30th June 1993, pages 2 and 6.

21 See: Willgerodt, *Ökonomische und soziale Folgen*, pages 154 et seq.

22 The Removal of Obstacles Act of 22nd March 1991 removed the postponing effect of objections and appeals against investment certificates (§ 4 section 3 of the Investment Act); the right of appeal against LAROV decisions concerning companies was also abolished. The 2nd Property Law Amendment Act of 14th July 1992 shortened the deadline, by means of § 12 section 2 of the Investment Priority Act, for applications to be placed before the Administrative Courts for the postponement of the effect of certificates to only two weeks, limited the facility for presenting new facts, and excluded the former owner's right to submit new investment plans.

The costs of "fresh" privatisation are probably higher than in comparable cases of reprivatisation, because bigger concessions have to be made to purchasers in terms of price and other conditions (restructuring, freeing of debt, subsidies, freeing of payments for the removal of historic environmental pollution, redundancy assistance, infrastructure, and development costs). In fiscal terms, "fresh" privatisation is only advantageous to the extent that the proceeds of the sale go to the THA and not, as with investment priority,[23] to the former owner. Although under § 6 of the Property Act in conjunction with the Restitution of Companies Ordinance of 13th July 1991 a payment has to be made to the returning owner for losses of assets and revenue, it is probably less generous than the concessions made to the privatisation buyer.

Former owners of real estate, particularly residential property, hardly shed any debt when the property is returned to them. If loans have been imposed by the state before 1990 they have to proof that none of the debt imposed on the buildings was actually used for building work; otherwise, although these loans are reduced by a percentage, these are added together with other land charges to arrive at a compensation amount which the owner has to deposit; he is then given his property free of encumbrances.[24] The question is left open as to whether he can produce this sum or has good reasons to retain the debt. If such reasons remain in effect, he has to replace the low-priced historic loan with a new one at a higher rate of interest. In such cases, the attempt made by the compensation process to take some of the work-load off the Land Registry Offices is unsuccessful; the hope had been that real collateral over historic debt would not have to be registered all over again. Nevertheless, the tendency is encouraged to dispense with restitution, to leave tumble-down old buildings for the municipality to look after, and to choose compensation instead unless the authorities will be successful in reducing this to a minimum. The tendency to waive restitution will be reinforced by the planned Property Levy Act, which provides for a property levy by reinstituted owners of one-third of the theoretical material value as of 1990, and which takes the often negative value of the future profit flow for residential buildings by rent freezing insufficiently into account. The charges raised are meant to feed into a compensation fund from which those former rightful owners not entitled to restitution will receive payment as will those who waive their rights to restitution.

If comprehensive "fresh" privatisation had gone ahead and restitution ruled out, the THA would have had to shoulder the burden of all the historic debt or else reduce the sale price to compensate. The proceeds from the sale of these properties would have been all the lower if privatisation had been faster and therefore the pressure to sell much greater. The way out into long-term leases has caused problems, even in agriculture.[25] If the sole policy had been "fresh" privatisation, the co-operation provided by the former owners in the task of reconstruction would have gone to waste, including the efforts of many entrepreneurs who had remained in East Germany. The money paid out in compensation would have flowed to the west, or been spent on consumption, but would have to paid out of funds which otherwise could have gone into invest-

23 § 16 section 1 of the Investment Priority Act.

24 §§ 18, 18a, and 18b of the Property Act.

25 The main problem is the financing of investments planned by the leaseholder. He cannot use the land as collateral. The other problem is the excessive use made of the land and the capital just before the lease comes to an end. The state as shareholder or lessor would have been exposed to demands for status guarantees.

ment in the east. The eastern capital supply would thus have been worsened to this extent. The endeavours by legislation and by the THA to pay off the former owners in money whenever possible, such as by paying them the proceeds of the sale of their property, already mean in most cases that the former owners' capital is not invested in the east but is expelled from there. Compensation for this procedure from higher proceeds flowing to the state from the sale of such property would only be successful if the former owner would not get the whole of it. It is hardly likely that investment undertakings signed by the new purchaser over and above the level he would have invested commercially anyway would even out the difference without compensatory concessions from the THA.

Administrative work in the Land Register, Real Estate, and Valuations Offices would not have been any the less if restitution had been ruled out, as all "fresh" privatisations have to be certificated in just the same way as restitution. As the former state-owned areas of land were and still are all muddled up geographically with private property and with "state" property in the narrower sense, there would have been no relief of any kind to the work-load, because in any case the necessity had arisen to re-organise the Land Registry Offices on the basis of the old documents in order to be able to separate out the areas of land for possible "fresh" privatisation. All in all, a process of total confiscation and "fresh" privatisation would have offered therefore no advantages; on the contrary, the abandonment of protection of ownership which this would have entailed would have tended to frighten domestic and foreign investors off.

III. The widening of investment priority

The *Bundesinvestitionsgesetz* (Federal Investment Act), which came into effect together with the *Vermögensgesetz* (Property Act) already in 1990, provided the possibility from the start, in the case of special and urgent investment projects, of forcing any refractory former owners of land and buildings down to a lower priority in favour of new buyers. The Removal of Obstacles Act of 1991 extended this regulation to include companies as well. The possibility of giving new buyers "right of way" for investments was further enlarged under the Investment Priority Act of 1992. The facility for trading claims for restitution, which was introduced only a short time ago with the 1991 Act, was robbed of its value by the exclusion of the buyer from the investment priority process.[26] The party entitled to restitution must express his views within two weeks on the investment plan to which priority is to be granted; his own plans are only taken into consideration if they are presented within six weeks; and the former owner can be denied a hearing altogether if it is to be expected that the proceedings will then take too long. Admittedly, he can himself apply for a notice of investment priority, but the authorised person is then allowed three months to look round for another investor; the former owner, "as a rule", will only be given precedence if he undertakes to make "the same or approximately the same" investments as

26 Tradability, if it were to make full restitution rights transferable, could transfer the competition for the property from the THA to the former owner as the decision-maker, and would turn into normal price competition such as was apparently not desired for the first transfer of public to private ownership, but which later on cannot be prevented anyway. For critical comments on tradability and with questionable interpretation of the concept of competition see: Keil, *Ungeklärte Eigentumsverhältnisse*, page 124.

the other would-be investor.[27] A particularly suitable means of neutralising the former owner is the open tendering procedure (§ 19 of the Investment Priority Act), under which he is only informed and is not given a hearing, and "as a rule" will only succeed if his offer is the same or approximately the same as the best alternative offer. This procedure is used frequently by the TLG because this gives it plenty of room for manoeuvre in making a decision. This makes the former owner's chances of success all the smaller.

Ownership law in a market economy is based on the supposition that it is in the interest of every private owner who competes with others to make good use of his property, and particularly that, unlike a government authority, he is stimulated or even compelled by competition to do so. Privatisation by THA is intended to lead finally to private owners' untrammelled decisions guiding the means of production, within the confines of the law and making use of the knowledge of innumerable suppliers and customers, to the best possible uses in the judgement of market participants who are free in their decision-making. In the transitional phase from "people's" property within a centrally planned economy to decentralised and thus to competitive private property, the THA can make its own judgement, replacing that of the market, and this is in effect a state judgement.[28] In the case of fresh privatisations, the state makes the decision on the choice of the future owner, on financial restructuring, and on the actual handling of the winding up (liquidation, bankruptcy). Proximity to the market results varies from case to case. The corporate strategy is judged on the basis of whether the largest possible number of jobs is preserved or created, and the relevant investment planned; the purchase price also plays a certain part, as on the other hand do attempts by many parties to enforce regional and other interests. Undertakings by the purchaser concerning jobs and investment are actually superfluous, if they match his commercial interests, because he will tend to keep to them anyway. If they go beyond the level of his interests they will have to be compensated for through subsidies from the Treuhand (e. g. by releasing a greater amount of debt, setting a lower purchase price, or providing assistance in restructuring); this is an expensive deviation from the market result, and as a rule is justified only by over-simplified economic or social policy arguments.

In the investment priority procedure the elements of new privatisation tend to dominate, where the scope for the application of judgement is far greater and liable to political influence, because the question of whose corporate strategy and offering is "the best" (see § 19 section 4 sentence 1

---

27 The difference in the periods of time set between § 5 sections 2 and 3 and § 21 section 4 sentence 1 of the Investment Priority Act is due to the assumption either that it must take a particularly long time for the former owner's investment plans to be examined or that a private person can decide more quickly than any state organisation. Moreover, the former owner's investments could not possibly be "the same", but only of the same value, as economic competition also expresses itself in the diversity of offerings, and the requirement that the investments be identical might possibly set off a conflict over the protection of intellectual property.

28 It is no easy matter to decide whether this is "a presumption of knowledge" in the sense in which F. A. von Hayek meant it. The obligation of a businessman to present his strategy to the THA can be a healthy one for him if it thus raises problems into his consciousness on which he would not otherwise have cogitated adequately. On the other side, skilfulness in presentation is not concomitant with the actual entrepreneurial ability, though it is indispensable even for a simple application for a loan and for motivating employees. The main problem lies in the question of whether civil servants are in any position to evaluate corporate strategies in the same way as the market does, and, assuming that they are, whether the state will permit any such "market" judgement instead of imposing "political" requirements on them.

of the Investment Priority Act), and whether the former owner has submitted one of equal value or not, cannot be judged with sufficient objectivity, particularly in the case of the majority of judgement criteria and because of the absence of any proper weighting between these factors. Although the public tendering procedure (§ 19 of the Investment Priority Act) creates competition on the purchaser's side, it does not remove the monopolistic position of the THA as a supplier and does not restrict its discretion of judgement. It is therefore greatly to be welcomed that the THA, at least, is not a normal government authority subject to orders from above, which would be subject to direct political pressure, but ensures that economic experts will be able to influence its decisions. However, even their judgement can later be set at nought by the market.

Investment priority can only relate to properties encumbered by restitution claims and not to the pure task of new privatisation which is dominating the Treuhand's work. In setting investment priorities it is assumed that investments that might otherwise be made will be dropped or postponed on account of the restitution procedure. Those entitled to restitution, however, have at least the same degree of interest in a profitable use being made of their property and in corresponding investment as does a new buyer. If they cannot or do not want to invest accordingly, they will respond to advantageous purchase offers made by investors.

What is the reason for the apparent failure of this normal procedure customary in a market economy to function properly? Firstly, restitution to former owners would have been necessary but was not handled quickly enough by the authorities competent to decide the ownership question. However, investment priority still does not absolve the deciding authorities from the duty of at least discovering the party reporting a restitution claim, if not of giving him a hearing (see § 5 and § 19 section 3 of the Investment Priority Act). Once the claimant has been identified and the justification of his claim established, restitution to the former owner so that he can make his own investments or to sell the property to some other investor would be simpler than the investment priority procedure. This requires additional administrative steps, namely an examination of whether a project has been submitted to justify priority and which investor deserves to be given preference, information to or a hearing with the claimant, promulgation of the notice of priority, later inspection to see whether the contractual conditions have been adhered to, and nullification if necessary, decisions on means of legal redress, and the amount of compensation to be paid to the former owner. Restitution by mutual agreement, as defined by § 30 section 1 of the Property Act, or the release of the property by the beneficiary for sale by the Treuhand acting in this case as a kind of broker, is altogether much simpler.

An important reason for the failure of the market to function properly in restitution proceedings could also lie in the fact that, although those entitled to a claim of restitution do raise it, they are postponing restitution until a law is passed on compensation. Previous drafts of this endeavoured to keep the compensation available as an alternative to restitution as small as possible. With the exception of completely run-down property (e. g. tumble-down buildings encumbered with historic debt and the liability to pay compensation for them) on which an additional tax for feeding the compensation fund is imposed, restitution or consent to an investment priority or sale can be more advantageous to the former owner than any minimal level of compensation. Shorter decision-making processes are thus no particular burden to him. The actual problem, however, has not been caused by him but by a state which has failed to produce a law on compensation.

The investment priority procedure offers the THA, and thus the state, opportunities to influence the choice of companies and investors and their plans in a dirigiste manner that would never have been possible to this extent with restitution. In comparison with the investment priority procedure the decision the competent LAROV has to make in restitution proceedings for companies, as far as the economic questions are concerned which are of sole interest to us here, is whether resumption of business operations can be expected "in the reasonable judgement of a businessman" (see § 4 section 1 sentence 2 of the Property Act). If this is not the case, the person entitled to restitution has the possibility under § 6 section 6a of the Property Act of demanding restitution of individual items of property; here the authorities are left with virtually no economic discretionary powers at all. In case of provisional management by the former owner the LAROV certainly decides whether there is any need for restructuring (see § 1 section 1 sub-section 2 of the Property Act), or whether a company could not be taken into consideration for profit equalisation after restitution because it is not capable of being restructured (§ 6 section 4 sentence 2). Apart from this, the authority has to check in the case of management by the former owner who only has to present a *prima facie* evidence for his entitlement to see whether there is any indication that the business managers appointed in this case are not conducting the company's business properly. It is only in this sense that the authority can exert influence on the appointment of managers by preventing it if necessary (§ 6a section 1 sub-section 1 of the Property Act). This is considerably less than the direct selection of the businessmen involved which is permitted to the THA in the case of investment priority and new privatisation. In negotiations to decide profit compensation in the case of provisional assignment, the Treuhand could try to impose requirements for investments and jobs which would be similar to the impositions in cases of investment priority. This principally applies when funds are to be used for the development of new products or if the profit compensation goes beyond the fixed rates laid down in § 6 section 2 of the Restitution Ordinance and therefore requires a check to be kept.

IV. The development of reprivatisation

1. Restitution of companies

In the reprivatisation of companies, the consideration was of great influence that they would be the prime motor of production and employment. It is for this reason that the Property Act provides for compensation payments when companies are returned to their owners. Although these normally fall short of the concessions made to new investors, they are relatively more generous compared with the treatment meted out to former owners of real estate, not to mention the cancellation of compulsory administration, under which the former owners receive the worst treatment. Whether this differentiation makes economic sense is a matter with which legislation does not appear to have concerned itself very deeply.

The effect of the resolution passed by the East German Council of Ministers on 9th February 1972 was that some 11,800 companies which were still partly or completely in private hands, most of them small to medium-sized industrial and commercial enterprises, were transferred into state ownership.[29] For these, the East German Companies Act of 7th March 1990 already provided for restitution. In those cases where the state had acquired compulsory equity in return for some compensation, or expropriated whole companies in return for a "purchase price", these

29 Schmidt and Kaufmann, *Mittelstand*, page 8.

transactions were now cancelled. State equity or debt would have to be accepted in return for increases in value over the time up to restitution. Private owners could then buy up these state shares. Losses in value would lead to state assistance, and not to any claim to a settlement of assets or revenue as under the later enacted Property Act. Because of the shortage of notaries, the prescribed notarised documentation of the conversion could not always been submitted ahead of the deadline of 3rd October 1990, the day on which the GDR ceased to exist. Not all the entries were even made in the Register of Companies. Nevertheless, 3,090 conversions and privatisations were achieved in barely seven months.[30] There were apparently no problems with possible claims from State or local government, and it would appear that the parts of the assets which each company was unable to make use of was not always taken back.[31] There was no right to choose compensation instead, and no investment priority, only the offer of acquiring equity or a whole replacement company if it was impossible to separate out the previously existing company. There was no withdrawal of liquidity with which to finance a compensation fund (see § 29a of the Property Act). The former owners were required to play their part in reconstruction, but no consideration was given to any more complicated kind of investment priority. If the previously existing company could not be carved out and handed back, compensation was paid in the form of ownership of the means of production and of equity capital. Unlike later regulations, the problem of the capital supply was taken into account.

All the same, the question did keep coming up of how to dispose the rest of unloved state equity holdings while at the same time having to provide funds even for an unfavourable value compensation, because assets tended to be valued far too high.[32] It was for this reason that, later, § 6 section 8 of the Property Act provided scope for restitution in the GDR to be adapted to the conditions of the Property Act, meaning that if the same conditions were met a claim to compensation for loss of assets and revenue could be raised (§ 6 sections 1, 2 and 4 of the Property Act, and the Restitution Ordinance).[33]

---

30 By the end of June 1993, 2,339 out of these 3,090 conversions had become final and absolute: THA (Reprivatisation Co-ordination), *Stand der Reprivatisierung von Unternehmen zum 30. Juni 1993*; see also: THA, press release dated 24th February 1993.

31 The only expedient course of action from the economist's or businessman's point of view is to take back those assets of which economic use can be made in the company; if objects have a greater value, or indeed a value at all, outside a company, they ought to be sold. If they have a negative value, e. g. because of the costs of demolishing them or clearing them of environmental pollution, they can only be charged up to the former company if the cost of removing them was allowed to be added into the production costs and charged up in the product price. Otherwise, this is a politically defined social liability of which the public sector would have to bear the cost.

32 Schmidt and Kaufmann, *Reprivatisierungsreport*, page 14.

33 Asset compensation is only possible if the company is over-indebted or fails to attain the minimum capital cover laid down for its type of company, DM 50,000 for a GmbH company or DM 100,000 for an AG company (§ 6 section 2 of the Property Act). The difference between equity capital at the moment the loss was sustained and at the present time is to be settled up, subject to a maximum of ten times these minimum capital amounts. This does not have to be done if the minimum capital is still present, however great the loss of original equity might be. Settlement of revenue requires substantial losses in turnover to be demonstrated, and can be used to promote the development of new products (§ 6 section 4 of the Property Act). It is defined under § 6 section 2 of the Restitution Ordinance as 6 multiples of the first half-year's losses incurred in the new DM accounts or 3 multiples of later annual losses, or higher if this can be demonstrated in individual instances (§ 6 section 3 of the Restitution Ordinance).

On 3rd October 1990, the reprivatisation of companies came to a complete halt, even though the Property Act had come into force on the same day; in the 4th Quarter of 1990 and first half of 1991, only 252 restitution claims were processed and completed.[34] Responsibility for this was placed on the inadequate manning and equipment of the Property Offices and the absence of any proper statutory regulations, particularly any covering compensation for loss of assets and revenue. However, the Property Offices could have been brought into a functioning condition earlier than this. The Restitution Ordinance submitted on 13th July 1991 finally brought in a basis for decisions, although the discrepancies caused by § 6 section 2 sentence 1 of the Property Act were not resolved.[35] In the six months from the date on which the Restitution Ordinance had been issued to January 1992, 629 cases of the restitution of companies had been decided on,[36] only a little more than one-fifth of the number the GDR had been settled in approximately the same period of time, although with all the shortcomings described. It is conceivable, even if it cannot be proved, that the restitution proceedings completed by the GDR had involved the rather simpler cases.

It was not until June 1992 that the pace of reprivatisation of companies appears to have started to pick up, apparently even before the Investment Priority Act, which was intended to have accelerated matters, came into effect on 14th July 1992. The number of investment priority decisions, however, does not appear to have increased very much. This is no great surprise, if one considers the complicated nature of the procedure, despite all the efforts made to push former owners into the background, and the fact that it cannot be simplified much further under the conditions of a free, law-abiding state. From August to October 1992 investment priority decisions account for a steady rate of about 15% of all completed reprivatisation cases.[37]

As companies were given back to their owners or parts of the firms released into an independent state, the relevant proportion of all completed cases of restitution claims (excluding investment priority) fell from 86% in January 1992 to about 74% at the end of that September, as the companies had had to get by somehow without any input from a private owner, which meant that they lost value; the applicants thus became more and more discouraged. The fact that the number of companies still capable of operation fell off as a proportion of all restitution cases can be seen from the increasing number of cases of restitution under § 6 section 6a of the Property Act; this limits restitution to individual tangible assets when the company has been closed down and is not going to be resuscitated. (The proportion rose from about 11% in January to about 20% in October 1992). It could be that the pressure on the decision-making bodies increased if a sound company was under discussion and a particularly active former owner had come forward to claim it, but it is an open question as to whether such cases were always successful. If the company was a sound one, the tendency was very marked to find a way booting the former

34 THA Resolution preparatory submission, *Bericht zum Stand von Rückübertragungen*, 4th March 1992, page 2.

35 See footnote 33, sentence 3.

36 As footnote 34.

37 The THA press release of 24th February 1993 gives only 7% to investment priority of all completed cases at the end of January 1993. In June 1993, after the reporting system and the data bank had been restructured, the proportion is given as 6.2%: THA (Reprivatisation Co-ordination), *Stand der Reprivatisierung von Unternehmen zum 30. Juni 1993*. The source of all the following figures is: THA documentation and author's own calculations.

owner out in favour of other interested parties. Apart from this, the Federal Office for the Regulation of Unsettled Property Questions states that, up to the end of June 1993, only 28.32% of the applications relating to companies were settled by the Property Offices.[38] The remainder cannot all have related to agricultural enterprises. Of the applications submitted to the THA for processing (and excluding agriculture), 60% had been decided by the end of June 1993, so that there was a considerable backlog here as well. The sense of resignation which overtook the former owners was also expressed in the fact that the proportion of cases in which they assented to the sale of the company had been rising since the beginning of 1992 (from 2.2 to 3.5%).

With some exceptions, the THA Central Office was responsible for all THA companies with more than 1,500 employees, whilst the branches had to look after the smaller ones. As the major companies had been expropriated under the occupational law, so that reprivatisation was ruled out for them, the branches had more to do with reprivatisation, at least as far as the number of claim registrations and their settlement is concerned; by the end of June 1993 the branches and branch offices had received 8,844 and the Central Office 4,259. Central Office had handed back 216 companies by the end of October 1992, and 1,476 by the end of June 1993; the corresponding figures for the branches were 3,613 and 6,500. This is a clear indication of the importance of the *Mittelstand* (small to medium-sized owner-operator companies) in the THA's restitution policy. More than two thirds of the restitution applications received by the branches related to Saxony and Thuringia. Most of those received by the Central Office went to the Corporate Divisions for the textiles, clothing, leather, toys and jewellery industries, but there were also high proportions relating to the chemical, construction, transport, wood and paper, mining and quarrying, and the specialist engineering and machine tool industries.

One particular problem was caused by the historic debt of the companies being reprivatised. When companies are privatised by selling them it can be assumed that the purchaser only pays for the company's net assets, meaning that the debts have to be deducted in full from the gross assets or in other words from the purchase price. If the THA asks a price equal to the gross assets, it first has to free the company from all debt so that gross assets and net assets come to the same figure. The acquiring party does not have to shoulder the burden of debt free of charge, and this places him on the same footing as if he had taken on a debt-free company or else one in which the debts are covered in full by assets. The new owner is thus only indebted to the extent that he can voluntarily accept the historic debt in return for a lower purchase price or get into debt in order to be able to pay this price.

The rules are different in the case of restitution to a former owner. The "authorised party" can stack up historic debts just to the point where the former owner decides he no longer wants to have his business back after all. If he is to take it back, its equity value must still be on the plus side of zero and also be of a certain minimum amount in relation to the commercial risk; at the same time, his emotional bond with his company can lead to his underestimating this minimum level. The former owner has to beg, whereas the buyer of a firm can afford to make demands.[39]

---

38 See: THA (Reprivatisation Co-ordination), *Stand der Reprivatisierung von Unternehmen zum 30. Juni 1993*; BAROV, press release, 11th August 1993.

39 For the former owner, restitution only starts to be less favourable than a purchase if the compensation would be sufficient for the purchase and better conditions could thus be negotiated.

The historic debt dating from GDR days bear little or no relation to the value of the assets still present in the company.[40] They were almost completely claims made by the state on the companies it had taken over, meaning demands the state is making on itself. If these companies still belong to the state today, as represented by the THA, and there is no claim for restitution, the state will become neither richer nor poorer by cancelling the debt, because the sale price always moves in the opposite direction.[41] However, if the companies are returned to their former owners, the fiscal authority loses out more and more as it cancels more and more debt, but gains on the other side if it thus secures viable companies as good, solid, future tax-payers. The more debt the state does not cancel, the less net assets it is giving back.

The compensation for assets and revenue described above served for reprivatised companies to lighten the burden of debt when insufficient equity capital was available, as did the DM Balance Sheet Act and the GDR Debt Cancellation Ordinance of 5th September 1990, which remained in force until 30th June 1991 and applied to all companies. No cases are known of the THA making use of the debt cancellation ordinance when companies were being handed back to their old owners, and bearing in mind the fiscal authority's interests it cannot be assumed that any use was made of it. Asset compensation requires that the equity capital in the business is less than the statutory minimum. Reaching this minimum, and thus obviating asset compensation, would in many cases have required a small amount of debt cancellation. Revenue compensation served as the only measure to be adjusted to the economic situation of a company, but this was based on a comparison with the past (namely, the point in time when the company was confiscated), and that was a time when the normal situation of a market economy did not exist. In cases of reprivatisation it is thus more difficult to cancel debts completely or to offer the equivalent than in the case of new privatisation.[42]

One particular kind of debt problem which the THA can avoid when negotiating a new privatisation is the joint and several liability borne by a company returned to its owners after having been hived off from a *Kombinat* under § 6b of the Property Act. It bears subsidiary liability for the debts of the other former member-companies of the *Kombinat* (§ 6 section 6 of the Property Act, but sentence 3 allows for the possibility of only certain people or the THA bearing liability). It is just possible that former owners bear legal liability for the debts of the new purchasers of other parts of the *Kombinat*, whose position is comparatively privileged anyway. Although the Splitting Act of 5th April 1991 (§ 11 section 1) covering the companies administered by the THA provided for a similar joint and several liability for separate legal entities carved off from the *Kombinate*, the party buying one up would insist that the THA should provide the necessary collateral or else satisfy the creditors.

---

40 See: Schmidt and Kaufmann, *Mittelstand*, page 79 et seq.

41 This is the justification for the cancellation of historic debt; see: Willgerodt, *Probleme*, pages 319 et seq.

42 For instance, the amount paid out as asset and revenue compensation in the Corporate Division for textiles, clothing, leather, toys, and jewellery was equal to DM 34,000 per employee; the financial commitments entered into in connection with new privatisation in the same Corporate Division at the end of 1992 was DM 104,950 per employee. Source: THA documents.

2. Restitution of parts of companies and plots of land

If market economy reform is to be successful it is not only necessary for existing companies to be privatised but also for markets to be opened to the means of production belonging to private owners, markets which will allow the factors of production to find their way to the party which will make best use of them and new companies to be created if they can obtain the means of production on such markets. It is also necessary to privatise here, and here once again privatisation and reprivatisation stand as alternatives to one another. It is the Property Offices that decide on restitution; former owners whose rights have been restored to them can then themselves make use of or sell the assets that have been returned to them. Harmful "speculative" restraint instead of selling is mainly based on the wrong overall institutional framework for which the state is responsible.[43] The Removal of Obstacles Act added § 6 section 6a to the Property Act which provided for the return of individual tangible assets one by one, thus opening up a further source for a private factor supply from the parts of companies no longer capable of survival. This means that the only debts to be taken over are those where the creditors are not legal entities under public law. It is also possible that a substitute plot of land is provided. Probably the right attitude formed the background to this, namely that offering compensation in kind in this way effectively privatises the commercial risk and also provides an incentive for new company units to be founded on this basis if that solves the location problem; apart from this, the need to pay compensation in cash is avoided which might so easily have drained away westwards.

The cessation of compulsory state administration, scheduled for the end of 1992 at the latest, should also be regarded as a form of restitution. If this did not affect entire companies, a higher level of private supply of real estate could have been created; this is hindered by the unsellability of property on which the rents do not cover the costs, and also the property transaction law,[44] and the law on planning procedures. Admittedly, though, every case of restitution means the state giving up direct rights of use over the property in question.

However, the THA is mainly influenced by the maxim that the selection of the private-sector first owner of previously collective assets, and the imposition of requirements over his behaviour, are primarily the task of the state, and that it can carry it out better through its experts than the market could do after having restored them to their original owner. This is the explanation for the tendency to grant priority to new privatisation, even when restitution would have been the administratively simpler route[45] and where the market is more efficient particularly for

43 In the case of land, hoarding out of fear of inflation, hopes of a higher price as the result of too little building land being released, uncertainty created by the state over possible investment opportunities for the proceeds of the sale, and differences in tax rates imposed can be considered as examples.

44 Real estate transactions are subject to official consent in eastern Germany, and this is only given if a kind of negative attestation has been issued to the effect that no restitution claims are pending or, if any are, that the claimant is in agreement.

45 The former owner of a plot of land for instance can himself plan a clear-cut project for the use of the land, and can have thought out the economic purpose of this in full detail. An attempt of government agencies at initiating an investment priority through a bidding competition assumes, in this case with a loss of time, that it might be possible to find some other and till then unknown use for the land and that the complicated mechanism should therefore be set in motion. Another point is that investment priority for the former owner himself is not exactly designed so as to be as kind as possible to him: § 21 of the Investment Priority Act.

parts of businesses and for real estate than for whole companies. In the state-organised competition arranged under § 19 of the Investment Priority Act, which is particularly suitable for real estate, the TLG is attempting, as explained earlier, to reduce the relative weakness of its negotiating position as the public seller under pressure to sell everything off by playing off one buyer against another. It is also trying to ensure that the "best" bidder, as judged by its own criteria, becomes the successful buyer. However, if the former owner joins in the bidding he is given a chance under § 19 section 4 sentence 3 of the Investment Priority Act to improve his offer in comparison with the bid the TLG would accept. This procedure is highly unusual for a public tender, and because it allows one bidder to examine the others' bids it is also highly dubious; it is probably rarely used, perhaps for these reasons. However, it shows the function of investment priority as a substitute for market forces; the former owner is to be placed under competitive pressure even if he wants to regain possession, whereas normal owners only come under this pressure if they have secured possession or the secured purchasing power to acquire it. The opposing bidders who come from the west have assets with the aid of which they are able to buy the property at auction, but the former owners do not know whether they will be given back the asset with the aid of which they intend to become competitive and are therefore at a built-in disadvantage in competing against other bidders even if they are let off paying the purchase price, as they have to compete with additional investment funds, because the bidding includes promises of future investment as criteria of the TLG decision.[46] On top of this, he has to contend with all the difficulties of furnishing proof of the justification of his restitution claim which the new purchaser does not have to worry about. Nevertheless, the TLG makes concessions to the former owners in advance of any outstanding decisions from the Property Offices by selling the property with a delayed payment clause or the possibility of cancelling the purchase price altogether if they can submit a convincing business strategy. It endeavours to act pragmatically in other cases as well. All the same, sale to a western purchaser seems to have become the general rule; former owners have been stimulated to agree with this by indicating that impressive sale proceeds are attainable. In any case, integrating a former owner and his assets to the reconstruction of eastern Germany is hardly part and parcel of the philosophy of those responsible for legislation or for administration.[47]

The sceptical attitude to former private owners and the market they are meant to supply applies less strongly when assets have to be returned, particularly real estate, to that part of the public sector which it once had owned. There is however a widespread lack of clarity over the matter of which body under public law is entitled as former owner to which asset. It is also not quite clear in many cases which of the companies under THA rule or which other institution is the "authorised party". It was for this reason that the Property Assignment Act handed over authority to make legally binding assignments to the *Oberfinanzdirektionen*, in effect the chief Tax Inspectors for a larger region, and to the THA (in this case a government authority). With regard to their nature and scope the administrative problems caused by this assignment appear to

46 The expectation that they could have amassed freely usable assets just like the other bidders ignores the fact that expropriation drastically reduced their ability to do so, particularly if they then remained in East Germany.

47 It is for this reason that attempts at replacing compensation in cash with a transfer of the ownership of physical assets or of equity holdings run into blank opposition and bitter resistance. Privatisation is generally understood to be the sale of former "collective" assets.

be hardly any smaller than those connected with the reprivatisation of private property. It is to be expected that applications will be made for the assignment of more than 2 million plots of land, and unsettled assignment questions are described as being one of the crucial impediments on investment. Because no decision is possible on privatisation or restitution until the "authorised party" has been definitely established, possibly by assignment, the problems of assignment and restitution overlap one another; in any case, the THA assignment department recommends assignment first and selling afterwards.[48] The THA companies however will hardly ever submit an assignment application in order to make reprivatisation possible. They will, instead, only take action if they intend via the TLG to sell off a plot of land not needed for operations in order to improve their financial position.

Bodies under public law have, in principal, an unlimited claim to restitution if the previously owned property was handed over free of charge to the central state apparatus or to States (*Länder*) or counties and communities (Article 21 section 3 and Article 22 section 1 sentence 7 of the Treaty of Unification). This applies both to "administrative" and to "financial" property. Considerations of the suitability to purpose of application strategies thus do not come into play as they do predominantly with former private owners.

It is, however, possible, but presumably not of great significance, that formerly state-owned assets held by the territorial bodies have been transferred to the state-owned companies and have thus come under the administration of the THA. If this is known to be the case, or comes out during assignment proceedings, the THA hands the asset back even if, for instance, it is a purely commercial item,[49] unless restitution is excluded through the appropriate application of the legal thinking behind §§ 4 and 5 of the Property Act. As this problem is still subject to legal controversy, a planned amendment to the Property Assignment Act intends to regulate the matter once and for all. However, part of the grounds for exclusion stated in the Property Act as applying to private persons are irrelevant to the public sector as it affects its own actions for which it has to accept responsibility. Apart from this, it is not only property and rights connected with real estate that are affected by restitution to public bodies but also companies as well (§ 1a section 1 of the Property Assignment Act). The "reasonable commercial judgement" required for the resumption of the business operations of a company must probably not be recognised for companies in the public sector. The problem is basically restricted to plots of land necessary for business operations which are also not being returned to private owners. It is not immediately clear why the public sector should have an urgent need for such plots of land although in GDR days the public sector itself handed them over for commercial use. Also, in such cases the customary procedures of a law-abiding state can be used to push through the public interest.

There is admittedly still the possibility that the THA could sell a property, with legally binding effect, in ignorance of a public-sector restitution claim over it. As a declaration from the local authority is necessary under § 24 (13) of the Building Act for the sale of commercial property,[50] such cases are fairly unlikely if the machinery of public administration is working properly. Even if the THA is aware of the public-sector restitution claim, it could still initiate invest-

48 Interview with Hans-Joachim Bange: "Erst zuordnen, dann verkaufen" ("Assign first, then sell"). In: Die Präsidentin der THA, Stelle für Vermögenszuordnung (department for property assignment): *PZ enthemmt ... Die Schnelle Stelle*, July 1992.

49 Treuhandanstalt, *Fragen und Antworten zur Übertragung von Vermögenswerten*, page 12.

50 op. cit., page 22.

ment priority proceedings if these were legally permissible. This point is contested legally, and in any case cannot be derived from the Property Act or the Investment Priority Act; § 1 sentence 1 of the latter only relates to restitution claims under the Property Act, and these do not include restitution claims from territorial authorities (at least, partly in this sense: see § 1 section 8d of the Property Act). All the same, investment priority proceedings are used by the THA in appropriate cases. The planned amendment to the Property Assignment Act, however, is to contain regulations which will lead to investment taking priority even ahead of restitution claims from public-sector bodies. It seems hardly likely that the interests of a former public-sector owner could be pushed any harder into the background than can be expected with a former private-sector owner, and the possibility can be virtually dismissed in view of the scope the state has for influencing such matters.

The question is also subject to controversy as to whether public bodies, in the event of the exclusion of restitution, have the same right to claim payment of the sale proceeds or the sale value as former private-sector owners. Up to now, the sale proceeds or substitute values have only been paid out under investment priority proceedings.[51] In other cases, the THA denies that there is any claim.[52] If it is granted unambiguously by the planned amendment to the Property Assignment Act, it is hardly likely to be encumbered with the planned property levy.[53]

It is still noteworthy that, in all the expert and public discussion of these problems, it is only restitution of property to former private owners that is held to blame for "unsettled property ownership situations" and never the unsettled assignment situations which are largely attributable to the public sector. The conclusion is also never drawn as it is for former private ownership that restitution to public bodies should be suspended instead of clarifying the ownership situation.

In addition to this, the public sector's scope for enlarging its assets above their present level has been widened on several occasions: under § 7a of the Property Assignment Act, the THA can transfer equipment, land and buildings (free of charge) to the communities for self-administration purposes if they are not needed for running a commercial company. Also, § 5 section 1 of the Property Act excludes the reprivatisation of land and buildings if they are dedicated to common use; no limit in terms of time is set for such dedication. Moreover, according to a report it issued in November 1992,[54] the TLG has sold a total of 1,111,698 square metres (1.33 million square yards) of land to the Federal and State governments and to counties, towns which are administrative districts in their own right, and communities for a total of about DM 770 million. There is likewise very little sign in eastern or western Germany of anyone thinking about

51 op. cit.; THA, Director for Communal Assets/Water Management, letter dated 12th November 1992 on "*Berücksichtigung kommunaler Belange bei der Privatisierung*", page 4.

52 See: Treuhandanstalt, *Handbuch Vermögenszuordnung*, page 48, where a decision on compensation is considered impossible for lack of any legal basis.

53 The draft text of a "Property Levy Act" does not indicate any obligation on public bodies to pay this levy, which would hardly make sense anyway, and neither does § 10 of the draft of a "Compensation Law", in which only 1.3 times the unitary value as of 1935 has to be paid if the restitution of administrative property to their former private owners is not possible on account of §§ 4 and 5 of the Property Act. The state would thus be able to retain the major part of the expropriated property and would not have to pay compensation for it.

54 TLG, *Erfolge, Erfahrungen, Probleme*, page 2.

whether this enormous public landed asset is being or has been put to the economically most beneficial use. Public purposes are regarded *per se* as being in conformity with public well-being.[55]

The possibilities for ignoring former owners have been extended not only by investment priority proceedings, which benefit external private investors, but also by widening of the authority given to the "authorised party". If this is the THA, it could make investments of its own with the aid of an investment certificate under § 1c of the Investment Act as modified by the Removal of Obstacles Act, thus excluding the possibility of restitution; it would, however, still be under an obligation to privatise. If some other state body was the "authorised party", it could increase the total of public assets by making its own investments. Under § 4 section 2 of the Investment Priority Act, the "authorised party" can issue an investment priority certificate to itself unless it is a private person. In conjunction with all the other possibilities the state has for adding to its gross assets, the limit set by private property rights to the extending or retaining of collective ownership over the previously expropriated property is greatly reduced.

This is sometimes expressed also in the case of agricultural and forestry land administered by the THA, or on its behalf by the BVVG. The THA held some 1.9 million hectares (4.7 million acres) of usable agricultural land, about 30% of the total in eastern Germany. Of this, 0.6 million has already been handed back, just under half of it to State and local government and the rest to the former owners expropriated after 1949. It also holds about 300 so-called people's-owned farms totalling 300,000 hectares (740,000 acres) which are available for privatisation along with the 1 million or so hectares previously used by the LPG's (Agricultural Production Co-operatives).[56] This total area is roughly equal to the agricultural land expropriated without compensation between 1945 and 1949, after deduction of the land used for new settlement (which remains in private hands). There is thus little scope left for reprivatisation in the narrow meaning of the term. However, the Federal Constitutional Court, in its judgement dated 23rd April 1991, left the question open as to whether those affected by expropriation without compensation should be granted repurchase of their former property. Occasional demands for this to be excluded would be contrary to the constitution.

In its Guideline dated 26th June 1992 the BVVG developed criteria for the sale of formerly state-owned agricultural and forestry land in deciding which would-be purchaser or leaseholder should be given preference to agricultural land. These guidelines have now been slightly modified by a paper (called the "Bohl Document") prepared in the Federal Chancellery, and presumably with the agreement of different private and political groups, on "the sale of formerly state-owned agricultural land". If the corporate strategies are of approximately equal value, preference should first be given to expropriated people living in or returning to the local area, or other persons intending to restore or set up an agricultural enterprise; then to the successors in office of the local LPG collective farms; and then to newcomers who were not local residents on 3rd October 1990. This will first apply to a 12-year lease. However, 70% of the land involved is

55 See in this context: Spoerr, *Treuhandanstalt*, page 164 et seq.

56 Derived from: the results of management consultancy work and decisions on the continuation of the restoration programme, *Verwertung ehemals volkseigener landwirtschaftlicher Flächen* (as of 1st December 1992), Gerster Commission. For further facts and figures see: *Frankfurter Allgemeine Zeitung*, 16th February 1993: "*Das 'volkseigene' Agrarland wird nur schleppend reprivatisiert*".

already leased on the basis of "husbandry notices" to the farmers who had previously used it.[57] The privatisation which is thus postponed is to be promoted by a land acquisition and settlement programme for natural persons. Leaseholders under the first phase of this programme, if they qualify according to the Bohl Document, will be given an option to purchase. Expropriated persons not entitled to restitution can receive compensation in the form of title over land and buildings instead of cash. Considerable opposition is being encountered from eastern German States against a programme to encourage the restoration of agricultural enterprises which would facilitate re-acquisition in this way,[58] because the return of former owners as active managers of their property is in many cases not generally desired.

Genuine reprivatisation to those people who have a claim to restitution are being held up by the back-log of claims awaiting processing at the Property Offices. Negative attestations are hard to obtain from them because the claims are listed by person and not by plot of land. The practical way out is for land to be leased subject to notice of termination being served by a former owner with a justified claim to restitution.

When the LPG's were broken down and converted into mammoth co-operatives or corporations, it proved possible for them to continue farming operations on about 75% of the usable agricultural land and to achieve an average farm size of 1,268 hectares (3,133 acres) as of February 1992. The other quarter of the land was accounted for by individual farms, the average size of which was 86 hectares (213 acres).[59] However, profit per employee measured as the owner's profit plus wages paid to outsiders was twice as high in the individual farms in 1991/92 as in the co-operatives that took over from the LPG's successors.[60] The world of yesterday will therefore hardly be able to hold its own in this area either.

V. Conclusion

The restitution of property to its former owners was regarded in public discussion, in contrast to the legal situation, as basically undesirable and at best a necessary evil. A number of amendment Acts, and proposals from the government on the Compensation Act, gave expression to this feeling. The THA has not been able entirely to escape from this general trend, all the more so since it is bound by every Act and every amendment. However, it has in many cases sought a practical, conflict-free, and mutually acceptable solution to reprivatisation problems and used the scope it has for by-passing former owners more as a means to the end of inducing them to come to a decision and overcoming delays resulting from inadequate legislation and administration. The THA has proved to be one of the very few government bodies which really urgently

57 Interview by Jutta Wietog on 2nd March 1993 with Dr Wolfgang Horstmann, THA, responsible for the BVVG.

58 See: speech before the State Parliament of Brandenburg on 28th October 1992 by the State Minister of Agriculture and his open letter to County Chief Executives and Presidents of County Councils and of County Land Commissions dated 7th January 1993; Decree issued by the Minister of Agriculture of Mecklenburg/West-Pomerania on 5th August 1992 on the responsibilities of the Agriculture Offices (*Ämter für Landwirtschaft*) in selling and administering former state-owned agricultural land.

59 *Agrarbericht* 1993, page 4, summary table 4.

60 op. cit., page 47, summary table 32.

strive to complete the tasks assigned to them. Many of its staff have attempted, successfully, to make the best out of an incomprehensible tangle of official bodies, lines of authority, and blockades wished on them by legislation often out of touch with reality, and to make use of the room for manoeuvre accorded to it to arrive at reasonable solutions. It was thus that a considerable number of reprivatisations were made possible.

All the same, the THA was dominated by the conviction that it would have to find the "best" company or user for the state property it was privatising. The THA staff had no option but to believe themselves to be up to this task in the case of "fresh" privatisation, but the former owner, if he can prove his entitlement, stands fore-square in front of them and is not subject to examination by them. The obvious course is to subject him to examination nonetheless, at least to a certain extent, as the changes to the law invite them to do. However, the highest court of appeal on the rightness of the decisions of the THA and of the new owners will always be the market.

VI. Literature

Agrarbericht 1991. Deutscher Bundestag, printed document 12/70.

Agrarbericht 1993. Deutscher Bundestag, printed document 12/4251.

Wissenschaftlicher Beirat beim Bundesministerium für Wirtschaft: Gutachten vom 16. Februar 1991, "Probleme der Privatisierung in den neuen Bundesländern". In: *Bundesanzeiger* No. 53, 16th March 1991.

Buck, Hannsjörg F., and Ute *Reuter*: *Das Scheitern des SED-Wohnungsbauprogramms und die infrastrukturellen und ökologischen Erblasten für die Wohnumwelt in den neuen Bundesländern. Vom Mißbrauch der Statistik unter dem SED-Regime*. Bonn 1991.

Bundesministerium für gesamtdeutsche Fragen: *SBZ von A-Z*. Bonn 1954.

Ehrenforth, Werner: Bodenreform und Enteignungsentschädigung. Ein Beitrag zum Urteil des Bundesverfassungsgerichts vom 23. 4. 1991. In: *Berichte über Landwirtschaft* 69/4, November 1991, pages 489 to 516.

Eucken, Walter: *Grundsätze der Wirtschaftspolitik*. Tübingen [6]1990.

Hamel, Hannelore (editor): *Bundesrepublik Deutschland – DDR, die Wirtschaftssysteme*. Munich 1983.

Statistisches Jahrbuch '90 der Deutschen Demokratischen Republik 35 (1990). Edited by the Statistisches Amt der DDR.

Keil, Martin: Ungeklärte Eigentumsverhältnisse als praktische Probleme bei der Privatisierung von Treuhandunternehmen. In: *Zeitschrift für Vermögens- und Investitionsrecht* 4/1992, pages 121 to 125.

Möschel, Wernhard: Strukturwandel in den fünf neuen Bundesländern. In: *Juristenzeitung* 41 (1992), pages 489 to 493.

Schmidt, Axel, and Friedrich *Kaufmann*: *Mittelstand und Mittelstandspolitik in den neuen Bundesländern: Rückgabe enteigneter Unternehmen*. Stuttgart 1992 (Schriften zur Mittelstandsforschung No 47 NF).

ditto: Reprivatisierungsreport. *ifm-Materialien* Nr. 84. Bonn, Institut für Mittelstandsforschung, May 1991.

Schrader, Jörg-Volker: Anpassungsprozesse in der ostdeutschen Landwirtschaft. Analyse und Bewertung. *Kieler Diskussionsbeiträge* 171/172. Kiel, August 1991.

Siebert, Horst: *Das Wagnis der Einheit. Eine wirtschaftspolitische Therapie*. Stuttgart 1992.

Sievert, Olaf: *Probleme des Übergangs von einer sozialistischen zur marktwirtschaftlichen Ordnung. Die Eigentumsfrage*. In: Werner *Dichmann* and Gerhard *Fels* (editors): *Gesellschaftliche und ökonomische Funktionen des Privateigentums*. Cologne 1993, pages 206 to 242.

Sinn, Gerlinde, and Hans-Werner *Sinn*: *Kaltstart. Volkswirtschaftliche Aspekte der deutschen Vereinigung*. Tübingen [2]1992.

Spoerr, Wolfgang: *Treuhandanstalt und Treuhandunternehmen zwischen Verfassungs-, Verwaltungs- und Gesellschaftsrecht*. Cologne 1993.

Treuhandanstalt: *Fragen und Antworten zur Übertragung von Vermögenswerten an Städte, Gemeinden und Landkreise*. June 1991.

ditto: *Monatsinformationen der THA* as of 30th June 1993.

TLG, Liegenschaftsgesellschaft der Treuhandanstalt mbH: *Erfolge, Erfahrungen und Probleme. Die Grundstückspolitik der Liegenschaftsgesellschaft der Treuhandanstalt (TLG)*. November 1992.

Willgerodt, Hans: Probleme der deutsch-deutschen Wirtschafts- und Währungsunion. In: *Zeitschrift für Wirtschaftspolitik 39* (1990), pages 311 to 323.

ditto: *Ökonomische und soziale Folgen der Beschränkung privater Eigentumsrechte*. In: Werner *Dichmann* and Gerhard *Fels* (editors): *Gesellschaftliche und ökonomische Funktionen des Privateigentums*. Cologne 1993, pages 139 to 184.

Communalisation and other forms of property transfer to the public sector

by Klaus König, with the assistance of Jan Heimann and Imke Junge

I. Publicly owned property in the divided Germany

Under German legal and administrative tradition, public property is fundamentally not "publicly-owned property" and thus falls outside the ambit of private civil law.[1] It is far more the case that this legal sphere is buried in the specific provisions of public law. To this extent, everything is counted as "administrative property" if it directly serves some public purpose. It is however not only administrative property that takes on the character of "property" in the public sector. Organisations forming part of public administrations can acquire property for a large number of different reasons, including even a legacy which a citizen bequeaths to his local municipality (the term being used here to cover the lowest tier or tiers of local government). Thus publicly owned property also consists of financial property, which only indirectly serves the purposes of public administration, namely by its asset and profit value rather than its use.[2] The law on budgets, as well as the law on municipal administration, does define certain limits with regard to profit-making companies. The Federal and State governments and the local authorities are only allowed to set them up or hold shares in them if the public interest requires them to and the aim being striven for cannot be better or more economically attained by any other means.[3] In political practice it is however easy to find reasons which permit an evaluation to be made in favour of the public sector: protection of the consumer, promotion of the economy, securing of jobs, etc. It is necessary to identify purely commercial interests, such as a public health insurance owning an optical business, to bring the public sector into legal difficulties.

After the Second World War, the Federal Republic pursued the time-honoured system of publicly owned property. As the public sector's responsibilities increased in a "welfare" state which had to provide for a totality of services for the public – from education to health policy, from transport to scientific research policy, and from social to communications policy – administrative property also expanded. With the growth in the economy, financial property also increased, as could and can be seen from such industrial-commercial complexes as *Volkswagen*, *VEBA*, *VIAG*, and such local legacies as mills, breweries, and salt-works.[4] Admittedly, the 1980's did bring a change in property policy. The organisations in the public administration showed clear signs of being overburdened, such as excessive labour costs, budget deficits, and an inundation of standards. The old ideological dispute over privatisation and deregulation had to be postponed. The public sector sold off large quantities of its holdings in industrial and com-

---

1 See Salzwedel, in: Erichsen and Martens (editors): *Allgemeines Verwaltungsrecht*, page 433 et seq.

2 op. cit., page 437.

3 See § 65 of the *Bundeshaushaltsordnung* (Federal Household Ordinance) dated 19th August 1969, published in *Bundesgesetzblatt* I, page 1284.

4 See Knauss, *Privatisierungspolitik in der Bundesrepublik Deutschland*.

mercial companies.[5] With the privatisation of activities which had traditionally been public responsibilities, however, property which had served these purposes also became up for sale: slaughterhouses, local transport undertakings, waterworks, etc.[6]

In contrast to this, developments in East Germany after 1945 and up to the East German Constitution of 1968/1974 marked a historical break with the concept of publicly owned property being limited by the legal system of private property. Ownership of the means of production could only be socialistic property, according to Marxist-Leninist doctrine. Constitutionally, this appeared in the form of *Volkseigentum* (ownership by the society as a whole, which will be signed as "state-owned property" in the following), common ownership of a co-operative by the Kollektiv (the people working in it), and the property of common social citizens' organisations.[7] The dominant element was statism managed by the Marxist-Leninist *Nomenklatura* (the self-perpetuating bureaucratic elite) with all-embracing state functions, particularly those connected with organising the economy.[8] In this "real-life socialism", publicly owned property was flattened into one level without any of the internal differentiation which would have permitted administrative bodies to function autonomously. The principle that applied to the organisation of the socialist state power was so-called democratic centralism; in reality, the whole system of power, economics, and social order was forced into a hierarchy under the leaders of the Party and the state.[9] Corresponding to this the original East German States were dissolved during the 1950's and the last remains of the independence of local authorities removed,[10] to become nothing more than the local branch offices of the central state power.[11]

For the remaining state organisations, which now were based on the division of labour and not on any separation of powers, there was nothing left of property rights but only a certain responsibility for its use. Although this was clad in the clothing of legal entities, the crucial point was the instrumental quality of socialist law. In this respect, not only the governmental organs and institutions could be legal entities but so could state-owned businesses and *Kombinate*, co-operatives, and social organisations.[12] Corresponding divisions of property were also made in the plans, quotas, and instructions issued to further the purposes of the Marxist-Leninist party and state leadership. Thus the legal position of the District Councils also governed the health, social, cultural, and educational organisations of more than regional significance, such as district hospitals, theatres, and museums.[13] The legal entities of the District Councils (*Räte der Bezirke*) covered schools and vocational training institutes, culture, youth welfare, and sport, as well as health and social affairs and children's affairs. The County Councils (*Räte der Kreise*) were thus

5 See: König, *Kritik öffentlicher Aufgaben,* pages 54 et seq.

6 op. cit., page 67.

7 See Article 10 of the East German Constitution dated 27th September 1974 published in *Gesetzblatt der DDR* I page 432.

8 See: König, *Zum Verwaltungssystem der DDR,* pages 9 et seq.

9 op. cit., pages 25 et seq.

10 See: Hauschild, *Die örtliche Verwaltung im Staats- und Verwaltungssystem der DDR,* page 57 et seq.

11 The position of the local organs of the governmental power was unified into a standard form of governmental organisation particularly in the Law on the local representatives of the people in East Germany dated 4th July 1985, published in: *Gesetzblatt der DDR* I, page 213.

12 See § 2 of the Regulations on the legal entity position of state-owned real estate dated 15th August 1969, published in *Gesetzblatt der DDR* I, page 433.

13 For the legal entity status of the District, County, County Towns and Parish Councils, see: Bartsch, *Aufgaben und Struktur der öffentlichen Verwaltung,* page 111 et seq.

legal entities responsible for some very important local facilities. The Town and Parish Councils (parish in the non-church sense) belonging to each county (*Räte der kreisangehörigen Städte*) represented the lowest rung of the administrative ladder in East Germany. They had no assets of their own with which to operate in their local economies or provide for essential needs. The reason for this was that all such assets had been shared out between the other organs of state. Thus the housing offices, health and children's institutions, service businesses, street-cleaning, and many other activities were apportioned to the county councils. For water and sewerage services, public local passenger services, and power supplies there existed special state-owned *Kombinate* managed by the *Bezirke* or Districts or managed centrally, and special state-owned companies. In addition to this, in the *Kombinate* and state-owned companies, regardless of the branch of industry involved, there was a large amount of local property allocated to the various legal entities; for instance, in 1989, 713 company vocational schools, 151 company polyclinics, 364 company out-patient departments, 851 company crèches, 1477 company kindergartens, and numerous sports facilities.[14] This all took the Marxist doctrine into account that social services should be organised in the places of production themselves.

II. Assignment of property under transformation and unification law

With the transformation of the "real-life socialist" social, economic, and state system and the unification of Germany, the time-honoured system of publicly owned property was recreated in eastern Germany. This applied just as much to the organisation of the economy with regard to the privatisation of the means of production as to the organisation of the state with regard to an internal and decentralised differentiation, meaning in particular federalism and communal self-administration. The change in the East German system took the form of a legal revolution.[15] The change-over to a system of private and publicly owned property did not take the form of a violent occupation of factories and government departments, but of laws, ordinances, contracts, and other legally binding acts.

Even before the unification of Germany, the legislative powers in East Germany had issued laws aiming at a new assignment of property. Whereas this was the Treuhandgesetz (Treuhand Act or THG) of 17th June 1990, with its Implementation Ordinances, for the field of companies, in the state and municipality field the change-over was effected by the *Kommunalverfassungsgesetz* (Communal Constitution Act) of 17th May 1990 and the *Kommunalvermögensgesetz* (Communal Property Act) of 6th July 1990.[16] The latter covers the transfer of formerly state-owned property to the municipalities. Although both bodies of law were created during the same period of time, there is very little co-ordination between them. The property in question, which under the Treuhand Act became the private property of the Treuhand companies, no longer belonged to the state-owned property. It therefore could not be covered by the Communal Property Act which came into force shortly afterwards. Because of this lack of co-ordination,

---

14 See: *Statistisches Jahrbuch '90 der DDR*, pages 336, 373 and 330.

15 See: Quaritsch, *Eigenarten und Rechtsfragen der DDR-Revolution*, pages 314 et seq.

16 Treuhand Act of 17th June 1990; 1st to 5th Implementation Ordinances to the Treuhand Act; Communal Constitution Act of 17th May 1990; Communal Property Act of 6th July 1990; for exact titles and sources see the summary of Acts and Laws in the introduction, pages XVI et seq.

and the short period of time during which the regulations were in force until the Treaty of Unification came into force,[17] only very few pieces of property changed owners under the Communal Property Act.[18]

Thus it was the law on unification in which the course was set in all important respects, and the most important clauses were Articles 21 and 22 of the Treaty of Unification. The Communal Property Act remained in force to the extent that property could only be transferred to municipalities in accordance with the above provisions.[19] The Treaty of Unification categorises state property along the traditional lines, into administrative and financial property. In addition to this, it defines "restitution" property. It thus adheres to a concept already used in the constitution of the Federal Republic of Germany (Article 134) for the transfer of German Reich property.

On the subject of administrative property, Article 21 section 1 sentence 1 of the Treaty of Unification says: "The property of the German Democratic Republic that directly serves definite administrative functions (administrative property) shall become the property of the Federal Government provided that the purpose determined for its use on 1st October 1989 is not principally for administrative functions which are to be exercised under the constitution by State governments, municipalities (and groups thereof), and other legal entities of public administration." The property of the German Democratic Republic (GDR) in this context is such state-owned property as was still on its books on 3rd October 1990. Those items of property which had already been transferred into private hands under the Treuhand Act or the Communal Property Act were thus not covered.[20] At this point a lack of co-ordination between transformation law and unification law becomes apparent. On the basis of the system of property ownership in East Germany a large amount of property used to belong to the former *Kombinate*, such as company-owned kindergartens or vocational schools, which under the (West) German constitution serves public tasks, mainly at municipality level. But they had become the private property of the THA companies when the Treuhand Act came into force on 1st July 1990. It was in order to cope with this lack of co-ordination that § 7a of the Property Assignment Act was created,[21] which states: "The President of the Treuhandanstalt shall be empowered to transfer the ownership of facilities, plots of ground, and buildings needed to fulfil the municipal self-administration tasks under the terms of Article 21 of the Treaty of Unification to municipalities, upon their application, by issuing a Notice, if such property is in the possession of companies whose shares are held entirely, directly or indirectly, by the Treuhand." The President of the Treuhandanstalt, acting as a federal authority, declared in an Order dated 28th September 1992 that use was to be made of this empowerment under § 7a of the Property Assignment Act and that a legal obligation to transfer property would be created if the conditions defined in the Order were met. Attention should also be drawn to the deadline set; its purpose was to make it possible to share out the property of a unitary state properly between the three constitutional levels of administration.[22]

17 Treaty of Unification of 31st August 1990.

18 See: Lipps, *Die Zuordnung ehemals volkseigenen Vermögens,* page 14.

19 See: Appendix II, Chapter IV, Section III, No. 2 of the Treaty of Unification.

20 See: Ipsen and Koch, *Zuordnung volkseigenen Vermögens,* page 2.

21 Property Assignment Act of 22nd March 1991, amended by the Second Property Law Amendment Act of 14th July 1992. Regarding § 7a, see: *Beschlußempfehlung und Bericht des Rechtsausschusses des Bundestages,* page 47.

22 See: *Denkschrift zum Einigungsvertrag,* page 365.

On the subject of financial property, Article 22 of the Treaty of Unification first says that this is subject to the trusteeship of the Federal government and must be legally shared out in such a way that half goes to the Federal government and half to the relevant government of the States (*Länder*): Brandenburg, Mecklenburg/West-Pomerania, Saxony, Saxony-Anhalt, Thuringia, and Berlin. The municipalities are to receive an appropriate proportion of their State governments' shares. State-owned property used for the provision of housing is exempted from this basic distribution, and is transferred into the possession of the municipalities with the aim of privatisation.[23] A further exemption, apart from the financial property of the social insurance and a proportion of the property of the Ministry of State Security (the Stasi), is mainly the property transferred to the THA.[24] This applies mainly to the shares in the corporations (*Kapitalgesellschaften*) created by the conversion of the former, state-owned Kombinate and companies which had thus become the owners of previously state-owned land.[25] Further areas are state-owned farms and plots of agricultural and forestry land and the assets of the Ministry of State Security.[26]

Municipalities' financial property creates a particular regulatory need as it is not subject to the trusteeship of the Federal government but has to be transferred to the parishes, towns, and rural counties. Under the terms of the Treaty of Unification regarding the Communal Property Act, the municipalities seem to be left with very little except their administrative property, if one ignores the residential property destined for privatisation and anyway heavily burdened with debt. The relevant Federal ministries and the representatives of national associations of local authorities have since agreed on a generous interpretation of the term "municipal financial property". "Municipalities' financial assets are the state-owned companies and facilities and the plots and areas of land which, if they do not directly serve the purposes of the municipality (administrative property), were in the possession of the legal entities of the former parish, town, or county councils as of 3rd October 1990 or were used by the municipalities under contract, and in both cases were foreseen for fulfilling the customary scope of municipal purposes. The situation in western Germany shall be taken as the basis for assessing customary scope in this context."[27] In defining this demarcation of municipal financial property, the aim was to equip the municipalities with an initial stock of assets.[28] To this one can add the shares in the corporations which emerged from the former state-owned companies, for instance in the field of water supply or traffic and transport, and certain state-owned plots of ground held legally by the former parish, town, and county councils.[29]

The difficulties in identifying municipal financial property – as well as in defining their public responsibilities in connection with administrative property – go to show that yet a third category of property has to be taken into account if property is to be assigned fairly. If a western German town is the owner of a salt-works, it is the fiscal situation, and not the administrative task, that determines the categorisation of the property, in this case as financial property. If a for-

23 See: Article 22 section 4 of the Treaty of Unification.

24 See: Article 22 section 1 of the Treaty of Unification.

25 See: § 1 sections 4 and 5 and § 11 of the Treuhand Act.

26 Regarding agricultural and forestry land, see 3rd Implementation Ordinance to the Treuhand Act, and the 4th Implementation Ordinance regarding *Stasi* property.

27 See: Bundesministerium des Inneren, *Arbeitsanleitung zur Übertragung kommunalen Vermögens*, page 11.

28 See: Lange, *Wem gehört das ehemalige Volkseigentum?*, page 335.

29 See: Decree by the Federal Minister of Finance, VIC-4–01002-172/91, page 14.

merly state-owned salt-works stands however in an eastern German town this town had been the owner before the salt-works had been transferred into state-owned property, then both the fiscal and the administrative categorisation criterion are absent. It is therefore understandable that in the negotiations on the Treaty of Unification the demand arose for the restitution of former municipal and State property which had been withdrawn from these bodies by the transfer into state-owned property to the benefit of the central state.[30] Article 21 section 3 of the Treaty of Unification therefore states, on the subject of administrative property, that property which had been made available free of charge to the central state or to the State governments or parishes (or groups of parishes) by a public body should be returned free of charge to this body or to its successor in law, and that the former property of the German Reich should now become the property of the Federal government. Under Article 22 section 1 of the Treaty of Unification, this regulation has to be applied correspondingly to financial property. A special category of restitution property was created by the level of priority of the property reversion.[31]

III. Transfer of publicly owned assets by the Treuhandanstalt

The Property Assignment Act creates the conditions for carrying out the material assignment of formerly state-owned assets under Articles 21 and 22 of the Treaty of Unification into the various state and municipal areas but does not alter the material distribution rules. Responsibility is divided by this Act for establishing the owners and the decisions that need to be taken.[32] If the THA itself is the owner, or administrator under trusteeship, its President is the person responsible. In all other cases, the decision rests with the *Oberfinanzpräsident* or highest-ranking Tax Inspector of the relevant State (*Land*). Their area of responsibility also includes state-owned property used to provide housing under the legal entity of the formerly state-owned residential property companies, as well as property necessary for the execution of municipal responsibilities. Also included is undeveloped land owned legally by the parishes, towns, and counties, and certain assets of the former apparatus of state security service.

The Treuhand, on the other hand, administers and utilises the following categories of property: the assets of former *Kombinate*, companies, and other organisations of the state-owned economy now converted into corporations and taking the form of buildings, plots of land, and machinery and equipment; also, the assets of the former state-owned agricultural and forestry companies, assets of the Parties and other mass organisations, the state security apparatus, and the East German armed forces; and in addition to this, on behalf of the Federal Minister of Finance, the firms formerly run by the parishes, towns, and counties forming a property in trusteeship of the Federal Government – not of the Treuhand – in accordance with the Treaty of Unification. (These firms are financial property.) Anyone who intends to form an overall impression of the scope of the THA's work, the following pointer may be of significance: the total area of eastern Germany is 10.8 million hectares (26.7 million acres).[33] The area under the administration of the THA totalled about 4 million hectares (9.9 million acres) of agricultural and forestry

30 See: Lange, *Wem gehört das ehemalige Volkseigentum?,* page 332.

31 See: Decree by the Federal Minister of Finance, VIC-4–1002-172/91, page 13.

32 See: § 1 section 1 of the Property Assignment Act.

33 *Statistisches Jahrbuch der DDR 1989,* page 1.

land, and about 2.5 million hectares (6.2 million acres) given over to mining, industry, and other purposes.[34] Thus the total area of the THA's responsibility, measured this way, covers more than half of eastern Germany.

If we now turn to the work of the Treuhand, the following data can be seen as of 19th February 1993: self-governing towns, rural counties, and parishes have made 170,347 applications for communalisation (transfer of ownership to the appropriate tier of local government) at the Treuhand, of which 111,436 were passed on to the competent authority, the relevant regional *Oberfinanzpräsident*.[35] This leaves 58,911 communalisation applications within the area of responsibility of the THA. 29% of these applications have so far been settled. As part of the process of communalisation, 12,472 assignment notices have so far been issued. 6,526 applications were decided positively, i. e. the applicants were granted ownership, so the rejection rate for communalisation application is about 50%. It can be seen that the rejection rate tends to be higher for the smaller municipalities.[36] 300 administrative appeals are pending against the negative notices, so that the "dispute rate" (the number of administrative appeals divided by the number of negative notices) is about 5%.[37]

The 6,526 positive assignment notices led in 2,434 cases to administrative property being transferred, and to "restitution" property in 3,283 cases. The total number of items of property involved was 6,663 (as one assignment notice can cover more than one item of property), including 157 waste disposals including disposal sites, 269 vocational schools, 136 apprentices' hostels, 629 company kindergartens, 125 polytechnic institutions, 112 office buildings, 745 sports facilities, 90 company polyclinics and out-patient departments, 98 arts centres, 60 ports and docks, and 1,772 other properties, as well as a total of some 70,000 hectares of land (173,000 acres) made up of 1,341 forestry and 998 agricultural areas. Whilst the properties listed above were principally single items, in many cases entire enterprises were handed over to municipalities,[38] including 15 water and sewerage companies, of which the municipalities were given 14, 215 public local transport companies, of which 162 were transferred, 4 river port companies which like the 3 seaport companies (in Rostock, Wismar, and Stralsund) all went to municipalities, not to mention a large number of other enterprises of which 223 were transferred.

As of 30th June 1993, the Federal government had placed 1,607 applications for the transfer of 6,790 plots of ground, and the State governments 3,426 applications for 32,536.[39] So far, 1,495 have been decided in the Federal government's favour and 4,551 properties transferred, and 2,201 for the State governments resulting in the transfer of 13,138 properties. Complete companies are also being transferred to the States, such as the airports of Berlin-Schönefeld, Leipzig-Halle, Dresden, and Erfurt; the relevant States have taken majority holdings in each of these. In addition to this, the Federal and State governments have also been granted minority holdings in enterprises of more than regional significance, such as the seaport of Rostock in which the State of Mecklenburg/West-Pomerania holds shares.

34 See: Schöneich, *Kommunale Wirtschaftsentwicklung*, page 17.

35 See: THA, Directorate for Municipal Property/Water Management, *Übersicht zum Stand der Antragsstellung*, dated 19th February 1993.

36 See: Schöneich, *Kommunale Wirtschaftsentwicklung*, page 11.

37 See: *Frankfurter Allgemeine Zeitung* of 28th January 1993, page 11.

38 See: Treuhandanstalt, *Monatsinformation der THA* as of 31st January 1993, page 19.

39 See: Treuhandanstalt, "PZ" statistics (on property assignment) dated 15th February 1993; Treuhandanstalt, *Monatsinformation der THA* as of 30th June 1993, page 9.

IV. Main problems in property transfer

Among the main problems in the transfer of property, of which only a few examples shall be examined here, there is the communalisation of water and sewerage companies, energy supply companies, and public local transport companies. In the German Democratic Republic there was a Kombinat or a state-owned company for each of these fields in every *Bezirk*, or District, making a total of 15 of them. This *Kombinat* structure, the expression of a striving for concentration, was typical of the centrally planned economy of the GDR. The Treuhand Act turned the district *Kombinate* and the state-owned companies into corporations, and since then their owner has been the THA. The areas supplied by the former *Kombinate* and state-owned companies still continued to cover the former Districts even after their conversion into corporations. The THA's job is to transfer shares in these companies to the municipalities. The decision on the communalisation of these companies is based on the "customary principle", which means that the communalisation of these companies depends on whether they serve municipal purposes to the customary extent. The criterion of customary practice is based on the situation in western Germany.[40]

The centralised water and sewerage undertaking in eastern Germany does not meet the criterion of customary practice in western Germany, where water management is mainly defined as a municipal responsibility. Thus in western Germany there are some 6,500 utilities, mainly owned by parishes and towns, that supply the population with water.[41] The water and sewerage utilities are therefore being transferred to the municipalities in eastern Germany, too. The difficulty in municipalising them has been in distributing the shares in these companies to the relevant municipalities within each of the old Districts. For this purpose early in 1991 the so-called "club-model" has been developed. According to this the municipalities within each catchment area of a water and sewerage company (i. e. within the former District) founded an ownership-club. Each of them got the shares in the relevant water and sewerage company. So far, 14 out of 15 water and sewerage companies have been transferred to ownership-clubs on the basis of this model. Afterwards, within these ownership-clubs the water and sewerage companies are broken up under municipal management, leading usually to a sharing out of the physical assets (including 5,200 water supply plants)[42] to smaller groupings of local communities, or to an individual town or city, and thus finally to their liquidation.[43]

Compared with other European countries, the sharing out of the task of water supply between a large number of companies, both in western Germany and in the near future in eastern Germany probably as well, represents the exception rather than the rule.[44] In France, for instance, water supply is mainly in the hands of two large private supply companies, whereas the population in Great Britain is supplied by some 40 private companies and in the Netherlands by about 50. This concentration on a small number of companies is justified in the countries concerned by such arguments as rationalisation and the greater efficiency of operation in these water supply companies.

---

40 See: Bundesministerium des Inneren, *Arbeitsanleitung zur Übertragung kommunalen Vermögens,* page 11.

41 See: Schmitz, *Die Trinkwasserversorgung in den neuen Bundesländern,* page 247.

42 op. cit.

43 See: Schöneich, *Kommunale Wirtschaftsentwicklung,* page 13.

44 See, for a European comparison of drinking water supply arrangements: Schmitz, *Die Trinkwasserversorgung in den neuen Bundesländern,* page 248.

By taking on these water and sewerage companies, the municipalities are shouldering considerable financial obligations for the future, because the European Union's Directive 90/656 EEC places Germany under an obligation to bring the quality of its drinking water completely up to conformity with current legal regulations by the end of 1995. Achieving this aim alone will give rise to a need for funds in eastern Germany of DM 21.7 billion.[45] Estimates for the modernisation of eastern German sewage disposal systems lie in the range between DM 100 and 150 billion.[46] In view of this order of magnitude, and the necessity of building up an environmental infrastructure very quickly in eastern Germany, the Ministers for Economic Affairs and for the Environment of the Federal government and the various eastern German State governments issued a joint declaration on 4th December 1991 fundamentally favouring greater involvement of the private sector in the field of water supply and sewerage.[47]

In the communalisation of public local passenger services, the focus of interest is on the motor traffic *Kombinate* (there was one in each District) which were firstly conglomerates covering public passenger services, goods traffic, taxis, and so on. The 15 former motor traffic Kombinate employed some 85,000 people, of which about a third worked in public local passenger services.[48] As the former *Kombinate* also contain companies that are being privatised, unbundling them is a job for the THA itself, unlike the water and sewerage companies. Subsequently, the public passenger traffic companies are being allocated to the geographically relevant rural counties or county boroughs, and the remainder are being privatised. This process of unbundling and assigning not only covers assets but also long-standing liabilities, contracts of employment, and the costs of removing historic environmental pollution. The process of assignment thus requires intensive negotiations with the municipalities, in order to bring about agreement on the points listed. The Treuhand has put its own special teams to work on these difficult problems of assignment; they are made up of local transport experts, lawyers, and auditors.

By 31st January 1993, the assignment of public local passenger services companies had been completed in 162 out of a total of 215 cases (this was the total number of rural counties and county boroughs), with more than 15,000 employees being taken on by the municipalities. Bearing in mind the total deficit of about DM 1.4 billion[49] being borne by public local passenger services in eastern Germany, and with uncertain finances at that, it was only to be expected that acceptance of responsibility for public local passenger services would have been somewhat cautious. In addition to this, it would have been up to the rural counties to establish their own traffic companies, which under certain circumstances would have been cheaper than taking over the existing companies "free of charge". There was therefore no way for biased (one-sided) solutions in favour of the Treuhand. Basically, mutual agreement with the municipalities was always the aim. Thus the privatisation of the remaining parts of the operation was always made conditional upon agreement being reached with the rural counties on the assignment of the assets of

---

45 See: ad hoc Gruppe der Fachkommission Soforthilfe Trinkwasser, *Bericht an den Bundesminister für Gesundheit über notwendige Sanierungsmaßnahmen*, page 14 et seq.

46 See: Bundesumweltministerium (editor), *Privatwirtschaftliche Realisierung der Abwasserentsorgung*, page 10.

47 op. cit.

48 See: Treuhandanstalt/Special Commissioner for Traffic and Transport, *Zwischenbilanz der Direktion Verkehr* as of 30th September 1992.

49 See: Bundesministerium für Verkehr, *Leitfaden zur Gestaltung des öffentlichen Personennahverkehrs* (ÖPNV), pages 14 et seq.

public local passenger services. In addition to this, a large part of the long-standing liabilities was simply cancelled.[50] In 7 cases, public passenger transport was privatised with the consent of the relevant rural counties.[51] In addition to this, it was left up to the municipalities after communalisation to decide whether or not to place public local passenger services in the hands of private companies. The THA estimates that the proportion of private operators working under contract from rural counties is 22% in Mecklenburg/West-Pomerania, 27% in Brandenburg, 18% in Saxony-Anhalt, 43% in Thuringia, and 9% in Saxony.[52]

Whilst the restructuring of ownership in the fields of water and sewage management and of public local passenger services has already made considerable progress, this is not the case for the regional energy supply companies. The entirety of their shares was still in the hands of the THA at the end of 1992. The cause of this was the reconstruction strategy of the whole of the eastern German energy supply industry, which finally took the form of the so-called *Stromverträge* or power contracts.[53] These contracts comprised one overall contract and 15 regional contracts. The substance of the overall contract was that a company should be established jointly by the three western German power generation groups, *RWE*, *Preußenelektra*, and *Bayernwerk*, which would be responsible for the business affairs of the power generation companies and for the companies in charge of regional distribution. 75% of the shares in these companies were to be taken over by them on 1st January 1991, and the remaining 25% were reserved for German national and, later, European integrated power groups.

The regional contracts stated that the three groups would first establish one business operations company in each of those 11 out of 15 Districts in which 60% of power is consumed, and would later retain at least 51% of the capital of the regional energy supply companies. The power-generating groups apparently made their majority shareholding in the regional energy supply companies a pre-condition for taking over and restructuring the whole power industry, in order to secure their channels of off-take. The agreements contained in the power contracts were also included in the Treaty of Unification, in which the municipalities are given an undertaking that they will be given a total of 49% of the shares in the regional energy supply companies.[54] By the middle of 1991, 146 municipalities had lodged constitutional objections against this provision of the Treaty of Unification for the transfer of a mere 49% of the shares in the regional energy supply companies, and on the other hand against their having been given nothing more than an undertaking to transfer shares in the companies, and no assets as such. They are thus attempting to have the local power generation plant handed over to them in order to be able to construct their own municipal electricity supply systems.[55] In response to this, the Federal Constitutional Court presented the following proposed settlement at the end of 1992:[56]

All the necessary plants should be transferred to the approximately 100 municipalities that wanted to set up their own municipal facilities, but they would then have to take over all the

---

50 See: Schöneich, *Kommunale Wirtschaftsentwicklung*, page 15.

51 See: Treuhandanstalt/Special Commissioner for Traffic and Transport, *Zwischenbilanz der Direktion Verkehr* as of 30th September 1992.

52 op. cit.

53 op. cit.

54 See: Appendix II chapter IV section III clause 2 sub-clause b) of the Treaty of Unification, which augments the Communal Property Act by adding § 4 section 2 sentence 2.

55 See: Harms, *Zwischen Privatisierung, Wettbewerb und Kommunalisierung*, page 79.

56 op. cit.

long-standing liabilities and to pay costs of historic environmental pollution; in some cases this would involve costs running into hundreds of millions. As compensation for the plant, the municipalities would have to give up their shares in the 14 regional energy supply companies (Berlin was not included), so that then 51% of all the shares could be privatised and 49% communalised. This settlement also included the agreement that all municipalities intending to set up their own facilities should only generate 30% of their power requirements themselves. This proportion could be higher in exceptional cases. The new regulation, which was also intended to ensure the off-take of brown coal (lignite) in eastern Germany, was to remain in force for 20 years. Whilst this settlement met initially with wide acceptance, a wave of protest broke out in early 1993. Some of the municipalities were complaining that they would have to take 70% of their current from the regional suppliers, mainly in order to support the local brown-coal industry.[57] However, this proposed settlement said nothing about the price of electricity, and the municipalities were not prepared to pay anything more than cost price.

The consequence of the delay caused by the argument over electricity is that the urgently necessary restructuring of the eastern German power industry has not even been started. The lack of clarity as to the areas of responsibility for power supply has hampered the approval of investments in power stations and distribution equipment totalling DM 30 billion.[58] These investments could on the one hand have swept some of the unemployment off the streets of eastern Germany, and were also urgently necessary from the ecological point of view. Also, no decisions could be made which would have settled the future of the eastern German brown-coal industry.

V. Transfer of property in the process of decision-making

Under the Property Assignment Act, the transfer of property takes the form of an administrative procedure which first requires an application from a potential rightful claimant (§ 1 section 6), and ends when an Assignment Notice is issued (§ 2). This administrative action has a constituent or a declaratory character, the latter being the case when the transfer of ownership is based on the force of law.[59] However, such a conventional view of straight-line administrative action is not in accord with the complexities of real-life property transfer. It is not only privatisation, with its difficult decisions on net sale proceeds, investment commitment, employment guarantees, and so on, that requires an intensive dialogue between the parties. In view of the principle of requiring an application, and the often very inadequate amount of information available to those who might possibly be involved, the THA pursued a policy of providing compendious information. In addition to this, no harm is done if an application is made to an authority which is not the competent one, as it is always passed straight on to the proper address.[60]

57 See: *Der Spiegel* of 18th January 1993, page 87.

58 See, for investment approval: Treuhandanstalt, *Monatsinformation der THA* as of 30th June 1993, page 5.

59 This applies to property used for the provision of housing within the meaning of Article 22 section 4 of the Treaty of Unification and for certain administrative assets which while the GDR was still in existence had already been in the possession of legal entities within public area bodies and mainly served administrative purposes.

60 See: Schöneich, *Die Kommunalisierung*, page 390.

On the other hand, little use has been made of the possibility[61] to decide *ex officio* in case of public interest.[62] "Compulsory" notices are being avoided. It is only the transfer of property as such that is carried out free of charge. The assignment can cover more than just the property itself, but also long-standing liabilities, contracts of employment, costs for historic environmental pollution, and so on.[63] Thus the style of negotiation is the distinguishing mark not only of privatisation but also of communalisation. The "co-operative" style of administration is practised, with preliminary negotiations, compromises, understandings, etc., which is typical of modern administration in many places and not only with major technical projects.[64] The THA can play more than the role of a mere participant in the "haggling" here, and can become an expert consultant, especially if the municipality involved does not have the whole picture of the subsequent costs likely to be incurred by the acquisition of the property. Once the negotiated solution has been reached, the final phase is a formal assignment notice, but it is also possible for a contract to be included under public law.

The basic idea of a fair process should not, however, be allowed to disguise the fact that there is a conflict of interests. Although the Treuhand Act (§ 1 section 1) defines both privatisation and communalisation as the job to be done, there is no ignoring the fact that the Treuhand regards itself primarily as a privatisation agency. This self-image stretches from its ideological rejection of the planned economy to its fiscal interest in the proceeds of sales, which cannot be attained with communalisation. Thus with a glance at the total assets of the Treuhand it is said: the free transfer of ownership to municipalities is the exception, and the general rule is commercial sale by the THA.[65]

A number of conflicts can be seen to be inevitable in this description of the main characteristics of property assignment under transformation and unification law. Admittedly, a number of controversies have been settled in the field of administrative property by § 7a of the Property Assignment Act in conjunction with the relevant instructions from the President of the Treuhand. But following the decision by the highest court we still have a "claim solution".[66] According to this, the municipalities have not become the owners by force of law; instead, claimants raise a claim to transfer of ownership and the THA has the corresponding obligation to make the transfer. The only exception is in the case of state-owned property used to supply residential accommodation and certain items of administrative property which was already owned by the municipalities while the GDR was still in existence and were also being mainly used for municipal purposes.[67]

In the cases of "claim solution", the municipalities can find that the consequences are unfavourable to them. If the item of property has been privatised with a THA company they will have no basis for entitlement.[68] It is even being assumed that no claims for damages or for shares in the

---

61 § 1 section 6 of the Property Assignment Act provides this possibility.

62 See: Schöneich, *Die Kommunalisierung,* page 390.

63 See: § 1a section 1 sentence 2 of the Property Assignment Act.

64 See: Bullinger, *Kooperatives Verwaltungshandeln,* pages 277 et seq.

65 See: Schöneich, *Die Kommunalisierung,* page 392.

66 See: Ruling of the Provincial High Court of Rostock of 27th August 1992, dossier no. 1 C 15/92; Judgement of the Federal Administrative Court of 18th March 1993, dossier no. 7 C 13.92.

67 See: Schöneich, *Die Kommunalisierung,* page 387.

68 § 7a of the Property Assignment Act refers expressly only to assets and property of the THA corporations in the possession of the Treuhand.

proceeds can be founded either.[69] Although precautions have been taken in the THA's privatisation hand-book to avoid putting the municipalities at a disadvantage,[70] but if one looks at the impetus which the privatisation work has built up then it is possible to produce facts.[71] Particular in its beginning the Treuhand thus sold off municipal property with Treuhand companies.

Claims for restitution, on the other hand, are regarded as more solidly based. They can be raised against the THA companies, and have precedence over other claims. They are regarded as being immune to bankruptcy proceedings.[72] In addition to this, the legal stance is taken that a claim for restitution is not invalidated when a company is sold,[73] meaning that an assignment notice can still be issued even after privatisation has been completed. This in turn throws up consequent problems, such as the treatment of assets necessary for the operation of the business. The legal practice of the Treuhand therefore assumes that both claims over administrative property and for restitution property can be countered by the objection of necessity for business operations, based on the legal ideas enshrined in §§ 4 and 5 of the Property Act. The municipalities thus excluded from the transfer of property are thus not even granted the possibility of suing for damages.[74]

Apart from this, ruling legal opinion holds that the precedence given to investments under the appropriate application of the Investment Priority Act[75] can also be used to counter claims to restitution by the public sector.

In proceedings for the transfer of property, the Treuhand and the municipalities (the Federal and State governments appear less often as rightful claimants) find themselves drawn into a configuration which is out of the ordinary run of German administrative matters. The THA is the embodiment of centralism in the decision-making mechanism, which is rather unusual in German tradition and can only be understood in relation to the history of its origination in the shadow of the unitary state system of the old GDR. On the other hand, it is only fair to bear in mind on behalf of the parishes, towns, and counties in eastern Germany that they are subject to political and administrative forces in which the weaknesses of the old local branches of the "real-life socialist" state power are still having their effect. On the other hand, municipalities are now organising themselves into interest groups, and can expect support from the States (*Länder*) case by case. The decision-making processes of the communalisation are in any case not only interesting as an expression of the law but also of power. The covetousnesses of the municipalities do admittedly have to be taken into account which are based on the fact that the transfer of property is carried out free of charge. The relatively high rejection rate suffered by the smaller municipalities has already been mentioned; it shows that wrong estimates were made of their chances of a successful and cost-free transfer of property, for both legal and economic reasons.

Communalisation and other forms of property transfer to the public sector have been encumbered, from the sheer weight of numbers, by many bottle-necks: difficulties in proving former ownership, disputes over the historic debts transferred with the property, claims for management

---

69 See: Schöneich, *Die Kommunalisierung,* page 390 et seq.

70 See: Treuhandanstalt, *Handbuch Privatisierung,* Chapter 3.6, as of January 1993, page 44.

71 See: Schöneich, *Die Kommunalisierung,* page 390.

72 See: Bundesministerium des Inneren, in: *Infodienst Kommunal* No. 61, page 10, Judgement of the Federal Administrative Court of 18th March 1993, dossier no. 7 C 13.92.

73 See: J. Grünwald, in the plenary protocol of the German Bundestag, 12/109.

74 See: Schöneich, *Die Kommunalisierung,* page 391.

75 For Investment Priority Act see summary of Acts and Laws in the Introduction, pages XVI et seq.

expenses by the THA, and finally a long drawn out procedure for the transfer itself until the claimant can finally be entered in the Land Register as the true and lawful owner.[76] The THA has only managed in a few exceptional cases to free itself of the procedural burden of such difficulties which have accumulated from the number and the diversity of the individual proceedings. One noteworthy case in this respect relates to water supply and waste-water disposal. With the development of the model of municipal ownership-clubs success has been achieved in escaping from the time-consuming operation of unbundling all the old regional water and sewerage utilities from one another. When one bears in mind that 7,565 individual parishes[77] formed the group of recipients to whom this work would have had to be charged up, one is once again faced by the "mass-production" nature of the work of the THA. It is then all the more remarkable that the "dispute rate" of 5% of rejections which go to the administrative courts should be so low, when fully half of all applications are rejected. This is a tribute to the Treuhand's pragmatic manner of dealing with this colossal problem.

However, the possibility cannot be excluded that the level of conflict will rise in the future. The THA has not only to grapple with the huge mass of about 70% of applications which have not yet been processed;[78] another 700 municipal applications are received on average every week.[79] The staff are preparing to see this flood of applications remain as high until the deadline for applications is reached on 30th June 1994. For this reason it must be assumed that the process of property assignment in the public sector is far from reaching its end, and the proceedings for the transfer of property to the municipalities will carry on until the end of the 1990's.[80]

VI. The new system of publicly owned property

The transformation of the state, the economy, and society in the former GDR and in the core of the old centrally planned economy is a historical process with a certain degree of finality about it. The situation in which this process started, the political and economic circumstances in eastern Germany as they existed up to 1989, were, although complex, at least historically stable because during the 1980's the symptoms of stagnation in the GDR had been increasing.[81] In contrast to the other "real-life socialist" states, there appeared to be no further possibility of the system reforming itself from within. The *Nomenklatura* even opposed the evolutionary intentions of the dominant power, the Soviet Union.[82] On the other hand, the end of the transformation process is a far less certain matter, and not only for the simple reason that it still lies in the future. Unlike Poland, Hungary, Russia, etc., in Germany the political and economic system of West Germany formed a constitutional point of reference once East Germany had entered into the jurisdiction of the Constitution, give or take a few treaty modifications. However, it is not possible to see the state and the economy in the old West Germany under any static approach as the target at which the transformation process has to aim. Too much in western Germany has

76 See: Schöneich, *Die Kommunalisierung,* page 391.
77 See: *Statistisches Jahrbuch '90 der DDR,* page 1.
78 See: Schöneich, *Die Kommunalisierung,* page 391.
79 op. cit., page 392.
80 See: *Frankfurter Allgemeine Zeitung* dated 28th January 1993, page 11.
81 See: König, *Zum Verwaltungssystem der DDR,* page 39 et seq.
82 op. cit., page 40.

now moved into a state of flux, and most particularly in the border area between the public and the private sectors.[83] Moreover, in view of the process of European integration it is now no longer possible even to define the area of responsibility of the public sector in terms of the simple national state.[84]

Communalisation and other forms of property transfer to the public sector as part of the process of transformation and integration seem, on the other hand, to be taking their line from the conventional German situation. Already the law on the self-administration of parishes and counties in East Germany of 17th May 1990 picked up the traditional definition of municipal responsibilities (in §§ 2 and 72). One particularly typical aspect is the interpretation of the term "municipal financial property", which refers to "the usual extent" and takes the situation in West Germany as the criterion for "customary practice".[85] It would also be fair to speak of a "customary principle" in the communalisation of assets.

Once such a principle has been adopted, the only points remaining to be resolved are whether the property assignment is "municipally friendly" or not. This term refers to the generous way of dealing with financial property, and basically also to the treatment of municipal administrative property within the context of § 7a of the Property Assignment Act. Less appealing to the municipalities, however, is the "claim solution", because it can lead to the extinction of a claim when THA companies are being privatised. Still less appealing is the rule that no claims for damages or for shares in the proceeds of sale can be grounded. This applies in particular when the municipality has to accept the objection of necessity for business operations with regard to assets. In the case of restitution claims, however, it does seem that the last word has yet to be spoken on the subject.

The "customary principle" ignores everything that has happened in the shift between public and private sectors at municipal level in West Germany just since the 1970's. The privatisation of traditionally municipal responsibilities can be seen in many fields of politics and administration: in traffic, with street cleaning and gritting in winter, parks, passenger traffic, etc., or in basic services such as electricity and gas supplies, refuse collection, sewerage, and so on.[86] In addition to this, facilities relating to culture, leisure, and education, and to health, youth and social affairs, have been hived off from the public sector. Urban council operations such as utilities, cattle yards, ports and railways, markets, meeting halls, tourists' and spa visitors' organisations, and many other activities have been privatised.[87] The whole picture can be summarised in statistics, but has not yet reached the situation in which it might be defined as "customary practice", perhaps with the exception of town slaughterhouses or arrangements for the cleaning of public buildings.

The question is constantly being asked, in connection with the unification of Germany, whether there was really nothing worth preserving in the old East Germany. Very little by way of an answer can be offered with respect to state and administration, including the centrally planned economy, in view of the bankruptcy to which the statism of the Marxist-Leninist inspired

---

83 See: König, *Systemimmanente und systemverändernde Privatisierung,* pages 280 et seq.

84 See: König: *Die Übertragung öffentlicher Aufgaben,* pages 438 et seq.

85 See: Bundesministerium des Inneren, *Arbeitsanleitung zur Übertragung kommunalen Vermögens,* page 11.

86 See: *Deutscher Städtetag* [standing conference of the municipal authorities] (editor), *Möglichkeiten und Grenzen der Privatisierung öffentlicher Aufgaben.*

87 See: König, *Systemimmanente und systemverändernde Privatisierung,* page 279.

Nomenklatura had led. Nevertheless, it is still fair to ask whether the Treuhand, with regard to the changes in the municipalities' areas of responsibility in eastern Germany and the situation existing prior to unification in East Germany, introduced any innovations for publicly owned property. This does not just refer to privatisation in the strictest sense, meaning the transfer of responsibilities previously assumed by the public sector and publicly owned assets to the private sector. We are referring to privatisation in the formal sense; that means that public administration, although it remains the owner of the corresponding property and responsible for the task, changes over to forms of organisation under private or civil law with certain consequences for rationalisation. Elsewhere the term privatisation is even used when publicly owned facilities use businesslike patterns of action.[88] It is basically fair to ask the question whether, with the new system for property traditionally perceived as being publicly owned property, whether administrative or financial, new economic organisational forms have been discovered which give rise to the expectation of a more efficient and effective way of producing goods and services.

As our report on the transfer of publicly owned property by the Treuhand has shown, particularly with regard to the main problem areas, innovative ideas for property ownership were not part and parcel of the THA's work. The higher rejection rate suffered by the smaller municipalities may have prevented parishes from taking on "assets" which ended up costing more than the use to be obtained from them, but even the development of the club model for water supply and waste-water disposal led only to the liquidation of the old utility companies in favour of supply and disposal units based on smaller operations. If one looks at the problems of know-how, utilisation of technology, personnel costs, etc., one may doubt whether one moves with such liquidations in direction of an optimal size of operations or whether, because of the need to invest, one is required to find a private operator. On the other side, the dispute over the restructuring strategy for the power industry in eastern Germany shows where plans will end up if they diverge from the tradition of municipal self-administration. Doubts are felt whether the highest bodies at federal level are in any way competent to pioneer new routes, almost in the manner of a centralist state, which go beyond the definition the municipalities apply to themselves and their areas of responsibility.[89]

Accordingly, one must come to the conclusion on behalf of the THA that it was never part of its job in transferring property to the public sector to deviate from the constitutional pattern of the division of responsibilities between the Federal, State, and municipal levels as laid down in the German Constitution. Even within the municipal level, the self-administration of the individual municipalities and counties has to be respected within each one's territorial boundaries. Solutions deviating from this pattern would at most have been possible by mutually agreement and within the parameters of the laws. In general terms, the scene presented by the inheritance of a centralist state power is nothing more than local organs which lacked even the material requirements for assuming local responsibilities with no outside help. With its transfer of property the Treuhand contributes material and indirectly financial resources to form the basic equipment which the municipalities need to fulfil their responsibilities.[90] Physical assets such as

---

88 See, on the definition of privatisation: von Loesch, *Privatisierung öffentlicher Aufgaben,* page 42.

89 See: catalogue of questions from the Federal Constitutional Court in Proceedings 2 BvR 1043/91, and others (Constitutional Complaint by the Municipalities against the power contract, referring to the regulations contained in the Treaty of Unification and the Municipalities' Property Act) in a letter of the THA/Directorate Law/Department 5 of 13th October 1992.

90 See: Schöneich, *Die Kommunalisierung,* page 384.

equipment for social, health, cultural and other basic provisions cannot be evaluated on efficiency criteria alone. The communal infrastructure makes an important contribution to the citizen's ability to identify himself with his local community politically and democratically. The transfers of property are, in this respect, contributions to the construction of a local system of independent self-administration in eastern Germany. This admittedly does not dispose of the innovation question altogether, but it should not be directed at the Treuhand but to the new municipalities and States. The assignment of property merely creates the necessary conditions.

If therefore the new system of property ownership in eastern Germany pursues the "customary principle", the final point to be examined is the demarcation of the private sector with regard to the state's economic activities. In the long history of our municipalities and States, a huge number of assets have somehow accumulated, from the Court Brewery of a well-known Free State (Bavaria) to the wine cellar of more than one well-known city.[91] A historic legacy of this kind has to be taken into account in considering claims to restitution. If, therefore, the State Porcelain Manufactory of Meissen was transferred to the Free State of Saxony, this is a symbol of mercantilist tradition which has fitted itself into the framework of political order and tolerance even in a society with private companies and a fully-fledged free-market system. The case of the former Zeiss optical industry Kombinat in Jena, which had 69,000 employees in GDR days,[92] has to be dealt with quite differently. It was considerations of regional, employment, and structural policy that led to this company being partly taken over by the State of Thuringia as early as 1991.

The question still keeps arising urgently for the THA as to how companies are to be dealt with that cannot be privatised at short notice. As of 30th June 1993, there were still 1,668 with 296,343 employees on the Treuhand's books.[93] Among them were more and more problem cases, as can be seen in the figure of 17% of these employees being on short-time working, or in particularly difficult areas like precision or optical engineering up to 38%.[94] In order to be able to continue these companies in operation – they are capable of being modernised but not immediately of being privatised – with the help of western managers, the model of the Management-Kommanditgesellschaft or "Management-KG" has been developed by the THA. A KG is a private partnership in which at least one partner carries unlimited, personal liability. The life of a Management KG is initially limited to three years. The major shareholder is still the THA. The task of the Management-KG is to restructure successfully in order to privatise quickly.[95] It is still a matter of some discussion whether, above and beyond this, any remaining eastern German companies, which mainly because of their size cannot be brought in under a Management-KG, would have to be sold off to the public sector. With regard to the "old industrial cores" of the former GDR, a state shareholding can be justified on the basis of public interest and proof can be found in the unavailing attempts of the THA to show that the aim being striven for cannot be attained better or more economically in any other way. Proponents of this course will be able to point to the state's ability to hold these companies off at arm's length by the possibility of becoming independent under company law and the competition provided by the market.

However, there is no getting round the fact that for all material purposes this is nationalisation in one form or another, which starts at a time when the whole assessment of the roles of the state

91 See: König, *Kritik öffentlicher Aufgaben,* pages 54 et seq.

92 See: *Frankfurter Allgemeine Zeitung* dated 7th December 1992, page 20.

93 See: Treuhandanstalt, *Monatsinformation der THA* as of 30th June 1993, page 10.

94 op. cit., page 29.

95 See: *Frankfurter Allgemeine Zeitung* dated 18th February 1993, page 13.

and the commercial sectors by west European (and other western) standards is running far more in the direction of privatisation, even including those fields of responsibility which have a long tradition of services provided by the state. It is therefore necessary at least to hold the problems of this kind of state economy in mind and to learn from experience. After the Second World War, the West German government took over a sizeable set of commercial-industrial assets in its capacity as the legal successor to the German Reich and the State of Prussia. It basically took up to the 1980's until the political intention and majority, social assessment and evaluation, and the economic conditions surrounding companies and markets coincided to such an extent that a window of opportunity opened for the widespread privatisation of the state's holding in commercial and industrial means of production of goods which in many cases had long ceased to be counted as part of the state sector.[96] In view of the inevitability of certain nationalisations, under the circumstances obtaining in the territory of the old German Democratic Republic, the question arises as what conceptional precautions could be taken to prevent such historical perseverances from being repeated over the decades in order that the modern welfare state does not overstrain itself with its burdens and that the necessary division of labour between the state, the free economy, and society is kept in sight.

VII. Literature

Ad hoc Gruppe der Fachkommission Soforthilfe Trinkwasser: *Bericht an den Bundesminister für Gesundheit über notwendige Sanierungsmaßnahmen bei der Trinkwasserversorgung der neuen Bundesländer,* dated July 1992. Berlin.

Bartsch, Heinz: *Aufgaben und Struktur der öffentlichen Verwaltung.* In: Klaus *König* (editor): *Verwaltungsstrukturen der DDR.* Baden-Baden 1991, pages 109 to 134.

Beschlußempfehlung und Bericht des Rechtsausschusses des Bundestages. In: *Bundestagsdrucksache* 12/2944.

Bullinger, Manfred: Kooperatives Verwaltungshandeln (Vorverhandlung, Arrangements, Agreement und Verträge) in der Verwaltungspraxis. In: *Die Öffentliche Verwaltung* 1989, pages 277 to 289.

Bundesministerium des Inneren: Arbeitsanleitung zur Übertragung kommunalen Vermögens und zur Förderung von Investitionen durch die Kommunen. In: *Infodienst Kommunal* no. 24, dated 19th April 1991, pages 1 to 72.

ditto: Übertragung kommunalen Vermögens. In: *Infodienst Kommunal* no. 61, dated 20th November 1992.

Bundesministerium für Verkehr: Leitfaden zur Gestaltung des öffentlichen Personennahverkehrs (ÖPNV) in den neuen Bundesländern. In: *Infodienst Kommunal* no. 51, dated 19th June 1992, pages 1 to 47.

Bundesumweltministerium (editor): *Privatwirtschaftliche Realisierung der Abwasserentsorgung – Erfahrungsbericht.* Bonn 1993.

Denkschrift zum Einigungsvertrag. In: *Bundestagsdrucksache* 11/7766, pages 355 to 378.

Deutscher Städtetag (editor): Möglichkeiten und Grenzen der Privatisierung öffentlicher Aufgaben. Reihe A, DST *Beiträge zur Kommunalpolitik,* volume 7. Cologne ²1986.

96 See: König, *Kritik öffentlicher Aufgaben,* pages 54 et seq.

Harms, Wolfgang: *Zwischen Privatisierung, Wettbewerb und Kommunalisierung.* Cologne 1992.

Hauschild, Christoph: *Die örtliche Verwaltung im Staats- und Verwaltungssystem der DDR.* Baden-Baden 1991.

Statistisches Jahrbuch der DDR 34 (1989). Edited by the Staatliche Zentralverwaltung für Statistik.

Statistisches Jahrbuch '90 der Deutschen Demokratischen Republik 35 (1990). Edited by the Statistisches Amt der DDR.

Ipsen, Jörn, and Thorsten *Koch:* Zuordnung volkseigenen Vermögens und Restitution früheren Eigentums der öffentlichen Hand. In: *Deutsches Verwaltungsblatt* 1993 no. 108, pages 1 to 9.

Knauss, Fritz: *Privatisierungspolitik in der Bundesrepublik Deutschland.* Cologne 1989.

König, Klaus: *Kritik öffentlicher Aufgaben.* Baden-Baden 1989.

ditto: Systemimmanente und systemverändernde Privatisierung in Deutschland. In: *Verwaltung/Organisation/Personal* 1992, pages 279 to 286.

ditto: Die Übertragung öffentlicher Aufgaben: Eine europäische Sicht. In: *Verwaltungsarchiv* 1990, pages 436 to 449.

ditto.: *Zum Verwaltungssystem der DDR.* In: Klaus *König* (editor): *Verwaltungsstrukturen der DDR.* Baden-Baden 1991, pages 9 to 44.

Lange, Manfred: Wem gehört das ehemalige Volkseigentum? In: *Deutsch-Deutsche Rechts-Zeitschrift* 1991, pages 329 to 336.

Law on the local representation of the people in the GDR of 4th July 1985. In: *Gesetzblatt der DDR* I, page 213.

Lipps, Wolfgang: Die Zuordnung ehemals volkseigenen Vermögens. In: *Zeitschrift für Vermögens- und Investitionsrecht* 1992, pages 14 to 16.

Loesch, Achim von: *Privatisierung öffentlicher Aufgaben.* Baden-Baden ^{2}1987.

Quaritsch, Helmut: Eigenarten und Rechtsfragen der DDR-Revolution. In: *Verwaltungsarchiv* 1992 no. 83, pages 314 to 329.

Salzwedel, Jürgen, in: H.-U. *Erichsen* and W. *Martens* (editors): *Allgemeines Verwaltungsrecht.* Berlin ^{9}1992

Schmitz, Michaela: Die Trinkwasserversorgung in den neuen Bundesländern – Ziele, Probleme, Lösungen. In: *Neue DELIWA-Zeitschrift* 1992, pages 247 to 250.

Schöneich, Michael: Die Kommunalisierung von öffentlichen Aufgaben in den neuen Bundesländern nach der Praxis der Treuhandanstalt. In: *Verwaltungsarchiv* 1993, pages 383 to 393.

ditto: *Kommunale Wirtschaftsentwicklung – Anforderungen an die Treuhandanstalt.* Manuscript of speech held on 1st October 1992 at the Forschungsinstitut für öffentliche Verwaltung bei der Hochschule für Verwaltungswissenschaften Speyer.

Treuhandanstalt: *Monatsinformation der THA* (various monthly news bulletins).

The Treuhandanstalt and the winding up of companies incapable of being effectively restructured

by Eckhard Wandel, with the assistance of Marcus W. Mosen

I. Introduction

Shortly after the Treuhandanstalt had started its undertaking, it became clear that many companies in eastern Germany were incapable of being restructured with any real effect. The way that the Treuhand chose to wind them up would therefore represent one of its most immense and controversial tasks. The media contributed to creating the public impression that "winding up" was tantamount to "demolition".[1] (The original German term, *Abwicklung*, was no doubt used because it sounds relatively innocent; it has the very broad and mundane meaning of "handling" or "despatching", and can in an everyday context be applied to the handling of passengers or freight departing from an airport or goods leaving a factory, although always with some connotation of finality.) People in eastern Germany in particular regard this phenomenon of winding up very critically. This is understandable when one bears in mind that employees in the old GDR had tended to spend their entire working lives in one company. For many of them, the closure of "their" companies therefore meant that a part of their lives had been wound up as well. It is therefore difficult for the employees to accept the decisions taken by the THA.

On closer examination, it soon becomes apparent that it is unjustified to equate the operations of the THA with "demolition" or the total closure of companies. Instead the process can be seen as providing a number of different creative possibilities, which can lead to the continuation of the firm or parts thereof. Some of the alternatives and the design parameters will be demonstrated in the following pages, with the prime emphasis on the liquidation process.

II. Winding up as a form of company liquidation in eastern Germany

1. The parameters of the Treuhandanstalt's mandate

The preamble to the Treuhand Act (that of 17 June 1990 empowering the Treuhandanstalt) defines its core task as being "to create in as many companies as possible the ability to compete, thus securing existing jobs and creating new ones". The THA fulfils this task through its privatisation work via the so-called "Industry Directorates". The Treuhand decides on winding up, in accordance with an established procedure, for companies which could not successfully complete

1 See: Köhler, *Wirtschaftliche Perspektiven,* page 10; "Die Plattmacher von der Berliner Treuhand", in: *Berliner Morgenpost* of 13th January 1992, page 1.

the privatisation phase in the respective Industry Directorate. It is also obliged to aim for job security and the creation of new jobs during the course of the winding-up process.

This process is only initiated for a company when it is obvious that all privatisation attempts have been to no avail. In other words, intensive efforts to privatise and attempts to reconstruct as a means of achieving privatisation have to take place before winding up would be considered.[2] It is only when these endeavours have failed that the company comes in line for "considerate closure".[3] The "considerate" way in which the Treuhand works is expressed in the objective that in the interest of the work-force, the labour market, and the local region, the largest possible number of jobs should be preserved and new approaches tried to create new jobs in the factory premises of the affected company.

From this requirement it soon becomes apparent that winding up, as carried out by the Treuhand, was far more extensive in breadth and depth of work than might be derived from the legal and economic definition of winding up.

2. Definition of winding up

The term "winding up" replaced the expression "closure" used by Rohwedder. In avoiding this term the THA intended to emphasise that the winding up of a company is not necessarily the same as the complete termination of its business activities.[4]

Subjecting the term winding up to closer scrutiny, one sees that it assumes a number of different meanings dependent on context. The three main types of usage are:

- winding up as a procedure to wind up a company,
- winding up as a process within a time-frame,
- winding up as a description of an organisational unit within the Treuhand.

The first usage is particularly common in the literature. Winding up is described here as the task of releasing a company, after it has been liquidated, from its obligations under labour and property law in order to bring about the final cessation of the company. The implication is that the procedure can just as well be described as liquidation. The characteristic feature is the methodical disposal of the existing assets in order to repay the company's debts from the proceeds and, when available, to distribute the residue amongst the shareholders or partners.[5]

In connection with the Treuhand's work, the term winding up is used to subsume the various alternative procedures involved in bankruptcy and liquidation. Whilst the procedure of bankruptcy is implemented by a sequestrator appointed by the court, in the case of liquidation the THA remains in charge of proceedings. The use of these terms shows that the previous, narrow interpretation given in the literature has been greatly enlarged in the practical work of the Treuhand.

---

2 Treuhand Guidelines on winding up, dated 22nd October 1991.

3 The term "considerate closure" *(behutsame Stillegung)* was used by Detlev Karsten Rohwedder in a memorandum dated 27th March 1991 addressed to the staff of the Treuhandanstalt, in which he formulated the guiding principles of the Treuhandanstalt: "Rapid privatisation – resolute restructuring – considerate closure."

4 See: Kemmler, *Die Entstehung der Treuhandanstalt,* page 277 et seq.

5 See: Heinen, *Handelsbilanzen,* page 496; Wöhe, *Allgemeine Betriebswirtschaftslehre,* page 916.

The winding-up process is carried out within a time schedule of several years. For simplification, this schedule is also referred to as winding up. Such an oversimplification ignores the fact that this process is made up of a number of phases each with its own required activities. Defining these parameters has a direct impact on the course and the outcome of the winding-up process.

Finally, the term winding up describes organisational units within the Treuhand. In the Central Office this unit is the "Winding-up Directorate", and in each of its 15 branches and later its branch offices as the "Winding-up Department". In contrast to the THA's Industry Directorates, both the Winding-up Directorate and the Winding-up Departments manage cases across all industrial directorates simultaneously. The Winding-up Directorate bears technical responsibility for implementing and monitoring the basic principles, guidelines, and working instructions relevant to winding up, both for the Central Office and for the Treuhand's branches and branch offices.

In this article, winding up is used to describe the process being applied. When the time-scale of this procedure is being considered, it is referred to as the "winding-up process".[6]

3. Liquidation and bankruptcy as winding-up alternatives

The Treuhand applies the procedures of (voluntary) liquidation and bankruptcy for the purpose of winding up companies. There are various arguments that can be presented favouring both alternatives.[7] The decision as to the winding up alternative is reached within the winding-up process. Regardless of which procedure is decided in any individual case, the legal guidelines currently in force have to be followed. The main provisions are described below.

In the event of the insolvency of a company – under German law, the inability to meet payments or in the case of overindebtedness – a statutory regulation comes into force which deviates from the law applicable in western Germany. In eastern Germany, the Compulsory Bankruptcy Order (*Gesamtvollstreckungsordnung*) applies as the legal basis for insolvency or bankruptcy proceedings.[8] If the application for enforcement is made (§ 1 of the Order) and bankruptcy proceedings opened, the relevant County Court entrusts a sequestrator with the task of selling off the assets (§ 8). Although his work is supervised by the Court and the creditors, he does it on his own authority and at his own discretion. As he is acting in the creditor's interest, his main objective is to achieve the maximum possible proceeds from these sales.[9]

---

6 See Point III.1.

7 These arguments are explained in more depth in the description of the winding-up process under Point III.2.

8 The Council of Ministers, while it was still the competent legislative body of the GDR, argued against the introduction of a uniform law on bankruptcy, insolvency, and arrangement for the whole of Germany. For this reason, the GDR insolvency law dating from 1975, the Compulsory Enforcement (= Bankruptcy) Ordinance, was adapted to meet the needs of the social market economy. The new Compulsory Bankruptcy Ordinance dated 6th June 1990 came into force on 1st July 1990 and superseded the previous Ordinance. The new Compulsory Bankruptcy Ordinance takes its line from western German insolvency law. Under the Treaty of Unification, the title of the Compulsory Bankruptcy Ordinance *(Gesamtvollstreckungsverordnung)* was altered to Compulsory Bankruptcy Order *(Gesamtvollstreckungsordnung).*

9 See: Hess and Binz, *Gesamtvollstreckungsordnung,* page 18.

The legal basis for the liquidation procedure as applied to THA companies is covered in §§ 262 et seq. of the *Aktiengesetz*, the German Companies Act covering public limited and joint-stock companies, and §§ 60 et seq. of the *GmbH-Gesetz*, the Act covering private limited companies.[10] Particular attention must be paid to the regulations referring to the purpose for which the company was established, its trading name, the way in which the proceedings are carried out, the executive bodies representing the company, its financial control, and its accounting methods. The Treuhand, as the sole partner, can call an Associates' Meeting (in the case of a GmbH) or as the sole shareholder a General Meeting (in the case of an AG) to pass a resolution liquidating the company (§ 262 section 2 no 2 of the Aktiengesetz and § 60 no 2 of the GmbH-Gesetz).

On entering into liquidation the aim of the company changes. The former aim of earning profits through its business operations is replaced by the goal of winding up. The commercial company turns into a winding-up company. This decision signifies the actual start of the winding-up process. During this process all remaining assets are liquidated in order to satisfy the creditors and to distribute any surplus to the shareholders or partners.[11] However, this cannot be done until a period of one year has elapsed after the publication of the public notice for creditors to come forward (§ 272 of the Aktiengesetz and § 73 of the GmbH-Gesetz).

The liquidation of a company should not be equated with its termination. It remains a legal entity until it is finally wound up and the entry removed from the Register of Companies.[12] It is not until winding-up proceedings have been completed and the deletion made that the company ceases to exist as a legal entity. In principle, all grounds for liquidation are capable of being resolved, and accordingly it is always theoretically possible that the liquidated company could continue in existence.

The company retains its trading name during winding-up proceedings, but the abbreviation "i. L." (in liquidation) is appended (§ 269 section 6 of the Aktiengesetz, § 68 sections 2 and 4 of the GmbH-Gesetz). This makes the change in company purpose apparent to all its business contacts. The law provides generally that the winding-up procedure will be carried through by the existing executive board (§ 265 of the Aktiengesetz) or management (§ 66 of the GmbH-Gesetz). When THA companies are being wound up, the Treuhand puts a sequestrator in the place of the existing board in the case of an AG (§§ 265 and 268 of the Aktiengesetz), and a liquidator takes the place of the management in a GmbH (§ 70 of the GmbH-Gesetz).[13] Lawyers in private practice who enjoy the confidence of the Treuhand are usually appointed for this work. In this function they take over the power to represent the company from its executive bodies, but without being thereby restricted by the purpose of winding up (§ 269 of the Aktiengesetz, § 70 of the GmbH-Gesetz). Their names and their authority to represent the company have to be entered in the Register of Companies (§ 266 section 1 of the Aktiengesetz, § 67 section 1 of the GmbH-Gesetz).

In the case of AGs, the Supervisory Board and the General Meeting remain in existence as company bodies (§ 264 of the Aktiengesetz). As a rule, when winding-up proceedings start, staff are seconded from the Winding-up Directorate of the Treuhand to the supervisory board, in order to ensure close collaboration and co-ordination between the liquidator and the THA. The

---

10 THA companies either have the legal status of an "AG" (joint-stock company) or of a "GmbH" (limited liability company). This description is therefore limited to the legal basis for corporations.

11 See: Geßler, *Aktiengesetz. Kommentar,* page 263, marginal note 1.

12 See: Heinen, *Handelsbilanzen,* page 496.

13 For simplicity's sake, the term "liquidator" will now be used to cover both instances.

controlling function of the supervisory board (§ 268 section 2 sentence 2 of the Aktiengesetz) is emphasised by the secondment of the THA staff.

The liquidators are under an obligation to make public appeals for creditors to come forward by placing three consecutive announcements in the *Gesellschaftsblätter*, an official Government publication (§ 267 of the Aktiengesetz, § 65 section 2 of the GmbH-Gesetz). The liquidator's prime responsibility consists of bringing on-going business to an end, collecting outstanding amounts receivable, and liquidating the assets. He is also permitted in this context to enter into new business commitment during the winding-up phase if this appears expedient (§ 268 of the Aktiengesetz, § 71 section 1 of the GmbH-Gesetz).[14]

The company is still under its normal obligation to present accounts. These include the drawing up of a balance sheet showing the situation at the opening of liquidation proceedings along with an explanatory report. The annual report and accounts also have to be prepared at the end of each company financial year (§ 270 section 1 of the Aktiengesetz, § 70 of the GmbH-Gesetz). With regard to establishing the balance, there is one special feature distinguishing this from the normal situation under the Aktiengesetz (§ 270 section 2), the balance sheet is not adopted by the supervisory board but always, as with GmbH-type companies, by the Treuhand as the sole shareholder/partner.

Closing accounts have to be drawn up for joint-stock companies (AG's) at the end of the winding-up procedure (§ 273 of the Aktiengesetz). Although it is not prescribed mandatorily in the case of limited liability companies (GmbH's), it is the duty of a conscientious liquidator to produce closing accounts.[15] For reasons of expediency, the Treuhand arranges for the final accounts to be prepared in the form of a closing balance sheet for both types of company.

III. Phases in the winding-up process: a process-orientated approach

1. Categorisation and preliminary investigation

The winding-up activities of the THA can, like any decision-taking process in business administration, be divided into the general phases of planning, implementation, and control.[16] These phases can be divided further into sub-phases in which the terminology specific to the Treuhand is used (Fig. 1).

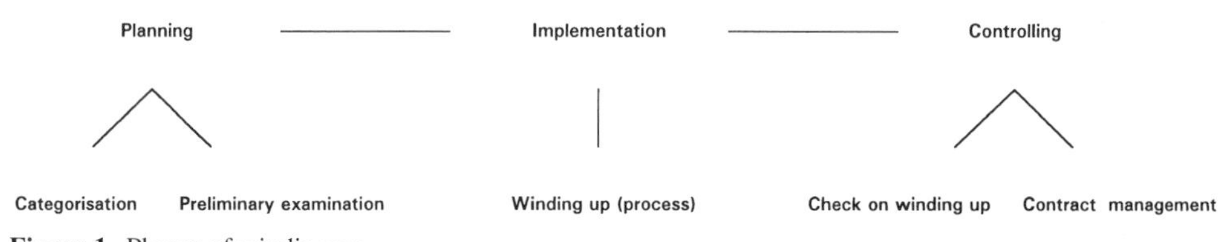

Figure 1 Phases of winding up

14 See Section IV.

15 See: Lutter and Hommelhoff, *GmbH-Gesetz Kommentar,* page 714.

16 See: Heinen, *Betriebswirtschaftslehre,* page 21.

The Treuhand subjects its companies to a permanent process of evaluation with regard to their suitability for privatisation and restructuring. This evaluation is carried out by the Management Committee (*Leitungsausschuß*).[17]

The evaluation leads to a judgement and to a numerical categorisation on a scale from "1" (company is operating profitably, no restructuring called for, privatise rapidly) to "6" (company is not capable of being restructured, decision must be taken on either bankruptcy or liquidation). The critical categorisation as "3.1.2" (a great need for cash, within a short period of time a partner has to be presented). For companies in this group, privatisation possibilities have to be identified as quickly as possible. If this is not done within a specified time-scale, the company immediately drops into category "6".

Category "6" entails wider responsibility within the THA for the company affected. In addition to the relevant Industry Directorate, the Winding-up Directorate is also drawn in to look after it. The joint action then to be taken is shown in the form of a "Resolution to initiate the preliminary investigation phase", under which the Winding-up Directorate is entrusted with the task of examining the options (voluntary liquidation or bankruptcy) and to take all the necessary steps, in co-ordination with the other parties involved, to prepare for winding up. At the same time, the Industry Directorate is asked to carry out a final examination and present its considered opinion on restructuring possibilities.

The examination of the alternatives of winding up is carried out by external experts (auditors) and takes the form of the preparation of a detailed assessment. This assessment is of cardinal significance for the subsequent action and can be divided into five sections:

The first part provides an overview, based on the company's own data, of its historical development, its legal position, and its personnel situation. Secondly, there is a section describing its business situation, e. g. the trends in its balance sheet and in its profit-and-loss account and a list of any court actions pending. In the third section, any unconcluded privatisation negotiations are listed. The fourth section contains notes on the company's assets and a comparison of costs. The available proceeds are based on the book value of assets and liabilities. This "liquid" amount is calculated as the "foreseeable distribution in bankruptcy proceedings" as defined in the Compulsory Bankruptcy Order. A detailed description of the derivation of this amount would go far beyond the bounds of this article, but to give the reader an impression of the substance of the cost comparisons an illustrative example is contained in the Appendix to this article.

In the cost comparison the two winding-up procedures are presented. As a rule, these costs differ from one another. The reasons for the differences can be circumstances such as the following:

- Any chance of privatisation still existing when the liquidation process starts will make it seem sensible to maintain production for a certain length of time. An immediate halt to production can under certain circumstances lead to lower costs, but would entail the immediate termination of all business relationships, which would be detrimental to any possible privatisation. A sequestrator carrying out the bankruptcy procedure, on the other hand, will only maintain production if this is compatible with the interests of the creditors.
- As a rule, the Treuhand offers both the *Deutsche Kreditbank*, as creditor for the historic liabilities, and the creditors for goods and services supplied, a composition quota of the liquida-

17 The Management Committee acts on behalf of the Federal Ministry of Finance as an independent body with a consultancy function for the Executive Board of the Treuhandanstalt and its Directorates. For this body's working methods, see: article by Schwalbach in this book, pages 183 et seq.

tion proceeds. This is as a higher percentage than that identified by the expert assessment in bankruptcy proceedings. The higher composition share in liquidation proceedings thus leads to higher costs than those in bankruptcy proceedings.

This higher percentage is intended to persuade the creditors to favour liquidation proceedings. If a sufficient surplus is available on liquidation, the creditors are entitled to full satisfaction of their payment demands. The Treuhand must first remove any inability of the company to pay its debts, so that no obligation remains to initiate bankruptcy proceedings. Insolvency is avoided by supplying additional liquidity in the form of a liquidator loan or by the THA conceding a lower priority for its payment demands.

The cost comparison is the main basis on which the expert gives his winding-up recommendation in the fifth part. In the illustrative example shown, it would not be difficult for the creditors to vote in favour of the liquidation alternative. The costs in the case of bankruptcy (DM 4,555,900) are DM 1,234,400 higher than in the case of liquidation (DM 3,321,600). However, even if the costs are lower in the case of bankruptcy, the expert is required to take other criteria into account in his recommendation, in addition to the costs aspect. A difference in costs disadvantageous to the liquidation route does not automatically lead to a vote in favour of bankruptcy proceedings. This aspect will be explained below in more detail in order to provide a better understanding and because of its cardinal significance for the winding-up policy of the Treuhand.

2. Winding up (as a procedure)

Once the winding-up recommendation has been received, the Treuhand takes the decision on the procedure to be followed. It takes its line, as required within its mandate, also from the criterion of securing or creating jobs. Hess perceives further criteria for this decision in the external effects of the Treuhand's actions, in the possibility of a loss of confidence in the event of bankruptcy, in the social compatibility of the measures being taken, and in acceptance by the population at large.[18]

The THA's decision mentioned here is the subject of lively debate. Bankruptcy sequestrators, in particular, regard the Treuhand's dominance of liquidation proceedings as not being crucial to their success. Kübler for instance argues that "the key to the success or failure" of winding-up proceedings depends more on the personal background and qualities of the sequestrator, and pleads in favour of a change in the Treuhand's existing policy. Instead of giving preference to liquidation, he would favour the initiation of bankruptcy proceedings. Compared thus, it is not possible to perceive any greater social compatibility in liquidation. He feels that the THA's scope for influence in bankruptcy proceedings is sufficiently taken into account by the "secondment of an expert representative" as a member of the creditors' committee.[19]

This line of argument needs to be countered by the fact that the actual scope for influence exerted by the creditor's committee is limited to checking up on the sequestrator and receiving his reports and accounts. Although any major legal transactions the sequestrator may enter into, such as taking out loans, accepting liabilities and obligations, acquiring and disposing of property, which all have a considerable impact on the value of the assets he is administering, require

18 See: Hess, *Rechtsfragen der Liquidation,* page 10.

19 See: Kübler, *Die Gesamtvollstreckung,* pages 92 et seq.

the assent of the creditor's committee, this committee cannot issue orders to the sequestrator with regard to his work (§ 15 section 6 of the Compulsory Bankruptcy Order). It is only in liquidation proceedings that the Treuhand remains the "master of ceremonies", and in practice this dominant position over liquidation proceedings is expressed in close, and usually very co-operative, collaboration between the liquidators and the Treuhand.[20]

Any decision by the THA to wind up all its relevant companies through bankruptcy would require a sufficient number of experienced bankruptcy sequestrators. However, the number of these people who can also act as trouble-shooters for eastern German companies is limited.[21] In the discussion of the alternative procedures it is also important not to overlook the Treuhand's political responsibility, which prevents it from taking all the actions which a major creditor would take in order to satisfy its claims. A major creditor can usually make full use of foreclosure proceedings without losing the respect of the business world, but this is tainted with a "condemnation" for the eastern German population and would "lead to a further loss of identification".[22]

The obligation to apply for the opening of bankruptcy proceedings is intended as a precaution against irregularities in the management of the business in cases of insolvency, and at the same time as a protection for the creditors. The lack of any scope for restructuring, on the other hand, is not to be equated with a state of insolvency, and the Treuhand therefore does not need any further justification for preferring a shareholders' or partners' resolution in favour of liquidation to the opening of bankruptcy proceedings. In this connection it should also be borne in mind that the creditors of a company which cannot be restructured are in many cases themselves THA companies, and the interests of these creditors and the debtor company thus ultimately lie with one and the same sole partner, the Treuhand.

Although the Treuhand is simultaneously one of the creditors, when liquidation is being carried out under company law it does not necessarily pursue the aim of maximising the proceeds. If a part of a company or a piece of property is being sold, it is not only the purchase price which is used as a criterion in the decision on disposal. The number of jobs preserved or created, and the amount of the planned investment, are also taken into account in deciding on the purchaser. It can make economic sense, particularly from the point of view of the labour market, to make concessions in setting the purchase price, if an investor with an plausible concept promises comparatively more jobs than another one.[23] This room for manoeuvre which the Treuhand has in setting the purchase price only exists in liquidation proceedings; in bankruptcy proceedings, on the other hand, the creditors will primarily put the sequestrator under pressure to produce the maximum proceeds or the highest purchase price.

A further aspect which favours liquidation from the Treuhand's point of view can be found in the contractual conditions under which other companies have been privatised. The privatisation procedures carried out in the various Industry Directorates can, for instance, conceal risks regarding their contestability (§ 10 of the Compulsory Bankruptcy Order). If, for instance, privatisation has taken the form of sale to one sole bidder, and not by public tender, the sequestrator in bankruptcy proceedings can contest this privatisation if assets have been sold for less than their

---

20 The active role of the Treuhandanstalt is examined in more detail in Section IV.2.

21 See: *Die Top-Sanierer Deutschlands,* pages 18 to 26.

22 See: Hess, *Rechtsfragen der Liquidation,* page 11.

23 See: Tränkner, *Abwicklung bedeutet Entwicklung,* page 3.

market value (§ 10 section 1 of the Order). In such an instance, the sequestrator has to supply evidence to the THA that the privatisation was carried out "in a manner not justified by the facts".[24]

Any attempt to evaluate the privatisations carried out by the THA must, however, be viewed against the background that investors, as a rule, were not prepared to pay the physical asset value of the company as the purchase price and at the same time to give comprehensive and undertakings on jobs covered by fines. These undertakings were in many cases "purchased" by the Treuhand in the form of concessions over the purchase price. If a final evaluation is to be made of any case of privatisation, however, the macro-economic benefit must also be taken into account, i. e. including the preservation or creation of jobs.

For the sequestrator in bankruptcy proceedings the only decisive factor, bearing the creditor's interests in mind, is any attempt to "reduce the value of assets", and he might be able to prove this if the net sale proceeds were low and the company had thus been sold "for less than its real value". However, the sequestrator will not be able to take any possible macro-economic benefits of privatisation into account, and the Treuhand can only avoid such contestation risks by avoiding bankruptcy proceedings.

3. Controlling and contract management in winding-up proceedings

The business management control function over the winding-up process takes two different forms. Firstly, a constant monitoring of all stages of winding up, and secondly, a controlling of all contractual obligations entered into by the THA's or the liquidating company's contractual partners.

Constant control is always exercised by two units which are independent of one another (on the principle that "four eyes always see more than two"). One is the Winding-up Directorate, and the other is the Winding-up Financial Control Department.[25] In organisational terms, the Winding-up Financial Control Department is integrated into a Commercial Directorate which does not report to the Winding-up Directorate. The main task of this department is a financial control function regarding flows of liquidity and the costs incurred by the winding-up proceedings. To do this, the Department makes use of monthly reports from the liquidators and undertakes immediate checks on deviations.

The area of responsibility of the Winding-up Financial Control Department also covers:

- examining the alternative procedures of liquidation and bankruptcy (decision-orientated financial control),
- comparing and evaluating purchase offers and corporate concepts,
- scrutiny of draft purchase contracts, and
- plausibility analyses during the winding-up process.

The Winding-up Financial Control Department thus becomes the "constant companion of the Winding-up Directorate, and contributes to increasing the efficiency, minimising the risk, and

---

24 See: Hess and Binz, *Gesamtvollstreckungsordnung*, page 215.

25 This division of responsibilities based on the "four eyes" principle is organised similarly in the Treuhandanstalt's branches and branch offices. In this Section reference is only made, however, to the Winding-up Financial Control Department in the Central Office of the Treuhand.

optimising the results of the winding-up process".[26] In addition to this financial control accompanying the winding-up process, the Treuhand has also established another control mechanism which monitors all the concluded privatisations.[27] This control function was taken over by the newly created "Contract Management" Division of the THA on 1st July 1993.

When assets are being sold during the course of the winding-up process, responsibility for contract control lies with the liquidators. When the shares are being sold, this control function passes to the Treuhand's Contract Management Division, which has to ensure on the THA's behalf that privatisation contracts are fulfilled and that the contracting parties' obligations (e. g. financial agreements, maintenance of the value of the assets, commitments of job preservation and investment) are monitored and implemented.[28] The Contract Management staff therefore makes a long-term contribution to the success of the THA's privatisation work.

IV. New practices, problem areas, and particular features of winding up

1. The liquidator's work

The actual winding-up process, and thus also the work of the liquidator, starts with the passing of the resolution to liquidate a company. The people selected by the THA for this task have to demonstrate a wide variety of abilities in addition to their professional qualifications: entrepreneurial capabilities, creativity, and sensitivity towards social and political questions. The liquidator's work covers the winding up of on-going business, the fulfilment of the shareholders' or partners' liabilities, the collecting of outstanding sums receivable, and the selling off of assets.

The area of responsibility of the sequestrators and liquidators working in eastern Germany cannot be totally described in terms of their original statutory duties. The Treuhand has widened the range of responsibilities to include "transfer-restructuring" (übertragende Sanierung). Knowing that the company entering liquidation is capable of being neither privatised nor restructured as it stands, the liquidator's task will include hiving off parts of the operation, selling assets, establishing individual sound production units as part of his liquidation work. These measures will first of all create smaller, competitive units which can be offered to investors. The work of restructuring will be transferred to the new owners.[29]

One factor of major significance for successful "transfer-restructuring" can be that new business commitments are entered into during the liquidation process. The liquidator has fundamental authority to do so if it is expedient to the closing of current business matters. He has to fulfil

26 B-Interview on 12th August 1993 with Dr Wolf Klinz, member of the Executive Board of the Treuhandanstalt, whose responsibilities include the Winding-up Directorate and the Winding-up Financial Control Department.

27 Financial control of winding-up activities is a sufficiently self-contained subject to deserve separate consideration within winding-up as a whole, but this would burst the bounds of this article. This description is therefore limited to its organisational position.

28 See: Resolution of the Administrative Board of the Treuhand dated 19th February 1993.

29 See: Tränkner, *Abwicklung bedeutet Entwicklung*, page 2.

existing contracts and orders to avoid any later claims for damages. The execution of new orders should as a rule only be undertaken if they bring in a net contribution, i. e. if the proceeds of such contracts exceed the costs relevant to cash flow. It is possible to deviate from this principle if an investor could be found by maintaining the existence of the loss-making company or sub-unit. If the Treuhand consents, it is even possible within the liquidation process to carry out an expensive restructuring programme if this means that the chances of privatising the business are thereby demonstrably enhanced, and the costs of the restructuring programme bear reasonable relationship to the number of jobs thus preserved.

2. The active collaboration of the Treuhandanstalt

The role of the THA in the winding-up process does not limit itself to merely supervising the liquidator's work. Its active collaboration is expressed not just in financial control but, in particular, in the provision of experience and creativity as well as other support services.

The operational activities involved in the winding-up process are initially managed and supervised by the executives of the process within the Winding-up Directorate or in one of the Treuhand's branches and branch offices. The liquidator normally has to agree all major plans and decisions with this executive, although as far as the outside world is concerned he then carries them out independently. This manager also initially solves all problems of co-ordination and synchronisation with other Treuhand departments indirectly involved in the liquidation process (e. g. the divisions in charge of company financing, labour market, and social affairs).

For the THA, the supply of information to all parties involved in the winding-up process has a very high priority. Once the liquidation of a company has been decided upon, the Winding-up Directorate calls the representatives of all interested groups together for a so-called "major meeting", at which the Winding-up Directorate informs the participants of the winding-up resolution and presents the planned method of working during the winding-up phase. Those invited then have the opportunity to draw the attention of the liquidator and of the executive responsible for this particular winding-up task to possible problems which could arise during the winding-up process. Similar meetings also take place in the various branches and branch offices.

The executives in the Winding-up Directorate are jointly responsible for a given number of companies. They thus become the contact person during the whole winding-up phase for works councils, trade unions, the representatives of political interest, and anyone else affected by any given winding-up procedure. The cumulative experience of the Winding-up Directorate is made available to the liquidators through the constant exchange of opinions with the local workforce. As a result of this collaboration, creative solutions can be found for problems occurring during the winding-up process. Furthermore the Winding-up Directorate summons liquidators to meetings at regular intervals in which it is possible both to develop new winding-up guidelines and to discuss problems encountered. Additionally, the Winding-up Directorate publishes a liquidators newspaper at regular intervals in order to inform liquidators of the latest developments.

This flow of information between the Treuhand and the liquidators is not one-sided. The so-called "Winding-up Advisory Board" was created as the consultative body for the Executive Board of the Treuhand.[30] In addition to its consultative function, this advisory board also repre-

30 This Winding-up Advisory Board has the following members: Professor Dr Wilhelm Uhlenbruck (chairman), Dr Wilhelm Schaaf, Joachim G. Brandenburg, Dr Volker Grub, and Dr Jobst Wellensiek.

sents the interests of the liquidators to the Executive Board of the Treuhand. This, for instance, also covers questions relating to the liquidator's contracts and remuneration, as well as problems connected with the reporting procedure and the liquidator's freedom of decision.

The services of other divisions within the THA (e. g. Investor Services and Environmental Protection/Historic Environmental Pollution) are also made available during the winding-up process. This contributes to a more efficient execution. Within this article illustrative examples of the service of two Treuhand holding companies deserve to be mentioned, *Liegenschaftsgesellschaft der Treuhandanstalt mbH* (*TLG*, the real estate company of the Treuhandanstalt) and *Maschinenhandel TechnoCommerz GmbH*, an "exchange and mart" for machinery.

The TLG assists in the winding-up process mainly by selling land which is not needed for business operations and the companies' residential properties. Generally speaking, selling off land and buildings is one of the most time-consuming parts of the liquidator's work but these sales represent an important inflow of cash into the winding-up process. Bottle-necks in the cash flow can in extreme circumstances lead to total insolvency, and thus to the mandatory obligation to declare the company bankrupt. At least they may restrict the creative possibilities of any "transfer restructuring".

The property of the companies being wound up that is not needed for business operations is marketed by the TLG. Neither the time when the TLG is informed that the property is available, nor the time this property is handed over determine, however, the day of sale. It is therefore not possible for the liquidator to plan the receipt of payment for the proceeds of the sale into his cash-flow plans. It was to overcome this delay that the TLG's "property pool" was created. It neutralises the critical time component of selling the property as a component of the winding-up process. If there is an urgent need for liquidity, the liquidator can sell the surplus property to the Property Pool and collect a provisional sale price.[31] The final purchase price is then calculated on the basis of an expert's assessment of the market value. The advantage of this procedure is that the provisional sale price is available to the liquidator at a very early stage, and the task of searching for an investor, which can under certain circumstances absorb a great deal of time, is passed over to the TLG.[32]

The establishment of the "machinery exchange" in August 1992 created an additional organisation to work particularly for the winding-up sector of the THA. Its task is to sell off machinery and equipment not needed for day-to-day operations from the THA companies which are in liquidation. This once again releases the liquidator from the time-consuming task of looking for investors. The "machinery exchange" has business connections in more than 40 countries. This is a considerable advantage, since the vast majority of interested parties looking for second-hand machinery comes from abroad, particularly from the eastern European countries and from developing countries.[33]

31 The provisional sale price is calculated on the basis of a quick and rough assessment by an expert, reduced by a safety margin to cover any selling risk and by a small commission to the TLG in respect of its services.

32 See: *TLG konkret,* Issue 4, June 1993.

33 B-interview with Dr Thomas Kettern, Managing Director of *Maschinenhandel TechnoCommerz GmbH,* the "machinery exchange", on 29th July 1993.

3. Problem areas in the winding-up process

When the winding-up process is being carried out, a considerable number of complex problems and risks can arise. Their extent cannot be foreseen or properly quantified either by the Treuhand or by the liquidator at the start of the process. To make this clearer in this article, a few of these problem areas are sketched in by way of example and to show their possible effect.

Actions deleterious to the assets of the company caused by previous managing directors or consultants but not visible until the liquidator works his way through the company's files during the liquidation process, for instance, can have a negative effect on the liquidation result which was calculated in the liquidation assessment. The ensuing actions which can be initiated against the culprits under civil and even criminal law take a considerable amount of time and expense, and the prospects of success in any such actions depend very heavily on a complete body of evidence being presented and, in most cases, this is difficult to obtain.

Risks of an entirely different kind can be cause by historic environmental pollution[34] on the premises. If there are definite grounds to suspect that such pollution on the site of a company in liquidation exists (e. g. in the case of chemical companies), the Winding-up Directorate calls for an expert's historic pollution assessment.[35] This assessment makes definite statements on the degree of contamination, possible measures to be taken to fend off the danger or minimise the risk, and the costs likely to be incurred. The environmental contamination discovered does not only enable the risks to the environment which had not previously been recognised to be quantified, but leads also to a reduction in the value of the property and thus to a different result from the liquidation process.

Legal problems can crop up for the liquidator in connection with questions of legal liability. The liquidator is in a similar position to the executive board or the sole director of a company in that he bears personal liability if he fails in his duty. In the context of liquidation proceedings, this duty includes the obligation to file a petition in bankruptcy when necessary, to favour all the creditors equally in proceedings for the compounding of debts, and to state the liability for any income tax or social insurance deduction made but not forwarded to the Tax Office or social insurance organisation. Liquidators, however, only bear legal liability if they violate their duty culpably, i. e. through gross negligence or with intent. The liquidator or sequestrator can take out legal liability insurance against claims for damages to assets, but these exclude cases of intent or gross negligence. The insurance policy covers violations occurring during the lifetime of the contract provided they are reported to the insurers no later than five years after the expiry of the contract.

A company can even have tax problems while it is in liquidation, as it is liable for taxation until it has been deleted as a legal entity. In winding-up proceedings, a number of special aspects arise with regard to value-added tax. In out-of-court settlements, for instance, for the compounding of debts any input tax already paid has to be balanced out. The creditor in such cases will correct his VAT statement accordingly. Otherwise he would have to record a bad debt. Consequently, the debtor must also balance out his input tax. This means that the proportion of outstanding debt finally paid out is, in effect, increased by the amount of the VAT at the level in force at that time.

---

34 Historic environmental pollution is any contamination of the soil by pollutants from earlier industrial or commercial use which can represent a danger to public health and safety.

35 In organisational terms, the preparation of the expert's assessment is handled by the Environmental Protection/Historic Environmental Pollution Directorate of the Treuhand.

Tax audits carried out on companies in liquidation often lead to unpleasant surprises and supplementary demands from the Tax Offices. In 1991 and 1992 it was often impossible to submit complete monthly advance notices of VAT returns to the tax offices, even though an additional period of grace of one month could be granted. In addition to book-keeping being in arrears, other difficulties arose. Because of postal delays bank statements took a long time to arrive and the processing of credit transfers by the banks was slow.

4. Particular features of the winding up of foreign trade companies

Because of the special features applying to the company purpose of the "foreign-trade companies of the GDR", a separate winding-up procedure has to be applied to them. There were 45 such companies in the GDR,[36] and each of them had a specific task which could be seen from its name: *VEB Schiffscommerz* as the shipping line, *VEB Außenhandel Chemie* for foreign trade in chemicals, as well as further companies for leisure and sport, transportation machinery, import/export of fish, export of books or medical equipment, etc. When the First State Treaty was signed on 18th May 1990 the foreign trade monopoly of these companies was abolished.[37] This removed their reason for existence and the necessity arose to develop a procedure to wind them up.

The task of winding up the foreign-trade companies was transferred from the Federal Ministry of Finance to the Treuhand,[38] which then developed a "concept for winding up former state-owned foreign-trade companies". The organisational framework was thus created which took into account both the statutory regulations and the economical and political aspects affecting the winding-up process.

The legal basis for the winding up of foreign-trade companies can be found in the Treuhand Act (§ 11 section 3) and in the Clearing Ordinance of 4th July 1990. The striking feature of these regulations is the statutorily standardised obligation of the THA to wind up companies with regard to the debtor and creditor accounts of these former foreign-trade companies. The aim of this legislation was to take account at an early stage of the particular circumstances surrounding these assets.

The foreign-trade companies had not been free in their decisions relating to the setting of prices, neither towards their domestic contractual partners nor towards those in other countries, but had been subject to the imposition of specific prices by the GDR Ministry of Foreign Trade, the relevant industrial ministries, and agreements resulting from the GDR's membership, and that

---

36 Foreign-trade companies (*Außenhandelsbetriebe*) are those within the currency area of the GDR-Mark that prior to 1st July 1990 operated on behalf of state authorities, and within the context of the monopoly on foreign trade and currency, in consort with companies or countries outside the currency area of the GDR-Mark. With regard to the assets being wound up, this also includes companies that have taken over part or all of these foreign trade operations for the purpose of the winding-up process.

37 State Treaty of 18th May 1990, Joint Protocol on Basic Principles, B II section 6.

38 It was laid down in the Treaty of Unification that the sums outstanding from debtors and to creditors of the foreign-trade companies would be settled on the instructions and under the supervision of the Federal Ministry of Finance (see Article 24 of the Treaty).

of its various organisations, of the "Council for Mutual Economic Assistance" (COMECON).[39] As these debtor and creditor accounts could be the object of separate agreements made by the Federal Republic of Germany, a separate procedure needed to be developed.

One source of considerable problems soon emerged: the statutory regulations did not provide for any transitional rules related to phasing-out business between the manufacturing companies and the foreign-trade companies to wind down. The managers of the manufacturing companies in eastern Germany were not prepared for the disappearance of the foreign-trade companies and the services they provided. The selling and trade experience accumulated in the foreign-trade companies (customer contacts, sales channels, execution of import and export orders, etc.) were not yet available in eastern German production companies.

The Treuhand was aware, in laying down the winding-up process, that the chances of survival of eastern German industry would be heavily dependent on the continued existence of functioning trade structures. As part of the winding up there are therefore two alternative ways of closing a foreign-trade company down:[40] at the instigation of the Winding-up Directorate, or on the basis of a management contract with a private company which takes over the business of the former foreign-trade company as a going concern. However, the liquidation process forms the basic form of winding up in both versions.

The scale and the amount of time and effort involved in winding up foreign-trade companies can be seen by looking at the debtor and creditor accounts that need to be wound up. On 1st July 1990 the foreign-trade companies had total debtor accounts of about DM 24.3 billion, and creditor accounts to DM 17.9 billion. The total amount receivable in convertible currencies from customers in the area outside the socialist economy was DM 5.6 billion; accounts payable amounted to about DM 4.3 billion.[41]

It is the job of the liquidators to collect the debts, but many of them were owed by other Treuhand companies and companies that had already been privatised. In order to avoid a long series of costly court cases against such companies, the debts were mainly settled with the aid of arbitration panels.

The collection of debts from certain debtors in so-called "problem countries" has been brought together at one point for organisational purposes to cover all the foreign-trade companies. Private debt-brokers were brought in who either bought the debts themselves or collected them in return for commission.[42] The implementation of the procedure always involved hand-in-hand co-operation between the THA, the Federal Ministry of Finance, the Federal Ministry for Economic Affairs, the (government-owned) Hermes Credit-Insurance Company, the State Bank, and the German Foreign Trade Bank DABA.

---

39 See: Kinze, Knop, and Seifert (editors): *Sozialistische Volkswirtschaft,* page 473.

40 See: Treuhandanstalt, *Konzeption der Abwicklung ehemaliger volkseigener Außenhandelsbetriebe* dated 3rd May 1991, page 2.

41 Collecting these debts proved increasingly difficult as the customers contested them or insisted the sums were not yet due for payment.

42 According to information from the Winding-up Directorate, up to June 1993 debts worth some US $ 140 million had been placed in the hands of debt brokers. This applies mainly to debts from customers in such countries as Egypt, Ghana, Yemen, Libya, and Tanzania. Of this total, some $ 20 million had been collected by June 1993.

5. Particular features of the winding up of formerly state-owned farms

A winding-up procedure, which differs from the "normal" procedure of the Treuhand, is applied to the selling off of some 300 state farms (*Volkseigene Güter*). The reasons for this difference lie partly in the method laid down by the Federal government for the selling off of formerly state-owned agricultural land, and partly in the legal status of these farms.

Awareness of the injustice behind the confiscation measures implemented between 1945 and 1949 in the Soviet Zone of Occupation[43] prompted the Federal government to determine the method of selling off state-owned agricultural land in line with a political strategy.[44] It provides for preferential treatment for the "victims of land-ownership reform" with the intention of giving them "reasonable prospects". The preferential treatment granted to these victims, or their legatees, includes:

- a certain priority in the newly initiated process of leasing out former state-owned land,
- possible compensation under the future Compensation Act not in the form of money but of agricultural land being assigned,
- the possibility of acquiring the agricultural land on preferential terms.[45]

In connection with the legal nature of the state farms, the Treuhand took the view that these had been converted into corporations (limited liability companies which have to be dissolved) on the strength of the law that took effect on 3rd October 1991.[46] However, adjudications have meanwhile been made reinforcing the view that state farms are mere assets of the THA with no independent legal status.[47] As no final ruling has yet been handed down, but it was necessary to reach a decision, the Treuhand decided that the only form of winding-up procedure applicable to former state farms would be liquidation.[48] This article will not go into any further detail on the opposing legal opinions.

The particular feature of the winding-up procedure is that all the farms are brought together into regional groups. One auditor is appointed to draw up the winding-up assessment for each group as well as one liquidator. The Treuhand hopes to see synergistic benefits (e. g. a more rapid flow of information through simpler channels, the use of interconnections in the physical

---

43 These confiscation measures were described by the Soviet Union as "Land-ownership Reform". During the negotiations leading up to the Treaty of Unification, both the GDR and the Soviet Union insisted that disappropriation based on the law or at least the sovereignty of military occupation would have to remain unchanged.

44 This strategy was prepared by the Minister for the Chancellor's Office, Friedrich Bohl, and is therefore known as the "Bohl document". It was agreed between the Federal government and the ministries of agriculture in the various eastern German States, with Brandenburg imposing certain reservations. The coalition partners in the German *Bundestag* gave their assent. On 2nd December 1992 the Federal Ministry of Finance requested the Treuhand to implement the strategy. Forestry land was exempted from this implementation because of its particular characteristics.

45 See: Written reply by the Federal Chancellor's Office to questions regarding the fate of the "victims of land-ownership reform".

46 See: Submission to the Executive Board of the Treuhandanstalt of 26th June 1991 and letter from the Federal Ministry of Finance of 29th May 1991.

47 Ruling of the Chamber Court *(Kammergericht)* of Berlin of 22nd January 1993, Dossier No. 7 U 3266/92-(79/93).

48 See: Concluding minutes of the Executive Board meeting of 3rd August 1993.

or geographical sense, etc.) from the "simplified and concentrated winding-up procedure" flowing from the sensible winding up of "farm groups".[49]

The winding up of former state farms has been made far more difficult, in many cases, by lack of clarity as to the identity of the true legal owners and even more so by the long-term tenancy agreements, some of them lasting up to 18 years. The winding-up process can thus prove to be a long drawn-out one.

V. Results achieved to date in winding up Treuhandanstalt companies

1. Interim balance of results to date

Figs. 2 to 5 show the increasing proportion of winding-up work in proportion to the total work of the Treuhand. Of a total of 13,136 companies, the THA still had 4,393 companies on its books as of 31st July 1993 with 311,092 employees. Of these, 2,880 companies (employing 44,237 people in total) were undergoing a winding-up procedure (Table 1).

Fig. 2 shows, for the two-year period from June 1991 to June 1993, the growing number of companies undergoing winding up.[50] As of 30th June 1993, 2,619 companies were undergoing

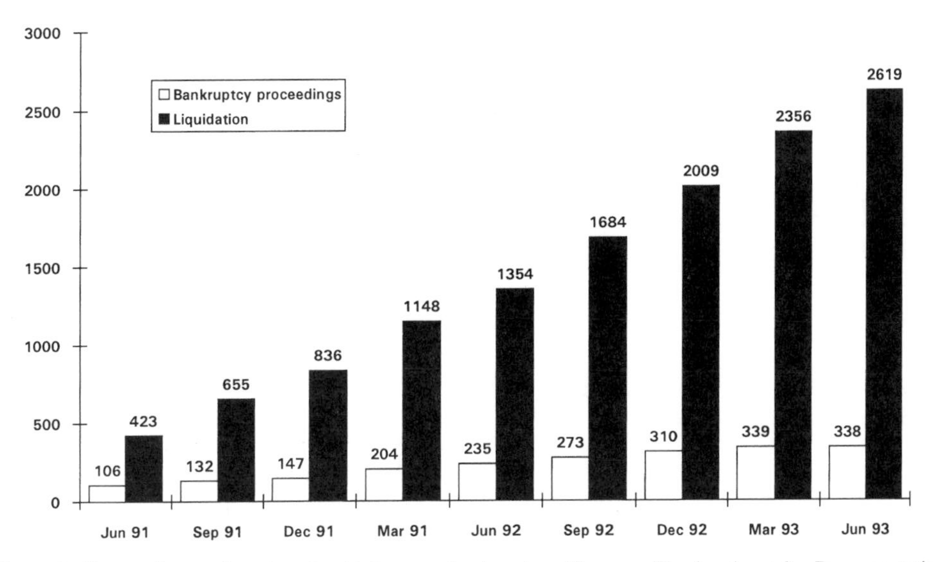

Figure 2 Companies undergoing liquidation or bankruptcy (Source: Treuhandanstalt, Documentation Department)

49 See: Submission to the Executive Board of the Treuhandanstalt of 29th July 1993 on state farms.

50 Of the 2,619 liquidation cases (as of June 1993), about 750 consisted of so-called "shell" or "vestigial" companies, in which the operational business has been closed down. Any debtor accounts still to be collected and creditor accounts to be settled are for small amounts, and these companies have no tangible assets, no employees, and are not involved passively or actively in any legal disputes.

liquidation, and bankruptcy proceedings had been opened against a further 338. Up to this point in time, a total of only 57 liquidation and bankruptcy proceedings had been brought to a conclusion with the deletion of the "dead" company from the Register of Companies.

Table 1:
Number of Treuhand companies and the number of employees, in total and those in liquidation, as of 31st July 1993

	THA-Companies		of which in liquidation	
Industry	No. of firms	No. employed	No. of firms	No. employed
Agriculture and forestry	440	7,215	95	865
Power & water supply	35	25,949	15	656
Mining	20	44,683	4	163
Chemical industry	97	31,793	66	1,964
Plastic, rubber, and asbestos processing	64	2,598	58	1,325
Quarrying, stone and earth processing, fine ceramics and glass	126	7,038	78	544
Ferrous & non-ferrous metal production, foundries & steel processing	110	21,287	62	4,991
Steel & light engineering	69	14,453	33	326
Mechanical engineering	443	47,530	268	4,849
Vehicle construction	114	15,268	77	4,608
Electrical and electronic industry	223	14,238	183	4,461
Precision and optical engineering	34	1,339	28	893
Iron, metal, sheet metal goods, musical instruments, sports & leisure equipment, games, jewellery	146	2,092	117	819
Wood industry	201	3,862	162	1,584
Paper and printing industry	84	3,933	67	903

Table 1:

	THA-Companies		of which in liquidation	
Industry	No. of firms	No. employed	No. of firms	No. employed
Leather and shoe industry	111	2,322	91	900
Textiles and clothing industry	318	13,540	237	4,037
Staple and luxury food & drinks industry	282	3,698	241	1,893
Construction (building) industry	154	9,553	108	786
Auxiliary building (extensions and conversions) industry	24	384	17	219
Wholesale and retail trade	499	6,431	359	3,106
Transport, information, transmission, haulage and storage	133	2,497	88	728
Finance and banking industry	1	446	0	0
Insurance industry	2	5	1	0
Services	621	27,091	407	3,526
Not categorised	42	1,847	18	91
Total	4,393	311,092	2,880	44,237

Source: THA-Documentation.

The fall-off in the percentage share of bankruptcy cases in the absolute winding-up processes, from 25% in June 1991 to 13% in June 1993, indicates the growing importance of liquidation as the form of winding up for THA companies.

The heavy responsibility borne by the Winding-up departments within the Treuhand for working people in eastern Germany can be seen from Figs. 3 and 4. These show the growing number of jobs affected by liquidation over the period from February 1992 to May 1993. The number of jobs at the beginning of the liquidation process is compared here with the number of jobs retained through liquidation.

When comparing the number of jobs affected and the number retained by liquidation, it is worth bearing in mind that the companies had usually undergone a drastic slimming down during the privatisation efforts before they even entered the liquidation phase. This was caused

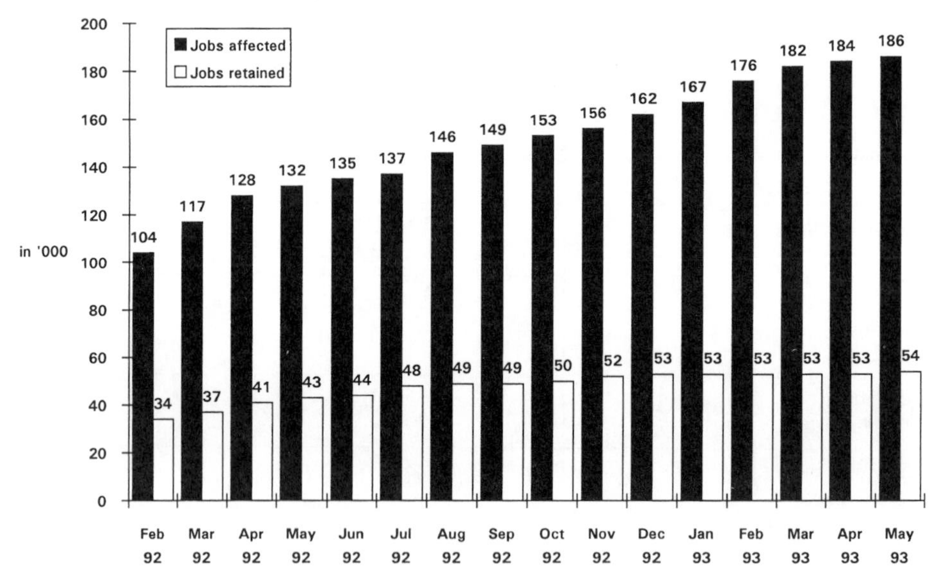

Figure 3 Number of jobs affected by liquidation and number retained as recorded by the Treuhand's Central Office (Source: Winding-up Directorate)

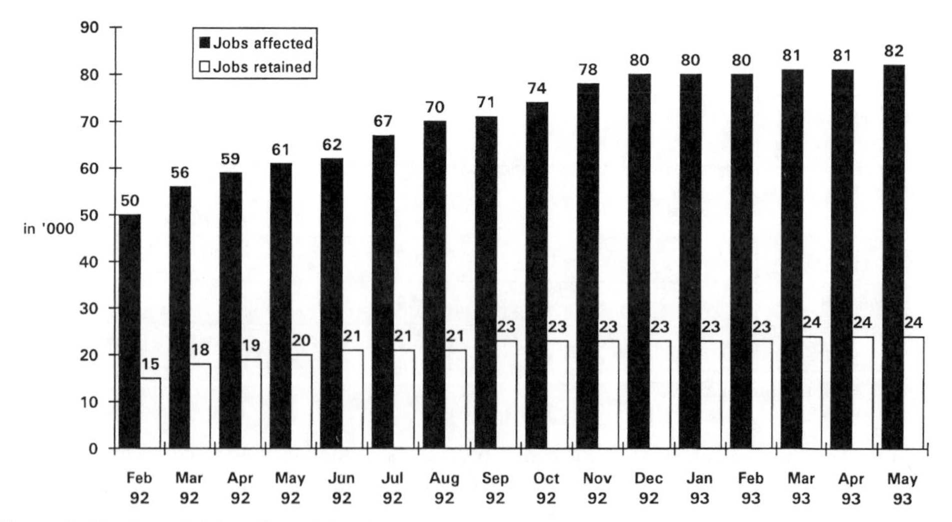

Figure 4 Number of jobs affected by liquidation and number retained as recorded by the Treuhand's branches and branch offices (Source: Winding-up Directorate)

both by the reduction in numbers employed and by the successful privatisations of parts of the companies.

As of May 1993 about 29% of the jobs were preserved through privatisation deals arising out of liquidation. This figure for the firms undergoing bankruptcy was about 16%. As of 31st December 1992, the success-rate for retaining jobs had still been about 31% for liquidations and

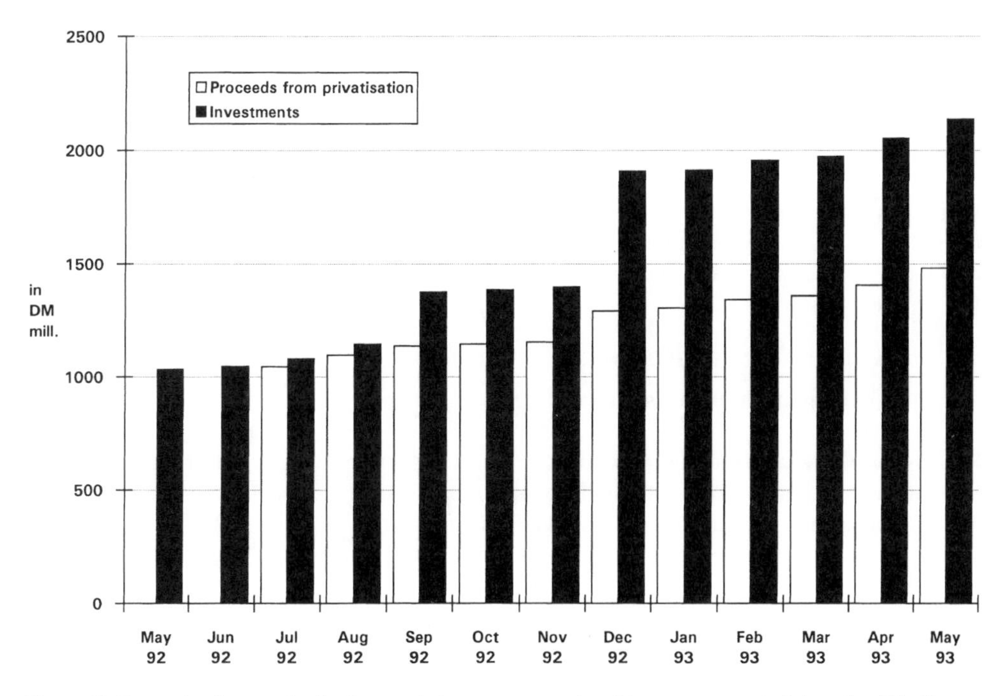

Figure 5 Proceeds from privatisation and investment undertakings as recorded by the Winding-up Directorate (Source: Treuhand, Winding-up Directorate. No figures were available for the proceeds of privatisation in May and June 1992, and no information was available from the branches and branch offices on the proceeds of privatisation or on investments.)

17% for bankruptcies. This downward trend is expected to continue because the companies entering the winding-up phase at this late stage have already been to a great extent part-privatised or sold off by the Industry Directorates.

Fig. 5 shows the growth in privatisation proceeds and contractually agreed investment undertakings that the Winding-up Directorate managed to achieve over the period from May 1992 to May 1993.

One result of the privatisation work of the Winding-up Directorate of the Treuhand, as of 31st August 1993, was the retention of 64,283 jobs. In the branches and branch offices, the figure at the same point in time was 25,900.[51] The proceeds from privatisation achieved in the liquidation proceedings supervised in the Central Office by the Winding-up Directorate amounted in August 1993 to about DM 1.68 billion, and the total investment undertakings made by purchasers was about DM 2.57 billion.[52] This level of success is counter-balanced by an enormous financial volume which has to be borne by the THA as part of the winding-up process. The 692 liquidations (figures for August 1993) carried out in the Treuhand's Central Office by the Winding-up Directorate are estimated to involve costs of about DM 8.3 billion.[53]

51 Winding-up Directorate of the Treuhand.

52 Ludwig M. Tränkner, Winding-up Director, press conference on 12th October 1993.

53 Treuhandanstalt, Winding-up Financial Control Department.

The Deutschmark opening balance sheet of the Treuhand as of 1st July 1990 contains reserves of DM 44.7 billion for the winding up of companies. Some DM 18.8 million of this is accounted for by winding-up costs for firms that cannot be restructured, and the remaining DM 25.9 million by costs for closing down and disposing of a nuclear power plant, *Kernkraftwerk Nord*, equity capital holdings of companies not capable of being liquidated, and interest charges on historic debt.[54] Based on information available today, DM 25 billion will have to be allowed for the winding-up costs for the companies that cannot be restructured.[55] The increase of DM 6.2 billion is caused by the number of liquidation proceedings, and thus the costs associated with them, having worked out higher than was expected at the time when the balance sheet as of 1st July 1990 was drawn up.

2. Examplary liquidation proceedings

Reports appear regularly in the press on spectacular examples of privatisation resulting from winding-up proceedings. The motor tyre manufacturer Pneumant Reifenwerke, the environment-friendly refrigerator manufacturer, dkk Scharfenstein, or the Zschopau motor-cycle works are some of the best-known. The sale of parts of companies undergoing liquidation to foreign investors, such as part of Renak-Werke to a Chinese bicycle manufacturer, or of Zellstoffwerke Pirna to a Russian investor, also deserve to be mentioned. The following examples will serve as illustrations, while making no claim to be representative.

a) Mitteldeutsche Beton- und Kieswerke GmbH i. L.

After this cement and gravel works had been written off as incapable of privatisation or restructuring, the liquidator succeeded in the spring of 1992 in preserving 968 jobs, and creating 724 new ones, by selling the company off in 15 pieces. The various purchasers gave assurances of investment totalling DM 80 million, and opened the prospect of investments of a further DM 10 million.

b) Sächsische Elektronikwerke GmbH i. L.

This electronics company was based near Klingenberg, in Saxony, and the liquidator succeeded within 12 months in creating some 1,000 new jobs in a series of 20 partial privatisation deals. At the beginning of the winding-up process the company was down to employing only 630 people. The investors have signed undertakings to carry out investment projects totalling DM 35 million, with newly founded companies ranging in size from the five employees in the privatised canteen to 200 employees taken on by a western German company to produce cable saddles for the motor industry. The successor companies include manufacturers of tools and jigs, craft enterprises, construction companies, and even a training centre.

---

54 Treuhandanstalt, *DM-Eröffnungsbilanz zum 1. 7. 1990*, pages 15 and 30. The reserves were calculated on the basis of estimates of winding-up costs made for each company individually by appointed experts representing 25% of the liquidation and bankruptcy cases. The values obtained were then extrapolated to cover the entirety of the companies on the Treuhandanstalt's books.

55 Ludwig M. Tränkner, Winding-up Director, press conference on 12th October 1993.

c) Baustoffe Porschendorf GmbH i. L.

This company used to produce asbestos panels for roofs and façades. Such materials are now no longer permitted for use in buildings. However, it proved possible during the winding-up phase to change production over to asbestos-free fibre-cement panels, and the historic environmental pollution caused by the old asbestos panel production was also removed. A haulage company and an engineering company founded by the management buy-out[56] of a company called Ratiomittelbau took over part of the factory site. The main works continued to produce small-format cement panels for sale via the newly founded sales company during the liquidation phase. Short-time working had to be imposed on only a small proportion of the staff.

It had not proved possible to bring the efforts at privatising this company to a successful conclusion during the 20-month liquidation phase, despite its economically favourable position as a supplier to the construction industry, because of the high level of investment needed subsequently. One disadvantage is that the market for products of this kind is dominated by a small number of major competitors. The only solution, once privatisation plans have collapsed, is finally to close down production and to put the location to a number of quite different uses.

d) Gummiwerke Rotpunkt GmbH i. L.

When liquidation proceedings started in the autumn of 1991, this location housed the largest plant for manufacturing sterile operating-theatre gloves in Europe, even if it was not quite complete at that state. At a cost of DM 15 million, which the THA made available to the liquidator as a loan, the construction of the plant was finished and privatisation is expected to be completed by the end of 1993.

As a result of splitting off land and buildings not necessary for business operations and selling them off individually to various different investors, including an American manufacturer of insulating materials, and by communalising the district heating plant, there will be more people employed on this site at the end of the liquidation process than there used to be before.

e) Märkische Milchwirtschaft GmbH i. L.

This dairy products company is based in Potsdam and is made up of seven former state-owned companies which used to operate as milk bottlers, creameries, and the like. On 1st June 1990 it employed 876 people. By the time liquidation started on 11th August 1992, a number of sections of the operation had been leased or sold off separately by the Industry Directorate. By that time the company only had six employees, and all remaining production locations had already been closed down.

The liquidator's prime task was to sell off the remaining inactive plants in Jüterbog, Oranienburg, Potsdam, and Rathenow in the most sensible manner possible. Within one year, in collaboration with the Treuhand, he managed to settle new commercial activities on all the former plant locations, preserving or creating a total of 375 jobs in the process. The total proceeds from privatisation amounted to DM 22.15 million, with investments agreed by contract totalling DM 62.5 million.

---

56 In a management buy-out (MBO) the managers, usually the previous directors or executives, of a company or of a unit splitted off buy it up and continue its operation as owner-managers.

f) Margarethenhütte Großdubrau GmbH i. L.

This company had once been a major producer of electrical porcelain. Because of lack of incoming orders and problems in achieving profitability the parent company, Tridelta AG, had decided to close it down. The decision could not be reversed despite political action which went as far as a parliamentary question in the Bundestag and sit-ins in the works. When liquidation proceedings began at the end of 1991, only 56 employees (out of an original total of 1,000) were still there. They maintained the heating system, kept the books, and provided security. In collaboration with a non profit-making "association for the promotion of Margarethenhütte" the liquidator was at last, after 18 months, successful in privatising parts of the company to investors in the same line of business.

The 40-hectare (100-acre) factory site was divided into separate plots and supplied with energy by an operating company. It is expected that 200 to 300 new jobs will be created, although not until 1994/95. The delay is not just due to the economy as a whole; one major reason was the worse than expected historic environmental pollution on the site. Some of this was removed as part of government job creation measures. The liquidation process suffered a setback when the County authorities ordered the closure of the company's waste disposal site, which had represented a major source of income to finance the liquidation itself.

This last example shows that it has only been possible to create a small number of new jobs during many liquidation processes. The reasons for this are, on the one hand, the geographical positions of these companies, and the lack of local infrastructure. On the other hand, however, there are also problem industries such as steel, shoes, and textiles/clothing, which are undergoing structural change in western Germany as well.

VI. Summary

Winding up in the sense in which the Treuhand uses the term is not limited to selling off all the assets of a moribund company and deleting the remnants from the Register of Companies. The THA practices a broad and flexible interpretation of the work of winding up as part of the winding-up process which it created; it is constantly being developed further and adapted to new tasks. It is therefore fair to speak of a dynamic winding-up process.

The winding-up policy of the Treuhand as the sole shareholder of the companies in liquidation places top priority on preserving and creating as many jobs as possible. It has been shown that the liquidation of old structures no longer capable of functioning profitably by means of liquidation creates good conditions for a successful new start. The Treuhand has based its winding-up policy for companies incapable of being restructured on the line laid down by Detlev Rohwedder, who always argued in favour of "turning close-down into the crystallisation core for new activities."[57]

57 Detlev Karsten Rohwedder in a letter to the staff of the Treuhandanstalt dated 27th March 1991.

VII. Literature

Geßler, Jörg: *Aktiengesetz. Kommentar.* Neuwied et al, June 1993.
Heinen, Edmund: *Einführung in die Betriebswirtschaftslehre.* Wiesbaden [9]1985.
ditto: *Handelsbilanzen.* Wiesbaden [12]1986.
Hess, Harald: *Rechtsfragen der Liquidation von Treuhandunternehmen. Abwicklung, Geschäftsführung, Unternehmenskauf, Haftung des Liquidators.* RWS-Skript 256. Cologne 1993.
Hess, Harald, and Fritz *Binz*: *Gesamtvollstreckungsordnung. Kommentar zum Konkursrecht für die Länder Brandenburg, Mecklenburg-Vorpommern, Sachsen, Sachsen-Anhalt und Thüringen.* Neuwied and Berlin 1991.
Kemmler, Marc: *Die Entstehung der Treuhandanstalt. Von der Wahrung der Privatisierung des DDR-Volkseigentums.* Diss. Tübingen 1993 (printed edition Frankfurt am Main and New York 1994).
Kinze, H.-H., H. *Knop* and E. *Seifert* (editors): *Sozialistische Volkswirtschaft. Hochschullehrbuch der DDR.* Berlin 1983.
Köhler, Claus: Die wirtschaftlichen Perspektiven in den neuen Bundesländern. In: Deutsche Bundesbank: *Auszüge aus Presseartikeln* Nr. 26 (1st April 1992), pages 6 to 13.
Kübler, Bruno M.: *Die Gesamtvollstreckung als Instrument zur Sanierung insolventer Unternehmen.* In: Peter *Hommelhoff* (editor): *Treuhandunternehmen im Umbruch. Recht und Rechtswirklichkeit beim Übergang in die Marktwirtschaft.* Cologne 1991, pages 79 to 99.
Lutter, Marcus, and Peter *Hommelhoff*: *GmbH-Gesetz Kommentar.* Cologne [13]1991.
TLG Konkret. Issue 4, June 1993.
Die Top-Sanierer Deutschlands. In: *Top Business Magazin* no. 4, April 1993, pages 18 to 26.
Tränkner, Ludwig M.: *Abwicklung bedeutet Entwicklung.* Berlin 1992.
Treuhandanstalt: *DM-Eröffnungsbilanz zum 1. Juli 1990.* Berlin, October 1992.
Wöhe, Günther: *Einführung in die Allgemeine Betriebswirtschaftslehre.* Munich [17]1990.

Appendix: Example of Expert's Liquidation Assessment

Costs comparison and winding-up recommendation Effective day: 31st December 1993

Company:	XY GmbH
Location:	Berlin
THA No.:	4711
Sub-unit:	0
No. employed:	100
Findings:	
Bankruptcy:	DM: –4,555,900
Liquidation:	DM: –3,321,500

Recommendation:
As liquidation is the less expensive alternative for the Treuhand, the Adlerauge Wirtschaftsprüfungsgesellschaft mbH (auditing company) recommends the liquidation of the company.

Auditor: Adlerauge Wirtschaftsprüfungsgesellschaft mbH Signature:

Assets status after liquidation/bankruptcy
as of 31st December 1992

Assets in DM '000	Book value 1	Liquidation proceeds from sale 2	Liquidation special rights 1) 3	Bankruptcy proceeds from sale 4	Bankruptcy special rights 1) 5	Bankruptcy residue (4–5)	Liquidation residue (2–3)
Fixed assets							
Land	5,000	6,500	2,500	6,500	2,500	4,000	4,000
Buildings	1,000	1,200	300	1,200	300	900	900
Machinery and equipment	500	2000	2000	200	200		
Equity holdings	0	0	0	0	0	0	0
Other fixed assets	0	0	0	0	0	0	0
Total fixed assets	**6,500**	**7,900**	**2,800**	**7,900**	**2,800**	**5,100**	**5,100**
Current assets							
Trade debtors	1,000	800	0	800	0	800	800
other outstanding debts	3,000	3,000	0	3,000	0	3,000	3,000
Total receivable	4,000	3,800	0	3,800	0	3,800	3,800
Other working capital (raw and auxiliary materials)	–	–	–	–	–	–	–
Finished products, goods in process, misc.	500	50	0	500	50	50	
Total current assets	**4,500**	**3,850**	**0**	**3,850**	**0**	**3,850**	**3,850**
Cash in hand	3	3	0	3	0	3	3
Bank balances	20	20	0	2	00	20	20
Total liquid assets	**23**	**23**	**0**	**23**	**0**	**23**	**23**
Total assets	**11,023**	**11,773**	**2,800**	**11,773**	**2,800**	**8,973** (A)	**8,973** (B)

1) Separation rights, and restitution rights if applicable

Assets status after liquidation/bankruptcy
as of 31st December 1992

Liabilities in DM '000	Book value 1	Special rights 2	Bankruptcy preferred debtors 3	Bankruptcy other debtors (1–2-3)	Liquidation settlement percentage 5	Liquidation corrected value ((1–2) × 5)
Liabilities to banks						
Historic loans	4,000	0	0	4,000	43.53	1,741.20
Unpaid interest on historic loans 3)	300	0	0	300	43.53	130.60
Liquidity loans from bank	5,000	0	0	5,000	43.53	2,176.50
Unpaid interests on liquidity loan until pay-off 4)	208	0	0	208	43.53	90.50
Other liabilities to own charge	0	0	0	0	0.00	0.00
Total liabilities to banks	**9,508**	**0**	**0**	**9,508**		**4,138.80**
Trade creditors	**1,000**	**0**	**0**	**1,000**	**43.53**	**435.30**
Other liabilities	–	–	–	–	–	–
Taxes	50	0	50	0	100.00	50.00
Social Insurance	20	0	20	0	100.00	20.00
Wages and salaries	300	0	300	0	100.00	300.00
Others	0	0	0	0	0.00	0.00
Total other liabilities	**370**	**0**	**370**	**0**		**370.00**
Total liabilities towards trade and other creditors	**1,370**	**0**	**370**	**1,000**		**805.30**
Reserves for compensation plan, new 5)	630	0	630	0	43.53	274.20
Other reserves	500	0	0	500	100.00	500.00
Ear-marked amounts, old (repayment claims)	2,500	0	0	2,500	43.53	1,088.30
Loans from THA (as shareholder)	0	0	0	0	0.00	0.00
Total liabilities	14,508	0	1,000	13,508		6,806.60
				(C)	(D)	(E)

2) from separation rights
3) if provisionally paid by THA since 1st July 1991
4) pay-off in second month of liquidation proceedings
5) amount corresponds to ear-marked funds, new

Cash flow calculation for liquidation procedure
excluding proceeds from sale and settlement of outstanding debts payable

Inflow of funds (excluding proceeds from sale)	
Turnover from production and services	0
Inflow from rents and leases	450
Other inflows	50
Total proceeds from business activity (I)	**500**
Outflow of funds (excluding settlement of outstanding debts payable)	
Liquidator's remuneration and expenses	
Consultancy/experts' assessments/auditing costs	400
Personnel/wages/non-wage labour costs	500
Operating expenses	50
Production expenses	0
Other expenses 6)	0
Total outflow of funds (excluding settlement of outstanding debts payable) (K)	**1,110**
Balance from liquidation proceedings (L=I-K)	**-610**

6) including financing expenses incurred during the liquidation process (excluding interest on liquidity loan)

Forecast distribution from bankruptcy proceedings

Residue (A)		**8,973.00**
Claims to be settled in advance (§ 13 Comp. Bankruptcy Order)		
Necessary administrative expenses	1,500.00	
Administrator's remuneration & expenses plus court costs	500.00	
Wages & salaries payable after deduction of paid bankruptcy wage guarantees	150.00	
Claims from social insurances and Federal Employment Office	0.00	
Total advanced claims (F)		**2,150.00**
Proceeds for distribution (G=A-F)		**6,823.00**
Preferred payments (§ 17 III Comp. Bankruptcy Order)		
Wages and salaries	300.00	
Claims from social insurances and Federal Employment Office	20.00	
Payable from compensation plan agreed with sequestrator	630.00	
Taxes and charges	50.00	
Total preferred payments (C)		**1,000.00**
Residual amount (H=G-C)		**5,823.00**
Not preferred payments (D)		**13,508.00**
Percentage pay-out for not preferred payments (H/D in %)		**43.11**

Outcome for the THA

Liquidation procedure	
Residue, Total assets (B)	**8,973.00**
Corrected value of liabilities (E)	**6,806.60**
Asset balance (M=B-E)	**2,166.40**
Balance from liquidation proceedings (L)	**-610.00**
Treuhand's bad debts 7)	
Unpaid interest on historic loans	69.40
liquidity loans from bank	2,823.50
Unpaid interest on liquidity loans	117.50
THA loan (interest-free)	0.00
Ear-marked funds, old	1,411.80
Ear-marked funds, new	355.80
Total bad debts (N)	**4,878.00**
Outcome on liquidation (O=M+L-N)	**-3,321.60**

Bankruptcy procedure	
Ear-marked funds, old (minus pay-out) (P)	**1,422.30**
Ear-marked funds, new (minus pay-out/return flow) (R)	**0.00**
Liquidity loan (minus pay-out) (S)	**2,844.60**
Interest on liquidity loan (minus pay-out) (T)	**118.30**
Historic loan interest (minus pay-out) (U)	**170.70**
(if already paid by THA)	
Miscellaneous	
THA guarantees (claimed minus pay-out)	0.00
THA loan (minus pay-out)	0.00
Bankruptcy grant	0.00
Other (bad debts to THA)	0.00
Total miscellaneous (V)	0.00
Outcome from bankruptcy proceedings (W=-P-R-S-T-U-V)	**-4,555.90**

7) 100% minus pay-out/return flow

The liquidity plan is normally drawn up for 24 months (month 1 to month 24). This example shows only month 1, 2, and 3, plus the total for all 24 months (in DM '000).

CN	Liquidity plan	Month 1	Month 2	Month 3	Total
A302	Turnover from production and services	0.00	0.00	0.00	0.00
A600	Income from rents and leases	81.00	81.00	81.00	450.00
A303	Other income	2.80	2.80	2.80	50.00
A601	Total revenue from business activity	83.80	83.80	83.80	500.00
A237	Land	0.00	0.00	0.00	4,000.00
A603	Buildings	0.00	0.00	0.00	900.00
A205	Machinery and equipment	20.00	0.00	0.00	200.00
A602	Equity holdings	0.00	0.00	0.00	0.00
A239	Other assets	0.00	0.00	0.00	0.00
A202	Total proceeds from sale of assets	20.00	0.00	0.00	5,100.00
A245	Proceeds from debtor accounts	0.00	0.00	200.00	800.00
A246	Other working capital (raw materials etc.)	0.00	0.00	0.00	3,050.00
A211	Total proceeds from working capital	0.00	0.00	200.00	3,850.00
A604	Total proceeds from all assets	20.00	0.00	200.00	8,950.00
A307	Total inflow of funds	103.80	83.80	283.80	9,450.00
A605	Liquidator's remuneration and expenses	0.00	0.00	64.00	160.00
A606	Consultancy and auditing fees	50.00	20.00	0.00	400.00
A607	Total liquidation costs	50.00	20.00	64.00	560.00
A309	Wages and non-wage labour costs	50.00	50.00	40.00	500.00
A608	Operating expenses (taxes, insurance. leasing)	5.00	5.00	5.00	50.00
A609	Production expenses	0.00	0.00	0.00	0.00
A308	Trade creditors	200.00	150.00	85.30	435.30
A231	Other liabilities	300.00	170.00	150.00	870.00
A234	Total settlement of creditor accounts	500.00	320.00	235.30	1,305.30
A310	Other expenses	0.00	0.00	0.00	0.00
A610	Interest paid on historic loans	0.00	0.00	0.00	0.00
A611	Interest paid on liquidation	0.00	0.00	0.00	0.00
A331	Total financing costs	0.00	0.00	0.00	0.00
A314	Total outflow of funds	605.00	395.00	344.30	2,415.30
A612	Liquidity balance 1	–501.20	–311.20	–60.50	7,034.70
A414	Cash in hand (opening balance)	3.00	0.00	0.00	3.00
A616	Cash at bank (opening balance)	20.00	100.00	100.00	20.00
A301	Total liquid assets	23.00	100.00	100.00	23.00
A625	Inflows/outflows	578.20	311.20	60.50	0.00
A613	Liquidity balance 2	100.00	100.00	100.00	7,057.70
A320	Ear-marked funds, new	630.00	630.00	630.00	630.00
A617	Liquidator loan	578.20	889.40	949.90	0.00
A618	Total theoretical winding-up items	1,208.20	1,519.40	1,579.90	630.00
A614	Liquidity balance 3	–1,108.20	–1,419.40	–1,479.90	6,427.70
A229	Historic loans (only with pay-out)	1,741.20	0.00	0.00	0.00
A619	Unpaid interest	300.00	0.00	0.00	0.00
A338	Liquidity loan from bank	5,000.00	5,000.00	0.00	0.00
A620	Unpaid interest on liquidity loan	208.00	208.00	0.00	0.00
A236	THA loan (interest-free)	0.00	2,041.20	7,249.20	7,249.20
A621	Ear-marked funds, old	2,500.00	2,500.00	2,500.00	2,500.00
A622	Total theoretical items prior to winding-up	9,749.20	9,749.20	9,749.20	9,749.20
A615	Liquidity balance 4	–10,857.40	–11,168.60	–11,229.10	–3,321.50
A624	Maximum exposure	–10,957.40	–11,268.60	–11,329.10	–10,957.40
A626	New exposure to be committed	2,949.40	1,519.40	1,579.90	2,949.40

Contract drafting and contract management by the Treuhandanstalt

by Hans-Ulrich Küpper, with the assistance of Robert Mayr

I. Aim and purpose of the investigation

For the privatisation of companies the Treuhand (THA) developed an original instrument in contract drafting; its purpose is to enable the THA to attain its statutorily defined aims to the greatest possible extent.

The purpose of this article is to investigate how this instrument developed and to what extent it contributed to the fulfilment of the stated aims. To this end, an analysis has first been made of the overall provisions built into each kind of contract and of the types of draft contracts, and the second part of the article describes the processes, organisation, and handling of contract management. Finally, an attempt is made to arrive at an initial, empirically founded assessment of contract drafting and contract management on the basis of a statistical analysis of the contracts.

II. Shape and dimensions of contract drafting

1. Overall conditions affecting contract drafting

a) THA's system of aims for contract drafting

Article 25 section 1 of the Treaty of Unification defines the ultimate goal of the THA as being to "structure and privatise the formerly state-owned companies so as to make them competitive". Under the motto: "Privatisation is the most effective form of restructuring",[1] the THA handed over the necessary restructuring work to the future owners of its businesses.

It is possible to derive the components of the various aims for the THA's tasks, and thus also for the drafting of contracts, from the preamble of the Treuhandgesetz or Treuhand Act (THG, the East German Act which set up the THA), which states:

"With the intention

- of reducing the entrepreneurial activities of the state through privatisation as quickly and as widely as possible,
- of creating competitive effectiveness for as many companies as possible, thus preserving existing jobs and creating new ones,
- of making land available for commercial purposes,
- that, after an inventory has been taken of the state-owned property and its profitability, and after priority has been given to its application in adapting the structure of the economy and

1 Detlev Rohwedder in his letter of 27th March 1991 to the staff of the THA.

restructuring the state budget, a certificated right to the ownership of shares in state-owned property can be granted to savers at a later point in time at the reduced amount as of the currency conversion on 2nd July 1990, the following Act is hereby passed into law."

The first paragraph of the preamble to the THG thus defines the first component in the THA's system of aims straight away. The reduction in the state's entrepreneurial activity is just the same as the far-reaching and the fast as possible privatisation. The second paragraph specifies the preservation of existing jobs and the creation of new ones as the second detailed aim, and also allows the third one to be derived. In order to "create competitiveness for as many companies as possible" it is necessary to generate investment in eastern Germany. § 2 section 6 of the THG pursues the same aim by covering the THA's influence over the development of companies capable of being restructured into companies which are competitive. Taken in conjunction with the requirement of profitability codified in § 7 of the Federal Budget Ordinance and placed on the THA, the Treaty of Unification can be seen to be prescribing the maximisation of the proceeds of the sale of state-owned properties within the parameters set by the THA's obligation to meet other aims at the same time.[2] In this way the fourth component of the THA's set of aims is defined and, if the text of the Act is taken into full account, the THA's system of aims can be itemised as follows:[3]

Table 1:
The THA's system of goals

Aim component	Level of preference	Time preference
Scope of privatisation	As far-reaching as possible	As rapid as possible
Jobs	Preservation/creation	As rapid as possible
Investments	Generation	As rapid as possible
Good proceeds from sale	Maximisation	As rapid as possible

Legislation did not provide any relative weighting for the various separate goals, and granted the THA plenty of scope for discretion and judgement.[4] Experience in contract management has shown that a fifth aim should be added to the first four: "minimisation of the THA's guarantee commitments".[5]

b) Economic environment of contract drafting

Although in October 1990 the expectation existed that the proceeds from the sale of state-owned companies could amount to some DM 600 billion,[6] recent projections based on proceeds realised to date[7] indicate a maximum of DM 46 billion. This serious miscalculation was caused by a

2 See: Treuhandanstalt, *Handbuch Privatisierung,* Section 2, Appendix 1, January 1993 version, page 3.

3 See: Sieben, *Zur Wertfindung bei der Privatisierung,* page 2048.

4 See: Treuhandanstalt, *Handbuch Privatisierung,* Chapter 2, Appendix 1, January 1993 version, page 3.

5 B-interview with Dr Zinken on 27th May 1993.

6 See: G. and H.-W. Sinn, *Kaltstart,* pages 88 and 70.

7 12,581 companies and parts of companies were privatised between 1st July 1990 and 30th June 1993, generating proceeds totalling DM 43.5 billion; Treuhandanstalt, *Monatsinformation der THA* as of 31st December 1992.

large number of overall economic factors, the significance and impact of which were not clearly or sufficiently recognised in early 1990, and which included the following in particular:[8]

- The collapse of the markets in the COMECON countries turned the capitalised value of potential return of the THA portfolio negative. Trading relations with the Eastern Bloc became almost totally unprofitable with the introduction of the Deutschmark into the German Democratic Republic, and it was hardly possible for East German companies to conquer new markets in the West quickly because of the lack of competitiveness on the part of their products and the lack of experience on the part of their managements.
- Companies were heavily subsidised and over-manned, and thus unable to set prices which would conform with the market and cover costs.
- As a result of the false system of incentives generated by the centrally planned economy, and the lack of funds for investment, the capital stock of East German companies was in a miserable condition.
- The market for companies is entirely subject to supply and demand, as is any other, so the over-supply of companies for sale led to their price declining still further.[9]
- Wage increases were negotiated which bore no relation to the level of productivity attained. "The collective wage agreements in eastern Germany are tantamount to outlawing employment in this part of the country."[10] In order to be able to ensure the continued existence of the companies under market conditions, an average of more than 35% of the employees in each firm had to be made redundant.[11]

A further factor adding to the general uncertainty in setting any price was the absence of any properly functioning real estate market in eastern Germany,[12] with the result that the customary valuation procedures could easily produce too low or too high a figure.

c) *Legal environment of contract drafting*

A large number of laws and ordinances have to be observed when privatisation contracts are being drawn up, in particular the Deutschmark Balance Sheet Act, the Property Act, the Investment Act, the Investment Priority Act, and the Outline Environmental Act.

The Deutschmark Balance Sheet Act regulates the unusual features which eastern German companies had to observe when preparing an opening balance sheet denominated in Deutschmarks. As the asset situation[13] of any company awaiting sale was a mass of uncertainties, legislation created the possibility of correcting the balance sheet retroactively (§ 36 of the Act). This possibility "endows the opening balance sheet with a slightly provisional character".[14] A correc-

8 See: G. and H.-W. Sinn, *Kaltstart,* pages 88 and 122 et seq.

9 See: op. cit., page 97.

10 op. cit., page 150.

11 Own calculation based on: Treuhandanstalt, *Monatsinformation der THA* as of 31st March 1993.

12 B-interviews with the financial control staff of the TLG (the THA real estate company) on 1st June 1993.

13 § 4 of this Act prescribes that the opening balance sheet has to provide a full and fair picture of the actual "asset situation". In the absence of any proper profit-and-loss statement it is not possible to state the profit situation, and the financial situation can only be assessed from the balance sheet by drawing conclusions from some of the key static data. On this point, see: Peemöller and Hüttche, *Zum Informationsgehalt von D-Markeröffnungsbilanz* page 210 et seq.

14 Kilgert and Großmann, *Notwendigkeit und Grenzen der Bilanzänderung,* page 497.

tion of individual balance sheet items can lead to various different changes, depending on the amount and the reason for it.

The Property Act[15] was passed by the *Volkskammer,* while the German Democratic Republic (GDR) was still in existence. However, the Investment Act made it clear that in certain exceptional cases the principle enshrined in the Property Act, "restitution before compensation", could be ignored in favour of investment activities. This set up an interlocking network of tension which the Removal of Obstacles Act should to resolve by amending the Property Act and the Investment Act. When the Second Property Law Amendment Act came into force on 15th July 1992, the Property Act was once again changed and the Investment Act (of 22nd March 1991) was repealed. The dilution of the principle of "Restitution before compensation" in favour of investment activities was placed on a new footing by the Investment Priority Act.[16]

Additional regulations to be observed during privatisation are to be found in the Outline Environmental Act and the resolution of the Executive Board of the THA of 21st September 1991, which lay down important procedures relating to historic environmental pollution.

2. Types of draft contracts

The contracts drafted and concluded by the THA can be categorised according to a number of different features, the most important distinction being made on the basis of the type of contract and the type of party with whom it is made. All the privatisation contracts, and thus the vast majority of all THA contracts, can be classified according to these criteria. There are also tenancy agreements and leases, contracts for the increasing of the registered capital of a company in order to take in additional partners, for the sale of mining property, and other contracts such as options.[17] These other contracts have not been included explicitly in this investigation because their significance for economic policy is relatively limited.

a) Differences reflecting purpose of contract

The THA concluded 12,581 company sale contracts between 1st July 1990 and 31st June 1993, covering the sale of 5,756 companies and 6,825 parts of companies. The TLG, which is responsible for the sale of real estate not required for the operations of the THA companies, carried through the sale of 16,405 pieces of real property during this time.[18] The privatisation contracts concluded by the THA can be categorised by the following characteristics:

- sale of a legally and commercially independent unit (share deal),
- sale of a legally dependent but commercially independent unit (borderline case between share and asset deal),
- sale of a legally and commercially dependent unit (asset deal, nearly always a real estate deal).

At the beginning of its work the THA was able relatively fully to meet the requirement for a programme that was as far-reaching as possible of privatisation as defined in the preamble to

---

15 For the titles and sources of the various laws and ordinances, see the Summary on pages XVI et seq.

16 A detailed statement of views on the Second Property Law Amendment Act is to be found in: G. and U. Dornberger, *Zum zweiten Vermögensrechtsänderungsgesetz,* pages 1613 et seq.

17 See: Treuhandanstalt, *Handbuch Privatisierung,* Section 10, January 1993 version, page 3.

18 See: Treuhandanstalt, *Monatsinformation der THA* as of 30th June 1993, page 5 et seq.

the THG, after negotiating with the investors almost exclusively for the sale of complete companies. The purchasers' idea that the acquisition of a THA company would be the first step towards opening new markets to the East probably played a certain part in this.[19] The asset value, at that point in time hard to estimate, and the immediate profitability of the companies were at the most secondary motives for investing.

Following the collapse of the eastern European markets, the acquisition of a THA company started to be viewed in a different light. The disappearance of this long-term prospect of success led to the asset value of a company being scrutinised much more closely, and the scope for restructuring it. Selected parts of companies now came up into the forefront of investors' interest, and those assets which could be restructured were removed from the shell companies and offered for sale on their own. This is in line with the more vigorous pursuit of the strategy of splitting up the big *Kombinate.*[20]

One typical characteristic of East German companies was their comparatively generous holding of land. In order to prevent speculation in real estate, the THA companies had to file lists of the land they held but did not need for operational purposes, and make it available for sale. The number of plots of land notified by 31st May 1993 was stated by the TLG to be about 50,000.[21] Lists of real estate were compiled by the TLG and put out for tender. This greatly increased the supply of real estate coming onto the market.

b) Differences reflecting the contracting parties

A further characteristic differentiating these contracts is the nature of the investor. Despite the wide range of possible draft contracts, it is possible to discern two specific types by applying this criterion, in addition to the basic type of sale to efficient companies and private individuals: the Management Buy-Out (MBO) and the Management Buy-In (MBI).

Under an MBO, the employees of eastern German companies were given the opportunity to take over responsibility for managing it. If a number of offers were on the table, all of roughly equal value, the THA always gave preference to the MBO. One particular feature of draft MBO contracts is a declaration to be signed by the new management in addition to the contract itself[22] and confirming the following:

- the absolutely definite origin of the funds necessary for the take-over and subsequent investment,
- that the management is not functioning as a "dummy" on behalf of a third party,
- that they never collaborated with the *Stasi* (the Ministry for State Security).

The THA also insisted on a clause preventing the company from being resold for a number of years, and one to the effect that if any information later proved to be incorrect this would give grounds for an action for damages or for the cancellation of the contract.

Under the MBI alternative form of privatisation, experienced managers from western Germany buy up the shares of a THA company. The fact that they can usually only bring in a

19 76% of all western German investors stated this as their reason in a survey conducted in 1991; see: *Treuhandanstalt Informationen* 6 (October 1991), page 18.

20 B-interviews with Contract Management staff on 27th May 1993.

21 B-interviews with TLG financial control staff on 1st June 1993.

22 See: Treuhandanstalt, *Handbuch Privatisierung,* Section 6, March 1992 version, page 13.

small amount of own equity capital is taken into consideration in the terms of the contract, and the purchase price is kept as low as possible by carving a large proportion of the real estate out of the company prior to privatisation and handing it over to a THA-owned real estate administration company established for this purpose. The investors, in taking over the shares of the company, also acquire an option to buy 100% of the shares of the real estate administration company, and at the same time also sign a tenancy agreement covering the property "parked" with the real estate administration company. If the new management team is successful in implementing its corporate strategy it can exercise the purchase option at a certain point in time and on pre-agreed conditions.[23]

3. The development over time of contract drafting[24]

The way these contracts are drafted has changed over a period of time that can be divided into three phases. The first of these began on 1st July 1990, when the THA took up its privatisation work. There is no longer any way of comparing the privatisation contracts of this "pioneer" phase with the present-day version. No guidelines had been issued on how they were to be framed, and there was usually no penalty imposed if undertakings given on jobs or investments were not adhered to. Of the contracts concluded during the second half of 1990, a mere 7% contained a penalty clause relating to jobs or investment.[25] In some cases the contracts only contained declarations of intent, worthy but not legally binding, of the investors' will to create jobs or to invest. There were very few cases of contracts providing for investigations to be made later regarding adherence to the commitments entered into.

Once the so-called Privatisation Financial Control organisation had been set up in the Financial Directorates, early in 1991, the second phase of contract drafting started. It is the task of these departments to analyse contracts for possible risks which the THA might have to bear. Before any contract is approved by the Executive Board it has to be endorsed by the Privatisation Financial Control departments. This inevitably generated tension between these departments and the Corporate Divisions in charge of privatisation, but this tension greatly improved the quality of the contracts. In the second half of 1991, 60% of the jobs and 64% of the investments promised were secured by penalty clauses.[26] Referring to the Financial Control Departments as the crucial control body within the THA also makes it easier to coerce the investors into accepting restrictive contract clauses. In drafting these contracts, the THA also attempts to achieve the highest possible degree of uniformity. If at all possible, risks are quantified or limited by clauses placing a maximum figure on the THA's exposure. Imprecise forms of words like "as soon as possible", "at the purchaser's free discretion", or "the purchaser intends" will now only be found in the preamble to these contracts, which has no legally binding effect. A minimum standard for privatisation contracts has been prepared in detail in the THA,[27] and covers virtually all eventualities. The contract clauses, which have been drafted in collaboration

23 This procedure is also used for MBO's; see: Birgit Breuel and Hero Brahms, Letter to all Directors and the Branch Managers, 9th November 1992.

24 These statements are based on data bank analyses and a survey carried out on employees.

25 Own surveys, as of 31st December 1992.

26 Own surveys, as of 31st December 1992.

27 See: Treuhandanstalt, *Handbuch Privatisierung,* Section 2, appendix 3, March 1992 version.

with external legal experts, only need the addition of the key figures on the individual privatisation project. A "modular" contract drafting system has led to many contracts being worded partly identically although they are used by various different Industry Directorates.[28] The THA only deviates from this rule in well justified exceptional cases, particularly if the privatisation project is likely to have substantial effects on social or structural policy or on economic order policy.

The third phase of contract drafting can be regarded as starting in 1991, when more and more problems became visible in the handling of privatisation contracts. This then led to the Contract Management team in individual departments bringing their influence to bear on the drafting of contracts. First follow-up negotiations indicate weak points in the wording of existing contracts, and experience gained through contract management shows that some clauses are hard to enforce and therefore need modifying. Agreements on periods of time (e. g. for raising objections or cancelling contracts) will in future take more account of the processing time required within the THA.

4. Systematisation of the individual contract components

The essential and typical clauses in a THA contract of sale are described below (Fig. 1). They represent the ideal contract, but in the initial period in particular it was not always possible to include them all.

a) Contractual clauses for ensuring the achievement of THA aims

THA companies are sold to the investor whose corporate strategy meets best the component aims in the THA's system of goals as shown above. In order to achieve this, clauses are included in the contracts to ensure that "quantifiable mutual relationships" are created which might have been agreed from the start without taking the unfulfilled "weak" aims into account.[29] Any culpable deviation by the purchaser from the number of jobs or amount of investment which he undertakes in the contract to provide leads inexorably to a retroactive increase in the purchase price. Contractual clauses of this kind are intended to ensure that the aims of preserving and creating jobs, generating investment, and realising reasonable proceeds from the sale are met. They are also intended to help in the search for buyers who intend to invest, and in preventing speculation. The clauses intending to secure the purchase price, to deal with dubious reserves, and to prevent speculative transactions relate to the last of the goals.

- *Securing jobs*

The purchaser undertakes, in an employment clause, "to create or secure and to fill" a set number of full-time job vacancies within a set period of time.[30] If the investor falls short of the agreed number of jobs within the prescribed period, and if he fails to take on workers and make good the shortfall, he has to pay a contractual penalty to the seller based on the number of jobs

---

28 The risk with standardised contracts is the non-validity of exclusion of guarantee clauses under the General Terms and Conditions of Business. This is taken into account in the wording of contracts.

29 Wächter, Kaiser, and Krause, *Klauseln in Unternehmenskaufverträgen,* page 298.

30 See: Treuhandanstalt, Letters from Directorate Law P R6 to the Directors in the Central Office, including the one dated 29th July 1992.

in the shortfall. It is due for payment after the end of the calendar year in which the shortfall occurred, and averages DM 24,000 per missing head.[31] If the vacancy remains unfilled for less than 12 months, the penalty is calculated in proportion to elapsed time. Another important point in the wording of employment clauses is that the full-time jobs must be created on the terms of employment customary in that industry, and that an assurance must given that, in the event of the works being relocated, the workers can reasonably be expected to remain with the firm. By the end of June 1993, undertakings covering 1,468,193 jobs had been agreed in the contracts and their preambles.[32] According to information from the THA, 20% of investors were unable to meet their commitments, but this is compensated for by some of the other 80% exceeding theirs.[33]

– *Investment obligations*
A further specific aim of the THA is that investment undertakings should be secured by contract in which the difference between the amount the investor undertakes to invest, and the amount he actually does invest, must be added to the purchase price and paid to the THA. On average, 33% of the amount promised but not spent has to be paid to the THA.[34] The nature of the planned investment, the financial resources of the purchaser, the company's current situation, and the provisions of the Investment Priority Act determine the length of time granted to the investor to meet his obligations.

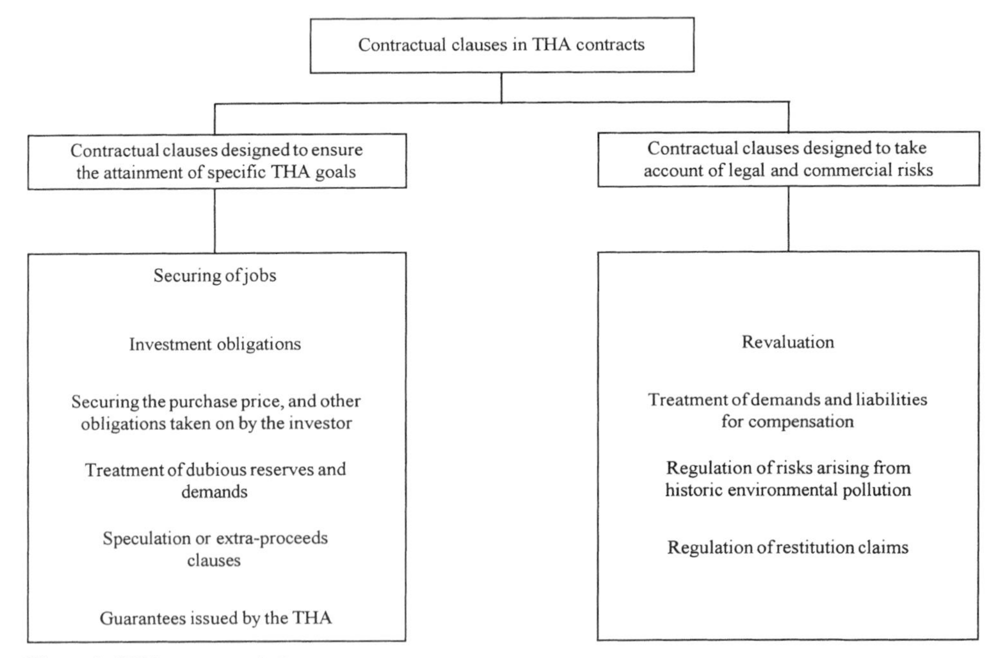

Figure 1 THA contractual clauses

31 Own surveys, as of 31st December 1992.
32 See: Treuhandanstalt, *Monatsinformation der THA* as of 30th June 1993, page 13.
33 B-interviews with Contract Management staff on 27th May 1993. See also: article by Hanau in this volume, page 441.
34 Own surveys, as of 31st December 1992.

Two aims are being pursued simultaneously with the investment obligation. One is that investment means fresh money flowing into the economies of the eastern German states, the other is that this regulation implies that the investor commits himself to a risk. The THA booked investment undertakings totalling DM 180.1 billion in the period of time up to 30th June 1993.[35] The only kind of investment allowed to count here is that made in buildings and movable production equipment in the company or part of a company that has been acquired.[36] In special cases, an agreed investment plan is attached as an appendix to the contract.[37] This is a very harsh restriction on the purchaser's room for manoeuvre, but makes the contract easier for the THA to supervise. The investor can only wriggle out of his obligations if this is forced upon him by compelling operational needs which could not have been foreseen at the time the contract was concluded.

– *Securing the purchase price and the investor's other liabilities*
In order to secure payment of the purchase price and the various individual instalments, the THA not only investigates the purchaser's credit rating but also requires the submission of an irrevocable guarantee, which is directly enforceable, payable upon first request, valid for an indefinite period, and drawn on a major German bank. If payment is to be made in instalments, the bank guarantee should cover accrued interest. In addition to this, the possibility exists for the transfer of the shares to be subject to the condition precedent that the purchase price be paid in full or that the THA's claims be secured under land registry law.[38] In order to limit its risk to no more than the purchase price, some investors establish a GmbH-company as a wholly owned subsidiary for the purpose of acquiring the THA company, so that in the most cases the liability borne by this company is limited to its registered and paid-up capital of DM 50,000; accordingly, the THA includes an agreement in many contracts imposing immediate foreclosures on the entirety of the investors' assets. This results in obtaining a maximum level of the investor's personal liability. If the company is being taken over by more than one investor, they all bear joint and several liability for any possible claims under the contract. This is intended to prevent the whole plan from ending in failure just because of the insolvency of one of the contracting parties.

– *Treatment of dubious reserves and outstanding payments*[39]
When opening DM balance sheets are being prepared, the auditors are required to include reserves on the balance sheet on the principle of the highest value. Uncertainty at the time the balance sheets were being drawn up led to the creation of enormous reserves. It is possible to distinguish between two alternative ways in which the contracts are drafted to cope with this aspect. One possibility is to value the reserves at "zero" in the hand-over balance sheet and to raise the purchase price accordingly. The THA absolves and redeems the purchaser in case one day a claim is made against him. The other is for the purchaser to undertake to demonstrate that

35 See: Treuhandanstalt, *Monatsinformation der THA* as of 30th June 1993, page 5.
36 See: Treuhandanstalt, *Handbuch Privatisierung,* Section 10, January 1993 version, page 31.
37 Since the end of 1992 most contracts have a so-called "project plan" attached to them as a consequence of the Investment Priority Act.
38 See: Treuhandanstalt, *Handbuch Privatisierung,* Section 10, January 1993 version, page 21.
39 op. cit., pages 23 et seq.

the reserves have been "ear-marked" for a specific purpose. The purchase price is then raised retroactively by the difference between the amount of the reserves and the claim actually made against it. Outstanding payments undergone an individually valuation adjustment are handled in a similar way. If the outstanding payments remain on the balance sheet as an in memoria item, the purchaser is required to pass all incoming payments to the THA. The investor can also be given an addition incentive in the form of "commission by results" as a fixed percentage of the payments received.

– *Speculation or extra proceeds of resale clause*
A speculation clause is intended to prevent the company shares or property assets acquired from being sold or leased in a manner contrary to the original plan within a certain minimum period of time. If the assets being purchased under the contract are sold off in violation of the strategy, this clause provides for the current market value to be calculated on the basis of a later valuation. The seller has to be paid a proportion, defined in the contract, of the profit from the extra proceeds of the resale; on average this is 88%.[40] The THA defines this extra profit as "the difference between the estimated value and the selling price actually achieved, at least the market value at the time of resale".[41] The extra proceeds of resale clause is intended to prevent companies being taken over and real estate sold for purely speculative reasons. The degree to which this clause is restrictive depends on the ability of the object being sold to gain in value. For the sale of some assets in and around Berlin, the THA was in some cases able to insist on an anti-speculation period of up to ten years, and on 100% of the proceeds being paid back in the event of speculative resale. As an additional form of security, the THA demands in certain circumstances also, for instance, prior right of purchase. In some cases it will dispense with the extra proceeds of resale if the purchaser can demonstrate that he is using the proceeds to re-invest in the company.

– *Warranty undertakings given by the THA*
The willingness of a purchaser to dispense with guarantees from the seller depends, among other things, on the possibilities granted to him to investigate, examine, and audit. The THA only makes undertakings in exceptional cases because they can give rise to an action for damages.[42] As the THA offers any party under consideration as a purchaser almost unlimited scope for examination and inspection,[43] they will have certain potential advantage through prior knowledge of the company. As a rule the THA only guarantees the following:[44]
- the company exists properly under all relevant laws,
- the THA is the owner of the shares and is free to dispose of them,
- the shares are not encumbered by any third party's rights,
- bankruptcy proceedings have not been opened, and,
- the THA is the owner of the land being sold.

40 Own surveys, as of 31st December 1992.
41 See: Treuhandanstalt, *Handbuch Privatisierung,* Section 10, January 1993 version, page 8 et seq.
42 See § 463 of the Civil Code.
43 The interested party merely has to sign a confidentiality declaration.
44 See: Treuhandanstalt, *Handbuch Privatisierung,* Section 10, January 1993 version, page 10.

In order to keep the risk manageable, the maximum extent to which any claim can be raised against the THA under any guarantee is in some cases the amount of the purchase price.

b) Contractual clauses for managing legal and economic risks

– Revaluation
The real estate market in eastern Germany is still subject to major fluctuations even two years after unification.[45] The opening of the frontier led in the conglomerations to some very wrong estimates of the value of land. This has created feelings of uncertainty, as a result of which revaluation clauses have been included in the contracts. Unlike the securing of jobs and investment, these are not specifically THA clauses. Revaluation means that any increase in value that has occurred since the property was sold is paid to the THA. An agreement of this kind can lead to financial constrictions, especially if the investor comes out of the small or medium-sized business, because in these cases, unlike those covered by extra proceeds of resale clauses, no funds flow in. In order to keep this risk manageable as well, a maximum level is sometimes agreed with the investor which sets a top limit on the amount he may have to pay. There are revaluation clauses in about 38% of all THA contracts.[46] In more recent contracts, the THA has been refraining more and more from revaluation clauses; the share of contracts containing such clauses fell from 54% in the first half of 1991 to 28% in the second half of 1992.[47]

– Treatment of compensation demands and liabilities
§ 36 of the DM Balance Sheet Act covers one possible way of amending the opening DM balance sheet retroactively which can lead to a changed compensation demand or liability. It is therefore necessary to take the amount of and the grounds for these balance sheet items into account in drafting the contract in order to avoid retroactive claims being made against the contracting parties.

– Dealing with the risk of historic environmental pollution
The problem of historic environmental pollution has a special position not only with regard to privatisation, as can be seen from the creation of a separate Directorate for "Environmental Protection/Historic Environmental Pollution" within the THA. This organisational unit is decisively responsible for the detailed preparation of standardised historic environmental pollution clauses, the central component of which is the distribution of the costs of disposal between the purchaser and the THA. As a rule, the following provisions are made:[48]

- The purchaser agrees to pay a basic amount.
- Any costs exceeding that basic amount are split between the THA and the investor.
- From a certain level upwards, any further risk is transferred back to the vendor.

In addition to this, a number of further rules have to be observed. No guarantee liability can be accepted by the vendor that the property is free of historic environmental pollution, and a set period of time must be agreed after which no report of historic environmental pollution will be accepted. In order to prevent any later claim against the THA based on "decontamination with

45 B-interviews with TLG financial control staff on 1st June 1993.

46 Own surveys, as of 31st December 1992.

47 Own surveys, as of 31st December 1992.

48 See: Treuhandanstalt, *Handbuch Privatisierung,* Section 10, January 1993 version, pages 39 et seq.

gold doorknobs", the contract has to include a precise definition of the term: "Historic environmental pollution shall be defined as meaning contamination of the soil by pollutants produced by industrial or commercial use which gives rise to any danger to public health or safety."[49]

Another condition which must be met before the THA will bear any part of the costs is an expert's assessment which meets certain criteria. If historic environmental pollution is discovered, the purchaser must submit an application for indemnity within a certain set period. If the investor is required by the authorities to dispose of existing pollution, the necessary decontamination measures must be agreed with the THA before they are carried out. The resultant disposal costs have to be properly substantiated. In order to prevent misunderstandings before they occur, the term "costs of disposing of historic environmental pollution" must be defined in the contract.

– *Settlement of restitution claims*

The treatment of restitution claims in purchase contracts raises two different kinds of problem:

- On the one hand, the excessive workload under which the Property Offices are suffering does not permit any inventory to be made of the actual situation.
- On the other hand, the continual changes in the law is making the process of privatisation more difficult.

A basic distinction needs to be made between restitution claims pertaining to the company and to parts of it. If it is not possible to reach amicable agreement between the rightful restitution claimant and the "authorised party" (the party who has the right of disposal of the property but is not its legal owner), the latter can make recourse to investment priority proceedings under § 3a of the Property Act. This defines the course of action when restitution claims are made against a company. If an investment priority decision is made, the former owner loses his claim to restitution of the company, but only on condition that the investor fulfils his obligations of creating and securing jobs and investment. When the 2nd Property Law Amendment Act came into force with the newly promulgated Investment Priority Act contained in it as Article 6, this area of activity was placed on a new legal footing.[50] The new Investment Priority Act mainly redefines the procedure to be followed in the sale of plots of land. Now a deadline has to be set within the promised investments have to be carried through. As it is possible for the investment priority notice to be rescinded, it is necessary to create an obligation of restitution. Finally, a penalty is to be imposed for any deviation from investment undertakings. In the case of share deals, the regulation that the investor has to undertake to make certain investments in the first two years after his contract takes effect remains unchanged. If the investor fails to fulfil his contractual obligations for reasons for which he is responsible, the company has to be transferred back into the vendor's possession. In addition to this reverse-transfer obligation, contractual penalties must also be built into the contract.

5. Assessment of contract drafting

The THA is averse to risks when it comes to drafting contracts. Potential risks have to be quantified and, unless historic environmental pollution is involved, held in check by a special clause

49 See: Treuhandanstalt, *Handbuch Privatisierung,* Section 7, January 1993 version, page 1.

50 See: THA: Letters from Directorate Law, Department 5: Zweites Vermögensrechtsänderungsgesetz, 30th June 1992.

imposing a top limit or are fully passed on to the investors. On the other hand, by the inclusion of revaluation clauses and/or extra proceeds of resale clauses the THA secures a share of the increases in value of land for itself.[51] In addition to this, the purchaser's future entrepreneurial room for manoeuvre is reduced by undertakings to make investments and create employment.[52] The contractual clauses described above limit the incentive effect for western investors. In order to be able to privatise some 80% of its portfolio of companies by 31st December 1992, the THA therefore had to create other forms of incentives, and these consisted of indirect subsidies for the investors from the THA. In order to get its way with regard to investment and employment undertakings, the THA made concessions in setting the purchase price.[53] The often cited losses of book value suffered in the course of privatisation were the price the THA had to pay for shifting the risks over to the investors.[54] The accusation that the THA was "flogging its companies off cheap" is therefore unfounded, as can be shown by the large number of cases in which the investors came and requested the re-opening of negotiations. This shows that the book losses were often less than the risks which the investors took on.

III. Methods and processes of contract management

1. Purpose and processes of contract management

a) Aims of contract management

It is after the privatisation processes have been completed and all the necessary documents handed over that the Contract Management department starts work.[55] In its relationships with the outside world for the investors and all other institutions the THA is also represented from this moment on by the Contract Management department. Initially, the THA defined the aim of this department as being the "recording of all privatisation contracts in a special EDP system, maintaining the 'four eyes' principle".[56] This definition is no longer adequate in light of its field of responsibility, which has now become very wide. As the THA's privatisation programme progressed, the Contract Management department gained steadily in significance. In addition to the recording of contracts, their fulfilment is now taking on an ever greater importance, as is any necessary adaptation work. This is reflected in the changing terminology used. The terms originally used such as "contract handling", "financial control of contracts", or "contract fulfilment" only ever covered a part of its spectrum of responsibilities at any one time.

The targets of contract management therefore have to be widened. The analysis of the contracts must reveal the risks they contain, and is therefore directed towards risk evaluation.

51 These only apply if the land is sold prematurely.

52 These undertakings are secured by hefty penalty clauses.

53 See: THA, slide presentation on *Die Treuhandanstalt und die Neuen Bundesländer,* 22nd September 1992, chart 24, and: THA, slide presentation on *Die Treuhandanstalt,* 6th February 1991, chart 27.

54 If the THA sells a company for less than its asset value, a book loss appears in the THA's balance-sheet.

55 See: Treuhandanstalt, *Handbuch Privatisierung,* Section 11, September 1992 version, page 1.

56 See: Treuhandanstalt, Organisational Instructions for the handling of contracts, dated 20th August 1992, page 4. Emphasis added by the author.

Adherence to agreed timings must be ensured by the recording of contracts. Adherence to agreements shall be ensured by applying the criteria of fulfilment. The goal of adapting the contract is the minimisation of expenditure and risk.

b) Detailed responsibilities and work phases of Contract Management

With regard to these specific aims, the detailed responsibilities shown in Fig. 2 can be broken down into the areas of analysis and collation, fulfilment, and adaptation, and can also be regarded as the steps in an ideal working sequence.

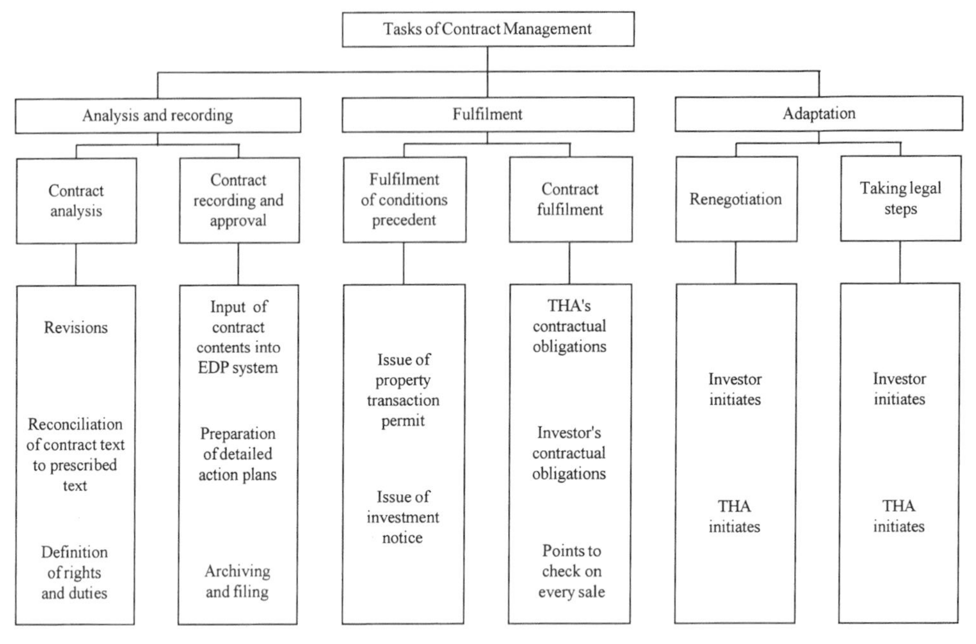

Figure 2 Detailed responsibilities and work phases of Contract Management

– Analysis and recording[57]

Contract analysis is started off when all the documents are passed to the Contract Management department which is responsible for the case. The total contents of the dossier are first documented as there are often important items missing which the THA executives responsible for privatisation have to provide later. The documents not only have to be checked for completeness but also to see whether they need any revision or not. Despite an efficient check-up system, there may be individual points which do not meet the THA's minimum requirements.

57 At the time of writing of this article, about 95% of all completed contracts had been analysed and recorded: own survey, as of 31st December 1992.

The contract is usually concluded after internal approval has been obtained from the Executive Board. Facts which have only recently come to light have to be taken into account. As major deviations are only made without authority it is necessary to obtain retroactive approval, which the Contract Management department has to request from the Industry Directorate concerned. The rights and duties of the THA imposed by the contract also have to be defined.

The contract is then entered on the data bank and approved for use there (see Fig. 2).

– *Fulfilment*

The payment of the purchase price and the transfer of the shares are conditional upon the fulfilment of the conditions precedent (see Fig. 2) and adherence to all approval and formal requirements. The THA's Administrative Board and the Federal Ministry of Finance must also add their consent to that of the THA's Executive Board if any two of the following criteria are met:[58]

- the number employed in the company being sold exceeds 2,000,
- the balance sheet totals more than DM 100 million,
- the forecast annual turnover is more than DM 300 million.

Once the contract has come into force, the Contract Management executive has to take on the responsibilities shown in Fig. 3. In addition to the general action to be taken on the sale of any company, specific responsibilities come into effect which are defined for the THA and the investor.

– *Adaptation*[59]

The dividing line between the activities which are necessary for the fulfilment of a contract and renegotiation of the contract is a fluid one. Renegotiations can therefore be defined as discussions between buyer and seller with the intention of arriving at an amendment to or an appropriate interpretation of the contract. The relevant Contract Management executives of the THA believe, on the basis of their own estimates, that about 10% of all privatisation contracts will have to be renegotiated at some stage. This figure is based on the sum total of all contracts concluded by the THA; if it were based on the more complex share deals, the renegotiation proportion would certainly be higher.

– *Factors necessitating adaptation*

A large number of factors give rise to the high proportion of contracts needing adaptation. The overall situation surrounding privatisation and contract drafting have changed continually during the course of time. Ambiguous wording in old contracts make renegotiation an almost urgent necessity. As shown under Point II.3, growing experience in privatisation has led to an improvement in the quality of the contracts, but the trends in the economy have meant that more generous concessions had to be granted in the more recent contracts. After the collapse of the COMECON the eastern German companies had to open new markets for themselves. Attempts to switch over into the recessionary markets in the west failed because of the high barriers to entry. One major problem, in addition to the way the markets were already divided up, was the

---

58 See: Treuhandanstalt, *Organisationshandbuch,* serial no. 1.7, as of July 1991. Approval requirements were amended in March 1993.

59 The factors which could make adaptation necessary and the strategies and forms of contractual adaptation were described in a number of B-interviews conducted in the Contract Management departments between 1st January and 1st April 1993.

lack of acceptance of eastern German products on the western German markets; also, many eastern German companies were excluded from western markets by the stringent quality and safety standards demanded there. These problems hit those companies particularly hard which had been privatised in an MBO, as these managers could not benefit from the west-east technology transfer which western German investors bring in. Co-operation and licence agreements signed on unfavourable terms also make it hard for privatised companies to establish themselves on a healthy basis.

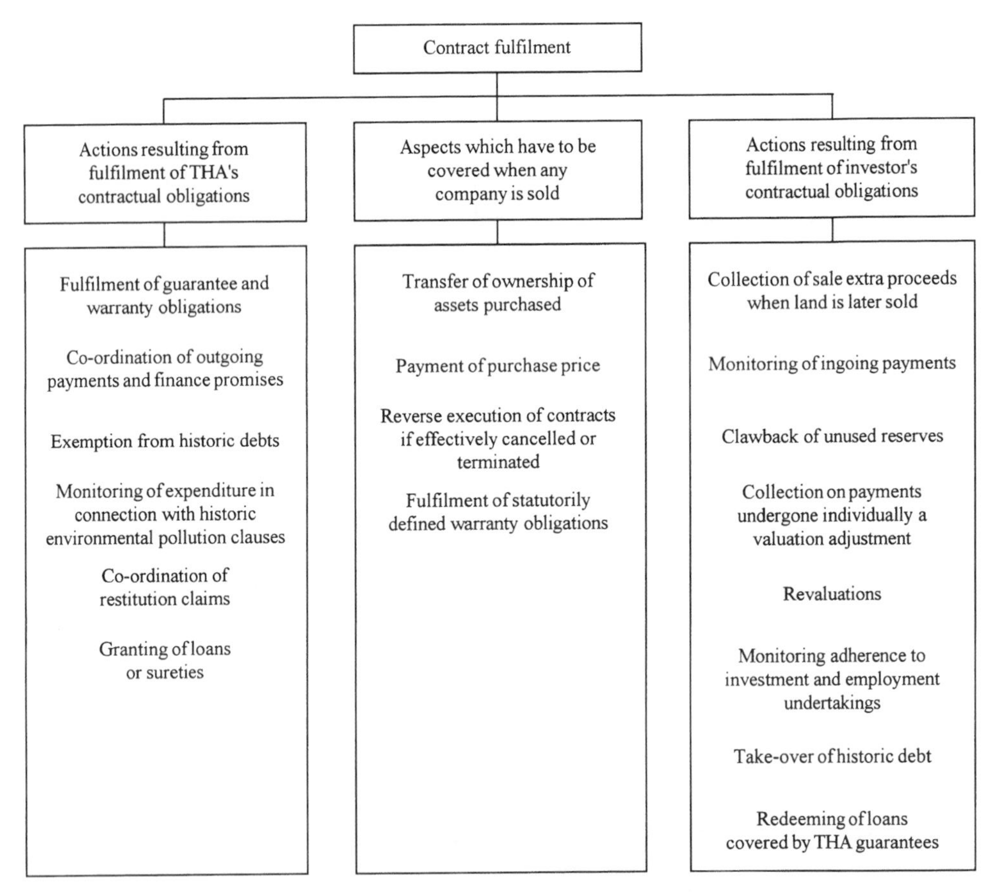

Figure 3 Detailed responsibilities of the Contract Management departments

The first signs of recession in western Germany became apparent in the first months of 1992, and many companies had to announce short-time working during the course of the year because their turnover was falling off. This situation had its inevitable effect on the eastern German states and even investors with excellent credit ratings found that the double burden caused by the recession in the economy and the costs of restructuring their new company in the east led to financial bottle-necks. Some investors in the most crisis-ridden industries were faced by threats to their very existence.

A further factor necessitating renegotiation of the older contracts was the fact that the THA was occupied not only with privatisation work but also with supporting the restructuring of companies on their way to privatisation. The on-going liabilities of the companies were covered by granting global guarantees. Individual guarantees had the character of direct restructuring. The restructuring risk had to be borne by the THA alone. Companies capable of benefiting from restructuring were converted, at great expense, into companies in a fit shape to compete on the open market. The later an investor decided to take over a THA company, the less the risk that he was investing in a company incapable of survival. Up to the point when a company was privatised, the selection process was in the hands of the THA. Experience to date with renegotiations show that it is in particular those managers who took over their former company as part of an MBO who tended to make a wrong estimate of the company's situation and of the market.

The prime requirement in investigating the investor's creditworthiness was to secure the purchase price. Under the older contracts a bank guarantee was the only requirement to cover the purchase price, and sometimes not even that. Just as little effort went into checking the investor's ability to meet his future obligations. Particularly in the case of share deals, the ability to meet the obligation of paying the purchase price gives little indication of the investor's creditworthiness in general. In order to keep the purchase price to a minimum, the companies were freed neither from historic debts nor from liquidity debts, so the purchase price was adjusted in line with the investor's ability to pay it. The future development of the firms, however, and the value of their assets were thus assessed much too optimistically. The additional financial obligations arising out of the contract had to be shouldered totally by the investors without their being able to realise any comparable revenue from the companies. In addition to redeeming liquidity loan guarantees and paying the interest on historic debt, the investors normally committed themselves in their contracts with the THA to carrying out investments. The amounts to be raised were often many times the purchase price.

– Strategies and forms of contract adaptation

The company sales carried out by the THA gave rise to a large number of issues regarding contract adaptation. In addition to the normal run of events, many renegotiations had to be conducted. Basically, the THA pursues a restrictive policy as the purchasers had been given unrestricted access to all information concerning the company prior to acquiring it. It is usually the investors that initiate renegotiation. But they do not attain specific negotiations in every instance, because some investors are merely using this method to optimise retroactively the results of privatisation. In order to be able to identify these "black sheep", the THA demands a comprehensive substantiation for the need to adapt the contract. However, distinguishing the deserving cases from the others is extremely difficult on account of the desperate economic situation which affects all investors to an equal extent.

Once discussions do start between the THA and the investor, any assessment of the scope for negotiation focuses primarily on the company's economic prospects. The THA is only ever prepared to make concessions if the company is capable of being restructured. In reaching his decision, the Contract Management executive is always caught between two fronts; in enforcing the THA's contractual rights he must always consider the economic consequences for the company. In order to achieve acceptable results from the negotiations, the THA always insists on some counter-performance from the investor. Renegotiations keep revolving around the investor's fulfilment of his financial commitments, adherence to his undertakings to provide jobs, and the contractual release of the THA from its guarantees. Investment obligations currently do not figure in these renegotiations as the period of time has not yet expired during which they have to be made. The THA usually declares its willingness to help the investor over liquidity difficulties by postponing payment of the purchase price or allowing it to be paid in a series of instalments. For instance, when jobs have been promised, the date by which this promise has to be honoured can be postponed beyond that agreed in the contract. The investigation of the company's ability to be restructured is of particular significance when the investor does not release the THA from its guarantees as agreed, because if the company does go into bankruptcy claims will be made against the THA under these guarantees.

If the parties are unable to come to an amicable settlement through such renegotiations, it is possible to make recourse to the courts. The initiation of legal steps has to be discussed and agreed with the THA's "Directorate Law" in advance. As the Contract Management departments have only just started on their work, there have not yet been many cases of this kind.

2. Organisation and financial control of contract management

a) Organisational integration of contract management at the Central Office

The period of time up to 1993 is characterised by the privatisation and restructuring of the companies belonging to the THA, which brought contract drafting forward to centre-stage. As the privatisation task moved towards completion, the centre of gravity shifted increasingly to contract management. This has its effects on the organisational structure surrounding the Contract Management departments; during the "privatisation phase" it was included under the Commercial Directorates of the various Corporate Divisions, as shown in Fig. 4, but by the middle of 1993 Contract Management had been promoted to a higher organisational position.

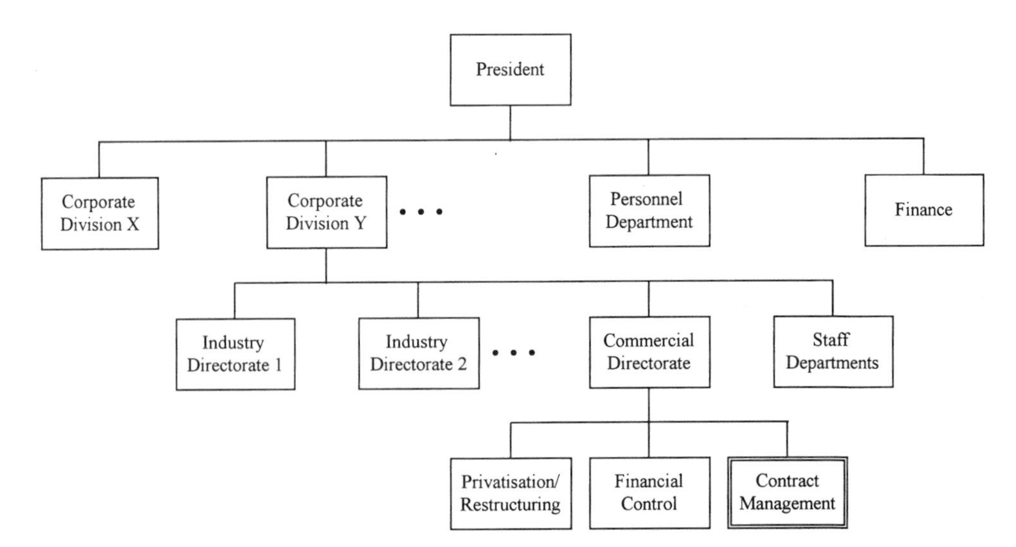

Figure 4 Organisational structure surrounding Contract Management in the THA Central Office

Source: Treuhandanstalt, Organisation der Treuhandanstalt as of 15th February 1992.

The Corporate, the Personnel and the Finance Divisions, each reports to their own Executive Board member, and each contains up to four Industry Directorates, one or two staff functions, and a Commercial Directorate. Whilst the Industry Directorates are entrusted with the sale and support of THA companies, the Commercial Directorate in each Corporate Division has a kind of staff function. In the organisational structure in force until the middle of 1993, the Commercial Directors had three departments under them: Privatisation/Restructuring, Financial Control, and Contract Management.

One advantage of integrating Contract Management into the Commercial Directorates in this way was that it ensured a direct exchange of information between this department and the Privatisation/Restructuring department, which supervised the on-going privatisation process. This information channel also provided an indirect feed-back from Contract Management to Privatisation.[60]

The growing importance of contract management also had its effect on the trends in numbers employed. Thus from August 1992 to January 1993 the number of employees in contract management almost doubled in order to cope with the unexpected rush of adaptation applications. By way of an example, staff numbers, professional qualifications, and the work-load of the Contract Management departments as it appeared towards the end of 1992 are shown in Table 2, which also indicates other aspects of the composition of the staff and the contracts dealt with. The differ-

Table 2:
Staff numbers, qualifications, and work-load in the THA Central Office Contract Management departments as of 31st December 1992

	U1	U2	U3	U4	U5	U6	THA
Numbers employed	10	7	21	30	30	29	127
Of whom fully qualified lawyers (in %)	20	0	29	13	37	10	20
Contracts in Corporate Division	340	378	1,681	921	796	586	4,702
Number of share deals	146	79	319	276	151	305	1,276

Source: Own surveys

ences in the number of contracts handled can be attributed to a very wide variation in the time taken to process one contract. One striking feature is the high level of qualification of the staff.

The Corporate Divisions are supposed to have completed their operational work on privatisation and restructuring by the end of 1993. On the other hand, contract management will be of considerable importance even in the future phases of the THA's work. The THA is assuming, on the basis of its own estimates, that the number of contracts requiring active work will reach its maximum of more than 32,000[61] in 1993/1994.

Coping with the resultant volume of work is only possible to a limited extent with the organisational structure outlined here. Following a detailed analysis, the THA's Administrative and Executive Boards decided in June 1993 to set up a "transitional organisation", to remain in force until early 1995 and designed to ensure uniformity in contract management, the provision of

60 B-interviews with Contract Management staff between 1st January and 1st April 1993. See also Section II.3.

61 This figure is based on the number of sales of companies, parts of companies, and real estate. Source: TLG, contract data-bank, and B-interviews with TLG staff.

management information relevant to decisions, and strict adherence to the "four eyes" principle. All the responsibilities of contract management will be "brought together into a Corporate Division, given a higher organisational position through the creation of Directorates, and supplemented by a Financial Control department"[62] as shown in Fig. 5.

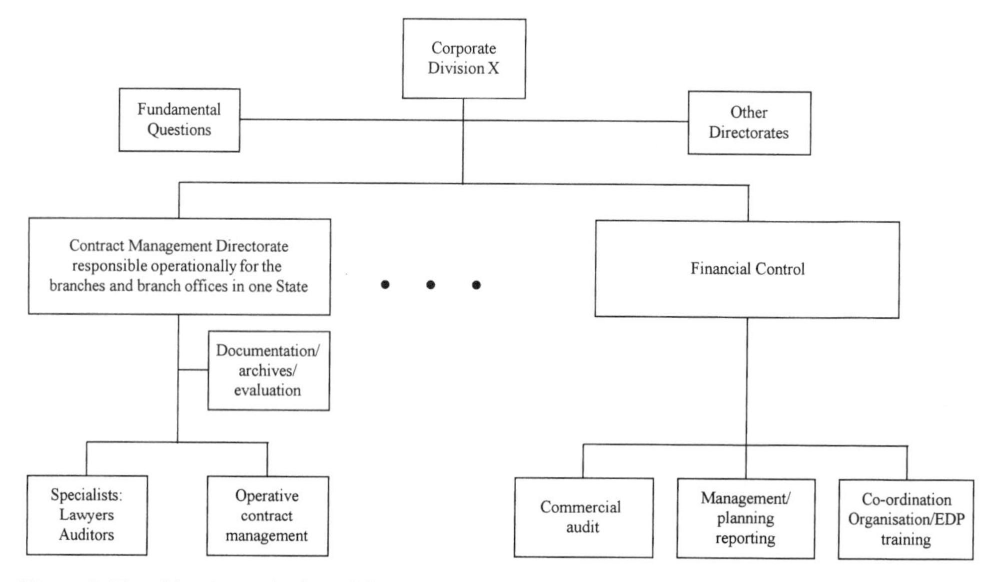

Figure 5 Transitional organisation of Contract Management from July 1993 onwards

The structure of Contract Management Directorates means the organisational separation of the operational day-to-day work from special problems. In addition to staff departments for "Documentation/Archives/Evaluation" and "Operational Contract Management", there are therefore several specialists allocated to the Directorate. They are responsible for conducting renegotiations in complicated and important cases. In order to facilitate the organisational transition, the new Directorates are organised by industry, as before. The central Financial Control Directorate safeguards the "four eyes" principle, and is broken down into three departments: Commercial Auditing, Management/Planning of Reporting, and Co-ordination of Organisation/ EDP Training.[63]

The Corporate Division responsible for contract management has the authority to issue guidelines to the TLG, the real estate company of the THA. Whilst contracts for the purchase of companies and "real estate contracts connected with companies" are supervised by the Contract Management Directorates, "other" real estate contracts, including tenancies and leases, come under the TLG's field of responsibility. If requested by the Contract Management departments, the "Historic Environmental Pollution" department takes on the technical and legal responsibility for handling obligations relating to historic environmental pollution arising from all the contracts handled by the Central Office.

62 Administrative Board submission dated 18th July 1993, page 5.

63 See: op. cit., page 8.

Despite far-reaching changes, the re-organisation of contract management has had no effect on the numbers employed by the THA. By far the largest proportion of the newly created positions have been filled by internal transfers.

b) Organisational integration of contract management in the Regions

In addition to its Central Office in Berlin, the THA had 15 branches in the five States *(Länder)* of eastern Germany. Each branch was organised into four directorates: Privatisation, Holdings (the companies in which the THA had an equity holding and for which it was therefore responsible), Personnel, and Finance. The tasks of contract management were carried out by a special department within the Finance Directorate, as shown in Fig. 6.

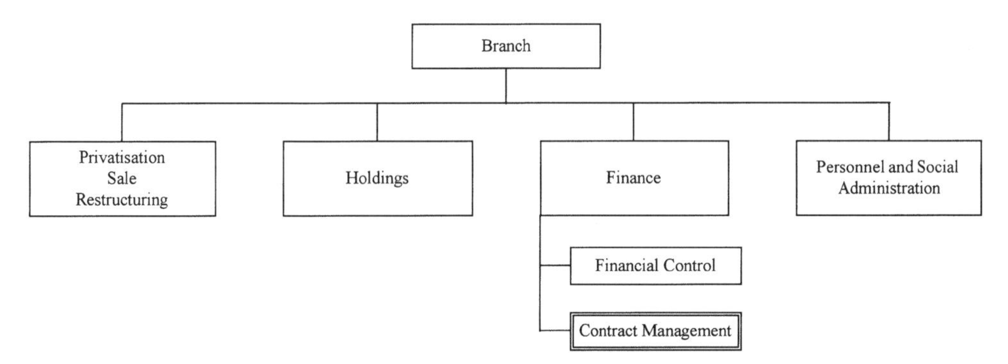

Figure 6 Organisational integration of Contract Management into the branches

Source: Treuhandanstalt, Organisationsprojekt Treuhand, as of 5th March 1991

The organisational position of contract management changed during the course of the change-over of the branches into branch offices following the conclusion of their privatisation work and thus also of their responsibility for companies. One of the priority tasks of the Contract Management department is to report directly to the Branch Manager, which thus gives it a higher organisational position. The position of the department within the entire organisation of a branch office can be seen from Fig. 7.

The organisation of contract management in the regions can be seen by taking the Berlin Branch Office as an example, where a staff of 17 (as of 30th June 1993) was looking after 690 contracts.[64] 367 of these were share and asset deals, and 323 real estate deals. Unlike those at the Central Office, the staff do not specialise in specific industries but on specific types of contract. Special attention is given to the handling of 124 contracts covering catering enterprises and dispensing chemists, which are dealt with separately by two employees. The degree of difficulty represented by a contract and the individual employees' professional qualifications are taken into account in sharing out the work-load. Of these 17 people in the Berlin Branch Office, 5 are qualified lawyers and 10 have commercial qualifications.

64 Treuhandanstalt, Geschäftsstelle Berlin, as of 30th June 1993.

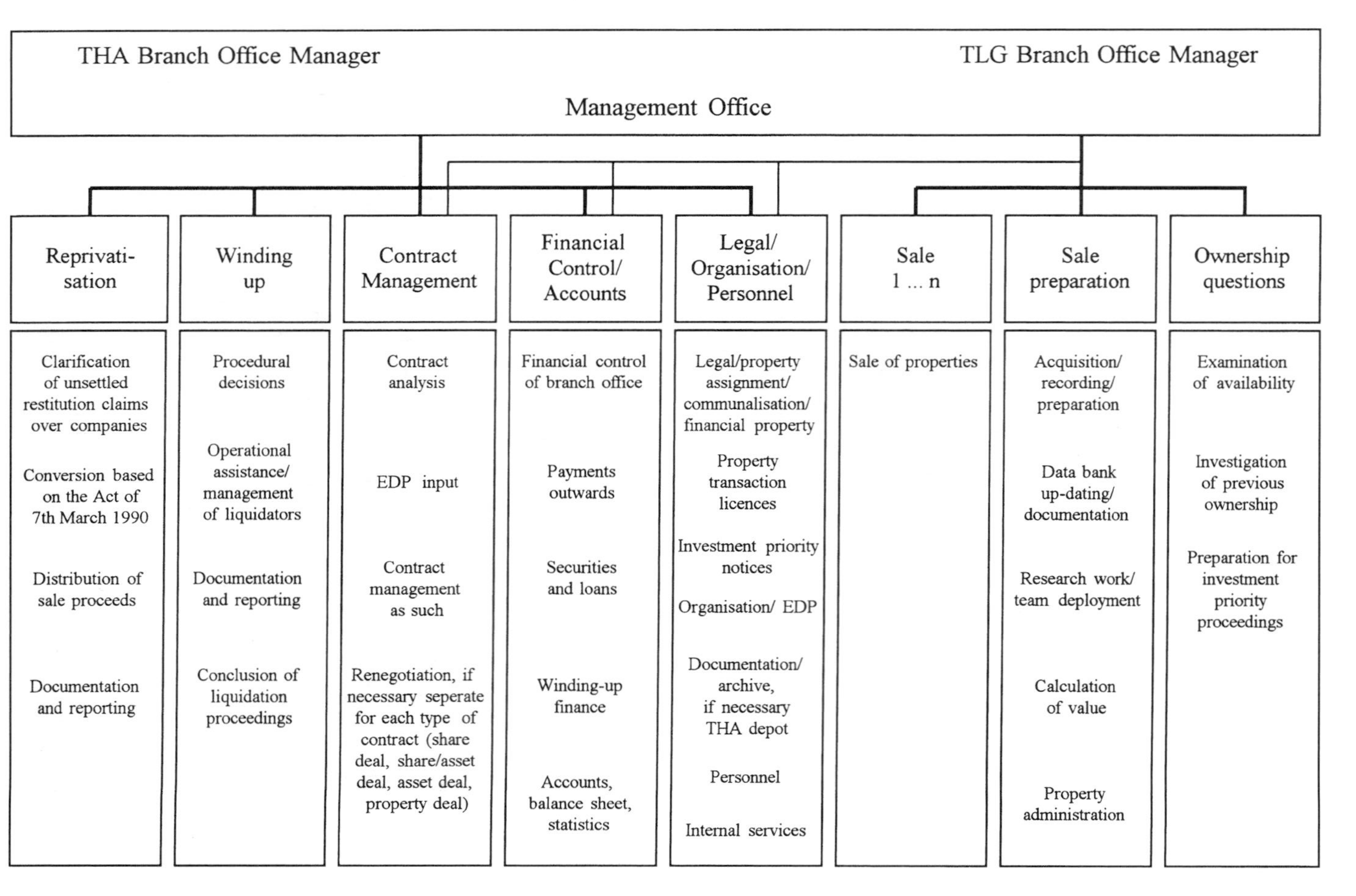

Figure 7 Organisational integration of Contract Management into joint THA/TLG branch offices

The organisational changes in the middle of 1993 also meant a new division of contract management responsibilities between the Central Office and the branches or branch offices, and placed operational responsibility for the branches and branch offices in each State with the relevant Corporate Division. In future, the only contracts to be managed directly from the Central Office will be:[65]

- those containing an undertaking to provide at least 500 jobs,
- those where the historic environmental pollution risk is at least DM 5 million, and
- those in which the company sold has a structure covering more than one region.

If any one investor has acquired more than one property from the THA, the relevant contracts will also be administered by the Central Office. On the basis of the new lines of responsibility, contract management will in future be extensively decentralised and handled by the branches/branch offices. Only a small proportion of them will then remain in the Central Office's sphere of responsibility.[66]

c) EDP-assisted information system for contract management

In order to make the mass of information contained in this multitude of contracts more transparent for decision-making, an EDP-assisted information system has been installed at the THA Central Office. This data bank is based on, and contains, all the privatisation contracts concluded by the THA. The relevant contract data is recorded on a decentralised basis by the Contract Managers at the Central Office or in the branches. A standardised mask allows up to 300 individual items of data to be inputted for each contract. The system serves the Contract Managers as an aid to ensuring that all obligations and rights given to the THA and the contractual partner by the various contracts are safeguarded and fulfilled. In addition to this, it can be used as the data basis for processes further down the line in the THA's accounting and financial areas.[67] In order to be able to manage and monitor the progress of contract management work, the system provides a number of standardised evaluation tables and statistics and makes cogent information available to those who have to make the decisions. For reasons connected with the data protection law, access is granted on a very restrictive basis and at the *Referent* (executive) level and in the department that needs the information.

For many Contract Managers, the recording of the information presents a problem, as can be seen by the unexpectedly demanding level at which the staff assess this task.[68] Despite the high degree of standardisation, not all contracts can be fitted into the pre-determined framework, resulting in the suitability of the data material for central evaluation often being called into question. In addition to this, the constant up-dating of the input masks is making the production of reliable chronological analyses very difficult. As a period of several weeks can elapse from the notarisation of a contract to its approval for use in the system, the reports cannot be guaranteed to be totally up to date. One indicator of the acceptance of the system (or lack of it) is the number of "insular" systems running parallel to the central data bank. In addition to the central compilation of contract data, many employees have set up a data bank on their own PC's because initially the central information system was not accessible and could not meet all information requirements.

---

65 See: Treuhandanstalt, *Organisationsprojekt Treuhand,* page 15.

66 Source: Contract data-bank.

67 See: Treuhandanstalt, *Vertragsabwicklung Benutzerhinweise,* November 1992 version, page 1.

68 Own surveys, as of 31st December 1992.

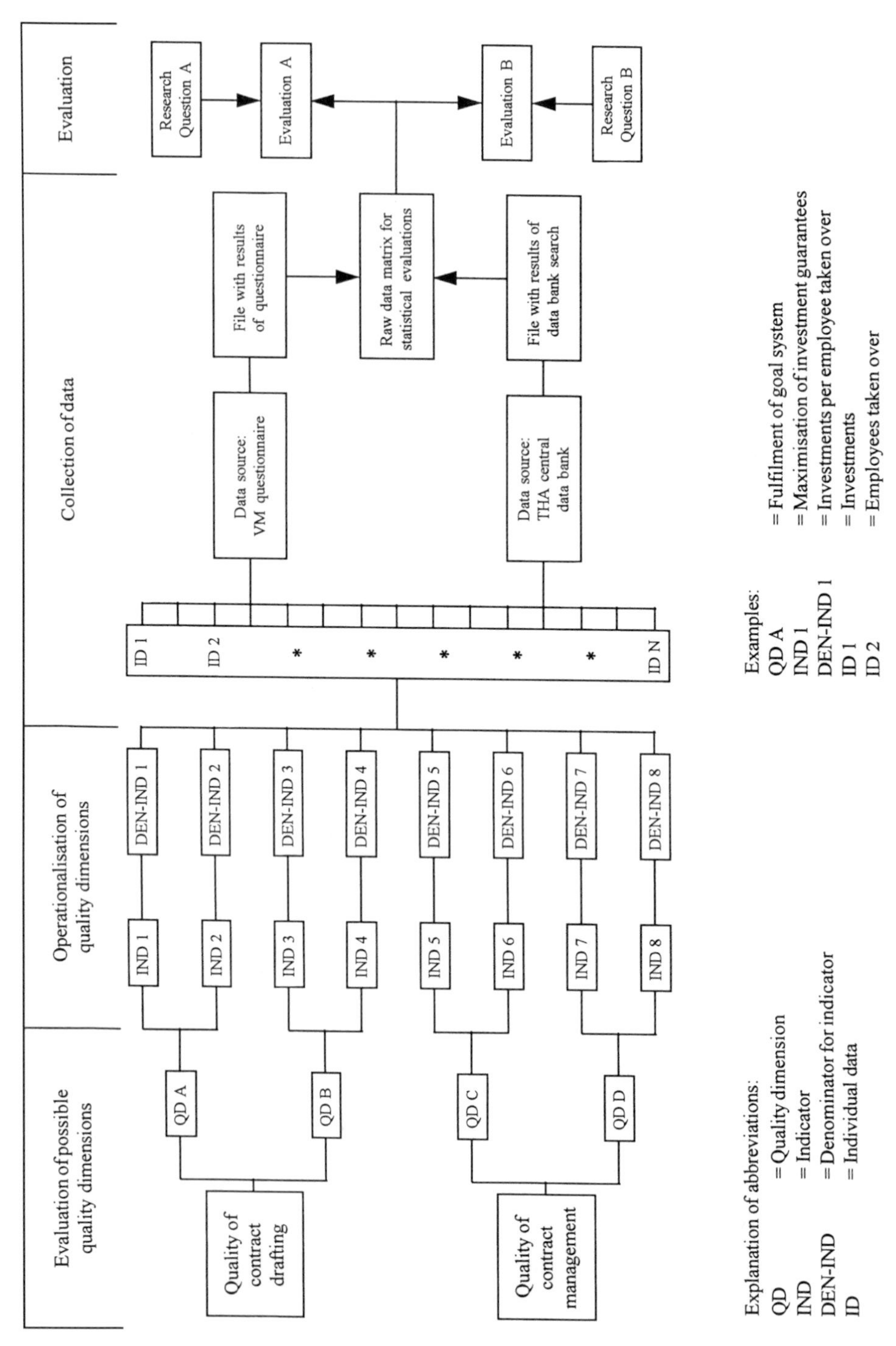

Figure 8 Research concept

IV. Initial considerations for an efficiency analysis of contract drafting and contract management

1. Basic concept of an efficiency analysis of contract drafting and contract management

It is necessary to ask which factors determine the quality of the drafting of a contract and what effect this potential influence has on the quality of contract management.

To answer these points, an empirical survey was carried out, the evaluation of which was based on the research concept shown in Fig. 8. The quality dimensions to be judged have to be evaluated against a number of different characteristics pertaining to contract drafting and contract management which can be measured against a number of indicators. These indicators relate to individual data stored in the THA central data bank or which were collected via a special questionnaire. It thus proved possible to analyse and quantify the influential factors by statistical evaluation.

2. Evaluation of possible quality dimensions

Because of the great diversity of requirements placed on contract drafting and contract management, a number of quality dimensions have to be differentiated from one another. Each of these only cover a certain aspect of the whole. Therefore the formation of any one individual dimension does not permit any valid conclusions to be drawn as to the quality of the contract or of contract management.

The most important quality dimensions for contract drafting are shown in Fig. 9: the fulfilment of the goal system, the limitation of valuation risk, securing the goal system, and the standardisation of contracts. The rapid recording and processing of contracts are the two quality dimensions for contract management.

3. Operationalisation of individual quality dimensions

In the following section a number of indicators are derived and formed by means of background hypotheses on the relevant quality dimensions. The latter define the direction of the relationship

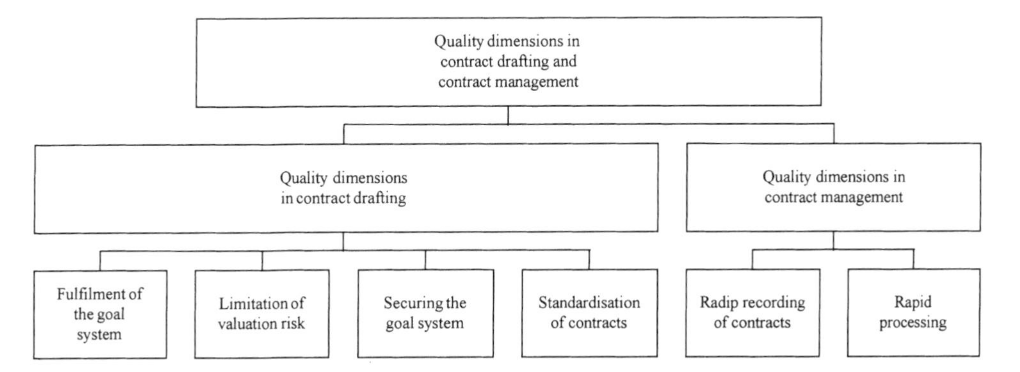

Figure 9 Quality dimensions in contract drafting and contract management

between the indicator and the quality dimensions. A denominator is allocated to each indicator to show the possible value of the indicator.

As shown in Section II.1.a, the THA's goal system embraces guarantees on investment and employment as well as proceeds from sales. The valuation risk can be limited by imposing a revaluation and/or extra proceeds resale clause. Penalties relating to employment and investment were imposed to secure the goals system. The standardisation of the contracts can be expressed in terms of the fulfilment of privatisation specifications. Contract management can be assessed approximately on the basis of the time taken to record contracts and the intensity of contacts.

In the first four dimensions, a higher value of the relevant indicator leads to a quality improvement, but the reverse is the case for the two last ones. Specific details of the denominators can be seen in Fig. 10.

4. Organisation of the data retrieval

The scope of the investigation covered all contracts concluded by the Central Office and the branches up to 31st December 1992. The total therefore comprised 11,043 contracts.[69] Questionnaire VM was first sent to all contract management departments and all branches. A

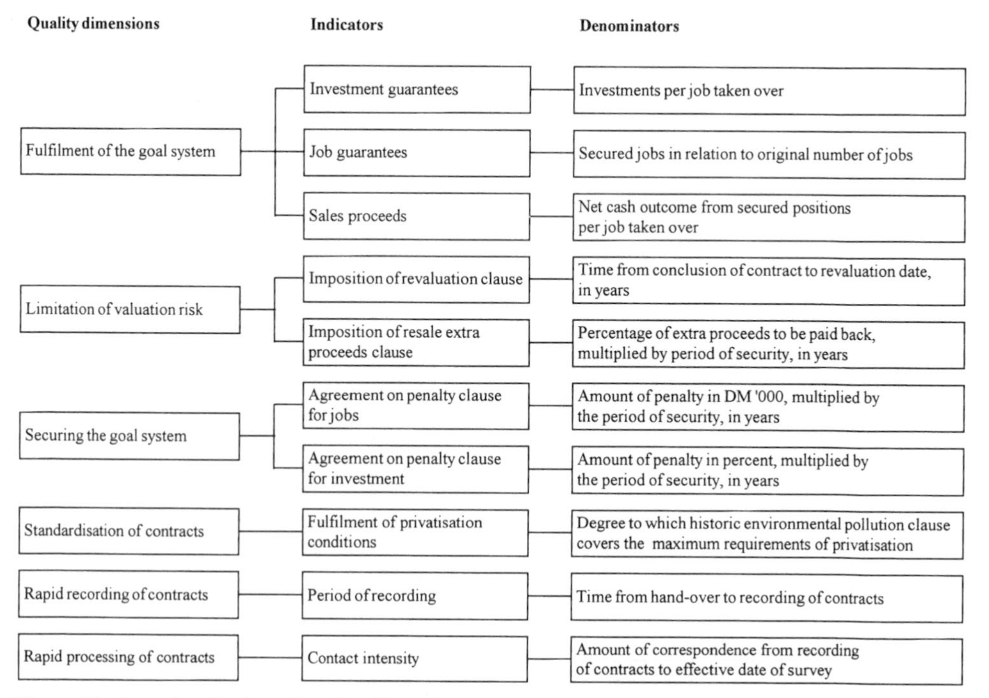

Figure 10 Operationalisation of quality dimensions

69 See: Treuhandanstalt, *Monatsinformation der THA* as of 31st December 1992, page 6.

maximum of 40 contracts was covered in each department or branch. One questionnaire was filled up for each contract included in the sample. This resulted in 312 contracts being suitable for evaluation and included in the survey, equal to a sampling rate of 3%.

5. Results of the statistical evaluation of the data

To produce an analysis of the empirical connections, the indicators relating to the denominators defined in Fig. 10 were calculated for each contract and compressed into the corresponding quality dimensions.

For each quality dimension, the average and the maximum value were calculated for each empirical value. The criterion for measuring the extent to which the goal had been attained was the maximum value for each quality dimension, which was given a value of 1. The "average degree of attainment per quality dimension" can be calculated from the relationship of the averages to the maximum figures. This represents a measure for the efficiency of contract drafting and contract management.

In Fig. 11, the horizontal axis represents the quality dimensions and the vertical axis the degree to which each goal was reached.

It can be seen from Fig. 11 that the degree of goal attainment was higher in those quality dimensions which were not affected by potential outside influence.[70] These include the standardisation of the contracts, the rapid recording of contracts, and the rapid processing of them. In the quality dimensions determined by external factors, the limitation of the valuation risk shows the highest degree of goal attainment.

The next step investigates the deviations between:
- contracts made in the branches and those from the Central Office,
- asset deals and share deals,
- "normal" contracts and MBO contracts, and between
- contracts where no renegotiation was necessary and those where it was

in terms of the evaluated quality dimensions.

In Figs. 12 to 15 the quality differences resulting from a splitting-up of the quality dimensions in the subgroups (i. e. Central Office versus Branches) are given as positive or negative deviations from the average values of Fig. 11. Positive deviations mean an above-average value of the quality dimension in the relevant subgroup; negative deviations point to a below average value of the quality dimension.

In Figs. 11 to 15, the horizontal axis shows always the quality dimensions and the vertical axis the positive/negative deviations from the average.[71]

The branches were better able to meet the requirements of the THA's goal system than the Central Office (Fig. 12). On the other hand, the Central Office contracts are characterised by a greater limitation of the valuation risk, more success in following the goal system, and a higher degree of standardisation. At the Central Office the contracts were recorded more quickly but took longer to process than in the branches.

---

70 In the sale negotiations the investors can exert direct influence on the first three quality dimensions.

71 Mathematical smoothing (standardisation) was used to bring the average value on each quality dimension to zero.

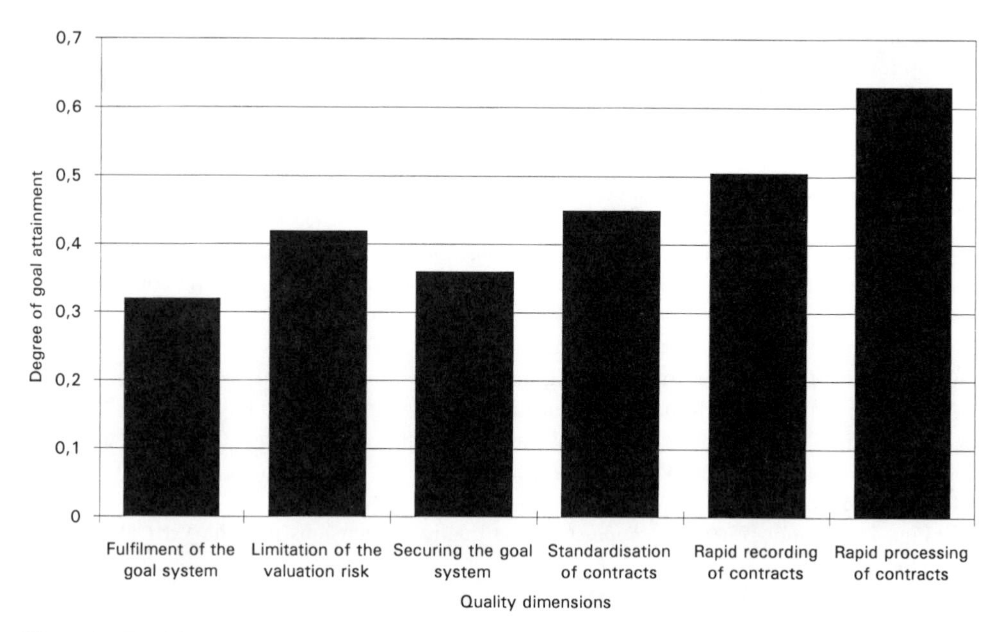

Figure 11 Empirical values for the individual quality dimensions

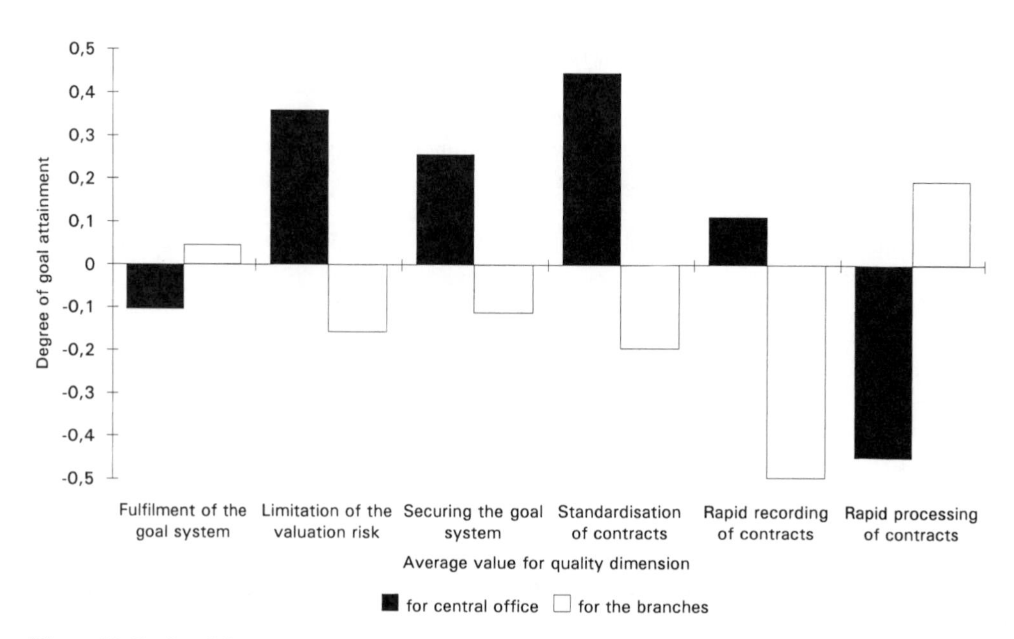

Figure 12 Quality differences between contracts made by the Central Office and those from the branches

Notes to Fig. 12:
The statistically significant differences between the group averages of the quality dimensions are:
– Limitation of valuation risk (r = 0.017)
– Standardisation of contracts (= 0.000)
– Rapid processing of contracts (= 0.000)

The low level of investors' willingness to take on risk in asset deals was compensated for by the THA achieving a better degree of fulfilment of the goal system (Fig. 13). Account is taken of the speculative aspect of the asset deals by a more restrictive limitation of the valuation risk. On the other hand, concessions were made regarding the securing of the goal system. As asset deals are less standardised than the sale of whole companies, it was possible to process them more quickly. The share deals appear to be accorded more importance, as they are given preference in the recording stage.

MBO contracts clearly show the THA's willingness to compromise when the company is being sold to its eastern German managers (Fig. 14). All quality dimensions are less restrictive from the THA's point of view with MBO's than with "normal" contracts. But the MBO contracts are recorded more slowly and processed more quickly than the "normal" contracts. This could be attributable to the relatively minor significance of the MBO's for employment and structural policy.

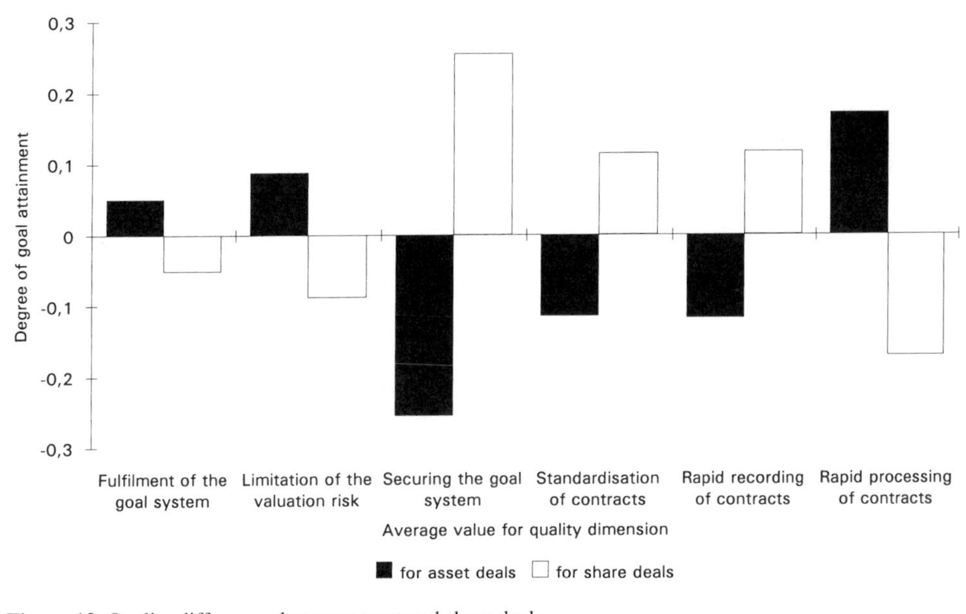

Figure 13 Quality differences between asset and share deals

Notes: The statistically significant differences between the group averages of the quality dimensions are:
– Securing the target concept ($\alpha = 0.010$)
– Standardisation of contracts ($\alpha = 0.042$)
– Rapid recording of contracts ($\alpha = 0.037$)
– Rapid processing of contracts ($\alpha = 0.002$)

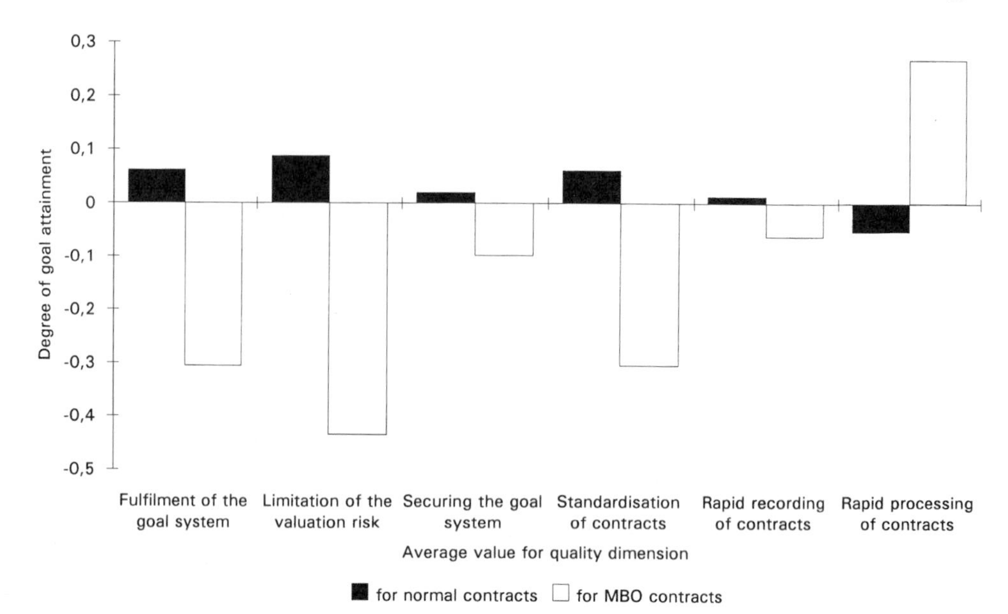

Figure 14 Quality differences between „normal“ contracts and MBO contracts

Nortes: The statistically significant differences between the group averages of the quality dimensions are:

- Securing the target concept ($\alpha = 0.000$)
- Limitation of valuation risk ($\alpha = 0.005$)
- Standardisation of contracts ($\alpha = 0.003$)
- Rapid processing of contracts ($\alpha = 0.013$)

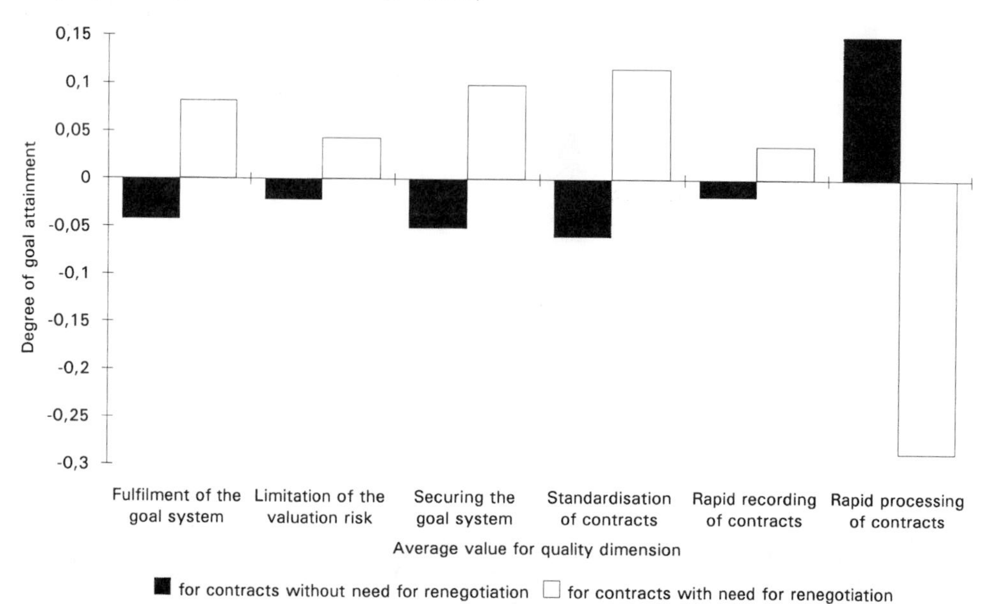

Figure 15 Quality differences between contracts with need and without need for renegotiation

Notes to Fig. 15: The statistically significant differences between the group averages of the quality dimensions are:
– Rapid processing of contracts ($\alpha = 0.003$)

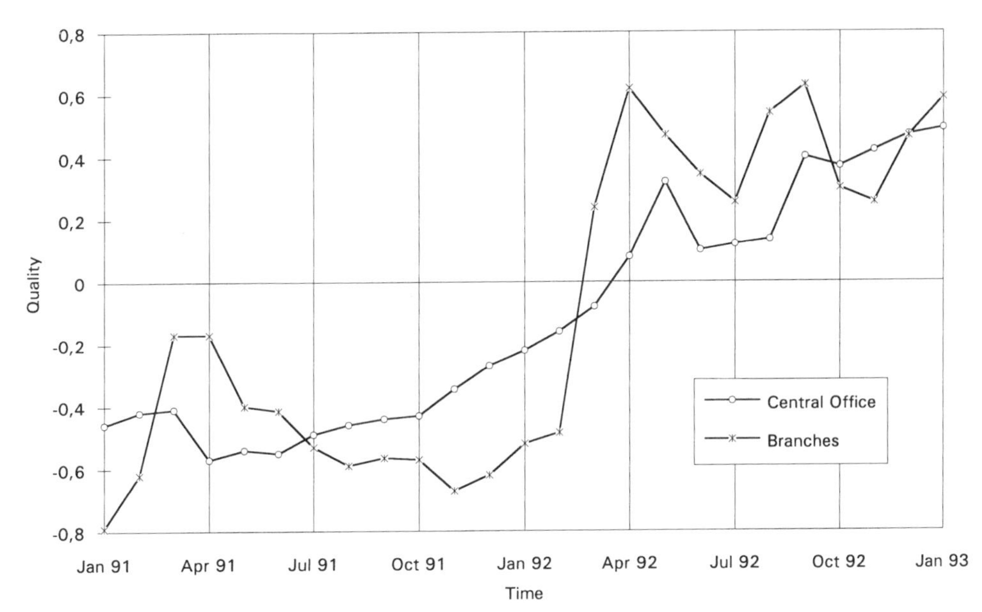

Figure 16 Trend over time in the quality of contract drafting in the THA Central Office and the branches

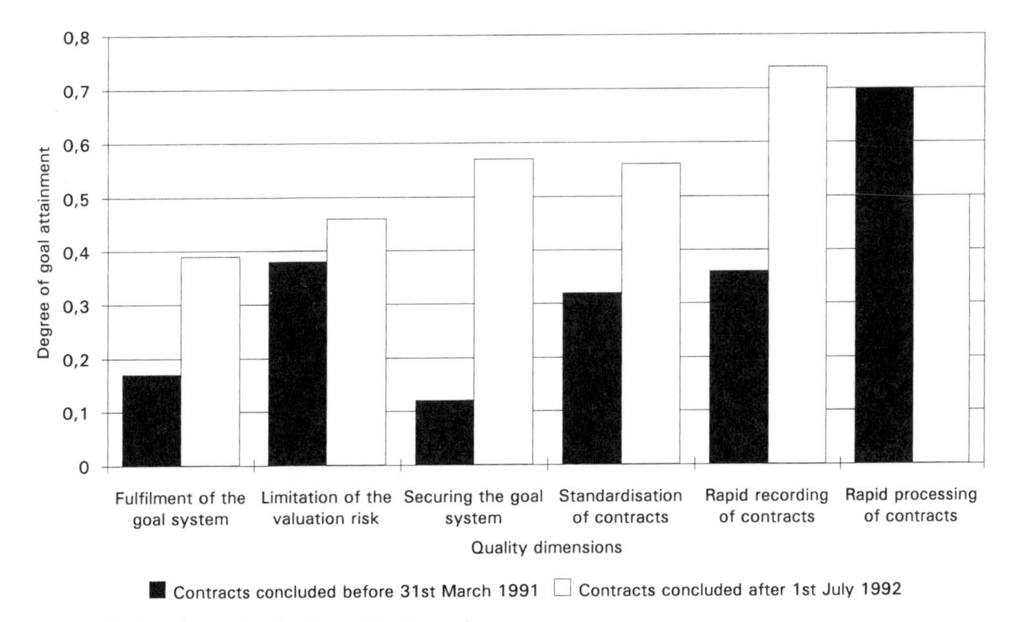

Figure 17 Trend over time in the quality dimensions

Table 3:
Correlation matrix of individual quality dimensions

	Fulfilment of goal system	Limitation of valuation risk	Securing the goal system	Standardisation of contracts	Rapid recording of contracts	Rapid processing of contracts
Fulfilment of goal system	1.0000	+	+**	+	+	–
Limitation of valuation risk	0.157	1.0000	+	+**	+	–
Securing the goal system	0.1846**	0.0664	1.0000	+**	+	–
Standardisation of contracts	0.0653	0.2826**	0.2686**	1.0000	+	–**
Rapid recording of contracts	0.0760	0.0156	0.0558	0.1119	1.0000	–
Rapid processing of contracts	–0.0736	–0.0016	–0.0983	–0.2368	–0.1252	1.0000

Explanation: The co-efficient of correlation (r) measures both the direction and the degree of correlation between two variables. It can accept all values from –1 to +1 ($-1 \leq r \leq +1$). In the event of $r = 0$, the variables do not correlate (there is no statistical connection between them).
+/–: There is a positive or negative correlation between the two quality dimensions.
**: This co-efficient of correlation is statistically significant (significance level = 0.001).

It can be seen from Fig. 15 that the increased need for renegotiation resulted from a more restrictive contract policy. For each quality dimension, the averages in the group of contracts which did need renegotiating were greater than in the control group which did not. As renegotiations are opened relatively soon after the contract is concluded, these contracts were recorded as soon as possible. The areas of disagreement between the contracting parties mean that rapid processing is not possible.

The graphs in Fig. 16 show the trend in the quality of contracts[72] broken down into Central Office and branches.

During the course of the privatisation activities, as Fig. 16 demonstrates, the quality of the contracts has improved steadily. While the trend in the Central Office contracts was fairly consistent,[73] the quality curve for the branches displays large fluctuations. These might possibly be attributable to the decentralised system for contract drafting in the 15 different branches. The clear improvement in the quality of the branches' contracts in the spring of 1992 can be attributed to the deployment of a "task force", in connection with which work was intensified on updating the central data bank.

72 The quality of the contract drafting was expressed by a linear combination of the quality dimensions in contract drafting.

73 One indicator for this is the variance of the chronological sequence. This is $\sigma^2 = 0.137$, which is almost half the size of the comparable value for the branches, where it is $\sigma^2 = 0.251$.

A similar analysis is shown in Fig. 17 regarding the trend over time in the individual quality dimensions, divided into the contracts concluded up to 31st March 1991 and those concluded from 1st July 1992 onwards.

A clear improvement can be seen in all the quality dimensions, with the sole exception of "Rapid processing of contracts". The slower processing of contracts of a more recent date can presumably be attributed to the more intensive contract management which was made possible by the increase in staff numbers.

The question finally needs to be examined as to the extent to which the various quality dimensions have any connection with one another. The correlation analysis shown in Table 3 indicates that there are statistically significant positive correlations between the following pairs: securing the goal system/fulfilment of the goal system; standardisation of contracts/limitation of the valuation risk; and standardisation of contracts/securing the goal system. A statistically significant negative correlation was discovered between rapid processing of contracts and standardisation of contracts.

V. Literature

Dornberger, Gerhard, and Ute *Dornberger:* Zum zweiten Vermögensrechtsänderungsgesetz. In: *Der Betrieb* 32 (1992), pages 1613 to 1614.

Kilgert, Theodor, and Phillipp *Großmann:* Notwendigkeit und Grenzen der Bilanzänderung nach § 36 DMBilG. In: *Die Wirtschaftsprüfung* 17, pages 497 et seq.

Peemöller, Volker, and Tobias *Hüttche:* Zum Informationsgehalt von D-Markeröffnungsbilanz und Folgeabschlüssen. In: *Die Wirtschaftsprüfung* 8 (1992), pages 209 to 221.

Sieben, Günter: Zur Wertfindung bei der Privatisierung von Unternehmen in den neuen Bundesländern durch die Treuhandanstalt. In: *Der Betrieb* 41 (1992) pages 2041 to 2051.

Sinn, Gerlinde, and Hans-Werner *Sinn: Kaltstart. Volkswirtschaftliche Aspekte der deutschen Vereinigung.* Tübingen 1991.

Treuhandanstalt: *Monatsinformation,* various months.

Treuhandanstalt Informationen 6 (October 1991).

Wächter, Gerd, Thomas *Kaiser,* and Michael *Krause:* Klauseln in Unternehmenskaufverträgen mit der THA. In: *Wertpapiermitteilungen* 8 (1992), page 298.

Part C

The effects of the Treuhand's work

The public image of the THA

by Hans Mathias Kepplinger, with the assistance of Christian Kolmer

I. Introduction

The THA finds itself at the intersection of a number of different interests, which can be described as lying along two axes. The tips of one of these axes represent the parties with whom the THA does business and those affected by its work in the widest sense of the term: the former owners of THA assets, the purchasers and new owners, the employees of all the companies affected, and their social environment. The tips of the other axis are formed by state organisations and individual citizens – the governments, parliaments, and courts involved – and the mass of the population not directly involved. These various protagonists and observers do not necessary all have the same view-point, and do not necessarily all act in accordance with the same maxims. Thus in many cases the investors and the workers in eastern Germany may have totally opposing interests, in the short term at least, the investors, for instance, may be interested in job cuts, the workers in job preservation. Even if their interests converge in the long term, they will possibly tend to judge the necessary activities by differing criteria, one group on the basis of economic requirements, the other on the basis of their welfare expectations. The result will be conflicts between those involved, sometimes massive ones, over the decisions that need making, and these will sometimes flood out over the public at large.

By far the largest proportion of the population only knows about the THA's work from reports in the press, radio, and television, or from what their friends tell them, and this in turn largely comes from the mass media. This makes the mass media, so to speak, the "hinge" between the THA's work and the population's point of view. The media include a number of specialist publications intended for readers with a more than average knowledge of and interest in economics, as well as those aimed at a broad audience to whom this does not apply. The question thus arises as to the point of view from which the media present the THA's work and the criteria for judgement which they infer in doing so. Is it the customers' point of view that dominates, or that of the people affected? Are the problems evaluated from an economic or a social point of view?[1]

The following study examines, on the basis of typical examples, the subjects and trends in the way the THA is described in newspapers and magazines. This is based, on the one hand, on three case studies which look at particularly striking THA activities, and on the other on a systematic analysis of the contents of reports on the important THA activities from 1st October 1990 to 30th September 1992. In parallel with this, and for the same period of time, the enquiries re-

---

1 On this aspect, see: Heinrich, *Forschungsstand Wirtschaftsjournalismus im deutschsprachigen Raum*; Kalt (editor), *Wirtschaft in den Medien*; Deetjen, *Industriellenprofile in Massenmedien*; Sondergeld, *Die Wirtschafts- und Sozialberichterstattung in den Fernsehnachrichten*; Klaue (editor), *Marktwirtschaft in der Medienberichterstattung*; Schröter, *Mitteilungs-Adäquanz*; ditto, *Qualität im Journalismus*; Friedrichsen, *Wirtschaft im Fernsehen*; Ruß-Mohl and Stuckmann (editors), *Wirtschaftsjournalismus*.

ceived by the THA's "Citizens' Telephone" service are analysed; the reasons which caused people to use it were many and varied, and can be taken as an indicator of the interests and problems of those people who were theoretically or practically affected by the THA's work.

The aim of this investigation is to answer the following questions:

1. How did newspapers and magazines present the liquidation, restructuring, and privatisation of three major companies?
2. Which subjects formed the focal point of reporting on the THA's activities?
3. How was the THA's work evaluated?
4. What points did the reports in the various newspapers and magazines have in common and what were the differences between them?
5. Which questions formed the focal point of the telephone enquiries received by the THA?
6. What points did the questions raised by callers ringing the THA have in common with the presentation of the priorities of its work and what were the differences between them?

II. The press response obtained by the THA

1. Qualitative analyses: case studies of liquidation, restructuring, and privatisation

The decision of the GDR government to entrust a state agency with the privatisation of the state-owned companies was based primarily on macro-economic considerations because the creation of private ownership was a pre-requirement for the establishment of a market economy. The THA's operational work, on the other hand, was far more determined by the considerations of business management. The THA had to decide from one case to the next whether and to whom a company was to be sold, whether financial resources were to be made available for any preceding restructuring, or whether the company was to be closed down. In this process the THA was exposed to influences of divergent interests, so that privatisation efforts could become the object of violent conflicts.

Three examples have been examined in order to show how the image of the THA was dominated by the way privatisation activities were presented in the press. Companies have been selected for this investigation which drew particular press attention to themselves because of the tradition behind them or because of their importance for the regional economic structure. A further criterion was that in each case the decision on privatisation, restructuring, or liquidation was a controversial one.

a) Liquidation (Robotron)

In the GDR, the *Robotron Kombinat* had been the sole manufacturer of micro-electronic devices such as personal computers. The largest part of its production, between about 35 and 40%, was exported to the COMECON countries. In 1989, the parent Robotron works in Sömmerda had had 13,800 employees, and in the autumn of 1990 there were still 11,000 of them left. Whilst Robotron's management believed, during the first months following monetary union in July 1990, that it could maintain the level of its exports to the Soviet Union, by the spring of 1991 the deterioration in the company's situation could no longer be ignored. At the end of July 1991 the THA decided to close the works down at the end of the year, and the last Robotron computer came off the assembly line on 5th December 1991.

A total of 208 articles on the development of Robotron between 24th December 1989 and 4th February 1993 are documented in the THA press archive. It is possible to identify three phases in these reports. The first ran from December 1989 to June 1991, when the press mainly reported on events in Robotron from the business economics point of view. The western German press, in particular, concerned itself with the company's market opportunities, possible joint ventures with western German companies, and Robotron's balance sheet, published in March 1991. The only paper to bring up any other point of view was an article in *Neues Deutschland* (an eastern German daily, once the official organ of the Party) on 12th February 1991 which bore the headline "For the lion now the coup de grâce?" and reported on a demonstration by the work-force in Erfurt.

The second phase ran from June 1991, when the subjects of imminent liquidation and mass redundancies started to be reported on, until the end of 1991. During this period of time the eastern German press gave Robotron more coverage than the western did, and the substance of the reports differed between east and west as well; more western German papers were concerned with the economic factors that had caused the redundancies and the closure of Robotron, whilst the eastern German papers, such as *Neues Deutschland*, *Tribüne*, and *Junge Welt*, as well as *Frankfurter Rundschau* (Frankfurt am Main) and the *tageszeitung* (Berlin), devoted more space to the unfavourable consequences of liquidation for the Robotron employees and the protests of the work-force against the THA and the company's management.

In September 1991 press reports were dominated by the demonstrations by Robotron employees in Berlin and Erfurt. The western German newspapers described these protests against the background of the desperate economic situation in which the company found itself, and treated it as a matter of peripheral importance. These reports did not present the THA as the party responsible for the closure of the works, but *Neues Deutschland*, *Tribüne*, and *Junge Welt* placed the full responsibility on the THA for the unfavourable consequences for the work-force and for the whole region. Criticism of the THA reached a climax with an article in *Junge Welt* on 25th October 1991 which accused the THA of deliberately destroying Robotron: the THA, the paper asserted, had closed the company down at the behest of western competitors and was now going to slice the "juiciest bits" out of it and toss them to companies in the west.

Eastern German newspapers and papers covering the whole region around Berlin mainly presented the arguments relating to social policy in favour of preventing mass unemployment. One member of the THA Executive Board, Mr Klinz, on the other hand, justified the authority's decision in an interview published in a leading western German daily newspaper, *Die Welt*, on 21st September 1991, with the business economics arguments; he said there had been no alternative but to close down this "mortally ill" company. Arguments in favour of preserving the works on account of its importance to the eastern German national economy, however, only appeared rarely in the press. The role of Robotron in the regional economic structure, and the danger for the eastern German work-force losing valuable skills, were mentioned in this context; one example was a commentary in the *Berliner Zeitung* of 5th September 1991, in which the author calls for Robotron to be kept in being in order to keep down the costs of re-entry into "the hi-tech field". In September, the press also reported in connection with Robotron on demands from the trade unions and the SPD opposition party (in the Federal government) for an "active structural policy". Taking up Robotron as an example, the SPD party manager Mr Blessing was reported in the Frankfurter Rundschau of 19th September as demanding that the THA should devote more effort to the restructuring of eastern German companies.

In the third phase, after the closure of the office equipment works and the heavy reporting on the protest demonstrations, the press returned with more concentration on the business-economic factors. Only one fifth of the reports covered protests against the THA. The regional press in Saxony dealt intensively with the fate of other Robotron subsidiaries, many of which were threatened with closure, even giving detailed coverage to the fate awaiting insignificant companies with few employees. The role of the THA is presented in negative terms in all these reports. Any positive developments, such as the privatisation of the Robotron subsidiary Comped in January 1993, were mainly covered by the western German press. But these events were not attributed to the THA's efforts, in contrast to the negative developments. The press devoted its praise to the investors, some of whom were given extensive editorial coverage.

b) Restructuring (Orwo)

Orwo is the brand name for products from the photographic film factory of Wolfen. Until 1990 this well-known photo-chemical company from the region in which many chemical companies are concentrated, around Halle, Bitterfeld, and Wolfen, used to employ 15,000 people. The *Wolfen Kombinat*, until 1945 one of the locations of the giant chemical concern IG Farben, used to produce viscose fibres and spun rayon, but in the THA's view it was only the photographic film production division that was capable of being restructured. It made DM 80 million available for this purpose in March 1992. The main obstacle to privatisation was the rectification of enormous environmental damage which no investor was willing to pay for.

The period under examination runs from 24th June 1991 to 6th December 1992. The reporting on Orwo mainly took the business-economics approach. The company manufactured competitive products, and accordingly almost one third of the articles examined dealt with the company's products such as a new colour film which was launched onto the market in 1991. The main element in these reports was the restructuring strategy and its implementation in the photographic factory. After the THA had declared the company capable of being restructured, the factory made 7,200 employees redundant in September 1991. Only eastern German newspapers reported on these redundancies, but without passing any judgement. However, *Junge Welt* published a report on 27th September 1991 that Orwo films would disappear from the market, and on the same day *Neues Deutschland* quoted the deputy chairman of the PDS (the successor-party to the once all-dominant SED) as saying that he suspected the influence of Orwo's western German competitors behind this decision. Although the THA was mentioned in these reports, nothing negative was held against it.

From February to August 1992 the press mainly covered the THA's decision-making process in restructuring the photographic film company. The nation-wide press described the various retructuring strategies and the one which the THA favoured, centring on the company's conversion into a property administration company for plots of land, some of which impossible to sell, and an entirely separate company for the production of photographic materials. These reports focused mainly on the company's potential for further development and sales, with the THA's activities only ever mentioned in passing. It was only the western German financial paper *Handelsblatt* that reported, on 12th March, on the extensive financial support the THA was giving to the company as the main part of an article on the THA's approval of the restructuring plan.

During this period of time, the press and in particularly the Saxon press gave plenty of space to the accusations made by Orwo's works council against the THA, principally that the THA was deliberately delaying reaching a final decision on the company, and also that the THA had given Orwo's competitors access to its customer lists during the course of sale negotiations. When the THA confirmed in May that the company was to be restructured, the eastern German press in particular represented this as a victory by the work-force over the authorities.

During the last half year of the period of time under investigation, press reports concentrated mostly on Orwo's new products and its sales potential. In September 1992, on the occasion of the *"Photokina"* trade exhibition, six articles appeared in eastern and western German papers contrasting the positive picture now presented by the company for itself and its products with the negative attitude of the THA. Junge Welt, for instance, in its report on the *"Photokina"* on 19th September 1992, mentioned the views voiced by the company's management which criticised the THA for lack of public support, but the THA was hardly mentioned at all in the other articles. Orwo was presented in most of the regional eastern German press and the nation-wide press as an independent company whose success in foreign markets was due solely to its own efforts.

c) Privatisation (Sächsische Edelstahlwerke Freital)

This company used to be the GDR's main supplier of speciality steels, and nine tenths of its output went to eastern German automotive manufacturers. After monetary union, therefore, the company was faced by serious difficulties. In March 1992 the THA announced that it had not proved possible to draw up a workable privatisation strategy for the steel works but that it hoped to be able to sell off individual parts of the business. The work-force fought against this decision, with sit-ins in September 1992 and a blockade of Dresden Airport, and succeeded in obtaining the support of Kurt Biedenkopf, the Minister-President of Saxony, for their cause. The THA backed down from its decision to liquidate, and at the end of 1992 approved the sale of the company to a medium-sized western German company.

Reporting on the high-grade steel factory was dominated by the work-force's protest demonstrations. The period of time under examination runs from 28th May 1991 to 18th January 1993, but the actual time of these upheavals was only from 22nd March to 2nd October 1992. 158 out of the total number of documented articles, 168, appeared during this phase, and only one in the whole of 1990 and 1991 which only mentioned the steel works in passing. The main item in all these reports was the sit-in at the airport, mentioned in 41 of them.

During the period from March 1992, when the *Neue Zeit* reported on the THA's intention of closing the works, to the airport sit-in in September 1992, the press reported on events in Freital mainly in terms of a conflict between the work-force and the THA. Semi-national eastern German newspapers, and the regional press in Saxony, reported extensively in April 1992 on the works sit-in with which the work-force demonstrated for the continued operation of their works. In western Germany it was the *Frankfurter Rundschau* that picked the subject up, whereas the *Handelsblatt* ran a story on the THA's decision to postpone liquidation without even mentioning the sit-in.

The climax of the conflict between the THA and the steel workers was reached in September 1992. As a reaction to the THA's decision to close the works, the Freital work-force staged a sit-in lasting several hours at Dresden Airport on 16th September 1992. This was reported on widely in the press. Newspapers like *Bild*, a leading popular national daily, and the *Dresdner Morgenpost* started with the airport sit-in and then went on to report in detail on the blockade with background information. The sit-in gained particular significance because the Minister-President, Mr Biedenkopf, "just happened" to be there at the time. 12 of the 41 articles, mainly those in the local Dresden papers, but also in *Bild*, centred their reports on Mr Biedenkopf's speech to the demonstrators. According to the version in the Dresdner Morgenpost, Mr Biedenkopf made serious allegations against the THA and promised the steel workers that Freital would be saved.

According to *Junge Welt* on 17th September, his accusations against the THA culminated in the words that the closure decision was an insult to all intelligent people. The THA reacted the next day by cancelling its closure decision.

A second main theme in the reporting on Freital was the description of the conflict between the THA and the State government of Saxony over the start-up capital for restructuring the steel works. In a special article in the *Leipziger Volkszeitung* on 26th September, Mr Biedenkopf called for the THA to be taken out of the area of responsibility of the Minister for Economic Affairs and to be given the job of modernising "companies vital to the economic structure". He at the same time made an attempt at "reconciliation" with the THA by warning against the dangers of making sweeping accusations against it.

The popular press, and the eastern German regional press, presented the THA as the antagonist of the steel workers. Its closure policy was described as the cause of the crisis in the high-grade steel company. One example is the headline in *Bild* on 8th September: "THA intends to roll Freital steel works flat". Economic arguments were pushed into the background, and were replaced in *Bild*, *Neues Deutschland*, and the regional press in Saxony with the accusation that the THA was exterminating the eastern German steel industry on the orders of the western German steel concerns. On 10th September the *Dresdner Morgenpost* raised the question, "High-grade steel from Freital – thrashed by its western competitors?"

The argument over start-up capital dragged out for a further month. Only the leading western German national daily, the *Frankfurter Allgemeine Zeitung*, and *Neue Zeit*, reported that the State of Saxony had declared its willingness to shoulder the financial burden. Since the end of this controversy, the Freital region has vanished from press reports. Although the steelworks was privatised on 1st January 1993, the only report was in the regional *Sächsische Zeitung* of 18th January on the company's general economic situation.

After the THA had climbed down from its liquidation decision, a more intensive discussion broke out as to the THA's actual task. The majority of newspapers in eastern and western Germany took up the arguments of the Saxon State government and the trade unions that the THA should change over to an active restructuring policy and that a state holding company for all companies capable of being restructured should be established. It was only *Die Welt* and the *Frankfurter Allgemeine Zeitung*, two leading "serious" western German dailies, as well as the business press that presented arguments against the retention of the works such as the disturbance of the market's ability to manage itself through the subsidising of unproductive companies.

One can summarise by saying that press reporting on this case of privatisation was dominated by the conflict between the work-force and the THA. Individual reports dealt primarily with the fate of the redundant workers, and their protests brought plenty of media attention. The mere fact that large numbers were being made redundant was not always presented in negative terms, and redundancies necessitated by restructuring programmes were hardly ever criticised. However, when protest did occur because eastern German companies were to be liquidated, the press always devoted plenty of space to the accusations hurled at the THA.

The role of the THA in privatisation was emphasised in the reports on individual companies mainly in connection with the less than happy events, and responsibility for them was usually placed with the THA. When more cheerful news was available, the newspapers mainly reported on the investors, restructuring strategies, products and their future prospects on the market, with the THA hardly even being mentioned. Any happy event was always attributed to someone else.

Little attention was devoted in these reports on privatisation to the economic causes of the eastern German crisis and the national economic circumstances determining the THA's scope for action. In individual cases, reports centred less on the national economic benefit of privatisation and more on the individual economic disadvantages suffered by work-forces and local communities in eastern Germany.

2. Quantitative analysis: subjects and trends of press reporting

From the 19 different publications studied (see Table 1), there is a total of 3,190 articles in the THA press archives for the period from 1st October 1990 to 30th September 1992 on the basic discussion of the nature of privatisation, the legal basis for the THA's work, the relative priorities accorded to the THA's various conflicting goals, reports on the Presidents, the structure and organisation of the THA, and the THA's sales policy. In addition to this, a further 419 articles have been collected on the eastern German economy in general in which the THA is at least mentioned. Most of these articles appeared in the national or semi-national dailies or in papers like the *Handelsblatt* which are sold mainly on subscription and delivered to readers' homes (popular papers like *Bild* are primarily sold from kiosks, and are therefore called "street" papers). However, there are major differences between these national and semi-national "subscription" papers in the intensity of their reporting. Whilst *Handelsblatt* and *Frankfurter Allgemeine Zeitung* dealt very frequently with this subject, the *Frankfurter Rundschau*, *Neues Deutschland*, and in particular *tageszeitung* only took it up relatively less often.[2]

The business press, with the exception of *Handelsblatt*, reported surprisingly little on the discussion of the stated goals and tasks of the THA and the legal basis for its work. This applies to the stock exchange paper, *Börsenzeitung*, and the business weekly *Wirtschaftswoche*, and most particularly to *Manager Magazin* and *Capital*, which dealt with this subject area less often than, for instance, *Die Zeit* or *Der Spiegel*. There are also clear differences in the importance placed on this subject by the three Berlin newspapers. *Tagesspiegel* printed a large number of articles, but the *Berliner Morgenpost* reported less often and, particularly, much shorter.

Most papers described the THA all in all in somewhat negative terms. The empirical total mean of the reports was 3.3 (the theoretical figure was 3.0). It was principally *Bild, Neues Deutschland, Der Spiegel,* the *tageszeitung*, and the *Superzeitung* that gave the THA a totally

2 A code book was developed for the quantitative analysis of press reports which basically conformed with the one developed for categorising the enquiries received on the Citizens' Telephone (see footnote 4), but in some instances covered wider fields. It was thus possible to combine the two parts of the study, and also to deal with questions not included in the Citizens' Telephone records. The press reports were collected by the THA and put into press files arranged by subject-matter which facilitated to relatively easy access to a large number of articles but did set limits to the analysis, because the filing system did not enable any statement to be made as to the total coverage given by individual publications. The selection of publications for investigation was based on two aspects: one was that they should represent various different types of newspaper and magazines, the other that they should include a certain minimum quantity of articles on the various subjects. The preliminary study enabled eight national or semi-national „subscription" newspapers to be selected for analysis (including two specialist business/financial papers) plus two „street" newspapers, three regional „subscription" newspapers, three weekly journals, and three business magazines. All articles were examined which covered the subjects defined under point II.2 and appeared between 28th November 1989 and 30th September 1992. The period of time preceding German unification was included in order to make statements possible on the earliest days of the THA, but in the interests of simplicity is not included here, particularly since the subject-matter of interest was hardly ever mentioned.

negative rating. At the other end of the scale, *Capital, Handelsblatt,* and *Wirtschaftswoche,* as well as *Frankfurter Allgemeine Zeitung* and *Die Welt* gave a more balanced picture or a slightly positive rating (Table 1).

The centre of interest in the reports under examination was the THA's sales policy, which was accounted for by 1,446 of the 3,609 articles covered. Two subjects dominated under this heading: the privatisation and the restructuring of companies. In comparison to them, reprivatisation

Table 1:
Number and length of reports recorded and general rating given to the THA

Newspapers and magazines examined	Number of articles	Length (standard lines)	Rating $\bar{x}$
Business press			
Handelsblatt	514	46,253	3.0
Börsenzeitung	76	7,725	2.9
Wirtschaftswoche	88	13,151	3.2
Capital	8	2,094	2.8
Manager Magazin	15	5,453	3.1
Total/average	701	74,676	3.0
National and semi-national subscription newspapers			
Frankfurter Allgemeine Zeitung	401	35,253	2.9
Die Welt	330	27,861	2.9
Süddeutsche Zeitung	281	27,623	3.1
Frankfurter Rundschau	249	27,691	3.3
tageszeitung (taz)	47	3,709	3.7
Neues Deutschland	293	19,133	4.0
Total/average	1,601	141,270	3.3
Weekly magazines			
Die Zeit	24	4,891	3.2
Der Spiegel	56	15,801	3.7
Stern	3	381	3.5
Total/average	83	21,073	3.5
Regional subscription newspapers			
Berliner Zeitung	352	25,369	3.3
Tagesspiegel	476	26,235	3.2
Berliner Morgenpost	348	18,615	3.1
Total/average	1,176	70,219	3.2
"Street" newspapers			
Bild	23	1,318	4.2
Superzeitung	25	741	3.4
Total/average	48	2,059	3.8
Grand total/overall average	3,609	309,297	3.3

Note: The "rating" given to the THA ranges from 1 = totally positive to 5 = totally negative.

and liquidation played a subordinate role. It is, however, necessary to put these findings into context: regardless of any specific intentions of the THA, there was a far-ranging and fundamental discussion in the press on the whole subject of privatisation. Together with the discussion of specific THA plans, the dominate theme in these reports was privatisation.

If the centres of interest are worthy of note, so also are the weak points in this reporting. Coping with historic environmental pollution, the communalisation of tangible assets, placing orders with THA companies, and a few other subjects as well received little attention in these reports. Possibly they were covered by other reports which it was not possible to pick up; the other possibility is that these subjects do not arouse much interest generally.

The THA is described in various different terms under these various headings, and in mainly positive terms in articles dealing with the basic questions of privatisation and with specific privatisation measures. The reports were nearly always negative when it came to articles on reprivatisation and the restructuring and liquidation of companies, which corroborates the results of the three case studies. The THA was also given a low rating in connection with nearly all reports on the discussion which kept flaring up on the priority of competing goals, and on the general economic situation in eastern Germany. This can be attributed, among other things, to the THA's being held at least partly responsible for the poor economic situation (Table 2).

Table 2:
Main subjects reported on and general rating given to the THA

Main subjects	Number of articles	Length (standard lines)	Rating $\bar{x}$
Basic discussion on privatisation	255	24,167	2.9
Legal basis of the THA	197	19,408	3.1
Priority of competing THA goals	163	17,026	3.4
Reports on the President of THA	62	6,327	3.0
Organisation and working methods of the THA	570	52,386	3.3
THA sales policy:			
– Reprivatisation	36	3,511	3.6
– Privatisation	837	58,198	2.9
– Restructuring	322	26,050	3.3
– Liquidation	120	8,415	3.3
– Other aspects of sales policy	131	8,408	3.1
Total/average for sales policy	1,446	104,537	3.2
Other subjects			
– Historic environmental pollution	10	851	3.0
– Employment companies	38	2,494	3.3
– Sale of special assets	54	3,375	3.4
– Communalisation	32	2,075	3.4
– Placement of orders with THA companies	9	415	2.8
– Accommodation for further vocational training	3	62	3.3
Eastern German economy in general	419	52,020	3.4
Other topics	351	39,029	3.1
Grand total/overall average	3,609	324,217	3.2

Note: The "rating" ranges from 1 = totally positive to 5 = totally negative.

Table 3:
Principle subjects of covering in publications with major or minor authority in business and economic matters (in % on the basis of n lines)

Main subjects	Business press n=79,798 in %	National "subscription" press n=145,452 in %	Weekly press n=21,181 in %	Regional "subscription" press n=74,667 in %	"Street" newspapers n=3,119 in %
Basic discussion on privatisation	9.8	6.8	7.4	6.5	3.0
Legal basis of the THA	8.4	6.1	6.0	3.3	0.9
Priority of competing goals	7.0	5.4	2.9	3.8	3.4
Reports on THA President	0.9	2.0	4.9	1.8	9.5
Organisation and working methods of the THA	12.5	17.8	28.8	12.7	30.8
THA sales policy:					
– Reprivatisation	1.3	1.1	0.9	0.8	–
– Privatisation	16.3	15.9	9.1	26.6	4.7
– Restructuring	8.8	8.2	4.1	8.3	2.9
– Liquidation	2.7	2.2	2.5	3.4	1.9
– other aspects of sales policy	2.8	2.1	1.1	4.0	1.1
Total for sales policy	31.9	29.5	17.7	43.1	10.6
Other subjects					
– Historic environmental pollution	0.5	0.2	–	0.1	–
– Employment companies	0.7	0.7	–	1.3	–
– Sale of special assets	0.1	1.1	–	2.2	4.5
– Communalisation	1.2	0.5	0.2	0.6	–
– Placement of orders with THA companies	0.1	0.1	–	0.2	–
– Accommodation for further vocational training	0.1	–	–	<0.1	–
Eastern German economy in general	14.5	18.9	21.2	10.6	14.2
Other topics	12.5	10.9	10.9	13.6	23.1
Total	100.2	100.0	100.0	99.9	100.0

The newspapers and magazines investigated deal generally with economic subjects, some more intensively than others. In addition to the business press in the narrower sense of the word, which reports principally or exclusively on this subject, there are the nation-wide and semi-national subscription newspapers with business editorial sections of great repute, weekly magazines with extensive background coverage, the regional press with regular business sections, and the "street" newspapers with more selective reports on business matters. In other words, the publications have a varying degree of specialisation, and thus a varying level of authority on the subject. This gives rise to two questions: firstly, did the specialist publications, with their greater authority, deal with the same subjects as or different subjects from those in the publications which only occasionally report on economic matters; and, secondly, was the public at large given the same picture of the

THA's work as those readers of publications which have special interests in economics and business or were they given an entirely different point of view on entirely different aspects?[3]

The answer to both questions is quite clear, as might have been assumed from the three case-studies. The publications with authority in business and economics matters featured quite different aspects of the THA from other publications. This becomes very clear when the two extremes are compared: the specialist business publications on the one hand and the "street" newspapers on the other. Thus the business publications reported far more intensively than the "street" newspapers on the basic discussion on privatisation of formerly state-owned companies, the legal basis of the THA, and the priorities accorded to its competing aims. On the other side, the "street" press reported far more intensively on the President and on the organisation and working methods of the THA. On the one hand the emphasis was on abstract principles, and on the other it was on specific people and organisations.

The regional subscription newspapers played a particular part here, as could also be sensed from the case-histories. They gave more intensive coverage than any of the other types of publication to the THA's sales policy and, within this, to privatisation in particular. This situation can probably be accounted for mainly by the fact that a relatively large number of people in these publications' circulation areas were or could have been directly affected by privatisation activities. Finally, it is noteworthy that the weekly press dealt relatively intensively with the general situation of the eastern German economy, mainly the structural problems; this is congruent with the character of the weekly press, which tends to put a number of issues together into their larger context rather than concentrate on individual events (see Table 3).

III. Comparison between the interests of callers using the "citizens' telephone" and the subjects of press coverage

After the THA had started work, it found itself inundated with telephone enquiries. The telephone exchange was able neither to connect the enquirer with the right person nor to provide the information itself. The President of the THA at that time, Detlev Rohwedder, therefore arranged for the "citizens' telephone" to be set up to be a point of contact in its own right within the THA Central Office and also to provide information directly on the various THA branches and other authorities concerned with the privatisation of formerly state-owned property in eastern Germany. The Citizens' Telephone was also intended to become a source of information for the Executive Board, which wanted to gain an overall picture of the questions raised most often in these calls. This was why the Citizens' Telephone department reported directly to the President himself (later herself), and the calls were logged and categorised by subject-matter as far as possible. From 21st May 1991, it proved possible to log and categorise about 60% of all calls in this way.[4]

---

3 On this aspect, see: Schröter, *Mitteilungs-Adäquanz*, pages 175 to 216; ditto, *Qualität im Journalismus*.

4 A code book was developed for the quantitative analysis of calls to the Citizens' Telephone and with the help of this book the available records were analysed. These records laid down the degree of differentiation in the code book and thus set limits on the analysis. All calls were included from 18th October 1990 to 30th September 1992. Up to 21st May 1991, the enquiries were only registered briefly, and only after that in detail, so that more precise data is only available on the subjects of the enquiries from that date onwards.

From the date it was set up on 18th October 1990 until 30th September 1992, the Citizens' Telephone was called 46,135 times. In 22,135 cases, specific subjects were raised on which a brief record was made and filed. The remaining 24,000 calls were of a general nature and were recorded only in figures, most of them in the time before 21st May 1991 when there was still no noting of the subjects.

There are differences, some of them substantial, between the subjects of interest to the callers on the Citizens' Telephone and those given prominence by the press (see Table 4). Callers' interest centred on the acquisition of THA real estate, THA special assets, and THA machinery and other material. This subject accounted for 24.5% of calls, but was hardly ever mentioned in the press, where reporting focused just as whole-heartedly on the acquisition of THA companies. This was covered in 23.3% of all articles, but only accounted for 15.5% of the phone calls. In addition to these divergences, there are two other differences of note: firstly, the placement of orders with eastern German companies came into 2.3% of all phone calls but was hardly ever mentioned in the press. Secondly, the press criticised the THA more intensively than the callers phoning the THA (5.5% against 3.3%).

The heavy concentration of press reports on the acquisition of THA companies, and the press' simultaneous neglect of the subject of the acquisition of other assets, can perhaps be attributed to three causes. Firstly, people affected by the sale of companies perhaps expressed themselves more succinctly, thus creating points suitable for reporting in the press which were missed in

Table 4:
Calls on the Citizens' Telephone and reports in the press

Subjects (from May 1991 to October 1992)	Citizens' telephone		Press (subjects of articles)	
	Number (n)	Share (%)	Number (n)	Share (%)
Acquisition of/investment in THA companies	2,088	15.5	1,331	23.3
Acquisition of THA real estate	1,899	14.0	104	1.8
Acquisition of THA special assets	800	5.9	64	1.1
Acquisition of THA machinery/material	601	4.4	2	<0.1
Property ownership questions not affecting THA (expropriations prior to 1949)	526	3.9	2	<0.1
Complaints against THA and/or its branches	443	3.3	314	5.5
Placement of orders with eastern German companies	311	2.3	31	0.5
Enquiries relating to severance/social plan payments	250	1.9	24	0.4
Enquiries relating to financial support and grants	201	1.5	149	2.6
Acquisition of residential property	193	1.4	3	<0.1
Reprivatisation	174	1.3	64	1.2
Complaints against authorities, particularly Offices for Unsettled Property Questions	73	0.5	18	0.3
Complaints of unfair advantage	67	0.5	39	0.7
Management Buy-Outs/Buy-Ins	59	0.4	94	1.6
Accommodation for further vocational training	54	0.4	–	–
Other matters	5,769	42.7	3,466	60.7
Total	13,508	99.9	5,705	99.7

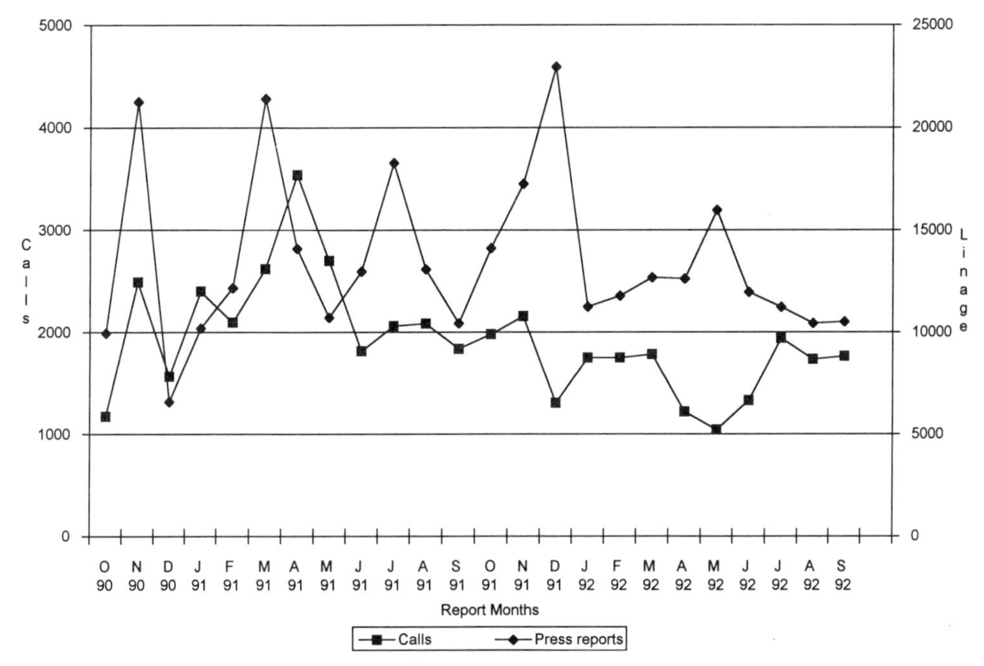

Figure 1 Calls on the Citizens' Telephone and reports in the press from October 1990 to September 1992

other cases, particularly since the THA reported primarily on the sale of companies in its press information. Secondly, it can be assumed that more people were affected directly by the acquisition of companies, so that the subject took on more relevance for the readers of newspapers and magazines. Thirdly, the mass media generally tend to concentrate on individual, noteworthy events such as accidents.[5] The consequence of this is that press reports give excessive coverage to a small number of noteworthy events, while the mass of less significant events are mentioned only relatively infrequently.

Calls on the THA Citizens' Telephone and media reporting on the THA were investigated for the period from October 1990 to September 1992. In the first year of this period, from October 1990 to September 1991, there was a remarkable conformity between the frequency of calls and the total linage of press reports. Two findings from the press analysis indicate that the reporting could have been a cause of the more frequent phone calls. One of these came in November 1990, when more intensive reporting was accompanied by a larger number of calls, and the second in the period of March and April 1991, when very intensive reporting was followed by a large number of calls (Fig. 1).

In the second year of this investigation, from October 1991 to September 1992, the trends in the number of calls and in the linage of press coverage diverged from one another. Press reporting continued to be relatively intensive, but the number of calls fell off fluctuating considerably. The declining number of calls could perhaps indicate that (potential) interest in doing business

5 On this point, see: Combs and Slovic, *Newspaper Coverage of Causes of Death,* pages 837 to 843 and 849; Kepplinger, *Künstliche Horizonte.*

with the THA was weakening. It can, however, also be connected with the fact that the questions which callers had been raising had now very largely been answered. The data available is not sufficient enough to decide which of these interpretations is correct. The relatively constant volume of press reports can probably be put down to the fact that problems caused by privatisation and the protests against the liquidation of companies continued to provide the press with sufficient material with which to fill its columns.

IV. Summary and interpretation

The analysis of the reports on three types of activity, the liquidation, the restructuring, and the privatisation of a company in each case has produced the following results:

Firstly, it is important in examining this subject to differentiate between normal phases and conflict phases. In normal phases, the press reported relatively infrequently on the THA's work, and concentrated more on the general and specific economic aspects of it. In conflict phases, the press reported far more intensively, pushing the parties affected into the limelight and principally raising social questions. This was especially the behaviour of the "street" newspapers and of the subscription newspapers in the regions affected.

Secondly, there were differences, sometimes major ones, between the western and eastern German press. Whilst the western German press, with some exceptions, regarded the THA's work as being objectively necessary and honourable, some parts of the eastern German press produced numerous articles in which the impression was aroused that the THA was bringing eastern Germany to slaughter in the interests of the western German competitors. Similar arguments could also be found occasionally in western German newspapers as well.

Thirdly, the THA is generally speaking only mentioned incidentally in reports on successful cases of the restructuring and privatisation of formerly state-owned companies, and the success is mainly attributed to the investors. In reports of unsuccessful cases, the THA's involvement is described in full detail and the THA is mainly held to blame for the failures.

The systematic analysis of the reports in 19 newspapers and magazines over the two-year period has produced the following results:

Firstly, the national and semi-national newspapers, and the subscription newspapers in Berlin, with one exception, reported very intensively on the THA's work but the purely business press gave it very little coverage, again with one exception.

Secondly, press reports concentrated on the sales policy of the THA, focusing on the privatisation and restructuring of companies. In addition to this, the press provided space for a broad, basic discussion on the whole subject of privatisation, but subjects like historic environmental pollution in eastern German companies, the communalisation of tangible assets, the placement of orders with THA companies, and a number of other topics were hardly ever mentioned.

Thirdly, the assessment made of the THA was related to the source from which it came and the thematic context in which it appeared. Publications specialising totally in business and economic affairs gave a more positive overall rating to the THA than publications of a more general nature. In the context of the discussion of basic principles on privatisation and the description of specific privatisation projects, the THA was mainly placed in a good light, but articles dealing with reprivatisation and the restructuring and liquidation of companies nearly always gave it a negative assessment.

Fourthly, the publications with a great level of specialisation on economic affairs concentrated on different aspects of the subjects from other journals. The former were more concerned with the abstract economic and legal principles which form the basis for the THA's work, and the latter more with the persons and personalities involved. The Berlin subscription newspapers played a particular role, concentrating entirely on the THA's sales policy.

Fifthly, there were sometimes major differences between the subject-matters covered in press reports and the interests of the people calling the THA on the Citizens' Telephone. The press dealt principally with the sale of companies; the telephone callers were primarily interested in the acquisition of real estate, special assets, machinery, and other material. The placement of orders with eastern German companies was also more important for the callers than for the press, which on the other hand tended to criticise the THA more intensively than did the callers.

Sixthly, in the first year of the period under investigation there was a relatively high correlation between the intensity of press reporting on the THA and the frequency of calls on the Citizens' Telephone. Two shorter periods indicate that the press reporting could have been the cause of the more frequent calls. A different trend emerged in the second year: reporting remained relatively intense, but the number of calls dropped off markedly, even though press reporting reached its highest level in December 1991.

It is possible to attribute at least part of the facts revealed to the situation of the THA at the intersection of the two axes described at the beginning. Four basic distinctions have to be made here.

The first distinction relates to the tasks of the THA and of the press. Whilst the THA principally acted on the basis of the macro-economic and the business economic point of view, and took a relatively long-term approach, the newspapers were working much more from the aims of social policy, concentrating on topical and clearly delineated events. This difference was an essential cause of the criticism raised against the THA's actions.

The second difference is that between the interests of the telephone callers ringing the THA and those of the readers of newspapers and magazines. Whilst the majority of callers, understandably enough, wanted information on the terms of acquisition of small and medium-sized tangible assets, the readers of most of the publications were at most interested in noticeable transactions with their social consequences for those directly affected. This particularly applied to the publications in the relevant regions, but also to the national "street" newspapers. This difference was an essential cause of the divergences between enquiries and reports.

The third distinction relates to the interests of the editorial staffs and readers of publications specialising heavily in economic affairs and those of a more general nature. Whilst the specialist publications presented events from the point of view of macro-economics and business economics, the general-interest publications far more often took the social point of view, and often preferred moral judgements to factual analysis.

The fourth difference relates to the interests of the editorial staff and readers of western German newspapers and those of newspapers in the east, particularly the opinion-leading publications of the former GDR. Whilst the western German explained events mainly in market economy terms, and emphasised the requirements of a social state, eastern German ones often explained them on the basis of conspiracy theories; this occasionally endowed their descriptions with an agitatory character.

As a result of the situations and actions outlined above, the broad mass of readers with no special interest in economics were given quite a different picture of the THA's work from the one presented to the specialised reader. This applied particularly to the readers of the national subscription newspapers, which dealt with this subject intensively. In addition to this, the readers of eastern German publications sometimes received a different picture of events from that given to the readers in the western German. The differences concerned the weighting given to the relevant subjects in the reports, the criteria applied to the assessment of problems, the explanations offered, and the assessments made of the THA's actions. It is hard to reconcile these findings with the widely held view that the press had been inundating the population with the one-sided views of the various protagonists involved and the autonomous laws in which they had been acting. It shows far more that the press has been presenting the events it reports on in a manner that reflects the autonomous laws of journalistic action, resulting in major or minor discrepancies between the points of view of the protagonists and the public or certain sections of it.[6]

V. Literature

Combs, Barbara, and Paul *Slovic*: Newspaper Coverage of Causes of Death. In: *Journalism Quarterly* 56 (1979), pages 837 to 843 and 849.

Deetjen, Gottfried: *Industriellenprofile in Massenmedien*. Hamburg 1977.

Friedrichsen, Mike: *Wirtschaft im Fernsehen. Eine theoretische und empirische Analyse der Wirtschaftsberichterstattung im Fernsehen.* Munich 1992.

Heinrich, Jürgen: *Forschungsstand Wirtschaftsjournalismus im deutschsprachigen Raum.* In: Siegfried *Klaue* (editor): *Marktwirtschaft in der Medienberichterstattung. Wirtschaftsjournalismus und Journalistenausbildung.* Düsseldorf 1991.

Kalt, Gero (editor): *Wirtschaft in den Medien. Defizite, Chancen und Grenzen. Eine kritische Bestandsaufnahme.* Frankfurt am Main 1990.

Kepplinger, Hans Mathias: *Künstliche Horizonte. Folgen, Darstellung und Akzeptanz von Technik in der Bundesrepublik.* Frankfurt am Main 1989.

ditto: *Lebensklugheit und wissenschaftliche Rationalität. Bemerkungen zum öffentlichen Konflikt verschiedener Denkstile.* In: Oscar W. *Gabriel*, Ulrich *Sarcinelli*, Bernhard *Sutor*, and Bernhard *Vogel* (editors): *Der demokratische Verfassungsstaat. Theorie, Geschichte, Probleme.* Munich 1992, pages 177 to 193.

Klaue, Siegfried (editor): *Marktwirtschaft in der Medienberichterstattung. Wirtschaftsjournalismus und Journalistenausbildung.* Düsseldorf 1991.

Ruß-Mohl, Stephan, and Heinz D. *Stuckmann* (editors): *Wirtschaftsjournalismus. Ein Handbuch für die Ausbildung und Praxis.* Munich and Leipzig 1991.

Schröter, Detlef: *Mitteilungs-Adäquanz. Studien zum Fundament eines realitätsgerechten journalistischen Handelns.* In: Hans *Wagner* (editor): *Idee und Wirklichkeit des Journalismus. Festschrift für Heinz Starkulla.* Munich 1988, pages 175 to 216.

ditto: *Qualität im Journalismus, Testfall: Unternehmensberichterstattung in Printmedien.* Munich and Mühlheim 1992.

Sondergeld, Klaus: *Die Wirtschafts- und Sozialberichterstattung in den Fernsehnachrichten.* Münster 1983.

6 Kepplinger, *Lebensklugheit und wissenschaftliche Rationalität,* pages 177 to 193.

Structural effects of privatisation by the THA

by Jürgen Müller, with the assistance of Georg Merdian and Donat von Müller[1]

I. Introduction

Ever since it was created, the THA has played an outstanding role in the reorganisation and restructuring of the eastern German economy. Its task of privatisation and restructuring made it the principal agent in the transformation of the centrally planned GDR economy into one that functions in accordance with the principles of a market economy.

Four consecutive but overlapping phases of the transformation process of the eastern German economy are distinguished from one another in the following article. First, the economic structure of the old GDR will be outlined as it existed in 1989. Particular attention should be paid to the structural comparison between East and West Germany. The second phase is delineated by the start of economic and monetary union on 1st July 1990 and the macro-economic and sectoral adjustment processes which this triggered off. The next phase was pre-occupied by the conversion of the *Kombinate*, the monolithic state-owned corporations, and smaller state-owned companies into private companies and the problems of the change in supervision which this entailed. The core of the fourth part is formed by showing the various instruments used by the THA for privatisation and restructuring. The last part of this article assesses the THA's work and summarises the results achieved so far in the process of restructuring.

II. Industry structure in the GDR (in 1989) and the importance of the main sectors

1. Kombinate and other forms of state-owned companies

The structure of the East German economy differed considerably from that in West Germany, with regard both to company forms and to the number and size of the various companies in each sector of the economy (see Figs. 1 and 2). The factor of outstanding significance to the East German economic structure was the presence of 152 *Kombinate*, very large combines, integrated both horizontally and vertically and often holding a monopoly position in their industries. This applies both to their proportion of value added they were generating in each of the branches and to the numbers they employed. There were also some 2,000 smaller companies, managed at the *Bezirk* or District level and mainly serving regional markets. In the field of tourism and other social facilities, the trade unions and the political parties are particularly worth mentioning as organisations which ran some sizeable operations.

---

1 Particular thanks are due for the assistance by Jutta Wietog in the THA and for the helpful criticism from Heike Belitz, Alexander Dyck, Wolfram Fischer, Frank Fleischer, Alfred Haid, Hans Karl Schneider, and Jörg Peter Weiß.

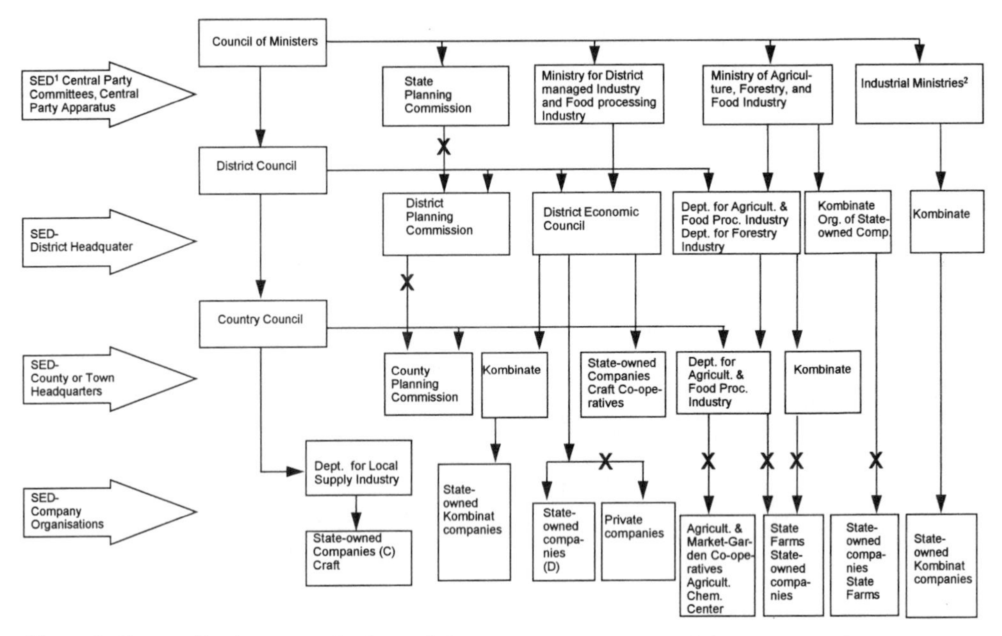

Figure 1 Forms of business organisation and the management structure of the economy of the GDR 1982 (simplified)

Source: Bundesministerium für innerdeutsche Beziehungen (editor), DDR Handbuch, Vol. 2, page 1501.

Notes: [1] SED = *Sozialistische Einheitspartei*, or „Socialist Unity Party", the sole party of government – made up of socialists, communists, and others, and often referred to simply as „the Party".

[2] There were also ministries: of finance, for foreign trade, retail trade and domestic supply, construction industry, science and technology, and materials management, a Prices Office, and so on.

[3] In interviews with former employees of the State Planning Commission and the *Kombinate* and companies it became obvious that there existed no relationship of subordination in those cases marked with (x).

On the other side, the importance of independent enterprises and co-operatives in the craft trades was far smaller than in West Germany. The East German agricultural industry was dominated by *Landwirtschaftliche Produktionsgenossenschaften* or LPG's (Agricultural Productive Co-operatives) and *Volkseigene Güter* or VEG's (State Farms); they had vastly bigger areas of land to manage than typical West German farms. Retail trade was entirely in the hands of the *Handelsorganisation* or HO (Trade Organisation) and the *Konsumgenossenschaften* (retail co-operatives). For export trade, largely concerned with capital goods, and imports, in which raw materials and fuel were the most important commodities, there were special foreign trade companies. Some of the large *Kombinate* were allowed to operate their own foreign trade, and were in some cases highly successful.[2]

2 However, they were subordinate to the Minister for Foreign Trade and were only independent to a limited extent.

2. Sectoral importance

There were substantial differences between East and West Germany with regard to the significance of the individual sectors of the economy. The East German economy was only integrated into the world economy to a very limited extent, and its integration into COMECON trade, which only held less than 10% of world trade, was unable to compensate for this. Also, the foreign trade structure was influenced in a very lop-sided way by the strict orientation towards the COMECON countries, and for this reason the structural adaptation to the requirements of western trade was only very slight. Thus the East German economy had a relative preponderance of basic raw materials, manufactured goods, and capital goods in comparison with con-

Table 1:
Sectoral employment structure in East and West Germany, 1989/1990

Selected branches of trade and industry	East Germany (1989)		West Germany (1990)	
	in '000s	in %	in '000s	in %
Agriculture, forestry, fishing	920	9.9	961	3.4
Energy and mining	295	3.2	466	1.6
Energy and water supply	120	1.3	286	1.0
Mining	175	1.9	180	0.6
Manufacturing industry	3,168	34.1	8,941	31.4
Chemical industry	152	1.6	644	2.3
Metal production and processing	183	2.0	687	2.4
Engineering	548	5.9	1,216	4.3
Motor vehicle construction	208	2.4	1,148	4.0
Electrical engineering	398	4.3	1,247	4.4
Clothing industry	197	2.1	230	0.8
Textile industry	217	2.3	238	0.8
Food industry	336	3.6	743	2.6
Others	929	10.0	2,788	9.8
Construction industry	563	6.1	1,914	6.7
Wholesale and retail trade	721	7.8	3,728	13.1
Wholesaling	258	2.8	1,369	4.8
Retailing	463	5.0	2,359	8.3
Transport and communication	628	6.8	1,588	5.6
Railways	245	2.6	255	0.9
Shipping and harbours	33	0.4	44	0.15
Other means of transport	233	2.4	751	2.6
Telecommunications	127	1.4	538	1.9
Banking and insurance	63	0.7	891	3.1
Hotel and catering trades	180	1.9	913	3.2
Services, public sector, defence, etc.	2,762	29,7	9,031	31.8
Total	9,300	100,0	28,433	99.9

Note: [1]Apprentices are not included; this would increase the total numbers employed in East Germany by 353,000.

Sources: Görzig and Gorning, Produktivität und Wettbewerbsfähigkeit der Wirtschaft der DDR; Statistisches Jahrbuch der DDR 34 (1989); Statistisches Jahrbuch der Bundesrepublik Deutschland 1989; Siebert, German Unification and the Economics of Transition; DIW (editor), Analyse der struktu-

sumer goods (Table 1). The proportion of employment accounted for by the manufacturing and construction industries, however, was similar to that in West Germany.

The retail trades and other services were heavily under-represented, with the exception of the transport and communications sectors (meaning the railways and the post office). The relative proportions accounted for by wholesale and retail trade, financial and insurance services, and

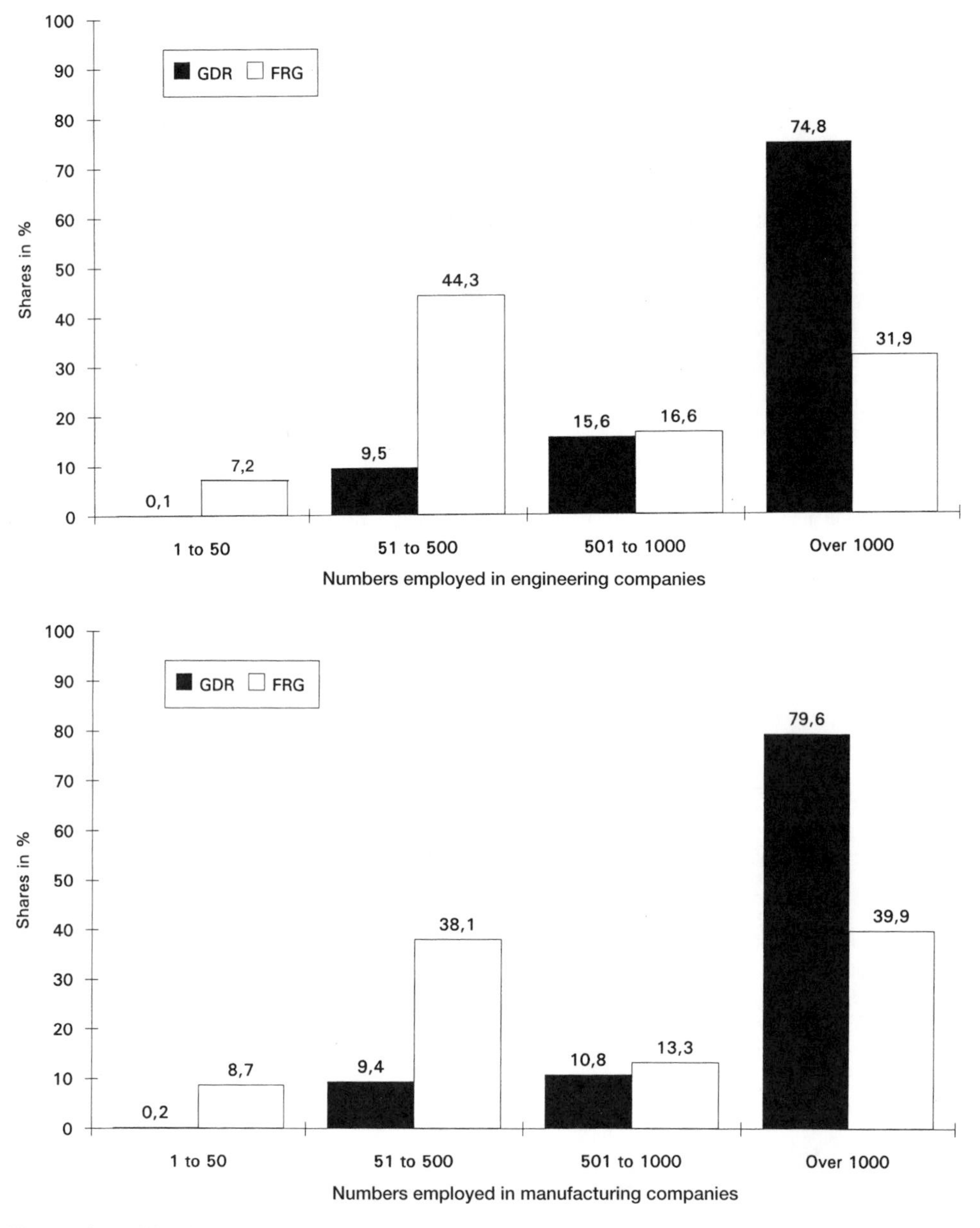

Figures 2a and 2b Comparison of company sizes

hotels and restaurants were in some cases less than half West German levels, and even the public sector was proportionately slightly smaller than in West Germany. This was certainly due to the fact that in West Germany many of the functions provided by the public sector were in East Germany supplied by the state-owned companies and *Kombinate*, e. g. children's, health or sports facilities, and arts centres.

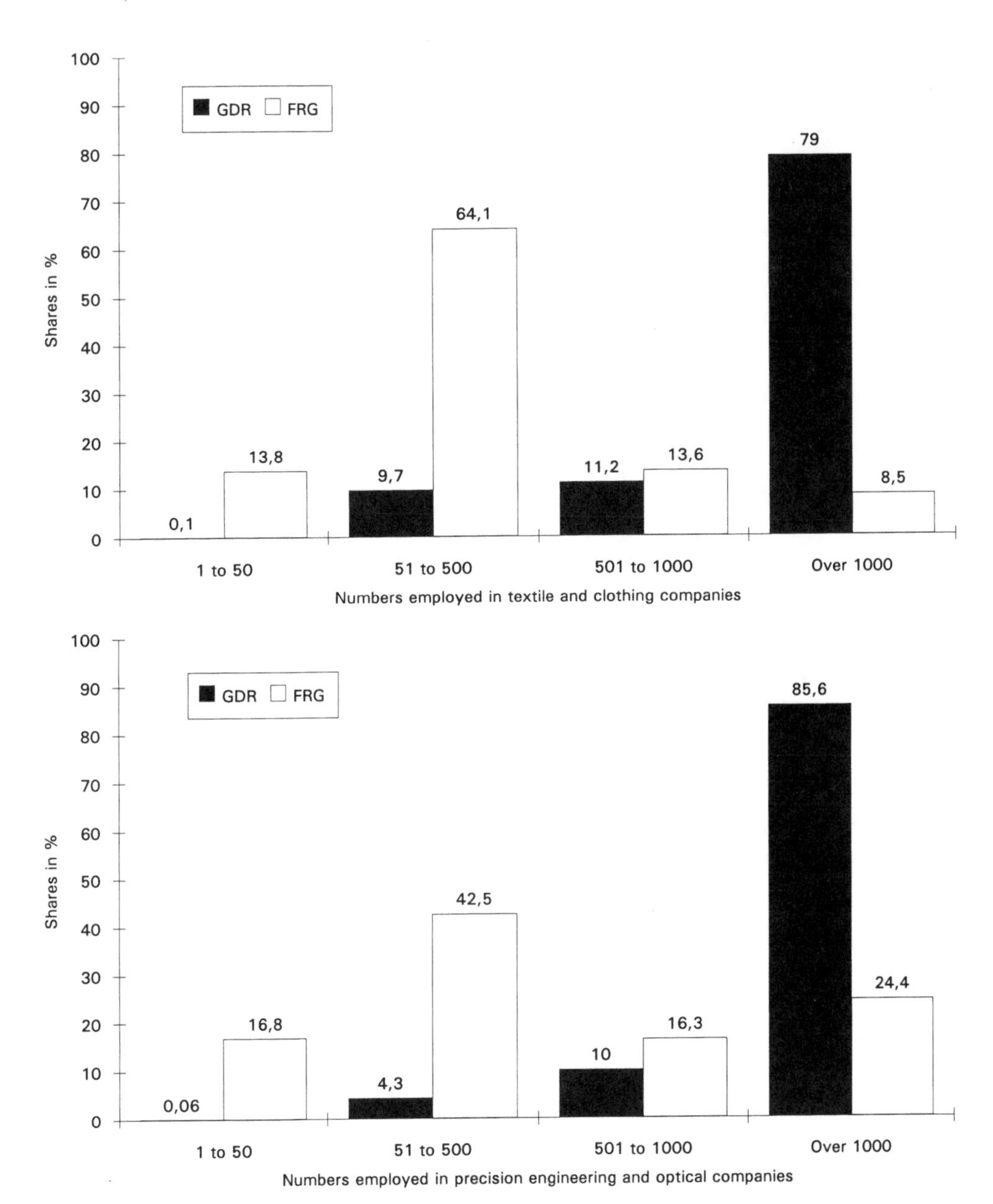

Figures 2c and 2d Comparison of company sizes

This comparison, based on the various proportions of sectoral employment,[3] shows the significance of agriculture, energy, and the production of basic raw materials, and that of heavy industry – exactly those sectors which have most lost importance in the course of the structural changes in West Germany in the last two decades, with the result that numbers employed in them also fell rapidly. On the other hand, the services sector, which in West Germany had provided the most powerful growth and employment impetus in the past decade, had taken a totally different line of development in East Germany. Part of the industrial services sector was integrated into production companies, such as the design of rationalisation means and construction and data processing. Because of the obsolete state of the plant and machinery, repair services were grossly inflated in size.

A comparison of this kind of course ignores the fact that major structural differences could have arisen between East and West Germany simply on the basis of their different endowment with the factors of production and income and without any elements of the planned economy intruding, but it does also clearly show the structural shortcomings of the old East German economy when compared with a modern economy capable of competing internationally. This will serve as a description of the sectoral context surrounding the privatisation strategy of the THA and within which its restructuring efforts need to be judged.

III. Sectoral adjustment from the macro-economic point of view

1. Effect on levels

The structure of the eastern German economy, and in particular of eastern German industry, has undergone a radical change since unification. Two effects can be discerned as a result. On the one hand there is the effect on levels of activity, expressed in the sharp drop in value-creation and employment, and on the other side the effect on industry structures, characterised by the shattering of the whole structure of production and employment and the resultant drastic changes in the relative significance of the individual branches of industry.[4]

At the start of economic and monetary union on 1st July 1990, and the accompanying immediate integration of the East German economy into the world market, the shortcomings in its productivity and its lack of ability to compete became blatantly apparent. The collapse of eastern German companies' markets to the East, combined with a substantial drop in employment and production, took its swift and merciless course. The heavy competitive pressure from western companies which set in at once was more than eastern German companies could stand in almost any industry. Shortcomings were nearly everywhere: in marketing, financial control, research and development, distribution, and finance. In addition to this, the cost disadvantage as a result of the introduction of the Deutschmark and of the large currency revaluation this implied, as well as of the rapidly rising wage costs was too great to cope with and led to a drastic fall-off in traditional exports to eastern European countries.

3 Measured in terms of proportion of employment, the significance of the food, forestry, and fishing sector, for instance, was almost twice as great as in West Germany. Such a distribution of employment, and the serious differences in productivity, naturally emphasise the importance of such low-productivity sectors as agriculture.

4 See: statistical appendix to this volume.

Against this background the question arises as to which sectors might be capable of survival at all, and to what extent. Companies which had enjoyed special significance in the GDR for reasons of self-sufficiency or because of supply commitments within the COMECON countries were scarcely capable of survival in a liberalised market such as the one that arose following economic and monetary union. Examples of this are the forced expansion of micro-electronics in Frankfurt/Oder and at Carl Zeiss in Jena, uranium mining in the region around Aue, the ship-building and ship-repair industry in Mecklenburg/West-Pomerania,[5] the production of radio and television sets, etc. Such "self-sufficiency planning" was the characteristic of individual industries or lop-sided trading relationships, but these are only part of sectors on which the changed trading regime had a negative influence.

Because of distorted prices[6] and the political orientation of foreign trade towards the COMECON countries, East Germany's foreign trade relations were not entirely based on its comparative advantages so that it was necessary to adapt these as well to changing circumstances such as radically different factor and goods prices. It was therefore necessary to swing trade round rapidly and orientate it towards western markets, even though initial struggles to gain market share ran into enormous difficulties because of the lack of time to facilitate adjustment, the lack of capital in the companies, the limited entrepreneurial experiences, the lack of any good product image, and in some cases considerable shortcomings in production technology, not to mention the cost disadvantage created by economic and monetary union.

A further negative effect arose from the new legal regulations, for example on the protection of the environment and on the health and safety at work. Because of the new overall situation (with different procedures and levels for licences, industrial standards, and standardisation), some companies found they were *de facto* producing illegally and therefore had to close down or totally change their product range and production methods (e. g. nuclear power stations, or the re-registration of pharmaceutical products).

2. Effect of structural adaptation

The approximately equal loss of domestic and export markets led to a landslide-like fall-off in production and, after a short time-lag, in employment. The pressure on companies to rationalise ensured a further reduction in employment. Whereas there were still about 9.6 million people in employment in East Germany at the end of 1989, by the end of 1992 it was only about 6.3 million, and 366,000 of these were on job-creation schemes and 233,000 on short-time working programmes partly financed by the national unemployment insurance. The gross national product fell from DM 286 billion in 1989 to DM 195 billion in 1991 before starting to rise again in 1992.[7] The fiscal transfers to the east took on greater significance, for structural development as

5 This industry was started in order to make post-war reparations to the USSR and ended up providing 80% of its requirements for fishing and transport vessels.

6 In the former GDR, energy was too cheap and housing, food, and textiles were heavily subsidised. Capital goods and consumer durables were in some cases heavily taxed.

7 See: Tables 1 and 2 in the statistical appendix.

well, rising from DM 141 billion gross (123 billion net) in 1991 to DM 164 billion gross (142 billion net) in 1992; these flowed via state benefits and social insurance from western to eastern Germany.[8]

Production initially shrank fastest in the product fields closest to the consumer: textiles, food, and light industry; the production fall-off in industries such as chemicals, engineering, motor vehicles, ship-building, and electrical engineering was initially somewhat less. The enormous *Kombinate* which dominated these industries still had nearly full order-books in 1990, mainly for orders from east European countries. The increasing payment difficulties, now in hard currencies, which the east European customers then began to run into led, however, to the cancellation of orders in these sectors as well. From the end of 1990 onwards, and once the very satisfactory trade based on "transfer roubles" had run out they also suffered a rapid fall-off in production and employment. This was particularly severe in engineering, which had always had a dominant position in manufacturing industry, and even worse in the textile and clothing industries and in office equipment industry. Restructuring and reconstruction is making great progress in many industries, as can be seen from the growing levels of investment,[9] but the decline in the core area of the economy, manufacturing industry, was still continuing in 1993.

The services sector was the only one to see, after a moderate fall-off in the second half of 1990, a steady growth in gross value creation starting as early as the beginning of 1991. However, even here the cutback in employment continued until the end of 1992, although at a comparative lower rate, from 2.72 million to 2.2 million employees. Nevertheless, the trend was very different from one industry sector to another. The situation was best in the construction industry, banks, insurance, and other services.[10] There has thus been a severe reduction on the supply side in the level of production within three years following the integration of the eastern German economy into the western German, whilst demand has grown as a result of large transfer payments. The sectors in most serious decline were mining, agriculture, and manufacturing industry, particularly in those branches which had been encouraged most by the division of labour within COMECON, and those which already had shrunk much earlier in West Germany, following the course of changes in the international division of labour.

IV. Adjustment of company structures within each industry

1. Components of change in market structure

In addition to the structural changes promoted by the privatisation programme, three components are of significance for the development of the market structure: entry to and exit from the market, internal growth, and mergers.[11]

8 The gross transfers included benefits paid by regional bodies, the „German Unity" fund, the social-security insurance organisations, and from the European Community (now Union). See: Meinhard et al, *Vorläufige Berechnungen zu den Transferleistungen in den neuen Bundesländern.*

9 On this point, see: Deutsche Bundesbank, *Bilanzrelationen und Ertragsverhältnisse ostdeutscher Unternehmen im Jahre 1991.*

10 See: Tables 2, 3, and 6 in the statistical appendix.

11 On this point, see: Müller, *The Impact of Mergers on Concentration.*

Market entry arises on the one hand through the business start-up of self-employed people, or those in the free professions, and on the other hand by the "green field" establishment of companies from another region or the transfer in use of land or machinery to another sector. *Market exit* relates to companies withdrawing from the market.

The role of *internal growth*, i. e. to gain a larger sectoral share for a leading company, can be neglected for the present purpose. The number of previously independent companies was too small to get any real sectoral significance through internal growth, and the huge former *Kombinate* and large companies initially lost much of their importance through rationalisation and "unbundling", with the result that their internal growth was usually negative.

The greatest significance in the adaptation of industry structures therefore went to *horizontal mergers*, the sale of THA companies to other firms in the same line of business (or, in the case of vertical mergers, further up or down the same chain of production).

2. Horizontal, vertical, and geographical unbundling

The old *Kombinate* or companies had been too large when viewed horizontally; in the most important industries there was often only one *Kombinat* which controlled everything. Also, viewed vertically, the depth of production in the individual companies was too great. Both the *Kombinate* and the individual companies had to be unbundled in both directions, which implied negative internal growth.

Horizontal unbundling of the *Kombinate* was often relatively easy to achieve. Although the individual plants of the companies had been earlier nationalised and brought together into *Kombinate* for administrative purposes, their production had often not been rationalised by closing down smaller scale locations on the one hand and creating central production locations on the other.[12] Breaking the *Kombinate* up horizontally into their individual historical units, encouraged by the *Treuhandgesetz* or THG (the Act setting up the THA – on this point, see § 11), was thus the easiest "autonomous" part of horizontal unbundling.[13]

The old *Kombinate* and their companies were generally very deeply integrated vertically. As there was *de facto* no market for any industry supplying components or semi-finished products, and none of the services associated with it, much had to be produced inside the company. When such companies were being slimmed and vertically unbundled, a balance had to be struck between the central "core" activities which were important to the company for its survival, and those which could be hived off. This included not only a large number of purely social activities (health services, old people's homes, holiday cottages), but also associated services such as

12 The companies within each *Kombinat* tended of course to specialise to a certain extent, but not to the extent that might have been expected on the basis of the corporate concentration that followed the centralisation of production in the *Kombinate*.

13 However, the horizontal unbundling of industrial monopolies was more difficult in newly created industries and sectors where the technical linkages within the *Kombinat* had been largely optimised. This also applied to the newly created industries in the other COMECON countries which had a central supply function for the whole COMECON.

transport, repair workshops, etc.[14] Vertical unbundling therefore resulted in a far greater splitting up of companies, meaning it created far more independent companies, than did the horizontal unbundling.

Geographical or *spacial unbundling* of business locations involves separating off the parts of the business sites not essential to its core operations. Vertical unbundling had of course already carved off many buildings and production locations from the former company sites. Geographical unbundling, often as a result of much smaller production volumes, continued the process by separating off the remaining buildings and the sites on which they stood until the minimum necessary for sustainable operations was achieved. The remaining land could then be made available to other companies.[15] This step also reduced the possibility of running assets down excessively during the restructuring process (as a result of insufficient supervision).[16]

The THA held a total of nearly 13,000 companies in all branches of the economy.[17] Initially, however, the number of companies belonging to the THA had been far smaller, as many new companies only came into being as a result of the unbundling of *Kombinate* and splitting off parts of companies. This resulted in an addition of about 3,000 companies between March 1990 and March 1993.[18] Other companies were not identified as belonging to the THA until some time later.

The THA companies grouped by status (communalised, reprivatised, liquidated or in liquidation, privatised, and still on the THA's books) in Fig. 3, however, are not weighted by numbers employed or value created, so that the structural effects of the THA's activities are only vaguely indicated by these shares.[19] Also, the status groups only partly match up with the three compo-

---

14 The vertically integrated activities of the Warnow shipyard in Rostock prior to restructuring covered such stages as steel processing, rust protection, insulation, scrap metal recycling, a factory kitchen, industrial cleaning, carpentry, repair work, plant construction, interior furnishing, upholstery work, transport services, staff training, kindergartens, and so on. After restructuring, only the central functions of planning and administration, ship-building and ship repair, and the production of several consumer goods were left within the company. All other activities were hived off as outside services and privatised separately; see: Albach, *The 1992 Uppsala Lectures in Business*.

15 The THA established the *Treuhand-Liegenschaftsgesellschaft mbH* or TLG (the THA real estate company) to handle these aspects of "site" unbundling separately from privatisation.

16 Experience in the eastern German states showed in fact that for the short term, if a company's assets were substantial, stripping off assets and consuming the proceeds was often more attractive to management than carrying out the necessary restructuring and dismissing redundant staff. The attraction was often very great for the THA companies because the company's chances of being categorised as capable of being restructured were increased the lower the losses it reported (or the fewer funds the THA had to guarantee it). However, such a strategy has no prospect of success in the long term and led to more negative value-creation and to further squandering of economic resources. All the same, if geographical unbundling is forced on a company, it is essential that the company should be supervised and assisted financially in the process in order to ensure liquidity through difficult times. An example for living off one's own assets was practised by Saxonia AG of Freiberg (a company processing precious metals) up to the end of 1991. They financed their on-going losses by selling their working capital of available silver. The company was thus only a tiny cash-gobbler, but it was also one of the THA's biggest loss-making companies.

17 See: Fig. 3, and in the statistical appendix Table 15.

18 This is in addition to the 3,000 companies already reprivatised by the Modrow government.

19 However, see also: Fig. 5 below.

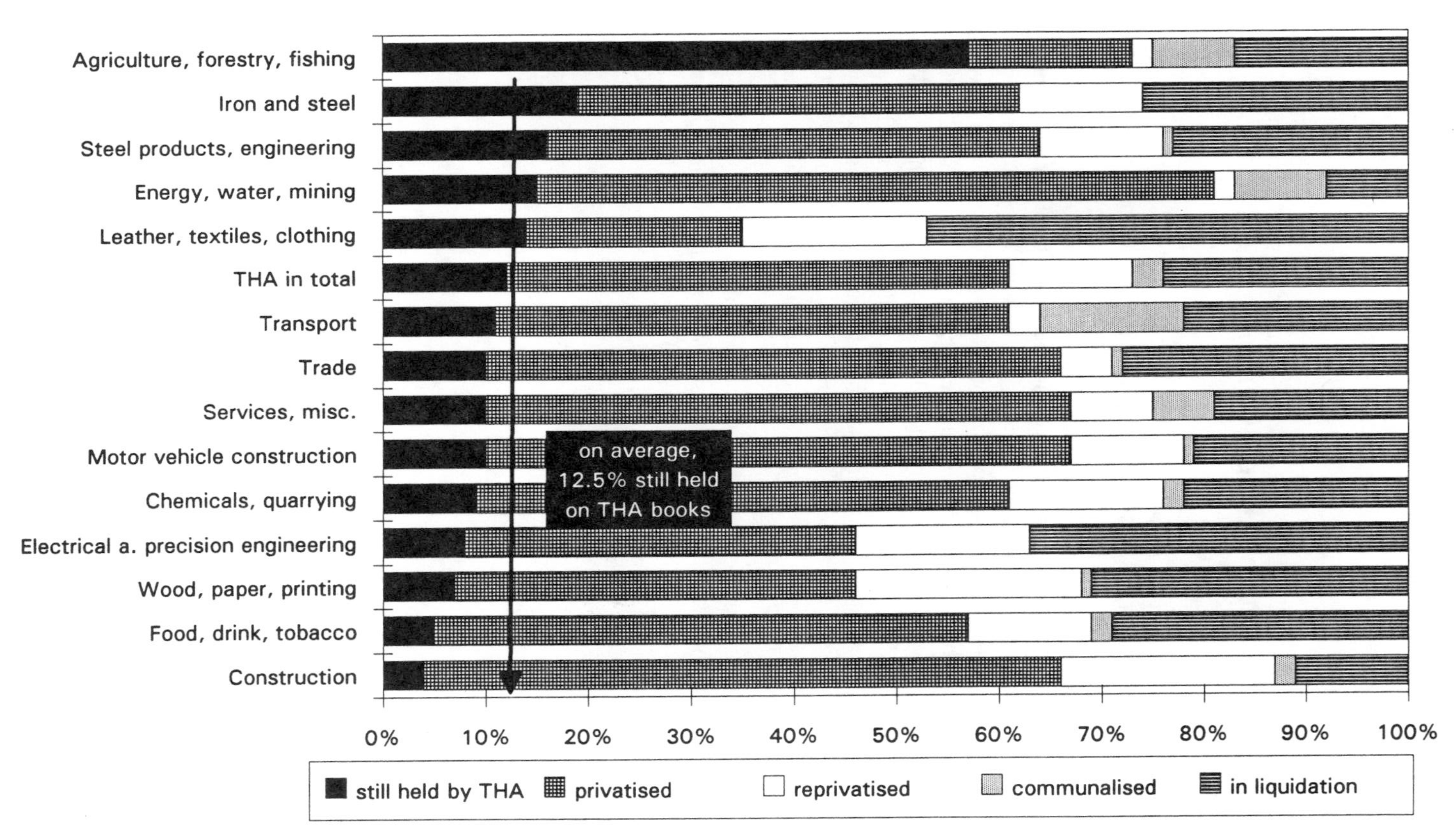

Figure 3 THA companies' status in early 1993 (Source: Treuhandanstalt Documentation Department)

nents of structural market change mentioned above. We will go into this problem in more detail in Section VI; but first, however, the THA's scope for exerting influence at the level of individual companies needs to be examined.

V. Commercialisation and the problem of supervision of companies

1. Autonomous structural change and passive privatisation

When it was founded, the THA took over almost all the companies in East Germany.[20] On paper, at least, it was the world's largest industrial conglomerate, and the supervision problems which this involved were thus enormous. It was, however, for some time not clear in what way the necessary control was to be exercised. The originally planned organisation for the 152 centrally managed *Kombinate* organised by industry[21] was abandoned in August 1990 by the THA President of the day, Mr Rohwedder. The matrix organisation adopted later, with 15 branches and a certain number of Industry Directorates in the Central Office, however, could not be put into effect until early 1991. Even in this form, the task was enormous. On 1st January 1991, the 1,231 THA employees had 3,826 companies to manage from Central Office and 6,718 from the branches.[22]

After German unification, therefore, the THA took on a dominant share of western German management personnel both at the Executive Board level and in the Industry Directorates and the 15 branches (see Table 2).[23] This enabled it to make use of western management within a relatively short time, at least at the THA management level, and to restructure the THA accordingly.

20 It took over all the VEB-companies and state farms, but not the socialist co-operatives.

21 The four "THA-AG's" (heavy industry, capital goods industry, consumer goods industry, and services) were to be structured so as to cover a number of branches of industry each; see: § 5 section 2 of the THA Statutes and appendix to the Statutes.

22 *Treuhandanstalt Informationen* 6 (October 1991), page 6; THA, PE T1/ih/ 19th March 1992. The word "manage" should be regarded here more in the legal sense because in the early days there was never much scope for exerting direct influence on the running of the companies. See also the figure in the statistical appendix, page 529.

23 The appeal from the Chancellor to major western German companies to second managers on loan for the rapid restructuring of the THA played a certain role here. See also: Letter from Hero Brahms to the Minister-Presidents of the States on 18th March 1993.

Table 2:
Extent of management transfer to the THA

	1. Permanent staff numbers (Central Office, branches, and TLG)				
	30th June 1990	31st December 1990	30th June 1991	31st December 1991	30th June 1992
Total numbers employed:	114	1,140	2,722	3,604	3,941
from eastern Germany	112	1,032	2,048	2,578	2,716
from western Germany/foreign countries	2	108	674	1,026	1,225
Administration Boards	18	22	24	24	24
from eastern Germany	8	5	4	3	3
from western Germany/foreign countries	10	17	20	21	21
Executive Board members	2	8	9	9	9
from eastern Germany	2	2	2	1	–
from western Germany/foreign countries	–	6	7	8	9
Branch Managers	15	15	15	15	15
from eastern Germany	15	–	–	–	–
from western Germany/foreign countries	–	15	15	15	15
Senior Managers	9	206	235	294	301
from eastern Germany	9	31	33	24	25
from western Germany/foreign countries	–	175	203	270	276
	2. Temporary staff numbers (Central Office, branches, and TLG)				
	30th June 1990	31st December 1990	30th June 1991	31st December 1991	30th June 1992
Managers on secondment	–	38	70	48	51
from eastern Germany	–	–	–	2	2
from western Germany/foreign countries	–	38	70	46	49

Note: [1]Administration Board started to be appointed on 15th July 1990.
Source: Treuhandanstalt

By April 1991 this reorganisation of the THA was more or less complete, so that the time previous to that date can be described as the passive privatisation and restructuring phase because the THA's control and management function on the companies was still in the process of creation. By that time, however, the *Kombinate* were to a large extent restructured and a large number of companies already privatised. This included the reprivatisation of 3,000 smaller companies under the Modrow government[24] and the privatisation of a number of particularly attractive properties. At this time well informed purchasers who were interested in specific parts of various *Kombinate*, and particularly in the lucrative fields of non-tradable goods such as energy, insurance, banks and hotels, were able to buy them at bargain prices. In some cases, there were co-operation agreements preparing mergers between eastern and western German companies, so

24 The East German Companies Act of 7th March 1990 covered the return to private ownership of the companies expropriated in 1972.

that the west German parties were able to exert influence even before an official purchase contract had been signed. In the energy sector, some of these privatisation contracts were signed even before German unification, e. g. in the power generation field, although because of legal objections these could not be implemented until the summer of 1994. The time gap was bridged by working with management contracts. Also, some 20 municipal utilities were established with the participation of western power companies. The same applies in the field of brown coal (lignite) and the gas industry. So far, about 20 western German companies have taken holdings in the newly independent regional gas supply companies.[25]

Some of the *Kombinate* were already converted into joint-stock companies during the time of the Modrow government and the necessary Supervisory Boards were appointed following the principles of codetermination laid down in West Germany for the so-called "Montan" industries (basically, major coal, iron, and steel concerns).[26] In some cases this first step towards commercialisation had been combined with a certain amount of unbundling, mainly horizontal but in some cases vertical as well.[27] Other companies preferred to remain under the roof of a holding company which had the legal form of an AG-company but retained the structure of the old *Kombinat*.

The horizontal and vertical unbundling of business and product divisions carried out "spontaneously" at that time did not always follow rationally comprehensible criteria, but were mostly designed to concentrate the company's activities on its core areas. Gripped to a certain extent by the feeling of "every man for himself", the core businesses often believed they could survive better on their own and therefore parted their companies from the *Kombinate*. This reduced the depth of production (vertical unbundling) and hived off separable parts of companies (e. g. social services, the vehicle fleet, repair and construction departments, and similar), but in some cases the companies did also lose important benefits of scope, such as from research and development or benefits of internal organisation, and the hived-off parts were not always capable of survival on their own. Even later the THA's more organised restructuring efforts, however, preceded by extensive managerial investigations, often ran into the same kind of problem.

This "spontaneous" restructuring often also involved the dismissal of members of the companies' management. Some managers in politically exposed positions, or those with a particularly authoritarian style, were not able to hang onto their jobs and were often replaced in a processed characterised by "grass-roots democracy" by those in the management level below them (e. g. production manager, works manager, senior managers in sales, export, or R & D, etc.). These were then the managers which the THA discovered when it took over and had to evaluate the company's management capability.

---

25 On this point, see: Frisch, *Unternehmenszusammenschlüsse in den neuen Bundesländern*, page 9.

26 From 1st July 1990 the THG converted all the remaining *Kombinate* into AG-companies and all VEB's into GmbH-companies.

27 The legal basis for the break-up of the *Kombinate* (or for hiving off parts of the former *Kombinate* or the converted AG-companies) was initially § 12 section 3 of the THG, and later the Splitting Act as applied to the companies administered by the THA, which included these possibilities:

a) splitting up the old companies and selling the shares, or
b) splitting off a new company from the old one which remained in existence but handed some of its assets to the new, small unit.

See: Priester, *Gesellschaftsrechtliche Zweifelsfragen*, pages 2373 et seq.

However, until the early summer of 1991 the THA tended more to operate in a passive role. It was not until the new organisation was more or less in place, and some of the legal hurdles to privatisation had been overcome by the necessary revisions to the Treaty of Unification or the Property Act,[28] that the THA was able to make an effective start on fulfilling its task of supervising, reorganising, restructuring, and privatising companies.

2. Controlled structural change by the THA

The THA had first to look at and sift through the companies which had landed in its lap and to examine their structures for economic and administrative practicability. Whenever possible, the THA acted as a holding company in the management of its companies. A Supervisory Board was installed in the larger ones, an Advisory Board in the smaller ones. The Supervisory Board examined the company (with the assistance of the THA's Central Office) and the management personnel, replaced some of it, issued new contracts, and assisted the management in the question of restructuring. The THA's Industry Directorates played a consultative role and were often asked for their views prior to any major investments or restructuring.

Nevertheless, the newly appointed Supervisory Boards had to intervene far more actively in the operational structure than is provided for in the German *Aktiengesetz*, the Companies Act for companies of the AG-type.[29] The THA had to appoint Supervisory Board Chairmen for about 550 companies; nearly all of them came from western Germany.[30] These chairmen then had to set up their Supervisory Board teams, with the assent of the THA, with half the seats being filled, under German codetermination law, by the employees side, meaning particularly by trade union representatives.

The restructuring proposals prepared by the Executive and Supervisory Boards were then discussed and agreed with the THA in order to ensure that the operational units thus created were capable of being sold. In particularly difficult restructuring cases, such as industries of great importance to their regions, the relevant Industry Directorate of the THA was also actively involved. Examples of this are the chemical industry, ship-yards, the steel industry, and microelectronics. In particularly complicated cases it was also necessary to consult the various State ministries, principally in order to permit the necessary accompanying measures to be taken in good time on the regional labour market.[31] However, as the States were not able to make any financial contribution to restructuring (except in the case of Carl Zeiss Jena), their direct influence remained relatively small.[32]

---

28 Legislation reacted to the difficulties caused to privatisation by the Property Act of 23rd September 1990 (restitution before compensation) with an amendment; see: new version of the Property Act dated 18th April 1991, and preamble to the Removal of Obstacles Act of 22nd March 1991.

29 The situation here is a little closer to that created by American company law, in which the "Chairman" often plays a very active part.

30 On this point, see: Müller, *Managementtransfer in die neuen Bundesländer*.

31 On this point, see: articles by Seibel and by Kern and Sabel in this volume.

32 The role of the States in maintaining "industrial cores" was somewhat more active, e. g. with such projects as ATLAS in Saxony.

The horizontal, vertical, and geographical restructuring process was in some cases highly complicated.[33] The most difficult step in preserving industrial locations was the decision as to whether the existing organisation could be restructured or should be closed down. Another crucial question was whether after liquidation[34] preference should be given to the establishment of a new, "green field" company or to the take-over of the old production locations from the bankruptcy estate by a third party.

3. Structural change through the Management-KG's

The THA originally intended to complete its operational business by the end of 1993, but even after that date it would still have companies on its books which, although rated as capable of being restructured, would not be immediately able to find a buyer (Fig. 4). This includes companies which are mainly hard to sell because of their enormous size, but which for the same reason and because of their resultant importance for their regions could not be considered for liquidation (e. g. *Deutsche Waggonbau AG* or *EKO-Stahl*).[35]

For the other companies in this category, which were mainly much smaller, the THA developed the concept of the Management-KG's.[36] The possibility of their being restructured depends mainly from their being given a highly qualified management team to work together with a motivated and trained work-force. The THA's first step is therefore to privatise the management of these companies; experienced "troubleshooters" will each look after a group of companies and help them along the way to privatisation. In June 1993, 58 such companies with a total work-force of almost 25,000 were organised into five of these Management-KG's.

VI. Different kinds of restructuring by the THA and by other parties

1. Privatisation or restructuring

After private ownership, contractual freedom, and protection of contracts (which principally affected the role of bankruptcy) had been created and legally underpinned, the crucial step towards creating a new structure is privatisation. The role of the state as the party ultimately responsible for the company is replaced by the supervision of a private provider of capital. This is particularly important in the implementation of corporate strategies by the companies that have been restructured; although bureaucrats can prepare the restructuring and the corporate strategies related to them, the question as to how much is to be invested and where in order to make

33 It was not until 11th March 1991 that the Companies Data Bank was complete, on the basis of which it was possible to categorise them; see: article by Seibel in this volume.

34 On this point, see: discussion in the article by Kern and Sabel and the article by Schmidt in this volume.

35 However, in September 1994 there were signs that a solution was in sight for both companies.

36 On this point, see: articles by Kern and Sabel, and by Schwalbach, in this volume.

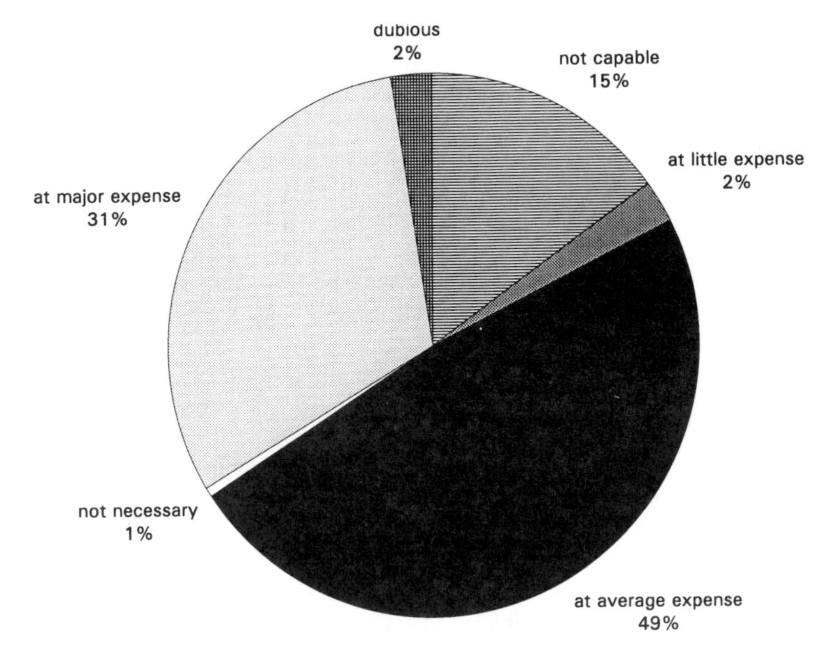

Figure 4 Companies in manufacturing industry on the THA's books rated by suitability for restructuring[1] (as of 31st December 1992) (Source: Treuhandanstalt)

Note: [1]440 companies allocated to the Central Office were categorised by the THA Management Committee. This categorisation of manufacturing companies is part of the categorisation of 999 companies, in which overall figures (in a clockwise direction on the above chart) were: 11.2%, 4.6%, 38.3%, 1.3%, 41.5%, and 3.0%.

the physical and human capital more productive can only be decided on a decentralised basis. Private capital is the natural choice for this function.[37]

A distinction needs to be made in privatisation between the first step, the *legal transfer*, i.e. the change of owner, and the subsequent stage of *implementation of the corporate strategy*. Legal transfer is strictly speaking the actual privatisation, and means that the existing company (or part of one) is handed over as it stands. The proceeds of privatisation (the "transfer price") do not depend on the companies previous turnover or its present stock of labour and capital, but far more on present and expected market conditions in which it has to operate. For some companies the transfer price was on the low side, and if there was a heavy burden of historic debt,

37 The THA pursued this idea in its policy of rapid privatisation to investors which offered a workable corporate strategy. In contrast to this there is the model based on the distribution of equity holdings through voucher-privatisation in which the shares are rapidly distributed (as in the Czech Republic) to the population at large, so that at least initially the share ownership is very widespread.

liability for environmental pollution, or obligations to employees under "social plans" (redundancy compensation) because of imminent lay-offs, the transfer price might even have been a negative quantity. The THA therefore sold many companies for the purely symbolic price of DM 1.00.[38]

On the other hand, the investments designed to re-activate the company and implement the corporate plan could be very high indeed.[39] However, only the two steps together will lead to the successful restructuring of the company.[40] It is therefore not fair to use the low prices attained for some companies under these circumstances as an argument against rapid privatisation. It was not until "real" owners – proprietors, in fact – could be found who had a long-term interest and sufficient control over the company that a sound corporate strategy could be implemented with the appropriate level of investment.[41]

The large number of privatisation cases to be handled naturally resulted in a time problem. For capacity reasons, it was not possible for the THA to privatise everything at once. While time was passing, decisions still had however to be taken on changes in production methods, reorganising the structure, and making investments. But as a rule, the THA only permitted "investor-neutral" investments, which over the course of time and without privatisation tended to worsen the companies' chances of survival.

There are also financial reasons for lengthening the privatisation phase.[42] The mass of companies awaiting privatisation – the "stock" – is faced by a limited amount of savings in the population, which represents a "flow". Theoretically at least, this could mean that the proceeds of a fast privatisation should be very low indeed.[43] This "stock/flow" problem can, however, be solved by the THA selling more slowly and privatising its companies only partly. In the case of agricultural land, long leases are one way of dealing with this problem.[44]

Another reason for the very low valuation of companies awaiting privatisation is their associated risk, as their economic developments are very hard to forecast with any certainty. If, however, the state holds on to part of a company via the THA, it has a stake both in the risks and in the possible increase in value that can arise when the individual companies improve. The demand for companies can then be increased by this policy of partial privatisation and therefore of easier market access. The THA pursues this policy, e. g. in the case of an MBO, when the payment of the purchase price can under certain circumstances be postponed, and also when particularly risky companies are being privatised.

38 On this point, see: article by Küpper in this volume.

39 If one compares the total proceeds realised up to 30th June 1993 of DM 43.5 billion with omitted investment undertakings totalling DM 180.1 billion, the proportion is about 1:4; see also: Table 16 in the statistical appendix.

40 On this point, see: Hax, *Privatization Agencies*.

41 If privatisation is carried out with vouchers, the concentration of decision-making into a small number of hands first has to be carried out through the secondary market, e. g. through banks or investment trusts.

42 On this point, see: G. and H.-W. Sinn, *Kaltstart*.

43 On this point, see: Neldner's discussion of G. and H.-W. Sinn's book *Kaltstart*. He does not consider this argument particularly convincing when looked at against the background of the THA's small revenue from sales; see also footnote 39 above.

44 It was for this reason that the BVVG, the THA's land sale and administration company, was established in September 1992. 75% of its capital is held by banks.

A further reason for the slack demand for THA companies, particularly those producing tradable goods, is that companies in western Germany and other EC countries often had ultra-modern production facilities, often not running at full capacity. It would therefore have made little sense for western German and west European companies to invest more heavily in eastern German companies in the same industries.

Another possibility for lengthening the period of time over which privatisation takes place is to keep companies for a longer time in state ownership and to work with management contracts. This was done, necessarily, in the management contracts signed with power utilities, because of the long legal delay in implementing their sale.[45] But under which criteria are the companies to be managed, and "investor-neutral" investment plans drawn up, if they are shortly to be privatised? Clear targets have to be set and supervised. This is difficult during the enormous structural changes which followed German unification, particularly in manufacturing industry.[46] How was the THA to design an incentive scheme for top management when even an insider finds it hard enough to distinguish between external factors affecting the company and the management's success in managing it?

A further reason for rapid privatisation instead of restructuring is the imperfect market for managerial talent. The THA's experience shows how difficult it is to "buy in" good managers to handle the restructuring of the company. There are more than enough opportunists and managers who were unsuccessful in the west, but really effective experts are very hard to come by. The THA is therefore thrown back mainly on the managers who are already in eastern Germany but first need to be familiarised with the new notions of a free market if it wants to pursue a policy of active restructuring.[47]

2. Privatisation by the THA

The quickest and most efficient way of restructuring and modernising a company's structure is usually to allow the purchaser to do it. The quicker companies are privatised, the sooner they will have access to capital, modern management knowledge, and technology. These are the crucial factors for achieving competitiveness under the new economic condition. It is these arguments which primarily justify the THA's theory that rapid privatisation means rapid restructuring.

The overall economic conditions brought about by the political precepts of the unification process only permitted one strategy for restructuring and unbundling: the fastest possible privatisation, coupled with the option, in well justified cases, of first restructuring individual companies.[48] By 1st August 1993, 7,247 of the 12,142 companies handed to the THA or created by conversion and unbundling had been handed back to their previous owners or handed on to new ones, with 1,481,000 jobs taken over or guaranteed and investments promised totalling DM

45 See Section V.1 above.

46 As compared to the case of public utilities referred to above.

47 See: Letter from Hero Brahms to the Minister-Presidents of the States dated 18th March 1993, and: Müller, *Managementtransfer in die neuen Bundesländer.*

48 For a slightly different view on this, see: G. and H.-W. Sinn, *Kaltstart*.

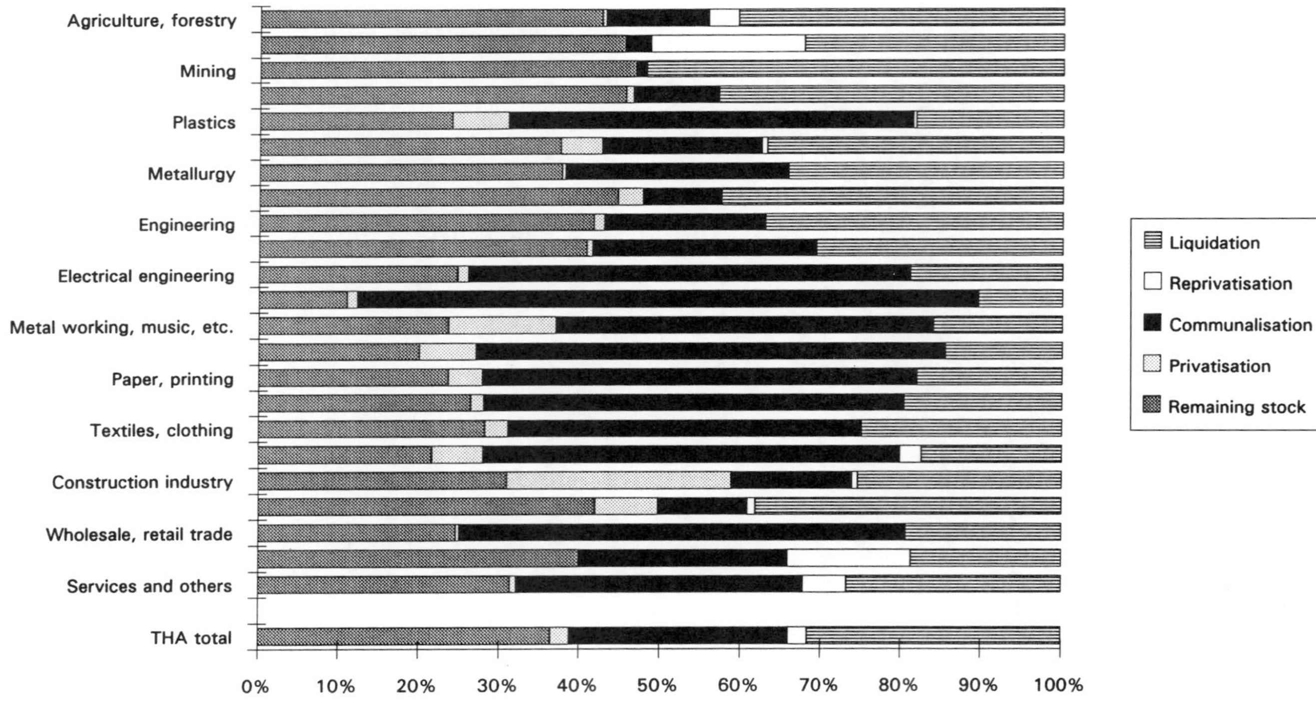

Figure 5 Progress in privatisation until June 1993 weighted by the number of employees[1] of the second quarter of 1991

Source: Treuhandanstalt Documentation Department

Notes: [1]Shares weighted by the number of employees as of the second Quarter of 1991 or, for those companies no longer on the THA's books on 30th June 1991, at an earlier point in time. Reference was not made to the figure available as of 30th June 1993 on numbers employed because, for instance, companies undergoing liquidation were shedding employees particularly rapidly and they would thus have been under-represented in these figures. Companies have not been included if they were only partially privatised or communalised, as this did not reduce the THA's stock.

180.1 billion.[49] This involved the reprivatisation (restitution to the previous owners) of 1,446 companies. 264 were "communalised", or handed over to eastern German regional administrative bodies, and 79 were assigned to new owners.[50] In almost 2,400 cases, privatisation took the form of management buy-outs (MBO's), an instrument of particular importance for creating a structure of small to medium-sized owner-operated businesses. The 1,513 companies for which the THA was still responsible on 1st August 1993 held a total work-force of 267,000. Liquidation proceedings had been started for 2,880 companies, but these often take a considerable amount of time and by that date had only been completed for 59 of them.[51]

Privatisation did not run at a uniform pace in all the individual sectors. Those in attractive sectors, such as those in which the competitive pressure was not as tough, for instance because their markets were regionalised, could be privatised more quickly than those in industries like textiles, engineering, and electronics where the need for adaptation was greater and competition more intensive.[52] Weighted by the number of employees, the progress of privatisation was greatest up to June 1993 in the fields of construction and its ancillary trades, food, quarrying, and wholesale and retail trade. The problem areas had always been, from the start of privatisation, in mining, agriculture and forestry, leather and shoes, and textiles and clothing (Fig. 5). Based on the number of companies being privatised, an above-average progress was achieved in the fields of energy, quarrying, and construction, and also in wholesale and retail trade and services. In the construction and ancillary industry, the rate of privatisation weighted by number of employees is greater than that weighted by the number of firms, but the proportions are the other way round in the energy field, wholesale and retail trade, and services.[53]

3. Mergers and diversification

By far the greatest proportion of eastern German companies created through privatisation arose from mergers with western German companies, and in some cases with foreign companies.[54] Not only the distribution of company acquisitions between western German and foreign firms is of interest, but also the distribution at the sectoral level and the horizontal, vertical, and conglomerate nature of these mergers. The THA's privatisation balance-sheet contains no indication of the sectoral origin of the purchasers of the various companies, but a statistical evaluation by the Federal Cartel Office allows these questions to be answered;[55] however, this only covers a proportion of the THA's privatisations because it sets a threshold of DM 500 million for the purchaser.

---

49 On this point, see: Fig. 3 above and Table 16 in the statistical appendix; Treuhandanstalt, *Monatsinformation der THA* as of 31st July 1993.

50 On this point, see: articles by König and by Willgerodt in this volume.

51 See: Treuhandanstalt, *Monatsinformation der THA* as of 31st July 1993; Table 16 in the statistical appendix.

52 See Figs. 5 and 6 in this text and Tables 14 and 15 in the statistical appendix, and: editors' introduction, page 2 et seq.

53 On this point, see: Gruhler, *Unternehmensbezogene Umstrukturierung in den neuen Bundesländern.*

54 By the end of July 1993, foreign investors had acquired 732 THA companies or parts of companies (5.7% of all privatisations), undertaking to invest a total of DM 18.9 billion (10% of the total) and guaranteeing 140,779 jobs (likewise 10%); Treuhandanstalt, *Monatsinformation der THA* as of 31st July 1993.

55 Frisch, *Unternehmenszusammenschlüsse in den neuen Bundesländern.*

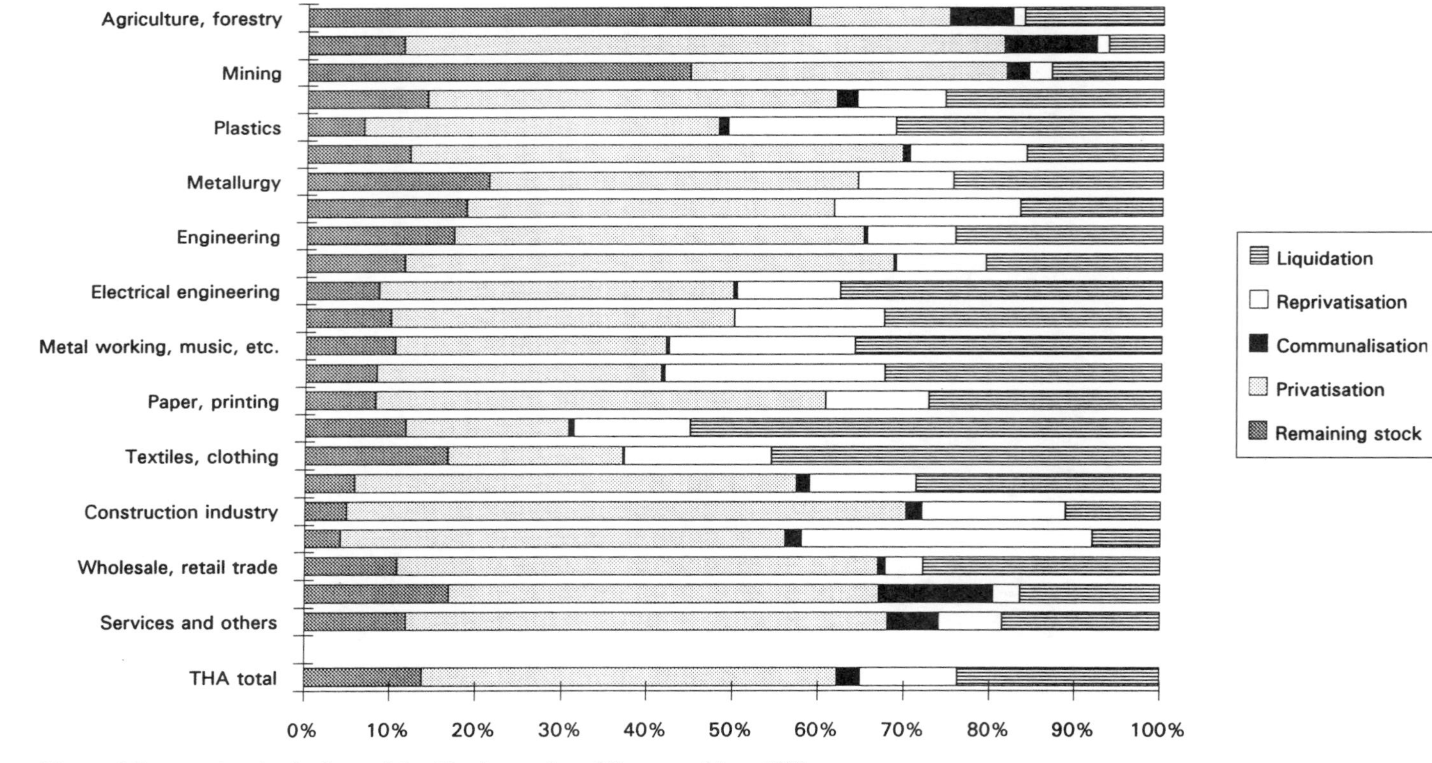

Figure 6 Progress in privatisation weighted by the number of firms, as of June 1993
Source: Treuhandanstalt Documentation Department

Table 3:
Distribution of mergers[1] by sectors

Sector	Mergers		Turnover acquired[2]	
	No.	in %	DM million	in %
Agriculture and forestry, animal husbandry, fishing	14	1.0	656	0.5
Power generation and distribution, gas and water supply	96	6.7	35,175	28.5
Mining	0		0	
Manufacturing industry in total	602	42.2	33,002	26.7
Raw materials and production goods	275	19.3	15,517	12.6
Capital goods	195	13.7	11,289	9.1
Consumer goods	37	2.6	1,117	0.9
Foodstuffs and food products incl. drinks	95	6.7	5,079	4.1
Construction industry including real estate	98	6.9	4,639	3.8
Wholesale and retail trade[2] in total	400	28.1	24,727	20.0
Food and drinks trade	198	13.9		
Petroleum and fuel trade	44	3.1		
Building materials trade	28	2.0		
Metal trade	17	1.2		
Chemical products trade	20	1.4		
General and mixed trade	26	1.8		
Service trades in total	190	13.3	25,083	20.3
Financial services[2]	29	2.0	6,470	5.2
Publishing and newspapers[2]	67	4.7	16,145	13.1
Services for environment and waste disposal	36	2.5	372	0.3
Transport and communications	26	1.8	276	0.2
Total	1,426	100.0	123,558	100.0

Notes: [1]Mergers completed with eastern German companies and reported to the Federal Cartel Office by the end of 1992.
[2]Based on turnover as defined by the Distortion of Competition Act: trade turnover reduced by a quarter; publishers rated at one-twentieth of their turnover, banks at one-tenth of their balance-sheet totals; insurance companies on their premium income; all taken from the most recent annual accounts. Turnover in East German Marks converted to DM at 2:1.

Source: Bundeskartellamt; Frisch, Unternehmenszusammenschlüsse in den neuen Bundesländern.

The sectoral distribution of mergers, weighted by the amount of turnover thus acquired, shows the following picture at the end of 1992: 28.5% of the total turnover was accounted for by the power generation and distribution and gas and water supply industries, 26.7% by manufacturing industry, 20.3% by the service sector, and 20.0% by wholesale and retail trading (Table 3).

The Federal Cartel Office's figures on mergers also permits the purchasers and the companies they acquire to be identified by sector of origin. Horizontal mergers dominate totally, with 92.6%, 95.9%, and 91.7% in the years 1990 to 1992 respectively. The proportion of vertical mergers fell from 5.8% in 1990 to 1.7% in 1991, rising slightly to 2.9% in 1992. Mergers of a conglomerate nature, meaning that the acquiring company was entering a totally new market, increased in the same period from 1.7% to 2.4% to 5.4%.

The dominance of horizontal mergers supports the theory of effective management and technological transfer through rapid privatisation. Companies acquiring others within their own industry are better able to evaluate its profit situation and to carry out the necessary restructuring more effectively than investors from outside the industry, and indeed better than the THA could. The very small but growing number of conglomerate mergers, however, gives rise to the assumption that it has become easier to evaluate the profit potential of companies and their management teams. The growing involvement of foreign companies in mergers, rising from 16.5% in 1990 to 16.7% in 1991 and to 23.8% in 1992, also appears to reflect a growing transparency in the evaluation of eastern German companies' potential profitability, and of course the redoubled efforts of the THA in finding buyers.

4. MBO/MBI

MBO's and MBI's have become significant forms of privatisation of the THA recently.[56] In an MBO, the employees or the managers in a company (and in an MBI from outside it) take over both ownership of and responsibility for managing the company or part of it having been unbundled before. This route enables a *Mittelstand*, a group of small to medium-sized independent company owner-managers to be created and strengthened in eastern Germany. Roughly one privatisation in six took this form; the total achieved by June 1993 was 2,364. This form of privatisation is however concentrated on a relatively small number of sectors of the economy, as Fig. 7 shows; most of them are engaged in services, and very few in manufacturing industry. MBO's are of significance mainly for small and medium-sized businesses.[57] In the case of MBO's the purchasers came mainly from inside the company, where 93% of them had had a leading position before. Only 7% came from outside the company, mainly in the case of MBI's; 74% of these purchasers were western Germans.[58]

The THA gave every possible support to this kind of privatisation. However, these newly-established business owners requested, and usually greatly needed, a more intensive consultancy assistance from the THA. This applied in particular to support and advice on financing and the prolongation of bank guarantees.

The use of the MBO/MBI as a novel instrument in the process of restructuring began under difficult conditions. The great majority of the buyers had very little market experience or knowledge and, in addition to this, the companies concerned were usually in a difficult economic situation anyway, as can be seen from the fact that no outside investor was interested in them. It therefore seems fair to say, in at least some of these cases, that the MBO teams took over the management of their company because they were forced into it.[59]

The success-rate achieved so far is surprisingly good, bearing the difficult initial circumstances in mind. Some 74% of these companies are currently in at least a satisfactory situation,

---

56 This applies at least when based on the number of companies being privatised.

57 According to: Friedrich, *Management Buy-Out*, 66% of the companies privatised by MBO/MBI have fewer than 50 employees, and only 16% of them employed more than 100 at the time they were taken over by their own management.

58 op. cit.

59 An investigation carried out on behalf of the Federal Ministry for Economic Affairs (see: Friedrich, *Management Buy-Out*) showed that in most MBO's the desire to preserve the participants' own job and those of their subordinates was the prime factor rather than any desire to become a self-employed business person.

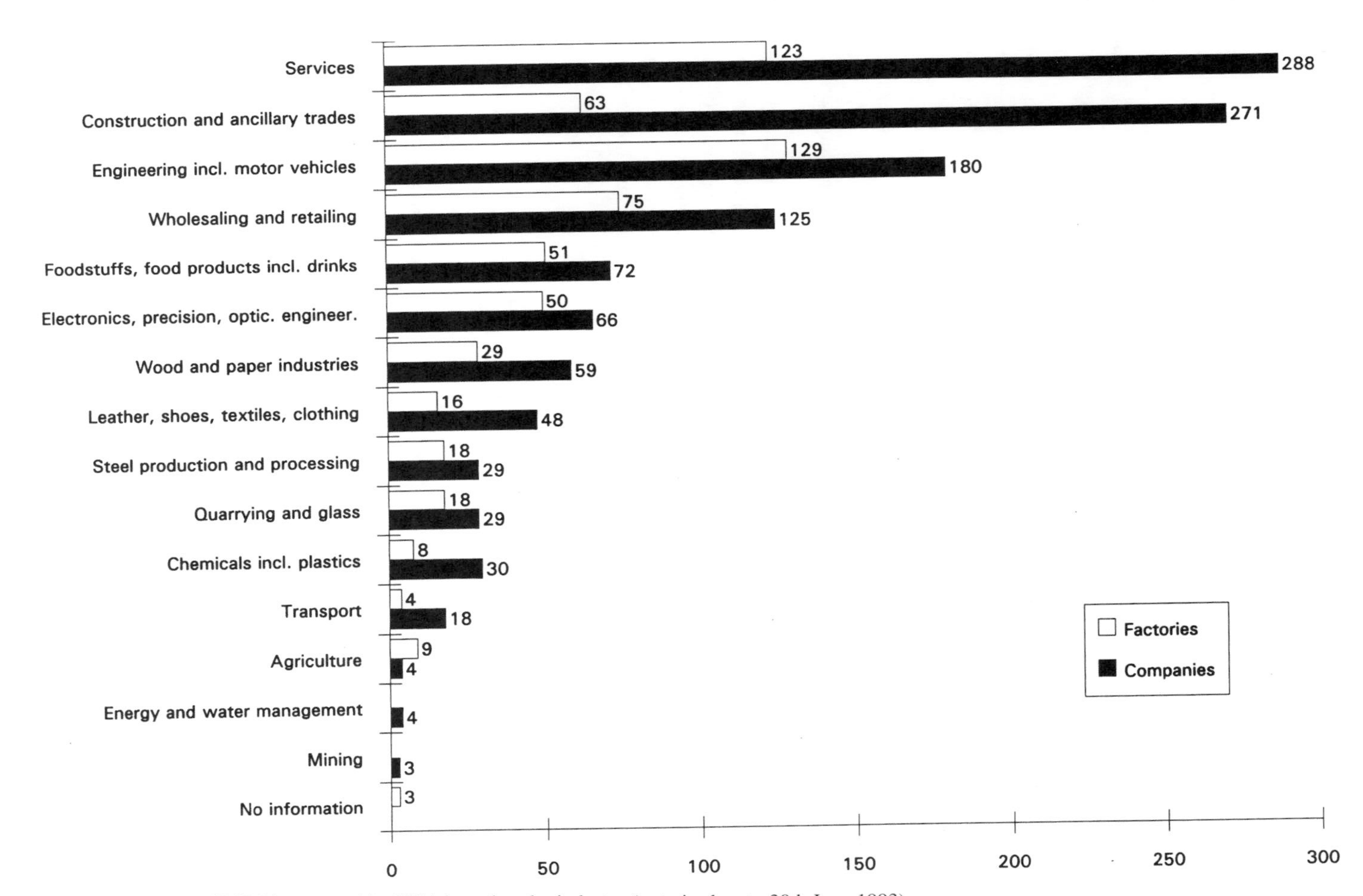

Figure 7 Number of MBO's arranged by THA branches, by industry (notarised up to 30th June 1993)
Source: Treuhandanstalt, Department U2 C2.

although in some cases there is still a certain amount of risk attaching to them. Only 5% of the MBO's/MBI's had failed, as of March 1993, although another 10% are in difficult economic straits.

5. Restitution

A further possible form of restructuring arose, in addition to that imposed "from above" and that carried out by the companies autonomously, and this was "reprivatisation" or restitution of firms or parts of them to their previous rightful owners. Thus individual factories or operating units were in some cases unbundled from their *Kombinat* with the aim of reprivatising them. In many cases, because of the great length of time during which the companies had been in state hands and because of changes in production methods and conditions, they were not capable of surviving in this form after reprivatisation, with the result that the former owners had to restructure them all over again, but this time under their own supervision.

In just the short time in which the Modrow government was in power, some 3,000 companies were handed back to their former owners. Up to August 1993 the THA had reprivatised another 1,360. Figs. 5 and 6 above show the sectoral importance of this form of privatisation. Weighted by number of companies, reprivatised companies play an important part in the building industry, printing works, and in the textiles field. No statement is possible on the restructuring measures and the expenditure incurred by the former owners on adaptation to changed times in comparison with the new owners of "freshly" privatised businesses,[60] but they complain that, because of their having to accept the historic debt and the risk of historic environmental pollution of their companies, they are often worse treated than investors in "fresh" privatisations; the latter are partly or completely let off these obligations by the THA in order to bring the purchase price up above zero. In order to ensure that all business owners start on comparable terms, however, the THA is prepared to improve the position of some reprivatised companies retroactively if they are having a particularly hard time of it.

6. Private and small and medium-sized enterprises (SME's)

Private companies, especially of the SME or *Mittelstand* category were of little significance in the old East Germany, and only occurred in a few areas of the economy. They only attained a certain prominence in the craft and catering trades, and even then were limited to small or family companies. Great hopes were therefore set in the newly created *Mittelstand* industrial and craft companies.[61]

In 1990, when the East German economy started to make its radical change, there were a good 80,000 craft enterprises employing about 400,000 people. A survey carried out by the German national association for craft enterprises showed that at the end of 1992 there were already 131,500 craft enterprises providing jobs for about 850,000 people.[62] The greatest growth in

60 On this point, see: article by Willgerodt in this volume.

61 The demarcation criteria for *Mittelstand* companies are supposed to be an upper limit of 500 employees, including the smallest companies with fewer than 20 employees and all craft enterprises.

62 On this point, see: *Süddeutsche Zeitung* of 8th June 1993.

employment came in the branches of the economy associated with construction. It is on the basis of these figures that it is fair to describe craft enterprises as the first to enjoy a dynamic upswing.

According to the results from questionnaires analysed by the DIW,[63] an economic research institute, *Mittelstand* companies have taken on considerable significance in the short time since the old East German economy collapsed. Apart from the establishment of new companies, this is mainly attributable to the shrinkage of the old companies and the process of vertical unbundling. According to this investigation, the description of *Mittelstand* fits two thirds of all companies in eastern Germany. In the manufacturing industry one of six employees is working in SME's. They have gained great significance in the food industry, particularly in the bakery and butchery areas, in wood-working, in plastic products, and in metal products and motor vehicles (particular motor repair workshops). There significance is small in those industries which produce in large-scale plant (chemicals, metals production); they are more important as small, mainly craft enterprises, and two thirds of them employ less than 20 people each.

The private companies which survived from GDR days, whether as independent companies or as members of a *Produktionsgenossenschaft des Handwerks* or PGH ("craft production co-operative"), are now in a minority. On the one hand, numerous new companies have arrived on the scene as a result of privatisation, reprivatisation, MBO's, and as newly established firms, and on the other hand many of the earlier East German SME's were unable to maintain their level of sales in the new competitive conditions and simply gave up. On the basis of numbers employed, the privatised and reprivatised companies, which were originally owned by the THA, form the largest group of all SME's. The new companies, established after 1989, employed only a slightly smaller number of people in the summer of 1992, according to the DIW survey quoted above, than the private businesses from the old GDR.

Both the unbundling of the old companies and access to the production capacity they no longer needed, sometimes in conjunction with liquidations, were particularly important for the rapid development of the *Mittelstand*. According to the DIW survey, a quarter of the existing craft enterprises had been founded after 1989; one in ten of them was a former THA company. The majority of the *Mittelstand* companies in manufacturing industry had previously been owned by the THA, but all the same no less than a quarter of east German industrial companies had been established after the collapse of the communist system.

All in all, these small to medium-sized companies have managed to re-establish themselves and take on considerable significance in eastern Germany since unification. Nevertheless, the process of restructuring in this field has not run its full course by a long way. One difficult problem for further development is bound to be the rapid decline of eastern German industry, which is leading to a fall-off in demand by larger, economically sound companies and thus failing to provide the necessary growth impetus for the smaller ones. As a result, most of the *Mittelstand* companies seem too be pinning too great hopes on their potential for growth.

7. Companies based on ABM and ABS job creation schemes

Because of the high level of unemployment in eastern Germany, particularly widespread use is being made of such labour market policy instruments as ABM and ABS. (ABM is *Arbeitsbe-*

63 On this point, see: DIW, *Wochenbericht* 11 (1992).

schaffungsmaßnahmen, "measures for creating jobs", and ABS is *Arbeitsförderung, Beschäftigung und Strukturentwicklung*, "promotion of work, employment, and structural development").[64] The aim of these temporary programmes and companies is to carry workers over their period of unemployment and to provide them with retraining and further training. The companies funded under those schemes took in nearly 400,000 employees in 1993. The THA's attitude to these labour market policy instruments is laid down in a joint declaration dated 13th April 1991 by the THA, the DGB (The German Federation of Trade Unions), and the DAG (Trade Union of German Employees, for salaried staff, the largest union not affiliated to the DGB) on regulations for redundancy compensation plan (the so-called social plans): the THA "will give particular support to companies in the use of the statutory instruments of promotion of work, especially in further vocational training, retraining, and work familiarisation, and in job-creation schemes in the companies in which the employees are threatened with the loss of their jobs".[65]

The main activity of these schemes is less training but more creating jobs (ABM) and implementing modernisation and restructuring (ABS). The main priority is the environmental and infrastructural area, followed by modernisation and restructuring companies. The main aim is thus to support public-sector activities in the environmental and infrastructural area until the situation on the labour market has returned to something near normal, and if these "artificial" organisations later develop into companies capable of survival this will at the same time be a contribution to creating a structure of private companies. However, this road is a long and hard one. It seems certain that greater support for hiving off parts of companies as part of the privatisation programme, e. g. through MBO or MBI, would have been more promising here than this indirect route.[66] The main point with THA activities in connection with ABM and ABS companies is therefore temporary material support in making redundancy easier to bear.

The THA regards these firms as an "employment policy catchment basin" for temporary employment in *Qualifizierungsgesellschaften (ABM)*, companies formed to train workers while employing them, and *Beschäftigungsgesellschaften (ABS)*, companies formed to employ workers mainly in social and environmental activities, with the aim of making the process of the privatisation of THA companies socially bearable. At the same time it did stress, however, repeatedly that employment policy was legally no part of its sphere of responsibility.

But increasingly, partly as a result of political pressure and public opinion, the THA had to show itself more willing to take financial responsibility for the companies within its ambit of responsibility. It supported major ABM projects by providing interest-free loans and bearing some of their costs (up to 10% of total costs, and recently up to 20%, to be used as a contribution to material costs). However, the THA would be glad if it could judiciously absolve itself from responsibility for the ABM companies if this can be done without jeopardising their existence. It regards the limited (negotiable) allocation of some property and tangible assets of THA companies to them as one measure designed to this end; these assets have as a rule already been transferred to the TLG. The THA positions are widely given a positive rating by the ABM and ABS companies.[67]

---

64 On this point, see: article by Kern and Sabel in this volume.

65 Reprinted in: *Treuhandanstalt Informationen* 3/4 (July/August 1991), page 23.

66 See: above, Section VI.4.

67 On this point, see: Outline agreement dated 17th July 1991; Härtel, Krüger, Seeler, and Weinhold, *Unternehmenssanierung und Wettbewerb in den neuen Bundesländern.*

The instigation of these companies was often an "reconciliation of interests" or "social plan", in other words the legal basis of a redundancy scheme. A study made by the Hans Böckler economic research foundation in 1992 showed that, in 57% of the cases investigated, the initiative for such companies came from works management, often in collaboration with works councils and local or county authorities. The trade unions and the State governments played only a minor role in establishing them.[68] The THA companies as shareholders are therefore almost always of major importance.

8. Liquidation

For companies and parts of them which even in the long term have very little prospect of becoming economically viable although much is spent on restructuring them, there is no other alternative but liquidation. The only exceptions to this rule are conceivable at most for reasons of structural and regional policy. By the end of July 1993, closure had been initiated for 2,880 companies because the THA no longer saw any prospect for effectively restructuring them, and completed for 59 of them. A total of 303,671 jobs were affected by liquidation up to that point in time. However, the hope existed for many companies that new commercial activities could arise out of the old structures after the close-down, e. g. through the establishment of new companies and by putting the old land, buildings, and equipment to new uses. The THA estimates that some 25 to 30% of the employees affected by liquidation would be able to find a new job at the old location. In some cases liquidation has even shown that the separate parts of the company would have been capable of being privatised (e. g. *Pentacon Dresden, MZ Zschopau*). In other cases, when liquidation was ordered it was road-blocked by the employees who thus forced a "normal" privatisation (e. g. *Addinol Mineralöl GmbH*).

Figs. 5 and 6 above show the distribution of liquidated firms by sectors; the loss of jobs through the liquidation of companies was particularly severe in the fields of electrical, precision, and optical engineering and the textiles and clothing industries. However, even in those areas where privatisation had already gone a long way, such as food and drink, paper and printing, and plastic and rubber, the THA regards the situation for most of the companies it is still left with as quite hopeless. On the other hand, there have been relatively few closures in quarrying, fine ceramics, and the glass industry, which is almost certainly connected with the positive trend in the eastern German building industry. Relatively few liquidations were set off in the steel and the chemical industries and in engineering, which are the industries in which THA companies still provide half the jobs. In such industries as steel structures, light engineering, and railway wagons, major THA companies still dominated the scene in 1993, as they did in motor vehicle construction and ship-building. In these cases, political reasons also militate strongly against closures, and this is why relatively few of these employees had been affected by liquidation up to that date.

68 See: Hans-Böckler-Stiftung (editor): *Qualifizierungs- und Beschäftigungsinitiativen*, page 3.

9. Restructuring and the retention of industrial core activities

The THA itself describes the relative priorities in its transformation work in one pithy motto: "rapid privatisation – resolute restructuring – considerate closure". The first and the last aspect of this strategy have indeed been implemented. The THA has sustained a pace of privatisation that few would have considered possible, but for a host of reasons has so far been rather more cautious with liquidation. However, controversy flared up, sometimes violently, over its restructuring work and the question of preserving jobs in the companies still on its books. Although the Federal government on more than one occasion emphasised its general support for the task of restructuring with the aim of "maintaining and further developing eastern Germany as a varied and diverse economic location", the question was left unanswered as to the extent to which the maintenance of "industrial core activities" was to be linked with the retention of "old" companies.

Two aspects based on structure political experience in West Germany over the past decades are worth considering here. It is easier to promote growth in regional centres than to hold back the deterioration of economically unattractive locations. On the other hand, it is more of a problem to create new centres of growth within a short time once the industrial infrastructure has completely disappeared. For this reason it is not possible to invoke economic criteria alone for the restructuring or close-down of companies, usually large ones, which are important for the whole economic infrastructure of a region (such as the shipyards in the north, *EKO-Stahl* near the river Oder, or *Zeiss-Jena*). The decision has to be supplemented by an examination of the macro-economic opportunity costs. As unemployment is anyway high in the economically weak regions in eastern Germany, the loss of each additional job is highly likely to lead to long-term unemployment.

The entire discounted costs of one permanently unemployed person, amplified by the so-called multiplier effect, is about DM 300,000.[69] A major German economic research organisation, the Institut der Deutschen Wirtschaft,[70] has put a figure of about DM 110,000 on the investment needed per job for a company categorised as capable of restructuring, i. e. one capable of survival in the long term under market conditions if given the appropriate support, if the company is in manufacturing and nearly DM 160,000 if it is in the field of transport and communications. In capital-intensive industries it is considerably higher even than this. The restructuring costs per job to be borne by the THA should therefore only exceed these figures as a result of giving special consideration to special structural and probably social policy angles. For instance, investment grants were given to the eastern German shipyards at the rate of DM 800,000 per job, some of it subsidised by the EC. The expenditure incurred at *Carl Zeiss Jena* was of a similar magnitude; part of it was borne by the State of Thuringia, but it is still not entirely clear here whether the jobs preserved will be profitable and capable of long-term survival.

Subsidies on this massive scale, based on political decisions for conserving the structure, can scarcely be justified in terms of the THA's task of restructuring.[71] A greater readiness to assume direct responsibility on the part of political forces, meaning the Federal and State governments, seems to be called for her. On the other hand, in those companies that have been on the THA's

69 See: McKinsey & Company, *Überlegungen zur kurzfristigen Stabilisierung.*

70 See: Gruhler, *Unternehmensbezogene Umstrukturierung in den neuen Bundesländern.*

71 On this point, see: article by Schwalbach in this volume.

books for rather longer it is possible to discern a something of a "wait and see" attitude to restructuring. All the usual restructuring programmes such as redundancies, unbundling, and principally investments in modernising the production plant have to be carried out in the interests of an unknown outside party and without any commercial risk. Thus the THA companies, in comparison with those already privatised, have invested far too little in proportion to their numbers employed. Because there is no proper incentive system, it is expected completely too much of the THA compared with an actively managed, private restructuring. It was in order finally to find a way out of the problem of these incentives, and to simplify institutional control, that the Management-KG's were founded. Experience to date indicates a change in behaviour, but time alone will tell whether this concept will allow the remaining THA companies to cope with their restructuring responsibilities or whether this is really only a transfer of the THA's control rights and responsibilities.

VII. Results of the process of structural change

It is necessary to take the macro-economic and sectoral effects over which the THA had no influence into account in analysing the process of structural change under its own control. At the beginning of this article we demonstrated the macro-economic and sectoral adjustment effects of German unification and the structural shortcomings which these brought to light. The decline of large parts of industrial production capacity as a result of their dependence on foreign trade, and also the lack of knowledge concerning the market economy within the companies, were the main characteristics of the environment in which the THA's privatisation strategy has to be evaluated. It played a dominant role in the conversion of *Kombinate* and VEB-companies under the old organisation of the planned economy in a decentralised economy functioning on market principles. Finally, the THA not only had to reconstruct the old structures and forms of organisation completely, but also supervise the companies during this process of transition and take on the huge task of giving them new, productive work to do. Nevertheless, the construction of a really independent and functioning privatisation institution was very difficult to begin with, as the problems of the "leaderless phase" up to the middle of 1991 have shown. The THA therefore had to work with highly simplified management instruments, such as the introduction of harsh budget restrictions in individual companies. This to a large extent led to the right, decentralised decisions. Principally for political reasons, however, these restrictions were sometimes circumvented, and this was very probably connected with a corresponding squandering of resources.

The horizontal, vertical, and geographical unbundling of the old *Kombinate* and companies then really was a far more radical and specific form of intervention on the company structures. The decentralised restructuring concept chosen by the THA, working through the appointment of Supervisory and Advisory Boards and decentralised support by the THA branches, has proved to be an effective management model for paving the way to privatisation, particular since the middle of 1991. In the eighteen months preceding this, however, uncontrolled, autonomous unbundling was of considerable significance and was usually based purely on criteria specific to that one company. At the same time, of course, the different forms of privatisation (e. g. reprivatisation, communalisation, or partial privatisation) changed corporate structures further; their indirect structural effects can, however, only be seen as a by-product of the privatisation process. Despite its enormous size and the scope of the legal measures it employed, the THA's ability to influence each sector's industrial structures was limited. This is partly connected with the fact that, although large parts of the economy were subservient to it, not all were,[72] and its scope for exerting influence of course declined as privatisation progressed. Compared with a total number of people in employment in eastern Germany of about 7.7 million on 1st January 1991, even during the phase of the "great" THA only about 3 million people were employed in its companies; by 1st April 1993 the proportion was 0.4 million out of a total of 6.2 million. Even in those sectors in which the THA had complete control its creative scope was partly limited by statutory requirements (such as communalisation and restitution). Even in the companies which were no longer capable of being restructured, because of statutory regulations and budget limitations the only possibility was often liquidation, and this could often be put off for a long time. The structural effects which we have described here thus resulted more often from the THA's reacting to sectoral developments and from the fulfilling of its statutory duties.

Through the policy of rapid privatisation, the equally important problem of changes in company supervision was pushed into the background. Although the problem of effective company supervision was solved in those companies that had already been sold, the question of the more active implementation of corporate strategies took on a growing significance in those companies that were left on the THA's books. The development of the concept of Management-KG's was an initiative in this direction, but it often covered a number of industries at once. Apart from this, corporate strategies specific to one industry were prepared more frequently under direct THA supervision, e. g. for the shipyards, the chemical and the steel industry.

The THA's task also included creating effective sectoral competitive structures. It was able to assume that there would be free market access for goods and services as part of the overall economic conditions resulting from German unification. Its privatisation also followed the goal, after a little gentle pressure from the Federal Cartel Office,[73] of creating effective competitive structures in the individual industries and reducing the barriers to market entry. The active search for foreign investors[74] not only improved the competitive situation in the various industries but also created additional demand for the companies still awaiting privatisation. The release of property no longer required for operations as a result of spacial unbundling was helpful in facilitating market access for new companies. It was not possible here to investigate the question in more detail as to whether any increased effort in liquidation would have made more sense in the direction.

The exit from the market, or liquidation, of companies no longer capable of being restructured is likewise part of the creation of an effective competitive structure. Although the THA has often been accused that it held individual companies above water financially for too long, thus distorting competition particularly for companies from western Germany,[75] this can be justified as part of the socially acceptable liquidation of moribund companies.

A further goal of privatisation was to raise the proportion of independent owners of capital in eastern Germany. However, the scope the THA had for influencing this on the ownership side

---

72 By way of a few examples: the railways, the post office, banks, health care, and libraries.

73 On this point, see: Härtel, Krüger, Seeler, and Weinhold, *Unternehmenssanierung und Wettbewerb in den neuen Bundesländern*; also: Frisch, *Unternehmenszusammenschlüsse in den neuen Bundesländern.*

74 See footnote 54 above.

75 For instance, the Bundesbank discovered in 1993, after analysing the balance sheets of 863 eastern German companies for 1991, that they had a return on sales of minus 13.5%; the figure in manufacturing industry was minus 23%.

was very small. There was too little capital in the form of savings available in eastern Germany, and even the banks tended to be cautious in financing the corporate strategies of eastern German company owners. This is why capital from western Germany and other countries became very dominant. The THA's initiatives to encourage the growth of a *Mittelstand* or SME, principally using the instruments of MBO and MBI, were only able to counter this trend to a certain extent. Nevertheless, these initiatives, together with so-called "mini" privatisation (retail trade, restaurants and cafés, hotels, etc.) became an important building block in the creation of a true, local business-owning class in eastern Germany.

The aim of also creating jobs through privatisation was a difficult one for the THA to reach. On the contrary, the rationalisation of companies connected with privatisation or with preparation for it tended to have just the opposite effect. On top of that came the macro-economic conditions of economic and monetary union under which the THA had to operate and the rapid levelling up, which was also politically intentional, of wages towards western German levels at a rate far beyond the growth in labour productivity. The result was an enormous fall-off in production and employment, particularly in manufacturing industry, which could hardly be compensated for by positive factors in the other sectors such as craft enterprises and the remaining services. By the middle of 1993, some 80% of the old industrial jobs were lost. The creation of new and more competitive jobs, however, is taking more time than the THA ever had available to it. Even the substantial assistance provided by ABM and ABS programmes only had the effect of softening the impact slightly.

The resolute and rapid restructuring of the remaining industrial core industries, accompanied by the liquidation of the ones that cannot be restructured, is therefore necessary, but so is also the further support of job creation schemes in order to be able to fill the gap in demand for labour during the transitional period. It is possible that the THA relied for too long on market forces and neglected to initiate an active restructuring programme in its key industries to accompany its very successful privatisation strategy. A typical sign of this is the totally inadequate rate of investment in the THA companies rated as worth to be restructured compared with the normal rate in companies already privatised.

Nevertheless, the THA's restructuring policy was a successful one particularly viewed against the background of the difficult macro-economic conditions of the time and the need to establish itself first as a functioning institution. This also applies in comparison with the situation in the other post-communist countries which might be held up as a comparative measure. The policy of rapid privatisation, pursued systematically, was crucial here, but also had major structural effects because it was based on normal business principles and had to be implemented in a decentralised manner. This is also showed by a glance at the sector privatisation summary given in Figs. 5 and 6, which make it clear that privatisation, measured by the number of companies involved, and even more clearly when measured by the number of employees involved, was extraordinarily difficult and time-consuming in exactly those areas in which, compared with western Germany, companies tended to have far too many employees anyway.[76] It was principally in the old industrial core areas of the East German economy, such as engineering, metal production, and steel processing that the rate of privatisation measured in terms of numbers of employees was still below 50% in June 1993 (see Fig. 5).

---

76 Agriculture and forestry, energy, mining, leather/textiles, see Table 1 above.

The THA will therefore be maintaining a major level of structural influence, in some sectors even after the end of 1993 but without having any long-term sectoral strategies for them.

The policy of restructuring, pursued ever more vigorously, is also a decentralised one if the initiatives from the States (*Länder*) such as "ATLAS" or "Anker" are ignored. The regional de-industrialisation could not for the time being be matched by any pioneering industries because of the tight time limit. When these problems were recognised, which was at a rather late stage, the scope for manoeuvre remaining to the THA had been greatly reduced by the restructuring and privatisation which had by then taken place and by its more restrictive budget conditions. Even this experience of the THA in learning a lesson late, as did the other parties involved, has to be seen as part of a painful but successful process of adaptation, particularly when viewed against the background of the difficult macro-economic conditions which we outlined at the start.

VIII. Literature

Albach, Horst: *The 1992 Uppsala Lectures in Business*. WHU, Koblenz 1992.

Bundesministerium für innerdeutsche Beziehungen (editor): *DDR Handbuch,* 2 volumes. Cologne [3]1985.

Deutsche Bundesbank: Bilanzrelationen und Ertragsverhältnisse ostdeutscher Unternehmen im Jahre 1991. In: *Monatsbericht* July 1993, pages 27 to 39.

Deutsches Institut für Wirtschaftsforschung (DIW, editor): *Analyse der strukturellen Entwicklung der deutschen Wirtschaft. Strukturberichterstattung 1992. Gutachten im Auftrag des Bundesministeriums für Wirtschaft*. Berlin 1992.

ditto: Gesamtwirtschaftliche und unternehmerische Anpassungsprozesse in Ostdeutschland, Berichte 1 bis 8. In: *Wochenbericht* 12 (1991), 24 (1991), 39 and 40 (1991), 51 and 52 (1991), 12 and 13 (1992), and 13 (1993).

ditto: Industrieller Mittelstand in Ostdeutschland. In: *Wochenbericht* 11 (1992).

ditto: Subventionierung und Privatisierung durch die Treuhandanstalt – Kurswechsel erforderlich. In: *Wochenbericht* 41 (1991).

ditto: Zur Politik der Treuhandanstalt. Eine Zwischenbilanz. In: *Wochenbericht* 7 (1992).

Dyck, Alexander: *Imperfect Information, Ownership and Incentives*. Dissertation Stanford University 1993.

Friedrich, Werner: *Management Buy-Out and Management Buy-In. Untersuchung im Auftrag des Bundesministers für Wirtschaft.* Cologne 1992.

Frisch, Thomas: Privatisierung und Unternehmenskäufe in Ostdeutschland. *HWWA-Report* No. 104, Hamburg 1992.

ditto: Unternehmenszusammenschlüsse in den neuen Bundesländern. *HWWA-Report* No. 119, Hamburg 1993.

Görzig, Bernd, and Martin *Gorning*: *Produktivität und Wettbewerbsfähigkeit der Wirtschaft der DDR*. Berlin 1991.

Gruhler, Wolfram: *Unternehmensbezogene Umstrukturierung in den neuen Bundesländern.* Cologne 1992.

Hans-Böckler-Stiftung (editor): *Qualifizierungs- und Beschäftigungsinitiativen. Bericht über eine Umfrage in den neuen Bundesländern*. Düsseldorf, May 1992.

Härtel, Hans-Hagen, Reinald *Krüger*, Joachim *Seeler*, and Marisa *Weinhold*: Unternehmenssanierung und Wettbewerb in den neuen Bundesländern. Fünfter und sechster Zwischenbericht gemäß dem Forschungsauftrag des Bundeswirtschaftsministeriums "Beobachtung und Analyse des Wettbewerbs in den neuen Bundesländern". *HWWA-Report* Nos. 100 and 103, Hamburg 1992.

Hax, Herbert: Privatization Agencies: The Treuhand Approach. In: Horst *Siebert* (editor): *Privatization Symposium in Honor of Herbert Giersch*. Tübingen 1992, pages 143 to 155.

Heseler, Herbert, and Heike *Löser*: *Die Transformation des ostdeutschen Schiffsbaus PIW/Büstro*. Rostock 1992.

Statistisches Jahrbuch der Bundesrepublik Deutschland (1989), edited by the Statistisches Bundesamt. Wiesbaden.

Statistisches Jahrbuch der Deutschen Demokratischen Republik 34 (1989), edited by the Staatliche Zentralverwaltung für Statistik. Berlin.

McKinsey & Company: *Überlegungen zur kurzfristigen Stabilisierung und langfristigen Steigerung der Wirtschaftskraft in den neuen Bundesländern*. Düsseldorf and Munich 1991.

Meinhardt, Volker, Bernhard *Seidel*, Frank *Stille*, and Dieter *Teichmann*: *Vorläufige Berechnungen zu den Transferleistungen in den NBL*. DIW, 1993.

Müller, Jürgen: The Impact of Mergers on Concentration. In: *The Journal of Industrial Economics*, December 1976, pages 113 et seq.

ditto: *Managementtransfer in die neuen Bundesländer. Schwerpunktthema zum Gutachten: Gesamtwirtschaftliche und unternehmerische Anpassungsprozesse im Gebiet der früheren DDR*. Berlin, July 1993.

Neldner, M.: Buchbesprechung. In: *Zeitschrift für Wirtschafts- und Sozialwissenschaften* 13 (1993), page 142.

Priester, Hans-Joachim: Gesellschaftsrechtliche Zweifelsfragen beim Umgang mit Treuhandunternehmen. In: *Der Betrieb* 1991, pages 2373 to 2378.

Siebert, Horst: German Unification and the Economics of Transition. *Institut für Weltwirtschaft, Working Papers* No. 468. Kiel 1991.

Sinn, Gerlinde, and Hans-Werner *Sinn*: *Kaltstart. Volkswirtschaftliche Aspekte der deutschen Vereinigung*. Tübingen [2]1992.

Treuhandanstalt Informationen, various issues.

Treuhandanstalt: *Monatsinformation der THA* as of 31st July 1993.

Regional aspects of the THA's privatisation work

by Paul Klemmer, with the assistance of Frank Aarts and Christian Cesar

I. Statement of problem

Under Article 25 section 1 of the Treaty of Unification, the ultimate aim of the THA consists of creating a competitive structure and rapidly privatising the formerly state-owned companies in eastern Germany. This is also expressed in the preamble to the *Treuhandgesetz* or THG (the East German law setting up the THA) of 17th June 1990, which after unification was passed almost unchanged into western German law. This law stresses the endeavours towards returning state commercial activities back into private hands with the same priority as the most far-reaching and rapid possible programme of privatisation. In response to this, the THA made rapid privatisation one of its core tasks and initially gave privatisation a higher working priority than restructuring.[1]

There were initially more than 8,000 *Volkseigene Betriebe* or VEB (state-owned) companies awaiting privatisation, with about 45,000 production locations and some 4 million jobs. This grew to a portfolio of almost 13,000 companies once the large *Kombinate* and the companies within them had been broken up into workable units.[2] From 1st July 1990 to 30th June 1993 a total of 12,581 of these latter had been privatised, a figure made up of 5,370 privatisations of complete companies, 6,825 of parts of companies, and 386 of mining rights.[3] Some 6,000 companies went to new investors, 1,360 were "reprivatised" (returned to their former owners), and about 300 made over to eastern German municipalities; liquidation proceedings were started, and in some cases completed, for more than 2,800 companies.[4] The portfolio remaining on the THA's books at the end of June 1993 comprised 1,668 companies.

Numerous studies and critical appraisals have now been produced on the THA's very impressive record of success, and are mainly concerned with the aims, the privatisation strategies, the financial expenditure, and the macro-economic effect on the economy of the THA's work. However, there is rarely any mention of any regional aspects, meaning that few questions are raised as to the geographical breakdown at any level below *Land* or State. Ignoring investigations conducted for individual counties or cities, there are also no complete cross-sectional anal-

---

1 This is stated in the THA's internal guidelines: „Privatisation has priority over restructuring. Restructuring should only be planned if it is demonstrably necessary in order to prepare the company for potential purchasers.“ Treuhandanstalt, *Organisationshandbuch*, serial no. 3.1.1, *Richtlinie für die Privatisierung von Betrieben*, page 1. See also: Dathe and Fritzsche, *Ziele, Tätigkeiten und Perspektiven der Treuhandanstalt.*

2 See: Treuhandanstalt, *Monatsinformation der THA* as of 30th June 1993, page 5; Dathe and Fritzsche, *Ziele, Tätigkeiten, und Perspektiven der Treuhandanstalt*, page 4.

3 See: Treuhandanstalt, *Monatsinformation der THA* as of 30th June 1993, page 6.

4 See: op cit.; Arbeitsgemeinschaft deutscher wirtschaftswissenschaftlicher Forschungsinstitute, *Die Lage der Weltwirtschaft und der deutschen Wirtschaft im Frühjahr 1993*, page 33.

yses for this regional level, although it would have been a particularly interesting question to ask to what extent overall regional conditions, as well as sectoral factors and those relating to the size of the companies, had any effect on the THA's privatisation success-rate.

The few articles which do go into regional aspects concentrate mainly on the State (*Land*) level, and the THA itself has issued plenty of regular information on this point. It can be seen, however, that there were no major differences at this level in the rate of privatisation defined as the proportion of already privatised companies to the number originally in the THA's possession.[5]

As statements made concerning the State level are very largely dominated by levelling-off effects, there is a need for a more profound break-down investigation, as this is the only way of analysing out regional regularity and other particular features. This is the aim of the present article, which to this end starts by operationalising the THA's targets and then sets up major hypotheses for evaluating regional privatisation tendencies; finally, it makes an analysis for all eastern German States of the privatisation success-rate at the county level.

II. Operationalisation of the THA's targets

1. General considerations

As already mentioned, one of the THA's main features is the complexity of its aims, which centre on rapid privatisation. Its main aim, apart from returning companies or parts of them to their previous rightful owners and making assets over to municipalities, is thus the swift and efficient sale of previously state-owned companies to commercially active investors. In other words, preference has so far been given to transferring the commercial risk to private owners, who in the ideal case contribute financial resources, markets, and relevant know-how. Therefore the THA saw it as its job to carry out "transitional restructuring", i. e. businessmen were sought of whom it could be expected that they would be able to carry out the restructuring of a factory more efficiently and to better effect than the THA itself could.

Privatisation as such took various different forms. The form which proved as a rule the most conducive to a rapid pace of privatisation was the "share deal". As it could not be in the THA's interest to remain as a minority shareholder, it usually endeavoured to sell 100% of the shares in any one company. A second form was the acquisition by an investor of the tangible assets alone of a company in an "asset deal", but this often entailed the disadvantage that it was then all the more difficult to find a buyer for the remaining rump of the company after the "juicy slices" had been sold off. On the other hand, pure share deals were also a rare occurrence in THA privatisations, as few investors were prepared to take on all existing liabilities. Those liabilities not taken over had to be met by the THA. Thus many share deals were in fact dressed up for tax purposes as asset deals.

Three possible routes are open in order to be able to understand and evaluate the THA's privatisation activities from the regional point of view. One initial approach pursued later in this article starts from the volume of privatisation, a second is guided by its effect on preserving and

5 See: Dathe and Fritzsche, *Ziele, Tätigkeiten und Perspektiven der Treuhandanstalt*, page 12 et seq., and the literature quoted there.

creating jobs, and the interest of a third approach focuses on the proceeds of company sales. The first measures the THA's success by the number of companies privatised or the number of jobs in them, or by the so-called degree of privatisation. In this connection, privatisation relates solely to the sales to which the THA gave its approval, and does not reflect the number of sales confirmed by notarised contract.[6]

This approach also plays an important part in the THA's reports, which usually give an overview of the so-called "portfolio development" or the stage reached by privatisation. This includes information on the net stock of companies still held by the THA broken down by branch of industry and size class of companies. Regional data relates only to the States. In order to analyse it at a lower regional level, the obvious approach is likewise to take the regional stock of companies still awaiting privatisation, or the number of jobs in these companies, at different dates and to compare them with one another. On the basis of the changing level of "stocks", it is then possible to make statements concerning the relative changes, i. e. reductions in the regional "stocks" of companies or employees in relation to the original figure for each region, and to make regional comparisons on this basis which provide information on the degree of privatisation success achieved in each region.

A further important criterion for the THA's privatisation decisions was and is the preservation and creation of jobs. Preservation means the transfer of existing contracts of employment to the investor, and creation relates to some future point in time (related to a predetermined date); this indicates the potential of the corporate strategy submitted by the potential buyer. The latter usually represents an important basis for sales negotiations between the THA and the investor, and is closely linked with specific plans for future investments. These result mainly from the corporate strategy, and correlate of course with the criterion of jobs, because rationalisation and modernisation are very closely linked to levels of employment.

Penalty clauses are built into the contract of sale in order to hold the purchaser to his obligation to provide the jobs and investment he has promised. If the contract is not adhered to, contractual penalties become due for payment to the vendor. Consequently, contractual penalties for failure to provide jobs are agreed fixed amounts for each job not provided; those for failure to make investments are a percentage, often on a sliding scale that increases over time, of the investment not made. A distinction needs to be made between an undertaking to provide jobs and investment against a penalty clause and any further undertaking with no such penalty; the latter represent pure declarations of intent and have no significance from the legal point of view. The THA has no recourse in the event of their not being adhered to.

Based on the information provided by the THA, from 1st July 1990 to 30th June 1993 undertakings totalling investments of DM 180.1 billion and jobs for 1,468,193 people were secured from privatisation.[7] Investment undertakings included DM 30 billion for modernising power stations and distribution networks, and DM 4.2 billion which cannot be allocated to individual States. The remaining DM 145.9 billion is distributed as follows: 30.4% in Saxony, followed in second place by Brandenburg with 21.7% and the eastern part of Berlin with 16.8%. In fourth place is Saxony-Anhalt with 14.1%, fifth is Thuringia with 9%, and last is Mecklenburg/West-Pomerania with 8%.[8] About 29% of the promised jobs that can be allocated to a specific State

6 See: Treuhandanstalt, *Monatsinformation der THA* as of 30th June 1993, page 11.
7 See: op. cit., page 3.
8 See: op. cit., page 14.

went to Saxony, just short of 20% to Brandenburg, 17% to east Berlin, and about 13% each to Thuringia and Saxony-Anhalt, leaving just short of 9% for Mecklenburg/West-Pomerania. This makes shows clearly that there are sharp quantitative differences to be observed just at State level with regard to the undertakings made to the THA to provide jobs and investment.

In considering aspects of regional and labour market policy, however, it seems urgently necessary to obtain information also on the jobs and investment undertakings (secured with penalty clauses) for a lower regional level. In order to obtain any indications of a need to take action on labour market and regional policy it would make sense, for instance, to work on the basis of regional labour markets (travel-to-work areas).[9] It would even be worthwhile, with regard to the active administrative units and regional idiosyncrasies, to take municipalities or counties as the unit for observation and analysis. Such information is not available, not only for reasons of data protection law, and anyway has very much the character of vague promises under which it is uncertain whether they can be also adhered to, or whether court action is possible if not, in a period of severe economic collapse such is currently to be observed. It is therefore of no use for a regional analysis and evaluation of the THA's work.

The third criterion of decision for assessing the THA's work focuses tightly on the proceeds realised from the sale of companies. These amounted to DM 43.5 billion for the period from 1st July 1990 to 30th June 1993.[10] It would be even more interesting to make a comparison between the effectively realised and potential proceeds, i. e. between the effective and the potential selling prices of the THA's portfolio of companies (including the acceptance of historic debt and liability). These criteria have taken on greater significance lately in light of budget restrictions and the THA's growing deficit. In practice, however, it is hardly ever possible to make a proper assessment of the sales proceeds and the potential market price of a company; for instance, the value of a company cannot be calculated as the value of its future profit flow cannot be estimated for lack of any historical profit flow. Thus the only basis for acquisition negotiations was often tangible asset value calculations, and even these had to be handled with care. Asset deals, on the other hand, were usually based on expert's assessments of their market value, and these were considerably more reliable.

These problems of valuation, and the problem of the lack of data at the regional level, make it advisable to dispense with this criterion. The following regional analyses therefore concentrate solely on the analysis of the companies portfolio and the degree of privatisation of the initial stock. As will be shown in a moment, even here the data basis has its deficiencies, but it will suffice for deriving regional trend statements and making an initial estimate of the influence of regional location factors.

9 See: Budde, Eckey, and Klemmer, *Vorschlag für die Abgrenzung von Arbeitsmarktregionen*; Budde, Hamm, Klemmer, Lagemann, and Schrumpf, *Übertragung regionalpolitischer Konzepte auf Ostdeutschland.*

10 See: Treuhandanstalt, *Monatsinformation der THA* as of 30th June 1993, page 12.

2. Operationalisation of the degree of privatisation at the regional level

Of the three criteria named for the regional analysis and evaluation of the THA's privatisation work, the first to be considered is thus the analysis of the degree of privatisation of the initial stock of companies awaiting privatisation, referring to stock-takings provided by the THA. These may be incomplete and not always fully compatible, but they do – and this is the decisive point – permit statements to be made on a regional basis concerning the THA's privatisation activities. It covers the companies offered for sale as of 10th March 1991 and on 26th January 1993 and the numbers of people employed by them. This basic information for which the author is most grateful was provided broken down geographically by postal code, and summed up to sub-groups representing the county level. This made it possible to couple it with information on regional economic conditions and factors of influence such as location, settlement structure, and infrastructural facilities.

It would certainly have been desirable also to include changes in stock from 1st July 1990 to 10th March 1991, as during this initial phase interest was very great, particularly in the services sector in major cities and conglomerations. Unfortunately, regional figures of this kind are not available for eastern Germany at this low level. Looked at the other way, this period under consideration of not quite two years can be regarded as the normal phase, both with regard to the THA's work and to the dissemination of information on the advantages and disadvantages of individual locations within the eastern German states. This latter aspect guarantees that the location factors affecting privatisation activities can be better taken into account.

Attention must, however, be drawn to a number of problems in the data material before it can be evaluated. The statistical basis of the portfolio stock, for instance, is the individual company, meaning that a company with more than one factory is only included under its registered or head office. This made it necessary to eliminate firms with facilities outside eastern Germany.

It should also be pointed out that, although this data permits a considerable depth of analysis in the regional respect, for some unknown reason it does not contain all the companies that were under the THA's administration and awaiting privatisation at the stated time. The figures thus do not provide a complete picture of the companies the THA was looking after at the relevant point in time, but they do represent a large part of the total and can be taken as representative. Thus the data for 1991 only includes 6,607 out of a recorded total of 9,000 relevant companies. This can partly be explained by the fact that this period from 1991 to 1993 saw on the one hand the establishment of a large number of new companies, and even more the unbundling of large state corporations and companies, with the result that the data on the portfolio stock in 1993 is by no means a sub-total taken from the 1991 data; there is merely a large area of overlap between the two, but its order of magnitude permits reliable trend statements to be made at the regional level.

It is also regrettable that no information at all is available from a few counties and cities. For instance, the cities of Dresden and Leipzig do not appear in the data on the number of companies or employees. The reason for this appears to lie in the different ways in which the THA Central Office in Berlin and the branches in Dresden, Leipzig, etc. collected their data. These few cases must therefore be excluded from the analysis; in some cases it is possible to draw conclusions regarding these cities from the data on the surrounding counties.

It is possible to compare and contrast data for 1991 and 1993 on most companies on the basis of their company numbers. Within this overlapping data there were, in some individual cases, differences in sectoral classification in 1991 and 1993, which increases the error quota with the depth of classification of the branches of industry. For this reason it was decided to dispense with sectoral analysis at any deeper level in the following study.

For some companies which appeared in the statistics of 1991 there was no data available for 1993, and for some which appeared 1993 the data for 1991 was missing. The companies mentioned first might have been privatised or unbundled; if the latter had happened, it proved impossible to reconstruct the process of unbundling. Therefore and because the data collected for a company with more than one factory was always assigned to its headquarters there occur regional as well as sectoral errors, and both of them are unavoidable. If there existed some data for 1993 but not for 1991 the company might have been a newly founded one or an unbundled one. When we calculated the privatisation success we assumed that the companies were unbundled since the number of the new companies has to be considerably lower than the number of unbundled ones because of the THA's specific tasks.

Calculation errors are thus unavoidable in view of these idiosyncrasies described in the available material. However, they keep within narrow limits provided no sectoral analysis is attempted at any deeper level, particularly since the regional errors are smaller than the distortions in the sectoral information. The evaluations of the available data therefore permit statements to be made on trends and conclusions to be drawn on the THA's degree of success in privatisation.

III. Possible regional influences

Before going into detail on the regional results obtainable from this material, it is necessary to pose the question as to the possible regional influences. The obvious course is first to look at regionally divergent sectoral and company size structures, and to expect that the asset deals completed will vary from one sector and one company size category to another. The mere fact that the enormous financial transfers from western to eastern Germany led to a stabilisation of purchasing power in eastern Germany and thus to a stabilisation, or even an expansion, of the mainly regional demand for tertiary activities will give grounds to the assumption that there was all in all a high level of willingness to take over companies in the services sector. It can also be assumed that small and medium-sized companies were easier to sell than huge corporations.

Hypotheses of this kind on the influence exerted by divergent sectoral and company size structures may be plausible, but hardly provide any information on the role or the significance of local factors. The latter are those that express of regional business characteristics or emphasise differences in regional structure, e. g. those defined by the infrastructure and the settlement structure, divergent factor stocks, transport costs, etc. In addition to this, the data material available does not permit any broadscale examination of the influence of regionally divergent sector and company size structures. It was therefore decided to look at other regional factors of influence.

Based on the results of structural reporting and more recent regional research,[11] it is for instance possible to say that regional development processes are usually successful if:

---

11 For the evaluation of the literature, see: Hamm and Klemmer, *Ansatzpunkte und Möglichkeiten einer Modifizierung der regionalen Strukturpolitik*; Klemmer, with the assistance of Eckey and Bremicker, *Zur Bestimmung kommunaler Industrialisierungsbesonderheiten.* See also: Klemmer, *Zum Entwicklungseinfluß sogenannter „harter" Standortgegebenheiten.*

- a fully functioning infrastructure,
- a favourable settlement structure,
- a sufficient potential work-force with adequate occupational qualifications,
- a good location,
- an adequate availability of land,
- an adequate supply of the services which companies need, and
- a good image or "economic climate" are all present.

Within the complex location factor of "infrastructure", a tendency of re-appreciation in the infrastructure of transport can be generally observed, mainly in the field of long-distance transport routes. On the one hand, the organisational and logistic demands made on the transport of goods are rising constantly, on the other an economy that operates world-wide and with an efficient division of labour is only possible if the transport infrastructure is adequate in quantitative and qualitative terms. The local or regional availability of access to long-distance transport routes is thus gaining constantly in significance as a location factor. Any given region or centre will for this reason only appear attractive in the long term if there is a fully functioning (and basically international) airport at least in the vicinity, if it is integrated into the European high-speed rail network, and if the trunk road capacity is sufficient. It can be assumed that this type of evaluation will be applied in full to eastern Germany, and that in particular the telecommunications infrastructure will be included.

Another factor of significance is the settlement structure, which can be described in terms of numbers of inhabitants and of density and centrality figures. Nearly all the empirical studies published to date permit the variable factor of "density of population" to be discerned as having a high explanatory value in statistics. It is an indirect indicator for summarising the so-called agglomeration advantages and the opportunities for achieving sales in the region, although increases in the density of population also entail conflicts on land use, jumble of property rights, and environmental pollution, meaning that once this factor passes a certain critical point it will tend to inhibit development. Closely connected with this is the availability of land, and this will be of particular importance if other characteristics can be taken into account such as property rights, the availability of freehold, infrastructural development, freedom from historic environmental pollution, processing of planning applications, and the shape of and proximity to areas of conflict (such as residential building).

Germany is a high-wage country. On the criterion of wage-rates, many other regions of Europe provide more attractive locations. The fact that the resultant trend to relocate production has so far remained within narrow limits can be explained, as the results of industrial and sectoral research[12] show, by the regional immobility of a highly qualified work-force, and this is why human capital tends to move centre-stage in most surveys of companies as one of the location factors with the highest value. Thus a large proportion of the commitment made by western German companies in the eastern German states can only be explained by bottlenecks in the market for skilled labour or by the availability of land in the traditional locations. However, difficulties usually arise in obtaining statistics on human capital as this can only be qualified on the basis of examination certificates and these are only to a limited extent comparable between eastern and western Germany.

---

12 See: Löbbe et al: *Analyse der strukturellen Entwicklung der deutschen Wirtschaft; Schwerpunktthema 1988: Standortqualität der Bundesrepublik Deutschland.*

Viewed against the background of current trends to internationalise the division of labour, to reduce vertical integration of manufacturing, and provide just-in-time deliveries, access to transport routes and the geographical position come even more into the centre of focus for explaining divergent regional development processes and thus development strategies for regional policy. The distinction has to be made here between the location factors affecting large areas and those affecting small areas. The former affect positioning within a large-area network (e. g. the whole of Germany or the European heartland), the latter the identification of the environmental significance of centres.

In all instances, location and transport infrastructure are heavily dependent upon one another. Although the location is defined geographically, for instance in terms of central selling markets defined by geography or which have arisen over time, the construction of the transport network is capable of influencing the accessibility ratios, defined in terms of time, and most particularly in connection with the construction and extension of long-distance routes. Thus the transport connections between a place of departure and a destination can be described as good if the destination can be reached within the shortest possible time. If one now considers all possible destinations in a broadly defined network of routes, one can describe the large-scale position of a region in terms specific to each mode of transport, for instance by adding up average journey times to all the counties in Germany or the European heartland weighted by their number of inhabitants, and thus make them accessible to numerical evaluation. More and more use is being made of digitalised transport networks for determining these location indicators; their edges are characterised by distance and speed of travel, and they have to contain both the place of departure and the destinations.[13]

In addition to these location factors, both wide-scale and those specific to each mode of transport, there are also aspects affecting the narrower choice of location. As finished products become more and more sensitive to time and transport, and the relevant consultancy intensity rises in step, the necessity also increases for finding a location close to the trading area. High-value, perishable products need proximity to a large market just as much as low-value mass goods sensitive to high transport costs (this applies to mining, quarrying, the furniture industry, the paper and printing industries, parts of the food and drink industry, and the construction industry). The significance of proximity to regional markets can increase as the size of the company becomes smaller; smaller companies are sometimes dependent upon regionally limited advertising media but do not want to build up any massive despatch organisation, and produce goods with a large service content (such as products requiring frequent maintenance, or the building industry). To make these components influencing location clear, it is possible to work with the definition of the population accessible within one, two, or three hours by predefined modes of transport.

It is also possible to demonstrate that the services selling directly to companies are increasingly taking on the character of an infrastructure which encourages higher productivity.[14] Also, this is a tertiary sector which in terms of numbers employed has been expanding rapidly in recent years. This sector includes legal counsel and services, tax consultancy, auditing, and management consultancy, architects, consultant engineers, advertising, data processing, and the

---

13 See: Eckey and Horn, *Lagegunst- und Verkehrsanalysen für die Kreise des vereinigten Deutschlands*; ditto, *Veränderung der Lagegunst und Erreichbarkeit der Kreise.*

14 See: Löbbe et al, *Technische Dienstleistungen, Technologietransfer und Innovation.*

many other small business such as typing and credit enquiry agencies. This very diverse range of services usually includes those which their corporate customers cannot themselves handle because their requirement is irregular or small, in relation to the size of the company, and within the company the problem of efficiency control can only be solved at great expense. These services depend crucially on the professional qualifications of the person providing them, and can thus only be delegated to a limited extent, and this is why small companies dominate here and often, particularly important, the orientation beyond the limits of the region. The latter makes the development of these organisations independent of the regional population basis but requires proximity to long-distance traffic routes of high quality (motorways, inter-city railway stations, and airports).

The most difficult aspect to quantify is the regional image or "economic climate". Image elements principally affect the region's international level of awareness and the estimates outsiders make of the local or regional quality of life. Cities with a highly urban character benefit here (measured, for instance, in terms of social diversity, density of population, or its general level of professional qualification) as do those with a historical tradition, major buildings and monuments, significant cultural amenities, or an attractive regional "aura". These factors are often summarised under the heading of "soft" location factors, and measuring them causes further difficulties because the synergistic effects of several of them together always require a summing of several subgroups for measurement.

The concept of economic climate is also connected with such aspects as the value placed on business activities in the local press, the support given by the local authorities to the existing economy when companies wish to expand or move to other premises, an adequate supply of land for commercial use, the accelerated handling of approval applications, etc. This also refers to the interrelationships between municipal administration and local companies, of the press to the companies, the attitudes of associations and institutions (such as the churches) to the business world, and the treatment of small companies by the existing large ones. These are only some of the important areas affecting the local identification with the wishes of the business world. They also determine the image of a region, depend on the personal efforts of individual people, and can only be changed over a long period of time. They also make it clear that municipalities are in many cases similar to modern companies. They offer their locations as their products, and they have to operate similar marketing strategies just as modern industries do. Just as a company will endeavour to discover the particular requirements of a specific group of users, the promotion of the municipal economy will have to develop a high level of technical competence and an all-embracing approach to solving problems in order to be accepted as an indispensable point of contact for local business. In this way, the disappearance of aid schemes at the state level can be more than compensated for.

If one tries, by means of the so-called "hard" location factors – such as density of population, the regional road and rail networks, the population accessible within one, two, or three hours by road and by rail, meaning nine independent variables –, to explain by regression analysis the variants in the distribution of employment (1987 employment census) to the regional labour markets in western Germany, and excludes the extremely densely populated Ruhr (6 regions out of a total of 166 travel-to-work areas) which distort nearly every attempt at analysing the labour market because of the internal delineation problems, it is possible to arrive at an explained vari-

---

15 Klemmer, *Zum Entwicklungseinfluß sogenannter „harter" Standortgegebenheiten.*

ance of about 50%.[15] If one takes the change in employment (of workers subject to compulsory social insurance) between 1982 and 1988 as variable to be explained, one arrives at an explained variance share of just under one quarter. In all instances, density of population has a positive influence, and for road access the smaller-area location dimension of the "3-hour population" and for rail access the "1-hour population" are of significance. Among the larger-area location dimensions (average distance in terms of time to all the counties in western Germany weighted by their populations in minutes) the location by rail has a statistically significant influence; for road the results are ambiguous, but this might be caused by the quality of the data.

Section V will later investigate the extent to which these "hard" location factors are also able to explain partly the THA's privatisation success rate.

IV. Selected regional results

Table 1 provides an over-view of the evaluation based on the analysis of the situation at the two selected points in time, 10th March 1991 and 26th January 1993, at the level of towns being administrative districts in their own rights and rural counties in eastern Germany. This makes it clear, for instance, that at the beginning, when many of the THA's privatisation efforts had already led to a positive conclusion, there were still 53 companies with 28,966 employees waiting for privatisation in the eastern city of Cottbus. By January 1993, this figure had been reduced to 10 units with only 1,525 employees. Expressed as an absolute change the THA's privatisation success rate amounted to 43 companies and 27,441 jobs. Based on the initial situation, this gives a relative change, which from now on will be referred to as the degree of privatisation, of 94.74% of the original total number of jobs and 81.13% of the companies in the initial year. Spaces in the columns for relative change marked with "–" refer to observation units for which there are no figures, or at least no comparable figures, for 1991 and/or 1993. One typical example is the city of Potsdam, which is shown in the source figures for 1993 as having one company awaiting privatisation, but had none in 1991. No attempt can be made to calculate the degree of privatisation when, as here, no comparable figures are available. A negative figure means that the number of employees or companies must have risen. This might have come about through a change in regional or sectoral categorisation resulting from unbundling, or through the establishment of new companies. The figures themselves provide no answer to the question of the causes.

Fig. 1 provides information on the counties and towns being administrative districts in their own rights in eastern Germany as the basis for the regional analysis. Fig. 2, using data as of 10th March 1991, shows the portfolio stock of THA companies awaiting privatisation. It is clear that large numbers (150 companies or more) were mainly to be found concentrated in the counties surrounding major cities, in the south-western part of Thuringia, the east part of Saxony, the group of counties from Bad Liebenwerda to Herzberg and Jessen, between Leipzig and Berlin, and the other group of counties near the northern city of Rostock: county of Rostock, Teterow, and Malchin. Where there are such prominent groupings of counties, it can be assumed that the core areas were characterised by similar features. Fig. 3 provides information on the numbers of employees and thus the number of jobs awaiting privatisation at the beginning of the period of time under investigation. Figures for counties with 30,000 or more employees awaiting privatisation conform with the trend figures for the numbers of companies. The group of counties from Jessen via Herzberg, Finsterwalde, Bad Liebenwerda, Senftenberg, and Spremberg to Cottbus

Table 1:
Selected companies and their employees in the THA portfolio by County (all sectors)

Regional code no.	County	Number of employees		Number of companies		Absolute change		Relative change (degree of privatisation)	
		10.3.91	26.1.93	10.3.91	26.1.93	Employees	Companies	Employees	Companies
11200000	Berlin (east), CB	9,892	644	28	5	9,248	23	93.49	82.14
12001000	Brandenburg/Havel, CB	16,995	2,973	38	7	14,022	31	82.51	81.58
12002000	Cottbus, CB	28,966	1,525	53	10	27,441	43	94.74	81.13
12003000	Eisenhüttenstadt, CB	15,998	8,007	21	7	7,991	14	49.95	66.67
12004000	Frankfurt/Oder, CB	22,607	99	48	3	22,508	45	99.56	93.75
12005000	Potsdam, CB	0	1	0	1	–	–	–	–
12006000	Schwedt/Oder, CB	14,675	1,096	15	4	13,579	11	92.53	73.33
12011000	Angermünde	99,864	17,523	134	498	82,341	–364	82.45	–271.64
12012000	Bad Freienwalde	5,997	50	97	4	5,947	93	99.17	95.88
12013000	Bad Liebenwerda	55,740	4,409	321	135	51,331	186	92.09	57.94
12014000	Beeskow	13,396	18,169	84	200	-4,773	–116	–35.63	–138.10
12015000	Belzig	782	255	7	3	527	4	67.39	57.14
12016000	Bernau	10,297	289	109	4	10,008	105	97.19	96.33
12017000	Brandenburg	26,042	2,299	210	103	23,743	107	91.17	50.95
12018000	Calau	8,654	5,499	138	131	3,155	7	36.46	5.07
12019000	Cottbus	67,004	1,038	356	51	65,966	305	98.45	85.67
12020000	Eberswalde	15,368	2,276	155	69	13,092	86	85.19	55.48
12021000	Eisenhüttenstadt	2,467	2,513	36	29	–46	7	–1.86	19.44
12022000	Finsterwalde	34,704	8,737	107	21	25,967	86	74.82	80.37
12023000	Forst	3,550	931	15	23	2,619	–8	73.77	–53.33
12024000	Fürstenwalde	46,529	5,830	181	46	40,699	135	87.47	74.59
12025000	Gransee	29,033	717	201	51	28,316	150	97.53	74.63
12026000	Guben	9,137	1,388	39	10	7,749	29	84.81	74.36
12027000	Herzberg	57,308	3,758	344	146	53,550	198	93.44	57.56
12028000	Jüterbog	11,185	1,749	52	91	9,436	–39	84.36	–75.00
12029000	Königs Wusterhausen	17,155	2,613	81	35	14,542	46	84.77	56.79
12030000	Kyritz	2,940	2,872	56	95	68	–39	2.31	–69.64

Table 1:

Regional code no.	County	Number of employees		Number of companies		Absolute change		Relative change (degree of privatisation)	
		10.3.91	26.1.93	10.3.91	26.1.93	Employees	Companies	Employees	Companies
12031000	Lübben	22,232	1,584	149	48	20,648	101	92.88	67.79
12032000	Luckau	3,084	8,749	54	194	–5,665	–140	–183.69	–259.26
12033000	Luckenwalde	27,926	568	61	17	27,358	44	97.97	72.13
12034000	Nauen	281,464	4,765	247	276	276,699	–29	98.31	–11.74
12035000	Neuruppin	35,514	9,999	203	302	25,515	–99	71.84	–48.77
12036000	Oranienburg	21,798	4,168	62	33	17,630	29	80.88	46.77
12037000	Perleberg	6,380	268	19	7	6,112	12	95.80	63.16
12038000	Potsdam	62,007	637	259	53	61,370	206	98.97	79.54
12039000	Prenzlau	13,086	6,363	58	175	6,723	–117	51.38	–201.72
12040000	Pritzwalk	6,900	4,511	58	146	2,389	–88	34.62	–151.72
12041000	Rathenow	29,596	1,600	100	91	27,996	9	94.59	9.00
12042000	Seelow	19,559	3,878	110	155	15,681	–45	80.17	–40.91
12043000	Senftenberg	66,528	37,114	67	10	29,414	57	44.21	85.07
12044000	Spremberg	39,305	24,194	74	67	15,111	7	38.45	9.46
12045000	Strausberg	8,899	2,417	57	52	6,482	5	72.84	8.77
12046000	Templin	23,068	1,094	88	53	21,974	35	95.26	39.77
12047000	Wittstock	3,168	569	12	32	2,599	–20	82.04	–166.67
12048000	Zossen	22,121	4,456	75	23	17,665	52	79.86	69.33
13001000	Greifswald, CB	11,255	2,761	19	4	8,494	15	75.47	78.95
13002000	Neubrandenburg, CB	27,514	1,168	64	8	26,346	56	95.75	87.50
13003000	Rostock, CB	87,264	7,308	58	14	79,956	44	91.63	75.86
13004000	Schwerin, CB	0	0	0	0	–	–	–	–
13005000	Stralsund, CB	12,277	4,104	35	5	8,173	30	66.57	85.71
13006000	Wismar, CB	10,490	0	15	0	10,490	15	100.00	100.00
13011000	Altentreptow	5,486	504	33	48	4,982	–15	90.81	–45.45
13012000	Anklam	2,169	2,765	10	105	–596	–95	–27.48	–950.00
13013000	Bad Doberan	5,494	1,886	45	59	3,608	–14	65.67	–31.11
13014000	Bützow	11,056	0	79	0	11,056	79	100.00	100.00

Table 1:

Regional code no.	County	Number of employees		Number of companies		Absolute change		Relative change (degree of privatisation)	
		10.3.91	26.1.93	10.3.91	26.1.93	Employees	Companies	Employees	Companies
13015000	Demmin	13,190	2,552	125	116	10,638	9	80.65	7.20
13016000	Gadebusch	8,658	0	31	0	8,658	31	100.00	100.00
13017000	Greifswald	2,949	504	57	56	2,445	1	82.91	1.75
13018000	Grevesmühlen	2,282	1,029	13	42	1,253	–29	54.91	–223.08
13019000	Grimmen	5,316	720	35	48	4,596	–13	86.46	–37.14
13020000	Güstrow	42,756	3,866	293	196	38,890	97	90.96	33.11
13021000	Hagenow	9,108	3,280	143	78	5,828	65	63.99	45.45
13022000	Ludwigslust	10,398	509	77	4	9,889	73	95.10	94.81
13023000	Lübz	11,262	2,096	58	27	9,166	31	81.39	53.45
13024000	Malchin	2,621	3,338	17	51	-717	–34	–27.36	–200.00
13025000	Neubrandenburg	123,890	175	67	64	123,715	3	99.86	4.48
13026000	Neustrelitz	12,101	779	131	59	11,322	72	93.56	54.96
13027000	Parchim	4,228	1,001	17	27	3,227	–10	76.32	–58.82
13028000	Pasewalk	11,812	6,240	129	120	5,572	9	47.17	6.98
13029000	Ribnitz-Damgarten	23,849	3,187	116	102	20,662	14	86.64	12.07
13030000	Röbel/Müritz	372	72	3	32	300	–29	80.65	–966.67
13041000	Wolgast	6,437	31	20	2	6,406	18	99.52	90.00
14001000	Chemnitz, CB	0	0	0	0	–	–	–	–
14002000	Dresden, CB	0	0	0	0	–	–	–	–
14003000	Görlitz, CB	9,206	2,602	19	5	6,604	14	71.74	73.68
14004000	Leipzig, CB	0	0	0	0	–	–	–	–
14005000	Plauen, CB	17,297	1,099	33	15	16,198	18	93.65	54.55
14006000	Zwickau, CB	4,773	855	12	4	3,918	8	82.09	66.67
14011000	Annaberg	17,665	2,357	106	19	15,308	87	86.66	82.08
14012000	Aue	22,066	2,709	74	20	19,357	54	87.72	72.97
14013000	Auerbach	12,349	2,721	54	42	9,628	12	77.97	22.22
14014000	Bautzen	114,147	25,205	278	199	88,942	79	77.92	28.42
14015000	Bischofswerda	8,295	1,281	45	10	7,014	35	84.56	77.78

Table 1:

Regional code no.	County	Number of employees		Number of companies		Absolute change		Relative change (degree of privatisation)	
		10.3.91	26.1.93	10.3.91	26.1.93	Employees	Companies	Employees	Companies
14016000	Borna	22,816	6,450	53	24	16,366	29	71.73	54.72
14017000	Brand-Erbisdorf	8,299	2,498	45	50	5,801	–5	69.90	–11.11
14018000	Chemnitz	15,780	876	61	13	14,904	48	94.45	78.69
14019000	Delitzsch	9,741	4,180	52	81	5,561	–29	57.09	–55.77
14020000	Dippoldiswalde	18,019	700	154	5	17,319	149	96.12	96.75
14021000	Döbeln	26,315	5,181	84	96	21,134	–12	80.31	–14.29
14022000	Dresden	14,465	1,519	51	13	12,946	38	89.50	74.51
14023000	Eilenburg	18,504	3,901	66	33	14,603	33	78.92	50.00
14024000	Flöha	16,593	2,843	55	30	13,750	25	82.87	45.45
14025000	Freiberg	21,839	5,681	75	77	16,158	–2	73.99	–2.67
14026000	Freital	15,611	2,062	48	23	13,549	25	86.79	52.08
14027000	Geithain	4,466	1,177	38	32	3,289	6	73.65	15.79
14028000	Glauchau	9,998	1,214	49	14	8,784	35	87.86	71.43
14029000	Görlitz	240	406	4	29	–166	–25	–69.17	–625.00
14030000	Grimma	18,918	1,944	153	43	16,974	110	89.72	71.90
14031000	Großenhain	11,463	2,073	99	49	9,390	50	81.92	50.51
14032000	Hainichen	11,509	1,530	59	10	9,979	49	86.71	83.05
14033000	Hohenstein-Ernstthal	12,153	1,988	41	26	10,165	15	83.64	36.59
14034000	Hoyerswerda	16,415	733	91	3	15,682	88	95.53	96.70
14035000	Kamenz	10,490	7,176	105	140	3,314	–35	31.59	–33.33
14036000	Klingenthal	5,937	1,523	31	28	4,414	3	74.35	9.68
14037000	Leipzig	46,793	18,232	178	76	28,561	102	61.04	57.30
14038000	Löbau	21,825	1,347	193	11	20,478	182	93.83	94.30
14039000	Marienberg	13,567	1,491	98	41	12,076	57	89.01	58.16
14040000	Meißen	15,048	1,098	59	13	13,950	46	92.70	77.97
14041000	Niesky	29,454	1,653	180	2	27,801	178	94.39	98.89
14042000	Oelsnitz	2,740	820	13	5	1,920	8	70.07	61.54
14043000	Oschatz	21,689	923	69	31	20,766	38	95.74	55.07

Table 1:

Regional code no.	County	Number of employees		Number of companies		Absolute change		Relative change (degree of privatisation)	
		10.3.91	26.1.93	10.3.91	26.1.93	Employees	Companies	Employees	Companies
14044000	Pirna	15,909	3,337	89	45	12,572	44	79.02	49.44
14045000	Plauen	408	3,264	34	68	-2,856	–34	–700.00	–100.00
14046000	Reichenbach	15,981	4,481	70	76	11,500	–6	71.96	–8.57
14047000	Riesa	19,164	6,439	52	115	12,725	–63	66.40	–121.15
14048000	Rochlitz	13,735	2,394	142	55	11,341	87	82.57	61.27
14049000	Schwarzenberg	10,373	556	30	7	9,817	23	94.64	76.67
14050000	Sebnitz	10,268	3,907	20	33	6,361	–13	61.95	–65.00
14051000	Stollberg	5,930	477	18	7	5,453	11	91.96	61.11
14052000	Torgau	12,855	660	84	4	12,195	80	94.87	95.24
14053000	Weißwasser	5,781	1,237	37	25	4,544	12	78.60	32.43
14054000	Werdau	13,107	2,164	37	14	10,943	23	83.49	62.16
14055000	Wurzen	5,998	1,011	32	22	4,987	10	83.14	31.25
14056000	Zittau	7,491	777	34	8	6,714	26	89.63	76.47
14057000	Zschopau	10,429	1,823	28	20	8,606	8	82.52	28.57
14058000	Zwickau	10,804	616	68	41	10,188	27	94.30	39.71
15101000	Dessau, CB	19,187	5,149	28	11	14,038	17	73.16	60.71
15112000	Bernburg	41,930	967	109	33	40,963	76	97.69	69.72
15113000	Bitterfeld	85,517	36,665	196	68	48,852	128	57.13	65.31
15118000	Gräfenhainichen	8,595	2,448	147	48	6,147	99	71.52	67.35
15124000	Jessen	49,820	3,315	303	128	46,505	175	93.35	57.76
15126000	Köthen	124,233	15,044	151	139	109,189	12	87.89	7.95
15134000	Roßlau	9,704	5,904	58	49	3,800	9	39.16	15.52
15144000	Wittenberg	16,144	7,626	108	55	8,518	53	52.76	49.07
15147000	Zerbst	2,297	511	13	3	1,786	10	77.75	76.92
15202000	Halle/Saale, CB	0	0	0	0	–	–	–	–
15211000	Aschersleben	6,683	1,591	16	39	5,092	–23	76.19	–143.75
15215000	Eisleben	11,334	3,195	42	59	8,139	–17	71.81	–40.48
15222000	Hettstedt	9,969	2,587	55	77	7,382	–22	74.05	–40.00

Table 1:

Regional code no.	County	Number of employees		Number of companies		Absolute change		Relative change (degree of privatisation)	
		10.3.91	26.1.93	10.3.91	26.1.93	Employees	Companies	Employees	Companies
15223000	Hohenmölsen	12,904	5,986	59	16	6,918	43	53.61	72.88
15227000	Merseburg	59,312	24,234	129	46	35,078	83	59.14	64.34
15228000	Naumburg	24,913	314	136	32	24,599	104	98.74	76.47
15229000	Nebra	17,304	375	101	25	16,929	76	97.83	75.25
15233000	Querfurt	5,928	1,192	39	25	4,736	14	79.89	35.90
15235000	Saalkreis	72,138	2,675	505	51	69,463	454	96.29	89.90
15237000	Sangerhausen	62,434	12,315	163	52	50,119	111	80.28	68.10
15242000	Weißenfels	26,017	8,506	109	27	17,511	82	67.31	75.23
15246000	Zeitz	13,193	8,387	49	35	4,806	14	36.43	28.57
15303000	Magdeburg, CB	0	0	0	0	–	–	–	–
15314000	Burg	22,350	5,736	95	97	16,614	–2	74.34	–2.11
15316000	Gardelegen	11,193	206	66	6	10,987	60	98.16	90.91
15317000	Genthin	5,500	678	27	2	4,822	25	87.67	92.59
15319000	Halberstadt	19,710	2,287	90	65	17,423	25	88.40	27.78
15320000	Haldensleben	66,090	280	334	57	65,810	277	99.58	82.93
15321000	Havelberg	2,133	178	23	17	1,955	6	91.65	26.09
15325000	Klötze	4,674	105	29	4	4,569	25	97.75	86.21
15330000	Oschersleben	4,142	1,901	13	36	2,241	–23	54.10	–176.92
15331000	Osterburg	2,198	2,133	18	95	65	–77	2.96	–427.78
15332000	Quedlinburg	36,562	2,409	109	28	34,153	81	93.41	74.31
15336000	Salzwedel	10,889	8,796	59	97	2,093	–38	19.22	–64.41
15338000	Schönebeck	16,834	4,044	67	32	12,790	35	75.98	52.24
15339000	Staßfurt	20,301	7,244	49	52	13,057	–3	64.32	–6.12
15340000	Stendal	24,455	2,229	141	54	22,226	87	90.89	61.70
15341000	Wanzleben	15,176	3,546	67	37	11,630	30	76.63	44.78
15343000	Wernigerode	22,238	4,232	83	38	18,006	45	80.97	54.22
15345000	Wolmirstedt	10,836	1,437	62	13	9,399	49	86.74	79.03
16001000	Erfurt, CB	0	0	0	0	–	–	–	–

Table 1:

Regional code no.	County	Number of employees		Number of companies		Absolute change		Relative change (degree of privatisation)	
		10.3.91	26.1.93	10.3.91	26.1.93	Employees	Companies	Employees	Companies
16002000	Gera, CB	25,157	1,799	65	12	23,358	53	92.85	81.54
16003000	Jena, CB	31,377	42	14	1	31,335	13	99.87	92.86
16004000	Suhl, CB	9,038	820	26	6	8,218	20	90.93	76.92
16005000	Weimar, CB	11,405	1,988	35	16	9,417	19	82.57	54.29
16011000	Altenburg	10,702	1,725	87	38	8,977	49	83.88	56.32
16012000	Apolda	6,386	5,003	56	88	1,383	–32	21.66	–57.14
16013000	Arnstadt	80,064	2,036	105	18	78,028	87	97.46	82.86
16014000	Artern	27,894	7,062	66	91	20,832	–25	74.68	–37.88
16015000	Bad Salzungen	30,640	9,584	71	27	21,056	44	68.72	61.97
16016000	Eisenach	19,021	7,392	142	130	11,629	12	61.14	8.45
16017000	Eisenberg	70,897	29,317	82	39	41,580	43	58.65	52.44
16018000	Erfurt	19,928	704	277	93	19,224	184	96.47	66.43
16019000	Gera	86,099	737	338	111	85,362	227	99.14	67.16
16020000	Gotha	76,201	3,825	590	81	72,376	509	94.98	86.27
16021000	Greiz	8,421	3,294	51	34	5,127	17	60.88	33.33
16022000	Heiligenstadt	34,673	8,527	159	155	26,146	4	75.41	2.52
16023000	Hildburghausen	16,177	344	247	98	15,833	149	97.87	60.32
16024000	Ilmenau	9,074	1,704	30	8	7,370	22	81.22	73.33
16025000	Jena	8,144	215	47	43	7,929	4	97.36	8.51
16026000	Langensalza	2,871	474	16	6	2,397	10	83.49	62.50
16027000	Lobenstein	3,699	1,542	15	32	2,157	–17	58.31	–113.33
16028000	Meiningen	60,807	3,825	368	59	56,982	309	93.71	83.97
16029000	Mühlhausen	23,321	13,959	128	107	9,362	21	40.14	16.41
16030000	Neuhaus a. Rennweg	8,629	195	33	15	8,434	18	97.74	54.55
16031000	Nordhausen	20,762	4,169	98	74	16,593	24	79.92	24.49
16032000	Pößneck	7,518	793	55	31	6,725	24	89.45	43.64
16033000	Rudolstadt	12,356	905	87	3	11,451	84	92.68	96.55
16034000	Saalfeld	48,296	18,838	136	89	29,458	47	60.99	34.56

Table 1:

Regional code no.	County	Number of employees		Number of companies		Absolute change		Relative change (degree of privatisation)	
		10.3.91	26.1.93	10.3.91	26.1.93	Employees	Companies	Employees	Companies
16035000	Schleiz	2,902	107	14	1	2,795	13	96.31	92.86
16036000	Schmalkalden	35,720	6,588	174	75	29,132	99	81.56	56.90
16037000	Schmölln	5,474	334	79	4	5,140	75	93.90	94.94
16038000	Sömmerda	15,957	408	21	46	15,549	–25	97.44	–119.05
16039000	Sondershausen	21,845	3,501	58	95	18,344	–37	83.97	–63.79
16040000	Sonneberg	18,761	1,744	131	12	17,017	119	90.70	90.84
16041000	Stadtroda	13,468	2,318	48	76	11,150	–28	82.79	–58.33
16042000	Suhl	13,468	3,758	78	22	9,710	56	72.10	71.79
16043000	Weimar	27,529	13,095	334	418	14,434	–84	52.43	–25.15
16044000	Worbis	12,198	1,845	61	55	10,353	6	84.87	9.84
16045000	Zeulenroda	6,474	860	48	5	5,614	43	86.72	89.58

Note: CB=county borough (*kreisfreie Städte*, being administrative districts in their own rights). The remainder are counties (with their county towns).

Figure 1 Counties and towns being administrative districts in their own rights in eastern Germany (Source: own calculations based on THA information)

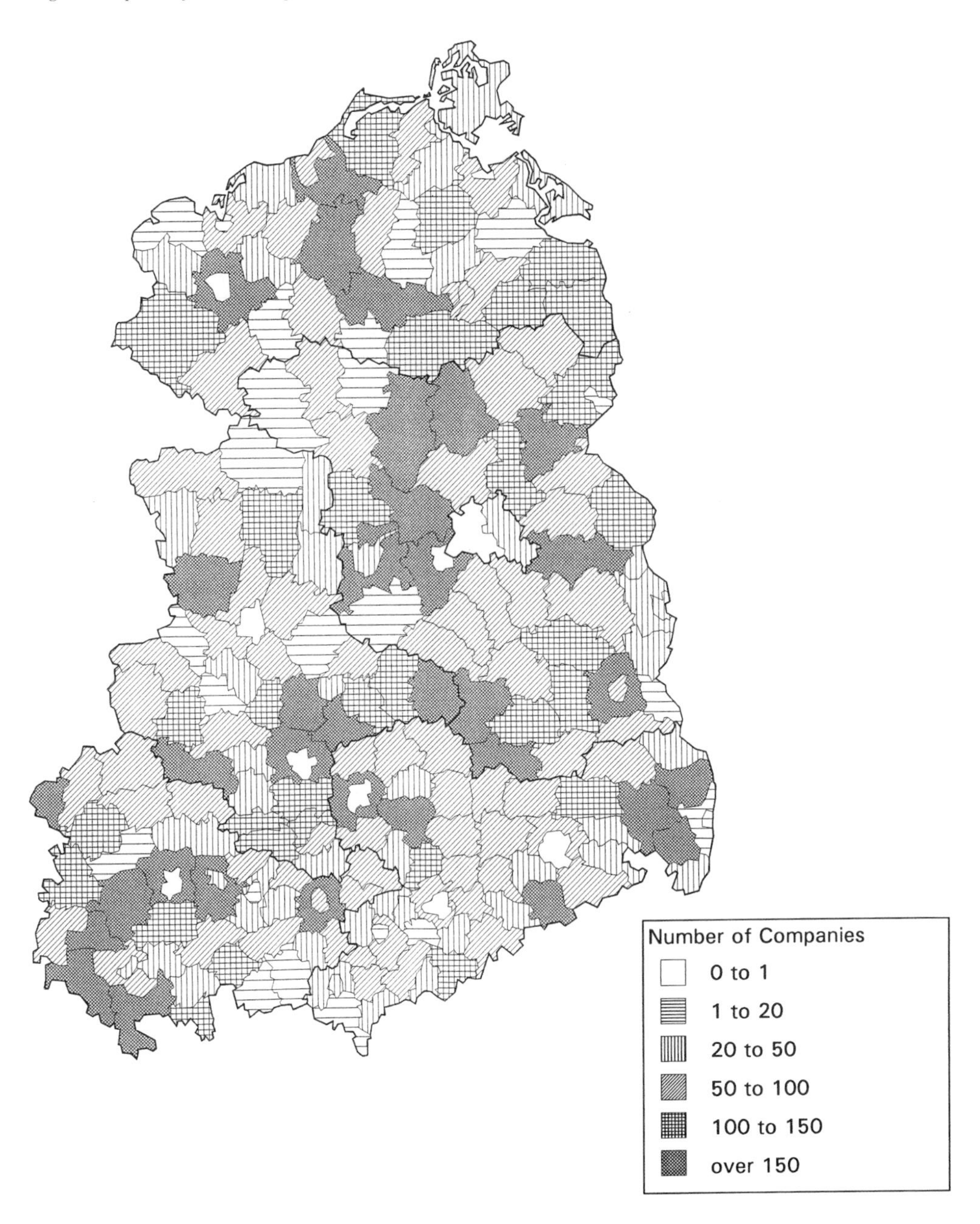

Figure 2 THA companies in the counties of eastern Germany as of 10th March 1991
(Source: own calculations based on THA information)

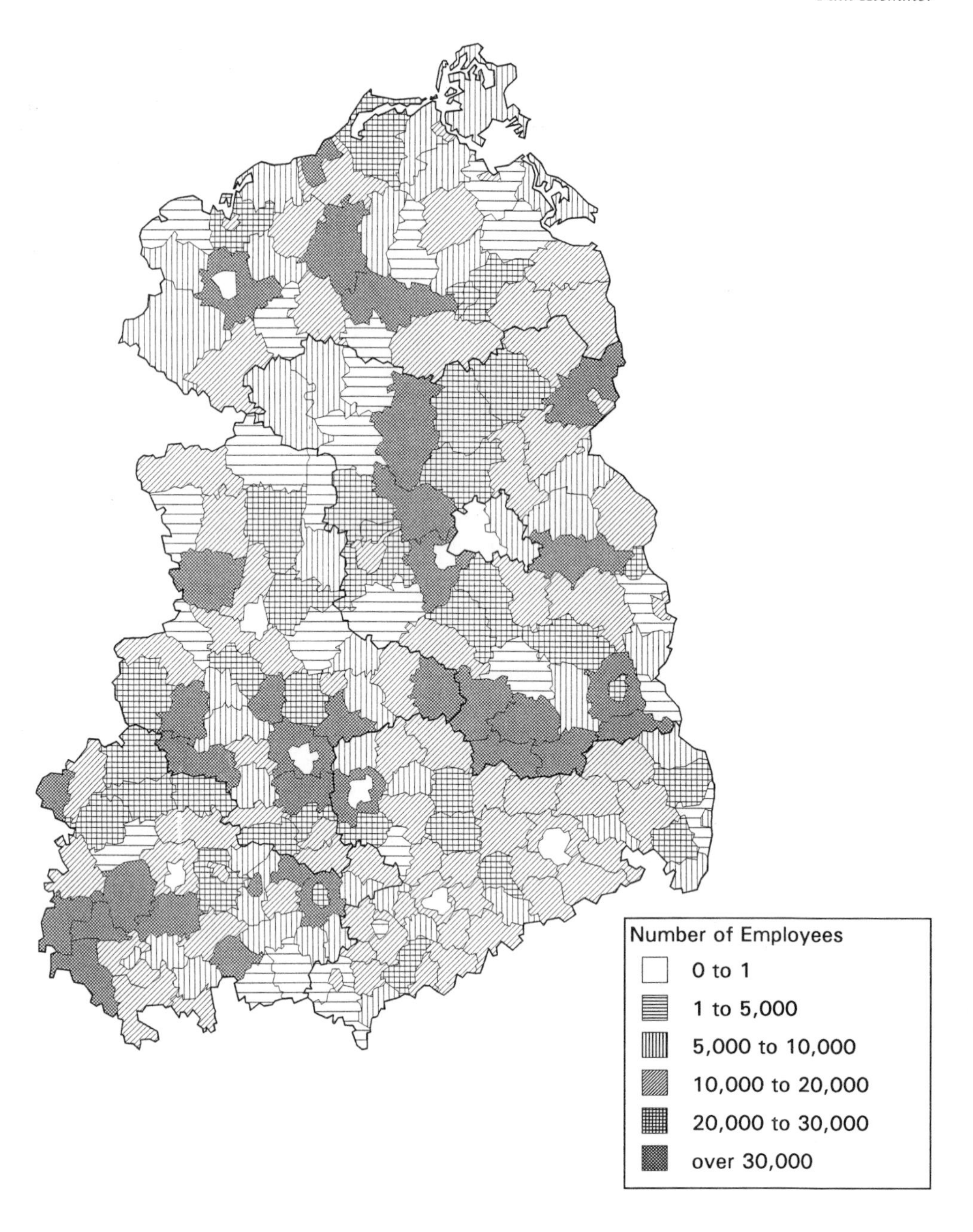

Figure 3 Number of employees in THA companies in the counties of eastern Germany as of 10th March 1991
(Source: own calculations based on THA information)

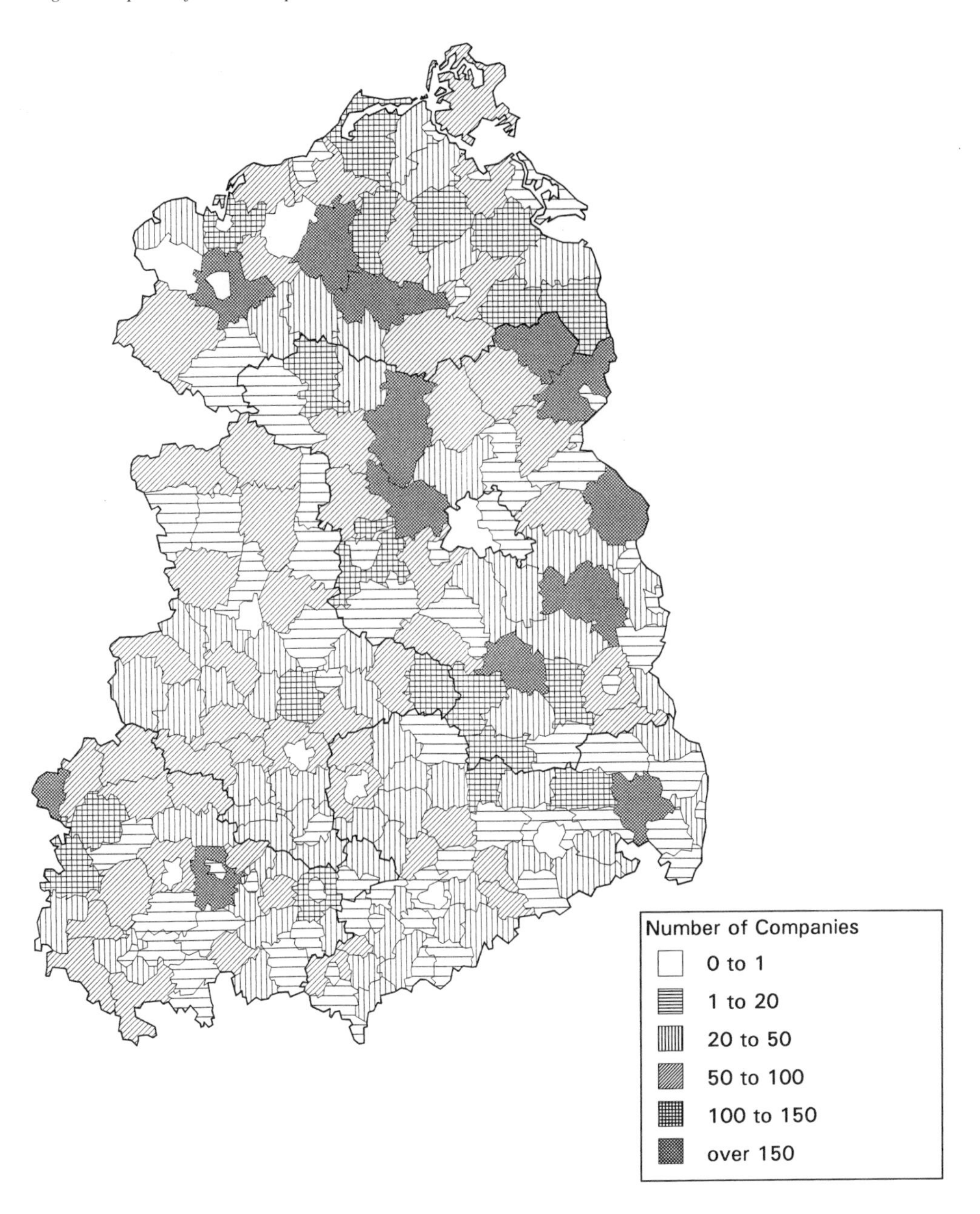

Figure 4 THA companies in the counties of eastern Germany as of 26th January 1993
(Source: own calculations based on THA information)

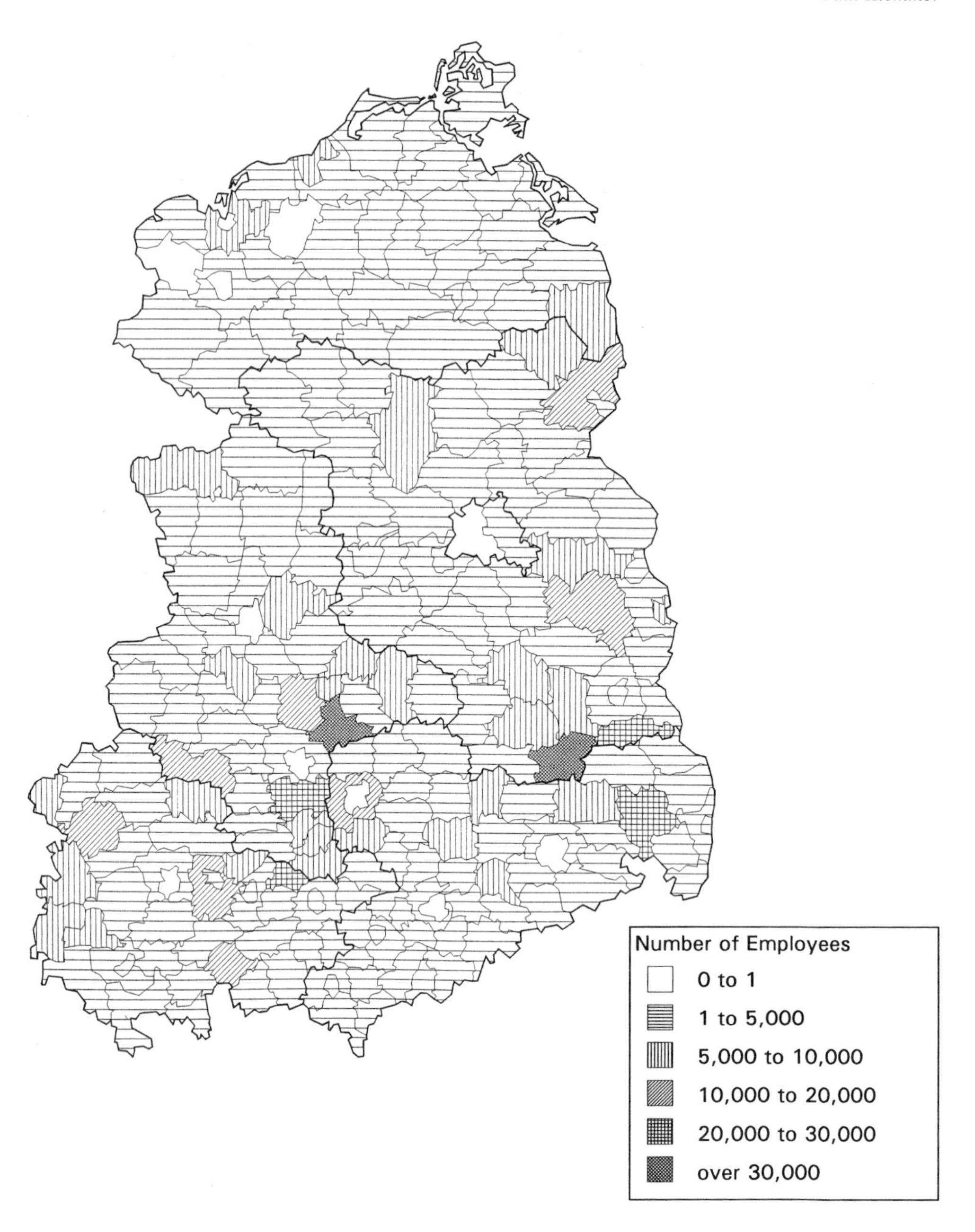

Figure 5 Number of employees in THA companies in the counties of eastern Germany as of 26th January 1993
(Source: own calculations based on THA information)

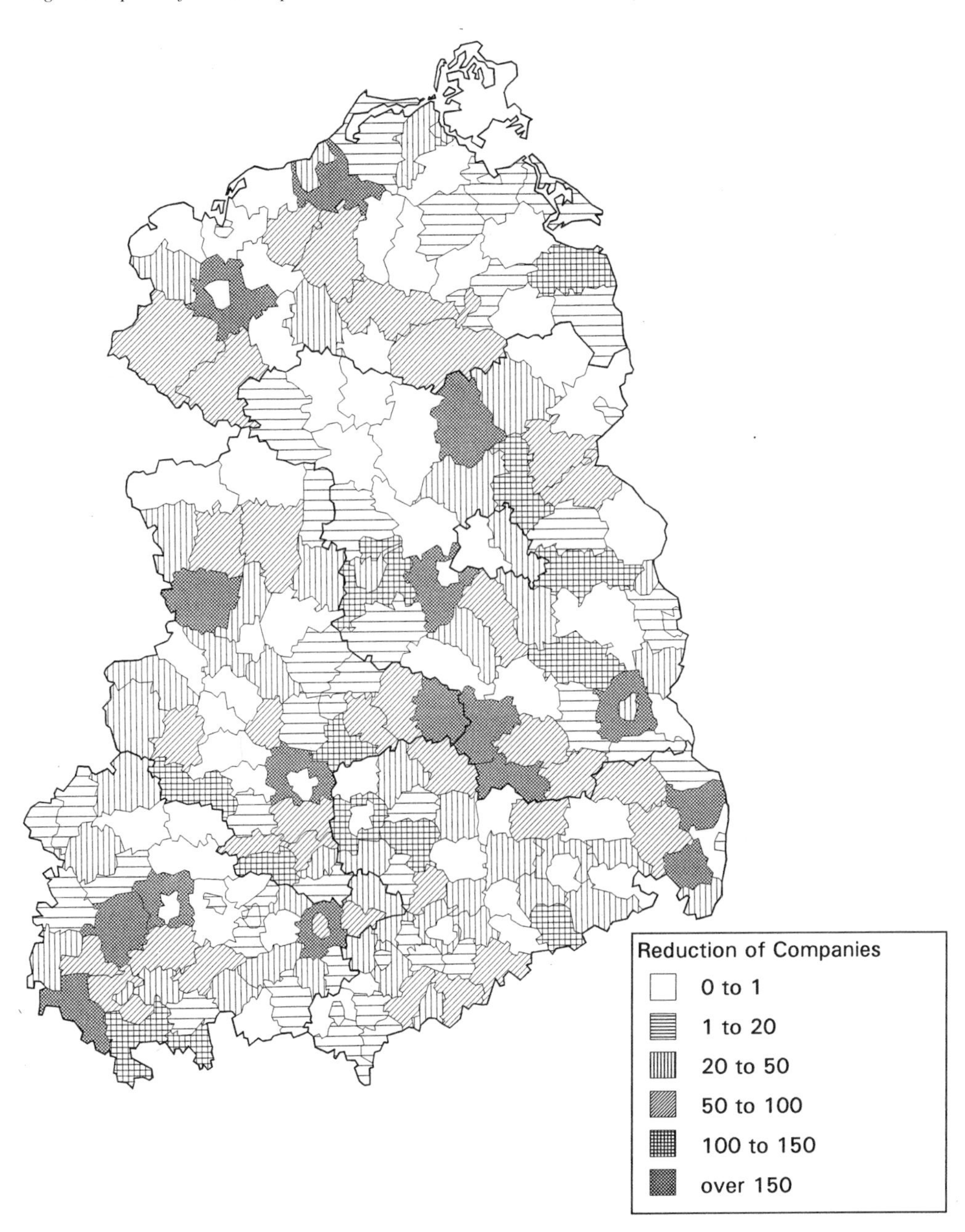

Figure 6 Absolute reduction in number of THA companies, 1991–1993, in the counties of eastern Germany (Source: own calculations based on THA information)

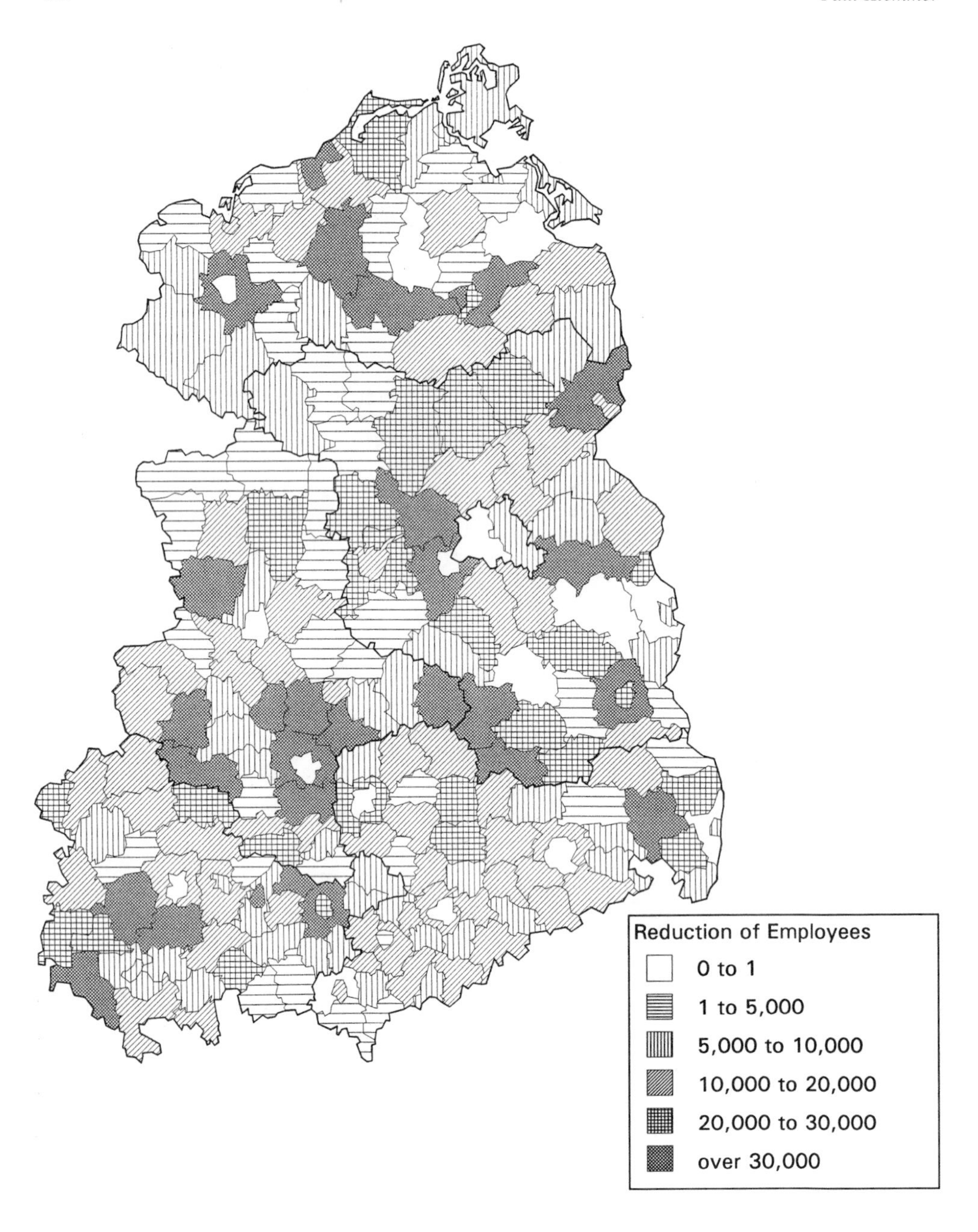

Figure 7 Absolute reduction in number of employees in THA companies, 1991–1993, in the counties of eastern Germany
(Source: own calculations based on THA information)

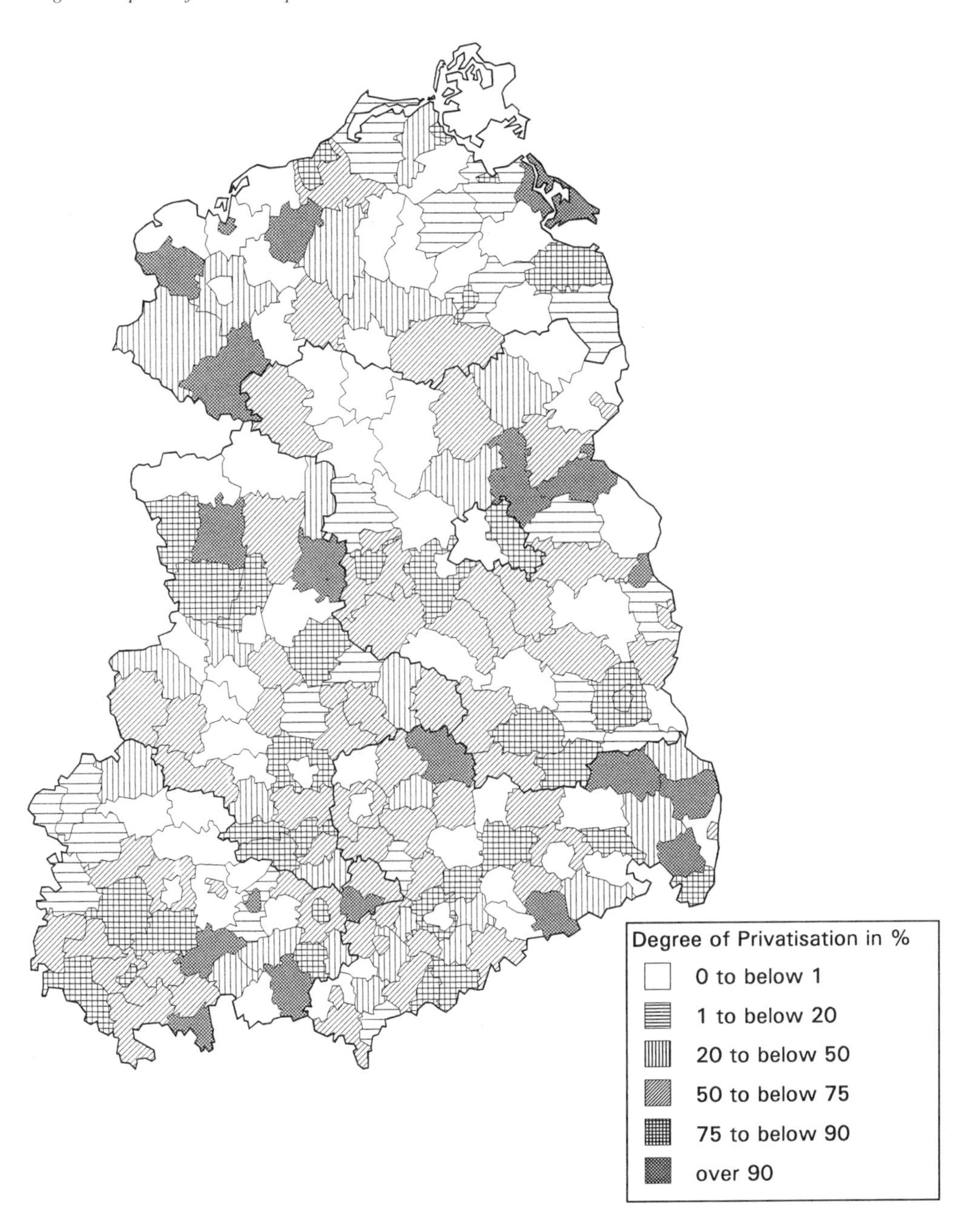

Figure 8 Degree of privatisation of THA companies, 1991–1993, in the counties of eastern Germany
(Source: own calculations based on THA information)

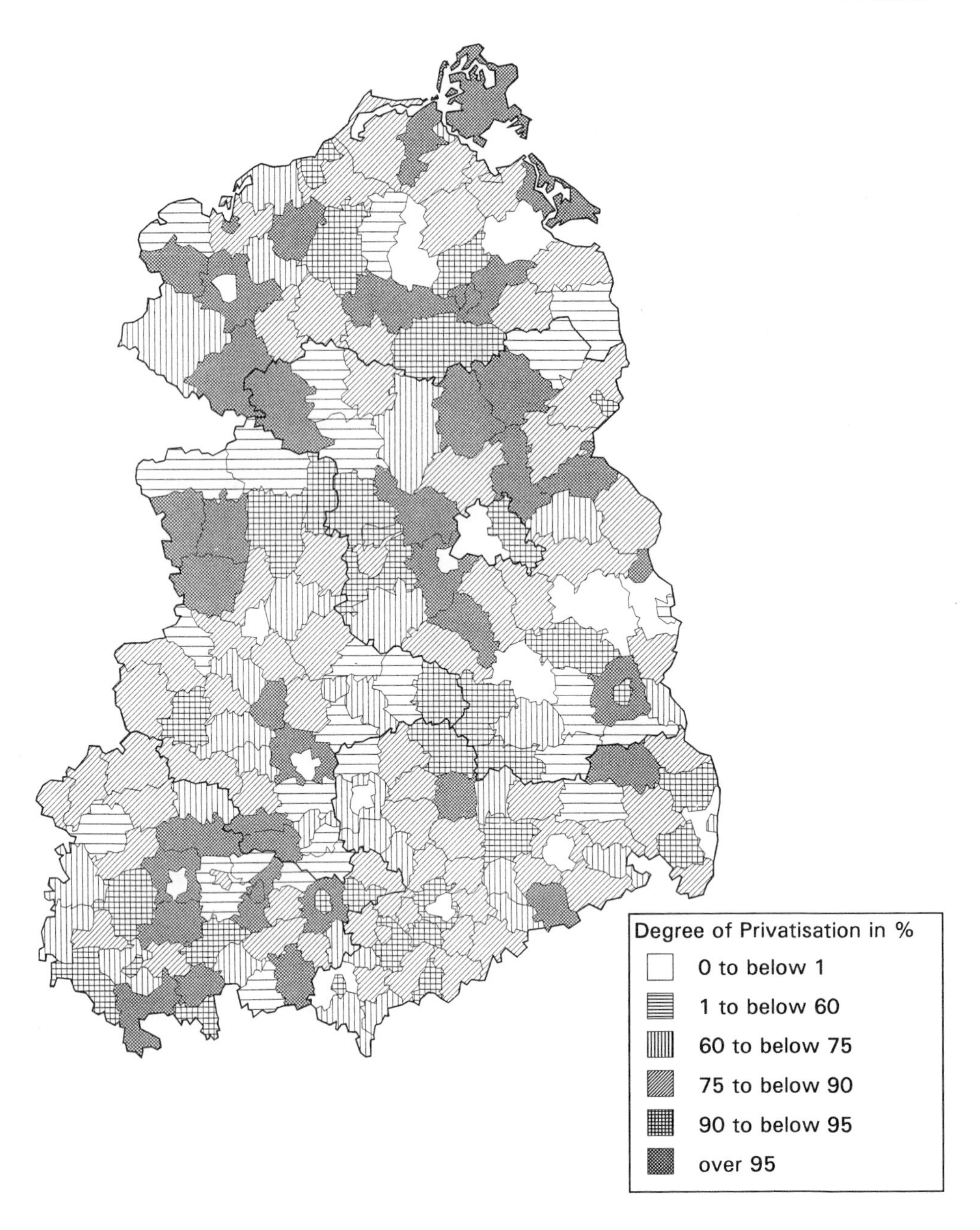

Figure 9 Degree of privatisation of employees in THA companies, 1991–1993, in the counties of eastern Germany
(Source: own calculations based on THA information)

now takes on even more prominence. Figs. 4 and 5 show the situation on 26th January 1993. Looking at the number of companies, it can be seen that the number of counties with 150 or more companies awaiting privatisation has dropped particularly rapidly in the southern part of eastern Germany. In the States of Thuringia and Saxony it is only the counties of Heiligenstadt, Weimar, and Bautzen that still have stocks at this level, but there are still high figures observable in the wider region around Berlin, in the counties of Angermünde and Prenzlau, Güstrow, and Waren, and in the Schwerin region.

Figs. 6 and 7 provide information on the absolute reduction in the number of THA companies in this period of time, from 1991 to 1993, and of the reduction of the number of jobs in them over the same period. Figs. 8 and 9 are particularly suitable for regional comparisons, as they show the degree of privatisation of companies and employees. Starting from the figures for employees, the greatest privatisation success was achieved in the cities of Erfurt, Weimar, and Jena, in the region all around Berlin, particularly the development belt stretching westwards from Berlin to Brandenburg-Havel, Klötze, and Haldensleben. All in all, most of the counties along the old German-German frontier show an above-average rate of privatisation.

V. The influence of regional factors

In order to define the influence of components specific to regions, the latter were described on the basis of data for counties and towns being administrative districts of their own rights in eastern Germany (see Fig. 1) in terms of the so-called "hard" factors: density of population, size of population, surface area of the county, position on the large scale (for road and rail in minutes the average distances in terms of time to all counties in the whole of Germany weighted by population) and for the small-scale position (1-hour, 2-hour, and 3-hour population for rail and road). As part of a multiple regression analysis, these variables were described as independent ones, and the degree of privatisation defined in terms of numbers employed (see Table 1, last column but one) as the variable requiring explanation.

As Table 2 shows, it is possible to explain just under 10% of the THA's privatisation success in terms of regional factors. When one bears in mind that barely a quarter of the change in the trend in employment from 1982 to 1988 in West Germany could be explained of similar facts, these results appear all in all to be plausible and interesting. In other words, it could be confirmed that the THA's privatisation work was affected favourable or unfavourably by regional factors of influence. As far as the individual components were concerned, the regression analysis shows that increasing density of population had a favourable effect on the THA's work but that high population figures on the other hand has the reverse effect. This might indicate problems connected with planning procedures and/or property rights in the major cities. Great importance was accorded to good connections to long-distance roads as one of the large-scale location characteristics, but for rail the results are less plausible and not statistically significant. This could have something to do with the quality of rail transport in eastern Germany. Of the small-scale location characteristics relating to road transport, the 1-hour population played a part in encouraging privatisation; relating to rail transport, the 2-hour and 3-hour populations were more significant.

By means of these results, which can be interpreted as cross-sectional regularity, it is possible to calculate expectation values for all observation units which explain that development which would have occurred if this regularity alone had been crucial for privatisation. These expected values can be compared with the effective value of each attribute and difference values calculated. If the effective values are higher than the expected ones, this indicates a high weighting for other factors not included in the analysis, and possible other regional influence factor components (such as a better image value).

Table 2:
Results of regression analysis

Measurements	Value of attribute (Regression co-efficient)	Standard error
R^2	9,96	
Constant term	111,58	12,13
Density of population	0,00423	0,00309
Surface area	0,00988	0,00477
No. of inhabitants in 1990	–0,000018	0,000036
Large-scale position (road)	–0,11009	0,04729
Large-scale position (rail)	0,051801	0,04296
Road		
1-hour population	0,0000014	0,0000023
2-hour population	–0,0000011	0,0000010
3-hour population	–0,0000017	0,0000007
Rail		
1-hour population	–0,0000009	0,0000029
2-hour population	0,0000006	0,0000012
3-hour population	0,0000005	0,0000007

Source: Own calculations

Table 3:
Comparative calculations for the counties in eastern Germany rated by the size of the differential values

Observation unit	Effective change	Expected value	Difference value
BERLIN (EAST)	93,49	73,94	19,55
JENA (C)	97,36	78,11	19,25
BERNBURG	97,69	78,84	18,85
POTSDAM (C)	98,97	81,04	17,93
HALDENSLEBEN	99,58	81,71	17,87
ARNSTADT	97,46	79,60	17,86
FRANKFURT (ODER) (CB)	99,56	82,26	17,30
NAUMBURG	98,74	81,61	17,13
GADEBUSCH	100,00	82,94	17,06
GERA (C)	99,14	82,36	16,78
JENA (CB)	99,87	83,22	16,65
SCHLEIZ	96,31	79,99	16,32
SAALKREIS	96,29	80,17	16,12

Observation unit	Effective change	Expected value	Difference value
WOLGAST	99,52	84,35	15,17
WISMAR (CB)	100,00	84,99	15,01
NEUBRANDENBURG (C)	99,86	85,07	14,79
NEBRA	97,83	83,28	14,55
GOTHA	94,98	80,51	14,47
MEISSEN	92,70	78,39	14,31
TORGAU	94,87	80,69	14,18
LUCKENWALDE	97,97	83,83	14,14
NEUBRANDENBURG (CB)	95,75	82,23	13,52
SÖMMERDA	97,44	84,58	12,86
NAUEN	98,31	85,54	12,77
SCHMÖLLN	93,90	81,29	12,61
BAD FREIENWALDE	99,17	86,74	12,43
RUDOLSTADT	92,68	80,33	12,35
STRALSUND (C)	95,84	83,50	12,34
BÜTZOW	100,00	87,69	12,31
OSCHATZ	95,74	83,55	12,19
SCHWERIN (C)	95,26	83,17	12,09
DRESDEN (C)	89,50	77,75	11,75
ZWICKAU	94,30	82,61	11,69
HOYERSWERDA	95,53	83,85	11,68
GRIMMA	89,72	78,49	11,23
NEUHAUS AM RENNWEG	97,74	86,70	11,04
ERFURT (C)	96,47	85,53	10,94
BAD LIEBENWERDA	92,09	81,32	10,77
BERNAU	97,19	86,49	10,70
RÜGEN	95,14	84,66	10,48
SCHWEDT (ODER) (CB)	92,53	82,28	10,25
COTTBUS (C3,)	98,45	88,27	10,18
HERZBERG	93,44	83,55	9,89
GERA (CB)	92,85	83,19	9,66
LÜBBEN	92,88	83,24	9,64
HAVELBERG	91,65	82,30	9,35
DIPPOLDISWALDE	96,12	86,84	9,28
RATHENOW	94,59	85,32	9,27
CHEMNITZ (C)	94,45	85,30	9,15
SCHWARZENBERG	94,64	85,62	9,02
KÖTHEN	87,89	78,95	8,94
ROSTOCK (CB)	91,63	82,84	8,79
LUDWIGSLUST	95,10	86,34	8,76
PLAUEN (CB)	93,65	84,91	8,74
PÖSSNECK	89,45	81,00	8,45
QUEDLINBURG	93,41	85,04	8,37
JESSEN	93,35	85,04	8,31
BRANDENBURG (C)	91,17	83,19	7,98
GARDELEGEN	98,16	90,56	7,60
GRANSEE	97,53	90,01	7,52
STOLLBERG	91,96	84,97	6,99

Observation unit	Effective change	Expected value	Difference value
WOLMIRSTEDT	86,74	79,95	6,79
HILDBURGHAUSEN	97,87	91,10	6,77
ZEULENRODA	86,72	80,22	6,50
TEMPLIN	95,26	88,87	6,39
PERLEBERG	95,80	89,55	6,25
LÖBAU	93,83	87,64	6,19
WITTSTOCK	82,04	76,12	5,92
COTTBUS (CB)	94,74	88,89	5,85
WURZEN	83,14	77,51	5,63
FREITAL	86,79	81,44	5,35
NIESKY	94,39	89,18	5,21
WAREN	95,19	90,18	5,01
GLAUCHAU	87,86	82,87	4,99
BRANDENBURG (CB)	82,51	77,69	4,82
MEININGEN	93,71	89,32	4,39
SUHL (CB)	90,93	86,69	4,24
GENTHIN	87,67	83,47	4,20
STADTRODA	82,79	78,63	4,16
BAD LANGENSALZA	83,49	79,69	3,80
ALTENTREPTOW	90,81	87,48	3,33
GÜSTROW	90,96	87,80	3,16
STRASBURG	88,68	85,58	3,10
ZITTAU	89,63	86,69	2,94
FÜRSTENWALDE	87,47	84,66	2,81
HAINICHEN	86,71	84,21	2,50
KLÖTZE	97,75	95,29	2,46
HALBERSTADT	88,40	86,09	2,31
WEIMAR (CB)	82,57	80,49	2,08
AUE	87,72	85,70	2,02
RÖBEL/MÜRITZ	80,65	78,65	2,00
SONNEBERG	90,70	88,70	2,00
GROSSENHAIN	81,92	80,10	1,82
BISCHOFSWERDA	84,56	83,11	1,45
MARIENBERG	89,01	87,70	1,31
ALTENBURG	83,88	82,85	1,03
GRIMMEN	86,46	85,63	0,83
STENDAL	90,89	90,30	0,59
WORBIS	84,87	84,41	0,46
NEUSTRELITZ	93,56	93,18	0,38
GUBEN	84,81	84,46	0,35
LÜBZ	81,93	82,02	-0,09
KOENIGS WUSTERHAUSEN	84,77	84,98	-0,21
EILENBURG	78,92	79,31	-0,39
HOHENSTEIN-ERNSTTHAL	83,64	84,08	-0,44
ROCHLITZ	82,57	83,39	-0,82
JÜTERBOG	84,36	85,21	-0,85
WERDAU	83,49	84,41	-0,92
EBERSWALDE	85,19	86,13	-0,94

Observation unit	Effective change	Expected value	Difference value
SONDERSHAUSEN	83,97	84,95	-0,98
FLÖHA	82,87	84,18	-1,31
PARCHIM	76,32	77,74	-1,42
ANNABERG	86,66	88,25	-1,59
WANZLEBEN	76,63	78,31	-1,68
ZSCHOPAU	82,52	84,60	-2,08
DESSAU (CB)	73,16	75,41	-2,25
QUERFURT	79,89	82,20	-2,31
ZWICKAU (CB)	82,09	84,46	-2,37
RIBNITZ-DAMGARTEN	86,64	89,22	-2,58
ZERBST	77,75	80,39	-2,64
ILMENAU	81,22	84,18	-2,96
GREIFSWALD (C)	82,91	85,98	-3,07
ASCHERSLEBEN	76,19	79,65	-3,46
SANGERHAUSEN	80,28	83,91	-3,63
ZOSSEN	79,86	83,87	-4,01
SCHÖNEBECK	75,98	80,07	-4,09
AUERBACH	77,97	82,87	-4,90
SCHMALKALDEN	81,56	86,51	-4,95
DOEBELN	80,31	85,36	-5,05
HEILIGENSTADT	75,41	80,71	-5,30
NORDHAUSEN	79,92	85,39	-5,47
WEISSWASSER	78,60	84,26	-5,66
BURG	74,34	80,47	-6,13
WERNIGERODE	80,97	87,24	-6,27
HETTSTEDT	74,05	80,57	-6,52
ANGERMÜNDE	82,45	89,30	-6,85
WEISSENFELS	67,31	74,39	-7,08
UECKERMÜNDE	78,48	85,58	-7,10
PIRNA	79,02	86,43	-7,41
GRÄFENHAINICHEN	71,52	79,31	-7,79
ORANIENBURG	80,88	88,71	-7,83
ARTERN	74,68	82,71	-8,03
BORNA	71,73	79,80	-8,07
FINSTERWALDE	74,82	83,54	-8,72
GREIFSWALD (CB)	75,47	84,83	-9,36
FREIBERG	73,99	83,37	-9,38
FORST	73,77	83,26	-9,49
DEMMIN	80,65	90,15	-9,50
GEITHAIN	73,65	83,19	-9,54
SEELOW	80,17	89,71	-9,54
KLINGENTHAL	74,35	84,01	-9,66
ROSTOCK (C)	76,23	86,05	-9,82
BAUTZEN	77,92	87,76	-9,84
WISMAR (C)	75,25	85,09	-9,84
REICHENBACH	71,96	82,71	-10,75
EISLEBEN	71,81	82,83	-11,02
RIESA	66,40	77,66	-11,26

Observation unit	Effective change	Expected value	Difference value
SUHL (C)	72,10	83,69	-11,59
STERNBERG	69,98	81,79	-11,81
NEURUPPIN	71,84	84,06	-12,22
OELSNITZ	70,07	82,57	-12,50
BELZIG	67,39	80,26	-12,87
BRAND-ERBISDORF	69,90	84,25	-14,35
BAD SALZUNGEN	68,72	83,11	-14,39
STRAUSBERG	72,84	87,81	-14,97
EISENACH	61,14	76,37	-15,23
STASSFURT	64,32	79,65	-15,33
EISENBERG	58,65	75,93	-17,28
STRALSUND (CB)	66,57	84,75	-18,18
LEIPZIG (C)	61,04	79,31	-18,27
MERSEBURG	59,14	78,88	-19,74
LOBENSTEIN	58,31	78,84	-20,53
SAALFELD	60,99	81,63	-20,64
BAD DOBERAN	65,67	86,49	-20,82
DELITZSCH	57,09	78,66	-21,57
BITTERFELD	57,13	79,17	-22,04
GREIZ	60,88	83,71	-22,83
HAGENOW	63,99	87,56	-23,57
HOHENMÖLSEN	53,61	78,13	-24,52
GÖRLITZ (CB)	71,74	96,48	-24,74
SEBNITZ	61,95	87,34	-25,39
OSCHERSLEBEN	54,10	79,64	-25,54
WITTENBERG	52,76	79,32	-26,56
WEIMAR (C)	52,43	80,25	-27,82
GREVESMÜHLEN	54,91	86,80	-31,89
ROSSLAU	39,16	74,99	-35,83
PRENZLAU	51,38	87,96	-36,58
EISENHÜTTENSTADT (CB)	49,95	87,46	-37,51
SENFTENBERG	44,21	82,44	-38,23
ZEITZ	36,43	77,46	-41,03
PASEWALK	47,17	88,68	-41,51
TETEROW	40,22	83,68	-43,46
SPREMBERG	38,45	82,33	-43,88
PRITZWALK	34,62	79,09	-44,47
CALAU	36,46	81,21	-44,75
MÜHLHAUSEN	40,14	86,19	-46,05
KAMENZ	31,59	82,57	-50,98
APOLDA	21,66	80,83	-59,17
SALZWEDEL	19,22	88,09	-68,87
KYRITZ	2,31	81,63	-79,32

Source: Own calculations
Note: C = County (*Landkreis*), BC = County Borough (*kreisfreie Stadt*, administrative district of its own right)

A comparative calculation of this kind is provided in Table 3, which contains only the observation units which have a plausible effective value. It shows that in many regions the effective degree of privatisation exceeded the statistically expected value. In the cases of eastern Berlin, Potsdam, Frankfurt an der Oder, Gera, Jena, Dresden (county), and the counties in the hinterland around Berlin this could be due to other regional factors such as the "capital city effect", location in the European heartland, as with Frankfurt an der Oder, or image factors. On the other side of the coin there are regions where the effective figure is below expectations, like Mühlhausen, Apolda, or the town of Suhl in Thuringia, the county of Riesa or the city of Görlitz in Saxony, or Bitterfeld in Saxony-Anhalt. In the cases of Suhl or Görlitz there could be location problems that have not yet been discovered which would be able to explain this idiosyncratic development, and in other cases, such as Bitterfeld and Riesa, there were specific privatisation problems connected with the sectoral and company size structure of the companies awaiting privatisation. This will make it clear that it can be the aim of a comparative calculation of this kind to reveal special factors in development which require further analysis before they can be explained.

VI. Literature

Arbeitsgemeinschaft deutscher wirtschaftswissenschaftlicher Forschungsinstitute: *Die Lage der Weltwirtschaft und der deutschen Wirtschaft im Frühjahr 1993.* Kiel 1993.

Budde, Rüdiger, Hans-Friedrich *Eckey*, and Paul *Klemmer*: *Vorschlag für die Abgrenzung von Arbeitsmarktregionen in den neuen Bundesländern. RWI-Gutachten im Auftrag der Gemeinschaftsaufgabe "Verbesserung der regionalen Wirtschaftsstruktur"*. Essen, January 1993.

Budde, Rüdiger, Rüdiger *Hamm*, Paul *Klemmer*, Bernd *Lagemann*, and Heinz *Schrumpf*: Übertragung regionalpolitischer Konzepte auf Ostdeutschland. *Untersuchungen des Rheinisch-Westfälischen Instituts für Wirtschaftsforschung* issue 2. Essen 1991.

Dathe, Dietmar, and Bernd *Fritzsche*: Ziele, Tätigkeiten und Perspektiven der Treuhandanstalt. *RWI-Papiere* No. 31. Essen 1992.

Eckey, Hans-Friedrich, and Klaus *Horn*: *Lagegunst- und Verkehrsanalysen für die Kreise des vereinigten Deutschlands im Straßen- und Schienenverkehr.* Kassel 1991.

ditto: *Veränderung der Lagegunst und Erreichbarkeit der Kreise im vereinigten Deutschland durch geplante Ausbau- und Neubaumaßnahmen.* Kassel 1991.

Hamm, Rüdiger, and Paul *Klemmer*: *Ansatzpunkte und Möglichkeiten einer Modifizierung der regionalen Strukturpolitik. RWI-Expertise im Auftrag des Bundesministers für Raumordnung, Bauwesen und Städtebau.* Essen 1993.

Klemmer, Paul: *Zum Entwicklungseinfluß sogenannter "harter" Standortgegebenheiten* (to be published shortly).

Klemmer, Paul, with the assistance of Hans-Friedrich *Eckey* and Burkardt *Bremicker*: Zur Bestimmung kommunaler Industrialisierungsbesonderheiten. *Schriftenreihe der Gesellschaft für Regionale Strukturentwicklung* e.V., volume 14. Bonn 1988.

Löbbe, Klaus, et al: *Analyse der strukturellen Entwicklung der deutschen Wirtschaft. RWI-Strukturberichterstattung.* Essen 1987.

Löbbe, Klaus, et al: Technische Dienstleistungen, Technologietransfer und Innovation. *Untersuchungen des Rheinisch-Westfälischen Instituts für Wirtschaftsforschung*, volume 7. Essen 1992.

Schwerpunktthema 1988: *Standortqualität der Bundesrepublik Deutschland und Veränderungen der Standortanforderungen im sektoralen Strukturwandel. RWI-Gutachten im Auftrag des Bundesministers für Wirtschaft*. Essen 1989.

Treuhandanstalt: *Monatsinformation der THA* as of 30th June 1993.

Regulation of the social effects of the THA's work by labour law

by Peter Hanau, with the assistance of Ralf Steffan

I. Introduction

Rapid privatisation, resolute restructuring, and considerate closure – these are the maxims of the THA for the transition from the socialist planned economy to the (social) market economy.[1] In abandoning the economic system of the GDR, the gigantic task of privatising the so-called people-owned property under the law of 17th June 1990[2] fell to the newly established THA, which became responsible for some 8,000 *Kombinate* and VEB-companies with a total of 45,000 operating units and more than 4 million employees.[3] It has described itself as being the world's biggest holding company and the only one with the overriding goal of terminating its own existence as quickly as possible.[4] Guidelines for those of its activities relevant to labour law were contained in the preamble to the THG and in § 2 of the THA Statutes of 18th July 1990.[5] In both of these sets of regulations, one of the aims is "to make as many companies as possible competitive, thus preserving existing jobs and creating new ones". In addition to this, § 3 of the Investment Priority Act[6] defines the preservation or creation of jobs as an investment purpose to which special attention must be paid. It soon became, however, apparent that the creation of companies' ability to compete and the creation and preservation of new jobs could not go hand in hand, at least for an initial period of time;[7] indeed, at this moment these two objectives are diametrically opposed to one another. In order to make eastern German companies at least roughly competitive, the number of employees has to be reduced drastically.

---

1 See: Bundesministerium der Finanzen (editor), *Die Tätigkeit der Treuhandanstalt*, covering letter; Gemählich, *Sozialverträglicher Beschäftigungsumbruch*, page 166.

2 *Treuhandgesetz* or THG; see: summary of laws on pages XVI et seq.

3 Bundesministerium der Finanzen (editor), *Die Tätigkeit der Treuhandanstalt,* page 8; Gemählich, *Sozialverträglicher Beschäftigungsumbruch,* page 166.

4 Treuhandanstalt, chart presentation, as of 26th August 1991; Koch, "*Eine Illusion müssen wir aufrechterhalten ...*", page 163.

5 *Gesetzblatt der DDR* 1990 I, page 809.

6 *Investitionsvorranggesetz*, promulgated as Article 6 of the 2nd Property Law Amendment Act; see: summary of laws on pages XVI et seq.

7 For the problems and requirements from the economic scientist's point of view see: BMWi Studienreihe No. 75, *Lohn- und Arbeitsmarktprobleme in den neuen Bundesländern. Gutachten des Wissenschaftlichen Beirats beim Bundesministerium für Wirtschaft.*

II. Trends in employment statistics as a result of privatisation, restructuring, and closure

1. Course of events

In the middle of 1990 there were about 4.1 million employees in the THA companies, amounting to about 42% of all those in employment in East Germany.[8] Privatisation, the break up of industrial combines and the formation of new companies, and redundancies caused a reduction in these numbers to 1.24 million by 1st April 1992.[9] This represents a reduction of about 70% in 21 months. The largest proportion was accounted for by job-changes on the basis of employment undertakings in ex-THA companies which had been privatised, reprivatised (returned to their former owners), or communalised (made over to the local authority), and job-changes to other companies. The second largest group consisted of the unemployed, most of them simply declared redundant because of operating conditions. By the second half of 1992 it became clear that the shedding of jobs in THA companies was increasingly leading to unemployment. According to a survey conducted by the labour market and occupational research unit of the Federal Institute for Labour on 3,177 THA companies, in the third quarter of 1992 37.7% of employees leaving THA companies had no new job to go to, and this number rose to 49.0% in the fourth quarter. Parallel to this development, it was still possible in the third quarter of 1992for 19% of departing employees to be found work in work-creation schemes (ABS companies providing restructuring work, work-creation and retraining outside the ABS scheme), but this figure dropped to 4.6% in the fourth quarter.[10]

As of 30th June 1993 there were still 296,343 people employed in 1,668 THA companies. The total portfolio of companies taken over or established by the THA amounted in June of that year to 12,993.[11] Employment trends varied from one industry to another. The work-force fell in the metal producing and metal-working industries to 10% of the original level, but in the chemical industry only to 21%. The reasons for the different rates at which numbers employed were reduced might be attributed to economic and political factors.

2. Possible courses of action

The figures quoted above clearly show the parameters within which the THA had to operate. They also substantiate the assumption the THA made when it started work that 50% of the more than 4 million employees which the THA took over with its companies would have to be dismissed. For those responsible this fact was clear from the beginning as it was confirmed repeatedly to us. This calculation was based on the general belief that, at the start of the THA's activity, there were *de facto* two employees doing every one job in East Germany.[12] One basis for this

8 See: Gemählich, *Sozialverträglicher Beschäftigungsumbruch*, page 166.

9 See: *IAB Kurzbericht* No. 15 dated 6th July 1992.

10 See: Wahse, Dahms, and Schaefer, *Beschäftigungsperspektiven von Treuhandunternehmen*, page 15.

11 See: Treuhandanstalt, *Monatsinformation der THA* as of 30th June 1993, page 6; ditto, *Monatsbericht* for May 1992, item 8.3.

12 See: Interview with Dr Koch, ex-member of the Executive Board, in: Koch, "*Eine Illusion müssen wir aufrechterhalten...*", page 160.

calculation was the fact that, despite the absence of a class of company owners running their own medium-sized businesses (the *Mittlestand*), half the population was engaged in employment in East Germany but only one third in West Germany.

There were a number of possible courses of action open for abolishing two million jobs. If carried out solely along the lines of conventional business management valuation procedures for establishing the capitalised value of potential returns or liquidation value of a company,[13] the aim of rapid privatisation would have led to the immediate closure of a very large number of THA companies. This would have meant neglecting the aim of preserving jobs. That the THA did not strictly follow this course is highly commendable from the point of view of social policy. Instead, it used the room for manoeuvre provided by legislation to delay in some cases the reduction in numbers employed, thus making redundancy socially more bearable. While it was looking for investors it kept running its companies for a certain time, and as a last resort sold them for a "negative purchase price", or less than the liquidation value. In view of the fact that the normal procedure for establishing the capitalised value of potential returns or liquidation value of a company is at best only of limited use to the THA for defining the lowest price limit, this does not necessarily represent a violation of the economic principle.[14] The conflict of aims that arose in the THA's work between rapid privatisation and the preservation of jobs precluded the use of conventional valuation methods, so that keeping the companies in operation for a limited period of time with later privatisation was the obvious alternative action to sale.[15] Where the closure of an insolvent company was inevitable, it was postponed in order to preserve jobs at least temporarily. The instrument used by the THA was liquidation after a preliminary phase during which assessments were made by relevant experts, thus avoiding the automatic machinery of bankruptcy proceedings and still retaining of other alternative courses of action with regard to securing jobs.[16]

In the opinion of Mr Meyer, who was at that time the president of the German Federation of Trade Unions,[17] it would have been possible and indeed desirable, within the existing financial limitations, to finance further restructuring programmes instead of mere liquidity subsidies. Run-down companies had been kept in existence for far too long in this way without any active restructuring.

III. Job security in the case of company disposal[18]

1. Undertakings to preserve or create jobs

Despite the necessary but massive reduction in numbers employed, the THA attempted to preserve as many jobs as it could within the parameters of its privatisation strategy. To this end, the purchase price was influenced by the potential buyer's undertakings to guarantee a given num-

13 See: Sieben, *Zur Wertfindung bei der Privatisierung*, page 2044.
14 op. cit., page 2045.
15 op. cit., page 2051.
16 See: article by Wandel in this volume.
17 B-Interview with Heinz-Werner Meyer on 12th May 1993 in Düsseldorf.
18 On the THA's privatisation strategy, see principally: article by Küpper, pages 317 et seq., and Schmidt, pages 212 et seq. in this volume.

ber of jobs for an agreed period of time. The standard form of disposal contract accordingly included clauses for guaranteeing jobs and employment, usually for a period of two to four years.[19] If the agreed undertakings are not adhered to, the purchaser has to pay a set sum per month for each employee he has failed to take on (e. g. DM 3,000), or in some cases a single payment increase in the purchase price (of about DM 20,000 to 30,000) is made for each missing employee. There are pre-defined exceptional circumstances applicable to the employment undertakings which vary from case to case: these regulations would not apply for instance if it is impossible for the purchaser to keep to his undertakings for reasons which he cannot influence and which fall outside his normal sphere of risk. In some cases a contractual penalty does not come into effect if the purchaser falls short of the promised number of jobs due to urgent operational requirements which could not have been foreseen at the time the contract was concluded. It proved possible to insist on these contractual penalties in about 70% of all privatisation and sale contracts, and they were far less frequently included in the initial phases of the THA's operational business than in more recent times. This is connected with the fact that § 8 section 3 of the Investment Priority Act now mandatorily prescribes the inclusion of contractual penalties in investment contracts. The THA was able to obtain employment undertakings for more than 1.46 million jobs up to 30th June 1993.[20] The THA describes the number of violations of these agreements as small. Statistical analyses are available for 1991 and 1992. For 1991, 3,550 investors had undertaken to employ a total of 265,000 people; for 1992 there were 6,405 contracts guaranteeing 411,519 jobs. 80% of these contracts have now been checked by the relevant contract management department of the THA, which revealed that in 1991 about 17% of the agreed undertakings had not been adhered to and 26% in 1992. Taking all these contracts together, the total number of jobs promised was however exceeded in 1991 by about 10% and in 1992 by 12%.[21] In those cases in which the requirements could not be fulfilled, the THA tends to be cautious in demanding the additional payments due to it in order not to drive these companies from their present economic difficulties into out-and-out bankruptcy.[22] Although the THA "on principal" does not waive any of its contractual rights, it does investigate each case individually to see whether postponement of the contractual claims could under certain circumstances provide help to the investor in difficulties.[23] This shows that in the long term undertakings to provide employment, backed by contractual penalties, could secure only profitable jobs which would have been preserved even without the undertakings and the purchase price reductions they entailed. Despite this limited effectiveness, the employment undertakings have proved to be a valuable means particularly of excluding potential purchasers who were not interested in continuing the company in operation but only in eliminating a competitor.

An interesting question in this connection is posed by the legal effect of the agreement and, in addition to that, whether individual employees can derive any legal claims from it. This is an application of a contractual penalty within the meaning of §§ 339 et seq. of the German Civil Code, but the relevant application of these regulations to the across-the-board increase in the purchase price is nonetheless dubious. The THA's claim to the penalty becomes null and void if

19 See: Wächter, Kaiser, and Krause, *Klauseln in Unternehmenskaufverträgen*, page 300.

20 See: Treuhandanstalt, *Monatsinformation der THA* as of 31st May 1993, page 13.

21 See: Press releases by THA contract management of 26th October 1992 and of 22nd June 1993.

22 See: *Handelsblatt*, 15th March 1993, page 4, and 17th May 1993, page 13.

23 See: Press release by THA contract management of 26th October 1992.

the purchaser can prove that his failure to adhere to the job guarantee was caused by factors outside his control. Whether this is the case, it is necessary to investigate and see whether the agreed circumstances justifying an exception apply. The contractual regulations take precedence here, and can go so far as to become a guarantee regardless of any question of responsibility. The acceptance of a "reconciliation of interests" (between employer and employees) under § 111 of the Industrial Constitution Act, on the other hand, will usually fail to apply because the works council is not party to the contract of sale between the THA and the purchaser. The individual employee would only have a claim under the job guarantee clause or for non-adherence to it if the contract is one for the benefit of a third party or one with a protective effect to the benefit of a third party within the meaning of § 328 of the Civil Code. This is a question of interpretation to which no general answer is possible. It can be generally assumed here that the parties concluding the contract, the THA and the purchaser, will be subject to reservation of authorisation under § 328 section 2 of the Civil Code for sharing out or altering the undertakings without the employee's assent if this appears to be necessary for economic reasons. One question left unanswered, and which at the time of writing could come to the top of the agenda in the case of the Oranienburg steelworks, is whether non-fulfilment of an undertaking to provide employment can only lead to an obligation to pay the contractual penalty or to repayment obligations, or to claims to performance of contract in creating or preserving jobs.

2. Management Buy-Out

The MBO system as practised by the THA can be categorised as a further means of preserving jobs,[24] as it secures existing jobs by selling the company or the factory to the senior managers who work in it. Bearing in mind the limited reserves of capital held by these employees, this method is most suitable for small to medium-sized enterprises. The THA supports MBO's in a variety of ways, e. g. by postponing payment of the purchase price for a certain period of time, permitting payment in instalments, and prolonging bank guarantees. In addition to the effect of preserving jobs, MBO's contribute to the important economic process of building up a class of owner-managers which had not so far existed in eastern Germany.[25] With the encouragement of the THA more than 2,360 MBO's had been set up in eastern Germany by 30th June 1993; this encouragement also covered mixtures of MBO's and buy-outs by a wider group of the company's workforce. This became known as the IMO model[26] of privatisation, and is based on 49.9% of the equity being held by a bank holding company, 25.2% by the MBO group of three directors, and 24.9% by an employees' holding company. The capital of this employees' holding company has to be pre-financed by a bank and paid back to the employees under the Wealth Formation Act, covered by a guarantee from the relevant State *(Land)*. In order to ensure that the employees' incentive is not diluted by the risk of a loss of value in the event of bankruptcy, the State has to bear the risk of paying back the loan in this eventuality. No other system of "Employee Buy-Out"[27] or other models in which the employees hold equity[28] appears to have established itself securely.

---

24 On this term, see: Otto, *Management-Buy-Out und Belegschafts-Buy-Out*, § 26, pages 834 et seq.; for the situation in eastern Germany see: Clausen, *Die Finanzierung des Unternehmenskaufs*, pages 1 et seq.

25 Gemählich, *Sozialverträglicher Beschäftigungsumbruch*, page 166.

26 First tried out in the privatisation of the firm of *Industriemontagen Leipzig GmbH* (IMO).

27 On this point, see: Wagner, *Management-Buy-Out und Belegschafts-Buy-Out*, § 26, pages 870 et seq.

28 On the possibilities open see: Schack, *Die partnerschaftliche Unternehmung*, pages 30 et seq.

3. Consequences of the passage of ownership

a) Basic area of application of § 613a of the Civil Code in the THA's sphere of influence

The regulations defined in § 613a of the West German Civil Code,[29] under which the legal transfer of ownership of a company or parts of one leads to the simultaneous transfer of the contracts of employment of the people working in it, took effect in East Germany as early as 1st July 1990. The applicability to eastern Germany of a standard which is constantly throwing up problems in practice[30] has been called into doubt.[31] It has been submitted that § 613a applies only to a passage of ownership within a market economy, but not for the transposition into such a system.[32] In view of the clarity of the statutory regulations, however, this view did not gain acceptance, but it is clear that § 613a of the Civil Code will only take effect when the legal ownership has been changed by means of a legal transaction. The mere conversion of formerly state-owned companies into corporations on the basis of the *Treuhandgesetz* or THG and the splitting up of individual companies by the THA itself are accordingly not a transfer of ownership within the meaning of § 613a.[33] This regulation is also inapplicable if privatisation takes the form of the take-over of shares (in a so-called share deal); in this case the employment contracts are not affected. But the regulation has to be observed if the THA has made over companies or parts of them to a purchaser by legal transaction (so-called asset deal), where privatisation under the laws of a market economy has already taken place at a previous stage, so that the statutory regulations of the market economy also have to apply.[34]

b) Amendment of § 613a of the Civil Code by the Splitting Act

In order to remove obstacles to investment, the Splitting Act[35] of 5th April 1991[36] permits the companies administered by the THA to transfer parts of themselves in their entirety. § 613a of the Civil Code thus underwent an amendment (in accordance with Article 232 § 5 section 2 of

---

29 From 1st July 1990 onwards as § 59a of the East German Labour Code in the version of 22nd June 1990, and since 3rd October 1990 directly under Article 8 of the Treaty of Unification.

30 Most recently by Hanau in: *Aktuelle Fragen zu § 613a*, pages 287 et seq.

31 It is contested by Hanau in: Adomeit, *Arbeitsrecht,* A III, page 25; Adomeit, Eiden, and Schack, *Arbeitsrecht und Privatisierung,* page 5; Heinze, *Betriebsübergang und Sozialplanpflichtigkeit*, pages 79 et seq.; Richardi, *Die Anwendbarkeit des § 613a*, page 289; Weimar and Alfes, *Neuregelung des § 613a*, page 1830.

32 Adomeit, Eiden, and Schack, *Arbeitsrecht und Privatisierung,* page 5; for a differing view: Richardi, *Die Anwendbarkeit des § 613a*, pages 289 et seq.; Oetker, *Übergang der Arbeitsverhältnisse*, page 7; Weimar and Alfes, *Betriebsbelegschaften als Investitionshemmnis*, page 18; Commandeur, *Die Bedeutung des § 613a*, page 710.

33 On this point, see: Heinze, *Betriebsübergang und Sozialplanpflichtigkeit*, page 80 et seq.

34 op. cit., page 82.

35 The concept of "splitting" subsumes two processes not previously codified in German company law, *Aufspaltung* (splitting up) and *Abspaltung* (splitting off). For a discussion *de lege ferenda* see: Lutter, *Zur Reform von Umwandlung*, page 403; Priester, *Strukturänderungen*, page 426.

36 *Bundesgesetzblatt* 1991 I, page 854; for more details on this point see: Weimar, *Spaltung von Treuhandunternehmen*, pages 182 et seq.; Ganske, *Spaltung der Treuhandunternehmen*, pages 791 et seq.

the EGBGB, the Introductory Act to the Civil Code) caused by § 16 section 2 of the Splitting Act as far as the territory of eastern Germany was concerned. Accordingly, the regulation was not applicable in bankruptcy proceedings up to 31st December 1992. The Amendment Act to the Introductory Act to the Civil Code of 21st December 1992 prolonged the special arrangements by two years, until 31st December 1994.[37] This is to an extent a relief compared with the situation in western Germany, as adjudication on the applicability of § 613a in bankruptcy proceedings permits limitations regarding legal liability, but not regarding the transfer of contracts of employment. The practical consequences of this regulation now appear to be slight so far, as the THA prefers out-of-court liquidation to bankruptcy proceedings.[38] This is often more favourable to the company's creditors because they usually receive more than at the end of bankruptcy proceedings.[39] By 30th June 1993, 2,857 THA companies had been affected by closure, and 57 of them already liquidated. Of the remaining 2,800 companies, bankruptcy proceedings have been opened for 343 of them and liquidation for 2,457.[40] The suspension of § 613a of the Civil Code during bankruptcy proceedings is thus probably less attributable to any request from the THA than to attempts being made from western Germany to legal policy attempts. It also said that only one potential buyer ever placed importance on bankruptcy proceedings in order to select employees without regard to § 613a. On the other hand, it was often possible, with the agreement of the trade union and/or the works council, to weaken the effect of § 613a and to define the group of employees to be taken over by mutual agreement. In this case it should probably taken into account that § 613a, particularly the law on dismissal defined in its section 4 sentence 2, has to be interpreted and used in the context of the THA's statutory task of privatisation.

§ 613a is basically applicable to the statutorily defined process of splitting in accordance with legislative regulation[41] and intention.[42] Opinions reported in the literature are divided. The validity of § 613a is denied in some cases with the justification that transfers of contracts of employment under the Splitting Act are cases of the complete succession in law and thus cannot be ssen as transfers by legal transactions.[43] Regardless of the controversial question of the legal

37 *Bundesgesetzblatt* 1992 I, page 2116.

38 See: Berscheid, *Konkurs, "Sanierung/Betriebsfortführung"*, marginal note 77; Kübler, *Die Gesamtvollstreckung*, page 90; Haarmeyer, Wutzke, and Förster, *Kommentar zur Gesamtvollstreckungsordnung*, introduction, marginal note 111. See also above, Section II.2, and the article by Wandel in this volume, pages 287 et seq.

39 On this point, see: Oberhofer, *Kurzstellungnahme*, page 122 et seq.; for a view concurring with "silent liquidation" see: Timm, *Die Sanierung der sogenannten "Treuhandunternehmen"*, page 420 (footnote 77).

40 See: Treuhandanstalt, *Monatsinformation der THA* as of 30th June 1993, page 20.

41 § 16 section 1 of the Splitting Act supplements § 613a of the Civil Code to the effect that it is only the later legal liability of the previous employer that does not take effect in the case of splitting. The result of this is that § 613a does otherwise apply in the case of splitting.

42 See Bundestag printed paper 12/254, page 23; Bundesrat printed paper 71/91, page 19.

43 See: Oetker, *Übergang der Arbeitsverhältnisse*, page 7; Oetker and Busche, *Entflechtung*, page 20; Schaub, *Einführung*, page 226; Commandeur, *Die Bedeutung des § 613a*, page 710 et seq.; a more cautious view is taken by: Commandeur, *Betriebsübergang*, page 169; Berscheid, *Konkurs, "Sanierung/Betriebsfortführung"*, marginal note 110; Weidner, *Neue Bestimmungen für Betriebsräte*, page 225.

nature of splitting,[44] it has recently been shown in the literature[45] that a legal transaction and complete succession in law are not mutually exclusive. The applicability of § 613a to the splitting process under the Splitting Act can therefore be endorsed.[46] The application of this regulation, when interpreted correctly, also allows for precedence over the distribution of the employees in accordance with the plan for splitting the company as defined in § 2 section No. 10 of the Splitting Act.[47]

The area of application of § 613a was subjected to a partial exception with regard to adjudications on the employees' recognised right of objection[48] which can exclude the transfer of the contract of employment to the purchaser. At the least when companies have been split up which is combined with their dissolution, the right of objection leads into a vacuum and is therefore not applicable.[49] In the case of splitting off, an admitted right of objection makes the statutory purpose of the Splitting Act of simplifying the splitting of THA companies and preparing them for sale harder to achieve.[50] In addition to this, a change of employer occurs legally but not economically in the THA's internal process of splitting companies.[51] Accordingly, a right of objection comes into force again if the company that has been split off, and therefore also the factory, is sold by the THA under an asset deal. In this event, the legal change of the employer brings with it the economic change which is far more important from the point of view of the work-force.

It is in the final phase of its operative business in particular that the THA will be tempted to close down loss-making companies but at the same time to continue its endeavours to sell them. § 16 section 2 of the Splitting Act gains in significance in this connection, as it modified § 613a

---

44 For the legal transaction as a modified form of individual legal succession ("partial succession"), see: Weimar, *Spaltung von Treuhandunternehmen*, page 182 et seq.; ditto, *Die Entflechtung von Treuhandunternehmen*, page 775; Weimar and Alfes, *Neuregelung des § 613a*, page 1831; Weimar and Alfes, *Widerspruchsrecht des Arbeitnehmers*, page 833; on complete legal succession see footnote 42 above.

45 Schmidt, *Universalsukzession*, page 517.

46 See: Weimar, *Spaltung von Treuhandunternehmen*, page 183; ditto, *Die Entflechtung von Treuhandunternehmen*, page 775; Weimar and Alfes, *Betriebsbelegschaften als Investitionshemmnis*, page 1831; ditto, *Widerspruchsrecht des Arbeitnehmers*, page 833; Ising and Thiell, *Der Übergang laufender Arbeitsverhältnisse*, page 2082; Mayer, *Zweifelsfragen*, page 1612; Scheifele, *Praktische Erfahrungen*, page 633 et seq.; *Das Bürgerliche Gesetzbuch (Kommentar)*, Ascheid, *§ 613a BGB*, marginal note 115; and probably also Belling and Müsgen, *Arbeitsrechtliche Aspekte der Sanierung*, page 17.

47 Ising and Thiell, *Der Übergang laufender Arbeitsverhältnisse*, page 2082; Weimar, *Spaltung von Treuhandunternehmen*, page 183; Mayer, *Zweifelsfragen*, page 1612; Oetker and Busche, *Entflechtung*, pages 19 and 21.

48 Consistent rulings since: Federal Labour Court, 2nd October 1974, *Arbeitsrechtliche Praxis* No. 1 on § 613a of the Civil Code. The European Court of Justice found, in its judgement dated 16th December 1992 (written up in *Neue Zeitschrift für Arbeits- und Sozialrecht* 1993, 169), that national adjudications on the subject of the right of objection do not oppose the Directive 77/187.

49 Ising and Thiell, *Der Übergang laufender Arbeitsverhältnisse*, page 2084; Weimar and Alfes, *Widerspruchsrecht des Arbeitnehmers*, page 835; but for a different view see: Mayer, *Zweifelsfragen*, page 1612.

50 Ising and Thiell, *Der Übergang laufender Arbeitsverhältnisse*, page 2084;Weimar and Alfes, *Widerspruchsrecht des Arbeitnehmers*, page 833, although they do tend to favour a right of objection.

51 This is also acknowledged by Weimar and Alfes, *Widerspruchsrecht des Arbeitnehmers*, page 834, although they do favour a right of objection also in this case.

section 4 sentence 2 of the Civil Code via Article 232 § 5 of the Introductory Act to the Civil Code in the eastern German area. Accordingly, the possibility of a dismissal for economic, technical, or organisational reasons (in short: redundancy) remains unaffected by the ban on dismissals in § 613a section 4 sentence 1 of the Civil Code. The formulation complies with Article 4 section 1 of EC Directive 77/187, and the wording it uses goes beyond the version of § 613a section 4 sentence 2 of the Civil Code as it applies in western Germany. To an extent, the regulation contained in Article 232 § 5 section 2 of the Introductory Act to the Civil Code is ascribed not only a clarifying character[52] but also a facility for making dismissal easier.[53] According to this view, dismissal is legally valid even if the transfer of the ownership of the business is a contributory factor to the dismissal provided that in addition to this at least one of the reasons for dismissal named in § 613a section 4 sentence 2 of the Civil Code has caused the dismissal.[54] A loosening of previous adjudications is also perceived from the fact that, according to a ruling handed down by the Federal Labour Court on 19th June 1991,[55] when dismissals are issued in connection with plans finally to close a plant down, they are not made invalid by § 613a section 4 of the Civil Code if the THA later does manage to sell the company after all.[56] The Court has since found that dismissal on the grounds of the transfer of ownership of the company is not deemed to exist if the dismissal notice was issued before the sale of the company is considered and carried out.[57] The Senate (the Bench which decided the case) has appositely enough drawn attention to its previous adjudications,[58] so that no change in adjudication appears to have taken place. Instead, if the exact wording of the justification of the ruling is examined, the situation that has emerged is rather awkward for the THA, as it has always endeavoured to put the sale of a company ahead of any plans to close it down: However, it is necessary to take the special responsibility of the THA for selling companies into account in the sense that, after long and weary endeavours at achieving a sale, a certain desire does arise to make a clean break. If it then decides in favour of closure and the dismissals that this entails, negotiations on a sale which start afterwards and lead to success cannot prevent dismissals at least on the basis of § 613a section 4 sentence 1 of the Civil Code. All that remains is the onus of showing proof, which under certain circumstances can be difficult, that the THA, despite the new sale negotiations, was still determined to close the company down.[59] The controversial question could then arise all over again

---

52 Hanau, Langanke, Preis, and Widlak (editors): *Das Arbeitsrecht der neuen Bundesländer*, I 2, page 21 et seq.; Ascheid, *Die betriebsbedingte Kündigung*, page 878; Landfermann, *Sanierungsförderung und Gesamtvollstreckung*, page 832.

53 Weimar and Alfes, *Neuregelung des § 613a*, page 1831; ditto, *Betriebsbelegschaften als Investitionshemmnis*, page 18; Commandeur, *Betriebsübergang*, page 169.

54 Weimar and Alfes, *Neuregelung des § 613a*, page 1831.

55 Written up in Neue *Zeitschrift für Arbeits- und Sozialrecht* 1991, 891, 893 = *Arbeit und Arbeitsrecht* 1992, 61.

56 Commandeur, *Betriebsübergang*, page 169.

57 Federal Labour Court, 19th June 1991, in: *Neue Zeitschrift für Arbeits- und Sozialrecht* 1991, 891, 893.

58 See notes in *Neue Zeitschrift für Arbeits- und Sozialrecht* 1991, 891, 893 to Federal Labour Court ruling of 28th April 1988, *Neue Zeitschrift für Arbeits- und Sozialrecht* 1989, 265, 267.

59 Federal Labour Court, 28th April 1988, *Neue Zeitschrift für Arbeits- und Sozialrecht* 1989, 265, 268; Federal Labour Court of 19th May 1988, *Arbeitsrechtliche Praxis* No. 75 on § 613a of the Civil Code; Hanau, *Aktuelle Fragen zu § 613a*, page 290 et seq.; Weimar and Alfes, *Betriebsübernahmen ohne § 613a BGB?*, page 159.

in this context as to whether a claim could arise from the retroactive change in the contract of employment for the (validly) dismissed employee to be re-instated in his contractual relationship.[60] This now leads us on to the issues concerning dismissal which need to be discussed.

IV. Necessity for and problems caused by mass redundancy

1. Basic principles

The treaty creating monetary, economic, and social union (the First State Treaty) of 18th May 1990, which ushered in the basic transfer of West German labour law to East Germany[61] also led to the far-reaching introduction of the grounds for dismissal, unknown up to then in East Germany but known in the West, of "urgent operational necessity"[62] (or: redundancy). The paramount significance of these grounds for dismissal, which are acknowledged in § 1 section 2 of the Dismissals Protection Act, can be seen from the following: of the approximately 3 million employees who lost their jobs in the two years following the setting up of the THA, the second largest group, making 30 to 40% of the total, are those who became unemployed, normally following redundancy.[63] Of the 3 million jobs in the eastern German manufacturing industry, less than 1 million were left over.[64] However, the introduction of substantive law did not mean the unlimited validity of the existing jurisdiction of the Federal Labour Court.[65] Despite the worthy aim of avoiding a division of adjudication between eastern and western Germany, people will continue to examine existing prejudices in adjudications for their substance with regard to the special situation in eastern Germany, and under certain circumstances it will be necessary to interpret them differently.[66]

2. Short-time working instead of dismissal

No dismissal, whether "through operational necessity" or for any other reason, is legally valid unless the basic and highly specific legal principle of "necessity" enshrined in § 1 section 2 of the Dismissals Protection Act is satisfied.[67] The principle of ultima ratio, or last resort applies:

---

60 On state of dispute, see: Stahlhacke and Preis, *Kündigung und Kündigungsschutz*, marginal note 645, and: vom Stein, *Wiedereinstellungsanspruch des Arbeitnehmers*, pages 85 et seq.

61 Article 1 section 4 sentence 2 and Article 17 of the State Treaty.

62 On this point see: Ascheid, *Die betriebsbedingte Kündigung*, page 873; Hanau, Langanke, Preis, and Widlak (editors): *Das Arbeitsrecht der neuen Bundesländer*, I 2, page 25; Stahlhacke and Preis, *Kündigung und Kündigungsschutz*, marginal notes 1338 et seq.

63 See: *IAB Kurzbericht* No. 15, 6th July 1992, page 2.

64 See: Interview with the Federal Minister for Economic Affairs Mr Rexrodt in *Die Zeit* 1993, no. 15, page 21.

65 See: County Court of Quedlinburg, 17th August 1990, *Neue Zeitschrift für Arbeits- und Sozialrecht* 1991, 73, 74; Labour Court of Berlin, 23rd January 1991, *Arbeit und Arbeitsrecht* 1991, 186.

66 On this point, see: Hanau, in Adomeit, *Arbeitsrecht*, A V 2b), page 28; Wolter, *Einige arbeitsrechliche Fragen*, page 44 et seq.; Adomeit, *Zum Betriebsübergang*, page 119.

67 For all aspects of this see: Stahlhacke and Preis, *Kündigung und Kündigungsschutz*, marginal note 616.

i. e. dismissal can only be considered as the last resort when all other possibilities such as putting the employee onto other work have been exhausted, even if, under certain circumstances, this means less favourable conditions of employment.[68] In this connection, it had always been a matter of dispute in West Germany as to whether the introduction of short-time working was to be regarded as a milder measure than declaring workers redundant.[69] Despite this unresolved dispute, the prerequisite for taking the milder of the two measure was always that there should be a temporary shortage of work for the employees to do within the meaning of § 63 section 1 sentence 1 of the Labour Promotion Act.[70] This has become topical again because § 63 section 5 of the East German Labour Promotion Act continued in force until 31st December 1991; this particularly and clearly emphasised the connection between short-time working and redundancy, and even stipulated that it applied regardless of whether the shortage of work was only temporary or not.[71] The discussion will not have been for nothing even after this regulation has ceased to apply. § 63 section 4 of the Labour Promotion Act rather remains in force in the version contained in the Employment Promotion Act of 22nd December 1989,[72] under which the regulations originally created to deal with the particular problems of the steel industry were extended to cover short-time working subsidies to all structurally related shortages of work in all branches of industry, likewise regardless of whether or not the shortage was temporary.[73]

3. Social responsible selection and operational needs under § 1 section 3 sentence 2 of the Dismissals Protection Act in the case of mass redundancies

§ 1 section 3 of the Dismissals Protection Act takes on particular significance in connection with the restructuring of companies in eastern Germany. An employer's dismissal of his staff which he accounted for operational needs, would be regarded under this paragraph as not socially justified if he fails to take the social consequences of his actions into account, or sufficiently into account, in selecting which of his staff are to be dismissed. This principal of social responsibility in selecting employees for redundancy is not limited even when mass redundancies are necessary, but the Federal Labour Court has admitted the notion of this responsibility applying

---

68 For a basic court ruling see: Federal Labour Court, 30th May 1978, *Arbeitsrechtliche Praxis* No. 70, on § 626 of the Civil Code.

69 For the latest state of this argument see: Stahlhacke and Preis, *Kündigung und Kündigungsschutz*, marginal note 641 (footnote 118); Hueck and von Hoyningen-Huene, *Kündigungsschutzgesetz, Kommentar § 1 KSchG*, marginal note 384; *Gemeinschaftskommentar zum Kündigungsschutzgesetz*, Becker, *§ 1 KSchG*, marginal note 397a.

70 Federal Labour Court, 17th October 1980, *Entscheidungssammlung zum Arbeitsrecht* § 1 KSchG, No. 15; State Labour Court of Schleswig-Holstein, 29th September 1988, *Neue Zeitschrift für Arbeits- und Sozialrecht* 1989, 275 et seq.

71 For a detailed discussion, see: Mallmann, *Kurzarbeit*, pages 202 et seq.; on subsidies for short-time working as a tool in active labour market policy, see: Völkel, *Kurzarbeit*, pages 1 et seq.

72 Promulgated in *Bundesgesetzblatt* 1989 I, page 2406.

73 For the prerequisites, see *Gemeinschaftskommentar zum Arbeitsförderungsgesetz, § 63 AFG,* Schmidt, marginal notes 37 et seq.; Völkel, *Kurzarbeit*, page 2 et seq.

to a whole group of people if the company is to continue properly in operation.[74] There has been no special regulation in respect of the complete structural change in eastern Germany, any more than there has been any more precise version of § 1 section 3 of the Dismissals Protection Act in respect of mass redundancies; and this paragraph gave rise to enough practical difficulties as it was.[75]

Redundancy dismissals therefore have to take their line from the law laid down (as mandatory) in the Dismissals Protection Act. Thus it is impossible, for instance, that in the case of redundancies according to the Dismissals Protection Act a compensation plan (the so-called "social plan", consisting mainly of compensation payments) is sufficient on its own to justify dismissals as socially responsible or to anticipate the employer's social selection as required by § 1 section 3 of the Act.[76] If a large proportion of the work-force is being dismissed, the necessary socially responsible selection can lead to an excessively high age profile in those remaining. This results, for one thing, on the fact that certain employees cannot even be considered for dismissal if their normal dismissal is protected by law (e. g. the severely handicapped, expectant mothers, members of the works council, and trainees) or by clauses[77] in the relevant Collective Agreement.[78] On the other hand, important factors for selecting employees will include their age, years of service with the company, and their prospects of finding new employment.[79]

One way out of this dilemma could be provided by the provisions of § 1 section 3 sentence 2 of the Dismissals Protection Act, under which the requirement of social responsibility in making the selection does not apply if well justified operational requirements dictate that one specific or a number of specific employees be kept on. The wording of this standard alone indicates that socially responsible selection can only be dispensed with if the retention of certain specially qualified employees is necessary in the interests of the proper running of the business.[80] Bringing in the point of view of the employee's individual performance as an "operational

74 Federal Labour Court, 16th December 1982, 18th October 1984, 25th April 1985; *Entscheidungssammlung zum Arbeitsrecht § 1 KSchG Betriebsbedingte Kündigung* No. 18, 34, and 35.

75 Hanau, Langanke, Preis, and Widlak, *Das Arbeitsrecht der neuen Bundesländer*, I 2, page 26.

76 For the legitimacy and substance of guidelines for selection see Federal Labour Court, 15th June 1989, 2 AZR 580/88; the same Court, 18th January 1990, 2 AZR 357/89.

77 Ruling opinion, for the present state of the discussion, see: Preis, *Handbuch des Arbeits- und Sozialrechts*, § 19F, marginal note 130. This led in particular, at a very close point in time to German unification, to far-reaching agreements protecting employees from the effects of rationalisation, with dismissal prevented under collective agreements. Possibly, redundancy under special operational conditions needs to be considered here, under which, and this opinion is right, employees affected by extraordinary dismissal have to be included in a socially responsible selection. See also: Preis, *Handbuch des Arbeits- und Sozialrechts*, § 19F, marginal notes 7, 122, with further references.

78 See: Preis, *Handbuch des Arbeits- und Sozialrechts*, § 19F, marginal note 129; Hueck and von Hoyningen-Huene, *Kündigungsschutzgesetz*, Kommentar, § 1 KSchG, marginal note 453; Berkowsky, *Die betriebsbedingte Kündigung*, marginal note 194.

79 For all aspects of this see: Berkowsky, *Die betriebsbedingte Kündigung*, marginal note 198.

80 Examples of this can be seen in: Preis, *Handbuch des Arbeits- und Sozialrechts*, § 19F, marginal note 129; Stahlhacke and Preis, *Kündigung und Kündigungsschutz*, marginal note 674; Rumpenhorst, *Das berechtigte betriebliche Bedürfnis*, page 215, where it is pointed out that this standard is not exactly designed to apply to mass dismissals.

necessity" has been met by a cautious jurisdictional approach, despite the many changes in view.[81] The recognition of the need to retain the existing age profile as another "operational necessity" is regarded critically in the literature[82] but is by and large accepted.[83]

The interest of companies no longer capable of operating efficiently and therefore undergoing radical restructuring must consist both of attaining an efficient and effective personnel structure with adequate qualifications and of retaining an appropriate age structure. The companies taken over by the THA, on the other hand, were characterised by over-manning and low productivity. The organisation of an efficient company capable of competing therefore dictates that a suitable structure of qualifications and age in the work-force has to be acknowledged as an operational necessity within the meaning of § 1 section 3 sentence 2 of the Dismissals Protection Act.[84] An appropriate balance between social demands and operational necessities can be achieved if both criteria are properly weighed against one another.[85]

4. Redundancies and reconciliation of interests

The highly contentious question as to whether the works council can prevent dismissals before the attempt at a reconciliation of interests has been completed, as provided for in § 112 sections 1 to 3 of the Industrial Constitution Act, has gained in topicality as the result of two court rulings from eastern Germany.[86] In the view of both Courts, it is possible for an interim injunction to be issued to prevent an employer from issuing redundancy notices before the process of reconciling interests has been completed. On the other hand, ruling opinion had up to now assumed that a violation of the obligations imposed by § 111 sentence 1 and § 112 sections 1 to 3 of the Industrial Constitution Act would have no effect on the permissibility of any operational changes that are carried through regardless.[87] The main argument revolves around the fact that the reconciliation of interests is not subject to the enforceable co-determination rights of the works council. Taking this view, the legal consequences defined in § 113 section 3 of the Industrial Constitution Act would then take effect. It is not possible to obtain any clarification of the matter from any higher court, desirable though this would be, as the interim injunction per-

81 For a summary of the relevant adjudications, see: Berkowsky, *Die betriebsbedingte Kündigung*, marginal notes 224 to 231; *Gemeinschaftskommentar zum Kündigungsschutzgesetz*, § 1 KSchG, marginal notes 361 to 363.

82 Stahlhacke and Preis, *Kündigung und Kündigungsschutz*, marginal note 673.

83 Hueck and von Hoyningen-Huene, *Kündigungsschutzgesetz*, Kommentar, § 1 KSchG, marginal note 476; Herschel and Löwisch, *Kommentar zum Kündigungsschutzgesetz*, § 1 KSchG, marginal note 240, with further references.

84 A similar view appears in Langanke, *Die soziale Auswahl*, page 219 et seq.; Rumpenhorst, *Das berechtigte betriebliche Bedürfnis*, page 215 et seq.

85 For a detailed discussion, see: Berkowsky, *Die betriebsbedingte Kündigung*, marginal notes 239 to 241.

86 County Court of Saalfeld, 2nd April 1991, *Der Betrieb* 1991, 919; Labour Court of Jena, 22nd September 1992, *Betriebs-Berater* 1992, 2223.

87 For a detailed summary of the state of opinion, see: Bengelsdorf, *Unzulässigkeit einer Untersagungsverfügung*, pages 1233 and 1282; Ehrich, *Einstweilige Verfügung*, page 356.

mitted by § 85 section 2 of the Labour Courts Act is debarred from appeal to the Federal Labour Court by § 92 section 2 sentence 3 of the same Act. However, legal disputes have not often arisen within the THA's sphere of activity on this complex of questions.

V. Social plan

1. Significance

As neither the laws on protection against unfair dismissal nor § 613a of the Civil Code have had much effect against brute economic reality, the social plan as defined in § 112 of the Industrial Constitution Act takes on a particular significance as an instrument of social support. The prerequisite for the preparation of a social plan is the submission of plans for operational changes within the meaning of § 111 of the same Act which could entail serious disadvantages for the work-force or for large parts of it. The central role within the THA's sphere of activity is played by § 111 sentence 2 clause 1 of the Industrial Constitution Act, under which the reduction and closure of an entire works or large parts of it count as operational changes. § 112a of the Act states that such operational changes can consist solely of the dismissal of employees. If an operational change is imminent, the works council can enforce the preparation of a social plan under § 112 sections 4 and 5 of the Act.[88] The essence of a social plan is that it compensates for or alleviates the economic disadvantages suffered by the employees as a result of the planned operational changes, and has the legal force of a works agreement. It can contain regulations which are normally the preserve of a collective agreement (see § 112 section 1 sentence 3 of the Industrial Constitution Act). In the THA's work, once-off compensation payments for loss of job have usually been in the forefront.

2. Existence of a works council

A social plan can only be drawn up, as a rule, if the company affected employs more than 20 people entitled to vote a works council into office, and if a works council already exists. For the transitional period it was important to note that the industrial constitution of the old East Germany did not provide for works councils. The interests of the work-force were supposed to be safeguarded under §§ 22 et seq. of the East German Labour Code (in the old version) by the company trade union committee. According to Appendix I Chapter VIII Item A Section III Clause 12b of the Treaty of Unification, initial works council elections had to take place under the terms of § 13 of the Industrial Constitution Act by 30th June 1991. This meant that, particularly in the case of the earliest sale and liquidation procedures carried out by the THA in 1990 and 1991, there was no works council then in existence properly elected under this Act. Various different judgements have been expressed in this connection on the mandate of the employees' representatives elected on democratic principles before the West German Industrial Constitution

88 A reconciliation of interests, in contrast to a social plan, cannot be enforced.

Act took effect (on 1st July 1990).[89] In the case of social plans concluded before 1st July 1990, in the view of the State Labour Court of Berlin these are not works agreements within the meaning of the Act.[90] Apart from problems such as these connected with the transitional phase following unification, works councils formed relatively swiftly in eastern Germany and, despite the difficulties, went to work on the tasks they were set with great commitment and understanding of economic necessities.

The works council must be in existence at the point in time when the company owner is required under § 111 sentence 1 of the Industrial Constitution Act to state his intentions.[91] If, on the other hand, a works council is elected after the company owner has already decided to carry out the organisational changes and has issued dismissal notices, the employees' right to be involved in the decision can no longer be enforced.[92] On the other hand, once such rights have arisen they do not necessarily expire when the works is closed down, but survive until the contract of employment has come legally to an end. In this case the works council retains a residual mandate in order to carry out all its duties in connection with the closure, and in particular with the drawing up of the social plan. It can also conduct any court actions connected with them.[93] In the view of the Federal Labour Court, the works council's mandate does not relate to any part of the works that has been split off .[94] For companies administered by the THA, however, § 13 of the Splitting Act disposes differently, and confers a transitional mandate[95] on the works council in the event of a THA company being split into smaller units, if the smaller unit has the number of employees defined in § 1 of the Industrial Constitution Act and has not been absorbed into some other unit in which there is a works council already in existence. The transitional mandate comes to an end as soon as the smaller units elect their works councils and the results of the election have been announced, or in no event later than three months after the splitting of the company has come into effect. If parts of a company which had previously been subordinate to various different works are brought together into one unit, the works council for the larger

---

89 On this point, see on the one hand: Engels, *Müssen alle Betriebsräte ... neu gewählt werden?*, page 3139 et seq.; Urban District Court of Berlin-Köpenick, 17th June 1990, *Arbeit und Arbeitsrecht* 1990, 234; or for a different view: Dänzer-Vanotti and Tyska, *Neuwahl von Betriebsräten*, pages 3186 et seq.; State Labour Court of Berlin, 25th September 1991, *Entscheidungen der Landesarbeitsgerichte § 112 BetrVG* 1972, No. 19.

90 State Labour Court of Berlin, 25th September 1991, *Entscheidungen der Landesarbeitsgerichte § 112 BetrVG* 1972, No. 19; a similar ruling from the Berlin Labour Court, 12th April 1991, *Arbeit und Arbeitsrecht* special issue 1991 page 36; supported by Düwell, *Betriebsverfassungsrechtliche Probleme,* page 196.

91 See: Federal Labour Court, 22nd February 1983, *Arbeitsrechtliche Praxis* No. 7 on § 113 of the Industrial Constitution Act, 1972.

92 Federal Labour Court, 20th April 1982, *Arbeitsrechtliche Praxis* No. 15 on § 112 of the Industrial Constitution Act, 1972; most recently, Federal Labour Court, 28th October 1992, in *Betriebs-Berater* 1993, 140 et seq., 224.

93 Federal Labour Court, 30th October 1979, *Arbeitsrechtliche Praxis* No. 9 on § 112 of the Industrial Constitution Act, 1972.

94 Federal Labour Court, 23rd November 1988, *Der Betrieb* 1989, 1194.

95 On this point, see: Engels, *Betriebsverfassungsrechtliche Aspekte*, page 966; Kissel, *Ein Jahr gesamtdeutsches Arbeitsrecht*, page 7; Düwell, *Betriebsverfassungsrechtliche Probleme*, page 197.

unit (measured in terms of numbers of employees entitled to vote) will take on the transitional mandate. The same applies in general terms if a number of firms are merged together into one bigger one. If the companies which have been split away from one another are then in competition with one another, the regulations on the works council's rights of involvement are not to be applied if they related to matters which could influence competition between the companies.

The concept of a transitional mandate, specially designed for the THA's sphere of activity, takes account of the employee's fundamental need for protection during the time when there was no works council, and could thus become the starting-point for a general principle of works constitution.[96]

3. Situations giving rise to a compulsory social plan

a) Introduction of short-time working

Firstly, the introduction of short-time working is not an operational change within the meaning of § 111 of the Industrial Constitution Act, so that the obligation to prepare a social plan does not arise until the contract of employment has finally come to an end. There is also nothing in the regulation already mentioned, § 63 section 4 of the Labour Promotion Act, to oppose this. Short-time work subsidy can therefore also be granted if, at last, the contract of employment will probably not be continued. This regulation does not permit any premature ending of the work or thus any permanent restriction on operations, as the aim and purpose of short-time work regulations are to ensure that an interruption in employment is not regarded legally as being the same as its termination.

b) Change of company ownership

The change of ownership of a company or part of one by legal transaction is not in itself an operational change within the meaning of § 111 of the Industrial Constitution Act and does not impose the duty of drawing up a social plan. Under these circumstances, § 613a of the Civil Code comes into force and ensures that the new owner assumes full liability for all contracts of employment.[97] However, the change of ownership can give rise to the kind of operational change in which it is obligatory to involve the employees if it is connected with other measures which the vendor or the purchaser intends to take. According to the Federal Labour Court's ruling of 26th May 1983,[98] and the dominant opinion in the literature,[99] the vendor can dismiss employees on the basis of the purchaser's restructuring strategy if the previous employer would have had to dismiss them if he had continued to manage the business. It is then the vendor who is under an obligation to draw up a social plan.

---

96 Fitting, Auffarth, Kaiser and Heither, *Betriebsverfassungsgesetz, Handkommentar*, § 21, marginal note 57.

97 Federal Labour Court, 4th December 1979, 21st October 1980, 16th June 1987, *Arbeitsrechtliche Praxis* Nos. 6, 8, and 19 on § 111 of the Industrial Constitution Act, 1972.

98 *Arbeitsrechtliche Praxis* No. 34 on § 613a of the Civil Code; for this, see: Hanau, *Zur Kündigung von Arbeitsverhältnissen,* page 141.

99 For the latest state of the dispute, see: Kreitner, *Kündigungsrechtliche Probleme*, pages 106 et seq.

This state of affairs must have arisen frequently in the THA's sphere of activity. During negotiations intended to lead to the take-over of a firm, the potential buyer presents the THA with a corporate strategy defining, among other things, the personnel structure with which he is contemplating continuing the management of the business. The THA examines this strategy and then, if necessary, reduces the numbers employed in the company it is still administrating to the level the potential purchaser is expecting.

Another variant is when the purchaser takes over the company with its existing work-force and gives the THA an undertaking to retain a certain number of them. The obligation to draw up a social plan for the others then falls upon the purchaser. However, this does also mean that his asset situation will be crucial and that the THA's social plan guidelines[100] cannot be applied. However, the THA indirectly pays part of the compensation payments by agreeing a correspondingly lower purchase price with the purchaser. In addition to this, the further question arises as to the extent to which the employees already working in the acquiring company have to be brought into the socially responsible selection of those to be dismissed.[101]

If the business is sold during bankruptcy proceedings, it is, however, worth considering whether the passage of ownership of the business constitutes one of the sets of circumstances which makes a social plan obligatory, as the protection provided by § 613a of the Civil Code is suspended in these situations until the end of 1994. The fact that § 613a of the Civil Code is systematically regarded as a substitute for the application of § 111 of the Industrial Constitution Act regarding changes in company ownership makes it all the more reasonable.[102] The practical importance of this consideration, however, is limited to instances in which only a small number of employees are not being taken on by the purchaser, because otherwise the situation is an operational change within the meaning of the Act and the obligation to prepare a social plan arises for that reason alone.

c) Establishment of new company

If a planned operational change consists only of dismissing employees, the provisions of § 112a section 2 of the Industrial Constitution Act can provide relief for the purchaser. It states that a social plan cannot be enforced if in the first four years after a company was established it carries out a reduction in numbers employed, either in its factory or in one of its factories, for which actually a social plan would be compulsory. Exemption from the obligations of drawing up a social plan under § 112a section 2 of the Act is intended to make the establishment of new companies easier, principally by ensuring that employers are not deterred from taking on new staff by the fear of having to bear the costs of a social plan if any operational changes are necessary later. The owner of a newly established company is not exempted from his obligations to consult with and to inform the employees of operational changes under § 111 of the Act, nor from his duty to try to achieve agreement on a settlement of interests under § 112 sections 1 to 3 of the Act and to negotiate on a social plan. The company owner must also be prepared for proceedings before the Conciliation Board.[103] The crucial factor for exemption under § 112a section 2 of

---

100 On this point, see under Point V.4, page 457.

101 On this point, see: Kreitner, *Kündigungsrechtliche Probleme*, page 117.

102 Landfermann, *Sanierungsförderung und Gesamtvollstreckung*, page 832.

103 Wlotzke, *Betriebsverfassungsgesetz (Kommentar)*, § 112a, footnote 2.

the Industrial Constitution Act is the age of the company itself, not of any factory or unit within it.[104] Exemption from the obligation to produce a social plan accordingly also applies when a newly established company carries out an operational change in a factory or unit which it has taken over and the unit itself has been in existence for more than four years.[105] However, § 112a section 2 of the Act will be circumvented if a factory or unit has been taken over by a newly established company solely for the purpose of closing it down without a social plan, and in these circumstances the company will not be able to invoke exemption.[106]

The provisions of § 112a section 2 sentence 2 of the Industrial Constitution Act are of significance for the restructuring of THA companies, whereby exemption is given from the obligation to produce a social plan in the event of the establishment of a new company together with legal restructuring. This applies if it is only the legal status of the company that changes while it remains within the THA.[107] However, exemption should not be withheld if a western German company establishes a new GmbH-company in eastern Germany which then takes over one factory or unit out of the THA's ambit. This does not result in an old company being artificially rejuvenated by legal restructuring, but in a new commercial activity developing from it.[108]

The "social plan privilege" can, however, have inappropriate consequences for the employees taken over by a new owner from former East German companies in that they lose their many years of entitlement to social plan subsidies by the transfer to a newly established company for four years. In such cases it is therefore appropriate for the THA, as the vendor directly or indirectly, to provide the employees with security, e. g. by undertaking to give a share at a later date in case the purchaser should be forced into an operational change without the obligation to produce a social plan during the course of those four years. This is the only way to avoid the interplay between § 613a of the Civil Code and §§ 111 et seq. of the Industrial Constitution Act going awry. The basic idea behind § 613a of the Civil Code is to avoid landing employees with a legal disadvantage when a company changes hands. This idea is still kept intact if the actual aim of § 112a section 2 of the Industrial Constitution Act, namely the creation of new jobs, is attained. One situation not provided for in legislation is when old firms are taken over and employees, without any own fault, are robbed of their many years' entitlement to social plan subsidies. In order to avoid this unacceptable situation for the employees, it is worth considering selling the company to a new owner, analogously to § 111 sentence 2 of the Industrial Constitution Act, as an operational change made by the vendor and automatically entailing the obligation of a social plan. The social plan might then consist of a contingent liability in the event of the

104 Ruling opinion; for a different view, see: Fitting, Auffarth, Kaiser, and Heither, *Betriebsverfassungsgesetz, Handkommentar*, §§ 112, 112a, marginal note 18 b; Rumpff and Boewer, *Mitbestimmung*, page 361 et seq.

105 Federal Labour Court, 13th June 1989, *Arbeitsrechtliche Praxis* No. 3 on § 112a of the Industrial Constitution Act, 1972.

106 Federal Labour Court, 13th June 1989, *Arbeitsrechtliche Praxis* No. 3 on § 112a of the Industrial Constitution Act, 1972.

107 As maintained by: Hanau, *Aktuelle Fragen zu § 613a*, page 294.

108 For a similar line of argument, see: Willemsen, *Anmerkung zu BAG vom 13. 6. 1989*; for a different view, see: Däubler, Kittner, Klebe, and Schneider, *Betriebsverfassungsgesetz, Kommentar*, §§ 112, 112a, marginal note 37.

purchaser making operational changes which under § 112a section 2 of the Act do not mandatorily entail a social plan.[109] However, in actual practice the THA does not seem to have encountered this problem very often.

4. THA social plan guidelines[110]

a) Events leading up to the agreement of 13th April 1991

Only a short time after taking up its work, the THA discovered that social plans had been signed in its companies between management and employees' representatives which, if put into effect, would have led inexorably to the companies becoming insolvent. The authors have also received confirmation of this assessment from the trade unions side. Mr Koch, a former member of the THA Executive Board,[111] offered one extreme example, in which a landscape gardener was to have been paid DM 156,000 in compensation. In the second half of 1990, average redundancy compensation was well over DM 12,000. An evaluation of the social plans of 16 companies effective from 1st January 1991 showed that the average social plan benefits in the individual companies lay between DM 5,000 and DM 21,000. The average for all the companies was DM 10,492. The companies were obviously assuming that the THA would foot the bill for any social plan they cared to write. As a reaction to this situation, the THA sent a circular out to all company managements on 11th December 1990 pointing out specifically that the THA would not be able to help, neither directly nor indirectly, in financing social plans. Social plans would fundamentally have to be paid for out of each company's own resources. It should also be noted, the circular said, that in view of general economic conditions redundancy pay should not exceed 25% of a month's income for each year of service.

The regulations laid down by this circular ran into opposition from the trade unions, which fought particularly hard against the 25% limit.[112] Recognising the necessity for a socially acceptable solution to this problem in order to have the consensus of all the forces involved behind it, initial negotiations started even at the end of 1990 between the THA, employers, trade unions, and representatives of the ministries for foreign affairs and of finance. It was in the THA's interests to draw up uniform criteria in the event of taking over redundancy payments. The guidelines were represented on the one hand by the economic tenability of the social plan benefits, and on the other hand by the need to soften the blow to a certain extent of mass redundancies which

---

109 See: Hanau, *Aktuelle Fragen zu § 613a*, page 295; but for an opposing view, see: Gaul, *Der Betriebsübergang*, page 133. On the compatibility of § 112a section 2 of the Industrial Constitution Act with EC Directive 77/187 see: Däubler, Kittner, Klebe, and Schneider, *Betriebsverfassungsgesetz, Kommentar*, §§ 112, 112a, marginal note 35.

110 For a basic discussion of THA Guidelines see: Schaub, *Die Rahmenvereinbarung der Treuhandanstalt*, pages 673 et seq.

111 B-Interview on 18th March 1993 in Frankfurt am Main.

112 See: Letter from the Deputy Chairman of the DGB (the German Federation of Trade Unions), Ms Engelen-Kefer, to Mr Rohwedder, the President of the THA, dated 11th January 1991; letter from Mr Klaus, a member of the executive board of IG-Metall, the metal-industries union, to Mr Koch, a member of the THA Executive Board, dated 14th January 1991.

were beginning to involve ever greater numbers. As a budget had been set up in agreement with the Federal Ministry of Finance of DM 10 billion to cover redundancy plans, it was possible to estimate compensation of DM 5,000 for each of the 2 million employees likely to be affected. The result of the negotiations was an agreement between the THA, the DGB (the German Federation of Trade Unions, and the DAG (Trade Union of German Employees) dated 13th April 1991, which formed the basis for the guidelines on social plans.[113]

b) "Ear-marking"

The core of the 13th April 1991 agreement is the financing by the THA of the social plans set up in its companies, subject to certain preconditions and using the instrument known as "ear-marking". In order to lay down the exact method of operation, the THA drew up its "Guidelines for Social Plans", of which there have now been three editions, and which are intended to take on the constantly changing problems of financing compensation schemes.

Basically, the THA was only prepared to admit any prospect of financing a social plan if the company itself was not able to do so. If a company is able to cover the costs of an imminent social plan from its own resources, it is not limited by the constraints of ear-marking. However, even in this instance the THA reserves itself the right it has under company law to give or withhold approval of the social plan. Following the joint declaration made between the THA, the DGB, and the DAG, it is normally regarded as appropriate to calculate the total volume of a freely financed social plan on the basis of four times the gross monthly income of the employee affected.[114] If the total volume exceeds this amount, the THA will not normally gives its approval to the plan, but will check carefully to see if the case can be regarded as an exception.[115]

The financial difficulties of the great majority of THA companies, however, rule out all hope of any freely financed social plan. Accordingly, it will not be possible for the company to draw up a social plan, as to do so would hurl the company straight into bankruptcy. In order to avoid this outcome, the THA makes ear-marked funds available to the companies if their works councils "co-operate positively in drawing up the whole package of the social plan".[116] The precondition for ear-marked funds is that a set maximum volume must not be exceeded for the benefits under the social plan. The basic figure suggested is DM 5,000 per employee affected. This is reduced to DM 3,000 for each employee who has drawn benefits from the labour administration for at least one year since his or her contract of employment came to an end as part of a retraining or work-creation programme, and DM 2,000 for those who will be entitled to a pension within one year of the contract of employment coming to an end.[117] The total volume (the maximum) of the social plan qualifying for ear-marked funds is calculated from the number of employees affected and by multiplying it by the relevant figure (DM 5,000/DM 3,000/DM 2,000). This total amount must not be exceeded if the company wants to qualify for ear-marked funds. On the other hand, the company is entirely free to decide how it will distribute the individual compensation payments within this maximum volume, so that different criteria can be

---

113 Published in (e. g.): *Zeitschrift für Wirtschaftsrecht* 1991, 691; *Arbeit und Arbeitsrecht* 1991, 178.

114 *Richtlinien der Treuhandanstalt für Sozialpläne*, Section IV clause 1.

115 op. cit., Section IV clause 4.

116 op. cit., Section III.

117 op. cit., Section II clause 4.

applied in individual cases such as years of service, age, or number of dependent relatives. According to the regulations laid down in the first Guideline in June 1991, the THA assumed that the ear-marked funds would be used on an "all or nothing" basis, and that if the social plan exceeded the maximum volume calculated according to the above rules the company would also be able to meet the costs without the THA's help. The ear-marked funds would then have been cancelled completely.[118]

In applying the first Guidelines for social plans in a total of 5,668 cases of ear-marked funds, a total of more than DM 6 billion was promised and paid out[119] until the end of April 1992, and the THA realised that it would have to adjust the volume of these funds because the numbers being declared redundant, particularly of older workers, was increasing constantly. Because of the retention of the multiplication factors it became unavoidable that in individual cases only smaller redundancy payments were granted, as more and more employees were being dismissed who had been with their companies for very many years. As the calculation of the maximum volume did not include any element for years of service, the total amount of ear-marked funds did not change even if a higher proportion of long-service employees had to be dismissed, with the result that individual payments were then smaller. There was as a result little room left for manoeuvre when companies tried to draw up autonomously, as the THA always emphasized their individual plans within the total volume of funds available. This was mainly regarded as being unjust. After the second edition of the Social Plan Guidelines had been issued in July 1992, the THA made additional sums available, retroactively for the period from 1st January to 30th September 1992 but subject to certain preconditions, in order to compensate for hardship when older employees with many years of service had to be dismissed.[120]

In parallel with this, the THA took up again negotiations with the DGB and the DAG, and these led to the agreement of 14th October 1992. The 3rd edition of the THA Social Plan Guidelines which appeared in January 1993 was based on this agreement, and is applicable to all employees leaving their companies after 30th September 1992. The core of the new Guidelines is a variable value which replaced the original system of fixed multiplicators (DM 5,000/3,000/2,000) and is intended to take better account of the dismissal of older workers with many years of service. Redundancy pay is now based on a basic amount plus a variable amount. The basic amount is the real variable, therefore companies which have a higher share of older workers with more service years are able to pay higher redundancy compensations. The basic amount is taken as DM 3,000, with an extra charge based on a number of factors such as age and years of employment, plus an additional amount for the handicapped. This total basic amount is not allowed to be lower than DM 5,000. The additional amount can reach a maximum of DM 1,800 per employee, and is mainly dependent on the company's work-creation programmes, but a minimum of DM 1,200 per employee can be set regardless of these.[121] Based on the new calculation method it is now certain that every employee dismissed after 31st September 1992 will receive a minimum compensation from the social plan of DM 6,200.

---

118 op. cit., Section III.

119 See: *Richtlinie der Treuhandanstalt für Sozialpläne*, 2nd edition, July 1992, Foreword.

120 See: op. cit., Section III.

121 For details of these preconditions see: Point IV of the Agreement between the THA and the DGB of 14th October 1992, reprinted in the 3rd Edition of the *Sozialplanrichtlinien der Treuhandanstalt*, page 34 et seq.

c) Persons entitled to make claims

The social plan applies to all employees affected by the operational change; this can also include those who have already been dismissed before the social plan has been drawn up because at the date of dismissal the company owner had already started putting his operational change into effect.[122] Employees are also covered who have themselves given notice and left the company in connection with the planned operational change, if this change was the cause of their leaving. This would apply, for instance, if the company owner informs his work-force that he intends to reduce the size of the operation and that certain employees can expect to be dismissed in the near future.[123] On this point, the THA generally assumed that the only employees entitled to social plan payments are those who have been served redundancy notices or have signed an *"Aufhebungsvertrag"* cancelling their contract of employment on account of operational necessities. Those who have given notice on their own initiative are expressly excluded. In the THA's view, this applies regardless of the reason for giving notice.[124] Since the agreement of 14th October 1992 between the THA, the DGB, and the DAG, however, employees have also been taken into account who had themselves given notice, if this was on or after 1st October 1992, if they had handed in their notice after already having been given notice by the employer.[125] It does seem to be problematic to make compensation dependent upon any preceding dismissal notice from the employer; the employees find themselves in the same difficult situation as if their employer informs them that because of operational changes he will not be able to keep them on much longer. If the employees then hand in their notice on account of the hopelessness of their situation, there is no reason to treat them differently from those who wait until the dismissal notice is in their hands. All that is necessary is an internal connection of such a nature that the employees can see with certainty, on the basis of information from the employer, that they are going to be affected by imminent redundancy. In the view of the Federal Labour Court, any social plan which differentiates merely in formal terms between the notice of dismissal from the employer and the notice of termination by the employee infringes the tenets of equal treatment for all enshrined in § 75 section 1 sentence 1 of the Industrial Constitution Act.[126] The decisive factor in the question as to whether an employee is entitled to compensation under the social plan is therefore not the technical legal form in which the contract of employment comes to an end, but the material reason for its ending.[127]

A further problem lies in the THA's way of working which makes social plan payments dependent on the employee not raising a dismissals protection suit. Adjudications and the relevant literature continue to regard such attempts at "buying off" dismissal protection as imper-

---

122 Federal Labour Court, 23rd April 1985, *Arbeitsrechtliche Praxis* No. 26 on § 112 of the Industrial Constitution Act, 1972.

123 On this point, see: Federal Labour Court, 15th January 1991, *Der Betrieb* 1991, 1526; the same Court, 28th October 1992, *Der Betrieb* 1993, 590 et seq.

124 See: *1. Sozialplanrichtlinie,* Section VI; *2. Sozialplanrichtlinie,* Section V.

125 See: Explanation on applications for ear-marked funds, *3. Sozialplanrichtlinie,* page 30.

126 Federal Labour Court, 15th January 1991, *Der Betrieb* 1991, 1526.

127 Federal Labour Court, 15th January 1991, *Der Betrieb* 1991, 1526 with further references.

missible.[128] The idea behind § 612a of the Civil Code here takes effect, under which the exercise of a right cannot be allowed to entail any disadvantage.[129] However, it is permissible to include an agreement in a social plan under which the due date for payment of redundancy compensation is postponed until any action for unfair dismissal has been concluded and any judgement has become final and absolute. Any compensation ordered by the court can be set off against the benefits under the social plan, according to §§ 9 and 10 of the Dismissals Protection Act.[130]

d) Effect of the Guidelines on social plans

As a result of the Social Plan Guidelines, the Central Office of the THA paid out a total of more than DM 4 billion in ear-marked funds on more than 2,100 social plans during the period from 17th June 1991 to the end of 1992. The THA Central Office only registered the social plans of companies with more than 1,000 employees, and it is not necessarily the case that one social plan equals one company; it often occurred that one social plan after another had to be drawn up for one company at a time when it emerged that the originally planned reductions in the workforce still did not make the company competitive. The THA branches processed 3,652 applications for ear-marked funds up to 30th September 1992 and approved a total volume of DM 1.7 billion. Of the total of DM 10 billion originally promised, the figure actually paid out was already heading for DM 8 billion by March 1993.

e) Legal nature and questions of liability

It is not possible to go into details here on the question of the legal nature of the agreement of 13th April 1991, and the effects in terms of legal liability of the Social Plan Guidelines, any more than it is possible to deal with the problem of any liability the THA might bear for payments under social plans which exceed the Guidelines' limits. The legal nature of the agreement has been discussed exhaustively elsewhere, to the effect that it cannot possibly be considered as a "collective agreement" (such as is usually made between trade unions and employers' associations), but might be regarded analogously to the "Resolutions" passed by the "Concerted Action" (the standing conference of employers and trade unions which operated in West Germany up to 1977 and settled wage disputes before industrial action broke out).[131] It is also worth considering whether the employees affected could be entitled directly to a claim under the

---

128 Federal Labour Court, 20th December 1993, *Arbeitsrechtliche Praxis* No. 17 on § 112 of the Industrial Constitution Act; same Court, 20th June 1985, *Neue Zeitschrift für Arbeits- und Sozialrecht* 1986, 258; Fitting, Auffarth, Kaiser, and Heither, *Betriebsverfassungsgesetz, Handkommentar*, §§ 112, 112a, marginal note 29; Däubler, Kittner, Klebe, and Schneider, *Betriebsverfassungsgesetz, Kommentar*, §§ 112, 112a, marginal note 43; Löwisch, *Betriebsrat und Arbeitnehmer*, page 1293; for a different view, see: Stege and Weinspach, *Betriebsverfassungsgesetz, Handkommentar*, §§ 111–113, marginal note 87; Hunold, *Ungelöste Probleme*, page 2282, for those cases when social plan benefits are paid without the employees having to substantiate that they have suffered a disadvantage.

129 Däubler, Kittner, Klebe, and Schneider, *Betriebsverfassungsgesetz, Kommentar*, §§ 112, 112a, marginal note 118.

130 Federal Labour Court, 20th June 1985, *Arbeitsrechtliche Praxis* No. 33 to § 112 of the same Industrial Constitution Act.

131 Däubler, *Sozialplan*, page 179 et seq.

Guidelines on the basic principle of a contract made between two parties to the benefit of a third as defined in § 328 of the Civil Code.

The question of legal liability was discussed at an early stage in the THA bodies responsible for such matters,[132] and reached a first climax with the ruling handed down by the County Court of Erfurt on 29th July 1991.[133] The Court found that the THA was a "company" within the meaning of §§ 15 et seq. of the *Aktiengesetz* (the German Companies Act covering AG-companies) and that it therefore exercised permanent and comprehensive influence on the management of its subsidiary companies. Accordingly, the THA and its companies together formed a so-called "qualified *de facto* concern", with the consequence that the THA, if § 303 of the *Aktiengesetz* is applied analogously, bears legal liability for the obligations of its subsidiaries. In the relevant case, a claim was made against the THA and the relevant THA company under joint and several liability for a social plan. A lively discussion has since broken out in the literature on company law on this complex of problems[134] which has not calmed down even after the introduction of § 28a of the *Einführungsgesetz zum Aktiengesetz* (the Introductory Act to the above Companies Act).[135] In the last analysis, this should not have a decisive effect on social plans, as the variable regulation now introduced for ear-marked funds has already led to the voluntary acceptance of liability and commensurability.

f) Possibilities for changing an existing social plan

If social plans exceed the volumes laid down in the Guidelines, the THA will definitely not provide any ear-marked funds. If the company is not able to finance it from its own resources, it can only obtain assistance from the THA if it is possible to reduce the volume of the social plan to bring it into line with the Guidelines. In order to modify any excessive social plan payments, the THA has been known to exert deliberate pressure by using the cogent argument of imminent insolvency against the company concerned. It is then usually possible to reach a consensus with the company on a reduction of the planned social plan scheme to bring it under the maximum limit for ear-marked funds.

It is basically possible to replace a social plan by mutual agreement with a new works agreement. It is not contested in adjudications or in the literature that it is possible to replace a works agreement with another which is less favourable to the employees.[136] The decisive factor here is

---

132 For instance, in the discussion conference held in Berlin on 8th February 1991 with the participation of Professor Dr Ulmer.

133 *Entscheidungssammlung zum Arbeitsrecht,* § 112 BetrVG 1972, No. 57, on § 112 of the Industrial Constitution Act.

134 For instance, see: Däubler, *Sozialplan*, pages 322 et seq.; Priester, *Gesellschaftsrechtliche Zweifelsfragen*, pages 2373 et seq.; Timm and Schöne, *Die Thesen der Treuhandanstalt*, pages 969 et seq., Weimar and Alfes, *Enthaftung der Treuhandanstalt*, page 1225 et seq.; Weisemann, *Zur Sozialplanpflichtigkeit der Treuhandanstalt*, pages 41 et seq.

135 *Bundesgesetzblatt* I, page 1257, under which the provisions of the *Aktiengesetz* on "dominant" companies are not applicable to the THA.

136 Federal Labour Court, 24th March 1981, *Arbeitsrechtliche Praxis* No. 12 to § 112 of the Industrial Constitution Act, 1972; same court (*Großer Senat*), 16th September 1986, *Arbeitsrechtliche Praxis* No. 17 to § 77 of the same Act, 1972; same Court, 25th February 1986, *Arbeitsrechtliche Praxis* No. 13 to § 6 of the same Act; Fitting, Auffarth, Kaiser, and Heither, *Betriebsverfassungsgesetz, Handkommen-*

the intention of the partners concerned, as this is the actual basis of the agreement. Accordingly, this basis can be changed by a later agreement.[137] When this later agreement comes into effect, it still only has the character from the start of a voluntary works agreement within the meaning of § 88 of the Industrial Constitution Act. So long as the social plan remains in force, the right of co-determination on the part of the work-force according to § 112 section 4 of the Act does no longer apply to the operational changes covered by the social plan.[138] A new, enforceable social plan cannot be considered until some further operational change becomes necessary. Despite the possible change to a works agreement through the collective intention of the parties concerned, they are subject to certain restrictions in compiling it up which result from the interests of the employees concerned. Interference with pending claims is subject to the principle of commensurability, and such action can only be restricted within the limits of right and reasonable judgement.[139]

In cases where no change to an existing social plan can be mutually agreed upon, the THA has recently taken to advising its company managements to terminate such social plans retroactively and without notice, with the alternative of normal termination, or to invoke the disappearance of the legal basis of the plan. However, the County Court of Suhl has now rejected these possibilities.[140] The Court found that it is incompatible with § 77 section 5 of the Industrial Constitution Act to terminate a works agreement retroactively. The standard provides only for termination at some future point in time. A notice to quit for cause could only be considered in the case of a social plan with a long-term effect, which hardly ever applies to THA companies, as only once-off redundancy payments ever came into the discussion. The Court also ruled out any termination with a normal period of notice if neither the possibility of termination nor any period of notice is defined in the social plan, stating that recourse to the period of notice defined in § 77 section 5 of the Industrial Constitution Act would then not automatically be possible. It must, instead, be noted that a social plan is a works agreement of a very special kind, and enjoys special protection on account of its aims. The Court also invoked the fact that, in the actual social plan in dispute, a period of validity had been agreed lasting until a new plan had been concluded.

The social plan appears to be a works agreement subject to the termination possibilities defined in § 77 section 5 of the Industrial Constitution Act. Ruling opinion in the literature, however, fundamentally does not permit the right of termination to apply to a social plan.[141]

---

tar, § 77, marginal note 40 et seq.; *Gemeinschaftskommentar zum Betriebsverfassungsgesetz*, § 77, marginal note 308; Däubler, *Nachträgliche Kürzung von Sozialplanansprüchen*, page 547.

137 Däubler, *Verschlechterung der Arbeitsbedingungen*, page 3 et seq.

138 Däubler, *Nachträgliche Kürzung von Sozialplanansprüchen*, page 547.

139 Federal Labour Court, 17th March 1987, *Arbeitsrechtliche Praxis* No. 9 on § 1 of the Industrial Constitution Act.

140 Judgement of 4th December 1991, in *Arbeitsrecht im Betrieb* 1992, 102; likewise, Berlin Labour Court, 11th May 1992, Case 82 Ca 21428/91, unpublished.

141 Fitting, Auffarth, Kaiser, and Heither, *Betriebsverfassungsgesetz, Handkommentar*, §§ 112, 112a, marginal note 31; Däubler, *Nachträgliche Kürzung von Sozialplanansprüchen*, page 545; Däubler, Kittner, Klebe, and Schneider, *Betriebsverfassungsgesetz, Kommentar*, §§ 112, 112a, marginal note 124; *Gemeinschaftskommentar zum Betriebsverfassungsgesetz*, Fabricius, § 112, marginal notes 63 and 74; for a less unambiguous view see: Stege and Weinspach, *Betriebsverfassungsgesetz, Handkommentar*, §§ 111–113, marginal note 98.

"Despite all the surprises of business life, it should be possible to rely at least on redundancy and other compensation payments".[142] As the one exception to this basic principle, termination at a normal period of notice should be permissible under § 77 section 5 of the Act if the social plan provides for a permanent flow of benefits for an indefinite period of time; however, termination is then only possible in respect of employee's claims that have not yet come into existence.[143] Accordingly, retroactive termination is not possible in any instance.

These principles, however, do not take us any further in the case of termination initiated by the THA when the maximum volume for ear-marked funds have been exceeded. No permanent flow of benefits was ever under discussion, but in most of the cases a one-off payment on account of redundancy. The employees' claims under the original social plan (when the maximum amount qualifying for ear-marked funds had been exceeded) had already come into existence and could not be affected by any termination of the social plan, which anyway could only affect the future. The requirements for qualifying for ear-marked funds could merely come into effect if a further social plan were to become necessary. If agreement is not reached on this new social plan, the Reconciliation Board would take the decision, and would then, unlike the companies and their employees, be bound by the calculation guidelines of § 112 section 5 clause 3 of the Industrial Constitution Act, meaning that it would have to take due note of the need for the company to survive. This is where the THA's guidelines gain in importance, as the ear-marked funds are financed by the THA, provided the maximum total volume is not exceeded, from the resources of the Federal Government and thus do not endanger the company's further survival if redundancy payments are based on them.

The termination at notice for cause of a social plan is only distinguished from termination at normal notice in that no period of notice needs to be observed. It is therefore only appropriate when there is a permanent flow of benefits, provided individual claims from employees have not yet come into existence.[144] The normal legal consequence of the disappearance of the legal basis of a contract (or "frustration") is that the contract then has to be adapted to suit the unforeseen change in circumstances.[145] It has to be decided in such cases whether the parties involved could have foreseen that the THA's financing of social plan benefits could only be expected if the Social Plan Guidelines had been observed, and this will only be relevant to those social plans which were concluded before the agreement of 13th April 1991 was made. In addition to this, the letter already mentioned from the THA Executive Board dated 11th December 1990 is a strong argument to support the view that the change was foreseeable. The Berlin Labour Court[146] found that a drastic worsening of the company's profit situation did not represent any "frustration", any more than did the expectation of ear-marked funds from the THA.

---

142 Däubler, *Nachträgliche Kürzung von Sozialplanansprüchen*, page 545.

143 Federal Labour Court, 24th March 1981, *Arbeitsrechtliche Praxis* No. 12 to § 112 of the Industrial Constitution Act.

144 State Labour Court of the Saarland, 3rd July 1985, *Entscheidungen der Landesarbeitsgerichte* No. 7 on § 112 of the Industrial Constitution Act, 1972; Labour Court of Berlin, 11th May 1992, case 82 Ca 21428/91, unpublished; Fitting, Auffarth, Kaiser, and Heither, *Betriebsverfassungsgesetz, Handkommentar*, §§ 112, 112a, marginal note 31; Däubler, *Nachträgliche Kürzung von Sozialplanansprüchen*, page 549.

145 On the basic effects of "frustration" see: Medicus, *Allgemeiner Teil des Bürgerlichen Rechts*, marginal note 861, on "foreseeability" see marginal note 868. On aspects of the social plan see: Fitting, Auffarth, Kaiser, and Heither, *Betriebsverfassungsgesetz, Handkommentar*, §§ 112, 112a, marginal note 31.

146 Labour Court of Berlin, 11th May 1992, case 82 Ca 21428/91, unpublished.

VI. THA's active labour market policy

1. Participation in job-promotion schemes

a) THA's standpoint

The THA's Social Plan Guidelines were able to a certain extent to place a social mattress under the necessary mass redundancies, but could not make a contribution to an active labour market policy, so the trade union side started insisting more and more on employment plans instead of social plans.[147] The aim of this was to replace the sole regulations on redundancy pay in social plans with a package of measures for preserving jobs and improving the qualifications of the work-force. As no early re-instatement in the relevant THA companies could be expected, the need arose to set up "employment companies" which could, in the trade unions' view, be attached to the THA companies. This was intended to preserve the close links of the employee with his or her firm, which was of particular significance in East Germany. On the other hand, the THA had always been opposed to the integration of employment companies into the firms as this would represent an obstacle to privatisation. Foreign investors in particular, and any others not acquainted with the idea of employment companies, would have found it hard to understand that organisations were attached to the firms which were above all administering unemployment. The THA always emphasized that by law it did not have any task under social or labour market policy.[148] The THA's guiding principle was far more to maintain a consultative and supportive function in the formation of employment companies and to provide the physical assets and accommodation, rather than to participate in any company law sense.[149] It was with this in mind that the THA then became active at an early stage and, even before 1990 was out, launched the *"Pentacon"* model and, in the spring of 1991, the *"Neuruppin"* model.[150]

b) ABS job creation programme – outline agreement of 17th July 1991

In order to achieve a mutually acceptable solution to all the different points of view, negotiations were held between the THA, the trade unions, the employers, and representatives of the States on the formation and maintenance of companies in which job creation schemes could be handled under the title of ABS (*Arbeitsförderung, Beschäftigung, Strukturentwicklung*, promotion of work, employment, structural development). The result was the outline agreement of 17th July 1991 between all concerned on the formation of these ABS-companies. The plan was to establish companies as initiators and supporters with GmbH status at the State or regional level in which all the parties to the agreement would hold stakes; the THA's shareholding was 10% of the nominal capital. The THA emphasised that it would urge its companies to support the ABS companies under the terms of this agreement with material, personnel, and finance,[151] and to this

---

147 See on this point: Klebe and Roth, *Beschäftigungsplan statt Sozialplan*, page 1518 et seq.

148 See *Berliner Morgenpost*, 28th June 1991, page 6; *Süddeutsche Zeitung*, same date, page 28.

149 Letter from the THA Personnel Executive Board member to the managements of all THA companies dated 7th June 1991; Gemählich in *Handelsblatt*, also 28th June 1991, page 9.

150 See: Gemählich, *Sozialverträglicher Beschäftigungsumbruch*, page 167 et seq.

151 For details, see: Section IV of the ABS outline agreement of 17th July 1991.

end concluded co-operation agreements with the ABS companies in which the exact method of operation was laid down for its participation. It was intended that employees of THA companies should be transferred into employment companies on the basis of the reconciliation of interests. It is a further prerequisite for the THA's participation that, before the employee is taken on by the ABS company, his or her contract of employment with the former THA company should be terminated. The social plan funds made available by the THA can, with the employee's express consent, be passed on to the ABS company.[152] The possibility of social plans "investing" rather than merely "consuming" is also provided for since the 2nd Edition of the THA Social Plan Guidelines.[153] If the employee is not entitled to benefits under a social plan as a consequence of being taken on by an ABS company until after the ABS scheme has come to an end, there are three versions of the application of social plan funds for ABS that can be considered: the payment of the ear-marked funds to a trust account, the assignment of the individual employee's claim to payment, or the later call-off of ear-marked funds from the THA, with the latter repaying the theoretical interest on them.[154] It was with the funds from the "investment" type of social plan that the *"Neuruppin Model"*, mentioned above, was financed. In this instance, the THA provided DM 12 million from social plan funds and an addition DM 0.5 million from a hardship fund and paid it into a trust account administered by an independent trustee.[155] On the basis of the outline agreement, the THA already agreed to provide about DM 175 million by the middle of 1992 to job creation programmes, thus enabling about 120,000 workers to be taken on by 145 ABS companies. Because the ABS projects were only designed to run for a limited period of time, the problem of unemployment is in many cases merely postponed for a while and not really solved. For this reason, the THA has been increasingly supporting the "hiving off", i. e. that the ABS companies should be converted into economically independent small or medium-sized companies. The THA had by November 1992 helped to set up 64 companies of this kind.[156]

c) Agreement between the THA and the chemicals and paper industry trade union

An outline agreement between the THA and *IG Chemie-Papier-Keramik*, the trade union for the chemicals, paper, and ceramics industry, bears the date of Wednesday 31st March 1993. It came into immediate effect the next day, and its main import is to encourage the measures provided for under § 249h of the Labour Promotion Act.[157] Under this Paragraph, work is encouraged until the end of 1997 (in the sphere of the THA until the end of 1994) by the Federal Labour Institute in the environmental field, such as cleaning up steel, chemical, and open-cast brown-coal industry sites and their surroundings as is work in the socially useful services or the youth welfare section. It was thus possible to provide a total of 17,000 jobs under § 249h for workers

---

152 See: op. cit., Section III.

153 See: *Richtlinie für Sozialpläne,* Section VIII, *Sozialplanmittel und ABS.*

154 For details, see: Section VIII clause 3 of the *Treuhandrichtlinien für Sozialpläne,* 2nd Edition (July 1992).

155 For a full description of this project, see: Heidemann and Maliszewski, *Qualifizierungs- und Beschäftigungsinitiativen,* pages 60 et seq.

156 See: Burian and Dehlinger, *Ausgründungen,* page 3 et seq.

157 This Act had come into force on 1st January 1993 (see *Bundesgesetzblatt* I, page 2044).

in chemical companies affected by redundancies up to 30th June 1994, or who leave current ABM (*Arbeitsbeschaffungsmaßnahmen* or work-creation) programmes, with a retraining component of 20% in each instance.[158] The finance came partly from social plan benefits and from revenue earned by the employees in an ABS company. As required by § 249h section 4 of this Act and § 4 section 4 of the Ordinance issued under it by the Federal Labour Institute,[159] the employees are not allowed to earn more than 90% of the net earnings they took home in their last month with their THA chemical company. The income from the restructuring company shall be covered by a uniform collective wage agreement between the unions for mining and energy and for chemicals, paper, and ceramics on the one hand and the employers' association for the restructuring companies on the other. The monthly wage subsidy "East" granted for programmes under § 249h of the Labour Promotion Act currently amounts to DM 1,260; of this, DM 969 comes from the Federal Labour Institute and DM 291 from the Federal Government.[160]

The total volume of this project amounts to DM 1 billion, and it is set to run for three to five years. The THA takes on 75% of the costs of the major projects.[161] This regulation complies with a decision from the Federal Government and the five eastern German State Governments (plus Berlin) of 22nd October 1992 covering the financial arrangements for the removal of historic environmental pollution. Despite all the encouragement given so far to cleaning-up work, particularly in the field of brown-coal mining (which is mainly open-cast, and particularly unsightly), the THA now appears to be making a change in tack. Bearing in mind that commitments in the ABM field have so far amounted to about DM 220 million, its 75% share of major projects seems altogether massive. The reason for this increased share could be that after the huge wave of redundancies so far, there is now a more manageable number of workers becoming eligible for ABS employment. Further developments should be followed closely.

2. Assistance with basic vocational training

In addition to its commitment to preserving and creating jobs, the THA started at an early stage to assist with basic vocational training. In a letter of the Executive Board member in charge of personnel issues dated 6th August 1991 it pledged its companies to continue apprenticeships and traineeships that had already been started and carry them through to the end (they usually last about three years), and if necessary to train more young people than the companies themselves would be needing (so that they would be well qualified for jobs with firms that do not do any training). The THA spent almost DM 1.5 billion in 1991 alone on assisting 90,000 trainees and apprentices. By the middle of 1992 there were still 52,000 of these youngsters in THA companies, and assisting them cost about DM 1 billion during that year. It can be expected that DM 600 million will be spent in 1993 on an average of 25,000 young people. A very steady figure of 6% has been maintained since 1992 for the proportion of the work-force undergoing full-time apprentice-type training. More than 40% of the financial assistance, above and beyond the companies' own resources, comes from the THA in the form of liquidity loans or other ear-marked

---

158 See: Section IV of the outline agreement between the THA and IG Chemie.

159 See: *Amtliche Nachrichten der Bundesanstalt für Arbeit* 1993, page 388.

160 See: Internal circular instructions of the Federal Labour Institute No. 28/93, 17th March 1993.

161 THA press release dated 31st March 1993.

funds. In privatisation contracts a high proportion of trainees is usually taken into account in setting the purchase price. Even when a company has been closed down, the continuation of training is usually assured by transferring the in-house training facilities to new organisations. The THA companies intend to take on larger number of trainees and apprentices in 1993 even in order to be able to assure the necessary supply of young talent for commercial occupations and the maintenance of eastern Germany's industrial cores.

In order to solve the problem of a training situation which all in all is very unsatisfactory in eastern Germany, the SPD has been proposing an "Apprenticeship Fund East" made up of contributions from western German companies who do not take on any apprentices, or too few, plus a contribution from the THA. This, they say, is necessary because at the beginning of 1993 there had only been 78,500 trainee places and apprenticeships for the 138,300 young people looking for them.[162] According to information from the DGB, there were still 34,000 too few trainee positions at the end of June 1993.[163]

VII. Works agreements and collective wage agreements

1. Co-operation with the trade unions

The THA has so far had a moderate influence on the shaping of works agreements and collective agreements, its motto being "exert influence through co-operation". Consensus with the trade unions and the works councils in this field was sought from an early stage. The crucial decisions on the THA's policy were made by the Administrative Board, with the participation and basically with the assent of the four trade union representatives (Meyer, Rappe, Issen, and Klaus). However, the authors of this article did not have access to the minutes of the Administrative Board meetings. The chairman of the DGB, Mr Meyer,[164] stated the following to have been the main fields of activity for the trade union representatives on the THA Administrative Board: social plan guidelines on the basis of a total volume of DM 10 billion; the introduction and financing of "short-time working with zero hours"; the continuation of trainee and apprenticeship arrangements; and the formation of the ABS companies with as broad an involvement by the THA as possible. A further field has recently been the special arrangements for the brown-coal and chemical industries, making use of § 249h of the Labour Promotion Act, which in Mr Meyer's opinion is not capable of being applied more generally.

A strike in the eastern German metal industry in the spring of 1993 seemed to show that battle-lines were being drawn with a vengeance.[165] The summary termination[166] by the employers of the collective agreement for the metal-producing and metal-working industry for the wage tarif area of Saxony on 18th February 1993 had led to bitter confrontation with the unions. In the employers' view, the 26% wage increase foreseen for 1993 in the eastern German states was

162 *Handelsblatt*, 7th/8th May 1993, page 7.

163 *Frankfurter Allgemeine Zeitung*, 28th July 1993, page 11.

164 B-interview with Heinz-Werner Meyer on 12th May 1993 in Düsseldorf.

165 On this point, see: Rüthers, *Die Verschränkung von Wirtschaft und Recht*, page 1628 et seq.

166 For one side of this dispute see: Zachert, *Möglichkeit der fristlosen Kündigung*, pages 299 et seq., for the other side: Buchner, *Kündigung der Tarifregelungen*, pages 289 et seq.

no longer feasible in light of the overall economic situation, and they were striving to reduce this to a 9% increase. The union, IG Metall, on the other hand, saw no evidence supporting this "sweeping assertion".[167] The THA wanted to make the same offer as the employers' side for the companies it was administrating. According to information from the Executive Board level, company managements were to lay down wage increases of "about 9%". At the beginning of 1993 there were still about 140,000 employees in THA companies in the metal industries affected by this dispute.[168] IG Metall considered that the THA's attitude represented unwarranted interference in free collective bargaining.[169]

On 14th May 1993, the two sides of the Saxon metal and electrical industries agreed on a new step-by-step plan which postponed the attainment of western wage levels until 1996. Under this plan, increases are scheduled which will result by 1st June 1993 in 75% of the wage levels agreed for Bavarian metal industries, 77% by 1st September 1993, 87% by 1st July 1994, and 94% by 1st July 1995. Full equality will be reached on 1st July 1996, although this date can be brought forward or postponed by six months depending on social and economic conditions. In addition to this, the dispute over the introduction of a general flexibility clause was settled in favour of a hardship clause (permitting companies in economic difficulties to pay less than the agreed wages), although IG Metall disputes its applicability to THA companies.[170] The THA's endeavours are directed towards making the provision of funds under § 249h of the Labour Promotion Act for the metal and electrical industries dependent upon IG Metall agreeing to the applicability of the hardship clause to THA companies as well.[171]

2. Guidelines on works agreements and collective wage agreements

The THA issued its "Guideline for Works Agreements and Local Wage Agreements" on 1st September 1992. The intended aim of these guidelines was to make the handling of such agreements by the THA companies, which up to then had been far from consistent in practice, "transparent and easy for an outsider to understand". They were intended to function as an aid to company managements, so that they could reach a judgement in difficult economic situations as to whether negotiations could be entered into regarding the demands of the works councils without neglecting the needs of the business. It was expressly emphasised that the Guidelines were not meant to interfere in the bargaining autonomy of the two sides of industry (or of any one company). They were not to cut down on the works councils' co-determination rights, nor to present any obstacle to the THA companies' commitment to collective agreements. The regulations were meant to cover the conditions under which the THA would be prepared to make use of public funds from its own budget to finance works and local wage agreements.[172] The THA nevertheless reserved its right under company law to give or withhold approval to those of its

167 *Frankfurter Allgemeine Zeitung*, 26th February 1993, page 17.

168 Dr Föhr, a member of the Executive Board, interviewed by *Frankfurter Allgemeine Zeitung* on 24th February 1993 in Berlin – see *FAZ* of 25th February 1993, page 15.

169 *Frankfurter Allgemeine Zeitung*, 26th February 1993, page 17.

170 See: *Frankfurter Allgemeine Zeitung*, 4th June 1993, page 15.

171 See: *Frankfurter Allgemeine Zeitung*, 6th July 1993, page 11.

172 See: Foreword in the *Richtlinie für Betriebsvereinbarungen und Haustarifverträge.*

companies entering into such agreements. The criticism that has been made up against this, to the effect that the reservation of rights under company law was a contradiction of free collective bargaining,[173] is described by the THA as being quite wrong. In its opinion, free collective bargaining protects the parties from interference by third parties, particularly the state, in their authority to make a legal contract, but does not thereby dictate that the shareholder of a corporation must stand helplessly aside and accept any agreement of the legal representatives if it is not compatible with the interests of the corporation or the shareholder. In the internal legal relationship between the legal representatives and the shareholder of a corporation it is not free collective bargaining that counts, but company law.[174]

On the other hand, if the company joins the relevant employers' association, this is not a matter on which the parent company has to give its approval. All the same, the THA points out that a merger between individual companies into some kind of grouping would not be accepted if the regulations concerning the THA's approval were thus circumvented.[175] The THA has a basically sceptical attitude towards the conclusion of local and supplementary collective agreements, justifying it on the one hand with its interest in the association membership of THA companies, and on the other hand with the fear that inappropriate conditions might be imposed (extremely long terms of notice or conditions of termination, excessively high fees, ancillary services, or periods of validity) which might in the end scare off a potential purchaser.[176] Besides this, local agreements were in the THA's opinion only possible if the company was likely to remain in the THA for a long period of time, and exactly this was not the intention.[177] Each company's Articles of Association, and the Rules of Procedure for its Supervisory and Management Boards, as well as the contracts of appointment of their members and managing directors, laid down in detail that works and other local agreements required the parent company's (the THA's) consent. In addition to this, the THA had drawn up for its companies a "catalogue of transactions requiring consent".[178] In the case of AG-companies and of GmbH-companies with Supervisory Boards, consent is given by the company's Supervisory Board, and for companies without them by the THA. The two regulations are combined with one another for subsidiaries of THA companies.[179] For local wage agreements, negotiations cannot even be started without prior consent, and consent is required again before any can be concluded.[180] There can never be any question of consent being given retroactively.

The employees' codetermination rights were of great importance even in the Supervisory Boards of the THA companies. Particularly in the branches of steel and mining which are covered by the Iron and Steel Codetermination Act, the Supervisory Boards came into existence at an early stage. A similar development can be seen in the shipyards which are covered by the

---

173 On this point, see: Köstler, *Die Treuhand gibt vor*, page 138 et seq.

174 Section 2 clause 2 of the *Richtlinie für Betriebsvereinbarungen und Haustarifverträge.*

175 op. cit., Section 2 clause 7.

176 See: op. cit., Section 2 clause 8.

177 Dr Föhr, a member of the Executive Board, interviewed by *Frankfurter Allgemeine Zeitung* on 24th February 1993 in Berlin – see *FAZ* of 25th February 1993, page 15.

178 For details, see: Section 3 clause 2 of the *Richtlinie für Betriebsvereinbarungen und Haustarifverträge;* for criticism, see: Köstler, *Die Treuhand gibt vor*, pages 138 et seq.

179 For details, see: Section 3 clause 2 of the *Richtlinie für Betriebsvereinbarungen und Haustarifverträge.*

180 For details, see: op. cit., Section 3 clause 5.

Codetermination Act. It was often possible to "reactivate" experienced people from western Germany to take on the position of the personnel director in the companies' representation bodies. Within the sphere of the THA this led to a very quick establishment of codetermination not only at the plant level but also at the company level; nobody denies that this supported, as far as possible, the structural change in eastern Germany.

VIII. Net outcome

1. Net outcome in social terms

The THA does not draw up a balance sheet to show the net outcome in social terms. This would in any case be difficult, but the following is a sketchy attempt to do so, which first has to take into account the THA's expenditure on privatisation, restructuring, and closures. The final figures on the 1992 annual plan can be taken by way of example.[181]

In 1992, a total of DM 25.5 billion was planned for these three above-named areas, and just short of DM 23 billion actually spent. The crucial factors for preserving jobs are investment grants and payments to compensate losses as part of the privatisation programme. Here the planned expenditure was DM 3.3 billion, and in fact almost DM 3.8 billion was spent. For the companies still on the THA's books, DM 5.25 billion was planned as part of the restructuring programme for investment loans, loss compensation, and raising registered capital, and the amount actually spent was close to DM 4 billion. For restructuring purposes under social plans there were benefits of almost DM 2.9 billion set aside as an estimate, but the actual expenditure was only DM 1.7 billion. Whilst the costs for the social plan benefits had been largely standardised by the Guidelines, there were no regulations which justified or defined the size of the expenditures devoted to preserving jobs because economic and social conditions varied from one company to another. The decentralisation of the privatisation programme contributed substantially to this differentiation, and served at the same time as a way of reducing political influence. The average expenditure per person employed was DM 11,400 in 1991 but rose to over DM 75,000 in 1993. In individual cases they are even considerably higher, with the range rising to DM 500,000 for each job preserved for example in the shipyards.[182]

The total figure for expenditure by the THA for 1992 was set at DM 42.3 billion, but it is possible that DM 6.5 billion less than this was actually spent. The planned deficit of DM 30 billion for 1992, on the other hand, was utilised almost to the full.

2. Net outcome in terms of social law

Any attempt at a balance sheet showing the net outcome in terms of social law must show the effects on the provisions of social and labour law. It has been shown here that the statutory regulations on the protection of the employee did not act as a curb on the THA's privatisation pro-

181 See: *Finanzbericht der Treuhandanstalt* for 1992, page 29.

182 See: Lichtblau, *Privatisierungs- und Sanierungsarbeit*, pages 24 and 40, and the article by Schmidt in this volume, page 238 et seq.

gramme. The regulations on dismissal discussed here could not and should not prevent the mass dismissals necessary during the transition from the planned economy to the social market economy. In the same way, the often criticised § 613a of the Civil Code does not represent any substantial obstacle to privatisation in the context of the THA's work. The protection of the employee (against unfair dismissal) as the actual aim of the regulations on the one hand and the recognition of operational necessities on the other set off a mechanism that forced works councils and managements to reach an agreement in which economic and social necessities were taken into account.

Not even use of the social plan as an instrument of social support was able to develop in a vacuum divorced from economic necessities. The social component of redundancy compensation payments, if defined without even a glance at their economic defensibility, would have had the immediate consequence of hurling the vast majority of THA companies straight into bankruptcy. Without the financial support of the THA, many social plans would have collapsed anyway for lack of liquidity. The consensus between the THA and the trade unions was able to make at least some contribution to providing a social safety-net beneath the unavoidable mass dismissals. Finally, the regulations of the Labour Promotion Act were and still are able to contribute the prevention of even higher level of unemployment, even though they were never intended to be anything more than a temporary measure.

In summary, it is possible to perceive that the THA has been pursuing a three-part concept, inevitably dictated by the tasks entrusted to it:

1. The only possible way of carrying through the privatisation programme was by making huge financial concessions to the investors, even reaching the point of agreeing on a "negative purchase price". In some cases it was not the companies that were being sold, but the investments that were being bought.
2. The THA paid the social plan costs up to a certain limit when mass dismissals were necessary as part of the restructuring programme and supported the process of transferring workers to ABS companies with financial, personnel, and material assistance.
3. As part of the programme of company closures, companies were kept in operation for a limited period of time and their liquidation postponed in favour of retaining jobs temporarily.

The THA's view of itself and the job it had to do always centred on privatisation. The sums of money spent to achieve this were enormous. Whether they were sufficient, and always spent effectively in every case, will always be a matter of contention, as events at the potash mine in Bischofferode showed.[183]

IX. Literature

Adomeit, Klaus, Stephan *Eiden*, and Axel *Schack*: Arbeitsrecht und Privatisierung von Unternehmen durch die Treuhandanstalt. In: *Arbeit und Arbeitsrecht* 1991, pages 5 to 7.

Adomeit, Klaus: Zum Betriebsübergang. In: *Arbeit und Arbeitsrecht* 1991, page 119.

Ascheid, Reiner: Die betriebsbedingte Kündigung – § 1 KSchG – § 54 AGB-DDR – § 613a IV2 BGB. In: *Neue Zeitschrift für Arbeits- und Sozialrecht* 1991, pages 873 to 879.

183 On this point, see: *Handelsblatt*, 2nd August 1993, page 5, and 3rd August 1993, page 4.

Belling, Detlev W., and Thomas K. *Müsgen*: Arbeitsrechtliche Aspekte der Sanierung von Betrieben in den neuen Bundesländern. In: *Neue Zeitschrift für Arbeits- und Sozialrecht* 1991, supplement 1/1991, pages 7 to 18.

Bengelsdorf, Peter: Unzulässigkeit einer Untersagungsverfügung bei Betriebsänderungen. In: *Der Betrieb* 1990, pages 1233 to 1238 and 1282 to 1286.

Berkowsky, Wilfried: *Die betriebsbedingte Kündigung*. Munich ^{2}1985.

Berscheid, Ernst-Dieter: *Konkurs – Gesamtvollstreckung – Sanierung*. Wiesbaden 1992.

Buchner, Herbert: Kündigung der Tarifregelungen über die Entgeltanpassung in der Metallindustrie der östlichen Bundesländer. In: *Neue Zeitschrift für Arbeitsrecht* 1993, pages 289 to 299.

Das Bürgerliche Gesetzbuch, mit besonderer Berücksichtigung der Rechtsprechung des Reichsgerichts und des Bundesgerichtshofs (Kommentar). Berlin ^{12}1992.

Bundesministerium der Finanzen (editor): *Die Tätigkeit der Treuhandanstalt. Schnelle Privatisierung, entschlossene Sanierung, behutsame Stillegung*. Bonn, 31st October 1991.

Burian, Walter, and Gabriele *Dehlinger*: Ausgründungen – Perspektiven für einen sicheren Arbeitsplatz. In: *Das neue Unternehmen* 1993, pages 3 and 4.

Claussen, Peter: Die Finanzierung des Unternehmenskaufs in den neuen Bundesländern. In: *Deutsche Zeitschrift für Wirtschaftsrecht* 1992, pages 1 to 6.

Commandeur, Gerd: Die Bedeutung des § 613a BGB im Bereich der ehemaligen DDR. In: *Neue Zeitschrift für Arbeits- und Sozialrecht* 1991, pages 705 to 711.

ditto: Betriebsübergang in den neuen Bundesländern. In: *Arbeit und Arbeitsrecht* 1992, pages 169 to 171.

Dänzer-Vanotti, Christoph, and Hans-Joachim *Tyska*: Neuwahl von Betriebsräten in den neuen Bundesländern. In: *Der Betrieb*, DDR-Report 1990, pages 3186 to 3188.

Däubler, Wolfgang, Michael *Kittner*, Thomas *Klebe*, and Wolfgang *Schneider*: *Betriebesverfassungsgesetz, Kommentar für die Praxis*. Cologne ^{3}1992.

Däubler, Wolfgang: Nachträgliche Kürzung von Sozialplanansprüchen? In: *Neue Zeitschrift für Arbeits- und Sozialrecht* 1985, pages 545 to 551.

ditto: *Ratgeber Arbeitsrecht*. Reinbek bei Hamburg 1991.

ditto: Sozialplan. In: *Arbeitsrecht im Betrieb* 1991, pages 322 to 325.

ditto: Verschlechterung der Arbeitsbedingungen durch Betriebsvereinbarung. In: *Arbeit und Recht* 1984, pages 1 to 28.

Düwell, Franz-Josef: Betriebsverfassungsrechtliche Probleme der Umstrukturierung von Unternehmen. In: *Arbeit und Arbeitsrecht* 1992, pages 196 to 199.

Ehrich, Christian: Einstweilige Verfügung gegen betriebsbedingte Kündigungen. In: *Betriebs-Berater* 1993, pages 356 to 360.

Engels, Gerd: Betriebsverfassungsrechtliche Aspekte des Spaltungsgesetzes. In: *Der Betrieb* 1991, pages 966 to 969.

ditto: Müssen alle Betriebsräte in der ehemaligen DDR im Frühjahr 1991 neu gewählt werden? In: *Der Betrieb*, DDR-Report 1990, pages 3139 to 3140.

Fitting, Karl, Fritz *Auffarth*, Heinrich *Kaiser*, and Friedrich *Heither*: *Betriebsverfassungsgesetz, Handkommentar*. Munich ^{17}1992.

Ganske, Joachim: Spaltung der Treuhandunternehmen. In: *Der Betrieb* 1991, pages 791 to 797.

Gaul, Dieter: *Der Betriebsübergang*. Cologne ^{2}1993.

Gemählich, Peter: Sozialverträglicher Beschäftigungsumbruch. In: *Arbeit und Arbeitsrecht* 1992, pages 166 to 168.

Gemeinschaftskommentar zum Arbeitsförderungsgesetz. Neuwied et al, as of November 1992.

Gemeinschaftskommentar zum Betriebsverfassungsgesetz, Volume II, §§ 74 to 132. Neuwied ^{4}1990.

Gemeinschaftskommentar zum Kündigungsschutzgesetz und zu sonstigen kündigungsschutzrechtlichen Vorschriften. Neuwied ^{3}1989.

Haarmeyer, Hans, Wolfgang *Wutzke*, and Karsten *Förster*: *Kommentar zur Gesamtvollstreckungsordnung*. Cologne ^{2}1992.

Hanau, Peter: *Aktuelle Fragen zu § 613a BGB*. In: *Festschrift für Dieter Gaul*. Neuwied et al 1992, pages 287 to 304.

ditto: *Sozialverträgliche Gestaltung bei der Umstrukturierung und Auflösung von Unternehmen*. In: Peter *Hommelhoff* (editor): *Treuhandunternehmen im Umbruch*. Cologne 1991, pages 101 to 119.

ditto: Zur Kündigung von Arbeitsverhältnissen wegen Betriebsübergangs. In: *Zeitschrift für Wirtschaftsrecht* 1984, pages 141 to 145.

Hanau, Peter in: Klaus *Adomeit*: *Arbeitsrecht* (textbook). Neuwied et al ^{10}1992.

Hanau, Peter, Annemarie *Langanke*, Ulrich *Preis*, and Harald *Widlak* (editors): *RWS-Dokumentation 6, Das Arbeitsrecht der neuen Bundesländer*. Cologne 1991.

Heidemann, Winfried, and Bärbel *Maliszewski*: Qualifizierungs- und Beschäftigungsinitiativen in Ostdeutschland. *Manuscript 46 of the Hans-Böckler-Stiftung*. Düsseldorf ^{2}1991.

Heinze, Meinhard: Betriebsübergang und Sozialplanpflichtigkeit – unter besonderer Berücksichtigung der Rechtslage in den neuen Bundesländern. In: *Das Arbeitsrecht der Gegenwart* 28 (1991), pages 79 to 88.

Herschel, Wilhelm, and Manfred *Löwisch*: *Kommentar zum Kündigungsschutzgesetz*. Heidelberg ^{6}1984.

Hueck, Götz, and Gerrick *von Hoyningen-Huene*: *Kündigungsschutzgesetz (Kommentar)*. Munich ^{11}1992.

Hunold, Wolf: Ungelöste Probleme im Recht der Personalanpassung. In: *Betriebs-Berater* 1984, pages 2275 to 2283.

Ising, Peter, and Marie-Theres *Thiell*: Der Übergang laufender Arbeitsverhältnisse nach dem Spaltungsgesetz. In: *Der Betrieb* 1991, pages 2082 to 2085.

Kissel, Otto Rudolf: Ein Jahr gesamtdeutsches Arbeitsrecht. In: *Neue Zeitschrift für Arbeits- und Sozialrecht* 1992, pages 1 to 8.

Klebe, Thomas, and Siegfried *Roth*: Beschäftigungsplan statt Sozialplan – Zwischenlagerung eines Problems oder Perspektive? In: *Der Betrieb* 1989, pages 1519 to 1521

Koch, Alexander: "Eine Illusion müssen wir aufrechterhalten..." Interview in: *Die Mitbestimmung* 1991, pages 158 to 163.

Köstler, Roland: Die Treuhand gibt vor. In: *Die Mitbestimmung* 1991, pages 138 to 139.

Kreitner, Jochen: *Kündigungsrechtliche Probleme beim Betriebsinhaberwechsel*. Heidelberg 1989.

Kübler, Bruno M: *Die Gesamtvollstreckung als Instrument zur Sanierung insolventer Unternehmen*. In: Peter *Hommelhoff* (editor): *Treuhandunternehmen im Umbruch*. Cologne 1991, pages 79 to 99.

Landfermann, Hans-Georg: Sanierungsförderung und Gesamtvollstreckung. In: *Zeitschrift für Wirtschaftsrecht* 1991, pages 826 to 834.

Langanke, Annemarie: Die soziale Auswahl bei betriebsbedingter Kündigung und der Zweck des Arbeitsverhältnisses. In: *Recht der Arbeit* 1993, pages 219 to 220.

Lichtblau, Karl: *Privatisierungs- und Sanierungsarbeit der Treuhandanstalt*. Cologne 1993.

Löwisch, Manfred: Betriebsrat und Arbeitnehmer in einem künftigen Sanierungsverfahren. In: *Zeitschrift für Wirtschaftsrecht* 1981, pages 1288 to 1296.

Lutter, Marcus: Zur Reform von Umwandlung und Fusion. In: *Zeitschrift für Unternehmens- und Gesellschaftsrecht* 1990, pages 392 to 415.

Mallmann, Luitwin: Kurzarbeit oder betriebsbedingte Kündigung. In: *Arbeit und Arbeitsrecht* 1991, pages 202 to 204.

Mayer, Dieter: Zweifelsfragen bei der Spaltung der Treuhandunternehmen. In: *Der Betrieb* 1991, pages 1609 to 1616.

Medicus, Dieter: *Allgemeiner Teil des Bürgerlichen Rechts.* Heidelberg [4]1990.

Oberhofer, Hermann: *Kurzstellungnahme zu den Referaten von Dr. Kübler und Prof. Dr. Dr. h. c. mult. Hanau.* In: Peter *Hommelhoff* (editor): *Treuhandunternehmen im Umbruch.* Cologne 1991, pages 121 to 131.

Oetker, Hartmut: Übergang der Arbeitsverhältnisse beim Betriebsinhaberwechsel in den neuen Bundesländern. In: *Zeitschrift für Vermögens- und Investitionsrecht* 1991, pages 7 to 12.

Oetker, Hartmut, and Jan *Busche*: Entflechtung ehemals volkseigener Wirtschaftseinheiten im Lichte des Arbeitsrechts. In: *Neue Zeitschrift für Arbeits- und Sozialrecht*, supplement 1/1991, pages 18 to 26.

Otto, Heinz-Dieter: *Management-Buy-Out und Belegschafts-Buy-Out.* In: Heinz-Dieter *Assmann* and Rolf A. *Schütze* (editors): *Handbuch des Kapitalanlagerechts.* Munich 1990, § 26, pages 834 to 870.

Priester, Hans-Joachim: Gesellschaftsrechtliche Zweifelsfragen beim Umgang mit Treuhandunternehmen. In: *Der Betrieb* 1991, pages 2373 to 2378.

ditto: Strukturänderungen – Beschlußvorbereitung und Beschlußfassung. In: *Zeitschrift für Unternehmens- und Gesellschaftsrecht* 1990, pages 420 to 446.

Richardi, Reinhard: Die Anwendbarkeit des § 613a BGB bei Betriebserwerb und Neugründung von Unternehmen in den neuen Bundesländern. In: *Neue Zeitschrift für Arbeits- und Sozialrecht* 1991, pages 289 to 293.

Rüthers, Bernd: Die Verschränkung von Wirtschaft und Recht – Zum Streik in Ostdeutschland. In: *Neue Juristische Wochenschrift* 1993, pages 1628 to 1629.

Rumpenhorst, Elmar: Das berechtigte betriebliche Bedürfnis i. S. d. § 1 III 2 KSchG bei Massenentlassungen. In: *Neue Zeitschrift für Arbeits- und Sozialrecht* 1991, pages 214 to 216.

Rumpff, Klaus, and Dietrich *Boewer*: *Mitbestimmung in wirtschaftlichen Angelegenheiten.* Heidelberg [3]1990.

Schack, Axel: *Die partnerschaftliche Unternehmung als Mittel zur Liberalisierung des Arbeitsrechts.* In: Klaus *Adomeit* (editor): *Arbeitsrecht für die 90er Jahre.* Munich 1991, pages 24 to 53.

Schaub, Günter: Einführung in das Recht der Betriebsnachfolge. In: *Arbeit und Arbeitsrecht* 1991, pages 225 to 229.

ditto: Die Rahmenvereinbarung der Treuhandanstalt mit den Gewerkschaften und ihre Richtlinie. In: *Neue Zeitschrift für Arbeitsrecht* 1993, pages 673 to 679.

Scheifele, Bernd: Praktische Erfahrungen beim Unternehmenskauf in den neuen Bundesländern. In: *Betriebs-Berater* 1991, pages 557 to 563 and 629 to 636.

Schmidt, Karsten: Universalsukzession kraft Rechtsgeschäft. In: *Archiv für die civilistische Praxis* 191 (1991), pages 495 to 525.

Sieben, Günter: Zur Wertfindung bei der Privatisierung von Unternehmen in den neuen Bundesländern durch die Treuhandanstalt. In: *Der Betrieb* 1992, pages 2041 to 2051.

Stahlhacke, Eugen, and Ulrich *Preis*: *Kündigung und Kündigungsschutz im Arbeitsverhältnis*. Munich [5]1991.

Stege, Dieter, and F. K. *Weinspach*: *Betriebsverfassungsgesetz. Handkommentar für die betriebliche Praxis*. Cologne [6]1990.

Stein, Jürgen vom: Wiedereinstellungsanspruch des Arbeitnehmers bei Fehlprognose des Arbeitgebers? In: *Recht der Arbeit* 1991, pages 85 to 94.

Timm, Wolfram: Die Sanierung der sogenannten "Treuhandunternehmen" zwischen Marktkonformität und Insolvenzrecht. In: *Zeitschrift für Wirtschaftsrecht* 1991, pages 413 to 425.

Timm, Wolfram, and Thorsten *Schöne*: Die Thesen der Treuhandanstalt zu Haftungsfragen – eine kritische Bestandsaufnahme. In: *Zeitschrift für Wirtschaftsrecht* 1992, pages 969 to 979.

Treuhandanstalt: *Monatsinformation der THA* as of 30th June 1993.

Völkel, Brigitte: Kurzarbeit in den neuen Bundesländern. In: *Arbeit und Arbeitsrecht* 1993, pages 1 to 3.

Wächter, Gerd H., Thomas *Kaiser*, and Michael *Krause*: Klauseln in Unternehmenskaufverträgen mit der Treuhandanstalt. In: *Wertpapier-Mitteilungen* 1992, pages 293 to 303 and 337 to 347.

Wagner, Klaus-R.: *Management-Buy-Out und Belegschafts-Buy-Out*. In: Heinz-Dieter *Assmann* and Rolf A. *Schütze* (editors): *Handbuch des Kapitalanlagerechts*. Munich 1990, § 26, pages 870 to 872.

Wahse, Jürgen, Vera *Dahms*, and Reinhard *Schaefer*: Beschäftigungsperspektiven von Treuhandunternehmen und Ex-Treuhandfirmen. Opinion survey, October 1992. *Beiträge zur Arbeitsmarkt- und Berufsforschung* 160.3. Nuremberg 1993.

Weidner, Norbert: Neue Bestimmungen für Betriebsräte in den neuen Bundesländern. In: *Arbeit und Arbeitsrecht* 1991, pages 224 and 225.

Weimar, Robert: Die Entflechtung von Treuhandunternehmen. In: *Zeitschrift für Wirtschaftsrecht* 1991, pages 769 to 777.

ditto: Spaltung von Treuhandunternehmen. In: *Deutsch-Deutsche Rechts-Zeitschrift* 1991, pages 182 to 184.

Weimar, Robert, and Jochen *Alfes*: Betriebsbelegschaften als Investitionshemmnis in den neuen Bundesländern. In: *Betriebs-Berater* 1991, supplement 9 to issue 12, pages 16 to 21.

ditto: Betriebsübernahmen ohne § 613a BGB? In: *Neue Zeitschrift für Arbeitsrecht* 1993, pages 155 to 161.

ditto: Enthaftung der Treuhandanstalt durch Gesetz? In: *Der Betrieb* 1992, pages 1225 and 1226.

ditto: Neuregelung des § 613a BGB für die neuen Bundesländer. In: *Der Betrieb* 1991, pages 1830 to 1832.

ditto: Widerspruchsrecht des Arbeitnehmers bei Umstrukturierung von Treuhandunternehmen. In: *Neue Zeitschrift für Arbeits- und Sozialrecht* 1991, pages 833 to 836.

Weisemann, Ulrich: Zur Sozialplanpflichtigkeit der Treuhandanstalt. In: *Arbeit und Arbeitsrecht* 1992, pages 41 to 43.

Weiss, Manfred, and Alexander *Gagel* (editors): *Handbuch des Arbeits- und Sozialrechts*. Baden-Baden, as of December 1991.

Willemsen, Heinz Josef: Anmerkung zu BAG v. 13. 6. 1989. In: *Arbeitsrechtliche Praxis* Nr. 3 zu § 112a BetrVG 1972.

Wlotzke, Otfried: *Betriebsverfassungsgesetz (Kommentar)*. Munich [2]1992.

Wolter, Henner: Einige arbeitsrechtliche Fragen des Einigungsvertrags. In: *Der Betrieb* 1991, pages 43 to 46.

Zachert, Ulrich: Möglichkeit der fristlosen Kündigung von Tarifverträgen in den neuen Bundesländern. In: *Neue Zeitschrift für Arbeitsrecht* 1993, pages 299 to 301.

The THA – a trials ground for developing new company forms[1]

by Horst Kern and Charles F. Sabel

I. Introduction

The THA's most difficult task from the beginning was the restructuring of those parts of the East German planned economy which no-one wanted to buy and which, being of major importance for the further existence of vital parts of the regional economy, could not have been closed down. Above all this refers to the core businesses of the giant industrial combines (the *Kombinate*) which produced large volumes of chemicals, steel, or textiles for the entire COMECON bloc and even manufactured the plant and machinery needed for them as well. In a period of expanding markets for mass market products it might have been conceivable for western companies to have regarded these mammoths as fossilised versions of their former selves, and modernising such factories might have appeared to them to be a cheap way of expanding capacity in a promising new territorial market. But production capacity for such goods vastly exceeds potential demand in western countries at the moment, and even companies which have up to now been the undisputed masters of the upper segments and niches of their market and would have considered themselves highly competitive even in the face of new challenges now find themselves in the throes of an unexpectedly deep recession. They find themselves to be suddenly confronted by competitors whom they are forced to take seriously and who were the first to push through the kind of organisational innovations which enabled them to produce high-quality products more cheaply and after a shorter development period than the established companies. The previous masters of the market are now forced to reduce their costs and their time-to-market as well. For these reasons, no-one is interested in any "modernised" version of the East German factories, and many companies hesitate at the idea of taking on the job of restructuring them when the necessity of reorganising their own factories keeps forcing its way to the forefront.

The THA itself, however, is not able to know which of the eastern German factories in which regional combination or in which combination of industries might be the promising candidates for reorganisation. As a central government institution it lacks the necessary knowledge of existing local resources. But, even if it could obtain all the necessary information, the selection of the right candidates would require the existence of a restructuring strategy to serve as the guiding principle for determining all criteria of selection. And clear, precise restructuring plans are in short supply at a time when even western firms are experimenting with new organisational forms.

The necessary information on existing resources can only be obtained in co-operation with other protagonists, and a number of possible ones can be considered: first the THA companies, whose (remaining) regular workforces have detailed knowledge of their company's resources,

1 We would like to thank the Harvard Center for European Studies for their assistance in our studies of the industrial restructuring of eastern Germany. This text is based on the Center's work.

having worked with them for many years, and whose managers, many of whom had to be appointed after the end of socialism, have learned to combine the knowledge of development, marketing, and financial control they brought with them from the west with the potential opportunities they find in the east. Other parties with whom the THA can co-operate fruitfully are: the eastern German State Governments (*Landesregierungen*) and their administrative departments, who not only know their regional economic structures very well from their proximity to them but can also provide assistance relevant to restructuring on the form of their programmes and economic promotion methods; potential investors, who know from their experience in competition and in industrial restructuring which organisational forms must first be developed for manufacturers to survive at all in modern competitive conditions; and finally the trade unions, which can be important not only as advocates of restructuring but also in improving the political management of the restructuring process.

The THA is faced by a dilemma when it tries to collaborate with these protagonists. In order to be sure of their co-operation it has to be prepared to grant the company selected for carrying out the restructuring a certain period of grace, as well as room for manoeuvre, and to bear a substantial part of the costs involved in the adaptation process while being, in the nature of things, unsure of the level these could reach. And it is of course highly problematical to promise open-ended support in a situation of extreme uncertainty. If the other parties involved draw the conclusion that the THA, as a generous company owner with no capacity for interfering in the running of the business, is going to act as its lifebelt come what may, then they would have little incentive to exert their full effort. If they even take any active part at all they will confine themselves to cosmetic operations which have no effect on the real substance of the firm. The outcome would have to be a new version of the state-owned company living entirely from a permanent flow of subsidies of a kind already discredited in the west long before the planned economies collapsed. If, however, the parties involved draw the reverse conclusion, that the owner will abandon their attempts at restructuring at the first sign of difficulties, they will for their part probably only decide to carry out short-term measures which can easily be cancelled and which may make the company's situation a little easier here and there but only have a random chance of improving its long-term ability to survive. If it is assumed that in the present economic situation a sudden and durable economic boom is rather unlikely, it can then also be assumed that this dilemma will become steadily greater as one firm after another collapses and the choice becomes all the more difficult between withdrawing all undertakings and conceding the necessity of providing further finance, even if the terms upon which the undertakings were made are not being adhered to. The first course of action would be the death-knell of the remaining industrial cores of eastern Germany; the latter would merely reinforce inefficiency.

The THA has not resolved this dilemma. It does not possess any organisational model with the aid of which the specific knowledge held by each of the protagonists involved in eastern German industry can be combined with the distant perspective of world markets in such a way that the joint learning process of all involved is stimulated and the mental barriers each has developed can be avoided. The THA, however, did at a relatively early stage provide *ad hoc* opportunities for experimental solutions despite the jumble of internal and public debate over the right relationship between privatisation and restructuring: co-operation concepts with external parties which determined both the selection of candidates for restructuring measures and the strategic direction of the restructuring itself. The double purpose of these projects consisted, as one can say with the benefit of hindsight, in a test of various different approaches to restructuring and subsequent privatisation as a way of solving the underlying dilemma.

These endeavours have two main features in common. They are firstly all based in one way or another on the knowledge that the THA cannot take the route to privatisation via restructuring without delegating substantial parts of its rights of involvement to outside parties, but that it will also not attain its goal if it delegates all its decision-making authority. Secondly, these arrangements came about as a reaction to an immediate danger (not least because of pressure from local politicians and trade unions), not as part of a comprehensive, far-sighted programme in which pilot projects based on various different concepts were tested out carefully for their durability. This is the reason for their *ad hoc* character. None of the solutions carries conviction in the sense that it can completely confirm or nullify the rightness of any given route. Looked at this way, the solutions are experimental and still open to further learning. Although they were organised as supplementary components or alternatives to the THA, and thus outside it or on its periphery, the results obtained by them will have a substantial influence on the final outcome of the THA's privatisation policy.

The main part of this essay will describe the three main experiments of this kind:

a) The ATLAS agreement, in which the THA co-operates with the State of Saxony in such a way that the State can apply its interests and its knowledge systematically to the selection of the companies to be restructured and to the decision on the restructuring strategy, but on the other hand has to bear part of the financial and political responsibility for the restructuring programme. An important role is played by the metal-processing and metal-working industry trade union IG Metall as a body which powerfully urges the preservation of the industrial cores and at the same time expertly monitors developments.
b) The EKO-Stahl project, in which the THA is attempting, together with the State of Brandenburg, to use co-operative development of basic technology as an instrument for the conception of creative companies. One crucial factor for the development of this strategy was the concept of a potential investor; another was the company itself which was awaiting restructuring, EKO Stahl AG.
c) Management-KG companies, in which the THA is attempting to create an intermediary organisation located between itself and the firms awaiting restructuring and which should prove more effective than the THA could be in carrying out the restructuring programme.

In each of these three experiments, a specific form of co-operation developed between the THA on the one side and various outside parties on the other. In no case were all the potential protagonists involved at once, but in all cases experience was gained which is important for determining more precisely the possibilities and the limitations of experimental forms of co-operation in restructuring and privatising the industrial cores of eastern Germany. We intend to deal in this article with the material gained through this experience in such a way that the empirical basis for drawing theoretical conclusions can be widened in respect of the methods for solving the more difficult cases of privatisation.

In addition to this point, the treatment of our three cases also promises to illuminate other unsolved problems relating to the classic concepts of economic restructuring policy. We are thinking primarily here of the interface problem between the state and the private sectors in periods of economic upheaval, as the detailed form of co-operation in each of the three experiments takes its distinctive character mainly from the self-critical endeavours of one central protagonist to define a division of labour between the private-sector and the public-sector bodies which takes this party's own mistakes in the past just as much into account as the mistakes which it can be assumed the other parties have been made as well.

In the second part we will be concentrating on discussing the specific characteristics of each of the three cases. We will withhold judgement as to which aspects of which case will actually work, but will instead attempt to describe the particular contours of each approach as fully as possible in case, as one would suppose, they all prove to work differently, so that our description can serve as the basis for explaining their later success or failure. In the concluding part we will return to the discussion opened at the start on the THA's basic dilemma. By examining in detail the problem of its finding a middle way between, on the one side, the necessity for stimulating experimental action and learning and on the other hand of maintaining a certain degree of control, we will then attempt to set up the initial criteria with the aid of which each approach's chances of success can be assessed, to the extent that these are already tangible.[2]

II. Co-operative experiments in the development of companies capable of privatisation

1. The ATLAS project in Saxony

If there was any one thing which the CDU government in Saxony did not want it was responsibility for restructuring those parts of the old East German economy that lay within its borders. The idea of returning a part of those economic institutions which the state had historically taken over for itself to the private sector of society was regarded as Saxony's sufficient contribution to the "new role of the state". Its "partner" state in the west was Baden-Württemberg, and many of the party faithful involved in this new role of the state were government officials from the south-west and other bearers of office who were mainly concerned to show the powerful statist groupings in the CDU back home that there are better ways and means for the state to do its business. The organisation of departments for promoting the economy was delegated to private-sector counsellors working under the supervision of political entities. In this way the State hoped to take account of the problem of "too much state" by means of a combination of "more market", meaning experts working on the terms customary in the market, and "more politics", meaning control of their activities by those parties most immediately affected by these activities.

The State government had therefore started by very readily sharing the THA's hope that most of the companies in eastern Germany could be privatised without prior intervention, and that restructuring could be left to the new owners. The State's policy therefore had the aim of encouraging this economic change by creating the labour market, financing, management consultancy, and other institutions that could reduce the costs of the privatised or newly established firms to provide them with the necessary services. The crucial characteristic of these institutions consisted, from point of view of the CDU government of the State that brought them to life, of their decentralised character and their positioning at the interface between the public and the private sectors. Instead of being operated as branch offices of the State authorities, they were set up as semi-autonomous organisations.

However, this approach was destined to produce less than the expected success. Above all, it was insufficient for the renewal of the industrial sector, as the THA found no purchasers for a large part of the industry in its hands. If the priority of privatisation had been maintained, the companies that could not be sold off would have had to be shut down completely. However, if

2 In this article we refer generally to the theoretical approach developed by Sabel, *Learning by Monitoring*.

the total de-industrialisation of Saxony was to be avoided it was therefore clearly necessary to change course. The step to take an active part in restructuring was thus unavoidable: stabilising the "industrial cores" by improvements to its very substance, thus increasing the chances to be privatised in the future.

In view of the great significance of the industrial sector to Saxony's economy – more than two-thirds of the THA companies are based in this State – the Saxon government had to face up more and more to the consequences. It became increasingly prepared to ease the THA's way to actively restructuring the industrial companies on its books by participating financially in selected cases in the restructuring costs and also by shouldering various other burdens. In return, it expected the THA to take full account of the State's interests in selecting companies for restructuring. The ATLAS project, agreed between the THA President Birgit Breuel and the State Minister for Economic Affairs Kajo Schommer on 23rd April 1992, provided documentary proof that both sides had changed tack.

Under this agreement, the State can give the THA the names of those Saxon industrial companies which from its point of view are of regional significance. The THA then announces which of them it categorises as being capable of effective restructuring, and is prepared to grant them the entrepreneurial and financial room for manoeuvre they need for this purpose, whilst the State for its part assists in the restructuring of these companies with the whole apparatus of support and promotion, thus departing from the previous principle of no support for THA firms; this means principally joint project funds and sureties, and also infrastructure projects and labour policy programmes. Any decision to close a company down is then not made by the THA until it has consulted the State government, but then both parties together support this decision.

Theoretically, the State is now faced with two possibilities open to it for adapting its economic policy in general and its economic promotion institutions in particular to this strategy of active restructuring. Expansive adaptation would have consisted in applying even "more market" and "more politics". The State would then have had to encourage the formation of a group of regional authorities capable of making and implementing decisions, shouldering responsibility for selecting the companies capable of restructuring, and supervising the restructuring process under the criteria of the various companies' relationships with one another and thus of their significance for the regional economy. Experts could have been given the job of scrutinising restructuring strategies, each individually and with regard to their suitability for integration into the overall strategy. Decisions to exclude certain firms from restructuring could have been fought politically through because all the local protagonists, unions, works councils, municipalities, and State representatives of the State parliaments *(Landtage)*, would have had to defend their joint decision, as to which firms were to be the victims as the price for the survival of the regional economy as a whole, an economy which they were then deeply involved in fashioning.

The systematic implementation of this expansive approach would have consisted of founding one or a number of State restructuring companies which would have been given the responsibility for the actual restructuring of groups of selected companies. It would probably have been best if the THA had remained the owner of these regrouped companies, on the same lines as with the Management-KG's, and would thus have retained the last word on all financial decisions. However, in return for taking on part of the financial burdens, the State might have got the right to appoint the managers of the restructuring companies if the THA would have retained the possibility of confirming appointments and periodically checking the financial position. If the expansive process within which the decision would have been made on which firms were to be restructured or not might also have helped to clarify who was good at what, the State then would have been in a very good position to make effective use of its operational responsibility. The Saxon branch of IG Metall, many representatives of the decision-making bodies in the new economic promotion organisations, and their opposite numbers in companies and local authorities all in one way or another favoured a strategy of this general type.

A policy of restrictive adaptation would on the other hand have meant to change the original programme of "more market and politics" into the paradoxical one of "more market by means of the state". Instead of expanding political participation, the State would have limited it for fear of promises being made by one side alone, which the other parties would then have had to out-bid, such as participation is likely to lead to. The role of the experts would then not have consisted in advising the local protagonists on their selection decisions but rather of supporting the State government in its negotiations with the THA. From this point of view, the THA's problem would have been its bureaucratic character which would have prevented it from grasping the opportunities the market offered. The State's aim would therefore have had to consist of bringing up market experts who would have had to underline the opportunities which the state-appointed managers had overlooked. Once this process of elucidation had led to the identification of firms that were suitable for restructuring, the function of the State would have been to monitor the progress of restructuring, making use of the same counsellors. This idea of "buying market" in the form of consultants in order to discipline the state in the form of the THA was preferred by certain high-ranking officials in the Finance and Economics Ministries, who were governed by the worry that anything more than this minimal definition of "more politics" would only encourage those etatist tendencies which they themselves opposed. One could suppose that the *Sächsische Aufbaubank* (the State bank for economic reconstruction) would have added its implicit support because it feared, more than anything else, that it would have to bear the brunt of the consequences of vague gestures of political generosity.

In the end, Saxony took the middle road. It took the restrictive route to the extent that decisions on restructuring were regarded as technical questions which were best left to the experts. Accordingly, little was done at the official level to bring the many networks of local protagonists which had sprung up in connection with the activities on the labour market and consultancy institutions into new units able to make decisions. Taking the expansive route of interpretation, however, assurances were given to the public that the State would do everything necessary to retain the base of the Saxon industrial economy. Thus the State took on responsibility for economic development, without defining it exactly and in such a way that it could share it with the experts or the social actors in various different combinations all according to the situation in each individual case.

This indecision is reflected in the organisation of the ATLAS team which, commissioned by the Saxon Economics Ministry, has since November 1992 the task of preparing and supporting the restructuring of regionally important THA companies in Saxony from the State's point of view. In formal terms, ATLAS is a working staff consisting of a "core team" and free-lance "company officers" linked to the political forces in the State (unions, employers' associations, and political parties) via consultative bodies. *De facto*, this is a new, semi-autonomous organisation which adds one more institution to the wide circle of economic promotion institutions already existing in Saxony. As if this ambivalent structure were not already precarious enough, the ATLAS team has even been appointed on the basis of equal representation for both sides of industry, so that control over the institution is split between the representatives of opposing strategies. One of its full-time directors is an expert for regional development with close links to the trade unions in general and to the leadership of the Saxon branch of IG Metall in particular, whilst the other has a highly sceptical attitude towards the political possibilities of influencing economic developments.

If an institution starts to speak with a divided voice it will have difficulties persuading anyone to listen, and this was indeed the fate awaiting ATLAS. On the other hand it expressed both strategic directions at once, and therefore the representatives of both sides were able to say, and with some justification, that ATLAS was living up to their hopes. Taking the expansive route, for instance, ATLAS co-operated with local bodies in Chemnitz in defining regional restructuring projects, thus laying the foundation stone for a possible restructuring company. Taking the more restrictive route, on the other hand, it took part in re-examining the THA's decisions regarding the selection of companies for restructuring. However, taking all things together, this institution is too severely split internally and too deeply integrated into the Economics Ministry to be able to provide any initial clarification one way or the other on Saxony's strategy towards the THA.

The upshot is a certain degree of confusion on the State government's side, both inwardly and towards the outside world, so it is not very surprising that the decisions previously made by this "middle course" system were just as indecisive as the design of the decision-making process itself.

By concentrating on the easy cases first, the ATLAS team has initially identified out of the total universe of THA companies in Saxony (at the beginning of 1993 there were 566 of them) 179 of them which, in the team's view, were without any doubt of regional significance. The Economics Ministry then handed this list on to the THA. Subsequent privatisations and liquidations have now reduced the number on it to 95, and the State and the THA have now started negotiating seriously on them. In 32 of these remaining cases, clarification will have to be obtained on whether the criteria for their suitability for restructuring are met; in 62, the THA has already confirmed that it categorises them as suitable. Discussions can now concentrate on the restructuring strategies and the contribution needed in advance from the THA and the State for them to be implemented. In five cases, positive decisions were reached until 9th July 1993; in nine others, a decision can be expected shortly. Further sub-groups of Saxon THA companies are to be worked on in tranches if it does not prove possible in the meanwhile to privatise them or wind them up.

The reason why already so much and yet so little has been achieved, with many firms acknowledged to be "regionally significant" and "capable of being restructured" but the financial arrangements definitely agreed between the THA and the State on so few of these projects, seems to us to be that the first of these decisions were affected by the intention, held both by Saxony and by the THA, of initially avoiding taking any clearly defined long-term responsibility onto themselves. Given this state of affairs, however, it is then difficult for the bodies which will in the end have to administer the restructuring finance to calculate the extent of the financial burdens they are letting themselves in for. Understandably enough, the reaction of these bodies is to allow themselves time, even in dealing with the potentially most successful projects, because this is one way of avoiding expensively wrong decisions. As an alternative, it is possible to exert pressure on the other parties which share the responsibility to specify the contributions they are prepared to make. The outcome is a situation in which it is so hard to distinguish progress from paralysis that they can virtually be taken to be two names for the same thing.

In order to discern the cumulative effects of this strategic ambiguity, it is first necessary to look at the precarious definition of the criterion of "suitability for restructuring" which is so important to the THA when it is basically willing to provide the appropriate financial support to the firms proposed by the State, and at the equally nondescript operationalisation of the criterion of "regional importance" which ATLAS uses on the State's behalf in categorising the suggested companies. The THA looks at each company as an individual case and not, as the alternative might be, as parts of any real or potential regional cluster. ATLAS, however, does not make good this gap, because its "criterion" of regional significance is, in our view, a highly bendable mixture of political considerations ("The minister already nominated it once before") and vague quantitative indications ("indispensable in this specific case because of the number of employees"). Consequently it is not possible to derive from it even rough officious rules on the connection between the "regional significance" of a company and any assessment of its possible suitability for restructuring.

However, there is no doubt that the context in general and the regional economic context in particular can make a crucial difference to the assessments that are needed. For instance, it only seems plausible that the Hirschfeld Linen and Textile Company was capable of being restructured if the company was regarded as part of a grouping of companies which could have covered everything from ready-to-wear clothing to retailing and could as one entity have been linked with a project, being supported by public funds under another heading, for reviving flax as a replaceable raw material. A similar example is the Grinding Machine Company in Chemnitz, which would have a better chance of success if looked at, not only as part of the THA's total capacity for such machines, but in its local surroundings, complemented by other machine-tool manufacturers in the Chemnitz region and making use of the available know-how resources in research and training which could make this local grouping attractive as a complete entity.

As the definition of the criterion of suitability for restructuring was left open with regard to the framework of reference to be selected, but the context was apparently allowed to count, the possibility always exists that either side could pass the buck to the other by changing the context. Thus, for instance, the State always had a good chance of turning a THA "No" into "Perhaps".

All the same, even a "Yes" in the sense of general acceptance that a company was suitable for restructuring was never anything more than a conditional "Yes, if", and thus not at all far away from "But then again perhaps No". As the capability of eastern German companies to be restructured starts, generally speaking, with the development of new products, and covers everything from improving production technology and the working organisation through to opening up new markets, and often includes the recruitment of new managers and the setting up of contacts with new customers and suppliers as well, it is extremely difficult to calculate what basic facilities the company is going to need and how long it will need as a minimum to show it can make the grade. Nevertheless, the THA and the State must together calculate the incalculable at least to the extent that both parties involved can perceive the length of time and the quantitative scale of the contributions they themselves must make in advance, and also can be sure that these advance contributions all taken together with those of the other party will produce an internally consistent basis for restructuring. It is already clear that the THA is tending to give a more restrictive and the State a less restrictive answer to this question. This dichotomy has so far mainly come out in differences of opinion over the minimum length of time for the company to show its mettle in the market; the State considers a period of several years to be necessary, and cites individual cases when three to five years seem to be necessary for a company to get started; the THA defines the period as being shorter, more likely 12 months. It was only possible to embrace a difference of this size in the implementation arrangement with a compromise formula: "As a rule, the THA will ... set a period of at least 12 months".

However, these differences of opinion over the relevant length of time are only a symptom of a deeper-seated problem: the difficulties in reaching agreement on the basic facilities a company needs to have to establish itself, and duties the parties involved have to accept to ensure that it does. Here, once again, worries about creating an expensive precedent are leading to deliberate delaying tactics.

Decisions on the financial magnitude and overall time-frame for specific restructuring projects were going to involve an enormous level of uncertainty anyway. They would be easier to handle if there was some system agreed between the parties for evaluating projects. However, there is none, and this once again has its effect on everyone's willingness to make decisions. So far, only one thing has become certain: attempts at restructuring which fail in their aim have to be terminated. The ATLAS agreement places the responsibility for making this decision with the THA, but the State is also given the possibility of examining alternatives and bringing them into the decision-making process. Primary responsibility for the examinations which have to accompany the restructuring process therefore lies with the THA, but with the State authorised to re-examine matters. And this is where we come full circle. Conflicts between the two examining bodies could be reduced to a tolerable minimum if agreement had been reached on the criteria for the examination. But, to make the point once again, this is exactly what was not done when such criteria as "regional significance" and "suitability for restructuring" were kept so vague and unrelated to one another.

Decision-making systems which produce decisions which then cannot be implemented are not likely to survive for long. If, as in this instance seems likely, the problems they are designed to address do not manage to solve themselves, either the barriers which are hindering the solution will be pushed aside or the latent conflicts which are making the solutions more difficult will erupt into open conflicts over the decisions themselves and the whole system that has produced them.

We can therefore imagine two possible lines of development for the ATLAS project. The first would be for the key participants to come with growing cynicism to the conclusion that the whole operation could deteriorate into a sophisticated arrangement for postponing decisions long enough for the spontaneous process of renewal or of decomposition to reduce the restructuring problem so far that the authorities responsible for it to say that they are hardly able to influence the course of events any longer and that the nature of the problem was such that events must be left to take their own course. In this instance, ATLAS would have become the name for a programme of palliatives which maintained social peace (and the existing political balance) until the *deus ex machina* of some future economic upswing takes effect. The other possible line of development would be for the key figures to become so alarmed over the dangers of procrastination that they manage after all to agree quickly on the criteria for the selection, financing, and supervision of a core group of companies the survival of which is assessed as being indispensable. Whether it would be able to work as a secretive group behind closed doors would be just as dubious on account of the public attention which the ATLAS project has drawn on itself and the expectations that have been aroused by this first wave of companies declared to be (perhaps) "suitable for restructuring" as on account of the political ambitions and survival instincts of some of the newer protagonists created by the State government as part of its "new role of the state" notions. However, when times are bad there is perhaps always a tendency to trust those in power; and when leading personalities stand shoulder to shoulder and give vent to their desperation they might just stand a chance of starting all over again.

The point which neither of the two lines of development produces is a route leading from the present confused situation to a stable version of ATLAS which might be a match for the original, earnest intentions which lay behind the origination of the project. In order to be able to understand the reason for this, it will be necessary to examine whether there was a defect in the design of this project; this could come to light if the project is compared with two other experiments in decentralised restructuring, which we will now start to do.

2. The Brandenburg EKO-Stahl project

Like ATLAS, the Brandenburg EKO-Stahl project has the aim of organising co-operation between the State and the THA in the management of major restructuring efforts. In Brandenburg, as in Saxony, an experiment is being conducted at the same time to define a new perspective of the role of the state, although in this case, admittedly, from the SPD point of view as it arises from its close partnership with one of the western German States which is the citadel of the SPD, North-Rhine/Westphalia. Instead of attempting to re-integrate the institutions of economic policy into the private sector of society, Brandenburg is endeavouring to find new ways for co-ordinating public-sector and private-sector interests in questions of economic development. New possibilities are being created for private companies to take part in key projects, and at the same time life is being given to new state organisations to manage this private-sector involvements.[3]

It is easier to understand this attempt at formulating a SPD variant of the new role of the state by bearing in mind how the party and industry learned to modify their view of the relationship between the state and the economy, and thus their relationships with one another, in North-Rhine/Westphalia from the 1960's to the 1980's. Their time-worn self-images became, on both sides, ever more questionable under the pressure of economic developments. The SPD came to feel that the conclusions it had drawn from the chronic problems of the "Montan" industries (the German coal and steel industry) had been confirmed as the right ones, namely that major corporations have severe difficulties in adapting themselves to changing market conditions. At the same time, the SPD also had to admit how unsuccessful attempts can sometimes be to control this process of adapting the business world directly through state holding companies, or of "buying" technological innovation directly through subsidies. These learning processes opened the way to a new approach.

On the side of the major corporations, the experience accumulated during those years had generated a growing level of awareness of the limitations of their own possibilities. Although the difficulties caused by adaptation in the Montan industries could be dismissed as the result of political interference, by the middle of the 1980's even the last remaining devotee of such "Stop-Thief" theories could see that this exculpation was nothing other than an attempt to wrap fog round the central and increasingly urgent problem of rising costs, increasing complexity, and the greater riskiness of technological innovation. In order to develop new products and production processes a choice has to be made between technical possibilities of which the final spectrum of

---

3 The fact that the SPD was governing Brandenburg in a coalition with other parties at this time – one the FDP, which tends to advocate the classic, liberal route of giving help to small and medium-sized companies, the other Alliance 90, which tries to cut a profile of its own in ecological questions – has the result in practice of blurring the contours of the new SPD approach, but does not change its basic substance and does not affect its underlying intentions. We therefore do not need to go into detail on the special characteristics of this coalition.

their uses is still unclear. At the same time, however, the reduction in development times becomes more and more important. For each technological solution there are, in the typical instance, several alternatives; any decision on the further development of a basic component presupposes a judgement as to which total system will be the most attractive, and these comparative judgements of the holistic entity in turn depend on assessment of the efficiency of the component parts. Deciding right at the start on one particular complete constellation is tantamount to playing a lottery with companies. If the whole project is being developed by units within one and the same company, institutional loyalties make it all the more difficult to admit that any one line of development has failed, and even more difficult to push colleagues aside in order to be able to look for an alternative solution in co-operation with competent external development organisations.

The new role of the state which the social democrats are attempting to form arose as an approach to these difficulties without running into the rigidity and "clientele-ism" that is so widespread in the management by state organisations.

The first assumption underlying this policy resulted directly from the analysis of the problem of arriving at decisions relating to basic technology. Because the development of new technologies can be too expensive and too risky even for mammoth companies, firms have to co-operate with one another in order to be able to explore the various versions of this basic technology. The result of this co-operation will then be made available to all involved as "pre-competitive knowledge", whilst specific applications of this knowledge will be marketed by the individual firms.

The second assumption expresses a more sober view of the possibilities really open to state politics. The state can play a conclusive role in this respect, but only by making co-operation between the parties actively involved easier by means of financial and organisational measures. If the state subsidises certain projects, this will reduce costs for all the companies taking part, but each of these companies will have to "buy" its right to involvement by making its own investments. The role falls as it was upon the state to sell options to private investors in the form of a right to participate in the multilateral co-operation. In organisational respect, the state is then serving as a kind of presenter, organising the discussion on potential co-operation between companies in the decision-making process of examining the financial arrangements when a long tradition of competitive relationships would have prevented them from even considering the possibility of complementary interests. To put it more exactly: by setting up a pool of know-how which also includes knowledge of the comparative strengths and weaknesses of the firms involved, the state assists the position of everyone within the companies which wish to co-operate straight across company boundaries. By creating such institutions, the state opens the way to co-operation agreements which breaks through the encircling bonds of the interested parties which had long become accustomed to think in their own company-egocentric way.

This model developed on the basis of a few technology centres and industrial parks in North-Rhine/Westphalia,[4] and it is experience such as this to which a few important people in the THA and the State of Brandenburg referred who had previously worked in North-Rhine/Westphalia.

EKO Stahl AG in Eisenhüttenstadt presented itself as just the ideal candidate for the application of a strategy of this kind when at the end of 1990 the discussion began in earnest on the company's future. The steel industry was still booming, and western steel concerns were in the

4 For more details see: Lütz, *Lokaler Technokorporatismus;* Heinze et al, *Strukturwandel und Strukturpolitik in Nordrhein-Westfalen.*

midst of a process of restructuring, a process which aimed both at a greater level of integration in the main stages of steel production and at a greater level of ability to produce steel to many different specifications and in such tiny quantities and so flexibly that any customer's particular requirements could be met quickly and effectively. The first technological pillar in this process of adaptation was miniature electrical steel furnaces which by using scrap iron could obviate the expensive production of raw steel which used iron ore and coke. This innovation had its effects. When electrical furnaces work with scrap iron, the quality of the steel produced and the ability to produce different kinds of steel depend on precise control of the composition of the scrap. The better the co-operation between the steelworks and its suppliers of scrap, the broader the range of products can be and the greater the reliability with which specifications can be adhered to. The quality and the degree of differentiation of the steel (and thus the profitability of the steelworks) can, however, also be increased in collaboration with the final user. The technological sea-change in the steelworks therefore has to go hand-in-hand with a redefinition of the relationship between the steel producer, its suppliers, and its customers all along the chain of production.

EKO Stahl AG offered comparatively favourable starting points in favour of restructuring, which were in line with the factors mentioned above. The cold-rolling mill in Eisenhüttenstadt was of recent date. The factory also enjoyed the general reputation of being technically competent and reliable to an extent that was unusual for East German factories. It is therefore not surprising that the THA received a number of offers during 1991 from western bidders interested in EKO, the seemingly most attractive being from Krupp Stahl AG; the THA concluded a preliminary agreement with Krupp in February 1992. Krupp submitted a business plan on the basis of developing a new, integrated production technology for the key processes and collaborating on the organisation of new customer-supplier relationships at the two crucial points in the production cycle.

It should be noted that this approach to restructure represented exactly the species of problems to which the SPD's new "role of the state" was directed. In the core production area, the Krupp plan provided for the construction of a mini-steelworks for flat-bar steel products, designed particularly for motor vehicle bodywork and domestic electrical appliances ("white goods"). EKO's old converter-steelworks was to be replaced by new plants using electric-arc technology more suitable for processing larger quantities of scrap in smaller batches. The previous gap in the warm wide strip steel would be made good by the installation of a thin-slab foundry rolling mill representing the latest technology of a compact conversion (and of which there was only one comparable example in the whole world, at Nucor). Moreover, the development of new firms further up and further down the production chain was to be assisted. In the region of the Rivers Oder and Spree, ecological disposal plant were to be set up for the State of Brandenburg and Berlin (car recycling, scrap-metal processing, thermal recycling, demolition operations). Any metal scrap would be processed in the electric steelworks, and was planned to account for 60% of the total volume of scrap. The existing capacities in plant engineering and construction were tried to be broken down into units of a more appropriate size for the market (this was a typical reaction to the high degree of vertical integration of the East German *Kombinate*), particularly in steel structures, mechanical engineering, and the production of building components. Ideas were mooted for the further processing phases such as construction parts, barrel components, electro-sheet metals, and plate bars panels. All these measures would produce a regional network of suppliers and customers for EKO.

The plan offered Krupp considerable advantages. Firstly it would have given the company the possibility of developing a highly integrated and flexible production system without having to take on too much of the risk. Although the details of the financial plan were still in a state of flux right up to the end of the negotiations with Krupp, the THA and the State of Brandenburg would in any case have financed not only the modernisation of the cold-rolling mill, with various different kinds of aid, but also, and principally, the mini-steelworks with its electric steel furnaces and the thin-slab foundry rolling mill. In return for making its technical knowledge available, Krupp would have been enabled to experiment with the possibilities and limitations of one of the most promising, but also one of the most difficult, steel technologies of the 1990's. In view of the experience being gained in more and more quarters that the only really effective laboratory for researching complex product and process technologies is the production line itself, this appeared indeed to offer attractive prospects.

Secondly, Krupp was able to use the State and its various institutions to improve its position in the rapidly changing market for steel products. The company was very well aware that its future, quite apart from all its cost-reduction strategies, depended on its ability to manufacture products with a high added value which had to meet the customer's specification so exactly that they could only be developed in collaboration with the customer himself. For this reason, Krupp was engaged at the time it made its offer for EKO in decentralising its downstream processing divisions in order to improve their ability to react to customer requirements. Involvement in the re-organisation of the downstream processing divisions in Eisenhüttenstadt offered the possibility of observing new developments, identifying potential customers, and developing criteria for success for its own sub-units at other locations. Here again, a substantial proportion of the costs of this improvement would be met from public funds, in the form of subsidies to Krupp's potential partners.

Finally, the State of Brandenburg was looking forward to advantages from the planned arrangement. The involvement of Krupp in this project and the precise plan which the company submitted offered Brandenburg the basis for a plausible regional development programme which would start with the steelworks project but could in principal be easily expanded beyond it.

The structure envisaged for EKO/Eisenhüttenstadt was called the "Oder Bridge Industrial Park" and was to be a network of independent companies locked on with EKO but also co-operating with other firms. The companies should have the quality of technically competent and efficient specialists with areas of specialisation which mutually complemented one another, thus allowing synergies to be exploited and more firms to be drawn in. In order to implement this industrial park plan, the State was willing to make use of its full range of promotional programmes (state programmes, administrative help with rules and regulations, placement of public-sector orders, establishment of a technical training college, and so on), and to use the State's own institutions for economic promotion such as the State investment bank, an agency for technology and innovation, a State development company, a State agency for structure and labour, etc. Other organisations, not owned by the State but promoted by it, were to play a role such as OSW (the Oder-Spree company for industrial location development and economic promotion) and the company for training and productive promotion of labour.

Despite all these potential advantages, Krupp withdrew from the project in November 1992, partly because the take-over of its major competitor Hoesch was imposing such an enormous load on its management (and financial) capacity that any other mammoth projects appeared to be dangerously undisciplined; partly also because other steel concerns had started to complain more and more in public about the "distortion of competition" that would result if Krupp realised its ambitions in Brandenburg; and partly also of course for reasons associated with the general crisis in the industry, which had recently started to take on unexpectedly massive dimensions. As there was little prospect, in view of the bad overall situation in the industry, of finding an alternative investor quickly, but at the same time the prospect of closing down EKO did not appear acceptable on account of its significance for Eisenhüttenstadt and the Oder-Spree region, the THA entrusted the EKO management with the task of drawing up their own restructuring strategy.

This has been submitted, and is mainly based on the Krupp plan. It has been approved by the THA, which is only prepared to finance the modernisation of the cold-rolling mill; decisions have been postponed on financing the electric steel furnaces and the thin-slab foundry rolling plant. However, the future of the project was still uncertain at the time of writing because the European Commission did not consider the EKO modernisation plan compatible with European regulations on coal and steel because of the public subsidies it required and because of the construction of additional capacity in the area of warm wide strip steel.

But the resistance coming from Brussels has taken nothing of the sturdiness out of the EKO restructuring project, which was based both on the Krupp original version and on its modified THA version.[5] It is therefore fair to assume that the THA and the State will be pursuing the project in one form or another. Two forms of continuation appear possible, which can be categorised according to their differing degrees of proximity to the original strategy.

An attempt would at least be conceivable at improving the chances of obtaining approval from Brussels by presenting the project more clearly for what it is: not an investment programme for the EKO company specifically but an experiment in complex technological and regional basic innovation in which learning processes can be organised which go far beyond the confines of the company itself. Since Krupp backed out of the project it is at least easier to place this aspect of the project fully into the limelight, and to this extent Krupp's negative decision is a misfortune which still contains something positive within it. So long as Krupp would have gained possession of the mini-steelworks and the innovative experience it would have generated, without any financial risk, it would always have been easy for Krupp's competitors to accuse it of potential distortion of competition and to mount campaigns against it, not least with the European Community. Even Krupp's potential partners in the project would have been able to voice concern that Krupp would be regarding their efforts as part of an experiment run free of charge for Krupp. At any rate, the possibility could not be ruled out that access to the new technology and to the new co-operation network would have been limited in such a way that it would have undermined exactly this kind of co-operation which would have given the project its special meaning. If, now, the THA company EKO, with the support of the State of Brandenburg, is to develop the technology further and then later invite other companies to participate on a broad, partner-like basis, the need would have been taken better into account to open access for all interested parties to the strategic information obtained. The special character of this project as a contribution to a public economic benefit would be far better expressed in this way. And as the know-how fund thus built up would be relatively easily accessible not only to German but also to other European parties interested in it, Brussels would have all the fewer good arguments for continuing to withhold its approval. If this approach would work in this way, it would in the end even be possible to attain better prices for participation rights, as the experimental group would be arousing more interest from more companies. The fact that a few companies, in

---

5 Even the expert assessment commissioned from Coopers & Lybrand by the European Commission and now submitted gives the plan an extraordinarily positive rating.

Germany and other countries, such as Hoesch Stahlwerke, Voest Alpine, and Tsherepovez have been thinking about these possibilities, and one of them, Riva, has already made a definite offer shows that we are not indulging here in pure speculation. If this development possibility really ends up crowned with success, the structuring of EKO would become the foundation for a major industrial park project which would then match up directly with the North-Rhine/Westphalian model. The experience with Krupp could then be written off as a lesson in the advantages and disadvantages of the restrictive versions of this very model.

As an alternative it is possible to imagine a bundle of further strategies all aiming at restructuring only one part of the steelworks – the cold-rolling mill – in the hope that this would be a pump priming for the further development of other activities related to steel and even of whole industries. Specific proposals have already been tabled by Thyssen and Preussag, who seem to be willing to take on the role of the organiser such as, in a more comprehensive strategy, would have fallen to Krupp and now will probably fall to Riva. Possibly, a strategy of this kind would enable the region to survive at least long enough until Brussels at last gets round to approve the larger steel project. In the best case, it might be possible to tap a hidden vitality which liberates Eisenhüttenstadt from its dependence on steel.

Let us bear one point particularly in mind: in contrast to Saxony, where the main protagonists, the THA and the State, do not have the courage of their own convictions, the EKO-Stahl model is mainly being held up by external circumstances, whilst the THA and the State of Brandenburg continue to profess their faith in their project. In the case of EKO, the external difficulties are resulting in increasing demands being made on the politicians which it is hard for them to meet. Having come to this conclusion, we will direct our gaze in the following section to the third form of experimental restructuring which could bring additional light to bear on the question of the circumstances under which new forms of co-operation between the state and the private sector could lead to a spiral of mutual benefits.

3. The Management-KG project

The THA was initially aiming to privatise as many parts of its portfolio as quickly as possible but without completely ruling out the possibility of restructuring if it appeared to be absolutely necessary. In formal terms, the THA's mandate was to ensure the transfer of the old East German companies into the market economy – a mandate broad enough to permit privatisation and restructuring. Detlev Rohwedder, the first President of the THA, also often said that for many firms the "initial restructuring" had to be started before they could be privatised.

In practice, however, efforts at privatisation nearly always came first before efforts at restructuring. If a specific restructuring plan was urgent in the sense that it provided for measures with which any hypothetical, reasonable investor would have to agree, it always ran into the objection: Why should the THA do something which the new private owner would do later anyway? If the plan was a risky one in that it pursued a plausible restructuring strategy at other people's expense, the objection then admittedly was: Why should the THA do something which the new private owner would later not agree with?

These objections were reinforced by the ambivalent attitude of the THA managers with regard to restructuring. Most of the top THA managers had spent the largest parts of their lives in big German companies, and most of these companies expanded almost throughout the post-war years. Many of these managers therefore knew a great deal about large organisations in general and major German concerns in particular, and were very well acquainted with the question of how to arrange matters when the company became larger. However, like Japanese companies which found out to their enormous cost when they attempted to set up production operations in the USA initially by taking over American firms, rather than setting up a "greenfield" plant, that the restructuring of existing resources is a fundamentally different matter from setting up new resources along the lines of a tried-and-trust model, the western German managers of THA companies had to learn exactly the same lesson. They also learned to develop more sensitivity to exactly this difference. They became gradually more and more inclined to leave matters to sort themselves out if it was possible to defend this as a course of action.

Towards the beginning of autumn 1991, the *de facto* priority of privatisation ahead of restructuring was running into more and more public criticism, particularly from the trade unions. Scepticism was growing within the THA itself as well. Small and medium-sized firms with secure local or regional markets found buyers soon enough; large western firms, mainly western German firms, took over units hived off from the old *Kombinate*. But it became clear that more and more "tough" cases were emerging which could neither be sold nor closed down, and at the same time that the THA in the form in which it had been constructed was not properly prepared for carrying out the radical restructuring needed before these tough cases could be transferred to the market economy.

Management companies of the *Kommanditgesellschaft* form (hence: Management-KG's) were created as one answer to this dilemma. They are designed to be restructuring companies into which firms are brought together which cannot be privatised for the time being and which require major expense to restructure them even though the THA does basically categorise them as being capable of restructuring. The first two Management-KG's were set up by the THA in 1992. Three more joined them in the spring of 1993 and a sixth is under development. The aim is to have a maximum of ten. In total, by June 1993 there were 58 THA companies in the first five Management-KG's, with a total work-force of nearly 25,000. It is envisaged that the Management-KG's will remain in existence for three years, but an extension of their life-time is not ruled out.

Each Management-KG contains an average of 12 companies, each of which will if possible have more than 250 employees. This will enable orders of magnitude to be attained which still make it possible for the managing director at the head of the Management-KG to keep track of everything, whilst at the same time representing an attractive field for a high-calibre manager. The management of the KG's was placed in the hands of experienced managers, some of whom had already been associated with the THA before they took up these positions. The portfolio of each Management-KG is not limited to any one industry, because it was feared that founding single-industry holding companies would lead to big-company (or even *Kombinat*) structures becoming fixed. It was definitely not intended that the Management-KG's should become the kernel of future state holding companies.

From the THA's point of view, the formation of Management-KG's is a step in the direction of "privatising" the THA's own restructuring activities. By organising THA companies into Management-KG's, it is intended that decisions on restructuring them will be brought closer to the ideal of free-market decisions. Freed from the restrictions of the state economy, and more independent of political influences, these Management-KG's should be as free in their actions as any private holding company. Because their order of magnitude is relatively small and their character decentralised, it is expected that their decision-making processes will be more transparent and will involve more personal responsibility, thus in turn leading to decisions being made more quickly and to better effect. By assigning the management of these companies to experienced business people ("someone is putting his own name behind them") and giving them management autonomy, it is hoped that real "entrepreneurial spirit" will be allowed to develop.

If one looks closely, these Management-KG's appear to be less of a solution on the lines of "more market" to the problem of "too much state", and more that they are heading toward the introduction of a new model of organisation which can be used in the public and in the private sector instead of the old one which has long been considered in both sectors to be needing improvement. Let us suppose for a moment that the THA were a very large private-sector concern. The introduction of Management-KG's would then be nearly indistinguishable from a change-over from hierarchical management structures to a form of organisation consisting of business divisions or subsidiary companies, independent in management but interwoven in ownership and organised into holding or sub-holding companies. Such structures have become typical of such well-known firms as IBM Deutschland or Siemens, to mention only two outstanding examples.

In these companies, as in the THA, the aim is to achieve greater flexibility by breaking away from time-worn traditions in which the hierarchically superior levels set targets for the subordinate levels, assign them as specific tasks, and then supervise their achievement. The alternatives consist, in both cases, of delegating as much responsibility as possible for setting and achieving targets to those who have the most direct experience with them, and thus the best knowledge of the consequences their actions will have. If one follows this route, the managers of the operating units set the general goals in consultation with the top management in the sub-holdings, but are then free to meet these goals by whatever route they consider most appropriate; nevertheless, they have to report at intervals to their sub-holding on their performance, just as these in turn, according to a similar cycle of consultations and autonomous action, have to report to the ultimate holding company. A brief glance at the way in which the THA companies are organised into Management-KG's, and also at the ownership arrangements in such firms and the relationship between a Management-KG and the THA on the one hand and the companies in its portfolio on the other, will confirm that the new organisation have everything to do with a new division of authority and responsibility on the road to the reform of management structures and nothing to do with the transfer of publicly-owned companies into private ownership.

To start with the composition of the portfolios: The companies are bundled together "bureaucratically" in just the same way as if company units were being integrated into the holding or sub-holding company of a private-sector concern: one member of the Executive Board is responsible for the selection and organisation of the firms taken from a list of those formally acknowledged to be "capable of restructuring". A manager or a management team is then offered the chance of operating the Management-KG thus created. Each Management-KG works with the companies allocated to it for six months under a management contract. If a company has not been handed back to the THA within this period of time, then it becomes legally subordinate to the Management-KG. A comparable reorganisation of the assets is known as well of the setting-up of holding companies, even when it is seldom recognised in such a formal way as in the case of building up the Management-KG's. An ordinary private firm which purchases assets will never be given the opportunity of X-raying its acquisition for six months before making its mind up. The period of time permitted under normal free-market rules during which a potential purchaser can inspect the company on site is usually measured in days, even for major take-over transactions.

However, even when the composition of a Management-KG's portfolio is finalised, the companies still remain in the possession of the THA as the limited partner in the KG. This represents a variation on the transformation of a department or unit in a large company into the subsidiary of a holding company, with the subsidiary and the holding company being partly or wholly owned by the parent. The fact that the top managers in the Management-KG's are remunerated by a complex bonus system connected both to the criterion of speed of privatisation and to those of the number of jobs secured and level of investment guaranteed does not mean that the managers are "owners" of their companies, just as the widespread use of incentive schemes to reward the performance of top managers in private-sector companies does not imply that they in any way own their businesses.

The way in which the Management-KG co-ordinates with the THA as the owner on the one side and with the firms in its portfolio on the other, finally, is reminiscent of the flow of information within the "flat", flexible organisation form of modern companies. As the Management-KG discovers in the first six months of its existence what it can expect from its portfolio, it negotiates on the adaptation of the balance sheets, its financial obligations, and the standards for its evaluation with the THA, and has to do this quickly, before it has become obvious whether restructuring is a good bet or a waste of time. Discussion on important "technical details" in this way redefine the situation of each company and, in cumulation, of each Management-KG.

When the former East German companies produced their opening Deutschmark balance sheets, it was for instance an obvious move to calculate the value of the assets with reference to the company's past turnover. The capitalisation of the historic profit flow thus brought the company to a nominal value which made its management at that time think it was sitting on a goldmine. However, this calculation ignored the necessity to write down the value of the assets, and therefore to finance this depreciation. The theoretical asset value then turned into an all too real minus value, meaning that debts had to be paid off. By modifying the declared asset value to bring it into line with the modified expectations of future turnover, the amount needed to service the company's debt was reduced and the chances that it would survive were increased – assuming, of course, that the THA was prepared to consent to the expensive process of reducing the value of its holding accordingly. Once the overall framework of expectations has been set up, there is then less to negotiate over and more to be examined jointly, although changes in the general situation will presumably lead, as in any holding company, to a re-opening of the discussion on financial support and the register of expectations.

The relationships between the Management-KG's and "their" companies follow similar lines. Because restructuring does not, as is often the case in western firms, involve simply correcting minor shortcomings in a company organisation which is basically functioning properly, but rebuilding the whole organisation itself, many problems relating to the restructuring process have to tackled at the same time. But this problem of simultaneity cannot be "organised" by the head office of the KG. As in a modern holding company, the KG's therefore have to create the overall conditions in which their companies can carry out the restructuring programme on their own: recruiting managers, obtaining know-how, arranging finance and such special functions as expertise on environmental pollution or working and evaluating company zones. This framework, however, institutionalises the pressure on the companies to restructure themselves. Implementation, and the continual detailed redefinition of the restructuring task, is thus left to the company itself.

One indication that the companies in the Management-KG's really have started to restructure themselves can be seen in the intensive exchange of experience on possible ways of cutting costs by combining purchasing or marketing; some occasional consideration has also been given to combined production projects. Apparently, the synergies thus discovered are credible enough to persuade the THA to deviate from its rule against arranging portfolios to cover individual industries. At least, when the last three Management-KG's were set up, strict adherence to this principle was *de facto* abandoned, and they now look more like the new-style holding companies which are formed in private industry from operating units.

However, if there should be a difference between the Management-KG's and these private-sector holding companies, it might consist of the fact that the former have the possibility open to them of modernising with the help of public funds during a recessionary phase in which private-sector companies' scope for investment is pinched, in the nature of things; this is "acyclical investment", in the jargon we have encountered in Management-KG's.

However, leaving this possible difference aside, it does appear that the THA is in the process of sorting itself out in such a way as to permit the public sector to become a seeding-ground for exactly those specialised but integrated units, which the Brandenburg SPD model of the new role of the state is trying to train up as partners of the state. And this is not all: over and above this characteristic, the different kinds of management structure appear to be converging so as to compel the state, in both situations, to help in the creation of such units. Such structural convergences should now be the central subject of our concluding attempt to learn something from the THA's efforts to break out of its own mould.

III. On the nature of experimental co-operation ideas

The co-operative solutions discussed here to the problem of the development of companies capable of being privatised are still at the experimental stage. Our description makes clear that the results are still open to modification and that it is not yet possible, at the time of writing, to pronounce any final judgement on the general potential or on the individual strengths and weaknesses of the various solutions. In order to take the first steps along the way towards a conclusion, we let our analysis aside in order to gain a broader view of the nature of the problems with which the THA has to cope with in the more difficult privatisation cases. From this vantage point we can give some thought to the conditions which have to be met if success is to be achieved.

Basically, all three approaches involve the THA's learning from co-operation with other protagonists, but without losing control over its own action. If the THA would know as the owner of the old East German factories which ones are going to be capable of restructuring, and how this has to be done, it would be able to act independently. However, this precondition does not exist in the difficult privatisation cases, so co-operation has to be the way for the THA to realise potential other than its own. Experience has now also shown that in "tough" cases the potential usefulness of the resources which the THA companies contain can only be discovered by making practical use of them. Processes of discovering the usefulness of specific resources for defined purposes can be called economic learning. Anyone who now maintains that the THA must restructure the "tough" cases in co-operation with external protagonists in order to be able to privatise them is thus also saying that the specific characteristic of the relationship between the THA and its partners is that of a learning association.

From here it is only a small step to a paradox. The pre-requisite for learning is the autonomy of the learner. If, for instance, a company does not possess sufficient freedom to pursue its own thoughts on those of its development possibilities which it considers to be the best, how can it ever discover which will be its most profitable strategy? Autonomy in economic questions, in turn, presupposes a certain degree of financial independence. But why should a firm make any effort to learn how to survive when its survival is guaranteed and financially secured anyway? This is why attempts at prompting to learn without monitoring are just as fruitless as monitoring without any encouragement to learn. The problem thus consists of developing a system of "supervised autonomy" in which the practical monitoring process does not strangle the ability and inclination to learn.

In this form, the dilemma is familiar and capable of resolution, even if the solution is less familiar than the problem it is supposed to address. Let us take the case of two firms which are trying to develop a new product in co-operation with one another, a product which neither could manufacture on its own. Either of the two companies might be motivated to terminate the interdependency created by their mutual co-operation by changing the relationship in its own favour as soon as it perceives a chance of doing so. This could take the form of plain blackmailing the other partner if the latter appears to be vulnerable. Mutual fear of any such blackmail attempt would inhibit co-operation and torpedo any chance of a successful development. The resolution of any such fatal barriers to co-operation is possible if standards of behaviour are institutionalised which enable either partner to observe (monitor) the actions of the other, and to do this in the form of collecting and distributing the information needed to evaluate and improve the other's behaviour (learning). Thus the key to ensuring co-operative development work would appear to lie in an agreement on the evaluation of the present situation and the aims of any attempt at improvement. Both parties could, at pre-set intervals, draw up a balance sheet of the costs of the services each has rendered to the other, and agree general targets for further improvements in costs and quality and a timetable for the next round of mutual check-ups. These examinations would also enable each of them to evaluate the services performed by the other and to redefine jointly the goals of their co-operation. Efficiency depends crucially on the application of this model.

It should be noted here that the point under discussion is not the limited or unlimited character of certainty. The obligations of one party towards the other are not invalidated by systems which combine learning with monitoring; they remain in force, but the substance of them are regarded as subject to revision, and will in fact be renegotiated periodically. Accordingly, J. Kornai's thought is only half-way correct that capitalism defeated communism because it lays down "hard" budget limits, thus preventing the capitalist owner from ignoring the losses which the market imposes on him, whilst communism is always at a disadvantage because companies always have the possibility of passing their losses on to the state. Indeed, communism failed because losses could be "nationalised". However, many highly innovative and competitive firms survive under capitalism precisely because of the possibility they have of repeatedly renegotiating with their partners on the distribution of costs, but not because there is a regime of fixed areas of responsibility which unambiguously governs the market.

It might now be possible to assume that the ability of such a system of co-operative rules to be institutionalised would be crucially dependent on specific background conditions and thus only feasible in exceptional cases. Mutual confidence, defined as the partners' mutual expectation that neither will exploit the vulnerability to which their co-operation subjects the other, could be one such pre-condition. If the shared culture and history of potential partners enable them to see their interests as being so closely intermeshed with one another that any form of deception would seem quite inconceivable, it must then be possible to arrive at learning through monitoring, as the protagonists can assume that the autonomy necessary for learning will not be misused to evade the rules of monitoring. Arguments of this kind have often been presented in the form of a cultural explanation of co-operation in the Japanese economy.

However, it is precisely the borderline case of privatisation that shows how this point of view shifts the perception of the importance of rules in the regulation of co-operation. It is, namely, important to understand also the potential disadvantages of a close link based on mutual confidence on the one side and the potential advantages of keeping a safe distance on the other. The disadvantage of too much intimacy generally consists of the indifference towards the world outside this intimate group. Two departments within the same company may be so closely intertwined in their relationships with one another that they fail to see the innovations produced by a third party. In the case of privatisation, this intimacy is doubly suspect because those involved, who know one another very well, presumably know a great deal either about parts of the former planned economy or parts of western industry, but none of them know everything about both. Accordingly, precisely these people could have a particular weakness with regard to the task in front of them in trying to combine the knowledge available about these two different worlds. In the worst case, their confidence in one another could turn into a conspiracy aimed at passing the costs of each one's own shortcomings onto other. On the other hand, the advantage of keeping a distance consists of a complementary value which can arise from the combining of a diversity of experience. The hope of achieving this effect is often the guiding force for companies when they decide in favour of developing products together with outside partners to whom they attribute more expert knowledge in a certain specialised field than to their own internal units. In the case of privatisation, diversity and distance are without any doubt indispensable for success; more of the same would be fatal.

Whether the start-point is to be confidence or distance, the problem will still always be that a development is possible. It is coping with this possibility that forms the function of the rules of learning through monitoring. These are meant to ensure that where an intimate relationship arises it is subject to outside observation which will prevent involution and conspiratorial exclusion. However, it should also guarantee that the various partners come under pressure to explore the potential complementary values in their areas of expertise. Looked at this way, the creation of a system of supervised autonomy aims to produce an auditing method which will oblige specific protagonists to create a practicable balance between intimacy and distance, and between homogeneity and diversity, in their mutual relationships, and will restimulate their endeavours if they are not initially successful.

Our three case histories demonstrate the converging function of the rules of learning through monitoring in different, self-contradictory initial situations.

The Management-KG's are closest in nature to the type of co-operation based on mutual confidence. This approach is based on the ability of those responsible for policy in the THA, and of the managers in the Management-KG's, to negotiate in a simple manner with one another, and this ability is in turn based to no small extent in an identical socialisation and co-operation experience in the past. The THA management suspects where the problems of the Management-KG's are hidden; the heads of the Management-KG's in turn think they know what kind of argument will carry weight in the THA. Thus their common backgrounds of experience create exactly the kind of mental synchronisation which is necessary for establishing systems of learning through monitoring. However, it is also exactly this kind of synchronisation which harbours the dangers of self-serving or collective self-deception.

It is the role of the recursive regulation system to avoid these dangers. The THA grants a Management-KG the basic financial resources in accordance with a provisional estimate of the potential of the firms in its portfolio. The Management-KG defines provisional performance standards for these firms. The evaluation of the firms' actual performance – their ability to develop new products, attain western standards of productivity, and set up reliable management information systems – will lead the Management-KG's to renegotiate their agreement with the THA and redefine their relationship with their own firms. The examination of individual firms, managers, strategies, and projects thus goes hand in hand with a re-examination of the firm's potential and of the funds needed to exploit it. Negative decisions are always possible because a large number of firms belongs to each Management-KG, and its managers can therefore permit individual firms to fail without endangering the overall success of their company; if things really do run badly, the willingness to sacrifice one unit in order to salvage the others is an important prerequisite for survival. The same logic also governs the relationship between the THA and the Management-KG's. Even if there is no clearly defined limit to the financial resources any one Management-KG can be given, no company or Management-KG can afford to go quietly off to sleep on the assumption that just its survival is assured. The mental co-ordination, if not to say *esprit de corps,* of those involved which makes the negotiating processes so much easier must not be allowed to deteriorate into over-cosy chumminess.

The Brandenburg EKO model lies closer to the second type of co-operation, typified more by distance. The density of integration in the social sphere within this model is set is less than in the case of the Management-KG's, and it is for this reason that this model's prospects of success depend crucially on whether a way can be found for recruiting potential partners to the project and motivating them to explore their potential complementarities. This is exactly the purpose of the sale of options on participation in technological developments. By acquiring such options, firms with the necessary technical competence demonstrate that they are motivated to enter into the risk with their own investments. If this proves successful, the start-point is created for a co-operation in the course of which durable rules can emerge of the exchange of complementary services. Only those firms that can offer expert knowledge about potential applications will allow themselves to be drawn in to participate. Each participant observe what the others are learning and will be prepared to contribute his own experiences as the price of the opportunity of being involved in the experience which the others are amassing. The periodic renegotiation of options forces those actively involved to make simultaneous assessments of the work produced so far and to evaluate the opportunities currently perceptible. In the original Brandenburg-EKO model, Krupp AG would have taken on the vital role of chairing in this development.

If this first model displayed dangers, these resulted ironically enough from its unadorned bluntness. The model made the implicit rules of the new form of economic co-operation explicit in an astounding way, before these rules could become absorbed as economic conventions. Compared with the standard models of free-market economic behaviour, this model looks like a vague agreement between a preferred investor on the one side and the THA and the State of Brandenburg on the other, although the parties involved had endeavoured to position the form of co-operation they were entering into as "pre-competitive collaboration" in the construction of normal market relationships. The difficulties they had with Brussels, looked at this way, were also a foretaste of the arguments which could arise from further developments of these forms of co-operation.

Exceptions confirm the rule. The ATLAS project, finally, seems to be the least suitable of our three cases of developing into the kind of co-operative learning which we have outlined above, precisely because the way in which general rules of co-operation were drawn up in the ATLAS procedure will divert the participants, in the process of decision-making on specific cases, into negotiation strategies which break down the interplay necessary for learning through monitoring. In order to prevent any precedence from being created which could narrow down later negotiating positions, each side is straining for a strict agreement which will leave little scope for interpretation and for the construction of binding obligations. The hidden ideal of this procedure could almost be described as decisions with no consequences: agreements which can be interpreted as progress in the direction of even more precise agreements but which do not in themselves entail any obligations or burdens. The worst result would then be outline agreements which bind the parties to continue negotiations indefinitely. Looked at this way, the tangible effects attained so far are close to this ideal: companies have been assessed as being worth to be restructured, without the State or the THA being under any obligation to say what financial consequences would result from this.

At this point, even a discussion must come to a halt which has been defined as a tentative one. The various different organisational models which emerged when the THA was beginning to learn how to organise learning display one decisive point in common with the company models which they would have to promote: Their usefulness will become clear through the process of application. The only point which is clear at the moment is that their success will already consist of their clarifying the conditions for success. Whether or not any one or all of them can be implemented so well that they will have any effect in countering the de-industrialisation of many eastern German regions is admittedly far from certain at the moment.

IV. Literature

Sabel, Charles F.: *Learning by Monitoring.* In: Neil *Smelser* and Richard *Swedberg* (editors): *Handbook of Economic Sociology.* Princeton N. J. 1994.
Lütz, Susanne: *Lokaler Technokorporatismus*. Manuscript. Duisburg 1988.
Heinze, Rolf G.: *Strukturwandel und Strukturpolitik in Nordrhein-Westfalen.* Opladen 1992.

The THA and Eastern Europe

by Günter Hedtkamp and Hermann Clement, with the assistance of Ludwig Koehne

I. The changed foreign trade environment in Eastern Europe for companies in the former German Democratic Republic

The decisive factors affecting the activities of companies in eastern Germany and the THA's work were the collapse of COMECON, the breakdown of the Soviet Union, and the incipient transformation process in Eastern Europe. These markets of the companies, by far the largest ones for customers and for suppliers, simply vanished as completely new options opened up for the partner countries and the companies in eastern Germany and processes of structural adaptation of enormous proportions took their course.

1. The collapse of COMECON

Since the beginning of the 1980's, the weakness of COMECON became more and more apparent. Up to 1987, however, its members had not drawn any real consequences to affect COMECON. Although since 1984 a somewhat hectic atmosphere[1] had permeated its organisation and its programmes which reached its climax in a document called "Complex-programme for promoting scientific and technical progress in the COMECON member states up to the Year 2000" and in an attempt at creating a "common market",[2] the organisation did not succeed in making any decisive changes, neither in the fields of organisation nor of economic policy. The COMECON pricing and accounting system led to more and more violent arguments over the exchange rates for barter trade. An improvement in the flow of capital and labour did not become perceptible until the most recent years, and then only to a limited extent, despite the individual countries giving approval to joint ventures.[3]

The 44th Council Session in Prague, in July 1988, was already showing clearly that COMECON was no longer capable of concerted action. The economic policy concepts had by then moved too far apart. With the renunciation by most of the member states of any binding economic planning, the elements of the internal economy which had implemented the bilateral trading regimes within COMECON had lost all effect and a new integration system became essential.

In the traditional manner of COMECON, a Commission was appointed to prepare a new form of organisation, a definition of its tasks, and a new working mechanism. However, it did not prove possible to carry these efforts, which were finally undertaken by the Hungarian Foreign Trade Minister Bela Kadar, through to their conclusion. "In 1989 and early 1990 it became clear

1 See, for instance: van Brabant, *The Demise of the CMEA*, pages 234 et seq.

2 See, for instance: Vincentz, *Produktion und Außenhandel.*

3 See, for instance: van Brabant, *The Demise of the CMEA*, page 242.

that the existing system would have to be abandoned."[4] Once German unification took effect, eastern Germany was no longer a member of COMECON and the remaining states were unable to reach agreement on any new integration mechanism.

2. Re-evaluation of the political significance of COMECON by the Soviet Union

In 1989, the Soviet Union began to re-evaluate the importance of COMECON to its foreign relationships. The strategic redesign of Soviet foreign policy under Gorbachev aimed at a constructive form of co-operation with the west, thus necessarily creating fundamentally new political conditions for relationships within COMECON. Most of its member states were now no longer striving only for reform within the system but for a transformation of the system in the direction of a market economy and integration with the west.

Internationally, this rapprochement to the rules of a market economy was sealed by the Final Act of the Bonn CSCE Economic Conference in April 1990.

3. Economic re-evaluation of trading relationships by the Soviet Union

This process also crucially affected the Soviet Union's security policy situation. The Warsaw Pact had reached the point of disintegration. COMECON thus also lost its significance as the economic basis of the military alliance. Once the Brezhnev doctrine, which claimed hegemony over Eastern Europe, had been abandoned, the integrative economic basis which had been necessary for its system of dominance also became redundant. It was therefore only a rational extension of these radical changes for the Soviet Union to start re-evaluating COMECON altogether. The political privileges of this trade were of no further benefit, and economic criteria took their place. Many Soviet scientists, and politicians as well to an increasing extent, endorsed the ruling opinion in the west that COMECON as it then stood represented a substantial economic burden for the Soviet Union.[5]

This inevitably had an alarming effect on the smaller member states, particularly East Germany. They became aware of their huge structural disadvantages: a bloated heavy-industry sector, excessive consumption of raw materials and energy, in conjunction with heavy dependence on supplies from the Soviet Union, and a spectrum of products of only limited suitability for the world market.

By the mid-1980's at the latest, the Soviet Union, despite joint investment projects, was neither able nor willing to meet the growing demand for raw materials and energy from the COMECON countries. Under these circumstances, the fact became an increasing nuisance to the Soviet Union that the East European states, including East Germany, were increasingly covering their need for hard currency by exporting finished products processed out of cheap Soviet raw materials, particularly "downstream" petroleum products, or even by simply reselling them unprocessed. This should be stopped, but to this end the existing COMECON trading regime would have to be redesigned or even abolished.

---

4 See: Sobell, *East European Economics*, page 41.

5 On this point, see: scientific discussion appended to the publication by Marrese and Vanous, e. g., Marrese and Wittenberg, *Implicit Trade*.

4. The collapse of COMECON and the termination of the accounting system based on "Transfer Rouble"

In view of the substantial economic advantages it expected to attain, the Soviet Union took over the position of Hungary and Poland and, at the 45th Session of the COMECON Council in Sofia, in January 1990, demanded a change-over to current world market prices and accounting in convertible currencies, thus abolishing the inefficient system of setting prices and accounting in "Transfer Roubles".[6] However, this made the whole existing trading system tumbling down like a house of cards. The successive expansion of trade in convertible currency and on the basis of world-market prices which they had hoped for, or the use of various transitional models as favoured by East Germany, were no longer acceptable by the partners.[7] It was the Modrow government in particular which had never reckoned with such radicalism.[8] Limitations which the Soviet Union placed on the supply of energy sources led to considerable tension in the COMECON accounting system and to delivery stoppages from the smaller states.[9] This was the final blow for COMECON. A planned successor organisation,[10] which many observers had ceased taking seriously,[11] came no nearer realisation than did any customs or payment union.[12] Poland, Hungary, and Czechoslovakia stoppages therefore started already in 1990 to change over their trade with the Soviet Union mainly to world-market prices and convertible currencies. Substantial shifts in relative prices in foreign trade, increasing freedom of choice, and excessive demand for western products gave reason to the expectation of huge structural shifts to the disadvantage of previous internal COMECON trade. The simultaneous abolition of state monopoly on foreign trade and the incipient independence and privatisation of companies also set the previous supply and sales channels into turmoil.

5. Changes in investment policy

A major shift in the demand and import structure of the East European countries was already felt in the 1980's. Investment levels fell off rapidly.[13] In the Soviet Union, for instance, net investment including military hardware in 1992 was 63% below its 1985 level and gross investment 40% below.[14]

---

6 See: Clement, *Transferrubel und Hartwährungsverrechnung.*

7 See: Sobell, *East European Economics*, page 42.

8 See: B-interview with Dr Wolfgang Lemke on 3rd March 1993.

9 See: van Brabant, *The Demise of the CMEA*, page 236.

10 See: *Financial Times*, 28th March 1990.

11 See: Sobell, *East European Economics*, pages 40 et seq. On the other side there were writers who saw the necessity of maintaining a successor organisation; e. g. see: Zschiedrich, *RGW*, pages 283 et seq.; van Brabant, *The Demise of the CMEA*.

12 It was not until 1993 that some of the COMECON countries took a step in this direction with the Visegard Convention, but these agreements are more in the nature of a "waiting room" for EC (European Union) membership than a genuine step towards integration. See: Sobell, *East European Economics*, page 42. Accordingly not all the participants regard them entirely positively. See: Csaba, *Economic Consequences*, page 18. Opinions expressed by the Czechs voice similar arguments.

13 See: Csaba, Economic Consequences.

14 See: *PlanEcon Report* nos. 5 and 6, 1993, pages 5 and 11.

In the revised version of its last five-year plan (1986 to 1990), the Soviet Union had still attempted[15] to increase investment again and to channel it primarily towards modernising the engineering industry.[16] However, a radical change already occurred in 1988. Investment was cut again, in favour of consumption, although the special priority given to petroleum and natural gas extraction was maintained.[17] The preference given to consumption became particularly obvious when the Soviet Union attempted to convert a 1989 loan provided by West Germany for the importation of capital goods for the consumer goods industries into pure consumer goods importation. The projects for the armaments industry, which included massive equipments and other supplies from East Germany, also dwindled in importance as *détente* and disarmament gained. East German companies, however, continued to rely for a long time on long-term contracts, although these had been based on an entirely different situation in the Soviet Union. The "enormous demand" from the Soviet Union was never examined to see if it was in fact at all realistic. One continued to believe in a market which would remain with hardly any changes in its demand structure and extremely large, profitable batch sizes. By the end of the 1980's, however, the production profile of East German firms was no longer in line with the effective demand from the former COMECON countries.[18] By then a large part of the market for capital goods from East German firms was already severely threatened or indeed lost.

With the introduction of market-economy rules, budget restrictions became tougher in all these countries' companies, and efforts started on dismantling structures that made no economic sense. A recession in the total economy therefore had to be expected.[19]

6. The collapse of the Soviet Union

The collapse of the Soviet Union and the rapid fall-off in petroleum output,[20] together with the long-term export and currency problems thus caused, led to a rapid decline in potential demand of the USSR. The individual republics and production regions started laying claim to the hard currency from their energy and raw materials exports for themselves, and used more and more of it to import consumer goods. In 1990 the USSR even lost part of its sovereign rights over the republics, and ceased to exist when the Commonwealth of Independent States (CIS) was founded at the end of 1991. The uniform market of the Soviet Union fell to pieces, and economic decline accelerated cumulatively in all its 15 successor states.[21] Their ability to import declined accordingly, particularly in the capital goods field.

---

15 See, for instance: Clement and Schrettl, *Inflationsstau plus Reformdefizit.*

16 See, for instance: Clement, *Umgestaltung*, page 133 et seq.; Vincentz, *Entwicklung der sowjetischen Konsumgüterindustrie.*

17 See, for instance: Vincentz, *Die Bedeutung des Konsums.*

18 See: Zschiedrich, *RGW*, page 290 et seq.

19 See, for instance: Csaba, *Economic Consequences*, page 6 et seq.

20 Contrary to popular assumption, this basic trend had been perceptible in the last years. See: Clement and Vincentz, *Sowjetische Wirtschaftskrise.*

21 See: Clement, *Zerfall und Neuaufbau*; ditto, *Die Neugestaltung.*

7. East Germany's slowness in understanding the changes

The radical changes resulting from the dissolution of COMECON were not fully appreciated at the time in the former GDR, especially neither in the new eastern German States after unification. The problems of maintaining sales levels in Eastern Europe, and in particular in the Soviet Union, were rather seen as a short-term political or economic event and not as a structural change of a radical nature.[22] But also many western economists, industrial managers, and politicians forecast that as soon as the planned economy had been abolished in the Eastern European countries they would immediately head into rapid economic growth and would be able to partake in an increasing level of trade and exchange.[23]

The foreign trade policy of the Modrow as well as the de Maizière governments was also subject to the same miscalculation. In addition to this, the suggestion made at the COMECON conference in Sofia to change its trade over to convertible currencies was not taken seriously enough because of the weakness of the Rouble.[24] Similarly, many of those actively involved in East as well as in West Germany simply could not imagine that the Soviet Union was prepared to abandon its empire, and particularly the sovereignty of the East German republic.[25] Many were still hoping in the early months of 1990 that it would be possible to continue trade with the COMECON at the existing volume, particularly as there were hardly any attractive alternatives.[26] It was completely clear only to a small number of people involved that a large proportion of East German products could be simply pushed out of the market, once exposed to world market conditions and bereft of their political preference.[27] For ten long years, attempts were made with heavy subsidies but no sign of success to raise the level of exports to the west; the failure was due to their inadequate quality.[28] Impressed by the pending introduction of the West German Deutschmark, however, the East German government fell in line, verbally at least, with the situation in COMECON. The Minister for Economic Affairs of the de Maizière government, Mr Pohl, announced on 22nd June 1990, that the intention was "to expand foreign trading relations with the COMECON countries on the basis of free-market principles".[29]

First tentative discussions on exports to the east took place between the West and the East German governments in Berlin in March 1990, and in the Federal Ministry for Economic Affairs in Bonn.[30] Also the government of de Maizière, which took office in April, thought that it would not be possible to replace exports to the east with exports to the west. As it assumed that this would also apply to the other COMECON countries, it favoured a "clearing system" (which would not include the USSR) to sustain solvency between the state-owned enterprises in the

---

22 See: Zschiedrich, *RGW*, page 284.

23 See, for instance: Collins and Rodrik, *Eastern Europe*; Sachs, *Poland and Eastern Europe*; Cohen, *The solvency*.

24 See: B-interview with Wolfram Krause on 2nd March 1993.

25 See: B-interview with Dr Wolfgang Lemke on 3rd March 1993.

26 See: B-interview with Wolfram Krause on 2nd March 1993.

27 According to Krause, considerations such as these were never even voiced. See: B-interview with Wolfram Krause on 2nd March 1993.

28 See: B-interview with Dr Wolfgang Lemke on 3rd March 1993.

29 MW-Informationen, *Die DDR-Industrie auf dem Wege zur sozialen Marktwirtschaft*, page 31.

30 See: B-interview with Axel Gerlach on 2nd May 1993.

smaller COMECON countries. However, these considerations did not fall on fruitful political soil any more in these states.

In the general East European euphoria of 1989 and 1990, East Germany was often regarded as the focal point for trade with Eastern Europe and the Soviet Union.[31] This thesis was still being upheld in 1992 by D. Gros and A. Steinherr.[32] It is probably not entirely wrong in the very long run, but is of not much use in solving the immediate and medium term problems. With the removal of the COMECON accounting system and of the split world market, the East German companies lost their bridgehead function to the eastern markets almost completely. Now that COMECON has fallen completely to pieces, as did the Soviet Union a year later, it was hardly possible any longer to talk of any such location advantages. All that remained were contact advantages and replacement business, and even the latter did not reach the level hoped for because investment levels declined and the balance of payments position worsened. The changes in the Russian and East European demand structures and the reduced volume of imports resulted in huge stockpiles of imported machinery and equipment building up. The situation which Csaba described for Hungary thus applied also to eastern Germany: "Firms were not told that it is not a liquidity problem, but rather a solvency problem (and an outcome from deep structural changes in the economy of the former Soviet Economy, H. C.) which they face on Soviet markets, which has nothing to do with the clumsiness of the bureaucracy in Moscow."[33]

II. Dependency of eastern German businesses on trade with Eastern Europe

These changes hit East German businesses particularly hard. The latest figures available at the time of writing from the Federal Office of Statistics[34] state the proportion of East German foreign trade accounted for by the European COMECON countries as being over two-thirds in 1987. Even in 1991, the figure was still 62%. A selection of THA companies representing one-fifth of the trade with East European countries by eastern German companies reported similar figures for 1992: 62.4% of all exports went to this region.[35] The Soviet Union alone accounted for some 40% of total exports and imports between 1987 and 1991.

---

31 Ms Birgit Breuel, the President of the THA, pointed this out explicitly at a meeting of about 200 representatives of small and medium-sized companies in Düsseldorf in November 1992. "The bridgehead function, which it had been hoped for the eastern German companies towards the East European markets, came to nothing when the markets in the former COMECON countries almost completely collapsed. The durable re-orientation of these companies in eastern Germany, however, has not yet been successfully implemented across the board." See: *Handelsblatt*, 6th/7th November 1992, page 13.

32 See: *Handelsblatt*, 22nd February 1992.

33 Csaba, *Economic Consequences*, page 13.

34 These are based on figures prepared by Department AB of the Federal Ministry for Economic Affairs. They are based in turn, however, on old East German figures and are simply converted into West German Deutschmarks at the relevant rate of exchange; they thus still contain serious structural errors.

35 The regional definition might be different here, as the figures were based on data for THA companies with a slightly different regional definition of East European trade.

Nevertheless, the figures in the statistics at least up to 1990 substantially exaggerate these companies' dependence on markets to the East. The Federal Office of Statistics has not corrected these structural defects yet either.[36] The cause of the exaggerated figures are discrepancies in rates of exchange and the price structure in Transfer Rouble (TR) trade and western trade. "Traditionally, the TR was artificially over-valued to inflate the importance of trade with 'fraternal' states, which was a political expectation."[37] For Hungary, for instance, Csaba estimates that one-third of the statistically stated re-orientation of trade towards the west after 1990 can be attributed to the change in exchange rates alone. The larger the proportion of COMECON trade was in a country, the greater was this statistical over-estimate. Drabeck demonstrated this already in 1988.[38]

This was also recognised in East Germany. Calculations based on product prices showed that the proportion of exports in the state-trading countries was only 53.9% in 1987, and sank to 50.6% in 1989.[39] This is also confirmed by a revaluation of the exchange rates and their standardisation, according to which the COMECON share of exports in 1985 was 40.9%, rising to 43.2% in 1989. The share of the USSR must therefore have been correspondingly lower. The west's share of exports, according to these calculations, was a little bit more than 48% in the second half of the 1980's, whilst the share of western imports rose from 40% to 53.1% and that of the COMECON countries fell from 49.3% to 39.4%.[40] But even these proportions are still very high. In 1987, 1.2 million workers in East Germany still depended for their livelihoods on exports to the state-trading countries.[41]

However, there were also great differences between the individual branches of industry. As a proportion of total exports, particularly high figures of more than 80% were attained by the building industry, vehicle construction, special engineering, and heavy engineering. This was an inevitable result of the particular nature of the relationships involved, because: "A major factor influencing the structure of East German exports was its involvement in the construction of large industrial projects in the USSR, particularly those connected with the securing of raw materials supplies."[42]

If the relationship of eastern trade to total turnover is taken as the more informative basis for employment and development facilities in the companies,[43] it becomes clear that East Germany was not excessively dependent on foreign trade as exports only accounted for 20% of the total production of goods; this figure had even fallen by 2.2 percentage points since 1985.[44] Exports to the state-trading countries, calculated in product prices as a proportion of turnover, was barely

---

36 See footnote 35.

37 Csaba, *Economic Consequences*, page 12.

38 Drabeck, *The East European Response*.

39 See: Wetzker, *Daten und Fakten*, page 265.

40 op. cit., page 277.

41 op. cit., page 265

42 op. cit., pages 281 et seq.

43 An input-output calculation would be even more reliable, but it is not possible to produce this on the basis of the figures available.

44 See: Wetzker, *Daten und Fakten*, page 265.

11%.[45] This figure is broadly in line with the results of the above-mentioned survey of THA companies, which gives a figure of 10.4% as the share accounted for by exports to the east of the total turnover of THA companies. Here, too, a high dependency rate is recorded for some important industry branches. Firms in heavy engineering, for instance, according to this survey, achieved 40% of their turnover in these markets, and relatively high figures were also recorded by companies in the armament industry (29.5%), machine tools (28.1%), and vehicle construction (24.4%). On the other hand there were many industries with a low proportion of their turnover in eastern exports: services (0%), food and drink (0%), electrical engineering (6.6%), and precision engineering/optical instruments/ceramics (7.9%).

Political actors, however, were still working on the exaggerated figures in 1990 and 1991 when making their decisions. The loss of existing markets to the east, after all, had serious consequences for a large number of industries and major companies.[46] The attempt had been made even in GDR days to escape from this position of dependency and to raise western exports instead.[47] The success actually achieved, however, remained at a low level. Even on the COMECON market, ability to export declined and the proportion of mechanical engineering, equipment, and means of transport exports, which in 1988 had represented almost half of total exports and about 70% of COMECON exports, fell away,[48] so that in mechanical engineering products East Germany fell to a ranking below those of Czechoslovakia and Poland.

For the USSR, however, East Germany was the "supplier by appointment" in some important areas (with 50 to 90% of total imports): railway carriages and refrigerated wagons, special equipment for micro-electronics, fisheries vessels, equipment for the petroleum processing industry, polygraphic equipment, and agricultural machinery.[49] As many East German companies were closely integrated into this division of labour, with more than a hundred co-operation agreements, they thought that their positions would be secure in the future. They also profited greatly from the COMECON accounting system,[50] but these agreements had been questioned even before 1990.[51] A real strategy for the dramatic changes in the structure of demand and the

---

45 op. cit., page 265. The main reason for this was that East Germany was relatively little integrated into the world economy. Exports per head of population lay in the range between US$ 700 to 1,500, placing it in the same group as the South European states and far behind such major exporting nations as West Germany, which achieve exports of more than $ 5,000 per head. See: Wetzker, *Daten und Fakten*, page 267.

46 A large number of THA companies were in June 1992 still dependent on the CIS market for a large proportion of their planned turnover, DM 5 billion out of a total of DM 8 billion, or 64%; See: Executive Board submission from Dr Hornef dated 8th July 1992.

47 "The economic relations [with COMECON] ... are for the majority of GDR enterprises an essential precondition for stable [business conditions] and [are] extremely important in terms of employment. Irrespective of the GDR enterprises' current intensive efforts to achieve industrial co-operation with, and the participation of, companies from the Federal Republic of Germany and other OECD countries, eastern trade in many cases will remain an important factor in the future development of these enterprises." Luft, *Economic Relations*, page 135. Note that heavy subsidies were applied in this context.

48 See: Wetzker, *Daten und Fakten*, page 268.

49 See: von Gusinski, *Chancen für Strategische Unternehmenskooperationen*, page 462 et seq.

50 See: Luft, *Economic Relations*, page 137.

51 op. cit., page 137.

accounting methods apparently did not exist in East Germany, however, neither at the government level nor that of the individual firms. There are merely indications that it was intended to counter these developments with financial regulations such as the promotion of "compensation" (barter) business and "clearing systems".[52]

The bonus of confidence which exports were given with the State Treaty on economic, monetary, and social union, and the possibility of concluding contracts in Transfer Roubles until the end of 1990, further postponed the need to adapt. Unlike eastern Germany, countries like Hungary, Poland, and Czechoslovakia were able to continue building up their share of trade with the west substantially without a collapse in the total quantity of trade.[53]

On the other side, after the introduction of the Deutschmark the East German firms drastically reduced their imports from the other East European states, in some cases violating existing contracts. They thus contributed to the reduced solvency of these countries. At the same time, the rate of exchange introduced for the Transfer Rouble of 1.00 = DM 2.34 proved to be highly favourable for exports.[54] This rate had been chosen on the basis of very intensive economic and also political considerations principally because it was thus intended to guarantee the assured exports to the Soviet Union covered by the confidence bonus. The rate was only a secondary consequence of the currency reform. In addition to this an export subsidy programme of DM 2 billion was provided for eastern German companies for the second half of 1990.[55]

The East European customers' payment difficulties which had so often been complained of were thus by no means the sole cause for the rapid collapse of eastern German trade with its eastern neighbours. This can be seen from a comparison of the trends in eastern trade of the other East-Central European countries and of western Germany; both were able to increase their exports to East Europe far more rapidly.[56] This even applies if the assumption is made that part of the trade might merely have been diverted. The crucial factor in this development was that eastern Germany, by changing over to world-market prices invoiced in convertible currency and with relatively high wage-rates,[57] had lost its competitiveness. Mr Kostrzewa, the chairman of the Polish banking association, declared in autumn 1992 that the reason for the lack of orders being received by eastern German companies was not Poland's shortage of hard currency but the poor value-for-money of eastern German goods.[58] When the THA published its opening DM balance sheet, its chief financial officer, Mr Hornef, also confirmed that a large proportion of the production plant fell short of the new requirements and that the level of productivity which it permitted was inadequate.[59] In addition to this, they were still hobbled rightly or wrongly with the negative image of "eastern products" (which were believed to be vastly inferior in quality to "western products").

---

52 On this point, see: Csaba's argumentation for Hungary in *Economic Consequences*, page 17 et seq.

53 See, amongst other sources: *iW-Trends* 20 (1993), volume 1.

54 The substantial undervaluing of the Deutschmark against the Transfer Rouble which this exchange rate represented can be seen approximately from the rate laid down by the GDR for 1989, which was based on DM 1.07 = 1 Transfer Rouble. See: Wetzker, *Daten und Fakten*, page 289.

55 See: B-interview with Axel Gerlach on 2nd May 1993.

56 See: Federal Ministry for Economic Affairs, *Der deutsche Osthandel 1991/92*.

57 See: *iW-Trends* 20 (1993), and 19 (1993) no. 7 of 18th February 1993.

58 See: *Handelsblatt*, 3rd November 1992.

59 See, amongst other sources: *Frankfurter Allgemeine Zeitung*, 16th October 1992.

III. The opening of the East-Central European market to goods and capital

Already in the 1980's, some of the East-Central European states had begun to open their markets to western capital, while East Germany had hesitated to do so. It meant that more and more rights were conceded to the western partners, and that these countries could be drawn more and more into the world-wide strategies of western investors. This trend took on a new quality when the process of transformation started. *Osteuphorie* – euphoria over Eastern Europe – was the order of the day, and first overwhelmed eastern Germany. However, the situation was soon to change radically. Industrial locations in Bohemia (the western part of the Czech republic), Poland, and Hungary started to compete more and more powerfully for investors with those in eastern Germany, and thus with the THA. With far lower wage rates but almost equally high productivity,[60] Poland, the former Czechoslovakia, and Hungary became attractive locations despite major language barriers and their lack of integration into the EC market. Their advantage in labour rates is likely to increase further.[61] A survey of opinion amongst joint ventures in the Czech Republic confirmed this; 80% of those questioned preferred investments in the Czech Republic to those in eastern Germany.[62]

Wage rates in eastern Germany, even while they were only 60% of those in western Germany, were still five times higher than the highest wage-rate country in the rest of Eastern-Central Europe. This makes eastern Germany comparatively unattractive for investment in labour-intensive production facilities. Eastern Germany's infrastructural advantages can largely be matched in those parts of the Czech Republic, Hungary, and Poland that are close to their western frontiers, and the level of education and training of their work-forces, particularly in Bohemia, is also very high.

The downward business cycle reinforced this trend and made the THA's privatisation efforts all the more difficult. Some investors who had initially settled in eastern Germany are now believed to have started moving on to locations further east, although no definite figures are available on the extent of these strategies. In May 1993 the chief executive of the German national association for the wood and plastics processing industries and associated branches of industry spoke of a broadscale relocation process affecting major investments towards the East-Central European states.[63] The sum total of western investment in these countries increased rapidly in 1991 and 1992.[64]

Out of the DM 6 billion of direct investment from the west in the east-central part of Europe in the years 1990 to 1992, 59% went to Hungary, 34% to the Czech Republic, and 5% to Poland. Of the sum total of direct investment from western Germany, the greatest preference was given to the Czech Republic,[65] which makes it the prime competitor to the eastern German production locations.

---

60 See: *Frankfurter Allgemeine Zeitung*, 20th January 1993.

61 See: *Direkt* 19 (1993), no. 16, 25th March 1993.

62 See: Kosta, Strouracova, and Konstantinov, *Deutsche Direktinvestitionen*, page 57.

63 See: *Süddeutsche Zeitung*, 14th May 1993.

64 See: *Volkswirtschaftlicher Dienst*, 2nd February 1993.

65 See: *Handelsblatt*, 3rd November 1992.

Considerations on the merits of production locations based on the prospects of entry into the huge East European market have to be revised; many western managers have made quite false assessments of the potential available here. They are now reconsidering their position.[66]

IV. The reaction of the THA and its companies to the changes occurring in Eastern Europe

1. The THA's tasks with regard to the eastern markets

In order to make the aims and tasks of the THA clear it is necessary to point out that it was given the job of privatising and restructuring its companies. The operational eastern trade activities of the companies were never a direct part of its responsibility. Specific items of business and the servicing of the market was a matter for the companies to look after on their own responsibility. Principally, the THA could only regard dependence on eastern European markets as a positive or negative valuation factor in the process of privatising or restructuring these companies.[67] This is how the THA defined its job at least until spring 1992.[68] It therefore has never developed any economic policy strategy of its own for maintaining eastern markets or for quickly reducing its dependence upon them,[69] and up to spring 1991 it would scarcely have been in any organisational position to do so. In addition to setting up its own internal organisation, the THA's main priority after monetary union was the reorganisation of its companies and the securing of their liquidity.[70] Moreover, developments in the eastern markets at that time, as many observers agreed, were not expected to turn out as dramatic as they later proved to be.[71] However, the fact that these eastern markets, which were vital for the very survival of some of these companies, then collapsed in the early months of 1992 forced the THA to take on a mediator role between its companies and the authorities responsible for making economic policy decisions. Only if the mass collapse of companies as a result of the lack of demand from Eastern Europe could be prevented it would be possible to pursue privatisation on reasonable terms. The simultaneous increase in the emphasis on restructuring activities and programmes pushed the question of the eastern markets sharply into the THA's focus. The eastern market was seen increasingly as the bridge for the western orientation of the companies.

---

66 The argument has been made for the location of commercial vehicle production in the Czech Republic that the collapse of trading relations between the former COMECON countries and their relations with the West have made all plans obsolete. See: *Süddeutsche Zeitung*, 2nd April 1993.

67 Nevertheless, privatisation is often regarded within the THA as a foreign trade restructuring exercise, expressed in the statement: "We are buying markets".

68 See: B-interviews with Dr Wolfgang Vehse on 18th May 1993, Erhard Bredenbreuker on 18th May 1993, and Dr Volker Charbonnier on 8th June 1993.

69 See: B-interviews with Rainer Maria Gohlke on 26th March 1993 and with Dr Wolfgang Vehse on 18th May 1993. If any such strategy had been developed, it was never implemented as an active policy. See also: B-interview with Dr Volker Charbonnier on 8th June 1993.

70 See: B-interview with Dr Franz Sack on 9th February 1993.

71 See: B-interview with Dr Volker Charbonnier on 8th June 1993.

However, the THA had technically supported the companies in their work on the eastern markets, both in the administrative handling of transactions and in financing them, handling each individual decision as a separate business matter. The setting up of a Directorate for exports to Eastern Europe, and allocating responsibility for East Europe to an Executive Board member, was not discussed before the first half of 1992 and, although the plan had the blessing of the Federal Ministry for Economic Affairs,[72] it was never put into effect. The THA was represented in an advisory capacity on the Inter-Ministerial Committee. When it was called upon to collaborate on the preparation of a Cabinet document on the problems of eastern trade, a working group was set up under the heading of eastern exports which also worked on more broadly based ideas for developing eastern markets and deriving strategies therefrom. However, these were never put into effect as policy because the THA never regarded itself as a policy-making body.[73] It was not until the end of 1992 that the THA modified its definition of its job and appointed a Special Officer for Eastern Europe.[74]

The THA pursues a double strategy in order to implement its goals of creating favourable conditions for privatisation or restructuring. Towards the government it strives to obtain plenty of financial support for exports to the East but without taking too much of a load onto its balance sheet. The instrument of "Hermes" (the government-owned export loan and credit guarantee insurance company) commended itself.[75] For at least some of the time it exerted influence on its companies to reduce their dependence on eastern markets as quickly as possible. However, this practically only happened in connection with the evaluation of corporate strategies, meaning once again that it took the purely business point of view, although the sanctions with which it backed up its influence were relatively small.[76]

2. The principal players and their knowledge of the situation

Up to 1991, eastern exports were regarded by the THA companies and their managers as being more on the assets than the liabilities side.[77] The consultants[78] commissioned by the THA were just as unaware of the explosive nature of the collapse of exports to Eastern Europe as were most of the leading figures in the THA itself, although some were beginning to perceive the risks; the financial departments were the first to draw attention to them. The Executive Board therefore began deliberating on the need to create a promotional instrument in order to maintain eastern exports at the highest possible level. However, the economic links and co-operation relationships which had grown up over the years were still in this phase regarded as a "market-

---

72 See: B-interviews with Fritz Hohmann on 30th April and 2nd May 1993.

73 See: B-interview with Dr Volker Charbonnier on 8th June 1993.

74 The position was filled by Hans-Georg Pohl, the former chairman of the executive board of Shell AG.

75 See: B-interviews with Fritz Hohmann on 30th April and 2nd May 1993 and with Dr Wolfgang Vehse on 18th May 1993.

76 See: B-interview with Erhard Bredenbreuker on 18th May 1993.

77 See: B-interviews with Rainer Maria Gohlke on 26th March 1993 and with Dr Volker Charbonnier on 8th June 1993.

78 In the first organigrams drawn up by consultancy firms, eastern trade was not even mentioned.

79 See: B-interview with Wolfram Krause on 2nd March 1993.

ing plus".[79] Once the special Hermes terms had been introduced in 1991, the THA assumed that in the medium term exports to the Soviet Union were as good as certain. Even with hindsight, few people considered that the collapse of the eastern markets could have been foreseen.[80]

The person of the THA who was responsible for eastern trade was Wolfram Krause, a member of the Executive Board who was in charge for financial affairs. He was the best informed on the complex links between the East German economy and the East European states, and therefore the most important person reporting on eastern export questions.[81] The financial division had already had to deal with eastern trade problems when monetary union came into effect, because the change-over from Transfer Roubles to convertible currencies was causing some companies to run up losses.

It was Krause's job to define the basic problem behind the situation in eastern trade and to influence the creation of possible cover with Hermes credit.[82] He always assumed that dependence on eastern markets would continue to be very high, and critically appraised the companies' competitiveness on eastern markets and the solvency of eastern customers, particularly the Soviet Union.[83] In October 1990 he was of the opinion that also in 1991 many companies would not be able to produce and export at prices which would cover their costs.

However, he apparently did not recognise the completely different situation in the Soviet Union, its interest in doing away with the disadvantages it had been suffering from COMECON trade, its new options, its rapidly sinking rate of investment, its high priority for food and other consumer products, ist strongly weakended economy, and its declining hard-currency revenue. Like many other observers, he assumed that the Soviet Union's interest would be in drawing further supplies from eastern German factories, bearing in mind the trend to long-term specialisation. Of the 150 companies which had been named in the appendix to the Executive Board submission of October 1990, in whose deliveries the Soviet Union allegedly had an unreserved interest, only a few still appear on the Russian priority list of 1992 which was reduced by the limits imposed on Hermes credit. This shows that the Russian priorities then changed rapidly officially as well.

A further important source of information on eastern trade was the corporate strategies of the THA companies, although their quality was highly dubious and the THA probably looked at them askance.[84] The Management Committee, however, which had the job of scrutinising corpo-

---

80 See: Birgit Breuel in a television discussion with Angela Merkel in February 1993, and documents from the Finance Department; also, Ms Breuel's opening address on the occasion of a businessmen's congress from 2nd to 5th December 1992 in Leipzig: "Eastern trade was intended to ensure that the basic production capacity of eastern German companies was fully utilised until they had established a foothold in the west." Later: "After the collapse of the eastern markets, we in the THA found ourselves face to face with this problem" of finding customer markets. See: *Hamburger Abendblatt*, 4th January 1993.

81 B-interview with Peter Bachsleitner on 7th March 1993: "Krause was the only person in the first Executive Board meetings (in 1990) who knew these companies and knew what on earth was going on there."

82 See: B-interview with Peter Bachsleitner on 7th March 1993.

83 Submission to the Executive Board of 22nd October 1990.

84 See: B-interviews with Dr Wolfgang Vehse on 18th May 1993, and Erhard Bredenbreuker on the same date.

rate strategies, evaluated eastern exports basically in terms of their financial backing from the Federal Government. One reason for this was that they were evaluated for conformity with preset targets exclusively in relation to the individual company. Before the special Hermes conditions came into effect, the Management Committee's scrutiny reports nearly always gave eastern exports a low rating, and the future of companies dependent on them was categorised correspondingly. After this point in time, the share of business labelled "SU" was more or less accepted.[85] Even the Management Committee seems to have regarded the cause of the collapse in export business more as a financing problem than as the result of structural changes on the demand side, as its April 1992 report states that "'good' companies have been able to defend their previous core markets".[86] Broken down by sales regions, companies with a high proportion of their sales in eastern markets and eastern Germany were categorised as being capable of restructuring. Sceptical voices only started to be heard when the DM 5 billion limit was set up when greater demands were made on the securing of these sales. Once the policy of judging each case separately had been brought in, CIS exports, with few exceptions, were no longer considered in corporate strategies.[87]

The THA Industry Directorates introduced at the beginning of 1991 were only peripherally concerned with eastern markets, and they were only able to acquire exact knowledge of their companies by about the middle of 1991. The proper reporting system in the form of a plan/actual comparison of eastern export figures did not start functioning until the fourth quarter of 1991. The arguments produced by directors and executive boards, according to which demand in the Soviet Union/CIS for precisely their products resulted from their particularly good contacts, the large quantities they had always delivered in the past, and the "ineluctable" import demand of the Soviet Union, were only rarely opposed even when they were urged to cut back the proportion of eastern market business in their sales plans. After the DM 5 billion limit had been introduced in 1992, the THA Executive Board and the directors in the working group took a greater hand on eastern exports to obtain Hermes cover for their firms' orders and possible alternative financing strategies.

The THA Economics Department, which was brought in during November 1991 when the THA was endeavouring to obtain a prolongation of the special Hermes conditions for USSR trade, was still placing a very high value on the significance of this trade, particularly on account of the specialisation agreements. The number of jobs at risk, however, was only assumed to be about 150,000,[88] which shows that this department was likewise only looking at the financing question and not at the structural changes which had started to take place and the massive devaluation of the specialisation agreements. This was why Hermes guarantees were regarded as an indispensable bridging aid; in the medium term, good sales opportunities were perceived to exist

---

85 Of a sample of 20 such scrutiny reports taken from this period in time on companies with a high proportion of eastern exports in their turnover, 14 recommendations contained no changes made by the Management Committee. Some of the figures were reduced in the reports on three of these companies.

86 "Re-examination of companies with a large liquidity requirement" by the Management Committee, page 26.

87 Result of the examination of Management Committee scrutiny reports and corporate strategies.

88 28th November 1991, Dr von Gusinski, Economics Department.

in Eastern Europe, Hermes cover was supposed to be less of a distortion of competition than a liquidity credit, and exports were regarded to counter the collapse of the USSR. The Executive Board endorsed this line of argument.[89]

3. Interplay between the THA and the Federal Government

As the THA regarded its job primarily as being the privatisation of its companies, its main expectations of the political world was the maintenance of favourable conditions for eastern exports and the solution of actual problems relating to eastern trade policy. At the same time, it regarded a powerful turning of its companies to the West as being urgently necessary.[90]

But not even the Federal Government was free in shaping its policy. The Soviet Union had only agreed to German re-unification on condition that it did not suffer any economic disadvantage thereby, meaning that the exports from eastern and western Germany would have to remain within their previous levels.[91] The eastern German politicians likewise tended to see the high proportion of eastern European business as a major plus which eastern Germany was contributing to re-unification.

It is possible to distinguish between five operative phases in the collaboration between the THA and the economic policy of the Federal Government.

In the first phase, directly after the introduction of the Deutschmark, the spotlight was on levelling out currency losses resulting from the new Transfer Rouble exchange rate.[92] DM 2 billion was therefore set aside in the budget for a currency compensation fund.[93] As the volume of applications rose to over DM 5 billion, a gap appeared in the financial plan. In this situation the THA managed to negotiate with the Federal Government an increase in the compensation amount, which was handled entirely via the THA in the case of five major suppliers, in the fields of railway rolling stock, ship-building, and vehicle construction, making a total volume of about DM 1.5 billion. 60% of the losses from the remaining companies were covered by the Federal Ministry for Economic Affairs via the compensation fund, and 40% by liquidity loans guaranteed by the THA for cases where it could be demonstrated that goods actually had been delivered.

---

89 See: B-interview with Wolfram Krause on 2nd March 1993.

90 See: B-interview with Dr Wolfgang Vehse on 18th May 1993.

91 See: B-interview with Axel Gerlach on 2nd May 1993.

92 The attempt was made to set the exchange rate at such a level that imports from the Soviet Union would not have to be subsidised and the promised exports could be guaranteed. It was then a secondary matter to arrive at the rate of 1.00 Transfer Roubles = DM 2.34 corresponding to 2:1 (the rate at which East German Marks were exchanged for Deutschmarks). See: B-interview with Axel Gerlach on 2nd May 1993.

93 The basis of this quasi-subsidy for exports was Article 29 of the Treaty of Unification, which postulated the confidence bonus for the long-established foreign trade relationships between the old East Germany and, in particular, COMECON countries.

In view of the difficulties in auditing compensation payments for Transfer Rouble transactions,[94] the THA backed the liquidity of its companies in December 1990 by providing intermediate finance.

However, it has turned out that the exchange rate set between the Transfer Rouble and the Deutschmark tended to represent a form of export promotion, and a compensation payment would not have had to be granted to the THA to this extent.[95]

In the second phase, the policy of the THA aimed primarily at creating a properly functioning financing instrument to back eastern exports. A number of models came up for discussion. One notion was to provide guarantees for 1991 to the companies which were most heavily dependent on eastern exports, loans with a limited repayment holiday, and a limited amount of export support. The Federal Ministry for Economic Affairs favoured the traditional form of export promotion, via the Hermes facilities, which was not subject to any international criticism, as the THA felt too much was being asked of it with a direct settlement of losses in each individual case[96] and the Federal Ministry of Finance tended to be hesitant while EC reactions had not been studied in full and the first negative signals had already been received. The Soviet Union's serious balance of payment problems, which would not have justified the use of Hermes facilities, were generally not yet regarded as existing. This procedure also suited the THA's interest in showing the smallest possible losses on its balance sheet, and that of the Federal Ministry of Finance in not having to provide the funds immediately.

The concept of special Hermes terms for trade with the Soviet Union, but not for the whole of eastern trade, was published on 6th December 1990. These special terms included waiving advance and interim instalment payments, a lengthened loan term, and a prolongation of the capital repayment "holiday" to three years. The THA collaborated particularly in formulating the outline agreement between the AKA Export Credit Company (which has a similar function to that of Hermes) and the Vnešekonombank. Limiting this agreement to the Soviet Union was definitely a mistake in view of the employment situation in eastern Germany, and can only be explained in terms of the particular contractual situation. Possible export opportunities in central European countries were not fully explored. One precondition for the granting of a Hermes guarantee was the "restructuring (suit)ability" of the company concerned, which had to be confirmed by the THA. However, there was no strict re-examination or audit to show that this criterion was met. All that was necessary to obtain Hermes cover was the ability of a company to document that it could fulfil the particular order in question. Virtually every application was thereforegiven this rating. In March 1991 it was assumed that contracts almost ready for signature would total DM 9 to 12 billion,[97] but by July 1991 the applications received already totalled DM 26.5 billion. The special terms agreed upon led to an export volume of DM 9 billion to the Soviet Union.

The third phase was mainly characterised by a high level of uncertainty. The putsch in Moscow in August 1991, and the Soviet Union's rapidly declining ability (and willingness) to pay its bills, were endangering the application of Hermes facilities. The general level of anxiety,

94 Ordinance of 16th October 1990. Payments were made without auditing up to 3rd October.

95 See: B-interview with Axel Gerlach on 2nd May 1993.

96 See: B-interviews with Axel Gerlach on 2nd May 1993 and with Fritz Hohmann on 30th April and 2nd May 1993.

97 Executive Board submission by Wolfram Krause dated 5th March 1991.

inflation, and confusion over lines of authority and responsibility in the Soviet Union also led to the delay or cancellation of a number of major projects.[98] At the same time, the Federal Government felt it had been swamped by the flood of applications, and that it was therefore compelled to act more cautiously. On 18th October 1991 it therefore laid down restrictive measures[99] which, as could be seen, would have a negative effect on employment, even if no exact figure was put on this.

The THA then attempted to prevent the special conditions from expiring in November and December 1991 without being replaced by anything else. The THA Executive Board argued in favour of a special promotional fund of DM 10 billion.[100] It was principally Mr Krause who emphasised that it would not be possible to carry out the privatisation and restructuring programmes and at the same time ensure political stability without measures to promote eastern exports. The re-orientation to other markets, he argued, would take too much time, and he suggested to undertake joint infrastructural projects with the Soviet Union.[101] The Federal Government, however, was only willing to decide on the limited cover policy practised in the fourth phase.[102] The Soviet Union had indicated that it would not accept the idea of a raw materials fund for financing measures of this kind. It was not borne in mind that a large proportion of the former level of exports had disappeared not because of any lack of financing facilities but because of structural changes.

A "brainstorming" meeting was held on 24th January 1992 with the top management of selected manufacturing and trade companies, and representatives of the Federal Ministries of Finance and for Economic Affairs, under the chairmanship of Ms Birgit Breuel, in which working groups were formed to investigate the possible financial arrangements for eastern trade.[103] The proposals which were made centred on project financing and barter and compensation transactions. This shows that it was financing and not the very real changes in eastern trade that were still regarded as the crucial aspects. However, the first signs did appear that greater efforts should be made to change the regional export structure.[104]

---

98 One major case, for instance, was the decision to delay concluding negotiations on the export of ships from Deutsche Maschinen- und Schiffbau AG on 27th August 1991.

99 All decisions were cancelled which the Inter-Ministerial Committee had taken on 9th October 1991 on granting cover for Soviet Union trade, and all applications had to be resubmitted. Those then decided positively on 23rd October 1991 were subjected to a moratorium until new decision criteria were available. All transactions of DM 30 million and more were to be thoroughly scrutinised. One criteria for western Germany was that transactions would improve the USSR's ability to export, and for eastern Germany the "economic significance of the export business for the company" and its effects on the labour market were to be looked at. The individual republics within the Soviet Union were to be asked to bear some of the legal liability.

100 See: B-interview with Wolfram Krause on 2nd March 1993.

101 For instance, in the fields of communication, energy management, petroleum, natural gas, coal, and agricultural technology.

102 See: submission to the Chancellor's Meeting on 11th December 1992.

103 The working groups set up were for: barter transactions, know-how transfer, joint ventures, and the promotion of sales activities.

104 See: B-interview with Wolfram Krause on 2nd March 1993.

Two days earlier, a cabinet meeting on 22nd January 1992 had made decisions which ushered in a fourth phase. Hermes cover was to be prolonged, but capped at DM 5 billion. Under this cap, contracts concluded up to the end of 1991 could still be fulfilled under the special terms if the contract covering the credit arrangements had been signed before 30th September 1992.

The imposition was now placed on the THA, however, to examine the companies' suitability for restructuring more minutely.[105] The responsibility for this was placed on the directors of the THA and on the Inter-Ministerial Committee. As no agreement could be reached on the legal nature of the guarantees to be granted from the Russian side, Hermes cover was delayed considerably. It was not until 11th June 1992 that the necessary agreement could be concluded with the Russian government.

It proved impossible to handle the exports under the DM 5 billion limit with any alacrity. The Russian side kept insisting on changes to the list of supply contracts and the cancellation of a number of projects. The Russians explained to the German delegation which was to negotiate the application of the "capped" sum that their preconditions and priorities had changed totally.[106] Although the goods provided for in the supply contracts between eastern German and Russian companies were desirable, they said, it was not possible to pay for them. All import contracts would therefore have to be re-examined, with priority being given and central resources devoted primarily to the importation of goods which could avert the imminent supply and production crisis. This included food and medicines, including in both cases the raw materials for producing them, raw and auxiliary materials for industrial production, machinery, equipment, and spare parts for agricultural machinery, certain kinds of freight and fishing vessels, the primary energy sector, and certain kinds of railway rolling stock. All other imports would have to be financed in Roubles at the open market rate of exchange. In view of the stockpile of capital goods that had been imported but not used, and which now represented a total value of DM 4 to 6 billion, and the rapidly falling rate of utilisation of industrial capacity, the Russian view was that no great import effect could be expected. The German Government, however, was not willing, on account of the lack of impact these deliveries would have had on employment, to accept the Russian demands. It regarded the business basis on which the Hermes cap had been negotiated as having disappeared. With regard to any revision of the contracts, the German stand-point was that they had been concluded between two independent legal entities and could not be changed or cancelled by any intervention from the state.

The Russian side confirmed its position once again, in the form of a second list of priorities. Traditional exports from eastern Germany like technical equipment, production lines, and products from the machine tool, heavy engineering, and chemical engineering fields which were favoured by the German side because of their employment effects were hardly included in this list.[107]

105 See Section 5 page 523.

106 This becomes particularly clear if the Russian priorities are compared with the Hermes applications in March 1992. See: THA Financial Division report of 18th March 1992.

107 See: memorandum from the THA Financial Division of 21st August 1992.

The funds made available were therefore drawn on only very slowly, and this had much less than the hoped-for effect on production in eastern Germany. The facility of DM 5 billion, initially seen as being far too small (after DM 10 billion in 1991, although contracts had been signed totalling DM 80 billion),[108] had been used by September 1992 only to 50 %.[109] Another factor which played an important role here was that the Russians failed to produce the letters of credit which had become due by then.

The critical situation which thus began to emerge apparently led to different assessments by the Federal Government and by the THA. The only area of agreement was the primary one: "The aim is to give the companies in eastern Germany more time and more opportunities to re-orientate their products towards western markets and to mobilise additional orders".[110] Even before the end of June, the chairman of the THA working group on eastern exports, Volker Charbonnier, emphasised the "bridging" function of eastern trade for gaining a larger share of world markets for nearly all machine-tool companies, and that this was a prerequisite for privatisation.[111] And one of the aspects described in an Executive Board submission of August 1992 as being indispensable to survival was "additional support, over and above the level of Hermes cover, for their exports to the CIS markets and central/ eastern Europe".[112] Looked at from the point of view of the THA and the job it had to do, and of the interests of companies in eastern Germany, these were logical considerations and they dominated also the "Emergency strategy for exports to Russia" drafted under the guidance of Charbonnier. It continued to be temporary and still believed in exports to Russia under tight requirements. However, it went far beyond the confines of Hermes cover by including a massive programme of promotion for trade with the CIS.[113] Thus, for instance, deliveries were planned that would be accounted for in Roubles and special regulations would apply to investment in Russia. Hopes that joint ventures and barter

108 By way of comparison: Total Russian imports in 1992 amounted to about DM 67 billion; see: *Vnešnjaja torgovlja* No. 2, 1992, page 44. Total imports fell by 5% compared with 1991.

109 Letter from Dr Charbonnier to Dr Hornef dated 7th September 1992.

110 Minutes on the conducting of a survey of eastern German companies dated 4th August 1992.

111 See: Letter from Dr Charbonnier to Wolfram Krause dated 11th June 1992.

112 Executive Board submission by Hero Brahms and Dr Charbonnier dated 10th August 1992. In addition to this, an early submission (by Dr Hornef, dated 8th July 1992) had already insisted that all companies with a particularly heavy dependence on CIS business should be checked to see "to what extent the fall-off or complete disappearance of eastern business would affect their prospects for being restructured and privatised".

113 1- Over and above the Hermes limit, Russia would be sold products from Priority List 1 (food, medicines: DM 3.6 billion) if eastern German companies could supply them; 2- Goods from List 2 (capital goods which the Russian government was prepared to subsidise: DM 4.3 billion) and List 3 (capital goods without subsidies) would be supplied by eastern German companies until the DM 5 billion limit was reached; 3- Products from List 2 exceeding the limit could be supplied at once in return for Roubles provided (a) the Rouble payments were in line with the current DM-Rouble exchange rate under the terms of payment, (c) Rouble balances (plus or minus) would bear interest and would be indexed to Russian inflation, (e) Roubles received by Russia would be used for the development of Russian infrastructure projects; 11- A Hermes facility would be opened for barter deals as well. See: Appendix to Executive Board submission dated 24th August 1992.

could be built up without additional financial help had proved to be illusory, at least with regard to the extent envisaged.[114] Besides this, however, the THA did start making hesitant moves in the direction of a rationalisation and modernisation concept for the world market. But the Federal Government turned down the idea of establishing a restructuring fund.[115]

The emergency strategy presented on 3rd September 1992, however, was not capable of convincing the representatives of the Federal Ministries of Finance and for Economic Affairs. The status report presented at the same time on eastern export dependency, which was meant to serve the purpose of selecting companies deserving extra assistance, inspired little confidence and also showed that only about half of the companies were booking a fall-off in eastern export shares. The fact that eastern trade in its previous form had no future[116] any more seems to have been broadly visible to the THA and to its companies, too. The logical conclusion, that all attempts should be abandoned at maintaining the production of goods for which there were no more customers and keep eastern exports as cheap as possible,[117] however, was not accepted. It was assumed that the almost total collapse of eastern trade within a period of only two years could not nearly be compensated for by exports to the west which was suffering a recession, too. It seems to make more sense to "bridge the gap" until markets could be resuscitated by prolonging subsidies for eastern exports for a certain time than the alternative of financing heavy losses and enormous levels of unemployment. The conditions under which this strategy could have worked would have been to believe in a resuscitation of the market for the products made in eastern Germany also in the East, and in the companies really being restructured under these subsidised conditions. Similar arguments, such as the THA used, were also forwarded by the representatives of many other interests such as the collective-bargaining experts in the chemical industry trade union IG Chemie,[118] the Economics working Group in the SPD parliamentary party[119] in Bonn, and some industrial associations.

The representatives of the ministries regarded the situation from a different point of view. Their assumption that the eastern German companies would hardly be able to adapt structurally even with a great amount of subsidy cannot be lightly dismissed. They believed that they could identify failures to take the appropriate prompt action in this connection during the preceding eighteen months.[120] They were unable to recognise any "bridging" function in eastern trade in the manner in which the THA laid claim to it, and preferred the necessary restructuring. Although the ministries' fears regarding delays in the process of adaptation were broadly accepted, the THA was forecasting the danger that "the whole core area of eastern German industry" would have to be liquidated if this export aid was refused and if purely business criteria continued to be applied.[121]

---

114 See: B-interview with Wolfram Krause on 2nd March 1993.

115 op. cit.

116 See: Otto Wolf von Amerongen as quoted in *Süddeutsche Zeitung*, 9th October 1992.

117 See: Helmut Schmidt, as quoted in *Handelsblatt*, 6th October 1992.

118 See: *Handelsblatt*, 25th January 1993.

119 See: *Süddeutsche Zeitung*, 13th January 1993.

120 Remark made on 24th August 1992 by Mr Hohmann, a senior ministry official regarding the sales problems.

121 B-interview with Dr Volker Charbonnier on 8th June 1993.

The cabinet paper drawn up and accepted on 23rd September 1992 focused primarily on the positions of the ministries to restructuring and adjusting the companies to face the western markets and on accelerated privatisation. The specific measures proposed, however, kept within very narrow confines. The special conditions for deliveries under contracts made in 1991 were extended to 31st March 1993. Decisions on which further exports were to be promoted were to be made on a stricter criterion and a case-by-case basis.[122] Also counter-party trade and project financial arrangements were from now on to be included in Hermes cover on terms which had yet to be worked out in detail, and this proved very difficult in practice. Measures were agreed and aid allocated to assist eastern German companies in orientating themselves towards western markets which even included development aid. Measures were also decided on for giving more consideration to eastern German companies in the placement of public-sector orders. Thus the fifth phase (case-by-case decisions) came to be ushered in.

According to the THA's point of view, however, these measures failed in a number of crucial points to meet the emergency and the premises on which the cabinet paper was based. The THA's view was that the analysis of the situation and the problem was somewhat divorced from real life with regard to the pace of restructuring, that the worldwide recession for key industries had not sufficiently taken into account, and that the THA companies' efforts at restructuring had been assessed too negatively. The THA's proposals regarding Rouble transactions, it felt, had not been taken into account at all. However, no protest was submitted to the Minister of Finance.[123]

This was nevertheless the phase in which the THA went over to active, global support for the regional restructuring of its companies' exports.

4. The THA companies' plans and ideas relating to developments in eastern markets

In 1990 the THA companies saw a bright future for themselves in eastern markets, mainly because of the confidence bonus provided for in the Treaty of Unification. This optimism was also expressed in the flood of applications for Hermes cover. By the end of 1991, the Hermes applications had reached a total of DM 61.5 billion, although the previous annual volume had been about DM 15 billion. Even bearing in mind the profit taking set off by the temporary special conditions, this volume of orders was overwhelming. 1992 exports resulted basically from running down the level of new orders taken onto firms' books during 1991. The export volume expected in 1992, at half 1991's level, does not completely reflect the actual reduction. Virtually only a few orders came in for 1993, and it was not even possible to realise all the remaining stock of orders.[124]

Companies trusted too much on their existing customers, although conditions had changed fundamentally. Although companies in the USSR or in Russia would have liked to continue importing at the old levels, their central authorities had other priorities and the companies them-

---

122 Agreement was necessary for such cases from the Federal Ministries of Finance or for Economic Affairs and from the Chancellor's Office.

123 B-interview with Dr Franz Sack on 9th February 1993.

124 See: B-interview with Dr Wolfgang Lemke on 3rd March 1993.

selves were hardly able to finance their imports. Those which had hard currency available mainly used it to pay for the imports of consumer goods for their employees.

Optimism therefore rapidly gave way to reality. It was not possible by a long way to achieve the figures written in to 1992 eastern-export plans.[125] Nevertheless, companies continued to base their turnover forecasts on the eastern market.[126]

The companies even at this late stage were still failing fully to recognise the real cause, as they were blaming the problems of eastern export volume on the "reduced willingness of the Russians to invest" but also, and primarily, on administrative problems getting in the way of financial arrangements.[127]

Even the structural shifts in priorities were interpreted as being only temporary.[128] This is supported by the fact that they were expecting an improvement in export business from the prolongation of Hermes cover and relief in barter business during 1993.[129] As late as the first half of 1992, they were still betting heavily on turnover in the eastern markets. The economic interest of the Russian trading partners must surely have played some part here, because they too had still not properly realised the changes in the situation of the Soviet Union.

The German Government's increased travelling activity in support of the Russian market must also have strengthened the companies' faith in the future in these markets. Particularly after the visit which the Federal Minister for Economic Affairs, Mr Möllemann, paid to Moscow and his announcement that the financial arrangements would soon be clarified, the THA companies started producing to meet the contracts already signed. As a result, in autumn of 1992 there was DM 1.5 to 2 billions' worth of machinery standing around in eastern Germany that had been produced for Russia.[130] Many western German and foreign investors who had taken over companies from the THA in the hope that they could do profitable business with Eastern Europe were making equally wrong assessments of the situation.[131]

In view of the problems that had come up, the THA companies took the initiative of their own in 1992 for rescuing the Russian business. Joint ventures and inclusion in infrastructure projects seemed to them to be the best ways to go, and it was planned to start 27 joint ventures, and 35 were initiated, but work was only completed on six, and the success rate was even lower with the similar number of planned or "envisaged" deliveries to key projects in the infrastructural area. It was not even possible to implement any significant proportion of barter projects to promote exports.[132]

---

125 Report by Central Financial Control Department in August 1992. In 272 selected THA companies, only 50.7% of the planned turnover had been achieved in the first half of 1992. Full and reliable statistics on the trends in eastern exports by THA companies were not available. The main causes of this were that the number of THA companies kept changing as the privatisation programme went ahead, the reporting system was incomplete, and the break-down was inexact into separate orders or parts of the year.

126 See: DIW, *Wochenbericht* 39/92, 24th September 1992, page 478.

127 Survey by L. Koehne, Spring 1993.

128 Survey by the Eastern Europe working group, August 1992.

129 Survey by L. Koehne, Spring 1993.

130 See: *Süddeutsche Zeitung*, 16th October 1992. Demands were made for the Federal Government to take responsibility for them to prevent them being sold off at "fire sale" prices and ruining the market.

131 See: DIW, *Wochenbericht* 39/92, 24th September 1992, pages 468 and 474.

132 Survey by the Eastern Europe working group, August 1992. The problems in barter trade were:
1. Russian products hard to sell, except for raw materials.
2. Russians in most cases expected prices above world price levels.

5. Co-operation by the THA and its companies with regard to secure export business in eastern markets and to restructure their turnover

The THA, mindful of its defined task and its corporate philosophy, did not interfere with its companies' business policies, but it was highly interested in maintaining the highest possible share of eastern trade. Therefore the measures it undertook were more of a supportive nature.

The THA's first precisely aimed action for its companies consisted, after the introduction of the re-examination of Transfer Rouble business, in granting intermediate finance for these transactions in order to maintain liquidity. The special terms acted as a trigger for the THA companies to get to grips in earnest with Hermes. The THA itself assisted them by providing the necessary technical knowledge.

In addition to this, the THA conducted central negotiations on terms with Hermes, the Federal Ministries for Economic Affairs and of Finance, and the banks, declared willingness to accept liability of last resort (contingent liability), and confirmed companies as being "suitable for restructuring".[133] There was for the moment no strict review of the companies' suitability, and the THA felt it was justified in doing so because the final decision was after all not for the THA to make. This confirmation would merely have served as one factor in the decision to be made by the Inter-Ministerial Committee.[134]

After the DM 5 billion limit had been introduced, co-operation in this area intensified between the THA and its companies. This cap forced everybody to make realistic assessments. In the interests of fulfilling its responsibility, the THA demanded from 1992 onwards that its companies had to include the possibility of a break-down of eastern markets in their corporate strategies.[135] Because of the cabinet's decision of 22nd January 1992, companies which had not yet been given definite approval from the Inter-Ministerial Committee were re-examined to see whether, "on the basis of provable facts, sufficiently good prospects exist for their becoming competitive under free-market conditions."[136] The companies were compelled to react quickly because the DM 5 billion available under the cap was being allocated on the "greyhound" principle (a speeded-up version of "first come, first served").[137]

---

3. Continuity of supply and delivery of the agreed quantity and quality cannot be guaranteed for products from the CIS.
4. Logistics problems: transport, transhipment capacity, approval for passage through the CIS republics – particularly with regard to raw materials.
5. Changing policy on customs duties, export bans, quantity limitations, lack of export licences.
6. No guarantee of co-ordination between Russian firms after the Ministry of Industry had been abolished. Lines of responsibility and authority unclear.
7. Russian firms' "retention quota" (the proportion of hard currency they could retain out of the total they had earned) was low and even then fluctuated.

133 Executive Board submission dated 10th December 1990: Involvement of the THA in the financing of exports by THA companies under Hermes cover. Worthwhileness of restructuring to be confirmed to the Hermes credit insurance company.

134 op. cit.; B-interview with Wolfram Krause on 3rd March 1993.

135 B-interview with Eberhard Bredenbreuker, 18th May 1993.

136 Executive Board minutes for 11th February 1992.

137 Internal memo, THA Financial Department, 22nd June 1992.

This financial support for modernisation from the THA was intended to contribute directly to strengthening the efficiency of the companies.[138] Its purpose was to bring them up to a level at which they could compete in the market.[139] According to the THA's point of view, most of their companies have now managed to start producing products which are technically competitive.[140] A survey carried out by the Eastern Europe working group in August 1992, however, showed that 22% of the companies had not achieved this goal. The main problem seems to have lain on the sales side.[141] One reason for this was that, after the foreign-trading companies had been wound up, a large proportion of their staff was unwilling to move away from Berlin to the companies "out in the provinces". Another was the tough competition for market share on western markets.[142] This can be seen clearly from the example of *Deutsche Waggonbau-AG* (or DWA for short), which has a monopoly on the supply of certain kinds of railway rolling stock to the CIS countries. The corporate strategy provided for securing the existing product and market segments up to 1992, and entering western markets step by step up to 1994 on the basis of holding cost-leadership. Accordingly, new products were designed such as rolling stock for the Berlin suburban electric railway. With the support of politicians and trade unionists, the order for the supply of new trains for this railway was retroactively split, although it had already been awarded to DWA, and parts given to a local competitor. The route to other countries in the west is similarly barricaded; foreign rail authorities always give preference to their own national suppliers. There is also excess capacity in the European rail rolling stock manufacturing industry.

From about the middle of 1992 onwards, the THA has been providing more and more marketing assistance,[143] particularly since western companies, having initially been more than willing to help, became reluctant to help their own competitors when the recession began to bite. The companies were provided with staff training and also assistance with their efforts in eastern markets,[144] as the THA is convinced that these should continue to be serviced even while companies re-orientate themselves towards the west. In both regions it is only possible to sell high-value

---

138 The investment rate particularly of those companies in the Engineering Directorate, which were the ones most dependent on eastern trade, were still on the low side (in engineering: 6.82% of turnover, or −4.42% after depreciation of tax and in vehicle construction 1.82% and -1.84% respectively). This was summarised by the Central Financial Control department from the monthly reports of 748 THA companies. The survey carried out in August 1992 by the Eastern Europe working group showed that 17% of the 143 companies questioned, all of which were heavily dependent on eastern exports, attributed their failure to build sales in western markets to insufficient investment, and 16% to their strategic orientation to eastern markets and excess capacity. (Multiple responses were possible in reply to this question.)

139 For reasons of space it is not possible to give a detailed description of the efforts made in the direction of restructuring. See: article by Schwalbach in this volume.

140 See: B-interview with Dr Wolfgang Vehse on 18th May 1993.

141 According to the survey referred to in footnote 138, 46% of the companies stated that they needed more time to build up a proper sales department, and 31% complained of image problems or of the negative effect of being part of the THA.

142 op. cit.; 14% of the companies questioned stated this reason.

143 See: B-interview with Dr Wolfgang Vehse on 18th May 1993.

144 B-interviews with Dr Franz Sack on 9th February and Hans-Georg Pohl on 8th April 1993.

goods, but the THA believes that the eastern German companies' long-standing contacts with eastern markets will enable them to gain an advantage for themselves.[145]

One of the initiatives of the THA was also a wide-ranging questionnaire campaign designed to bring eastern German suppliers and western German customers together. This campaign was a success. After 23rd September 1992, the THA took further steps to assist directly in promoting sales with, amongst other things, the "*Einkaufsinitiative Ost*" or eastern German campaign on western German purchasing departments.[146] It has now been extended to cover selected foreign countries in western and eastern Europe, and further strategies are now in preparation. For instance, it is being checked to see whether it is possible to build bridges into the CIS market with "triangular" business arrangements involving countries like India or Turkey, and whether there is any indication that mutual and common problems on the CIS market could be solved jointly in co-operation with Finland.[147]

The position of a Special Officer for Eastern Europe was created before the end of 1992 with responsibility for directly promoting the East European sales of THA companies, and all others in eastern Germany.[148] One campaign, however, that came under this person's responsibility was destined to achieve only a limited success. A list of 172 THA companies with significant shares of eastern trade was handed to the Russian side in Moscow in November 1992 with the aim of turning the DM 4 billion in Hermes cover still available into solid sales revenue. The Russians misunderstood it to be a list of firms willing to start co-operation agreements, and handed back a corresponding list of Russian firms.[149] The Special Officer for Eastern Europe selected four projects from it for implementation. When it later turned out that the Russian minister responsible for such projects had never heard of them, they all had to be cancelled abruptly on 29th April 1993. This shows the continuing administrative problems in Russia, and the increasingly deleterious effect they are having on trade relations.[150] The efforts being made to handle barter trade with the THA's assistance appear to be bearing first fruits in the Tyumen region.

6. Summary

The influence of relations with Eastern Europe on the THA's work changed dramatically over the first two years. Although they were initially entered on the assets side of the privatisation programme, it soon emerged when COMECON collapsed and the USSR fell to pieces that the totally different foreign trade situation, taken in conjunction with the economic policy decisions necessitated by German re-unification, represented a major liability to THA companies undergoing restructuring and privatisation. The THA's reaction to this challenge was at the beginning a somewhat passive one, but this was in conformity with its understanding of its responsibilities. Until the middle of 1992 it hardly developed any policy of its own for reducing its companies' dependence on eastern trade or restructuring their sales channels. However, it did exert its influ-

145 See: B-interview with Dr Wolfgang Vehse on 18th May 1993.

146 There are differing accounts of the origin of this idea. Even the Federal Ministry for Economic Affairs claimed it for its own. See: B-interviews with Fritz Hohmann on 30th March and 2nd May 1993.

147 See: B-interview with Dr Wolfgang Vehse on 18th May 1993.

148 op. cit.

149 See: B-interview with Hans-Georg Pohl on 8th April 1993.

150 See: B-interviews with Fritz Hohmann on 30th March and 2nd May 1993.

ence – with more or less energy, and varying success – to make the companies reduce their level of eastern exports rapidly, since these had only been regarded as a stop-gap measure within the restructuring programme. However, since eastern exports represented a sizeable dimension in the privatisation of the companies, the THA aimed its strategy at securing the financial arrangements for these exports at the political level. The THA itself made a contribution in the form of liquidity and modernisation loans. In many cases, the real opportunity for retaining these markets was, however, wildly overestimated. The German Government was also interested in maintaining the level of exports, particularly to the Soviet Union because of its political promises during the process of unification. In order not to conjure up any international trade problems, the measures it took were mainly concentrated on the tried-and-trusted instrument of Hermes guarantees.

No radically different strategies for securing jobs in eastern German companies, such as giving them a preferential rate of Value Added Tax or special restructuring strategies, ever reached any stage beyond initial considerations.

It was not until eastern trade finally and totally collapsed, in the spring of 1992, that a change of policy began to emerge. Once the emergency programme for eastern trade, which the THA had developed, had been turned down, its active assistance to its companies swung round to sales promotion and the construction of a sales organisation. It appointed a Special Officer for Eastern Trade; the establishment of Management-KG's and the concept of industrial cores were also closely bound up with the problems of eastern trade. Basically, the THA is still rating the chances on eastern markets higher than the German Government does, and is behaving accordingly. With hindsight, however, it is now being admitted that earlier action on eastern trade policy might possibly have favoured the restructuring and privatisation programmes of its companies, but then, if the German Government had had an eastern trade policy that was not so powerfully orientated toward Russia it might have been able to support the THA's work more effectively.

V. Literature

Bundesministerium für Wirtschaft: *Der Deutsche Osthandel 1991/92*, study series no. 82.

Brabant, Jozef M. van: The Demise of the CMEA – the Agony of Inaction. In: *Osteuropa-Wirtschaft* 36 (1991), issue 3.

Clement, Hermann: Die Neugestaltung der wirtschaftlichen Beziehungen zwischen den Staaten der GUS. In: *Arbeiten aus dem Osteuropa-Institut München*, No. 157, December 1992.

ditto: *Transferrubel- und Hartwährungsverrechnung im Intra-RGW- und im Ost-West-Handel.* Munich 1987.

ditto: *Umgestaltung der sowjetischen Investitions- und Strukturpolitik.* In: Bundesinstitut für ostwissenschaftliche und internationale Studien (editor): *Sowjetunion 1986/87. Ereignisse, Probleme, Perspektiven.* Munich 1987.

ditto: Zerfall und Neuaufbau der Arbeitsteilung zwischen den Republiken/Staaten. In: *Beiheft der Konjunkturpolitik*, issue 40, Berlin 1992, pages 134 et seq.

Clement, Hermann, and Wolfram *Schrettl*: Inflationsstau plus Reformdefizit gleich Erfolgslücke, die sowjetische Wirtschaft 1988/1989. In: *Arbeiten aus dem Osteuropa-Institut München* No. 132, May 1989.

Clement, Hermann, and Volkhart *Vincentz*: Sowjetische Wirschaftskrise: Tiefpunkt ist noch nicht durchschritten. In: *Arbeiten aus dem Osteuropa-Institut München* No. 138, May 1990.

Cohen, D: The Solvency of Eastern Europe. In: *European Economy,* 2nd special issue, June 1991.

Collins, Susan M., and Dani *Rodrik*: Eastern Europe and the Soviet Union in the World Economy. In: *Policy Analyses in International Economics* No. 32, Institute for International Economics, Washington DC, 1991.

Csaba, Laszlo: Economic Consequences of Soviet Disintegration for Hungary. *Kopint-Datorg, Discussion papers* No. 2, February 1992.

Drabek, Zadek: The East European Response to the Debt Crises: A trade diversification or a statistical aberration? In: *Comparative Economic Studies* 1 (1988).

Gusinski, Gerd von: *Chancen für strategische Unternehmenskooperation.* In: J. *Fischer*, F. *Messner*, and K. *Wohlmuth* (editors): *Osteuropa, Geschichte, Wirtschaft, Politik*, volume 3, November 1991.

iW-Trends 20 (1993), volume 1.

Kosta, Jiri, Judita *Strouracova*, and Michael *Konstantinov*: *Deutsche Direktinvestitionen in der Tschechischen Republik.* Friedrich Ebert Stiftung, Prague, April 1993.

Luft, Christa: Economic Relations between the German Democratic Republic and the CMEA Countries. In: *ECE, Economic Studies* No. 2, Reforms in the Foreign Economic Relations of Eastern Europe and the Soviet Union. Geneva 1991, pages 135 et seq.

Marrese, Michael, and Lauren *Wittenberg*: Implicit Trade Subsidies within the CMEA: A historical perspective. In: *Economic Systems* 16 (1992), issue 1, pages 1 to 32.

MW-Informationen: *Die DDR auf dem Wege zur sozialen Marktwirtschaft.* Edited by the Ministry for Economic Affairs, 22nd June 1990.

Plan-Econ Report Nos. 5 and 6, 1993.

Sachs, Jeffry: *Poland and Eastern Europe: What is to be done?* In: A. *Köves* and P. *Marer* (editors): *Foreign Economic Liberalization – Transformations in socialist and market economics.* Westview, Boulder Colorado 1990.

Sobell, Vlad: *East European Economics at a Turning Point.* RFE, Report on Eastern Europe, May 4, 1990.

Vincentz, Volkhart: *Die Bedeutung des Konsums in der neuen sowjetischen Wirtschaftspolitik: Bewertung und Perspektiven. Gutachten im Auftrag des Bundesministeriums für Wirtschaft.* Osteuropa-Institut München 1987.

ditto: *Entwicklung der sowjetischen Konsumgüterindustrie und Aussichten im Hinblick auf das Konsumgüter- und Dienstleistungsprogramm der UdSSR.* Gutachten im Auftrag des Bundesministeriums für Wirtschaft. Osteuropa-Institut München 1989.

ditto: *Produktion und Außenhandel der RGW-Staaten im Bereich der Hochtechnologie. Gutachten im Auftrag des Bundesministeriums für Wirtschaft.* Osteuropa-Institut München 1988.

Wetzker, K: *Daten und Fakten zur wirtschaftlichen Lage in Ostdeutschland.* Institut für Angewandte Wirtschaftsforschung. Berlin 1990.

Zschiedrich, Harald: RGW – Ende oder Neubeginn? In: *Osteuropa-Wirtschaft* 35 (1990), volume 4.

Statistical Appendix

Figure:

Tables:

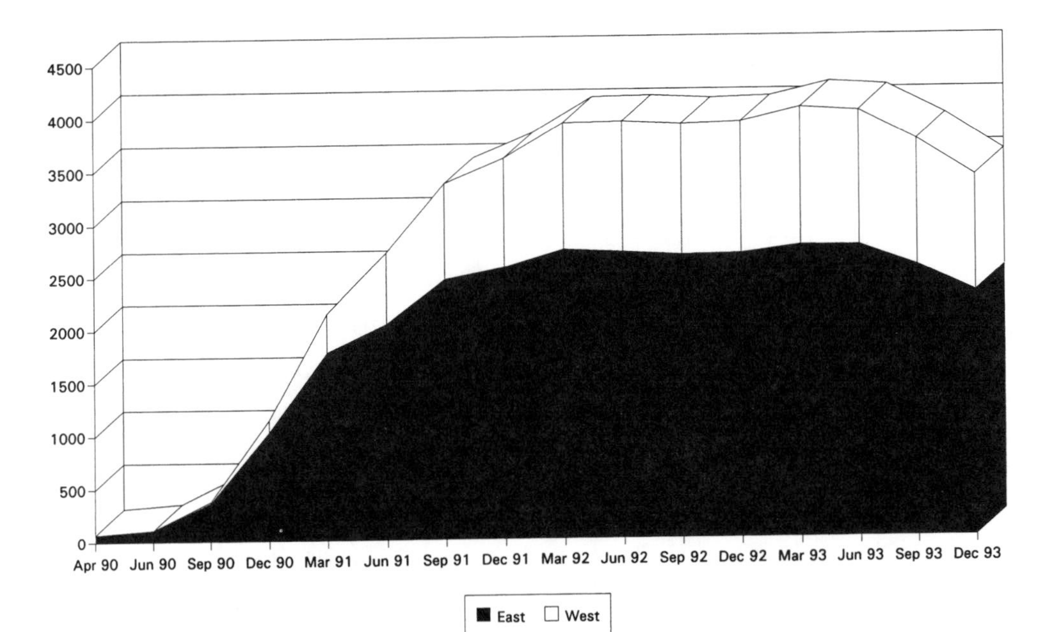

Figure: Numbers employed by the THA from 1990 to 1993

Source: Treuhandanstalt

Table 1:
Population, employment, and unemployment in Germany

Period	Germany	Of which		Share of eastern Germany[1])	Germany	Of which		Share of eastern Germany[2])
		Western Germany	Eastern Germany			Western Germany	Eastern Germany[1])	
	Population[3])				Working population[4])			
1986	77,780	61,140	16,640	21.4	.	26,960	.	.
1987	77,900	61,238	16,661	21.4	.	27,157	.	.
1988	78,390	61,715	16,675	21.3	.	27,366	.	.
1989	79,113	62,679	16,434	20.8	.	27,761	.	.
1990	79,753	63,726	16,028	20.1	.	28,495	.	.
1991	80,275	64,485	15,790	19.7	36,458	28,989	7,469	20.5
1992	...	...	...	...	35,816	29,115	6,701	18.7
1990 3.Qur.	79,671	63,560	16,111	20.2	37,398	28,625	8,773	23.5
4.Qur.	79,753	63,726	16,028	20.1	37,128	28,851	8,277	22.3
1991 1.Qur.	79,819	63,846	15,973	20.0	36,709	28,714	7,995	21.8
2.Qur.	79,951	64,036	15,915	19.9	36,529	28,940	7,589	20.8
3.Qur.	80,137	64,292	15,845	19.8	36,273	29,059	7,214	19.9
4.Qur.	80,275	64,485	15,790	19.7	36,321	29,243	7,078	19.5
1992 1.Qur.	80,372	64,618	15,755	19.6	...	29,033	...	...
2.Qur.	80,570	64,847	15,723	19.5	...	29,157	...	...
	Self-employed[4])[5])				Occupied[4])			
1991	3,531	3,041	490	13.9	32,927	25,948	6,979	21.2
1992	3,615	3,051	564	15.6	32,201	26,064	6,137	19.1
1990 3.Qur.	3,388	3,028	360	10.6	34,010	25,597	8,413	24.7
4.Qur.	3,448	3,036	412	11.9	33,680	25,815	7,865	23.4
1991 1.Qur.	3,477	3,028	449	12.9	33,232	25,686	7,546	22.7
2.Qur.	3,517	3,036	481	13.7	33,012	25,904	7,108	21.5
3.Qur.	3,551	3,047	504	14.2	32,722	26,012	6,710	20.5
4.Qur.	3,579	3,053	526	14.7	32,742	26,190	6,552	20.0
	Unemployed[6])[7]) total				Unemployed[6])[7]), women			
1990	2,124	1,883	241	11.3	1,042	915	127	12.2
1991	2,602	1,689	913	35.1	1,322	792	530	40.1
1992	2,979	1,808	1,170	39.3	1,567	826	741	47.3
1990 Sep	2,173	1,728	445	20.5	1,103	858	245	22.2
Dec	2,426	1,784	642	26.5	1,190	838	352	29.6
1991 Mar	2,539	1,731,	808	31.8	1,239	793	447	36.0
Jun	2,435	1,593	843	34.6	1,240	758	482	38.9
Sep	2,638	1,610	1,029	39.0	1,388	771	617	44.5
Dec	2,769	1,731	1,038	37.5	1,422	788	635	44.6
1992 Mar	2,988	1,768	1,220	40.8	1,554	793	761	48.9
Jun	2,839	1,715	1,123	39.6	1,509	794	715	47.4
Sep	2,894	1,784	1,111	38.4	1,550	831	719	46.4
Dec	3,126	2,025	1,101	35.2	1,600	896	704	44.0
1993 Mar	3,364	2,223	1,141	33.9	1,657	950	708	42.7
Jun	3,266	2,166	1,100	33.7	1,670	962	708	42.4

Period	Germany	Of which		Share of eastern Germany[1])	Germany	Of which		Share of eastern Germany[2])
		Western Germany	Eastern Germany			Western Germany	Eastern Germany[1])	
	Population[3])				Working population[4])			
	Employed, but seeking work [6])[7])				short-time workers [6])[8]), total			
1990	.	599	.	.	814	56	758	93.1
1991	1,276	651	626	49.0	1,761	145	1,616	91.8
1992	1,496	734	763	51.0	687	283	404	58.8
1990 Sep	743	601	141	19.0	1,761	32	1,729	98.2
Dec	917	618	299	32.6	1,845	50	1,794	97.3
1991 Mar	1,083	648	435	40.2	2,129	139	1,990	93.5
Jun	1,462	693	769	52.6	2,061	163	1,899	92.1
Sep	1,445	672	773	53.5	1,466	133	1,333	91.0
Dec	1,749	709	1,040	59.5	1,208	173	1,035	85.6
1992 Mar	1,533	757	776	50.6	760	266	494	65.0
Jun	1,607	785	823	51.2	646	229	417	64.6
Sep	1,463	743	720	49.2	456	204	251	55.2
Dec	1,557	830	727	46.7	883	650	233	26.4
1993 Mar	1,467	840	628	42.8	1,308	1,061	246	18.8
Jun	1,437	841	597	41.5	1,098	897	201	18.3

Notes: 1) including East Berlin; 2) percentage of all Germany; 3) as of the last day of each period, but 3rd quarter 1990 relates to 3rd October 1990; 4) German nationals, as defined by the national accounting system, averages; 5) including family members helping in the business; 6) source: Federal Labour Institute; 7) annual data: averages; monthly data: as of last day of month; 8) annual data: averages; monthly data: as of middle day of month

Sources: Federal Labour Institute, Federal Office of Statistics

Table 2:
Macro-economic trends in Germany, 1990-1993: Domestic product, employment and income[1])

	2nd half of 1990		1991		1992		1st half of 1993	
	Eastern Germany[2])	Western Germany	Eastern Germany[2])	Western Germany	Eastern Germany[2])	Western Germany	Eastern Germany[2])	Western Germany[2])
Use of domestic product	in 1991 prices (DM billion)							
Private consumption	93.0	705.2	179.4	1,428.3	192.5	1,452.1	93.9	702.0
State consumption	44.1	237.0	85.6	466.5	91.7	481.3	43.1	232.4
Gross investment	19.1	277.8	87.3	571.5	107.5	569.6	60.0	265.8
Fixed assets	36.6	280.7	87.2	564.9	108.1	571.4	57.6	256.9
Machinery, Equipment	13.5	130.2	41.8	262.8	46.3	252.6	22.5	103.2
Buildings	23.1	150.5	45.3	302.1	61.8	318.8	35.1	53.6
Changes in stock	-17.5	-2.9	0.1	6.6	-0.6	-1.8	2.4	9.0
Last domestic use of goods	156.2	1,220.0	352.3	2,466.3	391.8	2,503.0	196.9	1,200.2
Outward contribution (exports minus imports)[3])	-51.1	77.2	-171.4	168.7	-193.4	173.0	-98.3	86.6
Export of goods and services[3])	30.2	416.2	46.9	892.5	52.9	925.4	24.6	420.5
Import of goods and services[3])	81.3	339.1	218.2	723.9	246.3	752.4	122.9	333.9
Gross domestic product	105.2	1,297.1	180.9	2,635.0	198.4	2,676.0	98.6	1,266.8
	at current prices (DM billion)							
Private consumption	83.1	684.0	179.4	1,428.3	212.0	1,510.0	111.5	752.4
State consumption	38.1	236.7	85.6	466.5	105.8	500.6	50.6	235.5
Gross investment	22.7	265.6	87.3	571.5	113.2	589.0	63.4	278.6
Fixed assets	34.4	270.2	87.2	564.9	115.6	593.6	63.9	273.1
Machinery, Equipment	13.2	127.2	41.8	262.8	47.2	257.4	23.1	106.0
Buildings	21.2	143	45.3	302.1	68.4	336.2	40.7	167.1
Changes in stock	-11.7	-4.6	0.1	6.6	-2.4	-4.6	-0.5	5.5
Last domestic use of goods	143.9	1,186.2	352.3	2,466.3	431.1	2,599.6	225.5	1,266.5
Outward contribution (exports minus imports)[3])	-48.7	79.1	-171.4	168.7	-197.6	194.6	-101.3	102.0
Export of goods and services[3])	30.0	411.5	46.9	892.5	53.5	934.8	24.7	427.4
Import of goods and services[3])	78.7	332.5	218.2	723.9	251.1	740.2	126.0	325.3
Gross domestic product	95.2	1,265.3	180.9	2,635.0	233.4	2,794.2	124.2	1,368.5

	2nd half of 1990		1991		1992		1st half of 1993	
	Eastern Germany[2])	Western Germany	Eastern Germany[2])	Western Germany	Eastern Germany[2])	Western Germany	Eastern Germany[2])	Western Germany[2])
Income	at current prices (DM billion)							
Gross national income	.	1,141.5	191.0	2,362.5	236.3	2,481.4	123.4	1,207.7
of which income from employment	.	703.2	185.8	1,423.0	223.0	1,508.4	111.6	717.2
Gross total of wages and salaries received by natives	66.2	572.7	155.9	1,155.5	186.6	1,225.6	94.2	579.1
arising domestically	63.6	572.7	145.1	1,163.1	172.5	1,237.9	87.5	585.2
Disposable income of private households	83.1	791.9	193.8	1,650.5	244.2	1,732.3	125.7	857.1
received current transfers	.	194.6	71.9	401.5	93.0	430.7	50.4	221.6
Savings of private households	0.0	108.0	14.5	222.2	32.2	222.2	14.3	104.7
Employment	average in 1,000							
Working population	8,892	30,488	8,422	30,682	7,879	30,949	7,657	30,886
- unemployed	433	1,762	913	1,689	1,170	1,808	1,139	2,202
= nationals in employment	8,459	28,726	7,509	28,993	6,709	29,141	6,518	28,684
Self-employed and family members helping	288	3,035	362	3,044	411	3,055	437	3,058
Working population in employment	8,171	25,691	7,147	25,949	6,298	26,086	6,081	25,626
+ Foreign residents working in Germany minus German residents working abroad	-136	59	-290	234	-365	346	-359	347
= Working population in Germany	8,323	28,785	7,219	29,227	6,344	29,487	6,159	29,031
of which working population in employment in Germany	8,035	25,750	6,857	26,183	5,933	26,432	5,722	25,973
Average figures per inhabitant, per head of working population, per head of working population in employment	in DM							
Gross domestic product per inhabitant	5,900	19,900	11,400	41,100	14,800	43,100	...	...
per head of working population	11,400	44,000	25,100	90,200	36,800	94,800	20,200	47,100
Gross national product per inhabitant	6,000	20,100	11,900	41,400	15,600	43,100	...	...
Total gross wages and salaries per month and per head of national working population in employment	1,350	3,710	1,820	3,710	2,470	3,920	2,580	3,770

Notes: 1) as of September 1993; 2) includes East Berlin; 3) includes German-German transactions; 4) national income including depreciation

Source: Federal Office of Statistics

Table 3:
Structural change in eastern Germany[1])

Branch of economy	1990		1991				1992				1993
	3rd Qur.	4th Qur.	1st Qur.	2nd Qur.	3rd Qur.	4th Qur.	1st Qur.	2nd Qur.	3rd Qur.	4th Qur.	1st Half
	Gross added value (in DM billion) at current prices										
Agriculture and forestry[2])	4.2	0.1	–1.1	–0.7	4.1	0.1	–0.3	–0.1	3.4	0.6	–0.4
Manufacturing industry	21.6	18.9	16.6	16.7	17.4	18.5	19.2	21.1	22.1	22.9	45.2
Trade and travel	8.6	8.5	6.9	7.2	7.2	8.1	6.9	7.6	7.6	8.4	15.4
Service enterprises	7.6	8.3	9.2	10.3	11.4	15.1	15.5	16.7	17.3	17.0	38.1
State, private households, and similar	9.3	11.0	8.4	9.9	11.4	16.7	11.8	12.5	17.0	17.4	30.2
Gross added value (uncorrected)	51.2	46.9	40.0	43.4	51.4	58.6	53.0	57.7	67.3	66.3	128.5
Gross added value (corrected)[3])	46.8	41.9	34.7	38.1	45.8	52.9	47.3	51.9	61.4	60.4	116.5
Gross domestic product[4])	50.2	45.0	36.9	40.4	48.2	55.3	49.8	54.8	64.7	64.2	124.2
Gross national product[5])	50.5	46.3	38.3	42.4	50.7	58.8	52.4	57.7	67.5	67.7	129.5
	at 1991 prices										
Agriculture and forestry[2])	4.4	0.5	–1.1	–0.7	4.1	0.1	–0.6	–0.5	3.5	0.5	–0.6
Manufacturing industry	21.5	19.2	16.7	16.9	17.3	18.4	18.2	19.6	20.2	21.1	40.8
Trade and travel	9.2	9.0	7.1	7.1	7.3	8.0	6.6	7.1	7.0	7.7	14.1
Service enterprises	9.4	9.4	10.4	11.4	11.9	12.3	12.6	13.5	13.9	13.6	27.0
State, private households, and similar	11.9	13.1	12.2	11.4	11.4	11.4	11.4	11.5	11.6	11.7	23.3
Gross added value (uncorrected)	56.4	51.2	45.2	46.0	52.1	50.1	48.2	51.3	56.2	54.6	104.5
Gross added value (corrected)[3])	51.4	46.1	39.7	40.6	46.6	44.7	42.4	45.6	50.5	48.9	92.6
Gross domestic product[4])	55.4	49.8	42.0	42.9	49.0	47.0	44.7	48.2	53.3	52.3	98.6
Gross national product[5])	55.6	51.1	43.4	44.9	51.4	50.4	47.2	51.0	55.9	55.5	103.4

Branch of economy	1990		1991				1992				1993
	3rd Qur.	4th Qur.	1st Qur.	2nd Qur.	3rd Qur.	4th Qur.	1st Qur.	2nd Qur.	3rd Qur.	4th Qur.	1st Half
	Gross added value (branches of economy in %) at current prices										
Agriculture and forestry[2])	8.1	0.3	–2.8	–1.5	8.0	0.2	–0.6	–0.2	5.0	0.9	–0.3
Manufacturing industry	42.2	40.2	41.6	38.4	33.8	31.6	36.3	36.6	32.8	34.5	35.2
Trade and travel	16.8	18.2	17.2	16.5	14.0	13.9	12.9	13.1	11.3	12.7	12.0
Service enterprises	14.8	17.8	22.9	23.6	22.1	25.8	29.2	28.9	25.6	25.7	29.6
State, private households, and similar	18.1	23.5	21.1	22.9	22.1	28.4	22.2	21.7	25.2	26.2	23.5
Gross added value (uncorrected)	100.0	100.0	100.0	100.0	100.0	100.0	100.0	100.0	100.0	100.0	100.0
	at 1991 prices										
Agriculture and forestry[2])	7.9	1.0	–2.4	–1.5	7.8	0.2	–1.2	–0.9	6.2	0.9	–0.6
Manufacturing industry	38.1	37.5	36.9	36.7	33.3	36.7	37.8	38.2	36.0	38.6	39.0
Trade and travel	16.4	17.6	15.6	15.3	13.9	16.0	13.7	13.9	12.5	14.2	13.5
Service enterprises	16.6	18.3	22.9	24.7	22.9	24.4	26.1	26.2	24.7	24.9	25.8
State, private households, and similar	21.1	25.6	26.9	24.8	21.9	22.7	23.5	22.5	20.6	21.4	22.3
Gross added value (uncorrected)	100.0	100.0	100.0	100.0	100.0	100.0	100.0	100.0	100.0	100.0	100.0

Notes: 1) including East Berlin, as of September 1993; for 1993, only figures for the first six months have so far been published and not for the Quarters separately; 2) contribution to gross domestic product is negative if subsidies are higher than output during a given period of time; 3) total gross added value minus theoretical charges for bank services; 4) corrected added value plus non-deductible turnover tax and import charges; 5) including earned and unearned income received from, and plus earned and unearned income paid to, the rest of the world

Source: Federal Office of Statistics

Table 4:
Population, working population, and unemployment in eastern Germany and East Berlin

Period	Brandenburg	Mecklenburg/ West-Pomerania	Saxony	Saxony-Anhalt	Thuringia	East Berlin
	Population ('000) 1)					
1986	2,663.7	1,968.1	5,041.2	3,012.0	2,718.6	1,236.2
1987	2,669.1	1,978.8	5,014.4	3,004.5	2,723.3	1,284.5
1988	2,641.2	1,963.9	4,900.7	2,965.0	2,683.9	1,279.2
1989	2,578.3	1,924.0	4,764.3	2,874.0	2,611.3	1,275.7
1990	2,542.7	1,891.7	4,678.9	2,823.3	2,572.1	1,281.1
1991	2,527.3	1,883.3	...	2,810.0	2,551.1	1,287.5
1992 Jun						
	Employees required to hold social insurance ('000) 1) 2)					
1992 Jun	919.6	661.9	1,750.5	1,031.0	905.9	463.3
Sep	917.7	657.7	1,727.7	1,023.6	895.7	459.8
	Unemployed ('000) 1)					
1990 Dec	101.1	89.6	164.4	113.4	106.9	66.8
1991 Mar	124.4	120.5	210.6	143.7	133.0	76.2
Jun	130.2	122.7	214.9	156.8	136.5	81.4
Sep	159.8	137.5	274.3	193.2	164.3	99.7
Dec	161.9	141.7	276.8	192.8	165.5	99.0
1992 Mar	189.4	173.5	328.4	222.4	202.0	104.4
Jun	176.1	158.5	300.3	211.9	181.0	95.5
Sep	173.3	150.4	302.6	211.4	184.0	89.1
Dec	175.0	152.9	295.0	207.3	182.0	88.6
1993 Mar	178.5	155.9	309.7	219.8	190.6	86.2
Jun	177.4	145.7	298.1	217.5	182.6	78.5
	Unemployment rate (%) 3)					
1990 Dec	7.4	8.7	6.2	7.0	7.3	9.3
1991 Mar	9.1	11.7	8.0	8.9	9.1	10.7
Jun	9.5	11.9	8.1	9.7	9.4	11.4
Sep	11.7	13.4	10.4	12.0	11.3	14.0
Dec	11.8	13.8	10.5	11.9	11.4	13.9
1992 Mar	15.4	17.7	14.1	15.6	16.1	15.3
Mar II	16.0	20.0	15.5	17.0	17.1	17.2
Jun	14.4	16.2	12.9	14.9	14.4	14.0
Sep	14.1	15.4	13.0	14.8	14.7	13.0
Dec	14.2	15.7	12.7	14.5	14.5	13.0
1993 Mar	15.1	18.0	14.6	16.8	16.1	14.2
Jun	15.0	16.8	14.0	16.6	15.4	13.0

Period	Brandenburg	Mecklenburg/ West-Pomerania	Saxony	Saxony-Anhalt	Thuringia	East Berlin
	Short-time workers ('000) 4)					
1990 Dec	288.3	177.6	565.4	369.3	316.1	77.3
1991 Mar	295.2	228.6	639.3	383.1	368.6	86.8
Jun	290.7	214.6	595.7	368.6	350.7	88.5
Sep	208.0	142.7	402.6	274.1	249.1	56.0
Dec	164.9	118.4	313.2	205.6	190.1	42.4
1992 Mar	74.0	57.6	161.8	94.0	90.9	15.6
Jun	61.0	34.0	144.7	78.9	85.8	12.8
Sep	37.8	14.8	94.3	49.1	48.0	7.6
Dec	37.9	14.3	77.5	50.6	45.8	7.4
1993 Mar	35.1	16.4	83.5	51.6	52.0	7.5
Jun	27.6	10.4	68.3	48.2	40.9	5.2

Notes: 1) as of last day of period; 2) result of quarterly employment statistics based on total (waiting period for evaluation 6 months); 3) unemployed as % of working population (those required to hold social insurance, those in minor employment, civil servants, and the unemployed); up to 1991, the figures are based on a survey in September 1989, for 1992 on figures for November 1990, and for 1993 and March 1992 on figures for June 1992; 4) middle day of the reporting period.

Sources: Federal Labour Institute, Federal Office of Statistics

Table 5:
Mining and processing industry in eastern Germany[1])

Period		Total	Mining	Processing industries				
				Total	Raw materials and production goods	Capital goods	Consumer goods	Food, drink, tobacco
					Manufacturing industries			
				Companies (total number)				
1991		7,112	43	7,069	1,140	2,738	2,072	1,120
1992		6,375	40	6,335	1,051	2,671	1,673	940
1991	1st Qur.	7,254	44	7,210	1,152	2,763	2,157	1,138
	2nd Qur.	7,317	44	7,273	1,179	2,794	2,149	1,150
	3rd Qur.	7,016	41	6,974	1,126	2,699	2,033	1,116
	4th Qur.	6,861	41	6,820	1,101	2,697	1,947	1,076
1992	1st Qur.	6,435	40	6,395	1,033	2,630	1,725	1,007
	2nd Qur.	6,333	40	6,293	1,041	2,617	1,678	956
	3rd Qur.	6,347	40	6,307	1,058	2,683	1,658	909
	4th Qur.	6,385	40	6,345	1,073	2,753	1,631	887
1993	1st Qur.	6,111	28	6,083	1,011	2,710	1,514	848
	2nd Qur.	6,287	31	6,256	1,062	2,788	1,522	854
				Employees[2]) ('000)				
1991		1,759	121	1,638	341	848	316	133
1992		943	80	863	183	446	148	85
1991	1st Qur.	2,071	137	1,934	410	989	383	152
	2nd Qur.	1,955	129	1,826	374	965	347	141
	3rd Qur.	1,609	115	1,494	313	767	289	126
	4th Qur.	1,401	102	1,300	268	672	246	113
1992	1st Qur.	1,060	91	969	208	493	172	95
	2nd Qur.	973	84	889	190	459	155	86
	3rd Qur.	890	74	816	172	425	138	81
	4th Qur.	847	69	778	164	407	129	78
1993	1st Qur.	768	60	708	145	373	118	72
	2nd Qur.	749	54	695	143	364	116	72

Period		Total	Mining	Processing industries				
				Total	Raw materials and production goods (Manufacturing industries)	Capital goods (Manufacturing industries)	Consumer goods (Manufacturing industries)	Food, drink, tobacco
		of which hourly paid ('000)						
1991		1,176	91	1,085	229	526	236	95
1992		634	58	575	120	286	109	60
1991	1st Qur.	1,389	103	1,286	278	612	286	109
	2nd Qur.	1,306	97	1,209	252	597	259	100
	3rd Qur.	1,074	85	989	209	476	215	89
	4th Qur.	933	76	857	177	418	182	80
1992	1st Qur.	709	67	642	136	312	127	67
	2nd Qur.	653	61	591	125	292	114	61
	3rd Qur.	601	55	546	113	275	102	57
	4th Qur.	572	50	522	108	265	95	54
1993	1st Qur.	522	44	478	96	245	87	50
	2nd Qur.	509	39	469	94	240	86	50
		Total hours worked (millions)						
1991		1,417	128	1,288	289	590	267	142
1992		972	95	877	188	420	165	104
1991	1st Qur.	423	40	383	88	174	82	40
	2nd Qur.	371	33	338	77	154	71	37
	3rd Qur.	327	28	299	66	138	61	34
	4th Qur.	295	27	268	58	125	54	32
1992	1st Qur.	276	28	248	54	116	49	29
	2nd Qur.	247	25	222	49	105	42	26
	3rd Qur.	227	22	205	43	100	37	25
	4th Qur.	223	20	203	42	99	37	25
1993	1st Qur.	210	18	192	40	94	36	22
	2nd Qur.	201	16	186	38	91	35	22

Period		Total	Mining	Processing industries				
				Total	Raw materials and production goods	Capital goods	Consumer goods	Food, drink, tobacco
					Manufacturing industries			
		Gross total of wages and salaries (DM million)						
1991		29,596	2,923	26,673	5,957	13,835	4,525	2,357
1992		25,610	2,984	22,626	4,920	12,074	3,518	2,114
1991	1st Qur.	7,134	684	6,449	1,442	3,283	1,163	562
	2nd Qur.	7,798	798	7,000	1,616	3,659	1,137	589
	3rd Qur.	7,200	658	6,542	1,469	3,403	1,086	584
	4th Qur.	7,465	783	6,682	1,431	3,490	1,140	622
1992	1st Qur.	6,062	650	5,412	1,214	2,800	882	516
	2nd Qur.	6,333	708	5,624	1,250	2,970	888	516
	3rd Qur.	6,343	738	5,605	1,170	3,087	835	512
	4th Qur.	6,872	887	5,985	1,286	3,216	912	570
1993	1st Qur.	5,484	617	4,868	1,050	2,568	766	486
	2nd Qur.	5,952	667	5,284	1,145	2,798	824	518
		Turnover, total (DM million)						
1991		96,616	9,953	86,663	23,377	34,967	9,642	18,677
1992		92,969	6,987	85,981	21,298	35,957	9,994	18,732
1991	1st Qur.	24,073	3,278	20,794	5,963	7,805	2,391	4,635
	2nd Qur.	23,516	2,279	21,237	5,790	8,260	2,315	4,872
	3rd Qur.	23,429	2,123	21,306	5,867	8,608	2,330	4,500
	4th Qur.	25,598	2,272	23,326	5,756	10,294	2,605	4,670
1992	1st Qur.	22,027	2,068	19,958	5,315	7,774	2,502	4,368
	2nd Qur.	22,685	1,491	21,194	5,467	8,453	2,456	4,818
	3rd Qur.	22,956	1,627	21,329	5,206	9,121	2,370	4,633
	4th Qur.	25,302	1,802	23,500	5,311	10,610	2,666	4,913
1993	1st Qur.	21,830	1,703	20,127	4,938	8,036	2,563	4,590
	2nd Qur.	24,205	1,445	22,761	5,550	9,251	2,761	5,199

Period		Total	Mining	Processing industries				
				Total	Raw materials and production goods	Capital goods	Consumer goods	Food, drink, tobacco
					Manufacturing industries			
		of which: domestic turnover (DM million)						
1991		82,538	9,533	73,005	19,325	27,220	8,507	17,952
1992		80,090	6,640	73,451	18,024	28,796	8,962	17,668
1991	1st Qur.	21,620	3,175	18,445	5,203	6,740	2,086	4,416
	2nd Qur.	20,419	2,172	18,247	4,901	6,578	2,064	4,703
	3rd Qur.	19,854	2,018	17,836	4,846	6,530	2,091	4,369
	4th Qur.	20,645	2,168	18,477	4,376	7,371	2,267	4,463
1992	1st Qur.	18,755	1,981	16,775	4,236	6,177	2,208	4,153
	2nd Qur.	19,475	1,387	18,088	4,603	6,852	2,162	4,471
	3rd Qur.	19,747	1,541	18,206	4,565	7,076	2,142	4,423
	4th Qur.	22,113	1,731	20,382	4,620	8,691	2,449	4,622
1993	1st Qur.	19,231	1,630	17,601	4,170	6,769	2,329	4,334
	2nd Qur.	21,247	1,376	19,871	4,892	7,575	2,521	4,883
		of which foreign turnover (DM million)						
1991		14,079	420	13,658	4,052	7,746	1,134	725
1992		12,878	348	12,531	3,274	7,161	1,032	1,064
1991	1st Qur.	2,453	104	2,349	760	1,064	305	219
	2nd Qur.	3,097	107	2,990	889	1,681	251	169
	3rd Qur.	3,575	105	3,470	1,022	2,078	240	131
	4th Qur.	4,954	105	4,849	1,381	2,923	338	207
1992	1st Qur.	3,271	88	3,184	1,078	1,597	294	215
	2nd Qur.	3,210	103	3,106	864	1,601	294	347
	3rd Qur.	3,209	86	3,123	864	2,044	227	210
	4th Qur.	3,189	71	3,118	691	1,919	217	291
1993	1st Qur.	2,598	73	2,526	768	1,267	234	257
	2nd Qur.	2,959	69	2,890	657	1,676	240	316

Notes: 1) including East Berlin; figures for companies with 20 or more employees; 2) hourly paid and salaried

Source: Federal Office of Statistics

Table 6:
New orders and turnover booked by processing industry in eastern Germany[1]) (2nd Quarter of 1990 = 100)

Branch of economy	1990		1991				1992				1993	
	3rd Qur.	4th Qur.	1st Qur.	2nd Qur.	3rd Qur.	4th Qur.	1st Qur.	2nd Qur.	3rd Qur.	4th Qur.	1st Qur.	2nd Qur.
	Incoming order											
Processing industry, total	108.8	91.2	82.3	74.8	76.2	82.1	77.1	70.7	65.8	78.5	76.4	80.4
Domestic	108.5	91.4	77.3	70.7	71.7	72.7	79.0	75.2	72.7	82.8	83.2	86.0
Foreign	109.5	90.5	96.8	87.0	89.5	109.5	71.5	57.7	45.6	66.1	56.4	64.1
Raw Materials and production goods	119.1	80.9	73.3	62.8	60.8	68.9	63.5	52.4	55.2	53.2	58.0	60.6
Extraction and processing of stone and earth	119.0	80.9	38.9	64.5	73.2	67.2	78.0	93.5	109.2	109.6	93.2	139.7
Iron-producing industry	124.4	75.6	82.6	55.1	50.5	40.5	48.0	39.2	39.2	39.0	50.5	42.7
Chemical industry	118.6	81.4	77.5	64.7	61.5	86.4	62.8	45.0	48.3	48.8	54.1	54.1
Capital goods	100.1	99.9	92.0	88.7	94.8	98.7	89.2	87.8	75.1	102.2	90.5	98.3
Steel and light engineering, railway rolling stock	99.6	100.4	161.7	118.3	177.9	181.5	144.7	204.8	169.9	230.2	121.3	227.8
Mechanical engineering	92.1	107.9	109.6	123.2	126.2	120.8	102.7	90.7	76.9	100.2	83.9	78.8
Road vehicle construction and repair	121.0	79.0	51.8	42.0	31.6	33.3	64.9	72.1	65.2	133.3	134.8	148.0
Electrical engineering, repair of domestic appliances	104.7	95.3	68.8	57.1	48.7	64.4	52.4	42.4	46.6	53.7	66.1	58.6
Precision engineering, optical instruments, clocks and watches	106.3	93.7	104.1	55.7	67.7	54.0	76.3	78.0	73.8	107.4	75.8	87.9
Production of office equipment and automatic data-processing equipment	101.1	98.9	42.7	27.1	25.4	26.8	30.3	23.6	26.6	34.0	36.0	26.5
Consumer goods industry	109.6	90.4	74.7	63.7	59.9	66.1	74.2	65.0	64.1	70.3	78.8	75.4
Printing and duplicating	103.4	96.6	104.8	113.9	112.9	123.4	127.5	141.4	145.1	163.6	158.0	153.1
Textile	112.0	87.5	59.8	62.7	52.8	58.4	54.3	44.0	34.5	39.8	44.0	38.8

Branch of economy	1990		1991				1992				1993	
	3rd Qur.	4th Qur.	1st Qur.	2nd Qur.	3rd Qur.	4th Qur.	1st Qur.	2nd Qur.	3rd Qur.	4th Qur.	1st Qur.	2nd Qur.
	Turnover											
Processing industry, total	103.2	96.8	51.8	52.6	54.1	61.8	49.4	49.8	51.0	57.9	49.0	54.7
Domestic	105.4	94.6	68.1	65.1	64.3	68.3	59.2	60.9	62.0	73.8	63.0	69.8
Foreign	99.1	100.9	22.1	29.6	35.2	49.8	31.5	29.4	30.9	28.8	23.5	26.9
Raw Materials and production goods	106.2	93.9	65.7	64.2	66.6	70.7	61.5	57.4	54.4	56.0	54.5	59.2
Extraction and processing of stone and earth	118.0	82.0	46.3	68.0	79.3	76.3	66.9	94.7	110.9	116.0	80.8	142.4
Iron-producing industry	113.1	86.9	57.4	67.4	62.0	52.6	48.5	43.2	42.3	44.7	44.7	38.9
Chemical industry	98.9	101.2	74.3	64.2	70.1	85.4	66.5	53.8	45.6	50.4	53.2	51.7
Capital goods	102.5	97.5	44.2	47.0	48.1	57.8	41.2	43.9	48.1	57.5	43.2	49.7
Steel and light engineering, railway rolling stock	88.6	111.4	67.6	120.5	102.2	107.0	99.8	112.3	106.7	137.6	89.3	104.8
Mechanical engineering	104.6	95.4	43.3	42.5	48.3	55.0	32.2	32.4	41.2	45.0	29.1	32.8
Road vehicle construction and repair	106.7	93.3	25.1	24.0	14.4	16.1	31.7	35.9	35.1	66.6	63.5	68.9
Electrical engineering, repair of domestic appliances	104.3	95.7	46.3	38.8	41.4	45.2	33.4	33.4	35.4	40.4	38.1	40.8
Precision engineering, optical instruments, clocks and watches	102.5	97.5	27.5	22.4	22.0	26.0	23.5	28.1	35.8	45.8	27.1	29.9
Production of office equipment and automatic data-processing equipment	106.0	93.9	37.7	26.5	22.1	27.9	22.7	20.3	21.1	30.6	26.4	20.8
Consumer goods industry	100.3	99.6	56.7	53.6	54.8	61.1	60.1	59.2	56.3	63.2	62.5	66.4
Printing and duplicating	108.4	91.7	97.5	119.4	126.3	144.9	136.8	147.7	149.0	157.8	147.9	161.5
Textile	103.5	96.5	38.6	34.0	33.2	34.3	32.5	30.6	24.5	27.5	26.9	26.9

Notes: 1) value indices; excluding food and drinks industries; data includes East Berlin
Source: Federal Office of Statistics

Table 7:
Development and structural change in manufacturing industry in eastern Germany[1]) (net production[2]))

Branch of economy	Trend: 2nd half of 1990 = 100						Structural change: weighting in %[3])			
	1990		1991		1992		1990	1992	in western Germany	
	3rd Qur.	4th Qur.	1st half	2nd half	1st half	2nd half	2nd half[4])	2nd half	1985[5])	2nd half 1992
Manufacturing industry, total	102.5	97.3	76.3	77.4	75.6	82.2	100.00	100.0	100.00	100.0
Electricity and gas supply	97.5	102.6	107.7	98.3	94.6	98.8	12.42	14.9	6.37	6.1
Mining	91.4	108.8	78.7	61.3	51.9	48.9	9.56	5.7	2.87	1.9
Processing industry	105.7	94.1	64.5	67.0	62.5	66.7	59.95	48.6	84.69	84.7
Raw materials and production goods	107.5	92.3	72.4	78.7	79.0	77.9	11.51	10.9	22.78	21.4
of which										
Petroleum refining	108.9	91.1	117.7	130.6	129.4	134.5	1.27	2.1	3.22	3.1
Extraction and processing of stone and earth	123.4	75.9	52.4	71.1	81.3	111.9	2.51	3.4	1.92	2.2
Iron-producing industry	119.3	80.5	73.3	58.7	60.1	60.3	0.79	0.6	2.41	1.7
Metal foundries	109.3	90.4	60.7	49.5	49.0	36.3	1.07	0.5	1.20	0.9
Chemical industry	93.8	106.2	73.4	82.3	76.1	55.5	4.04	2.7	10.30	9.8
Capital goods producing industry	106.7	93.1	55.0	56.8	47.5	53.9	32.90	21.6	41.55	41.9
of which										
Steel and light engineering, railway rolling stock	100.0	99.7	93.3	124.4	124.5	156.0	2.93	5.6	1.67	1.9
Mechanical engineering	107.7	92.2	50.1	52.5	33.5	31.7	15.24	5.9	11.32	10.9
Road vehicle construction and repair	107.7	91.7	55.6	42.1	46.5	63.3	2.71	2.1	9.80	9.8
Electrical engineering, repair of domestic appliances	107.7	92.7	47.5	47.5	43.3	52.2	8.51	5.4	10.01	11.1
Precision engineering, optical instruments, clocks and watches	84.0	115.7	30.1	16.9	16.6	41.7	1.09	0.6	1.37	1.3
Production of office equipment and automatic data-processin equipment	120.0	79.2	42.1	25.5	24.2	16.3	0.88	0.2	2.10	1.5

	Trend: 2nd half of 1990 = 100						Structural change: weighting in %3)			
Branch of economy	1990		1991		1992		1990	1992	in western Germany	
	3rd Qur.	4th Qur.	1st half	2nd half	1st half	2nd half	2nd half 4)	2nd half	1985 5)	2nd half 1992
Consumer goods producing industry	104.2	95.6	67.8	70.8	73.4	74.4	7.22	6.5	12.19	12.2
of which										
Woodworking	96.1	103.9	77.5	72.7	79.8	78.2	1.53	1.5	1.76	1.9
Printing and duplicating	107.8	92.0	102.1	130.8	137.8	146.8	1.33	2.4	1.47	1.7
Textile trades	108.7	90.9	45.8	39.6	35.1	29.2	1.69	0.6	1.73	1.3
Food and drinks industry	100.2	99.6	90.4	90.0	91.7	96.9	8.32	9.8	8.17	9.1
of which										
Food and drink	104.7	95.6	84.2	85.3	93.9	96.5	6.90	8.1	5.82	6.7
Tobacco processing	80.0	120.2	117.9	111.0	82.3	99.3	1.42	1.7	2.35	2.4
Construction industry	101.4	98.3	92.3	105.6	117.7	139.7	18.07	30.7	6.07	7.4
of which										
Structures	102.9	96.7	102.7	104.4	116.1	130.6	8.79	14.0	3.17	4.0
Excavation	100.0	99.8	82.5	106.7	119.2	148.4	9.28	16.8	2.90	3.4

Notes: 1) data includes East Berlin; 2) index of net production in manufacturing industry, actual parts of companies, corrected for number of working days; 3) calculated from index of net production; 4) weighting in original index, 2nd half of 1990 = 100; the weighting in the individual branches of the economy to form sub-groups and groups in accordance with the system for manufacturing industry is based on the shares of gross added value (excluding VAT) from the costs structure survey carried out for the 2nd half of 1990 as separate statistics for eastern Germany and East Berlin; 5) weighting in original index, 1985 = 100

Source: Federal Office of Statistics

Table 8:
Trends in the construction industry in Eastern Germany[1])

Feature	Unit	1990		1991				1992				1993
		3rd Qur.	4th Qur.	1st Qur.	2nd Qur.	3rd Qur.	4th Qur.	1st Qur.	2nd Qur.	3rd Qur.	4th. Qur.	1st Qur.
		Construction industry (excluding ancillaries)										
Companies	number	1,463	1,599	1,711	1,881	1,959	2,348	2,474	2,582	2,650	3,404	3,521
Employees	'000	.	306	288	283	273	282	270	271	267	291	288
Gross total of wages and salaries	DM mill.	.	1,766	1,414	1,804	1,888	2,194	1,952	2,295	2,390	2,710	2,301
Hours worked, total of which	mill. hours	.	96.0	69.6	81.4	85.0	85.1	79.8	88.1	91.9	95.0	79.7
Structures	%	.	.	72.5	68.2	66.0	63.6	65.5	62.1	61.5	60.5	64.7
of which residential	%	.	.	21.1	20.5	18.0	16.1	15.2	15.9	15.8	16.8	17.1
Excavations	%	.	.	27.5	31.8	34.0	36.3	34.6	37.9	38.5	39.5	35.3
of which roads	%	.	.	6.6	8.5	10.3	11.2	8.6	10.0	10.2	10.3	6.8
Total turnover[2])												
Grand total	DM mill.	6,375	8,991	3,318	5,245	5,869	7,894	4,639	6,816	7,958	11,754	5,763
of which for construction	DM mill.	5,841	8,367	3,122	4,913	5,517	7,516	4,397	6,484	7,660	11,426	5,556
of which structures	%	73.3	72.2	74.9	65.0	61.2	56.0	63.0	58.1	56.8	55.4	61.1
of which residential	%	31.9	32.2	26.9	23.0	20.6	16.4	15.2	14.4	13.5	15.2	14.5
Excavations	%	26.7	27.8	25.1	35.0	38.8	44.0	37.0	41.9	43.2	44.8	38.9
of which roads	%	9.0	9.3	6.2	11.4	14.6	17.2	10.0	13.0	13.9	14.6	10.7
Incoming orders, total of which	DM mill.	3,199	3,303	2,800	4,373	5,904	5,568	5,370	6,807	7,454	7,968	6,746
Structures	%	71.0	65.6	65.7	61.4	54.5	57.1	63.1	59.6	56.9	57.9	62.5
of which residential	%	29.6	25.1	22.7	16.6	13.5	14.4	15.7	14.7	13.7	16.1	18.9
Excavations	%	29.0	34.4	34.3	38.6	45.5	42.9	36.9	40.4	43.1	42.1	37.5
of which roads	%	10.4	11.9	7.8	14.6	19.0	14.5	10.2	11.7	14.0	12.0	7.8
		Ancillary construction industry										
Companies	number	772	814	871	939	1,000	1,123	1,178	1,209	1,220	1,512	1,630
Employees	'000	.	59	59	60	62	67	68	69	69	79	81
Gross total of wages and salaries	DM mill.	.	331	317	358	403	496	470	509	542	669	621
Hours worked hours	mill.	.	6.8	19.4	19.9	20.9	22.6	23.7	23.1	23.6	27.0	27.0
Total turnover[2])	DM mill.	810	1,234	779	1,011	1,231	1,853	1,272	1,534	1,755	2,765	1,570
of which for construction work	DM mill.	722	1,132	710	920	1,122	1,713	1,164	1,425	1,632	2,590	1,448

Notes: 1) companies in the construction and ancillary industries with 20 or more employees; 2) turnover from construction work (construction turnover), turnover from other products manufactured, and from subordinate businesses; excluding turnover tax

Source: Federal Office of Statistics

Table 9:
Business starts and closures in eastern Germany 1)

Period	Total[2])				of which: industry			
	New business registration	Business registration withdrawn	Net increase[3])	Withdrawals as % of new registrations	New business registration	Business registration withdrawn	Net increase[3])	Withdrawals as % of new registrations
1990	281,096	26,694	254,402	9	.	.	.	.
1991	292,997	99,767	193,230	34	.	.	.	.
1992	213,832	120,555	93,277	56	8,857	2,977	5,880	34
1990 4th Qur.	85,241	14,419	70,822	17	.	.	.	.
1991 1st Qur.	81,060	20,257	60,803	25	.	.	.	.
2nd Qur.	81,121	22,362	58,759	28	.	.	.	.
3rd Qur.	69,256	27,174	42,082	39	.	.	.	.
4th Qur.	61,560	29,974	31,586	49	.	.	.	.
1992 1st Qur.	60,565	31,247	29,318	52	2,614	610	2,004	23
2nd Qur.	55,446	30,460	24,986	55	2,622	1,172	1,450	45
3rd Qur.	48,323	27,637	20,686	57	2,383	800	1,583	34
4th Qur.	49,498	31,211	18,287	63	2,185	809	1,376	37
1993 1st Qur.	50,800	32,413	18,387	64	2,288	735	1,553	32
2nd Qur.	49,273	28,913	20,360	59	2,301	749	1,552	33
1993 Jan	15,545	11,079	4,466	71	679	224	455	33
Feb	16,467	10,676	5,791	65	768	234	534	30
Mar	18,788	10,658	8,130	57	841	277	564	33
Apr	16,683	9,807	6,876	59	797	231	566	29
May	15,996	9,383	6,613	59	738	239	499	32
Jun	16,594	9,723	6,871	59	766	279	487	36
Jul	14,792	9,519	5,273	64	658	269	389	41

Period	Total[2])				of which: industry			
	New business registration	Business registration withdrawn	Net increase[3])	Withdrawals as % of new registrations	New business registration	Business registration withdrawn	Net increase[3])	Withdrawals as % of new registrations
1990	38,190	6,843	31,347	18	136,878	12,455	124,423	9
1991	27,207	12,109	15,098	45	138,009	48,091	89,918	35
1992	22,304	11,011	11,293	49	98,601	62,197	36,404	63
1990 4th Qur.	8,515	2,678	5,837	31	38,990	7,225	31,765	19
1991 1st Qur.	7,592	3,123	4,469	41	37,602	9,637	27,965	26
2nd Qur.	7,034	2,607	4,427	37	41,019	11,016	30,003	27
3rd Qur.	6,643	3,004	3,639	45	31,975	13,063	18,912	41
4th Qur.	5,938	3,375	2,563	57	27,413	14,375	13,038	52
1992 1st Qur.	6,310	3,211	3,099	51	27,283	15,927	11,356	58
2nd Qur.	6,115	2,625	3,490	43	25,594	15,550	10,044	61
3rd Qur.	4,738	2,354	2,384	50	22,441	14,159	8,282	63
4th Qur.	5,141	2,821	2,320	55	22,336	16,147	6,189	72
1993 1st Qur.	5,857	3,188	2,669	54	22,228	16,226	6,002	73
2nd Qur.	5,272	2,592	2,680	49	22,430	14,924	7,506	67
1993 Jan	1,719	1,105	614	64	6,882	5,593	1,289	81
Feb	1,871	1,060	811	57	7,177	5,261	1,916	73
Mar	2,267	1,023	1,244	45	8,169	5,372	2,797	66
Apr	1,882	926	956	49	7,436	5,003	2,433	67
May	1,623	805	818	50	7,342	4,873	2,469	66
Jun	1,767	861	906	49	7,652	5,048	2,604	66
Jul	1,553	874	679	56	6,897	4,859	2,038	70

Notes: 1) data includes East Berlin; 2) craft enterprises, wholesale and retail trade, hotel and catering trades, industry, other trades; 3) new business registrations minus withdrawals of registration

Source: Federal Office of Statistics

Table 10:
Average gross earnings per month of full-time employees in eastern Germany[1])

Branch of the economy	1990			1991			1992			Compared with western Germany[2])		
	Jan	Jul	Oct	Jan	Jul	Oct	Jan	Jul	Oct	Jul 1990	Oct 1991	Oct 1992
	GDR Mark	DM								in %		
Industry (including structures and excavation, and craft enterprises)	1,184	1,393	1,588	1,677	1,996	2,086	2,211	2,632	2,711	35.0	49.1	60.6
Industry (excluding construction industry)	1,183	1,350	1,525	1,606	1,886	1,950	2,119	2,504	2,559	33.8	45.7	56.9
Industry (excluding mining) including structures and excavation, and craft enterprises	1,178	1,396	1,587	1,661	1,992	2,088	2,184	2,586	2,684	35.1	49.2	60.0
Processing industry	1,172	1,341	1,498	1,584	1,842	1,902	2,009	2,354	2,437	33.7	44.8	54.5
Electricity, gas, district heating and water supply	1,286	1,568	1,705	1,697	2,168	2,294	2,690	3,055	3,182	35.7	48.8	63.2
Mining	1,302	1,372	1,607	1,685	2,053	2,066	2,554	3,218	3,107	32.9	46.9	66.8
Brown coal mining and briquette manufacture	1,322	1,365	1,587	1,743	2,044	2,048	2,616	3,327	3,125	30.2	42.7	61.8
Potash and rock-salt mining, salt basins	1,214	1,560	1,609		1,956	2,052	2,005	2,490	2,471	39.2	49.7	57.5
Basic raw materials and production goods industry	1,204	1,423	1,570	1,621	1,878	1,904	2,112	2,351	2,504	34.2	42.6	53.5
Petroleum refining	1,246	1,576	1,639	1,651	1,887	1,873	2,327	2,330	2,595	28.7	31.5	42.2
Chemical industry (excluding production of chemical fibres)	1,187	1,548	1,626	1,605	1,899	1,908	2,224	2,383	2,535	34.8	39.4	49.9
Production of chemical fibres	1,189	1,507	1,500	1,562	1,824	1,848	2,197	2,211	2,536	38.1	43.0	56.2
Capital goods industry	1,199	1,415	1,534	1,613	1,899	1,924	1,994	2,422	2,507	34.2	43.7	53.9
Ship-building	1,235	1,562	1,705	1,689	2,059	2,085	2,073	2,546	2,564	37.3	46.6	54.0
Electrical engineering 3)	1,159	1,381	1,367	1,563	1,868	1,894	1,946	2,399	2,498	34.2	43.8	53.5
Production of office machinery and automatic data-processing equipment	1,195	1,401	1,467	1,571	1,916	1,768	1,819	2,400	2,425	27.5	32.9	43.4

Branch of the economy	1990			1991			1992			Compared with western Germany[2])		
	Jan	Jul	Oct	Jan	Jul	Oct	Jan	Jul	Oct	Jul 1990	Oct 1991	Oct 1992
	GDR Mark	DM								in %		
Consumer goods industry	.	.	1,417	1,522	1,708	1,861	1,960	2,225	2,248	.	51.1	58.9
Production and processing of glass	1,155	1,218	1,495	1,615	1,790	1,863	1,914	2,309	2,404	33.4	47.6	58.5
Paper and board processing	1,079	1,140	1,400	1,507	1,706	1,735	1,785	1,925	2,012	33.0	47.1	52.4
Printing and duplicating	1,146	1,260	1,763	1,865	2,384	2,562	2,702	3,026	3,119	29.7	56.5	66.4
Textile trades	1,092	1,095	1,401	1,440	1,497	1,676	1,718	1,851	2,030	34.4	49.3	57.3
Food and drinks industry	1,101	1,183	1,456	1,479	1,701	1,858	1,908	2,240	2,265	32.4	48.2	55.6
Brewing and malt-making	1,127	1,254	1,475		1,948	1,979	2,075	2,481	2,544	30.2	46.0	55.0
Construction and ancillary industry	1,194	1,702	1,933	2,034	2,541	2,705	2,659	2,160	3,099	44.2	65.4	71,9
Wholesale and retail trades, banking and insurance industry[4])	1,500	1,565	1,807	1,994	2,159	2,572	2,658		50.5	62.6		
Wholesaling	1,076	1,169	1,516	1,640	1,847	2,048	2,164	2,494	2,590	29.7	48.9	56.7
Retailing	947	1,017	1,275	1,467	1,623	1,806	1,952	2,208	2,314	33.3	55.2	65.6
Banking	1,090	1,555	1,600	1,738	2,081	2,084	2,286	2,824	2,831	38.6	48.3	61.7
Insurance	1,072	1,369	1,675	.	.	.	.	.	3,257	31.9	.	67.1

Notes: 1) hourly-paid workers and salaried staff together; "gross monthly earnings" include all amounts which the employee receives regularly from the employer such as the wage or salary, whether freely agreed or laid down in a collective agreement, and including any bonuses or contributions for good performance or social factors, but do not include payments attributable to some other time than that covered in the survey, e. g. year-end or incentive bonuses and other delayed or once-off payments; 2) the area of the "Federal Republic of Germany" prior to 3rd October 1990 and including West Berlin; 3) including the repair of domestic electrical appliances; 4) only for salaried staff, but including hourly-paid workers in East Germany in January and July 1990

Source: Federal Office of Statistics

Table 11:
Trends in consumer and producer prices in eastern Germany[1])

Consumer prices (2nd half of 1990/1st half of 1991 = 100)

Period	All employee households	By category of expenditure[2])									4-persons employee household with average income
		Food, drink, and tobacco	Clothing and shoes	Rent for homes	Energy (excluding fuel)	Furniture and domestic appliances[3])	Goods for				
							Health and beauty	Travel and communications	Education, entertainment, leisure[4])	Personal outfitting[5])	
Weighting[6])	100.0	29.9	9.6	2.7	2.9	11.5	2.9	22.9	11.2	6.3	100.0
1991	108.3	102.7	104.1	176.6	159.2	102.8	104.1	105.3	106.0	115.7	108.2
1992	120.4	105.7	105.5	400.0	214.3	105.6	111.6	112.1	113.0	122.5	119.6
1990 3rd Qur.	94.3	98.7	90.6	97.1	63.8	96.7	96.0	96.0	92.0	85.0	94.3
4th Qur.	96.8	97.8	101.8	97.1	64.0	98.9	98.7	89.5	98.8	86.3	97.0
1991 1st Qur.	103.2	100.7	103.5	102.2	130.5	101.7	101.6	100.9	103.2	114.0	103.1
2nd Qur.	105.5	102.7	104.1	103.6	141.8	102.6	103.7	104.5	105.9	114.6	105.6
3rd Qur.	106.9	103.4	103.5	103.9	147.8	102.9	104.9	107.8	106.5	116.8	107.2
4th Qur.	117.8	103.9	105.4	396.8	216.5	104.1	106.3	108.2	108.4	117.3	117.0
1992 1st Qur.	119.3	105.4	105.2	398.4	216.1	104.9	108.7	110.1	112.1	118.1	118.4
2nd Qur.	120.5	106.4	105.3	400.2	213.3	105.4	111.4	112.3	112.5	121.9	119.7
3rd Qur.	120.7	105.7	105.4	400.2	213.7	105.8	112.7	112.8	113.0	124.2	119.9
4th Qur.	121.1	105.2	106.3	401.4	214.2	106.2	113.6	113.0	114.6	125.7	120.3
1993 1st Qur.	129.9	106.5	106.5	634.0	216.6	107.0	117.1	117.2	117.8	133.4	128.5
2nd Qur.	131.0	107.4	106.6	635.1	216.9	107.7	118.0	118.8	118.9	135.9	129.7
1993 Jan	129.4	106.1	106.4	631.7	216.2	106.9	116.7	116.3	117.3	133.4	128.0
Feb	130.1	106.7	106.4	634.1	217.5	107.0	117.2	117.3	118.0	133.4	128.6
Mar	130.3	106.6	106.6	636.1	216.2	107.2	117.5	117.9	118.1	133.5	128.8
Apr	130.8	107.1	106.7	634.1	217.3	107.6	117.9	118.5	118.7	135.4	129.4
May	130.9	107.3	106.6	635.4	216.7	107.7	117.9	118.4	118.9	135.5	129.6
Jun	131.4	107.8	106.5	635.7	216.6	107.8	118.1	119.5	119.0	136.9	130.0
Jul	131.4	107.4	106.3	634.8	216.2	107.9	118.2	119.7	119.3	138.2	130.0
Aug	131.3	107.0	106.3	634.3	216.7	107.9	118.3	119.6	119.5	138.3	129.9

Producer prices of industrial products (1989 = 100)

Period	Total	Mining products excl. natural gas	Electricity[7]), natural gas, district heating, water	Products from processing industry						Finished products	
				Total	Raw materials and production goods		Capital goods	Consumer goods	Food and drinks industry	Capital goods[8])	Consumer goods[8]) [9])
					Total	of which petroleum products	Producing sector				
Weighting[10])	100.0	3.0	5.1	92.0	30.1	3.5	28.5	17.2	16.3	9.3	17.3
1991	63.2	96.0	127.0	58.6	51.8	34.7	64.8	52.0	67.4	63.3	61.1
1992	63.8	102.1	134.3	58.7	51.3	34.8	64.3	52.1	69.7	63.9	62.9
1990 3rd Qur.	63.4	95.9	95.1	60.6	52.4	30.0	68.6	53.1	69.7	67.6	58.3
4th Qur.	62.5	97.2	95.4	59.6	52.6	39.1	66.8	52.3	67.6	65.5	57.5
1991 1st Qur.	63.3	93.7	123.3	59.0	52.4	34.6	65.7	52.0	66.9	63.8	60.4
2nd Qur.	63.1	95.7	126.1	58.6	51.8	32.6	64.7	52.1	67.2	63.8	61.4
3rd Qur.	63.1	95.5	129.3	58.4	51.7	35.7	64.2	52.0	67.4	62.5	61.3
4th Qur.	63.2	99.2	129.3	58.5	51.4	35.8	64.4	51.8	68.1	64.0	61.3
1992 1st Qur.	63.6	101.4	131.9	58.6	51.2	34.6	64.4	51.9	69.3	64.4	61.9
2nd Qur.	63.8	100.8	134.6	58.8	51.4	34.9	64.1	52.0	70.1	63.6	62.8
3rd Qur.	63.9	101.6	135.0	58.8	51.4	34.9	64.3	52.2	70.0	63.9	63.2
4th Qur.	64.0	104.6	135.9	58.7	51.1	35.0	64.4	52.4	69.4	63.8	63.5
1993 1st Qur.	64.1	104.4	138.1	58.8	51.1	36.4	64.7	52.5	69.3	64.2	63.7
2nd Qur.	46.4	102.8	140.3	59.0	51.2	37.7	64.9	52,7	69,5	64.3	64.1
1993 Jan	64.0	104.4	137.8	58.7	50.9	34.7	64.7	52.4	69.4	64.1	63.6
Feb	64.1	104.4	137.9	58.8	51.1	36.6	64.7	52.5	69.2	64.2	63.7
Mar	64.3	104.4	138.5	58.9	51.3	37.9	64.8	52.6	69.3	64.2	63.9
Apr	64.4	104.4	140.4	58.9	51.3	37.9	64.9	52.7	69.3	64.3	64.0
Ma	64.4	102.0	140.3	59.0	51.2	37.7	65.0	52.7	69.5	64.4	64.1
Jun	64.4	102.0	140.3	59.0	51.2	37.4	64.9	52.7	69.6	64.3	64.1
Jul	64.4	102.0	140.4	59.0	51.2	37.4	64.9	52.8	69.6	64.5	64.2

Notes: 1) data includes East Berlin; 2) classification according to the 1983 edition of the system for private households' income and expenditure; 3) including other goods for household maintenance; 4) excluding the service sector of the hotel and catering trade; 5) services of the hotel trade and goods of other kinds; 6) typical expenditure structure ("shopping basket") for in the household groups included in the calculations for 1989; 7) including distributors' sales in the case of electricity. natural gas. and water; 8) finished products grouped according to their principal purpose of use; 9) excluding food and drinks; 10) based on production figures for 1989, valuated at industrial selling prices in East German Marks

Source: Federal Office of Statistics

Table 12:
Income and expenditure for selected types of household in eastern Germany and East Berlin (monthly averages)

	Household with two children headed by salary or wage earner 3)						Pensioner households 2) Households of two persons					
	1990		1991		1992		1990		1991		1992	
	1st Half 4)	2nd Half	1st Half 4)	2nd Half	1st Half	2nd Half	1st Half 4)	2nd Half	1st Half 4)	2nd Half	1st Half	2nd Half
	Income/revenue in DM											
Gross income from employment	2,453	2,796	2,929	3,729	3,822	4,877	0	0	0	0	0	0
+ gross income from self-employment and unearned income	49	75	72	111	90	83	43	23	20	29	50	34
+ income from transfers and sub-tenancies	457	422	467	609	702	765	1,240	1,533	1,700	2,015	2,256	2,471
of which from the state 5)	348	345	387	464	560	605	1,140	1,506	1,682	1,977	2,207	2,394
Gross household income	**2,958**	**3,294**	**3,469**	**4,449**	**4,614**	**5,725**	**1,283**	**1,555**	**1,720**	**2,044**	**2,306**	**2,505**
– income and wealth taxes	236	144	179	324	334	533	0	0	0	0	0	0
– compulsory social insurance contributions	110	419	470	639	667	837	0	0	0	0	0	0
Net household income	**2,612**	**2,731**	**2,820**	**3,486**	**3,613**	**4,355**	**1,283**	**1,555**	**1,720**	**2,044**	**2,306**	**2,505**
+ other income 6)	43	12	0	2	2	13	25	8	0	10	7	10
Disposable income/revenue	**2,656**	**2,743**	**2,820**	**3,488**	**3,615**	**4,368**	**1,308**	**1,563**	**1,720**	**2,054**	**2,313**	**2,515**
	Use of disposable income/revenue in DM											
Expenditure of private consumption	1,858	2,407	2,272	2,828	2,718	3,271	1,090	1,325	1,491	1,708	1,855	2,122
Other expenditure	236	157	247	210	307	312	143	117	138	159	196	200
of which taxes 7)	26	7	36	11	34	20	13	5	16	5	18	9
contributions to voluntary supplementary pension	53	4	2	2	5	8	0	0	1	1	4	4
other insurance policies	39	37	94	67	138	81	19	14	35	19	56	30
subscriptions, donations, and other transfers	118	109	115	130	130	203	111	98	86	134	118	157
Savings 8)	562	180	300	450	590	785	74	121	91	187	262	193

	Household with two children headed by salary or wage earner 3)						Pensioner households 2) Households of two persons					
	1990		1991		1992		1990		1991		1992	
	1st Half 4)	2nd Half	1st Half 4)	2nd Half	1st Half	2nd Half	1st Half 4)	2nd Half	1st Half 4)	2nd Half	1st Half	2nd Half
	Structure of expenditure for private consumption in %											
Total, of which	100.0	100.0	100.0	100.0	100.0	100.0	100.0	100.0	100.0	100.0	100.0	100.0
Food, drink, and tobacco	38.5	30.1	31.6	27.8	29.7	26.6	44.9	37.0	31.9	31.1	28.6	27.5
Clothing and shoes	12.7	10.2	9.7	9.2	8.4	8.3	9.8	7.7	7.1	6.5	6.2	6.4
Rent for homes, energy (excluding fuel)	5.4	4.3	6.1	9.7	13.1	12.0	6.8	6.3	8.0	12.3	16.5	14.9
of which Rent	3.0	2.4	2.4	4.9	5.9	4.8	3.3	3.2	2.5	6.0	6.5	5.4
Fuel for domestic purposes	0.7	0.6	0.7	1.1	0.7	1.3	0.9	0.9	1.6	1.4	1.3	1.2
Electricity, gas, water, heating	1.7	1.2	2.9	3.5	5.0	4.5	2.3	2.0	3.6	4.6	6.7	6.1
Furniture and domestic appliances 9)	14.9	12.0	11.8	13.0	13.6	16.9	10.7	15.2	14.8	17.9	16.6	19.1
Health and beauty aids	2.5	2.6	3.0	2.8	3.2	3.1	3.7	4.5	5.1	5.5	5.3	5.4
Travel and communications	13.1	26.2	26.3	22.1	19.6	16.6	8.6	16.5	20.9	14.3	13.6	13.8
of which. motor vehicles and bicycles	5.1	18.1	17.6	13.1	10.5	8.6	1.1	9.0	14.3	7.3	6.9	6.8
Education, entertainment, leisure	8.0	12.0	9.4	10.7	8.5	10.6	10.1	8.6	7.7	7.9	7.5	7.3
of which television, radio, and sound reproduction	1.5	3.2	3.1	3.4	2.5	3.5	3.3	1.8	2.1	1.9	1.5	1.6
Personal outfitting and travel 10)	5.0	2.7	2.2	4.7	3.9	5.9	5.5	4.3	4.4	4.5	5.6	5.6
of which: travel	4.1	1.8	1.5	4.0	3.3	5.1	4.8	3.6	3.8	3.7	5.0	4.8

Notes: 1) results of statistics on budgets for households containing at least one hourly-paid or salary-earning person and for pensioner households with no income from employment; 2) households with no income from employment; 3) children under the age of 17; 4) excludes households in East Berlin; 5) pensions, child allowance (from the state), sick pay, maternity and post-natal allowances, unemployment pay, premature old-age pensions; 6) revenue from the sale of used goods and secondary raw materials, minor net income from goods produced in the home; 7) taxes on homes and households (e. g.: inheritance tax, property tax, dog licence, betting tax, or lottery tax); 8) net changes to asset and financial accounts; 9) includes other goods for household maintenance; 10) includes the purchase of foreign currency (etc.) for travel abroad

Source: Federal Office of Statistics

Table 13:
Privatisation – the THA's net achievement, 1991 to 1993

State	Privatised companies		Proceeds from sale		Jobs undertakings		Investment undertakings[1])		Companies under supervision	
	Number	%	DM bill.	%	Number	%	DM bill.	%	Number	%
	As of 30th June 1993									
Total, of which	12,581	100.0	43.5	100.0	1,468,193	100.0	150.1	100.0	12,993	100.0
Mecklenburg/ West Pomerania	1,609	12.8	2.8	6.4	128,725	8.8	11.7	7.8	1,455	11.2
Brandenburg	2,030	16.1	5.8	13.3	285,344	19.4	31.6	21.1	1,829	14.1
Saxony-Anhalt	1,958	15.6	4.5	10.3	184,656	12.6	20.6	13.7	2,101	16.2
Thuringia	2,372	18.9	4.0	9.2	194,809	13.3	13.1	8.7	2,129	16.4
Saxony	3,654	29.0	13.5	31.0	420,059	28.6	44.4	29.6	4,220	32.5
East Berlin	861	6.8	12.6	29.0	247,254	16.8	24.5	16.3	1,059	8.2
Not allocated[2])	97	0.8	0.3	0.7	7,346	0.5	4.2	2.8	200	1.5
	As of 30th June 1992									
Total, of which	8,175	100.0	30.7	100.0	1,223,709	100.0	114.0	100.0	11,926	100.0
Mecklenburg/ West Pomerania	1,125	13.8	1.8	5.9	100,494	8.2	6.7	5.9	1,372	11.5
Brandenburg	1317	16.1	4.5	14.7	254,190	20.8	25.2	22.1	1,696	14.2
Saxony-Anhalt	1,349	16.5	3.1	10.1	154,557	12.6	13.7	12.0	1,930	16.2
Thuringia	1,415	17.3	2.5	8.1	151,114	12.3	9.5	8.3	1,985	16.6
Saxony	2,352	28.8	9.6	31.3	332,717	27.2	33.9	29.7	3,805	31.9
East Berlin	581	7.1	8.8	28.7	213,778	17.5	19.2	16.8	994	8.3
Not allocated[2])	36	0.4	0.4	1.3	16,859	1.4	5.8	5.1	144	1.2
	As of 30th June 1991									
Total, of which	2,583	100.0	10.8	100.0	525,984	100.0	65.3	100.0	10,334	100.0
Mecklenburg/ West Pomerania	372	14.4	0.6	5.7	34,548	6.6	1.6	2.5	1,175	11.4
Brandenburg	342	13.2	1.9	17.9	93,568	17.8	7.8	11.9	1,375	13.3
Saxony-Anhalt	472	18.3	1.2	11.3	64,630	12.3	4.2	6.4	1,575	15.2
Thuringia	493	19.1	0.9	8.5	65,231	12.4	2.6	4.0	1,810	17.5
Saxony	748	29.0	4.1	38.7	158,028	30.0	15.0	23.0	3,400	32.9
East Berlin	156	6.0	1.7	16.0	95,847	18.2	3.0	4.6	903	8.7
Not allocated 2)	-	-	0.2	1.9	14,132	2.7	1.1	1.7	96	0.9

Notes: 1) the "total" figure includes DM 30 billion of investment undertakings for power generation and distribution; 2) proceeds from sales, and undertakings on jobs and investment, which cannot be allocated to a specific State from the sale of agricultural and forestry holdings and ancillary forestry enterprises, as well as plots of land not needed for operations

Source: THA

Table 14:
Trends in the total stock of companies in the THA's portfolio, as of 30th June each year

Main branches of industry[1])	Total portfolio			Reduction in portfolio[2])						Net portfolio[3])		
				Total			of which completely privatised					
	1991	1992	1993	1991	1992	1993	1991	1992	1993	1991	1992	1993
Total	10,334	11,926	12,993	2,391	7,586	11,325	1,145	3,798	5,370	7,943	4,340	1,668
Agriculture and forestry	567	734	726	61	263	379	23	104	a) 60	506	471	347
Energy industry and water supply	146	155	220	27	63	196	7	29	137	119	92	24
Mining	42	40	47	4	15	31	1	8	14	38	25	16
Chemical industry	223	237	257	54	151	221	31	90	116	169	86	36
Plastic, rubber, and asbestos processing	153	170	179	33	107	167	10	43	69	120	63	12
Extraction and processing of stone and earth; fine ceramics and glass	405	645	840	129	508	784	71	183	262	276	137	56
Ferrous and non-ferrous metal products, casting, steel products	215	232	249	41	127	196	16	68	102	174	105	53
Steel and light engineering	163	188	204	45	117	166	18	56	81	118	71	38
Mechanical engineering	1,001	1,070	1,114	181	559	921	100	327	509	820	511	193
Vehicle construction	331	361	373	68	217	330	44	147	201	263	144	43
Electrical engineering and electronics	453	499	514	108	327	471	46	132	188	345	172	43
Precision engineering and optical instruments	72	77	82	21	46	74	16	20	31	51	31	8
Iron, sheet metal and metal goods, musical instruments, sports equipment, toys, and jewellery	284	312	335	62	197	301	23	68	98	222	115	34
Wood industry	465	509	521	90	304	478	36	103	166	375	205	43
Paper and printing industry	234	240	248	48	152	228	28	86	124	186	88	20
Leather and shoe industry	158	167	169	17	93	149	3	15	31	141	74	20
Textile and clothing industry	493	505	529	74	258	442	16	52	101	419	247	87
Food and drinks industry	805	837	866	223	558	816	144	329	417	582	279	50
Construction industry	777	911	998	215	705	950	127	473	598	562	206	48
Ancillary construction industry	164	209	215	48	173	205	25	85	107	116	36	10

Main branches of industry[1])	Total portfolio			Reduction in portfolio[2])						Net portfolio[3])		
				Total			of which completely privatised					
	1991	1992	1993	1991	1992	1993	1991	1992	1993	1991	1992	1993
Wholesale and retail trade	1,208	1,366	1,493	284	941	1,349	127	437	653	924	425	144
Transport, communications, freight, and storage	310	363	420	77	176	350	25	90	183	233	187	70
Banks and other finance houses, insurance industry	9	12	17	7	10	15	1	5	6	2	2	2
Services	1,591	1,941	2,117	442	1,393	1,874	204	823	1,049	1,149	548	243
Not categorised	65	146	260	32	126	232	3	25	67	33	20	28

Notes: 1) THA definitions and categorisation; 2) total portfolio minus net number at end of period; the change is basically caused by privatisation, restitution, communalisation, assignment, and liquidation; 3) essential "companies on offer from THA", companies in the process of winding up, "purchase negotiations in hand or completed", companies undergoing assessment or similar, "shell" and "rump" companies, and farms.
a) Change of method.

Source: THA

Table 15:
Net stock of companies in THA ownership, with numbers employed, by branch of industry, as of 30th June

Main branches of industry[1])	Companies[2])						Employees					
	No.			Structure[3])			No.			Structure[3])		
	1991	1992	1993	1991	1992	1993	1991	1992	1993	1991	1992	1993
Total	17,943	4,340	1,668	100.0	100.0	100.0	2,593,577	830,792	296,343	100.0	100.0	100.0
Agriculture and forestry	506	471	347	6.4	10.9	20.8	38,695	19,318	7,407	1.5	2.3	2.5
Energy industry and water supply	119	92	24	1.5	2.1	1.4	72,355	67,311	25,887	2.8	8.1	8.7
Mining	38	25	16	0.5	0.6	1.0	147,141	91,211	55,275	5.7	11.0	18.7
Chemical industry	169	86	36	2.1	2.0	2.2	148,116	54,627	33,989	5.7	6.6	11.5
Plastic, rubber, and asbestos processing	120	63	12	1.5	1.5	0.7	29,963	7,036	664	1.2	0.8	0.2
Extraction and processing of stone and earth; fine ceramics and glass	276	137	56	3.5	3.2	3.4	70,708	19,322	7,339	2.7	2.3	2.5
Ferrous and non-ferrous metal products, casting, steel products	174	105	53	2.2	2.4	3.2	109,675	39,957	17,676	4.2	4.8	6.0
Steel and light engineering	118	71	38	1.5	1.6	2.3	47,722	23,711	14,570	1.8	2.9	4.9
Mechanical engineering	820	511	193	10.3	11.8	11.6	414,590	127,175	47,283	16.0	15.3	16.0
Vehicle construction	263	144	43	3.3	3.3	2.6	123,537	40,670	11,983	4.8	4.9	4.0
Electrical engineering and electronics	345	172	43	4.3	4.0	2.6	230,069	43,188	10,590	8.9	5.2	3.6
Precision engineering and optical instruments	51	31	8	0.6	0.7	0.5	26,529	4,640	622	1.0	0.6	0.2
Iron, sheet metal and metal goods, musical instruments, sports equipment, toys, and jewellery	222	115	34	2.8	2.6	2.0	43,894	11,408	1,554	1.7	1.4	0.5
Wood industry	375	205	43	4.7	4.7	2.6	52,629	15,789	2,898	2.0	1.9	1.0
Paper and printing industry	186	88	20	2.3	2.0	1.2	37,699	10,339	3,411	1.5	1.2	1.2
Leather and shoe industry	141	74	20	1.8	1.7	1.2	35,223	7,316	1,754	1.4	0.9	0.6
Textile and clothing industry	419	247	87	5.3	5.7	5.2	165,293	43,263	10,943	6.4	5.2	3.7
Food and drinks industry	582	279	50	7.3	6.4	3.0	87,705	21,049	2,674	3.4	2.5	0.9
Construction industry	562	206	48	7.1	4.7	2.9	185,995	56,916	9,176	7.2	6.9	3.1
Ancillary construction industry	116	36	10	1.5	0.8	0.6	9,015	3,072	245	0.3	0.4	0.1

Main branches of industry[1])	Companies[2])						Employees					
	No.			Structure[3])			No.			Structure[3])		
	1991	1992	1993	1991	1992	1993	1991	1992	1993	1991	1992	1993
Wholesale and retail trade	924	425	144	11.6	9.8	8.6	274,508	43,049	4,104	10.6	5.2	1.4
Transport, communications, freight, and storage	233	187	70	2.9	4.3	4.2	103,620	41,453	2,456	4.0	5.0	0.8
Banks and other finance houses, insurance industry	2	2	2	0.0	0.0	0.1	–	375	423	–	0.0	0.1
Services	1,149	548	243	14.5	12.6	14.6	138,896	38,268	21,383	5.4	4.6	7.2
Not categorised	33	20	28	0.4	0.5	1.7	–	329	2,037	–	0.0	0.7

Notes: 1) THA definitions and categorisation; 2) companies in which THA holds the majority of the shares and are not in the process of bankruptcy/liquidation; 3) proportion of companies/employees in the companies awaiting privatisation, in %

Source: THA

Table 16:
THA companies, 1991 to 1993

	Jan 1991		June 1991		Dec 1991		June 1992		Sept 1992		Dec 1992		June 1993	
	No.	%	No.	%	No.	%	No.	%	No.	%	No.	%	No.	%
Total portfolio of THA companies a)	8,489	100.0	10,334	100.0	10,979	100.0	11,926	100.0	12,313	100.0	12,599	100.0	12,993	100.0
In liquidation/ liquidated	120	1.4	520	5.0	1,014	9.2	1,869	15.7	2,057	16.7	2,249	17.9	2,857	22.0
Majority/entirety of holding privatised	574	6.8	1,789	17.3	2,996	27.3	4,590	38.5	5,040	41,0	5,456	43.3	5,831	44.9
(privatised parts of companies)					(1,895)		(3,585)		(4,679)		(5,258)		(6,363)	
Completely restored to previous owners	107	1.3	357	3.5	527	4.8	862	7.2	1,039	8.4	1,188	9.4	1,360	10.5
Completely transferred to municipalities	40	0.5	70	0.7	145	1.3	206	1.7	244	2.0	253	2.0	259	2.0
Remainder b)					160	1.5	59	0.5	482	3.9	878	7.0	1,018	7.8
Awaiting privatisation	7,648	90.0	7,598	73.5	6,128	55.9	4,340	36.4	3,451	28.0	2,575	20.4	1,668	12.8
Investment undertakings c) in DM billions	44.5		65.3		114.2		144		155.3		169.5		180.1	
Employment undertakings c) in '000 jobs	255		526		930		1,224		1,317		1,401		1,468	
Employees d) e) in '000														
in THA companies	2,937		2,115		1,404		1,070		560		458		296	
in ex-THA companies f)					254		529		885		836		815	
in total	2,937		2,115		1,658		1,599		1,445		1,308		1,111	

Notes: a) last day of each month; (b) communalisation applied for, ownership assigned, etc.; (c) according to THA, made at the time of privatisation, and including the privatisation of parts of companies; (d) first day of the next month; (e) according to survey (Wahse and others); (f) only fully privatised companies; (g) including assignments of ownership

Sources: Frank Stille, Sanierungsstrategien der Treuhandanstalt - politische Zwänge versus ökonomische Effizienz. In: Die Weltwirtschaft, 1993. The figures were summarised or derived from: Treuhandanstalt; Monatsinformationen (for various months); Jürgen Wahse, Vera Dahms, Sibylle Fitzner, et al, Beschäftigungsperspektiven von Treuhandunternehmen und Ex-Treuhandfirmen, survey, October 1991. In: Beiträge zur Arbeitsmarkt- und Berufsforschung 160, Nuremberg, 1992, page 79; Jürgen Wahse, Vera Dahms, and Reinhard Schaefer, Beschäftigungsperspektiven von Treuhandunternehmen und Ex-Treuhandfirmen, survey, October 1992. In: Beiträge zur Arbeitsmarkt- und Berufsforschung 160.3, Nuremberg, 1993, page 69

A chronicle of the THA

17 November 1989	Modrow's government declaration announces economic reforms.
6 January 1990	Draft Bill on joint ventures submitted to the East German Council of Ministers (maximum foreign holding 49 %).
7 February 1990	Cabinet committee on "German Unification" set up under the chairmanship of the (West) German Chancellor.
12 February 1990	"Round Table", in response to an initiative from Bündnis 90, proposes establishing a "Trustee Company" (in effect, the THA) to look after state-owned assets.
1st March 1990	East German Council of Ministers approves the establishment of an early form of the THA to administer state-owned companies and assets as a trustee. Dr Peter Moreth is appointed chairman of its *Direktorium*. An Ordinance is issued for the conversion of state-owned *Kombinate*, companies, and other organisations into joint-stock companies.
15th March 1990	East German Council of Ministers approves the Articles of Association of the original version of the THA. It is based in Berlin and has 15 regional offices, one in each *Bezirk* (the old administrative Districts) and in Berlin itself.
8th June 1990	Lothar de Maizière's government announces that a law will be passed converting the East German companies into GmbH or AG-companies with effect from 1st July 1990.
17th June 1990	East German *Volkskammer* (parliament) passes the *Treuhandgesetz* or THA Act.
1st July 1990	Treaty on economic, monetary, and social union between East and West Germany comes into force.
4th July 1990	The East German Council of Ministers appoints a leading West German businessman, Dr Detlev Rohwedder, as Chairman of the Administrative Board of the THA.
15th July 1990	Rainer Maria Gohlke replaces Peter Moreth as President of the THA (i.e. Chairman of its Executive Board).
20th August 1990	Gohlke resigns; Rohwedder takes his place.
29th August 1990	Jens Odewald, Chairman of the Executive Board of Kaufhof AG, becomes the new Chairman of the THA Administrative Board to replace Rohwedder.
13th September 1990	Rohwedder presents his first status report to the *Volkskammer*: out of 8,000 companies, 7,000 have been converted into GmbH or AG-

	companies, but the THA is facing a task "of terrifying proportions".
3rd October 1990	Germany is re-unified.
4th October 1990	Appointment of new managers to the 15 THA branches; the authorisation previously granted to these branches is withdrawn with immediate effect; and the branches take over responsibility for companies with up to 1,500 employees.
5th October 1990	Federal German Government appoints members to the Administrative Board: Hermann Rappe (president of the chemical workers' union IG Chemie), Horst Köhler (Secretary of State in the Federal Finance Ministry), and Dieter von Würzen (Secretary of State in the Federal Economics Ministry).
	The first Opel Vectra rolls of the production line in Eisenach, which used to produce the venerable little "Trabant".
6th October 1990	The *Gesellschaft zur Privatisierung des Handels* (GPH, or "company for privatising retail trade") is founded as a subsidiary of the THA for converting the *Handelsorganisation* (HO, or "trade organisation", virtually the entire East German retail trade).
9th October 1990	Top-level conference with the Chancellor. A call goes out to western German business to make managers available on secondment to the THA.
10th October 1990	Mercedes Benz AG, Stuttgart, announces it will be taking a holding in Ifa-Automobilwerk GmbH (a lorry manufacturer) in Ludwigsfelde.
15th October 1990	BASF takes over Synthesewerke Schwarzheide.
18th October 1990	Basic agreement with Volkswagen on extending the works at Mosel (near Zwickau).
	The THA sets up its "Citizens' Telephone".
22nd October 1990	The various economic research institutes present their regular "Autumn Assessment", which this year recommends that the THA should be relieved of its obligations to restructure companies.
24th October 1990	The THA sub-committee of the *Bundestag* (German parliament) Budget Committee is constituted.
16th November 1990	Approval of the Guiding Principles for Business Policy by the THA Administrative Board.
22nd November 1990	A first offer of tender goes out for 8,500 shops and 2,500 pubs and restaurants previously owned by the HO. A further 6,000 are to follow later. About 11,000 HO firms have already either been privatised or closed down.
28th November 1990	The German Government appoints further members to the Administrative Board: Heinz-Werner Meyer (chairman of the trade union federation DGB), Roland Issen (chairman of the salaried staff union DAG), and Horst Klaus (a member of the executive board of the metal-workers' union IG Metall).
3rd December 1990	Henkel buys up Waschmittelwerk Genthin, which had belonged to the Group before the two Germanies were separated.

18th December 1990	The Minister-Presidents of the five eastern German States become members of the THA Administrative Board. The State of Berlin is represented from 8th March 1991 by its Senator for Financial Affairs, Elmar Pieroth.
3rd January 1991	First progress report on privatisation: in 1990, about 500 companies and manufacturing locations were sold to private investors.
22nd January 1991	THA Executive Boards approves plans to establish the *Treuhand-Liegenschaftsgesellschaft* (or TLG) as its property management and sales company.
31st January 1991	The THA approves the final production runs, until March, of the "Wartburg" car.
8th February 1991	The THA accepts responsibility for liquidity funds totalling about DM 28 billion for its companies.
6th March 1991	Agreement between Mr Rohwedder, the THA President, and Mr Josef Duchac, Minister-President of Thuringia, under which the Carl Zeiss Foundation in Jena takes an 80% holding in Zeiss Jena in order to free the giant optical instruments company's of its debts; this Foundation is administered by the State of Thuringia.
8th March 1991	The German cabinet approves a promotional package under the name of *Gemeinschaftswerk Aufschwung Ost*.
14th March 1991	Outcome of talks chaired by the Chancellor: the basic principles of co-operation under *Aufschwung Ost* are agreed, and the Federal Government, the five eastern German States, and the THA decide, among other things, on the formation of "THA Economic Cabinets".
18th March 1991	Contract signed to establish the TLG, thus ushering in the sale of 1,000 plots of land.
20th March 1991	Some 15,000 people need to be recruited onto the Supervisory Boards of THA companies.
27th March 1991	Easter Letter from Mr Rohwedder, as President of the THA, to all his staff, with a 10-point plan for the THA's work summarised as: rapid privatisation – resolute restructuring – considerate closure. Prolongation beyond the original expiry date of the THA guarantees to cover liquidity loans to companies.
1st April 1991	Detlev Karsten Rohwedder is murdered at about midnight in the study of his home in Düsseldorf.
8th April 1991	First "stock exchange" for THA companies is opened in Berlin. The THA approves a strategy designed to make privatisation, new establishment, and unbundling from larger units easier for its small and medium-sized companies.
13th April 1991	Joint declaration by DGB/DAG and THA on social plans.
15th April 1991	THA Administrative Board elects Birgit Breuel to be the new President of the THA.
24th April 1991	GPH: the privatisation of the HO hotels will be completed by the end of June.
30th April 1991	The last "Trabi" rolls off the production line. Interflug, the East German State airline, ceases operation.

3rd May 1991	3,000 applications for debt cancellation have been received by the THA from agricultural enterprises.
15th May 1991	Orders from the Soviet Union account for 80% of the order-books of the shipyard companies with the Deutsche Maschinen- und Schiffbau AG.
17th May 1991	The THA calls on its companies not to reduce or abolish their facilities for training newcomers or their programmes for advanced training or retraining.
23rd May 1991	First MBO Congress held by the THA: "Purchase of Companies by their own Managers".
4th June 1991	EC promises support for eastern Germany.
7th June 1991	The THA calls on its company owners to provide assistance to "employment companies" with specialist personal and tangible facilities.
4th July 1991	First overall strategy for the eastern German chemicals industry based on the main locations of Leuna, Buna, and Bitterfeld.
16th July 1991	The THA starts examining the qualifications of members of its companies' Supervisory and Executive Boards.
17th July 1991	Conclusion of an outline agreement between the eastern German States, the trade unions, and the employers' associations, as well as the THA itself, on companies for promoting employment under the ABS programmes.
30th July 1991	End of the privatisation programme for the formerly state-owned HO. Of the original stock of 30,000 shops and other trading and catering firms, 22,300 have now found new owners.
1st August 1991	About 1,400 eastern German managers have been dismissed since September 1990. THA President Birgit Breuel gives the reasons as: overmanning of boards (500), political "pasts" (400), and embezzlement or other criminal actions (100).
13th August 1991	The Executive Board of the THA approves new rules on insider deals. The acquisition of THA companies by employees or their relatives will be subjected to strict supervisory conditions.
19th September 1991	15 THA employees are dismissed because of information provided by the Gauck commission on their previous informer activities for the *Stasi* (the secretive Ministry of State Security).
24th September 1991	Second MBO Congress in Berlin.
23rd October 1991	Franz Steinkühler, at that time chairman of the metal-workers' union IG Metall, proposes that the THA should be dissolved and regionally organised industrial holding companies set up.
30th October 1991	The THA Executive Board provides the eastern German States with an "early warning system" on forthcoming developments in major companies (meaning mainly warning of closure).
6th November 1991	The opening Deutschmark balance-sheets and the corporate strategies of the THA companies are evaluated. Seven out of every ten companies in the eastern German States are categorised as being suitable for restructuring.

8th November 1991	Carl Zeiss Oberkochen takes over the management of Carl Zeiss Jena with 51% of its shares.
21st November 1991	The Berlin Senate (the city-state's parliament) takes over 7,945 flats, 67 two-family houses, and 153 single-family (detached) houses previously provided to employees of the East German Ministry of State Security.
22nd November 1991	Deutsche Interhotel AG is sold for about DM 2.5 billion.
7th December 1991	The sale of the steel works in Hennigsdorf and Brandenburg to the Riva concern is approved by the THA Administrative Board.
31st December 1991	Status report on privatisation: the THA has handed 5,210 companies over to private investors, and the TLG has privatised 6,052 properties and 8,344 hectares of agricultural land.
16th January 1992	The THA Central Office building is renamed "Detlev Rohwedder House".
24th January 1992	Administrative Board approves an international solution to the privatisation of the ship-yards. MTW Schiffswerft GmbH is sold to the Bremer Vulkan Group, Neptun-Warnow Werft GmbH to the Norwegian Kvaerner Group.
18th March 1992	Congress on questions relating to management buy-outs (MBO's) in Frankfurt am Main. One THA privatisation in five involves a company being bought out by its own employees and managers.
25th March 1992	Birgit Breuel is nominated "Manager of the Year" by Forbes Magazine.
26th March 1992	Privatisation Congress held by the THA and the East Committee of German business in Berlin, with about 300 experts from 24 central, east, and south-east European states. Exchanges of experience are to be co-ordinated by a consultancy subsidiary, Treuhand Osteuropa Beratungs-GmbH.
24th April 1992	The agricultural property sales and administrative company is formed as Bodenverwertungs- und -verwaltungs-GmbH or BVVG, with one-quarter of the shares each held by: the THA, Deutsche Siedlungs- und Landesrentenbank Bonn, Landwirtschaftliche Rentenbank Frankfurt, and Landeskreditbank Baden-Württemberg, Karlsruhe.
7th May 1992	The THA holds an Information Congress and "open day" in Berlin.
19th May 1992	The THA approves the sale of DEFA to a German subsidiary of the French CGE group.
21st May 1992	New outline agreement on social plans between the THA and the trade unions.
22nd May 1992	The Directorate for Coastal Industries becomes the first part of the THA to complete its work and dissolve.
30th June 1992	The Schwerin branch becomes the first of the THA's 15 regional organisations to conclude its work.
3rd July 1992	The German *Bundestag* passes the Credit Acceptance Act into law limiting the THA's authority for taking out fresh loans to a normal limit of DM 30 billion for each of the years 1992 to 1994.

23rd July 1992 — The TED consortium, made up of the Thyssen Handelsunion and the French Elf group, sign a contract on the privatisation of Minol, the eastern German petrol-station company, and the construction of a refinery in Leuna to secure supplies of raw materials for the eastern German heavy chemicals industry.

4th September 1992 — Samsung takes over WF, the Werk für Fernsehelektronik GmbH, in the Oberschönweide district of (East) Berlin.

18th September 1992 — The THA's Administrative Board approves the privatisation of a highgrade steel factory, Edelstahlwerke Freital.

1st October 1992 — The THA Directorate for the food and drinks industry completes its privatisation work.

5th October 1992 — Government departments are urged to "go shopping" in eastern Germany. A special event to launch the marketing campaign is opened in the Berlin Congress Centre by the THA President, Birgit Breuel, and the Berlin Economics Senator Mr Meisner.

15th October 1992 — The THA presents its consolidated opening Deutschmark balance-sheet. Mr Theo Waigel, the Federal Finance Minster, explains that the THA will have taken on a total debt of about DM 250 billion when it finishes its work, but this deficit is only a fraction of the negative legacy left behind by the old East Germany.

3rd /5th December — THA Congress and Exhibition in Leipzig under the title of "Made in Germany".

16th December 1992 — The THA Directorate for the services sector completes its privatisation work.

31st December 1992 — Status report on privatisation: the THA has now handed 11,043 companies over to private investors, on top of which 10,311 properties and 27,807 hectares of agricultural land have been sold.

18th January 1993 — First working session of the delegates from 30 major western German companies on the "Go shopping in eastern Germany" campaign.

10th February 1993 — The Federal Finance Minister, Mr Waigel, declares: the *Gemeinschaftswerk Aufschwung Ost* has been a total success.
The *Bundestag* THA Committee is constituted under the chairmanship of Arnulf Kriedner (CDU) to replace the former sub-committee.

17th February 1993 — Three more Management-KG's are announced.

10th March 1993 — The THA issues its first five-year bonds, known as TOBL's.

25th March 1993 — Start of the public tendering process by the BVVG to sell forestry land.

31st March 1993 — Agreement between the THA and IG Chemie takes effect covering measures under the Labour Promotion Act.

8th April 1993 — Communalisation of waterworks and sewerage companies completed.

14th April 1993 — Jens Odewald resigns as Chairman of the Administrative Board.

19th June 1993 — IV International Eastern Europe Symposium, this time on the subject of: company conversion, privatisation, and investment in Eastern Europe and eastern Germany.

23rd June 1993 — The THA "Tour of eastern Germany" finishes in Berlin. Its motto was "Anyone who has booked orders does not need subsidies".

1st July 1993 — The Contract Management organisation of the THA starts work under its new organisation.

30th July 1993 — First portfolio privatisation of the THA (companies in the construction materials and building supplies field: Leipziger Beton Union GmbH, Naunhofer Kieswerke GmbH, Chemnitzer Baustoff- und Fertigteil GmbH, BB Beton und Bauwaren GmbH Zeulenroda, Systemelektronik Rostock and a further eight subsidiary companies in this group).

26th August 1993 — The Directorate for travel and transport completes its privatisation and communalisation work.

1st September 1993 — The 33 founder-companies in the "Go shopping" campaign have bought DM 850 million's worth of goods in eastern Germany over and above the planned amount.

13th September 1993 — Dessauer Gasgeräte privatised.

15th September 1993 — The THA's New York office completes it work.

30th September 1993 — The THA has now privatised 13,218 companies or parts of companies completely, and sold more than 35,000 hectares of agricultural and forestry land. The proceeds totalled DM 44.7 billion, and the THA was given assurances that DM 182.4 billion would be invested and 1,492,813 jobs preserved or created.

20th October 1993 — First meeting of the THA Committee of Enquiry of the German *Bundestag* under the chairmanship of Otto Schily.

27th October 1993 — The German Cabinet approves the plans for the restructuring of the THA once its core activities have been completed. A new THG (*Treuhandgesetz*) is announced for the summer of 1994.

Tables and figures

Tables

Figures

Index of authors

Dr Hermann Clement — Osteuropa-Institut, Munich

Professor Dr
Roland Czada — Fernuniversität Hagen

Professor Drs
Wolfram Fischer — Free University of Berlin

Professor Dr Peter Hanau — University of Cologne

Professor Dr Herbert Hax — University of Cologne

Professor Dr
Günter Hedtkamp — Osteruropa-Institut, Munich

Professor Dr
Hans M. Kepplinger — Johannes Gutenberg University, Mayence

Professor Dr Horst Kern — Georg August University, Göttingen

Professor Dr
Paul Klemmer — Rhenish Westphalian Institute for Economic Research

Professor Dr
Michael Kloepfer — Humboldt University of Berlin

Professor Drs Klaus König — Hochschule für Verwaltungswissenschaften, Speyer

Professor Dr Martin Kohli — Free University of Berlin

Professor Dr
Hans-Ulrich Küpper — University of Munich

Professor Dr Jürgen Müller — Fachhochschule für Wirtschaft, Berlin

Professor Charles Sabel — Massachusetts Institute of Technology, Cambridge, USA

Diplom-Volkswirt Klaus-Dieter Schmidt	Institute for World Economics, Kiel
Dr Harm Schröter	Free University of Berlin
Professor Dr Joachim Schwalbach	Humboldt University of Berlin
Professor Dr Wolfgang Seibel	University of Constance
Professor Dr Eckhard Wandel	Eberhard Karls University, Tübingen
Professor Dr Harm Peter Westermann	Eberhard Karls University, Tübingen
Professor Dr Hans Willgerodt	University of Cologne